Central European Economic History
from Waterloo to OPEC,
1815-1975

Central European Economic History from Waterloo to OPEC, 1815-1975

A Bibliography

Compiled by
Richard D. Hacken

Bibliographies and Indexes in Economics and Economic History, Number 6

GREENWOOD PRESS
New York • Westport, Connecticut • London

LIBRARY OF CONGRESS CATALOGING-IN-PUBLICATION DATA

Hacken, Richard D.
  Central European economic history from Waterloo to
OPEC, 1815-1975.

  (Bibliographies and indexes in economics and
economic history, ISSN 0749-1786 ; no. 6)
  Includes index.
  1. Central Europe—Economic conditions—Bibliography.
  2. Central Europe—Industries—History—Bibliography.
  3. Finance—Central Europe—History—Bibliography.
  I. Title. II. Series.
  Z7165.C42H33 1987 [HC244] 016.330943   86-27088
  ISBN 0-313-25460-5 (lib. bdg. : alk. paper)

Library of Congress Catalog Card Number: 86-27088
ISBN: 0-313-25460-5
ISSN: 0749-1786

First published in 1987

Greenwood Press, Inc.
88 Post Road West, Westport, Connecticut 06881

Printed in the United States of America

∞™

The paper used in this book complies with the
Permanent Paper Standard issued by the National
Information Standards Organization (Z39.48-1984).

10 9 8 7 6 5 4 3 2 1

Contents

2. History of Agriculture

3. History of Industry
(also includes historical productivity)

CONTENTS

4. History of Business and Commerce
   (also includes histories of entrepreneurship, customs, integration efforts,
   cooperatives, capitalism, economic growth, crises and business cycles)

5. **History of Finance**

   (also includes histories of money and banking, the stock market, taxes, social insurance and reparations)

Preface

On the thirtieth day of March in 1815 a minor play by the great Goethe, entitled <u>The Awakening of Epimenides</u>, premiered on the stage in Berlin. Uncharacteristic of its author, the obscure script strayed into plump melodrama ("...freed at last from the bonds of slavery") and undisguised chauvinism ("We Germans...the noblest of races"). Although this play has now justly fallen into the shadows of forgetfulness, at the time it did reflect a crucial turning-point, the awakening of Central Europe after Napoleon.

In the decades following 1815, the hopes for progress in the broad midlands of the European continent probably found their best realization in the economic realm. Even while the political structures largely returned to what they had been before the Bonapartist era, the first great steps were already being taken in the metamorphosis from an agrarian to an industrialized society.

The year 1815 thus forms a logical starting point for this bibliographic guide to the modern history of economic conditions in Central Europe. The history of its economic life offers illuminating and complementary views to the political and social happenings of the region. It helps to explain the German-speaking world in context from the first efforts at economic development and political unification, through full industrialization and the disasters of war, to the complexities of a re-divided Central Europe and two competing economic systems.

Geographic Scope:

Although the scope of coverage has been limited for practical reasons to the German-speaking world, the historically mixed-language areas such as Hungary, Bohemia and Silesia are also selectively covered. The result is a "Central Europe" with borders that have shifted throughout the years, but which excludes predominantly non-German-speaking areas. Though a number of relevant works exist in Romanian, Hungarian, and the Slavic languages, they have somewhat reluctantly been deleted in favor of the more familiar western languages (primarily German and English). A notation is made where English-language summaries are available.

Particular emphasis has been placed on regional and local economic conditions, with their various border shifts and name changes thoughout the 19th and 20th centuries. The locales which are now within the borders of the Federal Republic of Germany are listed under the name of the present state rather than as former entities, e.g., Stuttgart under "Baden-Württemberg", not just "Württemberg", Oldenburg under "Lower Saxony", not "Oldenburg", etc. "Alsace-Lorraine" is included for the years 1871-1918. Works on the "Rhineland" are generally categorized within North Rhine-Westphalia. The areas of the present German Democratic Republic plus the formerly German lands of the east are divided into: Brandenburg, Thuringia, Saxony (including Saxony-Anhalt), Mecklenburg, Danzig (including the area of Pomeralia) until 1945, Pomerania, Silesia until 1945, West and East Prussia until 1945, in addition to the generic term "Eastern Germany," which reflects the Pre-World War II concept of the lands east of the main Reich as "Ostdeutschland". The relevant areas of the former Austro-Hungarian Empire are divided as follows: the provinces of the Austrian Republic under their present names, plus "Bohemia and Moravia" to 1918, and "Hungary", "Rumania" and "Transylvania" to 1945.

The German-speaking cantons of Switzerland and the countries of Liechtenstein and Luxemburg prove considerably less troublesome regarding historic change.

Works covering all of Europe or comparing continental European economic conditions with those of America, Britain, Japan or other areas of the world are listed under "Central Europe."

Bibliographic Scope:

It goes without saying that a bibliographic guide to Central European economic history from Waterloo to OPEC requires a good deal of selectivity, since a plethora of material exists.

As a general rule, the titles chosen describe economic conditions from a historic perspective; *i.e.*, they do not offer contemporaneous, on-the-scene reports except for those chronicles that include comparison with the past. This is one reason an end date of 1975 was chosen as far as subject matter is concerned, though imprint dates after that year are included. The available wealth of primary source material is ignored in favor of secondary works in economic historiography.

For the same reason, listings of theoretical treatises on economic questions are missing here. The time in question was assuredly an epoch-making one in the evolution of economic theory, but the aim of this collection of titles is to present a variety of views on Central European historical--rather than theoretical--economics. Certain works have used considerable facts taken from elapsed economic history to illustrate their theories, and these works are included.

In order to devote close attention to regional and local economic conditions without lapsing over into the unmanageable, it was necessary to exclude biographies and histories of individual companies or branches of industry. Likewise, works on predominantly legal, political, or social matters are deleted, unless they represent a valuable contribution to the history of economic conditions as well.

Monographs, bibliographies and dissertations are included, as well as articles from journals and Festschriften. An attempt has been made to avoid duplicate listings through the use of cross-referencing.

This bibliography distinguishes geographic and chronological subdivisions within the following broad subject areas:

1. The History of Economic Conditions (includes general works)
2. The History of Agriculture
3. The History of Industry (also includes historical productivity)
4. The History of Business and Commerce (also includes histories of entrepreneurship, customs, integration efforts, cooperatives, capitalism, economic growth, crises and business cycles)
5. The History of Finance (also includes histories of money and banking, the stock market, taxes, social insurance and reparations)

Labor history is a far-ranging topic which is consciously excluded here. The existence of excellent bibliographies on the history of the German labor movement precludes the need for a redundant listing of labor titles in this work.

Any bibliography is of necessity a reflection of its compiler's subjective priorities, and this one will prove no exception. This list of titles takes a broad approach to documenting the historic literature on economic conditions of modern Central Europe, especially with its accent on regional and local histories. I hope it may assist in the search for new sources and insights.

Sources

Card catalogs and holdings of the following libraries were consulted for relevant works on the economic conditions of Central Europe between 1815 and 1975 (listed in order of importance for volume of entries):

Kiel. Bibliothek des Instituts für Weltwirtschaft.
Berlin (West). Staatsbibliothek Preussischer Kulturbesitz.
Lawrence. Kansas University. Watson Library (Howey Collection).
Vienna. Universität. Seminarbibliothek des Instituts für Wirtschafts- und Sozialgeschichte.
Munich. Bibliothek des Instituts für Zeitgeschichte.
Zürich. Zentralbibliothek.
Zürich. Universität. Seminarbibliothek des Instituts für Wirtschafts- und Sozialgeschichte.
Stuttgart. Bibliothek für Zeitgeschichte.
Berlin (East). Staatsbibliothek.
Luxembourg. Bibliothèque Nationale.

Among the bibliographies consulted were the following:

Aldcroft, Derek H. and Richard Rodger. Bibliography of European Economic and Social History. Manchester: Manchester University Press, 1984. 293 pp.

Dapper, Karl-Peter and Gerhard Hahn, eds. Bibliographie zur Sozialen Marktwirtschaft. Die Wirtschafts- und Gesellschaftsordnung der Bundesrepublik Deutschland 1945/49-1981. Baden-Baden: Nomos Verlagsgesellschaft, 1983. 269 pp.

Fout, John C., ed. German History and Civilization 1806-1914. A Bibliography of Scholarly Periodical Literature. Metuchen, NJ: The Scarecrow Press, 1974. 243 pp.

Institut für Zeitgeschichte München. Bibliographie zur Zeitgeschichte 1953-1980. Band I: Allgemeiner Teil. Munich: K.G. Saur, 1982. 445 pp.

International Bibliography of Historical Sciences. Ed. International Committee of Historical Sciences. (1929-1983).

Keyser, Erich, ed. <u>Bibliographie zur Städtegeschichte Deutschlands</u>. Vienna: Böhlau, 1969.
    404 pp.

Rausch, Wilhelm, ed. <u>Bibliographie zur Geschichte der Städte Österreichs</u>. Linz: Wimmer,
    1984. 329 pp.

Sachse, Wieland. <u>Bibliographie zur preussischen Gewerbestatistik 1750-1850</u>. Göttingen:
    O. Schwartz, 1981. 392 pp.

Wehler, Hans-Ulrich, ed. <u>Bibliographie zur modernen deutschen Wirtschaftsgeschichte.
    (18.-20. Jahrhundert)</u>. Göttingen: Vandenhoeck & Ruprecht, 1976. 239 pp.

Journal Abbreviations:

<u>Schmollers Jahrbuch für Gesetzgebung. Verwaltung und Volkswirtschaft im Deutschen Reiche</u>
                                                                    = <u>Schmoller</u>

<u>Schweizerische Zeitschrift für Volkswirtschaft und Statistik</u>   = <u>SZVS</u>

<u>Vierteljahrschrift für Sozial- und Wirtschaftsgeschichte</u>   = <u>VSWG</u>

All other journals are listed by either their full title or by a recognizable truncated version of the full title.

Subject headings for which relevant entries were extracted at the library of the Institut für
 Weltwirtschaft, Kiel (West Germany):

Agraraussenhandel
Agrargenossenschaft
Agrargeschichte
Agrarkonjunktur
Agrarverfassungsgeschichte
Aussenwirtschaftsgeschichte
Ausstellungsgeschichte
Bankgeschichte
Börsengeschichte
Einkommensteuergeschichte
Finanzgeschichte
Finanzgeschichte der Landesteile
Gebirgswirtschaft
Geldgeschichte
Gemeindefinanzgeschichte
Genossenschaftsgeschichte
Gewerbegeschichte
Gewerbepolitik
Goldgeschichte
Handelsgeschichte
Industrialisierung
Industrieaussenhandel
Industriegeschichte
Juden im Wirtschaftsleben
Kapitalismus
Konjunkturgeschichte
Konjunkturbeschreibung
Kriegsbedingte Änderungen ... (several subjects)
Kriegsentschädigung
Marktgeschichte
Maschinenindustriegeschichte
Münze
Münzunion
Nahrungsmittelversorgung der Stadt
Preisstatistik
Produktionsgenossenschaft
Produktivität
Silbergeschichte
Sozialgeschichte
Sozialversicherung
Sparkassengeschichte
Standortpolitik
Steuergeschichte
Technikgeschichte
Unternehmer

Verbrauchergenossenschaft
Versicherungsgeschichte
Werbungsgeschichte
Wirtschaft der Landesteile
Wirtschaft und Staat
Wirtschaftsgeschichte
Wirtschaftskammerbeschreibung
Wirtschaftsunion
Wirtschaftswachstum
Zollgeschichte
Zollunion

Acknowledgments

Compiling a bibliography may be the greatest strain on an optic nerve short of eye surgery. Any aid in the search, selection, and proofing procedures is very welcome. Therefore, I am most grateful to those individuals and institutions that assisted me.

Dr. Erwin Heidemann of the Institut für Weltwirtschaft in Kiel was particularly helpful in granting advice, insight, and easy access to both the subject catalog and indispensable copy facilities. Similar help was given by Frau Olsen and W. Limacher of the Zentralbibliothek in Zurich and by the staff of the seminar library of the Institut für Wirtschafts- und Sozialgeschichte at the University of Zurich. Dr. Sauer of the Viennese Wirtschaftsuniversität sent me on a fruitful trail that led to Dr. Roman Sandgruber and the seminar library at the University of Vienna. Gratitude is also due the staff of the Staatsbibliothek Preussischer Kulturbesitz in West Berlin and the staff of the Staatsbibliothek in East Berlin, especially Frau Reulke.

A research trip of 1982 was made possible by grants from the German Academic Exchange Service and the Brigham Young University Library Professional Development Fund, both of which are gratefully acknowledged. The latter fund also covered essential costs of copying, word processing, and student assistance. My thanks to Dean Larsen and Randy Olsen of BYU--as well as Tony Ferguson, now at Columbia University--for granting the funds and time necessary to make this project a reality.

Staff and former colleagues of the University of Kansas library, notably Mr. Jim Neeley, offered the use of their facilities and their valuable economic history collection to me.

Special kudos and thanks go to Mr. Oscar Nobles for his dedicated evening and weekend hours at the console of a CPT 8100 word processor and to my daughter Kristin for her help with the Author Index.

Love and appreciation extend to my father, Nephi R. Hacken, and grandfather, John R. Hachen, through whom I trace a uniquely personal interest in Central European industriousness back to Rüeggisberg, Canton Bern, Switzerland.

Fault for errors or omissions rests partly with the vagaries of an optical scanner that selectively digested or distorted bits of the manuscript. All further blame rests on my own shoulders.   I would appreciate receiving any correspondence regarding possible corrections or additions for any future updated edition.

1.
History of Economic Conditions

CENTRAL EUROPE

Bibliographic References

1. Aldcroft, Derek H. and Richard Rodger. Bibliography of European Economic and Social History. Manchester: Manchester University Press, 1984. 243 pp.
2. American Economic Association. Index of Economic Journals. 5 vols. Homewood, IL: Irwin, 1961-62.
3. Bibliographie der Sozialwissenschaften: internationale Dokumentation der Buch- und Zeitschriftenliteratur des Gesamtgebiets der Sozialwissenschaften. Göttingen: Vandenhoeck & Ruprecht, 1905-1967.
4. Bibliographie der Wirtschaftspresse. Hamburg: Welt-Wirtschafts-Archiv, 1949- .
5. Bibliographie der Wirtschaftswissenschaften. (formerly: Bibliographie der Sozialwissenschaften.) Göttingen: 1967-
6. Bibliographie zur Zeitgeschichte. Munich: Institute for Contemporary History, 1953- .
7. Bibliothek des Instituts für Zeitgeschichte. Sachkatalog. 6 vols. Boston: G. K. Hall, 1967.
8. Boehm, Eric H., ed. Historical Abstracts. (1775-1945). Santa Barbara, CA: ABC-Clio, 1955- .
9. Braeuer, Walter. Handbuch zur Geschichte der Volkswirtschaftslehre. Ein bibliographisches Nachschlagewerk. Frankfurt a. M.: Klostermann, 1952. 224 pp.
10. Brussels. Université libre. Centre d'économie régionale. Bibliographie Internationale d'Économie Régionale. Brussels: Université libre de Bruxelles, 1964. 757 pp.
11. Caron, Pierre and M. Jaryc, eds. World List of Historical Periodicals and Bibliographies. Oxford: Macon, 1939. 391 pp.
12. Clapham John H. et al., eds. The Cambridge Economic History of Europe from the Decline of the Roman Empire. Cambridge: Cambridge University Press, 1942- .
13. Dahlmann, Friedrich C. and Georg Waitz. Dahlmann-Waitz Quellenkunde der deutschen Geschichte. 10th ed. Stuttgart: A. Hiersemann, 1965- .
14. Documentation Économique: Révue Bibliographique Trimestrielle. Paris: Presses Universitaires de France, 1947- .
15. Dubester, Henry J., ed. National Censuses and Vital Statistics in Europe, 1918-1939: an Annotated Bibliography. Washington, D. C.: Library of Congress, 1948. Rpt. Detroit: Gale Research Co., 1967. 48 pp.
16. Economic Abstracts: a Semi-monthly Review of Abstracts of Economics, Finance, Trade and Industry, Management and Labor. The Hague: M. Nijhoff, 1953- .
17. Economics Selections: an International Bibliography. Series I: New Books in Economics. Pittsburgh: University of Pittsburgh, 1966- . (formerly: International Economics Selections Bibliography).

18. Flora, Peter et al. State, Economy, and Society in Western Europe 1815-1975. A Data Handbook in Two Volumes. Frankfurt a. M.: Campus, 1983.
19. Gay, Edwin F. List of References in Economics. 2nd Ed. Cambridge: Harvard University, 1920. 73 pp.
20. Gilbert, Victor F. Economic and Social History: a Guide to Sources of Information. 2nd ed. Sheffield: University of Sheffield Library, 1974. 21 pp.
21. Gray, Richard A. Serial Bibliographies in the Humanities and Social Sciences. Ann Arbor, MI: The Pierian Press, 1969. 345 pp.
22. Hall, Laura M. et al., eds. A Bibliography in Economics for the Honour School of Philosophy, Politics, and Economics. 2nd ed. Oxford: Oxford University Press, 1959. 82 pp.
23. Harvard University. Library. Economics and Economics Periodicals. 2 vols. Cambridge, MA: Harvard University Press, 1970.
24. Harvard University. Library. Kress Library of Business and Economics. Catalogue; with Data Upon Cognate Items in Other Harvard Libraries. 3 vols. Boston: Baker Library, 1940-67.
25. Howe, George F. et al., eds. Guide to Historical Literature. New York: Macmillan, 1961. 962 pp.
26. Hutchinson, William K. History of Economic Analysis. Detroit: Gale Research Co., 1976. 243 pp.
27. Institut für Zeitgeschichte München. Bibliographie zur Zeitgeschichte 1953-1980. Vol. I: Allgemeiner Teil. Munich: K.G. Saur, 1982. 445 pp.
28. International Bibliography of Economics. Bibliographie Internationale de Science Economique. London: Tavistock, 1955- .
29. International Bibliography of Historical Sciences. Washington, D. C.: ICHS, 1926- .
30. International Index: A Guide to Periodical Literature in the Social Sciences and Humanities. New York: H. W. Wilson, 1907- .
31. Journal of Economic Abstracts. Cambridge, MA: Harvard University, 1963- .
32. Kellenbenz, Hermann. "Firmenarchive in ihrer Bedeutung für die europäische Wirtschafts- und Sozialgeschichte." Tradition, 14 (1969), 1-20.
33. Kiel. Universität. Institut für Weltwirtschaft. Bibliothek. Behördenkatalog. 10 vols. Boston: G. K. Hall, 1967.
34. Kiel. Universität. Institut für Weltwirtschaft. Bibliothek. Körperschaftenkatalog. 13 vols. Boston: G. K. Hall, 1966.
35. Kiel. Universität. Institut für Weltwirtschaft. Bibliothek. Personenkatalog. 30 vols. Boston: G. K. Hall, 1966.
36. Kiel. Universität. Institut für Weltwirtschaft. Bibliothek. Regionenkatalog. 52 vols. Boston: G. K. Hall, 1966.
37. Kiel. Universität. Institut für Weltwirtschaft. Bibliothek. Sachkatalog. 83 vols. Boston: G. K. Hall, 1967.
38. Kiel. Universität. Institut für Weltwirtschaft. Bibliothek. Standortskartei der Periodika. 10 vols. Boston: G. K. Hall, 1968.
39. Kiel. Universität. Institut für Weltwirtschaft. Bibliothek. Titelkatalog. 15 vols. Boston: G. K. Hall, 1968.
40. Kipp, Laurence J., ed. Source Materials for Business and Economic History. Cambridge, MA: Harvard University, 1967. 154 pp.
41. Melnyk, Peter. Economics; Bibliographic Guide to Reference Books and Information Sources. Littleton, CO: Libraries Unlimited, 1971. 263 pp.
42. Mitchell, Brian R. European Historical Statistics, 1750-1975. 2nd ed. Cambridge: Cambridge University Press, 1981. 868 pp.
43. Neuss, Erich. Aktenkunde der Wirtschaft. 2 vols. Berlin: Rütten & Loening, 1954-56.
44. Organization for Economic Cooperation and Development. Catalogue des Périodiques. 3 vols. Paris: O. E. C. D., 1966.
45. Osaka S. Daigaku and Keizar Kenkyujo. Bibliography of Economic Science. 4 vols. Tokyo: Maruzen, 1934-39.
46. Pehrsson, Hjalmar and Hanna Wulf, eds. The European Bibliography. Leyden: A. W. Sijthoff, 1965. 472 pp.
47. Quarterly Check-List of Economics & Political Science: an International Index of Current Books, Monographs, Brochures and Separates. Darien, CT: American Bibliographic Service, 1958- .
48. Revue Economique Internationale. 32 vols. Brussels: Bibliographia Economica Universalis, 1904-1940.

49. Schleiffer, Hedwig and Ruth Crandall. Index to Economic History, Essays in Festschriften, 1900-1950. Cambridge, MA: Harvard University Press, 1953. 68 pp.
50. Seusing, Ekkehart. Wirtschaftswissenschaftliche Bibliographien 1974-1981. Kiel: Institut für Weltwirtschaft, 1983. 294 pp.
51. Studenski, Paul. The Income of Nations; Theory, Measurement and Analysis, Past and Present; a Study in Applied Economics and Statistics. New York: New York University Press, 1958. 554 pp.
52. Vesenyi, Paul E. European Periodical Literature in the Social Sciences and the Humanities. Metuchen, NJ: Scarecrow Press, 1969.
53. Weltwirtschaft. Kiel: Institut für Weltwirtschaft, 1950- .
54. Winschuh, Josef. Männer. Traditionen. Signale. Berlin: Osmer, 1940. 361 pp.

CENTRAL EUROPE

55. Abhandlungen zur Rechts- und Wirtschaftsgeschichte. Festschrift Adolf Zycha zum 17. Oktober 1941. Weimar: Böhlau, 1941. 638 pp.
56. Aldcroft, Derek H. The European Economy 1914-1980. London: Croom Helm, 1980. 251 pp.
57. Alpert, Paul. Twentieth Century Economic History of Europe. New York: Schuman, 1951. 466 pp.
58. Ambrosi, Christian and Max Tacel. Histoire économique des grandes puissances à l'époque contemporaine, 1850-1964. Paris: Delagrave, 1965. 782 pp.
59. Anderson, Eugene N. Modern Europe in World Perspective. 1914 to the Present. New York: Rinehart, 1958. 884 pp.
60. Anderson, J. L. "Climatic Change in European Economic History." Research in Economic History 6 (1981), 1-34.
61. Ashworth, William. A Short History of the International Economy since 1850. 3rd ed. London: Longmans Green, 1975. 318 pp.
62. Bairoch, Paul. "Europe's Gross National Product 1800-1975." Journal of European Economic History 5 (1976), 273-340.
63. Baldwin, Robert E. Economic Development and Growth. 2nd ed. New York: J. Wiley, 1972.150 pp.
64. Barnes, Harry E. An Economic History of the Western World. New York: Harcourt, Brace & Company, 1937. 190 pp.
65. Below, Georg von. Probleme der Wirtschaftsgeschichte. Eine Einführung in das Studium der Wirtschaftsgeschichte. Tübingen: Mohr, 1920. 711 pp.
66. Bettelhelm, Charles. Esquisse d'un tableau économique de l'Europe (depuis 1928). Paris: Domat-Montchrestien, 1949. 356 pp.
67. Birnie, Arthur. An Economic History of Europe, 1760-1930. London: Methuen, 1930. 289 pp.
68. Blodgett, Ralph H. and Donald L. Kemmerer. Comparative Economic Development. New York: McGraw-Hill, 1956. 557 pp.
69. Blum, Jerome et al. The Emergence of the European World. London: Routledge & Kegan Paul, 1975. 539 pp.
70. Blum, Jerome et al. The European World since 1815. Triumph and Transition. London: Routledge & Kegan Paul, 1975. 585 pp.
71. Bogart, Ernest L. Economic History of Europe, 1700-1939. London: Longmans, Green & Company, 1942. 734 pp.
72. Borchardt, Knut. Europas Wirtschaftsgeschichte, ein Modell für Entwicklungsländer? Stuttgart: Kohlhammer, 1967. 32 pp.
73. Bowden, Witt et al. An Economic History of Europe Since 1750. New York: American Book, 1937; rpt. New York: 1970. 948 pp.
74. Brenner, Y. S. A Short History of Economic Progress. London: F. Cass, 1969. 304 pp.
75. Brome, Vincent. We Have Come a Long Way. London: Cassel, 1962. 278 pp. (German: Wiesbaden, 1964.)
76. Brusatti, Alois. Wirtschafts- und Sozialgeschichte des industriellen Zeitalters. 2nd ed. Cologne: Verlag Styria, 1968. 312 pp.
77. Buchanan, Norman S. and Howard S. Ellis. Approaches to Economic Development. New York: The Twentieth Century Fund, 1955. 494 pp.
78. Cairncross, Alexander K. Factors in Economic Development. London: Allen & Unwin, 1962. 346 pp.

79. Chaloner, William H. and Barrie M. Ratcliffe, eds. Trade and Transport. Essays in Economic History in Honour of T.S. Willan. Manchester: Manchester University Press, 1977. 293 pp.
80. Chandler, Alfred O., Jr. and Louis Galambos, eds. "Economic History, Retrospect and Prospect." The Journal of Economic History, 31 (1971), 1-258.
81. Cipolla, Carlo M., ed. The Fontana Economic History of Europe. 6 vols. London: Fontana Books, 1976-78. (German: Stuttgart, 1980).
82. Cipolla, Carlo M. Literacy and Development in the West. Harmondsworth, England: Penguin, 1969. 143 pp.
83. Clark, Colin. The Conditions of Economic Progress. 3rd ed. London: Macmillan, 1957. 720 pp.
84. Clough, Shepard B. The Economic Development of Western Civilization. New York: McGraw-Hill, 1959. 540 pp.
85. Clough, Shepard B. and Charles W. Cole. Economic History of Europe. 3rd ed. Boston: Heath, 1952. 917 pp.
86. Clough, Shepard B. et al., eds. Economic History of Europe. 20th Century. London: Macmillan, 1969. 384 pp.
87. Cole, George D. H. Introduction to Economic History, 1750-1950. London: St. Martin's Press, 1952. 232 pp.
88. Conze, Werner. "Der Wandel der Wirtschaftsordnung." in W. F. Mueller, ed., Die europäische Lebensordnung im Wandel, von der Zeitenwende bis zum 1. Weltkrieg. Stuttgart: Kohlhammer, 1959. pp. 83-103.
89. Craig, Gordon A. Europe Since 1815. 3rd ed. New York: Holt, Rinehart & Winston, 1974. 867 pp.
90. Crouzois, François. "The Economic History of Modern Europe." Journal of Economic History 31 (1971), 135-52.
91. Cunow, Heinrich. Entwicklung der kapitalistischen Wirtschaft in Deutschland, Frankreich, England und den Vereinigten Staaten von Amerika. Berlin: Dietz, 1931. 452 pp.
92. Daitz, Werner. "Die europäische Grossraumwirtschaft. Geschichtliche Grundlagen und näturliche Voraussetzungen." Diplomaten-Zeitung 14 (1940), 1-7.
93. Davis, Ralph. The Rise of the Atlantic Economies. London: Weidenfeld & Nicholson, 1973. 352 pp.
94. Day, Clive. Economic Development in Europe. A Revision and Extension of Economic Development in Modern Europe. New York: Macmillan, 1942. 746 pp.
95. Ellsworth, Paul T. The International Economy. 5th ed. New York: Macmillan, 1975. 564 pp.
96. Eyre, Edward, ed. Economic History of Europe Since the Reformation. London: Humphrey-Milford, 1937. 1328 pp.
97. Falkus, Malcolm E., ed. Readings in the History of Economic Growth. London: Oxford University Press, 1968. 391 pp.
98. Fischer, Wolfram. Wirtschaft und Gesellschaft im Zeitalter der Industrialisierung. Göttingen: Vandenhoeck & Ruprecht, 1972. 547 pp.
99. Friedlaender, Heinrich E. and Jacob Oser. Economic History of Modern Europe. New York: Prentice-Hall, 1953. 611 pp.
100. Gerschenkron, Alexander. "Approach to Economic History." in E. Henderson and L. Spaventa, eds. Guest Lectures in Economics. 20 Lectures ..., 1956-1961. Milan: Giuffre, 1962. pp. 3-18.
101. Gerschenkron, Alexander. Continuity in History and Other Essays. Cambridge, MA: Harvard University Press, 1968. 545 pp.
102. Gerschenkron, Alexander. Europe in the Russian Mirror. Four Lectures in Economic History. Cambridge, MA: Harvard University Press, 1970. 158 pp.
103. Gould, John D. Economic Growth in History. Survey and Analysis. London: Methuen, 1972. 460 pp.
104. Habakkuk, H. John. "Economic History of modern Europe." Journal of Economic History 18 (1958), 488-501.
105. Häpke, Rudolf and Erwin Wiskemann. Wirtschaftsgeschichte. 2 vols. Leipzig: Glöckner, 1928-33.
106. Harrison, Anthony. The Framework of Economic Activity. London: Macmillan, 1967. 189 pp.
107. Heaton, Herbert. Economic History of Europe. New York: Harper, 1936. 775 pp.
108. Heckscher, Eli F. The Continental System. An Economic Interpretation. Oxford: Clarendon, 1922. 420 pp.
109. Heilbroner, Robert L. The Making of Economic Society. 5th ed. Englewood Cliffs, NJ: Prentice-Hall, 1975. 299 pp.
110. Helleiner, Karl F., ed. Readings in European Economic History. Toronto: University of Toronto Press, 1946. 437 pp.

111. Henke, Rudolf. Geschichte und Theorie der Grossraumwirtschaft. Diss. Vienna, 1937. Pirna: Ostermann, 1939. 94 pp.
112. Hippel, Eike von. Grundfragen der Weltwirtschaftsordnung. Munich: Beck, 1980. 165 pp.
113. Hobson, John A. The Evolution of Modern Capitalism. 4th ed. New York: Macmillan, 1949. 510 pp.
114. Hoffmann, Walther G. et al. Das Wachstum der deutschen Wirtschaft seit der Mitte des 19. Jahrhunderts. Berlin: Springer, 1965. 842 pp.
115. Hohenberg, Paul M. A Primer on the Economic History of Europe. New York: Random House, 1968. 241 pp.
116. Hughes, Jonathan R. T. Industrialization and Economic History. Theses and Conjectures. New York: McGraw-Hill, 1970. 336 pp.
117. Jennings, Walter W. A History of the Economic and Social Progress of European Peoples. Lexington, KY: Kernel Press, 1936. 713 pp.
118. Jones, Eric L. The European Miracle. Environments, Economies, and Geopolitics in the History of Europe and Asia. Cambridge: Cambridge University Press, 1981. 276 pp.
119. Jusenius, Carol L. Economic Development and Political Change in a Labor Surplus Model. Diss. New York University, 1973. 232 pp.
120. Kellenbenz, Hermann, ed. Handbuch der europäischen Wirtschafts- und Sozialgeschichte. Stuttgart: Klett-Cotta, 1981. 79 pp.
121. Kemp, Tom. Historical Patterns of Industrialization. London: Longman, 1978. 183 pp.
122. Kenwood, A. G. and A. L. Lougheed. The Growth of the International Economy, 1820-1960. London: Allen & Unwin, 1971. 319 pp.
123. Kindleberger, Charles P. Economic Response. Comparative Studies in Trade, Finance and Growth. Cambridge, MA: Harvard University Press, 1978. 308 pp.
124. Kindleberger, Charles P. The Formation of Financial Centers. A Study in Comparative Economic History. Princeton, NJ: Princeton University Press, 1974. 82 pp.
125. Knapp, Vincent J. Europe in the Era of Social Transformation. 1700-Present. Englewood Cliffs, NJ: Prentice-Hall, 1976. 253 pp.
126. Knight, Melvin M. et al. Economic History of Europe. Boston: Houghton Mifflin, 1982. 813 pp.
127. Knittler, Herbert, ed. Wirtschafts- und sozialhistorische Beiträge. Festschrift für Alfred Hoffmann zum 75. Geburtstag. Munich: Oldenbourg, 1979. 480 pp.
128. Kranzberg, Melvin and Carroll W. Pursell, eds. Technology and Western Civilization. 2 vols. New York: Oxford University Press, 1967.
129. Kulischer, Josef. Allgemeine Wirtschaftsgeschichte des Mittelalters und der Neuzeit. 3rd ed. 2 vols. Munich: Oldenbourg, 1965.
130. Kurth, James R. "Industrial Change and Political Change. A European Perspective." in The New Authoritarianism in Latin America. Joint Committee on Latin American Studies. Princeton, NJ: Princeton University Press, 1979. pp. 319-62.
131. Kuske, Bruno. "Treibende Kräfte in der Entwicklung der wirtschaftlichen Teilräume Europas." in Nationale Wirtschaftsordnung und Grossraumwirtschaft. Beiträge der Gesellschaft für europäische Wirtschaftsplanung und Grossraumwirtschaft. Dresden: Meinhold, 1942. pp. 28-42.
132. Kuznets, Simon. Economic Growth of Nations. Total Output and Production Structure. Cambridge, MA: Harvard University Press, 1971. 363 pp.
133. Kuznets, Simon. Modern Economic Growth. Rate, Structure and Spread. New Haven, CT: Yale University Press, 1966. 528 pp.
134. Kuznets, Simon. Six Lectures on Economic Growth. Glencoe, IL: Free Press, 1959. 122 pp.
135. Lander, J. E. International Economic History. Industrialisation in the World Economy, 1830-1950. London: Macdonald & Evans, 1967. 298 pp.
136. Landes, David S., ed. The Rise of Capitalism. New York: Macmillan, 1966. 150 pp.
137. Landes, David S., ed. Western Europe. The Trials of Partnership. Lexington, MA: Lexington Books, 1976. 406 pp.
138. Levy, Hermann. England and Germany. Affinity and Contrast. Leigh-on-Sea, Essex: Thames Bank, 1949. 167 pp.
139. Lévy-Leboyer, Maurice and Paul Bairoch, eds. Disparities in Economic Development since the Industrial Revolution. New York: St. Martin's Press, 1981. 428 pp.
140. Lewis, W. Arthur. The Evolution of the International Economic Order. Princeton, NJ: Princeton University Press, 1978. 81 pp.

6   HISTORY OF ECONOMIC CONDITIONS

141. Ludat, Herbert, ed. Agrar-, Wirtschafts- und Sozialprobleme Mittel- und Osteuropas in Geschichte und Gegenwart. Wiesbaden: Harrassowitz, 1965. 503 pp.
142. Lutz, Burkart. Der kurze Traum immerwährender Prosperität. Eine Neuinterpretation der industriellkapitalistischen Entwicklung im Europa des 20. Jahrhunderts. Frankfurt a. M.: Campus, 1984. 272 pp.
143. Maczak, Antoni and William N. Parker, eds. Natural Resources in European History. Baltimore: Johns Hopkins University Press, 1979. 226 pp.
144. Maddison, Angus. "Economic Growth in Western Europe, 1870-1957." Banca Nazionale del Lavoro Quarterly Review 12 (1959), 58-102.
145. Maddison, Angus. Economic Growth in the West. London: Allen & Unwin, 1964. 246 pp.
146. Maddison, Angus. Phases of Capitalist Development. London: Oxford University Press, 1982. 274 pp.
147. Magdoff, Harry. "European Expansion Since 1763." in Imperialism. From the Colonial Age to the Present. Essays. New York: Monthly Review Press, 1978. pp. 17-75.
148. Maitra, Priyatosh. The Mainspring of Economic Development. London: Croom Helm, 1980. 162 pp.
149. Mauersberg, Hans. Wirtschafts- und Sozialgeschichte zentraleuropäischer Städte in neuerer Zeit. Dargestellt an den Beispielen von Basel, Frankfurt a.M., Hamburg, Hannover und München. Göttingen: Vandenhoeck & Ruprecht, 1960. 604 pp.
150. Moulin, Léo. L'aventure européenne. Introduction à une sociologie du développement économique de l'Occident. Bruges: De Tempel, 1972. 242 pp.
151. Mühlpfordt, Günter. "Der Übergang von Feudalismus zum Kapitalismus auf dem 'preussischen Weg.' Eine Gemeinsamkeit der russischen, polnischen und deutschen Geschichte." in E. Donnert, ed. Beiträge zur russischen, polnischen und deutschen Geschichte. Halle a. d. S.: Niemeyer, 1956. pp. 135-70.
152. Myrdal, Gunnar. An International Economy. New York: Harper, 1956. 381 pp.
153. North, Douglass C. "A New Economic History for Europe." Zeitschrift für die gesamte Staatswissenschaft 124 (1968), 139-47.
154. Nussbaum, Frederick L. A History of the Economic Institutions of Modern Europe. An Introduction to "Der moderne Kapitalismus" of Werner Sombart. New York: Crofts, 1933. 448 pp.
155. Obermann, Karl, ed. Probleme der Ökonomie und Politik in den Beziehungen zwischen Ost- und Westeuropa vom 17. Jahrhundert bis zur Gegenwart. Berlin: Rütten & Loening, 1960. 304 pp.
156. Ogg, Frederic. Economic Development of Modern Europe. New York: Macmillan, 1928. 861 pp.
157. Oppenheimer, Franz. Abriss einer Sozial- und Wirtschaftsgeschichte Europas von der Völkerwanderung bis zur Gegenwart. 3 vols. Jena: Fischer, 1929-35.
158. Parker, William N. Europe and the World Economy. Cambridge: Cambridge University Press, 1984. 270 pp.
159. Pollard, Sidney. European Economic Integration, 1815-1970. New York: Harcourt, Brace & Co., 1974. 180 pp.
160. Pollard, Sidney. The Integration of the European Economy since 1815. London: Allen & Unwin, 1981. 109 pp.
161. Pommery, Louis. Aperçu d'histoire économique contemporaine 1890-1945. Paris: De Médicis, 1947. 473 pp.
162. Post, John D. The Last Great Subsistence Crisis in the Western World. Baltimore: Johns Hopkins University Press, 1977. 240 pp.
163. Postan, Michael M. et al., eds., The Cambridge Economic History of Europe. 7 vols. Cambridge: Cambridge University Press, 1978.
164. Pounds, Norman J. G. An Historical and Political Geography of Europe. 2nd ed. London: G. G. Harrap, 1947. 540 pp. (German: Braunschweig, 1950).
165. Radandt, Hans, ed. Handbuch Wirtschaftsgeschichte. 2 vols. Berlin: Das Europäische Buch, 1981.
166. Renard, Georges F. and G. Weulersse. Le travail dans l'Europe moderne. Paris: Alcan, 1920. 524 pp.
167. Rostow, Walt W. How It All Began. Origins of the Modern Economy. London: Methuen, 1975. 264 pp.
168. Rostow, Walt W. The World Economy: History and Prospect. Austin: University of Texas Press, 1978. 833 pp.
169. Roth, Günter D. Kurze Wirtschaftsgeschichte Mitteleuropas. Munich: Oldenbourg, 1961. 272 pp.

170. Schambach, Joseph. Die Rolle des Staates in den verschiedenen Wirtschaftssystemen seit dem 17. Jahrhundert bis heute und über die Notwendigkeit ihrer Erweiterung zur endgültigen Verhinderung von Massenarbeitslosigkeiten. Frankfurt a. M.: R. G. Fischer, 1980. 188 pp.
171. Schmidtchen, Volker and Eckhard Jäger. Wirtschaft, Technik und Geschichte. Beiträge zur Erforschung der Kulturbeziehungen in Deutschland und Osteuropa. Festschrift für Albrecht Timm zum 65. Geburtstag. Berlin: U. Camen, 1980. 392 pp.
172. Scoville, Warren C. and J. Clayburn La Force, eds. The Economic Development of Western Europe. 5 vols. Lexington, MA: Heath, 1969-70.
173. Senghaas, Dieter. Von Europa lernen: entwicklungsgeschichtliche Betrachtungen. Frankfurt a. M.: Suhrkamp, 1982. 355 pp.
174. Soltau, Roger H. An Outline of European Economic Development. London: Longmans, Green, 1935. 307 pp.
175. Sombart, Werner. Der moderne Kapitalismus. Historisch-systematische Darstellung des gesamteuropäischen Wirtschaftslebens von seinen Anfängen bis zur Gegenwart. 3 vols. Munich: Duncker & Humblot, 1928.
176. Stearns, Peter N. The European Experience Since 1815. New York: Harcourt Brace Jovanovich, 1972. 476 pp.
177. Stearns, Peter N. European Society in Upheaval. Social History Since 1800. New York: Macmillan, 1967. 425 pp.
178. Studenski, Paul. The Income of Nations. Theory, Measurement and Analysis, Past and Present. New York: New York University Press, 1958. 554 pp.
179. Svennilson, Ingvar. Growth and Stagnation in the European Economy. Geneva: United Nations, 1954. 342 pp.
180. Tilly, Charles and Richard H. Tilly. "Agenda for European Economic History in the 1970s." Journal of Economic History 31 (1971),184-98.
181. Treue, Wilhelm. "Das wirtschaftliche und soziale Gefüge." in F. Valjavec, ed. Historia mundi. Bern: Francke, 1961. X, 546-652.
182. Treue, Wilhelm. Wirtschaftsgeschichte der Neuzeit 1700-1965. 3rd ed. 2 vols. Stuttgart: Kröner, 1973.
183. Tuma, Elias H. European Economic History. Tenth Century to the Present. Theory and History of Economic Change. New York: Harper & Row, 1971. 384 pp.
184. Usher, Abbot P. et al. An Economic History of Europe since 1750. New York: American Book, 1937. 948 pp.
185. Viljoen, Stephan. Economic Systems in World History. London: Longman, 1974. 313 pp.
186. Vries, Johan de. "Kooplieden en bankiers, de Europese dimensie." Maandschrift Economie 42 (1978), 61-79.
187. Weber, Max. Gesammelte Aufsätze zur Sozial- und Wirtschaftsgeschichte. Tübingen: Mohr, 1924. 556 pp.
188. Weber, Max. Wirtschaftsgeschichte. Berlin: Duncker & Humblot, 1924; rpt. Washington, D. C.: 1981. 348 pp.
189. Wexler, Imanuel. The Marshall Plan Revisited: The European Recovery Program in Economic Perspective. Westport, CT: Greenwood Press, 1983. 327 pp.
190. Woodruff, William. The Impact of Western Man: A Study of Europe's Role in the World Economy 1750-1960. New York: St. Martin's Press, 1966; rpt. Washington, D.C.: 1972. 375 pp.
191. Youngson, Alexander J., ed. Economic Development in the Long Run. London: Allen & Unwin, 1972. 256 pp.

SEE ALSO: 2702, 2709, 2719, 4194.

CENTRAL EUROPE--1815-1918

Bibliographic References

192. Bullock, Alan L. C. and Alan J. P. Taylor. Select List of Books on European History, 1815-1914. 2nd ed. Oxford: Clarendon Press, 1957. 79 pp.
193. Enser, A. G. S. A Subject Bibliography of the First World War. Books in English. 1914-1978. London: A. Deutsch, 1979. 485 pp.

194. Mitchell, Brian R. The Fontana Economic History of Europe. Statistical Appendix 1700-1914. The Fontana Economic History of Europe, 4. London: Fontana Books, 1971. 87 pp.
195. Reeves, Dorothea D., ed. Harvard Unversity. Graduate School of Business Administration. Resources for the Study of Economic History: A Preliminary Guide to Pre-Twentieth Century Printed Material in Collections Located in Certain American and British Libraries. Boston: Baker Library, 1961. 62 pp.

CENTRAL EUROPE--1815-1918

196. Adelman, Irma and Cynthia T. Morris. "Patterns of Industrialization in the Nineteenth and Early Twentieth Centuries." Research in Economic History 5 (1980), 1-84.
197. Ahr, Wilhelm. Kriegswesen und Volkswirtschaft der Grossmächte während der letzten 30 Jahre. 2nd ed. Berlin: Verlag Vossische Buchhandlung, 1910. 44 pp.
198. Ashworth, William. "Typologies and Evidence; Has Nineteenth-Century Europe a Guide to Economic Growth?" Economic History Review 30 (1977), 140-158.
199. Bakeless, John. The Economic Causes of Modern War. A Study of the Period 1878-1918. New York: Williams College Dept. of Political Science, 1921. 265 pp.
200. Barnes, Thomas G. and Gerald D. Feldman. Nationalism, Industrialisation and Democracy, 1815-1914. Boston: Little Brown, 1972. 317 pp.
201. Berend, Iván T. and György Ránki. The European Periphery and Industrialization 1780-1914. Cambridge: Cambridge University Press, 1982. 180 pp.
202. Berend, Iván T. and György Ránki. "Underdevelopment in Europe in the Context of East-West Relations in the Nineteenth Century." Etudes Historiques Hongroises (1980), 687-710.
203. Binkley, Robert C. Realism and Nationalism 1852-1871. New York: Harper & Row, 1963. 338 pp.
204. Blanqui, Adolf. "Histoire de l'économie politique en Europe depuis les anciens jusqu'à nos jours." in Cours d'économie politique. Brussels: Société typog. belge, 1843. pp. 1-213. (German: Karlsruhe, 1840-41).
205. Brinkmann, Carl. "Weltpolitik und Weltwirtschaft im 19. Jahrhundert." Weltwirtschaftliches Archiv 16 (1920-21), 186-211.
206. Brunn, Geoffrey. Nineteenth Century European Civilization, 1815-1914. London: Oxford University Press, 1959. 256 pp.
207. Bury, John P. T., ed. The Zenith of European Power, 1830-1870. New Cambridge Modern History, 10. Cambridge: Cambridge University Press, 1960. 766 pp.
208. Cameron, Rondo E. France and the Economic Development of Europe 1800-1914. Conquests of Peace and Seeds of War. Princeton, NJ: Princeton University Press, 1961. 586 pp.
209. Clapham, John H. The Economic Development of France and Germany, 1815-1914. 4th ed. Cambridge: Cambridge University Press, 1955. 420 pp.
210. La crisis europea de 1848, aspectos politicos, sociales y economicos. Madrid: Real Academia de ciencias morales y politicas, 1949. 96 pp.
211. Crouzet, François et al., eds. Essays in European Economic History 1789-1914. New York: St. Martin's Press, 1969. 280 pp.
212. Fieldhouse, David K. Economics and Empire, 1830-1914. Ithaca, NY: Cornell University Press, 1973. 527 pp.
213. Fuchs, Rudolf. Die Kriegsgewinne der verschiedenen Wirtschaftszweige in den einzelnen Staaten an Hand statistischer Daten dargestellt. Diss. Zurich. Zurich: Müller, 1918. 162 pp.
214. Gülich, Gustav von. Geschichtliche Darstellung des Handels, der Gewerbe und des Ackerbaus der bedeutendsten handeltreibenden Staaten unsrer Zeit. 5 vols. Jena: Frommann, 1830-45.
215. Hamerow, Theodore S. The Birth of a New Europe: State and Society in the Nineteenth Century. Chapel Hill: University of North Carolina Press, 1983. 447 pp.
216. Hartwell, Ronald M. "Economic Change in England and Europe 1780-1830." in New Cambridge Modern History. Cambridge: Cambridge University Press, 1965. IX, 31-59.
217. Haussherr, Hans. Wirtschaftsgeschichte der Neuzeit. Vom Ende des 14. bis zur Höhe des 19. Jahrhunderts. 3rd ed. Graz: Böhlau, 1960. 544 pp.
218. Henderson, William O. Britain and Industrial Europe, 1750-1860: Studies in British Influence on the Industrial Revolution in Western Europe. 3rd ed. Leicester: Leicester University Press, 1972. 267 pp.

219. Herkner, Heinrich. Die wirtschaftliche Annäherung zwischen dem Deutschen Reiche und seinen Verbündeten. 3 vols. Munich: Duncker & Humblot, 1916.
220. Herkner, Heinrich. "Die wirtschaftlichen und sozialen Bewegungen von der Mitte des 18. Jahrhunderts bis in die zweite Hälfte des 19. Jahrhunderts." in Die Französische Revolution. Napoleon und die Restauration 1789-1848. Propyläen Weltgeschichte, 7. Berlin: Propyläen Verlag, 1929. pp. 331-406.
221. Hinsley, Francis H., ed. Material Progress and World-Wide Problems, 1870-98. The New Cambridge Modern History, 11. Cambridge: Cambridge University Press, 1962. 732 pp.
222. Hobsbawm, Eric J. The Age of Capital. Europe 1848-1875. London: Weidenfeld & Nicolson, 1975. 354 pp.
223. Hobsbawm, Eric J. The Age of Revolution. Europe 1789-1848. London: Weidenfeld & Nicolson, 1962. 356 pp.
224. Industrial Power and National Rivalry 1870-1914. London: Arnold, 1972. 509 pp.
225. Jindra, Zdenek. "Uber die ökonomischen Grundlagen der 'Mitteleuropa'-Ideologie des deutschen Imperialismus." in Probleme der Ökonomie und Politik in den Beziehungen zwischen Ost- und Westeuropa vom 17. Jahrhundert bis zur Gegenwart. Berlin: Rütten & Loening, 1960. pp. 139-62.
226. Knowles, Lilian C. A. Economic Development in the Nineteenth Century. France, Germany, Russia, and the United States. London: Routledge, 1932. 368 pp.
227. Kuske, Bruno. Die Bedeutung Europas für die Entwicklung der Weltwirtschaft. Cologne: O. Müller, 1924. 114 pp.
228. Landes, David S. "Technological Change and Development in Western Europe 1750-1914." in Cambridge Economic History of Europe. Cambridge: Cambridge University Press, 1965. VI, 274-601.
229. Lewis, W. Arthur. Growth and Fluctuations, 1870-1913. London: Allen & Unwin, 1978. 333 pp.
230. McManners, John. European History 1789-1914. Men, Machines and Freedom. Oxford: Blackwell, 1966; rpt. New York: 1969. 438 pp.
231. Milward, Alan S. and S. B. Saul. The Development of the Economies of Continental Europe, 1850-1914. London: Allen & Unwin, 1977. 555 pp.
232. Milward, Alan S. and S. B. Saul. The Economic Development of Continental Europe 1780-1870. 2nd ed. London: Allen & Unwin, 1979. 548 pp.
233. Morazé, Charles. Les bourgeois conquérants. Paris: Colin, 1957. 492 pp. (German: Düsseldorf, 1959).
234. Nachimson, Miron. Imperialismus und Handelskriege. Eine volkswirtschaftliche Untersuchung über die Entwicklungstendenzen der modernen Wirtschaft und der Handelspolitik. Bern: Wyss, 1917. 167 pp.
235. Nef, John U. "War and the Early Industrial Revolution." in Economic Problems of War and its Aftermath. Chicago: 1942; rpt. Freeeport, NY: Books for Libraries Press, 1972. pp. 1-53.
236. Pönicke, Herbert. Die wirtschaftliche und soziale Entwicklung Europas im 19. Jahrhundert. Paderborn: Schöningh, 1974. 111 pp.
237. Roth, Günter D. Kurze Wirtschaftsgeschichte Mitteleuropas. Von den Zünften zur industriellen Revolution. Munich: Oldenbourg, 1961. 272 pp.
238. Shotwell, James T., ed. Economic and Social History of the World War. Washington, D. C. : Carnegie Endowment for International Peace, 1926- . (German: 12 vols. Stuttgart: 1927-37).
239. Théry, Edmond. L'europe économique. Paris: Economiste Européen, 1911. 332 pp.
240. Viallate, Achille. L'impérialisme économique et les relations internationales pendant le dernier demi-siècle (1870-1920). Paris: Colin, 1923. 316 pp.
241. Waller, Bruce. "Bismarck, the Dual Alliance and Economic Central Europe, 1877-1885." VSWG 63 (1976), 454-67.
242. Woodruff, William. "The Emergence of an International Economy, 1759-1914." in C. M. Cipolla, ed. The Emergence of Industrial Societies. Fontana Economic History of Europe, vol. 4, pt. 2. Glasgow: Fontana, 1973.

CENTRAL EUROPE--1919-1945

References

243. Enser, A. G. S. A Subject Bibliography of the Second World War. Boulder, CO: Westview Press, 1972. 592 pp.
244. Lewis, W. Arthur. Economic Survey, 1919-1939. London: Allen & Unwin, 1960. 221 pp.

CENTRAL EUROPE--1919-1945

245. Aldcroft, Derek H. From Versailles to Wall Street, 1919-1929. London: Allen Lane, 1977. 372 pp.
246. Arndt, Heinz W. The Economic Lessons of the Nineteen-Thirties. London: F. Cass, 1963. 314 pp.
247. Aubert, Louis. The Reconstruction of Europe. New Haven, CT: Yale University Press, 1925. 180 pp.
248. Boettler, H. E. "Significant Economic Developments Since the Armistice." Journal of Accountancy 41 (1926), 341-52.
249. Brunner, Karl, ed. The Great Depression Revisited. The Hague: Nijhoff, 1980. 360 pp.
250. Davis, Joseph S. The World Between the Wars, 1919-39. An Economist's View. Baltimore: Johns Hopkins University Press, 1975. 436 pp.
251. Day, John P. An Introduction to World Economic History Since the Great War. London: Macmillan, 1939. 161 pp.
252. Eichholtz, Dietrich. "Kriegswirtschaftliche Resultate der Okkupationspolitik des faschistischen deutschen Imperialismus, 1939 bis 1944." Militärgeschichte 17 (1978), 133-51.
253. The End of the Old Europe, 1914-1939. London: Arnold, 1973. 623 pp.
254. Feldman, Gerald R. "Socio-Economic Structures in the Industrial Sector and Revolutionary Potentialities 1917-22." in C. L. Bernard, ed. Revolutionary Situations in Europe 1917-22. Montreal: Interuniversity Center for European Studies, 1977. pp. 159-69.
255. Fischer, Wolfram. Weltwirtschaftliche Rahmenbedingungen für die ökonomische und politische Entwicklung Europas 1919-1939. Wiesbaden: Steiner, 1980. 33 pp.
256. Friedman, Philip. "An Econometric Model of National Income, Commercial Policy and the Level of International Trade. The Open Economies of Europe, 1924-38." Journal of Economic History 38 (1978), 148-80.
257. Friedman, Philip. The Impact of Trade Destruction on National Incomes. A Study of Europe, 1924-38. Gainesville: University Presses of Florida, 1974. 150 pp.
258. Haberler, Gottfried. The World Economy, Money, and the Great Depression 1919-1939. Washington, D. C.: American Enterprise Institute for Public Policy Research, 1976. 48 pp.
259. Hill, Martin. The Economic and Financial Organization of the League of Nations. A Survey of Twenty-Five Years' Experience. Washington, D. C.: Carnegie Endowment for International Peace, 1946. 168 pp.
260. Kaiser, David E. Economic Diplomacy and the Origins of the Second World War: Germany, Britain, France, and Eastern Europe, 1930-1939. Princeton: Princeton University Press, 1981. 346 pp.
261. Kapp, Karl W. The League of Nations and Raw Materials, 1919-39. Geneva: Geneva Research Center, 1941. 64 pp.
262. Kindleberger, Charles P. The World in Depression, 1929-39. Berkeley: University of California Press, 1973. 336 pp.
263. Lawson, William R. Europe After the World War. A Financial and Economic Survey. London: "Financial News," 1921. 276 pp.
264. Leffler, Melvyn P. The Elusive Quest. America's Pursuit of European Stability and French Security, 1919-33. Chapel Hill: University of North Carolina Press, 1979. 409 pp.
265. Maier, Charles S. Recasting Bourgeois Europe. Stabilization in France, Germany and Italy in the Decade after World War I. Princeton, NJ: Princeton University Press, 1975. 650 pp.
266. Recker, Marie-Luise. England und der Donauraum 1919-1929. Probleme der europäischen Nachkriegsordnung. Stuttgart: Klett, 1976. 324 pp.
267. Samhaber, Ernst. Die neuen Wirtschaftsformen 1914-1940. Berlin: Neff, 1940. 364 pp.

268. Silverman, Dan P. Reconstructing Europe After the Great War. Cambridge, MA: Harvard University Press, 1982. 347 pp.

SEE ALSO: 15.

CENTRAL EUROPE--1945-1975

References

269. United Nations. Department of Economic and Social Affairs. World Economic Survey. New York: Columbia University Press, 1948- .
270. United Nations. Economic Commission for Europe. Economic Survey of Europe. Geneva: United Nations, 1947- .

CENTRAL EUROPE--1945-1975

271. Bayer, Kurt. Economic Conditions and Social Services in Europe, 1970-1975. Vienna: European Center for Social Welfare Training and Research, 1976. 19 pp.
272. Dillard, Dudley. Economic Development of the North Atlantic Community. Historical Introduction to Modern Economics. Englewood Cliffs, NJ: Prentice-Hall, 1967. 747 pp.
273. Engel, Ernst. "Die wirtschaftlichen Integrationsbestrebungen in der freien Welt nach 1945." Geschichte in Wissenschaft und Unterricht 10 (1959), 556-66.
274. Fanfani, Amintore. Età contemporanea. Storia economica, 2. Turin: Unione Tipograf., 1970. 528 pp.
275. Figueroa, Emilio de. "Hegemonía y declinación económica de Europa." in Estudios sobre la unidad económica de Europa. Madrid: Espasa-Calpe, 1952. II, 1-104.
276. Gimbel, John. The Origins of the Marshall Plan. Stanford, CA: Stanford University Press, 1976. 344 pp.
277. Hennessy, Josselyn et al. Economic Miracles. London: A. Deutsch, 1964. 228 pp.
278. Hoffmann, Stanley and Charles S. Maier, eds. The Marshall Plan: A Retrospective. Boulder, CO: Westview Press, 1984. 139 pp.
279. Kenney, Elinor M. The Origin of the Marshall Plan. Los Angeles: Bookman Press, [after 1950]. 107 pp.
280. Kindleberger, Charles P. Europe's Postwar Growth, the Role of Labor Supply. London: Oxford University Press, 1967. 288 pp.
281. Kulshreshtha, S. S. Economic Development of Modern Powers, U. S. S. R., U. S. A., Great Britain, Germany, and Japan. Allahabad: Kitab Mahal, 1966. 483 pp.
282. Lüdemann, Ernst, ed. Die Wirtschaft kapitalistischer Länder in Zahlen. Berlin: Institut für Internationale Politik und Wirtschaft der DDR, 1982. 175 pp.
283. Postan, Michael M. An Economic History of Western Europe, 1945-1964. London: Methuen, 1967. 382 pp.
284. Waterlow, Charlotte and Archibald Evans. Europe, 1945 to 1970. London: Methuen, 1973. 316 pp.
285. Wee, Herman van der and Paul M. M. Klep. "New Economic History of Europe Since the Second World War." in Michael D. Intriligator, ed. Frontiers of Quantitative Economics. New York: American Elsevier, 1977. IIIb, 417-28.
286. Wee, Herman van der and Paul M. M. Klep. "Quantitative Economic History in Europe Since the Second World War." Recherches Economiques de Louvain 41 (1975), 195-218.
287. Wilson, Theodore A. The Marshall Plan, 1947-1951. New York: Foreign Policy Association, 1977. 64 pp.

SEE ALSO: 189.

12   HISTORY OF ECONOMIC CONDITIONS

AUSTRIA

Bibliographic References

288. Malina, Peter and Gustav Spann. Bibliographie zur österreichischen Zeitgeschichte 1918-1978. Eine Auswahl. Vienna: Verlag für Geschichte und Politik, 1978. 70 pp.
289. Rausch, Wilhelm, ed. Bibliographie zur Geschichte der Städte Österreichs. Linz: J. Wimmer, 1984. 329 pp.

AUSTRIA

290. Berend, Iván T. and György Ránki. Economic Development in East Central Europe in the Nineteenth and Twentieth Centuries. New York: Columbia University Press, 1974. 402 pp.
291. Brusatti, Alois. Betrachtungen zur Wirtschafts- und Sozialgeschichte. Ausgewählte Schriften von Alois Brusatti aus Anlass seines 60. Geburtstages. Ed. Herbert Matis et al. Berlin: Duncker & Humblot, 1979. 226 pp.
292. Carlen, Louis and Fritz Steinegger, eds. Festschrift Nikolaus Grass. Zum 60. Geburtstag. 2 vols. Munich: Wagner, 1974-75.
293. Dittrich, Erich. Staatszerfall, Staatsneubildung und Wirtschaft. Eine Untersuchung über die Probleme der Volkswirtschaftsbildung in Österreich und der Tschechoslowakei. Leipzig: Noske, 1937. 162 pp.
294. Endres, Robert. Handbuch der österreichischen Staats- und Wirtschaftsgeschichte. Leipzig: Hasse, 1922. 156 pp.
295. Gerschenkron, Alexander. An Economic Spurt that Failed. Four Lectures in Austrian History. Princeton, NJ: Princeton University Press, 1977. 172 pp.
296. Gülich, Wilhelm. "Wirtschaftliche Entwicklung und volkliche Eigenständigkeit in Südosteuropa." Südosteuropa-Jahrbuch 3 (1958), 1-15.
297. Herbert, Walther H., ed. Österreich-Kunde. Land, Volk, Geschichte, Kultur, Bildung, Landwirtschaft, Gewerbliche Wirtschaft, Energie- und Verkehrswirtschaft, Aussenhandel, Währung, Kreditwesen, Verschuldung, Rechtswesen. Stuttgart: Wirtschaft und Verkehr, 1938. 246 pp.
298. Hertz, Friedrich. The Economic Problems of the Danubian States. A Study in Economic Nationalism. New York: H. Fertig, 1970. 223 pp.
299. Hoffmann, Alfred. Studien und Essays. Ed. Alois Mosser. Vienna: Verlag für Geschichte und Politik, 1979. 371 pp.
300. Hofmann, Victor. Beiträge zur neueren österreichischen Wirtschaftsgeschichte. 3 vols. Vienna: Archiv für Österreichische Geschichte, 1919-1932.
301. Knittler, Herbert, ed. Wirtschafts- und sozialhistorische Beiträge. Festschrift für Alfred Hoffmann zum 75. Geburtstag. Munich: Oldenbourg, 1979. 480 pp.
302. Kramer, Helmut, ed. Österreich im internationalen System. Vienna: Braumüller, 1983. 190 pp.
303. Lampe, John R. and Marvin R. Jackson. Balkan Economic History, 1550-1950. From Imperial Borderlands to Developing Nations. Bloomington: Indiana University Press, 1982. 728 pp.
304. Lendl, Egon. "Die alpine Wirtschaftslandschaft Österreichs in den letzten Jahrzehnten." Geographische Rundschau 8 (1956), 400-406.
305. Macartney, Carlile A. The Danube Basin. Oxford: Clarendon, 1941. 32 pp.
306. Mayer, Hans, ed. Hundert Jahre österreichischer Wirtschaftsentwicklung 1848-1948. Vienna: Springer, 1949. 714 pp.
307. Mentschl, Josef. Österreichische Wirtschaftspioniere. Vienna: Birken, 1959. 178 pp.
308. Mentschl, Josef and Gustav Otruba. Österreichische Industrielle und Bankiers. Vienna: Bergland, 1965. 184 pp.
309. Mitscherlich, Waldemar, ed. Die Ostmark. Eine Einführung in die Probleme ihrer Wirtschaftsgeschichte. Leipzig: Teubner, 1911. 153 pp.
310. Okey, Robin. Eastern Europe, 1740-1980. Feudalism to Communism. London: Hutchinson, 1982. 264 pp.
311. Otruba, Gustav. Die österreichische Wirtschaft im 20. Jahrhundert. Vienna: Bundesverlag, 1968. 113 pp.
312. Papesch, Josef et al., eds. Verwaltung, Wirtschaft und Technik. Graz: Steirische Verlagsanstalt, 1941. 212 pp.

313. Pasvolsky, Leo. Economic Nationalism of the Danubian States. New York: Macmillan, 1928. 609 pp.
314. Reiter, Ludwig. Kulturgeschichte und Wirtschaftsgeschichte Österreichs. Salzburg: Österreichischer Kulturverlag, 1952. 280 pp.
315. Rothschild, Kurt W. "Wurzeln und Triebkräfte der Entwicklung der österreichischen Wirtschaftsstruktur." in W. Weber, ed. Österreichs Wirtschaftsstruktur gestern, heute, morgen. Berlin: Duncker & Humblot, 1961. I, 1-157.
316. Spulber, Nikolas. The State and Economic Development in Eastern Europe. New York: Random House, 1966. 179 pp.
317. Tautscher, Anton. "Die Entwicklung der österreichischen Staatswirtschaft." Schmoller 89 (1969), 267-311. (English summary)
318. Tautscher, Anton. Wirtschaftsgeschichte Österreichs auf der Grundlage abendländischer Kulturgeschichte. Berlin: Duncker & Humblot, 1974. 811 pp.
319. Toch, Josef. Vergesellschaftung in Österreich. Von den Anfängen bis heute. Vienna: Verlag der ÖGB, 1962. 123 pp.
320. Tremel, Ferdinand. "Die Entwicklung der österreichischen Wirtschaft in der Ersten und Zweiten Republik." in B. Zimmel, ed. Hundert Jahre im Dienste der Wirtschaft. Vienna: Bundesministerium für Handel und Wiederaufbau, 1961.
321. Tremel, Ferdinand. Wirtschafts- und Sozialgeschichte Österreichs. Vienna: Deuticke, 1969. 486 pp.
322. Weber, Wilhelm, ed. Österreichische Wirtschaftsstruktur--gestern, heute, morgen. Strukturwandlungen der österreichischen Volkswirtschaft in der Vergangenheit und ihre Bedeutung für Strukturprobleme der Gegenwart und Zukunft. 2 vols. Berlin: Duncker & Humblot, 1961.
323. Die Wirtschaftsgeschichte Österreichs. Vienna: Hirt, 1971. 223 pp.
324. Zimmel, Bruno, ed. 100 Jahre im Dienste der Wirtschaft. Eine Festschrift. 2 vols. Vienna: Bundesministerium für Handel und Wiederaufbau, 1961.

SEE ALSO: 2896-97.

AUSTRIA-HUNGARY--1815-1918

Bibliographic Reference

325. Spann, Othmar. Bibliographie der Wirtschafts- und Sozialgeschichte des Weltkrieges. Vienna: Hölder-Pichler-Tempsky, 1923. 167 pp.

AUSTRIA-HUNGARY--1815-1918

326. Benedikt, Heinrich. Die wirtschaftliche Entwicklung in der Franz-Joseph-Zeit. Vienna: Herold, 1958. 200 pp.
327. Beurle, Carl. Die staatswirtschaftliche Bilanz eines Jahrhunderts. Linz: Steurer, 1910. 16 pp.
328. Breisach, Herma. Grundzüge der wirtschaftlichen Entwicklung Österreich-Ungarns 1909-1914. Diss. Vienna, 1950. 214 pp.
329. Brenman, Andrew H. Economic Reform in Neuzeit Austria 1852-1859. Diss. Princeton, 1966. 341 pp.
330. Brusatti, Alois. Österreichische Wirtschaftspolitik vom Josephinismus zum Ständestaat. Vienna: Jupiter-Verlag, 1965. 164 pp.
331. Brusatti, Alois. "Die wirtschaftliche Situation Österreich-Ungarns." in Österreich am Vorabend des Ersten Weltkriegs. Graz: Stiasny, 1964.
332. Brusatti, Alois. "Die wirtschaftlichen Folgen des Ausgleichs von 1867." in Der österreichisch-ungarische Ausgleich von 1867. Vienna: Forschungsinstitut für den Donauraum, 1967. pp. 127-42.
333. Brusatti, Alois, ed. Die wirtschaftliche Entwicklung. Vienna: Österreichische Akademie der Wissenschaften, 1973. 666 pp.

334. Charmatz, Richard. Österreichs innere Geschichte von 1848 bis 1907. Leipzig: B. G. Teubner, 1909. 128 pp.
335. Czoernig, Carl Freiherr von. Österreich's Neugestaltung 1848-1858. Stuttgart: Cotta, 1858. 728 pp.
336. Engel-Janosi, Friedrich. "Über die Entwicklung der sozialen und wirtschaftlichen Verhältnisse im deutschen Österreich 1815-1848." VSWG 17 (1924), 95-108.
337. Entwicklung von Industrie und Gewerbe in Österreich in den Jahren 1848-1888. Vienna: Niederösterreichischer Gewerbeverein, 1888. 407 pp.
338. Freudenberger, Herman. "State Intervention as an Obstacle to Economic Growth in the Habsburg Monarchy." Journal of Economic History 27 (1967), 493-517.
339. Good, David F. The Economic Rise of the Habsburg Empire, 1750-1914. Berkeley: University of California Press, 1984. 309 pp.
340. Gratz, Gustav and Richard Schüller. The Economic Policy of Austria-Hungary During the War in its External Relations. New Haven, CT: Yale University Press, 1928. 286 pp. (German: Vienna, 1925)
341. Gratz, Gustav and Richard Schüller. Der wirtschaftliche Zusammenbruch Österreich-Ungarns. Die Tragödie der Erschöpfung. Vienna: Hölder-Pichler-Tempsky, 1930. 307 pp.
342. Gross, Nachum T. "Die Stellung der Habsburgermonarchie in der Weltwirtschaft." in A. Wandruszka and P. Urbanitsch, eds. Die Habsburgermonarchie, 1848-1918. Vienna: Österreichische Akademie der Wissenschaften, 1973. I, 1-28.
343. Haber, Franz. Österreichs Wirtschaftsbilanz. Ein Vergleich mit der Vorkriegszeit. Munich: Duncker & Humblot, 1928. 169 pp.
344. Hertz, Friedrich. The Economic Problem of the Danubian States. New York: H. Fertig, 1970. 223 pp.
345. Huertas, Thomas F. Economic Growth and Economic Policy in a Multinational Setting (The Habsburg Monarchy, 1841-1865). New York: Arno Press, 1977. 114 pp.
346. Kann, Robert A. The Multinational Empire. Nationalism and the National Reform in the Habsburg Monarchy, 1840-1918. 2 vols. New York: Columbia University Press, 1950.
347. Komlós, John, Jr. The Habsburg Monarchy as a Customs Unions: Economic Development in Austria-Hungary in the Nineteenth Century. Princeton, NJ: Princeton University Press, 1983. 347 pp.
348. Krizek, Jurij. "Die Kriegswirtschaft und das Ende der Monarchie." in Die Auflösung des Habsburgerreiches. Munich: Oldenburg, 1970. pp. 43-52.
349. Krizek, Jurij. Die wirtschaftlichen Grundzüge des österreichisch-ungarischen Imperialismus in der Vorkriegszeit (1900-1914). Prague: Ceskoslov. akad. ved., 1963. 122 pp.
350. Lopuszanski, Eugen. Die Volkswirtschaft Österreichs in den Jahren 1900 bis 1904. Vienna: A. Hölder, 1904. 111 pp.
351. Macartney, Carlile A. The Habsburg Empire, 1790-1918. London: Weidenfeld & Nicolson, 1971. 908 pp.
352. Macartney, Carlile A. The House of Austria: The Later Phase, 1790-1918. Edinburgh: Edinburgh University Press, 1978. 306 pp.
353. März, Eduard. "Einige Besonderheiten in der Entwicklung der österreichischen Volkswirtschaft im 19. Jahrhundert." Sozialwissenschaftliche Annalen des Instituts für Höhere Studien 1 (1977), 87-107.
354. März, Eduard. "Some Economic Aspects of the Nationality Conflict in the Habsburg Empire." Journal of Central European Affairs 13 (1953), 123-35.
355. Marx, Julius. Die wirtschaftlichen Ursachen der Revolution von 1848 in Österreich. Graz: Böhlau, 1965. 207 pp.
356. Marx, Julius. "Die Wirtschaftslage im deutschen Österreich vor Ausbruch der Revolution 1848." VSWG 31 (1938), 242-82.
357. Matis, Herbert. "Leitlinien der österreichischen Wirtschaftspolitik." in A. Wandruszka and P. Urbanitsch, eds. Die Habsburgermonarchie 1848-1918. Vienna: Österreichische Akademie der Wissenschaften, 1973. I, 29-67.
358. Matis, Herbert. Österreichs Wirtschaft 1848-1913. Konjunkturelle Dynamik und gesellschaftlicher Wandel im Zeitalter Franz Josephs I. Berlin: Duncker & Humblot, 1972. 490 pp.
359. Matis, Herbert, ed. Von der Glückseligkeit des Staates. Staat, Wirtschaft und Gesellschaft in Österreich im Zeitalter des aufgeklärten Absolutismus. Berlin: Duncker & Humblot, 1981. 558 pp.

360. May, Arthur J. The Hapsburg Monarchy, 1867-1914. Cambridge, MA: Harvard University Press, 1960. 532 pp.
361. Mitrany, David. The Effect of the War in South-Eastern Europe. New Haven, CT: Yale University Press, 1936. 282 pp.
362. Neck, Rudolf. "Wirtschaftliche und soziale Probleme während der Regierungszeit Kaiser Franz Josephs I." Österreich in Geschichte und Literatur 10 (1966), 462-69.
363. Neydl, Anton W. Die wirtschaftlichen Verhältnisse und Zustände Österreichs, 1848-1876. Vienna: Hartleben, 1876. 64 pp.
364. Otruba, Gustav. "Wirtschaft und soziale Lage Österreichs im Vormärz." Österreich in Geschichte und Literatur 10 (1966), 161-76.
365. Palotas, Emil. "Ziele und geschichtliche Realität: Wirtschaftsbestrebungen Österreich-Ungarns auf dem Balkan zur Zeit des Berliner Kongresses im Jahre 1878." Etudes Historiques Hongroises (1980), 651-85.
366. Pistor, Erich. Die Volkswirtschaft Österreich-Ungarns und die Verständigung mit Deutschland. Berlin: G. Reimer, 1915. 175 pp.
367. Putz, Franz. Die österreichische Wirtschaftsaristokratie von 1815-1859. Diss. Vienna, 1975. 504 pp.
368. Reimann, Paul. "Die grundlegenden Entwicklungstendenzen des Imperialismus in Österreich-Ungarn. Jahrbuch für Geschichte der UdSSR und der Volksdemokratischen Länder Europas 4 (1960), 122-73.
369. Rudolph, Richard L. et al. "Social Structure and the Beginning of Austrian Economic Growth." East Central Europe 7 (1980), 207-24.
370. Sandgruber, Roman. "Lebensstandard und wirtschaftliche Entwicklung im österreichischen Neo-absolutismus (1848-1859)." in H. Knittler, ed. Wirtschafts- und sozialhistorische Beiträge. Festschrift für Alfred Hoffmann zum 75. Geburtstag. Munich: Colloguium, 1979. pp. 372-94.
371. Stadler, Karl R. "The Disintegration of the Austrian Empire." Journal of Contemporary History 3 (1968), 177-90.
372. Stavrianos, Leften S. The Balkans, 1815-1914. New York: Holt, Rinehart & Winston, 1963. 135 pp.
373. Stojanovic, Mihailo D. The Great Powers and the Balkans, 1875-78. Cambridge: Cambridge University Press, 1939; rpt. 1968. 296 pp.
374. Studien zur Wirtschaftsgeschichte Grossbritanniens, der USA und der ehemaligen Habsburgischen Monarchie. Leipzig: Grundstoffindustrie, 1983. 128 pp.
375. Taylor, A. J. P. The Habsburg Monarchy, 1809-1918. New York: Harper & Row, 1965. 279 pp.
376. Thalmann, Friedrich. "Die Wirtschaft in Österreich." in H. Benedikt, ed. Geschichte der Republik Österreich. Vienna: Verlag für Geschichte und Politik, 1954. pp. 487-572.
377. Todorov, Nikolai. "The Genesis of Capitalism in the Balkan Provinces of the Ottoman Empire in the Nineteenth Century." Explorations in Economic History 7 (1969-70), 313-24.
378. Tremel, Ferdinand. "Die wirtschaftlichen Folgen der Revolution." in Österreich, 1848-1918. Graz: Stiasny, 1959. pp. 46-57.
379. Die Volkswirtschaft der Nationalstaaten. Vienna: Allgemeine Depositenbank, 1921. 80 pp.
380. Wandruszka, Adam et al., eds. Die Donaumonarchie und die südslawische Frage von 1848-1918. Vienna: Österreichische Akademie der Wissenschaften, 1978. 184 pp.
381. Wandruszka, Adam and Peter Urbanitsch, eds. Die Habsburgermonarchie 1848-1918. 3 vols. Vienna: Österreichische Akademie der Wissenschaften, 1973-80.
382. Warriner, Doreen, ed. Contrasts in Emerging Societies. Readings in the Social and Economic History of South-Eastern Europe in the Nineteenth Century. Bloomington: Indiana University Press, 1965. 402 pp.
383. Wegs, Robert. Die österreichische Kriegswirtschaft 1914-1918. Vienna: Schendl, 1979. 194 pp.
384. Wessely, Kurt. "Österreich-Ungarns Wirtschaft vor dem Ersten Weltkrieg." Donauraum 12 (1967), 13-37.
385. Wisshaupt, Erhard. Die wirtschaftliche und soziale Lage in Oesterreich von 1830-1939. Nach amtlichen Berichten. Diss. Vienna, 1952. 260 pp.
386. Wysocki, Josef. Infrastruktur und wachsende Staatsausgaben. Das Fallbeispiel Österreichs 1868-1913. Stuttgart: G. Fischer, 1975. 257 pp.

SEE ALSO: 2112.

AUSTRIA--1919-1945

387. Andics, Hellmut. Der Staat, den keiner wollte. Österreich 1918-1938. Vienna: Herder, 1962. 562 pp.
388. Bardy, Roland. "Die österreichische Wirtschaft während des Zweiten Weltkrieges (Ein Überblick)." Österreich in Geschichte und Literatur 10 (1966), 213-222.
389. Bayer, Hans. Strukturwandlungen der österreichischen Volkswirtschaft nach dem Kriege. Vienna: F. Deuticke, 1929. 176 pp.
390. Butschek, Felix. Die österreichische Wirtschaft, 1938-1945. Stuttgart: Fischer, 1978. 160 pp.
391. Edelstein, Robert. Vienne et la situation économique de l'Autriche de 1918-1928. Diss. Neuchâtel, 1930. 145 pp.
392. "Die Entwicklung der ostmärkischen Wirtschaft seit der Wiedervereinigung mit dem Reich." Monatsberichte des Wiener Institutes für Wirtschafts- und Konjunkturforschung 13 (1939), 29-107.
393. Gulik, Charles A. Austria from Habsburg to Hitler. 2 vols. Berkeley: University of California Press, 1948.
394. Hasslacher, Franz. Die wirtschaftliche Entwicklung in der Ostmark im ersten Jahre nach dem Anschluss. Vienna: Hasslacher, 1939. 15 pp.
395. Lovin, Clifford R. "Food, Austria and the Supreme Economic Council, 1919." East European Quarterly 12 (1979), 475-89.
396. Romanik, Felix. Der Leidensweg der österreichischen Wirtschaft 1933-1945. Vienna: Bundesverlag, 1957. 142 pp.
397. Rothschild, Joseph. East Central Europe Between the Two World Wars. Washington, D. C.: American University Publishers Group, 1975. 420 pp.
398. Rothschild, Kurt. Austria's Economic Development Between the Two Wars. London: F. Muller, 1947. 108 pp.
399. Schausberger, Norbert. "Der wirtschaftliche Anschluss Österreichs 1938." Österreich in Geschichte und Literatur 15 (1971), 249-73.
400. Seton-Watson, Hugh. Eastern Europe Between the Wars, 1918-1941. Hamden, CT: Archon Books, 1962. 425 pp.
401. Tremel, Ferdinand. "Die wirtschaftliche Situation der ersten Republik." Österreich in Geschichte und Literatur 2 (1958), 138-57.

SEE ALSO: 385.

AUSTRIA--1945-1975

402. Ausch, Karl. Erlebte Wirtschaftsgeschichte. Österreichs Wirtschaft seit 1945. Vienna: Europa, 1963. 359 pp.
403. Ausch, Karl. Licht und Irrlicht des österreichischen Wirtschaftswunders. Vienna: Wiener Volksbuchhandlung, 1965. 380 pp.
404. Brusatti, Alois and Karl Bachinger. "Österreichs Wirtschaft in der Zweiten Republik. Wirtschaftsentwicklung, Wirtschaftspolitik, Sozialpolitik." in K. Gutkas et al. Österreich 1945 bis 1970. 25 Jahre Zweite Republik. Vienna: Bundesverlag, 1970. 364 pp.
405. Butschek, Felix. "Österreichs Wirtschaft. Vom Zusammenbruch zum Staatsvertrag." Europäische Rundschau 8 (1980), 67-77.
406. Haberler, Gottfried. "Austria's Economic Development After the Two World Wars: A Mirror Picture of the World Economy." in S. W. Arndt, ed. The Political Economy of Austria. Washington, D. C.: American Enterprise Institute for Public Policy Research, 1982. pp. 61-75.
407. Hollerer, Siegfried. Verstaatlichung und Wirtschaftsplanung in Österreich (1946-1949). Diss. Hochschule für Welthandel Vienna, 1972. Vienna: VWGÖ, 1974. 258 pp.
408. Jeglitsch, Helmut. "Die österreichische Wirtschaft nach Bundesländern 1969 bis 1972." Monatsberichte. Österreichisches Institut für Wirtschaftsforschung 46 (1973), 455-72.
409. März, Eduard. Österreichs Wirtschaft zwischen Ost und West. Vienna: Europa, 1965. 293 pp.
410. Matis, Herbert. "Das Jahr 1945--die wirtschaftliche Ausgangsituation." Österreich in Geschichte und Literatur 19 (1975), 289-98.

411. Nemschak, Franz. Österreich's Wirtschaft in den sechziger und siebziger Jahren: Rückschau und Ausblick. Vienna: Österreichisches Institut für Wirtschaftsforschung, 1970. 28 pp.
412. Nemschak, Franz. "Österreichs Wirtschaft seit Kriegsende." Schweizer Monatshefte 33 (1953), 1-10.
413. Nemschak, Franz. Ten Years of Austrian Economic Development, 1945-55. Vienna: Association of Austrian Industrialists, 1955. 87 pp. (German: Vienna, 1955)
414. Rothschild, Kurt W. The Austrian Economy Since 1945. London: Royal Institute of International Affairs, 1950. 82 pp.
415. Seidel, Hans et al. Die regionale Dynamik der österreichischen Wirtschaft. Vienna: Österreichisches Institut für Wirtschaftsforschung, 1966. 69 pp.
416. Tremel, Ferdinand. "Landeskundliche Literatur zur Wirtschafts- und Sozialgeschichte Österreichs 1943-1951." VSWG 40 (1953), 146-73.
417. Weber, Wilhelm. Wirtschaft in Politik und Recht. Am österreichischen Beispiel 1945-1970. Vienna: Europaverlag, 1972. 533 pp.

SEE ALSO: 376.

AUSTRIAN AND AUSTRO-HUNGARIAN REGIONS

Bohemia and Moravia

418. Basch, Antonin. Germany's Economic Conquest of Czechoslovakia. Chicago: Czechoslovak National Council of America, 1939. 29 pp.
419. Douglas, Dorothy W. Transitional Economic Systems. The Polish-Czech Example. New York: Monthly Review Press, 1972. 375 pp.
420. Gruber, Josef, ed. Czechoslovakia. A Survey of Economic and Social Conditions. New York: Macmillan, 1924; rpt. New York: Arno Press, 1971. 256 pp.
421. Heilig, Bernhard. Urkundliches zur Wirtschaftsgeschichte der Juden in Prossnitz. Brno: Jüdischer Buch- und Kunstverlag, 1929. 32 pp.
422. Medinger, Wilhelm. Wirtschaftsgeschichte der Domäne Lobositz. Diss. Halle a. d. Saale. Vienna: C. W. Stern, 1903. 203 pp.
423. Nachtmann, Erich. "Die wirtschaftliche und soziale Lage Brünns im Revolutionsjahr 1848/49." in Heimat und Volk. Forschungsbeiträge zur sudetendeutschen Geschichte. Festschrift für Wilhelm Wostry. Brno: R. M. Röhrer, 1937. pp. 521-43.
424. Necas, J. "Economic and Social Problems in German Bohemia." Slavonic and East European Review 15 (1937), 599-611.
425. Spiesz, Anton. "Die Slowakei in der Sozial- und Wirtschaftsgeschichte Mittel- und Osteuropas." Bohemia. Jahrbuch des Collegium Carolinum 10 (1969), 256-69.
426. Teichova, Alice. An Economic Background to Munich. International Business and Czechoslovakia, 1919-1938. Cambridge: Cambridge University Press, 1974. 422 pp.
427. Teichova, Alice. Forty Years After. An Economic Reassessment. Norwich: University of East Anglia, 1978.
428. Udalzov, I. I. Aufzeichnungen über die Geschichte des nationalen und politischen Kampfes in Böhmen im Jahre 1848. Berlin: Rütten & Loening, 1953. 235 pp. (Original: Moscow, 1951).

Burgenland

429. Bodo, Fritz, ed. Burgenland 1921-1938. Eine deutsches Grenzland im Südosten. Vienna: Österreichischer Landesverlag, 1941. 54 pp.
430. Fünfundzwanzig Jahre Burgenland. Eine Rückschau auf seine politische, kulturelle und wirtschaftliche Entwicklung. Vienna: Volksbildungswerk für das Burgenland, 1946.
431. Fünfzig Jahre Wirtschaft im Burgenland. Eisenstadt: s.n., 1971.
432. Rauhofer, Otto. "Handel, Gewerbe und Industrie im Burgenland." in 10 Jahre Burgenland, seine politische, kulturelle und wirtschaftliche Entwicklung in den Jahren 1921-1931. Vienna: Amt der burgenländischen Landesregierung, 1931.

433. Wessely, Alois. "Die Entwicklung der burgenländischen Wirtschaft 1921 bis 1951." in Burgenländische Freiheit, 11 November 1951.
434. Zehn Jahre Burgenland, seine politische, kulturelle und wirtschaftliche Entwicklung in den Jahren 1921-1931. Vienna: Amt der burgenländischen Landesregierung, 1931.

Carinthia

435. Dinklage, Karl and Alfred Wakolbinger. Kärntens gewerbliche Wirtschaft von der Vorzeit bis zur Gegenwart. Klagenfurt: Leon, 1953. 493 pp.
436. Fünfundzwanzig Jahre Kärntner Wirtschaftsgeschichte, 1951-1976. 125 Jahre Handelskammer Kärnten. 2nd ed. Klagenfurt: Heyn, 1976. 255 pp.
437. Jausz, Fritz. Kärnten. Vienna: Verlag für Geschichte und Politik, 1967. 31 pp.

Hungary

438. Berend, Iván T. and György Ránki. "Economic Factors in Nationalism. The Example of Hungary at the Beginning of the Twentieth Century." Austrian History Yearbook 3 (1967), 163-86.
439. Berend, Iván T. and György Ránki. Hungary. A Century of Economic Development. Newton Abbot: David & Charles, 1974. 263 pp.
440. Berend, Iván T. and György Ránki. "Ungarns wirtschaftliche Entwicklung 1849-1918." in A. Wandruszka, ed. Die Habsburgermonarchie 1848-1918. Vol. I. Vienna: Österreichische Akademie der Wissenschaften, 1973. pp. 462-527.
441. Ecker-Racz, László. The Hungarian Economy, 1920-1954. Washington, D. C.: Council for Economic Industry Research, 1954. 114 pp.
442. Fellner, Frédéric. "Die volkswirtschaftliche Entwicklung Ungarns unter der verfassungsmässigen Regierung Franz Joseph I. (1867-1916)." Ungarische Jahrbücher (1927), 186-93.
443. Gratz, Gustav. The Economical Situation in Hungary. Budapest: Pallas Printing Co., 1925. 30 pp.
444. Hanák, Péter. "Economics, Society and Sociopolitical Thought in Hungary During the Age of Capitalism." Austrian History Yearbook 11 (1975), 113-35.
445. Hanák, Péter. "Hungary in the Austro-Hungarian Monarchy. Preponderancy or Dependency." Austrian History Yearbook 3 (1967), 260-302.
446. Hanák, Péter. "Die Stellung Ungarns in der Monarchie." in Probleme der Franzisko-Josephinischen Zeit 1848-1916. Munich: Oldenburg, 1967. pp. 79-93.
447. Horváth, Robert. "The Interdependence of Economic and Demographic Development in Hungary (From the Mid-Eighteenth to the Mid-Nineteenth Centuries)." Proceedings of the International Economic History Conference 4 (1968).
448. Ivanyi, B. G. "From Feudalism to Capitalism. The Economic Background to Szechenyi's Reform in Hungary." Journal of Central European Affairs 20 (1960), 270-88.
449. Katus, László. "Economic Growth in Hungary During the Age of Dualism, 1867-1918." in Social-Economic Researches on the History of East-Central Europe. Budapest: Academy of Sciences, 1970. pp. 34-127.
450. Komlós, János. "Economic Growth and Industrialisation in Hungary, I880-1913." Journal of European Economic History 10 (1981), 5-46.
451. Lers, Wilhelm von. Volkswirtschaftliche Entwicklung Ungarns. Pest: Pester Buchdruck, 1909. 13 pp.
452. Macartney, Carlile. A History of Hungary, 1929-1945. 2 vols. New York: Praeger, 1956-57.
453. Matolcsy, Mátyás and S. Varga. The National Income of Hungary, 1924/25-1936/37. London: P. S. King, 1938. 116 pp.
454. Mérey, Klára T. Wirtschafts- und Gesellschaftsverhältnisse eines Komitats in Transdanubien, 1867-1918. Pécs: Magyar Tudományos Akadémia, 1975. 93 pp.
455. Miskolczy, Julius. Ungarn in der Habsburger-Monarchie. Vienna: Verlag Herold, 1959. 210 pp.
456. Nagy, Tamas. "The Hungarian Economic Reform. Past and Future." Austrian Economic Review 61 (1971), 430-35.
457. Ránki, György. "Some Problems of Capital Accumulation and Industrialisation in Hungary, 1867-1914." Proceedings of the Second International Economic History Conference, Aix en Provence, 1962. Paris: Mouton, 1965.

458. Tremel, Ferdinand. "Die Industrielle Entwicklung in Ungarn." VSWG 45 (1958), 242-50.
459. Wolf, Franz. Die Tulpenbewegung in Ungarn: wirtschaftliche und politische Auseinander-setzungen zwischen Oesterreich und Ungarn. 2 vols. Diss: Vienna. Vienna: VWGÖ, 1979. 593 pp.

Lower Austria

460. Firnberg, Hertha et al. Die wirtschaftliche und soziale Entwicklung Niederösterreichs von der industriellen Revolution bis zur Gegenwart. Vienna: Arbeiterkammer fur Niederösterreich, 1957.
461. Gerhartl, Gertrud. Wiener Neustadt: Geschichte, Kunst, Kultur, Wirtschaft. Vienna: Braumüller, 1978. 594 pp.
462. Die Kalkbrenner am Ostrand der Alpen: Beitrage zur Volkskunde, Wirtschafts- und Sozialgeschichte Niederösterreichs. Augsburg: Perlach, 1977. 127 pp.
463. Knittler, Herbert. "Abriss einer Wirtschafts- und Sozialgeschichte der Doppelstadt Krems-Stein." in Ausstellung 1000 Jahre Kunst in Krems. Krems: Kulturverwaltung, 1971. pp. 43-73.
464. Wiltschegg, Walter. Niederösterreich. Vienna: Verlag für Geschichte und Politik, 1967. 31 pp.
465. Zündel, Helmut. Die wirtschaftliche Entwicklung Wiener Neustadts 1841-1918. Diss. Vienna, 1951. 176 pp.

Rumania

466. Constantinescu, N. N. and V. V. Axenciuc. "The Economic Development of Romania in the Period between 1919-1939." Papers in East European Economics (1972).
467. Cristea, Gheorghe. "L'expansion economique austro-hongroise en Roumanie et la reaction de la bourgeoisie autochtone. 1886-1891." Revue Roumaine d'Histoire 19 (1980), 313-32.
468. Economic Development of the Rumanian People's Republic. Bucharest: Chamber of Commerce of the Rumanian People's Republic, 1954. 151 pp.
469. Grünberg, Karl. Wirtschaftszustände Rumäniens vor dem Kriege. Vienna: A. Holzhausen, 1916. 54 pp.
470. Logio, George C. Rumania, Its History, Politics and Economics. Manchester: Sherratt & Hughes, 1932. 4 pp.
471. Marguerat, Philippe. "L'Allemagne et la Roumanie à l'automne 1938: économie et diplomatie." Relations International (1974), 173-79.
472. Müller, Carl. Beiträge zur Wirtschaftsgeschichte der deutschen Siedlungen bei Sathmar in Rumänien. Stuttgart: Ausland und Heimat, 1932. 159 pp.
473. Riker, Thad W. The Making of Roumania. A Study of an International Problem, 1856-66. London: Oxford University Press, 1931; rpt. New York, 1971. 592 pp.
474. Royal Institute of International Affairs. The Balkan States. A Review of the Economic and Financial Development of Albania, Bulgaria, Greece, Roumania and Yugoslavia since 1919. London: Oxford University Press, 1936; rpt. New York, 1970. 154 pp.
475. Seton-Watson, Robert W. A History of the Roumanians. Cambridge: Cambridge University Press, 1934. 596 pp.
476. Stahl, Henri H. Traditional Romanian Village Communities. The Transition from the Communal to the Capitalist Mode of Production in the Danube Region. Cambridge: Cambridge University Press, 1980. 227 pp.
477. Welzk, Stefan. Nationalkapitalismus versus Weltmarktintegration? Rumänien 1830-1944. Ein Beitrag zur Theorie eigenständiger Entwicklung. Saarbrücken: Breitenbach, 1982. 199 pp.

Salzburg

478. Klein, Herbert. Beiträge zur Siedlungs-, Verfassungs- und Wirtschaftsgeschichte von Salzburg. Festschrift zum 65. Geburtstag von Herbert Klein. Salzburg: Gesellschaft für Salzburger Landeskunde, 1965. 720 pp.
479. Lendl, Egon. "Salzburg, vom Erzstift zum Bundesland. Der Wertwandel eines Landes." Berichte zur Deutschen Landeskunde 21 (1958), 16-47.

Styria

480. Beiträge zur Sozial- und Wirtschaftsgeschichte der Steiermark und Kärnten. Ferdinand Tremel zur Vollendung des 65. Lebensjahres. Graz: Historischer Verein für Steiermark, 1967. 167 pp.
481. Brunner, Karl et al., eds. Die Steiermark. Land, Leute, Leistung. Graz: "Styria," 1956. 772 pp.
482. Ibler, Hermann. "Steirische Wirtschaftsgeschichte." in Die Steiermark. Graz: Imago, 1971. pp. 841-61.
483. Kosch, Friedrich W. "Stadt der Generale--Graz in der zweiten Hälfte des 19. Jahrhunderts." Zeitschrift des historischen Vereins für Steiermark 64 (1973), 17-46.
484. Muchar, Albert von. Geschichte des Herzogthums Steiermark. 3 vols. Graz: Damian & Sorge, 1844-46.
485. Posch, Fritz, ed. Siedlung, Wirtschaft und Kultur im Ostalpenraum. Festschrift zum 70. Geburtstag von Fritz Popelka. Graz: Steiermärkisches Landesarchiv, 1960. 385 pp.
486. Rüdegger, Erika. Steiermark. Vienna: Verlag für Geschichte und Politik, 1968. 31 pp.
487. Tremel, Ferdinand. "Die wirtschaftliche Entwicklung des Landes Steiermark seit der Mitte des 13. Jahrhunderts." Zeitschrift des historischen Vereins für Steiermark (54) 1963.
488. Tremel, Ferdinand. "Die wirtschaftliche Entwicklung in der Franz-Joseph-Zeit, vornehmlich in der Steiermark." Zeitschrift des historischen Vereins für Steiermark 50 (1959).
489. Tremel, Ferdinand, ed. Festschrift für Otto Lamprecht. Graz: Historischer Verein für Steiermark, 1968. 199 pp.
490. Zehn Jahre steirische Wirtschaft. Graz: Handelskammer Steiermark, 1955. 29 pp.

Tirol

491. Ager, Walter. Tirol, einst, jetzt und in der Zukunft. Eine Darstellung der Wirtschaftsentwicklung im Land Tirol. Innsbruck: Tiroler Handelskammer, n.d. 90 pp.
492. Grass, Nikolaus, ed. Beiträge zur Wirtschafts- und Kulturgeschichte des Zisterzienserstiftes Stams in Tirol. Innsbruck: Wagner, 1959. 243 pp.
493. Huter, Franz. Herzog Rudolf der Stifter und die Tiroler Städte. Festgabe der gewerblichen Wirtschaft Tirols zum 600-Jahr-Jubiläum der Vereinigung Tirols mit Österreich. 3 vols. Innsbruck: Wagner, 1971.
494. Huter, Franz, ed. Aus Wirtschaft und Gesellschaft. Festschrift für Ferdinand Ulmer anlässlich der Vollendung des 60. Lebensjahres. Innsbruck: Wagner, 1963. 292 pp.
495. Pan, Christoph and Gerhard Marinell, eds. Wirtschafts- und Sozialforschung in Tirol und Vorarlberg. Festschrift für Univ. Prof. Dr. Ferdinand Ulmer anlässlich der Vollendung seines 70. Lebensjahres. Vienna: Braumüller, 1972. 587 pp.
496. Pfaundler, Wolfgang. Innsbrucks Wirtschaft im Spiegelbild der Annoncen 1822-1981. Innsbruck: Wagner, 1982. 412 pp.
497. Stolz, Otto. Geschichte des Zollwesens, Verkehrs und Handels in Tirol und Vorarlberg von den Anfängen bis ins 20. Jahrhundert. Innsbruck: Wagner, 1953. 315 pp.
498. Stolz, Otto. Die Schwaighöfe in Tirol. Ein Beitrag zur Siedlungs- und Wirtschaftsgeschichte der Hochalpentäler. Innsbruck: Deutscher und Österreichischer Alpenverein, 1930. 197 pp.
499. Stolz, Otto. "Wattens und Umgebung im Rahmen der Tiroler Landesgeschichte." in Wattner Buch. Beiträge zur Heimatkunde von Wattens, Wattenberg und Vögelsberg. Innsbruck: Wagner, 1958. pp. 69-108.
500. Tiroler Wirtschaft in Vergangenheit und Gegenwart. Festgabe zur 100-Jahrfeier der Tiroler Handelskammer. 3 vols. Innsbruck: Wagner, 1951.

SEE ALSO: 1535-36.

Transylvania

501. Göllner, Carl. Die siebenbürgische Militärgrenze. Ein Beitrag zur Sozial- und Wirtschaftsgeschichte 1762-1851. Munich: Oldenbourg, 1974. 264 pp.
502. Leon, Gheorghe N. Siebenbürgen und die rumänische Wirtschaftspolitik. Bucharest: Analele economice, 1942. 44 pp.

503. Moga, Ioan. Siebenbürgen in dem Wirtschaftsorganismus des rumänischen Bodens. Geschichtlicher Rückblick. 2nd ed. Bucharest: National Printing Office, 1942. 91 pp.
504. Rothbächer, Ernst. Heldsdorf. Monographie einer Burzenländer Gemeinde. Bucharest: Kriterion, 1977. 221 pp.

Upper Austria

505. Beiträge zur Rechts-, Landes- und Wirtschaftsgeschichte. Festgabe für Alfred Hoffmann zum 60. Geburtstag. Graz: Böhlaus Nachf. in Kommission, 1964. 561 pp.
506. Bittner, Margarethe. Die wirtschaftliche und soziale Entwicklung von Linz. Diss. Innsbruck, 1957. 150 pp.
507. Hofmann, Viktor. "Beiträge zur neueren österreichischen Wirtschaftsgeschichte." Archiv für österreichische Geschichte 108 (1920), 345-778.
508. Kotzina, Vinzenz, ed. Wirtschaftsgeschichte des Landes Oberösterreich. 2 vols. Salzburg: Müller, 1952.
509. Lackinger, Otto. Die Veränderung der Bevölkerungs- und Wirtschaftsstruktur des Bezirkes Linz-Land. 1934-1954. Wels: Oberoesterreichischer Landesverlag, 1955. 214 pp.
510. Meixner, Erich M. "Abriss der Linzer Wirtschaftsgeschichte." Historisches Jahrbuch der Stadt Linz (1960), 515-619.
511. Pisecky, Franz. Oberösterreich. Vienna: Verlag für Geschichte und Politik, 1968. 31 pp.
512. Pisecky, Franz. Wirtschaft, Land und Kammer in Oberösterreich 1851-1976. Linz: R. Trauner, 1976. 292 pp.
513. Trathnigg, Gilbert. "Beiträge zur Verwaltungs- und Wirtschaftsgeschichte von Wels im 19. und 20. Jahrhundert." Jahrbuch des Musealvereins Wels 11 (1964-65), 51-91.
514. Wilflingseder, Franz. "Die Linzer Mitbürger. Ein Beitrag zur Verfassungs- und Wirtschaftsgeschichte der Stadt Linz." Historisches Jahrbuch der Stadt Linz (1966), 61-149.

SEE ALSO: 1547.

Vienna

515. Baltzarek, Franz et al. Wirtschaft und Gesellschaft der Wiener Stadterweiterung. Wiesbaden: Steiner, 1975. 432 pp.
516. Banik-Schweitzer, Renate et al. Wien im Vormärz. Vienna: Kommission-Verlag Jugend und Volk, 1980. 216 pp.
517. Czeike, Felix. Wirtschafts- und Sozialpolitik der Gemeinde Wien in der 1. Republik (1919-1934). 2 vols. Vienna: Verlag für Jugend und Volk, 1958-59.
518. Lichtenberger, Elisabeth. Wirtschaftsfunktion und Sozialstruktur der Wiener Ringstrasse. Vienna: Böhlau, 1970. 268 pp.
519. Mayer, Sigmund. Die Wiener Juden. Kommerz, Kultur, Politik, 1700-1900. Vienna: Löwit, 1918. 531 pp.
520. Spiesz, Anton. "Die Wirtschaftspolitik des Wiener Hofes im 18. Jahrhundert und im Vormärz." Ungarn-Jahrbuch 1 (1969), 60-73.
521. Tietze, Hans. Die Juden Wiens. Geschichte-Wirtschaft-Kultur. Vienna: Tal, 1933. 301 pp.
522. Walter, Friedrich. Die neueste Zeit. (1790-1918). Die Geschichte einer deutschen Grosstadt an der Grenze, 3. Vienna: Holzhausens Nachfolger, 1944. 476 pp.
523. Zapf, Johann. Die Wirtschafts-Geschichte Wien's unter der Regierung . . . des Kaisers Franz Joseph 1. (1848-1888). Vienna: Braumüller, 1888. 337 pp.

SEE ALSO: 391.

Vorarlberg

524. Bilgeri, Benedikt. Bregenz: Geschichte der Stadt: Politik, Verfassung, Wirtschaft. Vienna: Jugend & Volk, 1980. 760 pp.

525. Hundert Jahre Handelskammer und gewerbliche Wirtschaft in Vorarlberg, 1850-1950. Feldkirch: Unterberger, 1952. 514 pp.
526. Ilg, Karl. Geschichte und Wirtschaft. Landes- und Volkskunde, Geschichte, Wirtschaft und Kunst Vorarlbergs, 2. Innsbruck: Wagner, 1968. 544 pp.
527. Ilg, Wolfgang. Vorarlberg. Kleines Land mit grosser Wirtschaftskraft. Ein Überblick über Aufbau und Leistungen der Vorarlberger Wirtschaft. Bregenz: Russ, 1972. 285 pp.
528. Kathan, Klaus. Das Rheintal-Dorf Mäder im Wandel seiner Wirtschaftsstruktur. Innsbruck: Wagner, 1970. 69 pp.
529. Sinz, Josef. Wirtschaftsgeschichte Vorarlbergs. Bregenz: Russ, 1955. 311 pp.

SWITZERLAND

530. Bächtold, Hermann. "Die geschichtlichen Entwicklungsbedingungen der schweizerischen Volkswirtschaft (1903-1924)." in H. Bächtold. Gesammelte Schriften. Aarau: Sauerländer, 1939. pp. 65-87.
531. Bächtold, Hermann. Die schweizerische Volkswirtschaft in ihren Beziehungen zu Deutschland in Vergangenheit und Gegenwart. Frauenfeld: Huber, 1927. 92 pp.
532. Bauer, Hans. The Growth of the Swiss Economy. Facts, Causes and Consequences. Basel: Swiss Bank Corp., 1964. 38 pp.
533. Behrendt, Richard Fritz et al., eds. Strukturwandlungen der schweizerischen Wirtschaft und Gesellschaft. Festschrift für Fritz Marbach zum 70. Geburtstag. Bern: Stämpfli, 1962. 618 pp.
534. Bergier, Jean-François. Histoire économique de la Suisse. Paris: Colin, 1984. 376 pp.
535. Bergier, Jean-François. Problèmes de l'histoire économique de la Suisse. Population, vie rurale, échanges et trafics. Bern: Francke, 1968. 94 pp.
536. Bickel, Wilhelm. Die Volkswirtschaft in der Schweiz. Entwicklung und Struktur. Aarau: M. Sauerländer, 1973. 464 pp.
537. Biucchi, Basilio M. "I fattori determinanti dello sviluppo nella storia economica della Svizzera." Economia e Storia 18 (1971), 482-501. (English and French summaries.)
538. Biucchi, Basilio M. "Tendenze liberiste nella storia economica svizzera." Rivista internazionale di scienze sociali 42 (1934), 523-34.
539. Bodmer, Walter. Die Entwicklung der schweizerischen Textilwirtschaft im Rahmen der übrigen Industrien und Wirtschaftszweige. Zurich: Berichthaus, 1960. 579 pp.
540. Brüschweiler, Carl. "Strukturwandlungen der schweizerischen Bevölkerung und Wirtschaft." SZVS 70 (1934).
541. Bürgin, Alfred. "The Growth of the Swiss National Economy." in H. G. J. Aitken, ed. The State and Economic Growth. New York: Social Science Research Council, 1964. pp. 213-36.
542. Dürr, Emil. Neuzeitliche Wandlungen in der schweizerischen Politik, eine historisch-politische Betrachtung über die Verwirtschaftlichung der politischen Meinungen und Parteien. Basel: Helbing & Lichtenhahn, 1928. 120 pp.
543. Etter, Walter. Die Entwicklung von Wirtschaft und Bevölkerung in der Nordostschweiz seit Beginn des 19. Jahrhunderts. Diss. Zurich, 1969. 242 pp.
544. Feldmann, Alfred. "Die schweizerische Wirtschaft--gestern, heute, morgen." Sozial. Studienkommission Schweizer reform. Pfarrver. 76 (1946), 435-442.
545. Fueter, Eduard. Die Schweiz seit 1848. Geschichte, Politik, Wirtschaft. Zurich: Füssli, 1928. 305 pp.
546. Gruner, Erich. "100 Jahre Wirtschaftspolitik. Etappen des Interventionismus in der Schweiz." SZVS 100 (1964), 35-70.
547. Gruner, Erich. Die Wirtschaftsverbände in der Demokratie. Vom Wachstum der Wirtschafts-organisationen im schweizerischen Staat. Erlenbach-Zurich: E. Rentsch, 1956. 131 pp.
548. Haene, Max. "Die schweizerische Volkswirtschaft (vor dem Kriege)." in H. Dommann and E. Vogt, eds. Volk und Werk der Eidgenossen. Lucerne: Rex Verlag, 1941. pp. 237-69.
549. Handbuch der Schweizerischen Volkswirtschaft. 2nd ed. 2 vols. Bern: Schweizerische Gesellschaft für Statistik und Volkswirtschaft, 1955.
550. Hauser, Albert. Schweizerische Wirtschafts- und Sozialgeschichte. Erlenbach-Zurich: E. Rentsch, 1961. 400 pp.

551. Huber, Jakob. "Wirtschaftliche Zusammenhänge 1913-1943." Gewerkschaftliche Rundschau der Schweiz 36 (1944), 94-111.
552. Hughes, Christopher. "The Swiss Economic Miracle." in Switzerland. London: Benn, 1975. pp. 173-180.
553. "Ein Jahrhundert schweizerischer Wirtschaftsentwicklung." SZVS 100 (1964), 1-368.
554. Keller, Paul and Roger Nordmann. Wohlstand aus dem Nichts. Das Abenteuer der Schweizer Wirtschaft. Bern: Hallwag, 1973. 164 pp.
555. Kleinewefers, Henner and Regula Pfister. "Geschichte der schweizerischen Volkswirtschaft." in Die schweizerische Volkswirtschaft. Eine problem-orientierte Einführung in die Volkswirtschaftslehre. Frauenfeld: Huber, 1977. pp. 37-92.
556. Laur, Ernst. Erinnerungen eines schweizerischen Bauernführers. Ein Beitrag zur schweizerischen Wirtschaftsgeschichte. 2nd ed. Bern: Verbandsdruckerei, 1942. 331 pp.
557. Schaffner, Hans. Dauer und Wandel in der schweizerischen Wirtschaft. Zurich: Schweizerischer Handels- und Industrieverein, 1970. 14 pp.
558. Schweizer Pioniere der Wirtschaft und Technik. 16 vols. Zurich: Verein für wirtschaftshistorische Studien, 1955-65.
559. Seiler, Eduard. Das Schweizervolk und seine Wirtschaft, gestern, heute, morgen. Zurich: Aktionsgemeinschaft Nationaler Wiederaufbau, 1944. 176 pp.
560. Stalder, Arnold. Geschichte, Kultur und Wirtschaft. Lucerne: Keller, 1937. 75 pp.
561. Stucki, Lorenz. Das heimliche Imperium. Wie die Schweiz reich wurde. Frauenfeld: Huber, 1981. 354 pp. (English: New York, 1971)
562. "Zwei Säulen. Kapital und Qualität. Wie aus der Schweiz ein 'heimliches Imperium' wurde." Werkzeitung schweizerischer Industrieller 37 (1969), 82-83.

SEE ALSO: 4456.

SWITZERLAND--1815-1918

563. Emminghaus, Arwed. Die Schweizerische Volkswirthschaft. 2 vols. Leipzig: G. Mayer, 1860-1861.
564. Freudiger, Hans. "Die oekonomischen Lebensbedingungen in der Schweiz. Ein Beitrag zur Frage der Teuerung der Lebenshaltung 1800-1880, resp. 1880-1914." Schweizerische Blätter für Wirtschafts- und Sozialpolitik (1913), 1-289.
565. Gariel, Georges. La centralisation économique en Suisse: l'oeuvre économique de la Confédération depuis 1848. 2 vols. Paris: A. Rousseau, 1912-13.
566. Geering, Traugott. Grundzüge einer schweizerischen Wirtschaftsgeschichte. Bern: Stämpfli, 1912. 48 pp.
567. Hauser, Benedikt. Wirtschaftsverbände im frühen schweizerischen Bundesstaat (1848-1874). Diss. Basel. Basel: Helbing & Lichtenhahn, 1985. 205 pp.
568. Ochsenbein, Heinz. Die verlorene Wirtschaftsfreiheit 1914-1918. Methoden ausländischer Wirtschaftskontrollen über die Schweiz. Diss. Bern, 1969. Bern: Stämpfli, 1971. 349 pp.
569. Rappard, William E. Le facteur économique dans l'avènement de la démocratie moderne en Suisse. Geneva: Georg, 1912. 230 pp.
570. Weckerle, Eduard. "Die Schweiz vor hundert Jahren." in Die Schweiz der Arbeit, 1848-1948. Zurich: Schweizerischer Gewerkschaftsbund, 1948. pp. 26-52.

SWITZERLAND--1919-1975

571. Bickel, Wilhelm. "Wachstum und Strukturwandel der Wirtschaft." in Die Schweiz seit 1945. Bern: Francke, 1971. pp. 56-76.
572. The Economic Situation of Switzerland 1939-1945. Basel: Société de Banque Suisse, 1945. 42 pp.
573. Fischer, Georges. Die Entwicklung der kantonalen Volkswirtschaften seit 1965. Bonn: Haupt, 1981. 124 pp.
574. Halpérin, Jean. Politik und Wirtschaft in den Entscheidungsjahren 1936-1946. Bern: Francke, 1947. 280 pp.

575. Masnata, Albert. "Switzerland's Economic Evolution Since the Second World War." Swiss Industrial Trade 33 (1954), 3-4.
576. Nabholz, Hans. Ausgewählte Aufsätze zur Wirtschaftsgeschichte. Zurich: Schulthess, 1954. 207 pp.
577. Schmid, Hanspeter. Wirtschaft, Staat und Macht. Die Politik der schweizerischen Export-industrie im Zeichen von Staats- und Wirtschaftskrieg (1918-1929). Diss. Basel. Zurich: Limmat, 1983. 432 pp.
578. Siegenthaler, Hansjörg. "Switzerland 1920-70." in C. M. Cipolla, ed. Contemporary Economies. Fontana Economic History of Europe, vol. 6, pt. 2. Glasgow: Fontana, 1976. pp. 530-76
579. "Die wirtschaftliche Entwicklung in der Schweiz im [2.] Weltkriege." In Bericht der Bundes-kommmision des Schweizerischen Gewerkschafts-Bundes, 1939-1946. Bern: Schweizerischer Gewerkschafts-Bund, 1947. pp. 33-52.
580. Wittmann, Walter. "Die Take-off-Periode der schweizerischen Volkswirtschaft." Zeitschrift für die gesamte Staatswissenschaft 119 (1963), 592-615.

SWISS CANTONS

Aargau

581. Lauchenauer, Eduard. Die wirtschaftliche Entwicklung des Kantons Aargau seit der Gründung der Aargauischen Bank (1855-1955). Ein Rückblick der Aargauischen Kantonalbank. Aargau: Aargauische Kantonalbank, 1956. 226 pp.
582. Siegrist, Jean J. Beiträge zur Verfassungs- und Wirtschaftsgeschichte der Herrschaft Hallwil. Diss. Zurich. Aarau: Sauerländer, 1952. 533 pp.

Appenzell

583. Eugster, Arnold and Albert Koller. Heimatgeschichte und Wirtschaft des Appenzellerlandes. Zollikon-Zurich: Bosch, 1949. 144 pp.
584. Gmür, Klaus. Staatliche Aktivität und wirtschaftliche Entwicklung im Kanton Appenzell-Ausserrhoden nach dem Zweiten Weltkrieg. Diss. Fribourg, 1967. 128 pp.
585. Preisig, Ernst. "Die Volkswirtschaft von Appenzell-Ausserrhoden in den letzten 40 Jahren." Appenzeller Zeitung 117, 300, 306 (1944-45).
586. Schläpfer, Walter. Wirtschaftsgeschichte des Kantons Appenzell-Ausserrhoden bis 1939. Herisau: Appenzell-Ausserrhodische Kantonale Buchdruckerei, 1984. 476 pp.
587. Schürmann, Markus. Bevölkerung, Wirtschaft und Gesellschaft in Appenzell-Innerrhoden im 18. und frühen 19. Jahrhundert. Diss. Basel. Appenzell: Genossenschafts-Buchdruckerei, 1974. 356 pp.

Basel

588. Banderet-Lüdin, Elisabeth. Obrigkeitliche Marktpolitik im 19. Jahrhundert. Eine Studie zur Basler Wirtschaftsgeschichte. Diss. Basel. Weinfelden: Neuenschwander, 1944. 77 pp.
589. Bauer, Hans. Basel. Gestern, heute, morgen. Hundert Jahre Basler Wirtschaftsgeschichte. Basel: Birkhäuser, 1981. 303 pp.
590. Beiträge zur Entwicklungsgeschichte des Kantons Basel-Landschaft. Herausgegeben von der Basellandschaftlichen Kantonalbank aus Anlass ihres 100-jährigen Bestehens, 1864-1964. Liestal: Basellandschaftliche Kantonalbank, 1964. 575 pp.
591. Bruckner, Albert, ed. Wirtschaftsgeschichte Basels mit besonderer Berücksichtigung der Gegenwart. Basel: Linthescher, 1947. 674 pp.
592. Bütler, Kurt. Die wirtschaftliche Entwicklung der Stadt Liestal. Diss. Bern. Basel: Arnaud, 1954. 91 pp.

593. Kaegi, Werner. "Die Geisteswissenschaft und die Geschichte des baslerischen Wirtschaftslebens." in Wissenschaft und Wirtschaft. Basel: Helbing & Lichtenhahn, 1943. pp. 34-38.
594. Sarasin, Hans F. "Die Basler Wirtschaft und der Gotthard. Beitrag zu Basels Wirtschaftsgeschichte aus Anlass des 75jährigen Bestehens der St. Gotthardbahn." Strom und See 52
(1957), 263-65.
595. Stolz, Peter. Basler Wirtschaft in vor- und frühindustrieller Zeit. Zurich: Schulthess, 1977.
178 pp.

SEE ALSO: 1582.

Bern

596. Geiser, Karl. "Rückblick auf die Entwicklung der wirtschaftlichen Verhältnisse im Kanton Bern."
Berufliche Ausbildung (1953) I, 38-46.
597. Scheidegger, Urs. Werden und Wachsen der bernischen Wirtschaft. 2 vols. Bern: Kantonalbank
von Bern, 1983.
598. Spörri, Werner H. Die volkswirtschaftliche und wirtschaftspolitische Entwicklung im Kanton
Bern in der Zeit der Mediation und Restauration. 1803-30. Diss. Bern. Bern: Grunau, 1940.
239 pp.
599. Strahm, Hans et al. "Die Amtsbezirke des Kantons. Bern: Behörden Geschichte, Wirtschaft und
Verkehr in den Ämtern, Fremdenverkehrsentwicklung im Berner Oberland." in Berner Staatsbuch.
Bern: Buchdruck Berner Tagblatt, 1945. pp.163-734.

Fribourg

600. Hattemer, Herman C. Die wirtschaftliche Entwicklung des Kantons Freiburg 1941-1966. Diss.
Fribourg, 1968. Munich: Schön, 1968. 245 pp.

Glarus

601. Bodmer, Walter. Das glarnerische Wirtschaftswunder. Glarus: Neue Glarner Zeitung, 1952.
53 pp.
602. Dürst, Elisabeth. Die wirtschaftlichen und sozialen Verhältnisse des Glarnerlandes an der Wende
vom 18. zum 19. Jahrhundert. Der Übergang von der Heimindustrie zum Fabriksystem. Diss.
Zurich. Glarus: Tschudi, 1951. 144 pp.
603. Das Land Glarus. Chronik seiner Landschaft, Geschichte, Kultur und Wirtschaft. Zurich: Bosch,
1945. 300 pp.

Graubünden

604. Oswald, Werner. Wirtschaft und Siedlung im Rheinwald. Diss. Zurich, 1931. Thusis: Roth,
1931. 158 pp.
605. Sprecher, Georg. Die Bündner Gemeinde, ihre wirtschaftliche und finanzielle Entwicklung und
heutige Struktur. Chur: Sprecher, Eggerling, 1942. 221 pp.

Lucerne

606. Dubler, Anne-Marie. Geschichte der Luzerner Wirtschaft: Volk, Staat und Wirtschaft im
Wandel der Jahrhunderte. Lucerne: Rex-Verlag, 1983. 312 pp.
607. Dubler, Anne-Marie. Luzerner Wirtschaftsgeschichte im Bild. Bilder als Quelle zur Geschichte
der wirtschaftlichen Entwicklung des Kantons bis 1900. (Festschrift 125 Jahre Luzerner
Kantonalbank). Luzern: Luzerner Kantonalbank, 1975. 118 pp.

608. Gubler, Konrad R. Bevölkerungsentwicklung und wirtschaftliche Wandlungen im Kanton Luzern (seit dem Ende des 18. Jahrhunderts). Diss. Zurich. Stans: Matt, 1952. 224 pp.
609. Schnellmann, Meinrad. "Luzern in Geschichte und Wirtschaft." Textil-Rundschau 8 (1953), 457-60.
610. Zimmermann, Basil. Das Rigigebiet und seine durch Verkehrsveränderung bedingte Umgestaltung in Siedlung und Wirtschaft. Lucerne: Haag, 1955. 142 pp.

St. Gallen

611. Häne, Johannes. Zwei Abhandlungen zur Kultur- und Wirtschaftsgeschichte der Stadt St. Gallen. St. Gallen: Fehr, 1932. 55 pp.
612. Jöhr, Walter A. "Die Wirtschaft des Kantons St. Gallen im Rahmen der schweizerischen Volkswirtschaft." in Denkschrift zum 75jährigen Bestehen des Handels- und Industrievereins. St. Gallen: Zollikofer, 1950.
613. Keller, Theo. "Die wirtschaftliche Entwicklung des Kantons St. Gallen." St. Galler Tagblatt 115 (1953), 217.
614. Schönenberger, Karl et al. Chronik des Kantons St. Gallen, Geschichte, Kultur, Wirtschaft. Lucerne: Winkelried, 1950. 614 pp.
615. Thürer, Georg. "Entstehung und Entwicklung des Kantons St. Gallen 1803-1953." Verwaltungs-Praxis 7 (1952/53), 199-209.
616. Thürer, Georg. St. Galler Geschichte, Kultur, Staatsleben und Wirtschaft im Kanton und Stadt St. Gallen von der Urzeit bis zur Gegenwart. 2 vols. St. Gallen: T. Schudy, 1953-72.

Schaffhausen

617. Bächtold, Kurt and Hermann Wanner. Wirtschaftsgeschichte des Kantons Schaffhausen. Schaffhausen: Schaffhauser Kantonalbank, 1982. 289 pp.
618. Ott, Bernhard. Die Verwandlung einer Stadt: Schaffhausen einst und jetzt. Schaffhausen: Schaffhauser AZ, 1983. 67 pp.
619. Traupel, Richard. Die industrielle Entwicklung des Kantons Schaffhausen (mit besonderer Berücksichtigung der allgemein-wirtschaftlichen Entwicklung des Kantons). Diss. Basel. Thayngen: Augustin, 1942. 246 pp.

SEE ALSO: 2222.

Schwyz

620. Kistler, Robert. Die wirtschaftliche Entwicklung des Kantons Schwyz. Diss. Bern, 1961. Stans: Matt, 1963. 215 pp.

Thurgau

621. Häberlin-Schaltegger, Jacob. Der Kanton Thurgau in seiner Gesamtentwicklung vom Jahr 1849-1869 geschildert. Frauenfeld: J. Häberlin, 1876. 396 pp.
622. Schmid, Ernst. Beiträge zur Siedlungs- und Wirtschaftsgeographie des Kantons Thurgau. Diss. Zurich. Frauenfeld: Huber, 1918. 168 pp.
623. Schoop, Albert. Der Kanton Thurgau, 1803-1953. Ein Rückblick auf 150 Jahre Kantonaler Selbständigkeit. Frauenfeld: Huber, 1953. 214 pp.
624. Schoop, Albert, ed. Wirtschaftsgeschichte des Kantons Thurgau. Festgabe zum hundertjährigen Bestehen der Thurgauischen Kantonalbank 1871-1971. Weinfelden: Thurgauische Kantonalbank, 1971. 410 pp.
625. Seeger, Walter. "Die geschichtliche und wirtschaftliche Entwicklung." Thurgauer Jahrbuch 27 (1952), 3-19.

Unterwalden

626. Bauer, Felix. Die Wirtschaft und der Finanzhaushalt des Kantons Nidwalden. Diss. Fribourg. Bern: Herbert Lang, 1972. 105 pp.
627. Kaiser-Kägi, Josef. "Nidwaldens Volkswirtschaft einst und jetzt. Das Erwerbsleben früher und heute." Vaterland 118 (1951), no. 273.

Zug

628. Brandenberg, Rolf. Die Wirtschafts- und Bevölkerungsentwicklung des Kantons Zug 1850-1960. Diss. Zurich, 1970. 188 pp.

Zurich

629. Bernhard, Hans. Wirtschafts- und Siedlungsgeschichte des Tösstales. Diss. Zurich. Zurich: Lohbauer, 1912. 186 pp.
630. Brüschweiler, Carl. "Die wirtschaftliche Struktur des Kantons Zürich 1900 und 1950." Neue Zürcher Zeitung 175 (1954), No. 3113, 3137, 3176.
631. Dejung, Emanuel et al. Chronik Bezirke Winterthur und Anderfingen. Wintherthur: Vogel, 1945. 292 pp.
632. Duttweiler, Max. Eine Züricher Wirtschaftrechnung 1883-1910. Tübingen: s.n., 1915.
633. Ganz, Werner. Beiträge zur Wirtschaftsgeschichte des Grossmünsterstiftes in Zürich. Diss. Zurich. Zurich: W. Coradi-Maag, 1925. 141 pp.
634. Hauser, Albert. Die wirtschaftliche und soziale Entwicklung eines Bauerndorfes zur Industrie-gemeinde. Neuere Wirtschaftsgeschichte der zürcherischen Gemeinde Wädenswil. Wädenswil: Stutz, 1956. 276 pp.
635. Hermann, Eugen. Ein Jahrhundert Zürich und die Entwicklung seiner Firmen. 2 vols. Zurich: Müller, 1946.
636. Hermann, Eugen. Zürcher Quartierchronik: Wiedikon, Aussersihl, Industriequartier. Zurich: Verlag Zürcher Quartierchronik, 1952.
637. Kläui, Paul. Zürich: Geschichte der Stadt und des Bezirks. Zollikon: Bosch, 1948. 244 pp.
638. Schoch, Franz. Aus den Winterthurer Wagbüchern. Ein Beitrag zur lokalen Wirtschafts-geschichte. Winterthur: Handelskammer Winterthur, 1932.
639. Weisz, Leo. Die wirtschaftlichen Gegensätze zwischen Zürich und Winterthur vor Entstehung der Fabrikindustrie. Zurich: Orell Füssli, 1929. 76 pp.
640. Weisz, Leo. Wirtschaftsgeschichte [Winterthurs] bis 1900. Winterthur: Schönenberger & Gall, 1935.
641. Widmer, Jakob. 100 Jahre Wirtschaft und Gewerbepolitik im Kanton Zürich. Festschrift zum 100-jährigen Bestehen des Kantonalen Gewerbeverbandes. Horgen: Kantonaler Gewerbeverband, 1954. 71 pp.
642. Witzig, Paul. Beiträge zur Wirtschaftsgeschichte der Stadt Winterthur im 19. Jahrhundert. Diss. Zurich. Zurich: A. Vogel, 1929. 158 pp.

28 HISTORY OF ECONOMIC CONDITIONS

LIECHTENSTEIN

643. Dommer, Hermann. Die wirtschaftliche Entwicklung des Fürstentums Liechtenstein unter spezieller Berücksichtigung der gegenwärtigen Verhältnisse in der Landwirtschaft. Diss. Bern. Vaduz: Buch und Verlagsdruckerei Vaduz, 1954. 96 pp.
644. Das Fürstentum Liechtenstein und seine wirtschaftliche Entwicklung. Zurich: F. Brun, 1954. 168 pp.
645. Kraetzl, Franz. Das Fürstentum Liechtenstein und der gesamte Fürst von und zu Liechtensteinsche Güterbesitz. Brünn: 1914; rpt. Vaduz: Topos, 1984. 383 pp.
646. Ospelt, Alois. "Wirtschaftsgeschichte des Fürstentums Liechtenstein im 19. Jahrhundert. Von den napoleonischen Kriegen bis zum Ausbruch des ersten Weltkrieges." Jahrbuch des Historischen Vereins für das Fürstentum Liechtenstein 72 (1972), 5-423. (Diss. Fribourg)
647. Sarasin, Alfred. Das Fürstentum Liechtenstein und die Schweiz: Währungs-, Wirtschafts- und Schicksalsgemeinschaft? Vaduz: Verwaltungs- und Privat-Bank Aktiengesellschaft, 1981. 30 pp.
648. Vogt, Alois. "Die Entwicklung der liechtensteinischen Wirtschaft." Ostschweiz 83 (1955), no. 419-20.

LUXEMBURG

649. Augustin, Christian et al., eds. Die wirtschaftliche und soziale Entwicklung im Grenzraum Saar-Lorraine-Luxembourg. Saarbrücken: Saarbrücker Druck, 1978. 651 pp.
650. Calmès, Albert. "Aperçu de l'histoire économique de 1839 à 1939." in Luxembourg. Livre du centenaire. 2nd ed. Luxembourg: Saint-Paul, 1949. pp. 127-67.
651. Calmès, Albert. "L'évolution économique du Luxembourg dans les temps modernes." Academia 49 (1949), special issue.
652. Calmès, Albert. Le Grand-Duché de Luxembourg dans le Royaume des Pay-bas (1815-1830). Brussels: Ed. universelle, 1932. 163 pp.
653. Kirsch, Raymond. "Luxembourg 1870-1970. Un siècle de mutations économiques et sociales." Reflets Economiques 10 (1973), 4-12.
654. Weber, Léon. L'économie luxembourgeoise contemporaine. Diss. Nancy. Nancy: Tollard, 1939. 150 pp.
655. Weber, Paul. Histoire de l'économie luxembourgeoise. Publication à l'occasion du centenaire de la Chambre de commerce. Luxembourg: Buck, 1950. 431 pp.
656. Widung, André. Der Anschluss des Grossherzogtums Luxemburg an das Zollsystem Preussens und der übrigen Staaten des Zollvereins. Ein Beitrag zur Wirtschaftsgeschichte des Grossherzogtums Luxemburg. Luxembourg: Schamburger, 1912. 167 pp.
657. Witlox, Henricus J. M. Schets van de ontwikkeling van welvaart en bedrijvigheid in het Verenigd Koninkrijk der Nederlanden. "Benelux 1815-1830". Diss. Tilburg. Nijmegen: Centrale Drukkerij, 1945. 232 pp.

GERMANY

Bibliographic References

658. Baumgart, Winfried. Bücherverzeichnis zur deutschen Geschichte. Hilfsmittel, Handbücher, Quellen. 4th ed. Frankfurt a. M.: Ullstein, 1978. 248 pp.
659. "Bibliographie wirtschaftsgeschichtlicher Literatur der DDR." Jahrbuch für Wirtschaftsgeschichte 1972- .
660. "Bibliographie zur deutschen Zeitgeschichte." Zeitschrift für Geschichte 1952- .
661. Bog, Ingomar. "Wirtschaftgeschichte." in Dahlmann-Waitz Quellenkunde der deutschen Geschichte. Stuttgart: A. Hiersemann, 1969. Sec. 37.
662. Deutsche Bibliographie. Frankfurt a. M.: Deutsche Bibliothek, 1951- .
663. Deutsche Wirtschaft in Fest- und Denkschrift. Eine Bibliographie des Besitzes von Wirtschafts-Hochschule Tokio von Jahre 1973 ab. Tokyo: Tokyo College of Economics, 1973- .
664. Eichenhofer, H. et al. "Übersicht über Wirtschaftsarchive." Archivar 13 (1960), 291-334.
665. Giersiepen, Elisabeth. "Die deutsche Wirtschafts- und Sozialgeschichte in der Forschungsarbeit der Wirtschaftshistoriker der DDR." Zeitschrift für Geschichte Sonderheft (1960), 229-44.
666. Günther, Renate. "Hochschulschriften zur Wirtschaftsgeschichte." Jahrbuch für Wirtschaftsgeschichte 1971- .
667. Historische Forschungen in der DDR, 1949-1960. Berlin: Rütten & Loening, 1960. 634 pp.
668. Historische Forschungen in der DDR, 1960-1970. Berlin: Deutscher Verlag der Wissenschaften, 1970. 836 pp.
669. Historische Forschungen in der DDR, 1970-1980. Berlin: Deutscher Verlag der Wissenschaften, 1980. 884 pp.
670. Keyser, Erich, ed. Bibliographie zur Städtegeschichte Deutschlands. Vienna: Böhlau, 1969. 404 pp.
671. Köllmann, Wolfgang. "Wirtschafts- und Sozialgeschichte. Literaturbericht." Geschichte in Wissenschaft und Unterricht 19 (1968), 700-09.
672. Oberschelp, Reinhard. Die Bibliographien zur deutschen Landesgeschichte und Landeskunde im 19. und 20. Jahrhundert. 2nd ed. Frankfurt a. M.: Klostermann, 1977. 106 pp.
673. Otto, Frieda. Bibliographie wirtschafts- und sozialwissenschaftlicher Bibliographien . . . 1962 bis 1967. Kiel: Institut für Weltwirtschaft, 1968. 592 pp.
674. Otto, Frieda. Bibliographie wirtschafts- und sozialwissenschaftlicher Bibliographien . . . 1968 bis 1973. Kiel: Institut für Weltwirtschaft, 1975. 783 pp.
675. Radandt, Hans et al., eds. "Spezialverzeichnis ausgewählter Nachschlagewerke für die wirtschaftshistorische Forschung aus den Beständen Berliner Bibliotheken." Jahrbuch für Wirtschaftsgeschichte (1962), II, 257-61.
676. Redlich, Fritz. "Recent Developments in German Economic History." Journal of Economic History 18 (1958), 516-30.
677. Tilly, Richard. "Soll und Haben: Recent German Economic History and the Problem of Economic Development." Journal of Economic History 29 (1969), 298-319.
678. Wehler, Hans-Ulrich. Bibliographie zur modernen deutschen Wirtschaftsgeschichte (18.-20. Jahrhundert). Göttingen: Vandenhoeck & Ruprecht, 1976. 242 pp.
679. Wutzmer, Heinz. Zeittafel zur Wirtschaftsgeschichte Deutschlands. Berlin: Volk und Wissen, 1960. 104 pp.

GERMANY

680. Abelshauser, Werner and Dietmar Petzina, eds. Deutsche Wirtschaftsgeschichte im Industriezeitalter. Konjunktur, Krise, Wachstum. Düsseldorf: Athenäum, 1981. 396 pp.
681. Aus Sozial- und Wirtschaftsgeschichte. Gedächtnisschrift für Georg von Below. Stuttgart: Kohlhammer, 1928. 369 pp.
682. Baudis, Dieter and Helga Nussbaum. Wirtschaft und Staat in Deutschland. Eine Wirtschaftsgeschichte des staatsmonopolistischen Kapitalismus in Deutschland vom Ende des 19. Jahrhunderts bis 1945. 3 vols. Berlin: Akademie, 1978-1980.
683. Bechtel, Heinrich. Wirtschaftsgeschichte Deutschlands im 19. und 20. Jahrhundert. Wirtschaftsgeschichte Deutschlands, 3. Munich: Callwey, 1956. 488 pp.

684. Bechtel, Heinrich. Wirtschafts- und Sozialgeschichte Deutschlands. Wirtschaftsstile und Lebensformen von der Vorzeit bis zur Gegenwart. Munich: Callwey, 1967. 573 pp.
685. Berding, Helmut, ed. Wege der neuen Sozial- und Wirtschaftsgeschichte. Göttingen: Vandenhoeck & Ruprecht, 1980. 161 pp.
686. Bernstein, Daniel. "Wirtschaft. Handel und Industrie." in S. Kaznelson, ed. Juden im deutschen Kulturbereich. Ein Sammelwerk. Berlin: Jüdischer Verlag, 1959. pp. 760-97.
687. Beutin, Ludwig. Einführung in die Wirtschaftsgeschichte. Cologne: Böhlau, 1958. 179 pp.
688. Beutin, Ludwig. "Wirtschaftsgeschichte." in Handbuch der Wirtschaftswissenschaften. Berlin: Verlag "Die Wirtschaft", 1959. II, 1405-43.
689. Beutin, Ludwig and Hermann Kellenbenz. Grundlagen des Studiums der Wirtschaftsgeschichte. Cologne: Böhlau, 1973. 247 pp.
690. Blaich, Fritz. Staat und Verbände in Deutschland zwischen 1871 und 1945. Wiesbaden: Steiner, 1979. 151 pp.
691. Böhme, Helmut. An Introduction to the Social and Economic History of Germany. New York: St. Martins, 1978. 171 pp. (German: Frankfurt a. M., 1968)
692. Borchardt, Julian. Deutsche Wirtschaftsgeschichte von der Urzeit bis zur Gegenwart. 2 vols. Berlin: E. Laub, 1922-24.
693. Borchardt, Knut. Grundriss der deutschen Wirtschaftsgeschichte. 2nd ed. Göttingen: Vandenhoeck & Ruprecht, 1985. 105 pp.
694. Borchardt, Knut. "Trend, Zyklus, Strukturbrüche, Zufälle. Was bestimmt die deutsche Wirtschaftsgeschichte des 20. Jahrhunderts?" VSWG 64 (1977), 145-78.
695. Born, Karl E., ed. Moderne deutsche Wirtschaftsgeschichte. Cologne: Kiepenheuer & Witsch, 1966. 535 pp.
696. Brinkmann, Carl. Wirtschafts- und Sozialgeschichte. 2nd ed. Göttingen: Vandenhoeck & Ruprecht, 1953. 194 pp.
697. Brook, Warner F. Social and Economic History of Germany 1888-1938. 2nd ed. New York: Russel & Russell, 1962. 291 pp. (See also: Brück, Werner F. below)
698. Brück, Werner F. Social and Economic History of Germany from Wilhelm II to Hitler, 1888-1938. London: Milford, 1938. 292 pp.
699. Brusatti, Alois. Betrachtungen zur Wirtschafts- und Sozialgeschichte. Berlin: Duncker & Humblot, 1979. 226 pp.
700. Brusatti, Alois. Wirtschafts- und Sozialgeschichte des industriellen Zeitalters. 3rd ed. Graz: Styria, 1979. 323 pp.
701. Cornelius, Friedrich. Wirtschaftsgeschichte. Stuttgart: Schwann, 1950. 118 pp.
702. Corsten, Hermann. 100 Jahre deutsche Wirtschaft in Fest- und Denkschriften. Cologne: K. Schroeder, 1937. 428 pp.
703. Curth, Hermann. Volk und Wirtschaft in Lehre und Geschichte. Hamburg: Hanseatische Verlagsanstalt, 1934. 190 pp.
704. Dahrendorf, Ralf. Society and Democracy in Germany. New York: Doubleday, 1969. 457 pp.
705. Deutsche Wirtschaftskunde. Berlin: Reimar Hobbing, 1930. 398 pp.
706. Dopsch, Alfons. Beiträge zur Sozial- und Wirtschaftsgeschichte. Ed. E. Patzelt. Vienna: Seidel, 1928. 360 pp.
707. Droege, Georg. Deutsche Wirtschafts- und Sozialgeschichte. Frankfurt a. M.: Ullstein, 1973. 223 pp.
708. Eisermann, Gottfried. Die Grundlagen des Historismus in der deutschen Nationalökonomie. Stuttgart: Enke, 1956. 249 pp.
709. Engelsing, Rolf. Sozial- und Wirtschaftsgeschichte Deutschlands. Göttingen: Vandenhoeck & Ruprecht, 1976. 223 pp.
710. Facius, Friedrich. Wirtschaft und Staat. Die Entwicklung der staatlichen Wirtschaftsverwaltung in Deutschland vom 17. Jahrhundert bis 1945. Boppard am Rhein: Boldt, 1959. 271 pp.
711. Federau, Fritz. Von Versailles bis Moskau. Politik und Wirtschaft in Deutschland 1919-1970. Ein Dokumentar-Bericht unter Verwendung von vertraulichem, internem und ehemals geheimem Material. Berlin: Haude & Spencer, 1971. 248 pp.
712. Fischer, Wolfram. "The Role of Science and Technology in the Economic Development of Modern Germany." in Science, Technology, and Economic Development. New York: Praeger, 1978. pp. 71-113.
713. Friedensburg, Ferdinand. Politik and Wirtschaft. Aufsätze und Vorträge. Berlin: Duncker & Humblot, 1961. 988 pp.

714. Gattineau, Heinrich. Durch die Klippen des 20. Jahrhunderts: Erinnerungen zur Zeit- und Wirtschaftsgeschichte. Stuttgart: Seewald, 1983. 269 pp.
715. Gruner, Erich. "Wirtschaftsverbände und Staat. Das Problem der wirtschaftlichen Interessenvertretung in historischer Sicht." SZVS 90 (1954), 1-27.
716. Hallbauer, Wilhelm. Unsere Umwelt. Versuch einer Rechenschaft über 2000 Jahre deutscher Wirtschafts- und Stadtentwicklung. Weinsberg: Rock, 1962. 44 pp.
717. Hardach, Gerd. Deutschland in der Weltwirtschaft 1870-1970. Eine Einführung in die Sozial- und Wirtschaftsgeschichte. Frankfurt a. M.: Campus Verlag, 1977. 179 pp.
718. Hardach, Karl W. Germany, 1914-1970. The Fontana Economic History of Europe, 6. London: Fontana, 1975. 90 pp. (German: Stuttgart, 1980)
719. Hardach, Karl W. The Political Economy of Germany in the Twentieth Century. Berkeley: University of California Press, 1980. 235 pp. (German: Göttingen, 1976; 2nd ed. 1979)
720. Harms, Bernhard, ed. Strukturwandlungen der deutschen Volkswirtschaft. 2 vols. Berlin: Reimar Hobbing, 1928.
721. Heinrich, Walter. Wirtschaftspolitik. 2 vols. Vienna: Sexl, 1952. 303 pp.
722. Henning, Friedrich-Wilhelm. Das industrialisierte Deutschland, 1914 bis 1976. Wirtschafts- und Sozialgeschichte, 3. 4th ed. Paderborn: Schöningh, 1978. 292 pp.
723. Hentschel, Volker. Deutsche Wirtschafts- und Sozialpolitik, 1815 bis 1945. Düsseldorf: Droste, 1980. 103 pp.
724. Herbig, Rudolf. Notizen aus der Sozial-, Wirtschafts- und Gewerkschaftsgeschichte vom 14. Jahrhundert bis zur Gegenwart. 6th ed. Wolframs-Eschenbach: RMG, 1978. 295 pp.
725. Hoffmann, Walther G. et al. Das Wachstum der deutschen Wirtschaft seit der Mitte des 19. Jahrhunderts. Berlin: Springer, 1965. 842 pp.
726. Holborn, Hajo. A History of Modern Germany. 3 vols. Princeton, NJ: Princeton University Press, 1982.
727. Hubatsch, Walther. Entstehung und Entwicklung des Reichswirtschaftsministeriums 1880-1933. Berlin: Duncker & Humblot, 1978. 190 pp.
728. Handbuch Wirtschaftsgeschichte. Ed. Institut für Wirtschaftsgeschichte der Akademie der Wissenschaften der DDR. 2 vols. Berlin: Deutscher Verlag der Wissenschaften, 1981.
729. Jecht, Horst. Deutsche Wirtschaftsgeschichte seit dem Ausgang des 18. Jahrhunderts. Salzgitter: Freymark, 1949. 67 pp.
730. Kaltefleiter, Werner. Wirtschaft und Politik in Deutschland. Cologne: Westdeutscher Verlag, 1968. 190 pp.
731. Kehr, Eckart. Economic Interest, Militarism, and Foreign Policy. Berkeley: University of California Press, 1977. 209 pp.
732. Keil, Erika. Das Bewirtschaftungssystem im Ersten und Zweiten Weltkrieg. Thesis: Vienna, 1948. 334 pp.
733. Kellenbenz, Hermann. Deutsche Wirtschaftsgeschichte. 2 vols. Munich: Beck, 1977-1981. (vol. I: Von den Anfängen bis zum Ende des 18. Jahrhunderts; vol. 2: Vom Ausgang des 18. Jahrhunderts bis zum Ende des Zweiten Weltkrieges.)
734. Kellenbenz, Hermann. Grundlagen des Studiums der Wirtschaftsgeschichte. Cologne: Böhlau, 1973. 247 pp. (Reworking of Beutin's Einführung in die Wirtschaftsgeschichte. Cologne, 1958.)
735. Kelter, Ernst. "Die Juden in der deutschen Wirtschaftsgeschichte." in Abhandlungen zur Rechts- und Wirtschaftsgeschichte. Adolf Zycha Festschrift. Weimar: Böhlau, 1941. pp. 551-88.
736. Klein, Burton H. Germany's Economic Preparations for War. Cambridge, MA: Harvard University Press, 1959. 272 pp.
737. Knapp, Georg F. Einführung in einige Hauptgebiete der Nationalökonomie. Munich: Duncker & Humblot, 1925. 390 pp.
738. Kocka, Jürgen. Die Angestellten in der deutschen Geschichte 1850-1980. Göttingen: Vandenhoeck & Ruprecht, 1981. 235 pp.
739. Kuczynski, Jürgen. Die Bewegung der deutschen Wirtschaft von 1800 bis 1946. Meisenheim an Glan: Hain, 1948. 217 pp.
740. Kuske, Bruno. "Leistungs- und Arbeitsentwicklung in der deutschen Wirtschaft." Soziale Welt (1949), 12-28.
741. Laum, Bernhard. Deutsche Wirtschaftsgeschichte. Berlin: Spaeth & Linde, 1936. 53 pp.
742. Lestschinsky, Jakob. Das wirtschaftliche Schicksal des deutschen Judentums. Aufstieg, Wandlung, Krise, Ausblick. Berlin: Selbstverlag der Zentralwohlfahrtsstelle der Deutschen Juden, 1932. 172 pp.

743. Lütge, Friedrich. Beiträge zur Sozial- und Wirtschaftsgeschichte. Gesammelte Abhandlungen. Stuttgart: G. Fischer, 1970. 305 pp.
744. Lütge, Friedrich. Deutsche Sozial- und Wirtschaftsgeschichte. Ein Überblick. Berlin: Springer, 1966. 4th ed. 644 pp.
745. Mauersberg, Hans. Wirtschafts- und Sozialgeschichte zentraleuropäischer Städte in neuerer Zeit. Göttingen: Vandenhoeck & Ruprecht, 1960. 604 pp.
746. Mayer, Theodor. Deutsche Wirtschaftsgeschichte der Neuzeit. Leipzig: Quelle & Meyer, 1928. 142 pp.
747. Michels, Roberto. Sunto di storia economica germanica. Bari: Laterza & Figli, 1930. 119 pp.
748. Michels, Roberto. "Die Wirtschaft." in W. Hofstaetter and F. Schnabel, eds. Grundzüge der Deutschkunde. Leipzig: B. G. Teubner, 1929. II, 113-52.
749. Morsey, Rudolf. "Wirtschaftliche und soziale Auswirkungen der Säkularisation in Deutschland." in Festgabe für Kurt von Raumer. Münster: Aschendorff, 1966. pp. 361-83.
750. Mottek, Hans. Wirtschaftsgeschichte Deutschlands: ein Grundriss. 3 vols. Berlin: VEB Deutscher Verlag der Wissenschaften, 1975-76.
751. Nageshrao, S. Modern Economic Development of Great Powers. U.K., U.S.A., U.S.S.R., Germany & Japan. Baroda: Good Companions, 1962. 408 pp.
752. Nöll von der Nahmer, Robert. "Weltwirtschaft und Weltwirtschaftskrise." in Propyläen-Weltgeschichte. Berlin: Propyläen, 1960. IX, 353-88.
753. Nürrenberg, Renate and Hermann Meyer. Wirtschaftsordnungen des 19. und 20. Jahrhunderts. Donauwörth: Auer, 1977. 111 pp.
754. Nussbaum, Helga and Lotte Zumpe. Wirtschaft und Staat in Deutschland: eine Wirtschaftsgeschichte des staatsmonopolistischen Kapitalismus in Deutschland vom Ende des 19. Jahrhunderts bis 1945. 3 vols. Vaduz, Liechtenstein: Topos Verlag, 1978-1980.
755. Passant, Ernest J. A Short History of Germany, 1815-1945. Cambridge: Cambridge University Press, 1959. 255 pp.
756. Petzina, Dieter. "Materialien zum sozialen und wirtschaftlichen Wandel in Deutschland seit dem Ende des 19. Jahrhunderts." Vierteljahrshefte für Zeitgeschichte 17 (1969), 308-38.
757. Pinson, Koppel S. Modern Germany. Its History and Civilization. 2nd ed. New York: Macmillan, 1966. 682 pp.
758. Price, M. Philips. The Economic Problems of Europe, Pre-War and After. London: Allen & Unwin, 1928. 218 pp.
759. Pritzkoleit, Kurt. Das kommandierte Wunder. Deutschlands Weg im 20. Jahrhundert. Vienna: Desch, 1959. 802 pp.
760. Proesler, Hans. Die Epochen der deutschen Wirtschaftsentwicklung. Nuremberg: Krische, 1927. 173 pp.
761. Reinhardt, Kurt F. The Second Empire and the Weimar Republic. Germany, 2000 Years, 2. 2nd ed. New York: Ungar, 1961. 341 pp.
762. Riedel, Manfred. "Vom Biedermeier zum Maschinenzeitalter." Archiv für Kulturgeschichte 43 (1961), 10-23.
763. Seraphim, Peter-Heinz. Deutsche Wirtschafts- und Sozialgeschichte. Von der Frühzeit bis zum Ausbruch des zweiten Weltkrieges. 2nd ed. Wiesbaden: Gabler, 1966. 248 pp.
764. Sieveking, Heinrich. Grundzüge der neueren Wirtschaftsgeschichte vom 17. Jahrhundert bis zur Gegenwart. 5th ed. Leipzig: Teubner, 1928. 127 pp.
765. Sieveking, Heinrich. Wirtschaftsgeschichte. Berlin: J. Springer, 1935. 209 pp.
766. Simpson, Amos. "The Struggle For Control of the German Economy." Journal of Modern History 31 (1959), 37-45.
767. Spiethoff, Arthur. Die wirtschaftlichen Wechsellagen. 2 vols. Tübingen: Mohr,1955.
768. Steitz, Walter. Schwerpunkte der deutschen Sozial- und Wirtschaftsgeschichte im 19. und 20. Jahrhundert. Heidelberg: Groos, 1979. 183 pp.
769. Stolper, Gustav. German Economy 1870-1940. Issues and Trends. New York: Reynal & Hitchcock, 1940. 295 pp. (German: Stuttgart, 1940)
770. Stolper, Gustav et al. The German Economy, 1870 to the Present. New York: Harcourt, Brace & World, 1967. 353 pp. (German: Tübingen, 1966)
771. Storm, Ernst. "Staat und Wirtschaft." Geist der Zeit 19 (1941), 193-203.
772. Tilly, Richard H. "Los von England: Probleme des Nationalismus in der deutschen Wirtschaftsgeschichte." Zeitschrift für die gesamte Staatswissenschaft 124 (1968), 179-96.

773. Totomiano, Bachan F. Geschichte der Nationalökonomie und des Sozialismus im Zusammenhang mit der Wirtschaftsgeschichte. Jena: Thüringer Verlags-Anstalt, 1925. 192 pp.
774. Treue, Wilhelm. Konzentration und Expansion als Kennzeichen der politischen und wirtschaftlichen Geschichte Deutschlands im 19. und 20. Jahrhundert. Dortmund: Gesellschaft für westfälische Wirtschaftsgeschichte, 1966. 24 pp.
775. Treue, Wilhelm. Wirtschaftsgeschichte der Neuzeit. 2 vols. Stuttgart: Kröner, 1962.
776. Weber, Adolf. Deutsches Wirtschaftsleben. 3rd ed. Berlin: Duncker & Humblot, 1949. 295 pp.
777. Weber, Max. Gesammelte Aufsätze zur Sozial- und Wirtschaftsgeschichte. Tübingen: Mohr, 1924. 556 pp.
778. Weber, Max. Wirtschaftsgeschichte. Abriss der universalen Sozial- und Wirtschaftsgeschichte. Aus den nachgelassenen Vorlesungen. ed. S. Hellmann and M. Palyi. Munich: Duncker & Humblot, 1924. 348 pp.
779. Weinryb, Bernard D. "Prolegomena to an Economic History of the Jews in Germany in Modern Times." Leo Baeck Institute of Jews from Germany. Year Book 1 (1956), 279-306.
780. Winkler, Heinrich A. Liberalismus und Antiliberalismus. Studien zur politischen Sozialgeschichte des 19. und 20. Jahrhunderts. Göttingen: Vandenhoeck & Ruprecht, 1979. 376 pp.
781. Wurm, Franz F. Wirtschaft und Gesellschaft in Deutschland, 1848-1948. Opladen: Leske, 1969. 317 pp.
782. Zorn, Wolfgang. Einführung in die Wirtschafts- und Sozialgeschichte des Mittelalters und der Neuzeit. Munich: Beck, 1974. 126 pp.
783. Zorn, Wolfgang. "Wirtschaft und Politik im deutschen Imperialismus." in W. Abel, ed. Wirtschaft, Geschichte und Wirtschaftsgeschichte. Stuttgart: Fischer, 1966. pp. 340-70.
784. Zorn, Wolfgang, ed. Handbuch der deutschen Wirtschafts- und Sozialgeschichte. 2 vols. Stuttgart: Klett, 1976.

SEE ALSO: 3271, 4663.

GERMANY--1815-1918

References

785. Fout, John C., ed. German History and Civilization, 1806-1914. A Bibliography of Scholarly Periodical Literature. Metuchen, NJ: Scarecrow Press, 1974. 342 pp.
786. Giersiepen, Elisabeth. "Die deutsche Wirtschafts- und Sozialgeschichte des 19. Jahrhunderts in der Forschungsarbeit der Wirtschaftshistoriker der DDR." in Historische Forschungen in der DDR. Berlin: Zeitschrift für Geschichtswissenschaft, 1960. pp. 229-44.
787. Hasbach, Wilhelm. "Recent Contributions to Economic History in Germany." The Economic Journal 1 (1891), 509-19.
788. Lötzke, Helmut. "Quellen zur Wirtschaftsgeschichte in der Epoche des Imperialismus im Deutschen Zentralarchiv Potsdam." Jahrbuch für Wirtschaftsgeschichte (1961), I, 239-83.
789. Steitz, Walter, ed. Quellen zur deutschen Wirtschafts- und Sozialgeschichte im 19. Jahrhundert bis zur Reichsgründung. Darmstadt: Wissenschaftliche Buchgesellschaft, 1980. 470 pp.
790. Steitz, Walter, ed. "Quellen zur deutschen Wirtschafts- und Sozialgeschichte im 19. Jahrhundert im Rahmen der sich auflösenden Feudalstrukturen 1806-1850." VSWG 63 (1976), 145-79.
791. Steitz, Walter, ed. Quellen zur deutschen Wirtschafts- und Sozialgeschichte von der Reichsgründung bis zum Ersten Weltkrieg. Darmstadt: Wissenschaftliche Buchgesellschaft, 1985. 553 pp.

GERMANY--1815-1918

792. Armin, Otto, ed. Die Juden in den Kriegs-Gesellschaften und in der Kriegs-Wirtschaft. Munich: Deutscher Volksverlag, 1921. 156 pp.
793. Arnold, Wilhelm. Zur Geschichte des Eigentums in den deutschen Städten. Basel: Georg, 1861. 486 pp.
794. Aubin, Gustav. "Der deutsche Wirtschaftsraum im Osten vor 1918 und seine Zerstörung." Volk und Reich 7 (1931), 410-22.

795. Augel, Pierre. "Les structures économiques et sociales de l'Allemagne Bismarckienne." Revue d'histoire économique et sociale 41 (1963), 374-90.
796. Ballod, Carl. "Deutschlands wirtschaftliche Entwickelung seit 1890." Schmoller 24 (1900), 493-516.
797. Banze, Angelika. Die deutsch-englische Wirtschaftsrivalität. Berlin: E. Ebering, 1935. 105 pp.
798. Barclay, David E. "A Prussian Socialism? Richard v. Möllendorff and the Dilemmas of Economic Planning in Germany 1918-1919." Central European History 11 (1978), 50-82.
799. Baudis, Dieter. "Wirtschaft und Kriegführung im imperialistischen Deutschland 1914 bis 1918. Zur Darstellung der Rolle der Wirtschaft bei der Vorbereitung und Führung des Ersten Weltkrieges in einigen neueren historischen Publikationen in der BRD und der DDR." Jahrbuch für Wirtschaftsgeschichte (1974), III, 235-51.
800. Beiträge zur deutschen Wirtschafts- und Sozialgeschichte des 18. und 19. Jahrhunderts. Berlin: Akademie-Verlag, 1962. 287 pp.
801. Bentler, Wilhelm et al. Der Staat und die Verbände. Heidelberg: Verlag 'Recht und Wirtschaft', 1957. 84 pp.
802. Berg, Werner. Wirtschaft und Gesellschaft in Deutschland und Grossbritannien im Übergang zum 'Organisierten Kapitalismus.' Unternehmer, Angestellte, Arbeiter und Staat im Steinkohlenbergwerkbau...1850-1914. Berlin: Duncker & Humblot, 1984. 888 pp.
803. Bergmann, Jürgen. "Ökonomische Voraussetzungen der Revolution von 1848. Zur Krise von 1845 bis 1848 in Deutschland." in H.-U. Wehler, ed. 200 Jahre amerikanische Revolution und moderne Revolutionsforschung. Göttingen: Vandenhoeck & Ruprecht, 1976.
804. Bissing, Wilhelm M. "Geschichte der deutschen wirtschaftswissenschaftlichen Ostforschung bis 1945." Schmoller 86 (1966), 179-215.
805. Bläsing, Joachim F. E. Das goldene Delta und sein eisernes Hinterland, 1815-1851. Von niederländisch-preussischen zu deutsch-niederländischen Wirtschaftsbeziehungen. Leiden: Stenfert Kroese, 1973. 276 pp.
806. Blaich, Fritz et al. Vom Kleingewerbe zur Grossindustrie. Quantitativ-regionale und politisch-rechtliche Aspekte zur Erforschung der Wirtschafts- und Gesellschaftsstruktur im 19. Jahrhundert. Berlin: Duncker & Humblot, 1975. 259 pp.
807. Böhme, Helmut. Deutschlands Weg zur Grossmacht. Studien zum Verhältnis von Wirtschaft und Staat während der Reichsgründungszeit 1848-1881. 2nd ed. Cologne: Kiepenheuer & Witsch, 1972. 728 pp.
808. Böhmert, Victor. "Deutschlands wirtschaftliche Neugestaltung." Preussische Jahrbücher 18 (1866), 269-304.
809. Böhmert, Wilhelm. "Wandlungen der deutschen Volkswirtschaft 1882-1907. Ein Blick auf die Ergebnisse der Berufs- und Betriebszählungen." Der Arbeiterfreund (1910).
810. Bondi, Gerhard. "Zur Vorgeschichte der 'kleindeutschen Lösung' 1866-1871. Eine wirtschaftshistorische Betrachtung." Jahrbuch für Wirtschaftsgeschichte (1966), II, 11-33.
811. Borchardt, Knut. "Regional Differentiation in Development of Germany throughout the Nineteenth Century with Special Regard to the East/West Differential." in Papers Presented to the Third International Conference of Economic History, Munich, 1965. Paris: Mouton, 1974.
812. Born, Karl E. "Der soziale und wirtschaftliche Strukturwandel Deutschlands am Ende des 19. Jahrhunderts." VSWG 50 (1963), 361-76.
813. Born, Karl E. Wirtschafts- und Sozialgeschichte des deutschen Kaiserreichs (1867/71-1914). Wiesbaden: Steiner, 1985. 175 pp.
814. Brinkmann, Carl. "The Place of Germany in the Economic History of the Nineteenth Century." Economic History Review 4 (1933), 129-46.
815. Buckhard-Wuhrmann, W. "Über Goethes Anteilnahme und Mitwirken am wirtschaftlichen Geschehen seiner Zeit." Mitteilungen der List Gesellschaft 3 (1960), 155-226.
816. Burchardt, Lothar. Friedenswirtschaft und Kriegsvorsorge. Deutschlands wirtschaftliche Rüstungsbestrebungen vor 1914. Boppard am Rhein: Boldt, 1968. 277 pp.
817. Caro, Georg. Neue Beiträge zur deutschen Wirtschafts- und Verfassungsgeschichte. Leipzig: Veit, 1911. 156 pp.
818. Caspary, Adolf. Wirtschafts-Strategie und Kriegsführung. Wirtschaftliche Vorbereitung, Führung und Auswirkung des Krieges in geschichtlichem Aufriss. Berlin: Mittler, 1932. 166 pp.
819. Clapham, John H. Economic Development of France and Germany, 1815-1914. 4th ed. London: Cambridge University Press, 1937. 420 pp.
820. Dawson, William H. The Evolution of Modern Germany. London: T. Fisher Unwin, 1908. 503 pp.

821. Delbrück, Clemens von. Die wirtschaftliche Mobilmachung in Deutschland 1914. Munich: Verlag für Kulturpolitik, 1924. 322 pp.
822. Dix, Arthur. Wirtschaftskrieg und Kriegswirtschaft. Zur Geschichte des deutschen Zusammenbruchs. Berlin: Mittler, 1920. 369 pp.
823. Dreyfus, François-G. "Bilan Économique des Allemagnes en 1815." Revue d'histoire économique et sociale 43 (1965), 433-64.
824. Ehlert, Hans G. Die wirtschaftliche Zentralbehörde des deutschen Reiches 1914 bis 1919. Das Problem der 'Gemeinwirtschaft' in Krieg und Frieden. Wiesbaden: Steiner, 1982. 597 pp.
825. Fischer, Wolfram. "Das Verhältnis von Staat und Wirtschaft in Deutschland am Beginn der Industrialisierung." Kyklos 14 (1961), 377-63.
826. Fischer, Wolfram. Wirtschaft und Gesellschaft im Zeitalter der Industrialisierung. Aufsätze, Studien, Vorträge. Göttingen: Vandenhoeck & Ruprecht, 1972. 547 pp.
827. Franz, Eugen. Der Entscheidungskampf um die wirtschaftspolitische Führung Deutschlands (1856-1867). Munich, 1933; rpt. Aalen, 1973. 464 pp.
828. Freytag, Gustav. Aus neuer Zeit. 1700-1848. Bilder aus der deutschen Vergangenheit, 5. Leipzig: List, 1924. 587 pp.
829. Gall, Lothar. "Der Staat und Wirtschaft in der Reichsgründungszeit." Historische Zeitschrift 209 (1969), 616-30.
830. Gellately, Robert. The Politics of Economic Despair. Shopkeepers und German Politics 1890-1914. London: Sage Publications, 1974. 317 pp.
831.   Goebel, Otto. Deutsche Rohstoffwirtschaft im Weltkrieg einschliesslich des Hindenburgprogramms. Stuttgart: Deutsche Verlags-Anstalt, 1930. 195 pp.
832. Gradnauer, Georg and Robert Schmidt. Die deutsche Volkswirtschaft. Eine Einfuhrüng. Berlin: Vorwärts, 1921. 231 pp.
833. Groh, Dieter. "L'Echec de la 'Fondation interne du Reich': institutions, économie et politique sociale du Deuxiéme Reich." Revue d'histoire moderne et contemporaine 19 (1972), 269-82.
834. Hamerow, Theodore S. Restoration, Revolution, Reaction. Economics and Politics in Germany, 1815-1871. 2nd ed. Princeton, NJ: Princeton University Press, 1967. 347 pp.
835. Harms, Bernhard. "Die Entstehung der modernen Volkswirtschaft. Grundzüge eines Vortrages." Arbeiten der Landwirtschaftskammer für die Provinz Hannover 25 (1909), 46-51.
836. Harms, Bernhard. Über die Anfänge der kapitalistischen Wirtschaftsordnung in Deutschland. Jena: Vopelius, 1906. 16 pp.
837. Haussherr, Hans. Wirtschaftsgeschichte der Neuzeit vom Ende des 14. bis zur Höhe des 19. Jahrhunderts. 5th ed. Cologne: Böhlau, 1981. 544 pp.
838. Helfferich, Karl T. Deutschlands Volkswohlstand 1888-1913. Berlin: G. Stilke, 1913. 127 pp. (French: Berlin, 1914)
839. Helmreich, Ernst C. "Prussian Economic Policy Foundations of German Unification." Current History 16 (1949) 151-55.
840. Henning, Heinz. Die Situation der deutschen Kriegswirtschaft im Sommer 1918 und ihre Beurteilung durch Heeresleitung, Reichsführung und Bevölkerung. Diss. Hamburg, 1957. 301 pp.
841. Hentschel, Volker. "Erwerbs- und Einkommensverhältnisse in Sachsen, Baden und Württemberg vor dem Ersten Weltkrieg (1890-1914). VSWG 79 (1966), 26-73.
842. Hentschel, Volker. Wirtschaft und Wirtschaftspolitik im wilhelminischen Deutschland. Organisierter Kapitalismus und Interventionsstaat? Stuttgart: Klett-Cotta, 1978. 303 pp.
843. Herrmann, Walther. "Wirtschaftszustände in Preussen 1815-1825. Bemerkungen zu einer retrospektiven Kritik liberaler Wirtschaftspolitik des angehenden 19. Jahrhunderts." Finanzarchiv, Neue Folge 5 (1937-38), 504-14.
844. Hesse, Friedrich. Die deutsche Wirtschaftslage von 1914 bis 1923. Krieg, Geldblähe und Wechsellagen. Jena: Fischer, 1938. 498 pp.
845. Hirsch, Julius. "Deutsche Wirtschaftswissenschaft und Praxis im letzten Menschenalter." in Die Wirtschaftswissenschaft nach dem Krieg. Munich: Duncker & Humblot, 1925. II, 146-97.
846. Huber, Frank C. Fünfzig Jahre deutschen Wirtschaftslebens. Stuttgart: C. Grüninger, 1906. 136 pp.
847. Inama-Sternegg, Karl. Deutsche Wirtschaftsgeschichte. Leipzig: Duncker & Humblot, 1909. 755 pp.
848. Jastrow, Ignaz. Geschichte des deutschen Einheitstraumes und seiner Erfüllung. Berlin: Allgemeiner Verein für Deutsche Litteratur, 1890. 400 pp.

849. Jöhlinger, Otto, ed. Deutsche Wirtschaft im Kriege. Berlin: Deutsche Export-Revue, 1917. 123 pp.

850. Kaufhold, Karl H. "Wirtschaft und Gewerbe in Preussen 1817. Ein Überblick nach einem Bericht von G. J. Ch. Kunth," in Auf dem Weg zur Industrialisierung. Stuttgart: Klett-Cotta, 1978. pp. 265-79.

851. Kindleberger, Charles P. "Germany's Overtaking of England, 1806-1914." Weltwirtschaftliches Archiv 111 (1975) 477-504.

852. Kirchgaessner, Bernhard. Einführung in die Wirtschaftsgeschichte. Grundriss der deutschen Wirtschafts- und Sozialgeschichte bis zum Ende des alten Reiches. Düsseldorf: Werner, 1979. 230 pp.

853. Kitchen, Martin. The Political Economy of Germany 1815-1914. London: Croom Helm, 1978. 304 pp.

854. Klein, Fritz. Deutschland von 1897-98 bis 1917. Deutschland in der Periode des Imperialismus bis zur grossen sozialistischen Oktoberrevolution. Berlin: VEB Deutscher Verlag der Wissenschaften, 1961. 408 pp.

855. Knapp, Theodor. Gesammelte Beiträge zur Rechts- und Wirtschaftsgeschichte vornehmlich des deutschen Bauernstandes. Tübingen: Laupp, 1902. 485 pp.

856. Krings, Wilfried and Wolfgang Zorn. "Nachtrag zur historischen Wirtschaftskarte um 1820." Rheinische Vierteljahrsblätter 35 (1971), 274-87.

857. Krüger, Dieter. Nationalökonomen im Wilhelminischen Deutschland. Göttingen: Vandenhoeck & Ruprecht, 1983. 336 pp.

858. Kügelgen, Werner von. Kriegswirtschaft und Sozialismus. Die sozialistische Ordnung der deutschen Volkswirtschaft im Weltkrieg. Diss. Heidelberg, 1935. Tallinn: Estländische Druckerei, 1936. 84 pp.

859. Lamprecht, Karl. "Die Entwickelung des wirtschaftlichen und geistigen Horizonts unserer Nation." Handels- und Machtpolitik 1 (1900), 39-62.

860. Lichtenberger, Henri. L'Allemagne moderne, son évolution. Paris: E. Flammarion, 1907. 399 pp. (English: London, 1913; German: Dresden, 1908)

861. Lotz, Walther. "Wandlungen im deutschen Wirtschaftsleben und Wandlungen in der deutschen Wirtschaftswissenschaft seit Bismarcks Rücktritt." in Hauptprobleme der Soziologie. Munich: Duncker & Humblot, 1923. pp. 309-16.

862. Martin, Günther. "Der Staatsauftrag. Seine Problematik, dargestellt an einem ausgewählten Kapitel preussischer Wirtschafts- und Sozialgeschichte." Tradition (1972), 314-321.

863. Mendelssohn-Bartholdy, Albrecht. The War and German Society. 1937; rpt. New York: H. Fertig, 1971. 299 pp.

864. Meyer, Rudolph. Politische Gründer und die Corruption in Deutschland. Leipzig: Bidder, 1877; rpt. Ann Arbor, MI: University Microfilms International, 1980. 240 pp.

865. Mone, Franz J. Beiträge zur Geschichte der Volkswirtschaft aus Urkunden. Karlsruhe: Braun, 1859. 219 pp.

866. Mottek, Hans. "Zur historischen Entwicklung der ökonomischen Rolle des bürgerlichen Staates bis zum ersten Weltkrieg." Jahrbuch für Wirtschaftsgeschichte (1974), III, 65-71.

867. Müller, Alfred. Die Kriegsrohstoffbewirtschaftung 1914-1918 im Dienste des deutschen Monopolkapitals. Berlin: Akademie, 1955. 138 pp.

868. Müller, Ernst F. "Zur Wirtschaftsgeschichte des Preussenlandes von der Errichtung des Herzogtums Preussen (1525) bis zum Ausbruch des Weltkrieges." in Deutsche Staatenbildung und deutsche Kultur im Preussenlande. Königberg: Gräfe & Unzer, 1931. pp. 471-535.

869. Müller-Jabusch, Maximilian. So waren die Gründerjahre. Düsseldorf: Becker & Wrietzner, 1957. 69 pp.

870. Neuhaus, Georg. Deutsche Wirtschaftsgeschichte im 19. Jahrhundert. Munich: J. Kösel, 1907. 182 pp.

871. Perlo, Victor. "Partners in Plunder." International Affairs 7 (1961), 48-57.

872. Pietri, Nicole. Evolution économique de l'Allemagne du milieu du XIXe siècle à 1914. Paris: CDU & SEDES, 1982. 565 pp.

873. Pingaud, Albert. Le développement économique de l'Allemagne contemporaine (1871-1914). Paris: Berger-Levrault, 1916. 108 pp.

874. Pohl, Hans. "Die Entwicklung der deutschen Volkswirtschaft (1820-1880)." in Wissenschaft und Kodifikation des Privatrechts im 19. Jahrhundert. Frankfurt a. M.: Klostermann, 1977. II, 1-25.

875. Pohl, Hans. "Wirtschafts- und sozialgeschichtliche Grundzüge der Epoche 1870-1914. Einführung in die Problematik." in Sozialgeschichtliche Probleme in der Zeit der Hoch-industrialisierung (1870-1914). Paderborn: Schöningh, 1979. pp. 13-55.

876. Pohle, Ludwig. Die Entwicklung des deutschen Wirtschaftslebens im letzten Jahrhundert. 5th ed. Leipzig: Teubner, 1923. 144 pp.

877. Poidevin, Raymond. "Economic Aspects of Franco-German Negotiations, June-October 1871." Revue d'Histoire Moderne et Contemporaine 19 (1972), 219-234.

878. Prinz, Arthur. Juden im deutschen Wirtschaftsleben. Soziale und wirtschaftliche Strukturen im Wandel, 1850-1914. Tübingen: Mohr, 1984. 202 pp.

879. Radloff, Anneliese. Hardenbergs Stellung im Rahmen der preussischen Sozial- und Wirtschafts-reform. Diss. Berlin, 1957. 153 pp.

880. Richter, Siegfried and Rolf Sonnemann. "Zur Problematik des Übergangs vom vormonopolisti-schen Kapitalismus zum Imperialismus in Deutschland." Jahrbuch für Wirtschaftsgeschichte (1963), II, 39-78.

881. Roscher, Carl. Zur Kritik der neuesten wirthschaftlichen Entwickelung im Deutschen Reiche. Zittau: Menzel, 1876. 518 pp.

882. Roscher, Wilhelm G. F. Geschichte der National-Ökonomik in Deutschland. Munich: 1874; rpt. New York, 1965. 1085 pp.

883. Rosenberg, Howard R. et al. "The Economic Impact of Imperial Germany." Journal of Economic History (1973), 101-34.

884. Sartorius von Waltershausen, August. Deutsche Wirtschaftsgeschichte 1815-1914. 2nd ed. Jena: Fischer, 1923. 636 pp.

885. Schmoller, Gustav. Preussische Verfassungs-, Verwaltungs- und Finanzgeschichte. Vols. 3-5. Berlin: Reimar Hobbing, 1948-51.

886. Schnabel, Franz. Deutsche Geschichte im 19. Jahrhundert. 3th ed. 3 vols. Freiburg i. B.: Herder, 1954.

887. Schneider, Franz. Geschichte der formellen Staatswirtschaft von Brandenburg-Preussen. Berlin: Duncker & Humblot, 1952. 197 pp.

888. Schneider, R. Hundert Jahre deutscher Wirtschaftsgeschichte. Berlin: Linden, 1914. 23 pp.

889. Schoeps, Hans J. Von Olmütz nach Dresden 1850-51. Ein Beitrag zur Geschichte der Reformen am Deutschen Bund. Cologne: Grote, 1972. 230 pp.

890. Schultze-Grossborstel, Ernst. Weltanschauung und Wirtschaftsleben in der deutschen Kultur-entwicklung des 19. Jahrhunderts. Hamburg: Gutenberg, 1910. 103 pp.

891. Schumacher, Hermann A. Weltwirtschaftliche Studien: Vorträge und Aufsätze. Leipzig: Veit & Comp., 1911. 574 pp.

892. Seeber, Gustav. Zwischen Bebel und Bismarck. Zur Geschichte des Linksliberalismus in Deutschland 1871-1893. Berlin: Akademie, 1965. 226 pp.

893. Silbergleit, Heinrich. Freistaat Preussen. Die Bevölkerungs- und Berufsverhältnisse der Juden im Deutschen Reich, 1. Berlin: Akademie, 1930. 348 pp.

894. Sombart, Werner. Die deutsche Volkswirtschaft im neunzehnten Jahrhundert und im Anfang des 20. Jahrhunderts. Eine Einführung in die Nationalökonomie. 7th ed. Berlin: Bondi, 1927. 532 pp.

895. Sombart, Werner. Die Juden und das Wirtschaftsleben. Munich: Duncker & Humblot, 1918. 476 pp.

896. Steglich, Walter. "Beitrag zur Problematik des Bündnisses zwischen Junkern und Bourgeoisie in Deutschland 1870 bis 1880." Wissenschaftliche Zeitschrift der Humboldt-Universität zu Berlin 9 (1959), 323-40.

897. Stern, Fritz. "Money, Morals, and the Pillars of Bismarck's Society." Central European History 3 (1970), 49-72.

898. Stoehle, H. "Remarques sur la politique économique et sociale de la Prusse." Révue d'économie politique 60 (1950), 141-56.

899. Stutzer, Emil. Grundzüge der deutschen Wirtschaftsgeschichte insbesondere der neuesten Zeit. 2nd ed. Dresden: Ehlermann, 1925. 95 pp.

900. Stutzer, Emil. Skizzen zur deutschen Wirtschaftsgeschichte insbesondere des 19. und 20. Jahrhunderts. Dresden: Ehlermann, 1925. 126 pp.

901. Théry, Edmond. Histoire économique de l'Angleterre, de l'Allemagne, des Etats Unis et de la France. Paris: Economiste Européen, 1902. 451 pp.

902. Thwaite, Benjamin H. The Rise of Germany 1870-1905. London: P. S. King, 1906. 28 pp.

903. Treue, Wilhelm. "Deutsche Wirtschaftsführer im 19. Jahrhundert." Historische Zeitschrift 167 (1943), 548-65.
904. Treue, Wilhelm. "Expansion und Konzentration in der deutschen Volkswirtschaft (1866/71-1914)." in Wissenschaft und Kodifikation des Privatrechts im 19. Jahrhundert. Frankfurt a. M.: Klostermann, 1977. II, 26-46.
905. Treue, Wilhelm. Gesellschaft, Wirtschaft und Technik Deutschlands im 19. Jahrhundert. 9th ed. Munich: Deutscher Taschenbuch Verlag, 1975. 301 pp.
906. Treue, Wilhelm. "Wirtschafts- und Sozialgeschichte Deutschlands im 19. Jahrhundert." in Von der französischen Revolution bis zum 1. Weltkrieg. 9th ed. Stuttgart: Union Verlag, 1970. pp. 376-541.
907. Treue, Wilhelm. Wirtschafts- und Technikgeschichte Preussens. Berlin: de Gruyter, 1984. 657 pp.
908. Treue, Wilhelm. Wirtschaftszustände und Wirtschaftspolitik in Preussen 1815-1825. Stuttgart: Kohlhammer, 1937. 256 pp.
909. Treue, Wilhelm, ed. Studien zu Naturwissenschaft, Technik und Wirtschaft im Neunzehnten Jahrhundert. 3 vols. Göttingen: Vandenhoeck & Ruprecht, 1976.
910. Troeltsch, Walter. Über die neuesten Veränderungen im deutschen Wirtschaftsleben. Stuttgart: Kohlhammer, 1899. 156 pp.
911. Veblen, Thorstein. Imperial Germany and the Industrial Revolution. New York: MacMillan, 1915. 324 pp.
912. Vogel, Barbara, ed. Preussische Reformen 1807-1820. Königstein: Verlag Gruppe Athenäum, 1980. 331 pp.
913. Weber, Max. Der Nationalstaat und die Volkswirtschaftpolitik. Freiburg i. B.: Mohr, 1895. 34 pp. (Max Weber's academic inaugural address.)
914. Winkel, Harald. Die deutsche Nationalökonomie im 19. Jahrhundert. Darmstadt: Wissenschaftliche Buchgesellschaft, 1977. 193 pp.
915. "Die wirthschaftliche Reformbewegung in Deutschland." Preussische Jahrbücher 6 (1860), 563-83.
916. Die wirtschaftlichen Kräfte Deutschlands im Kriege. Berlin: Dresdner Bank, 1916. 31 pp.
917. Wiskemann, Erwin. Wirtschaftsgeschichte. 1800-1933. Leipzig: Glöckner, 1933. 183 pp.
918. Wittenberg, Max. Ein Blick auf den wirthschaftlichen Aufschwung am Ende des 19. Jahrhunderts. Berlin: Simion, 1900. 58 pp.
919. Wolff, Emil. Grundriss der preussisch-deutschen sozialpolitischen und Volkswirtschaftsgeschichte von 1640-1900. 2nd ed. Berlin: Weidmann, 1904. 240 pp.
920. Wygodzinski, Wilhelm. "Staat und Wirtschaft." in Handbuch der Politik. 3rd ed. Berlin: W. Rothschild, 1920. I, 107-12.
921. Wygodzinski, Wilhelm. Wandlungen der deutschen Volkswirtschaft im neunzehnten Jahrhundert. Cologne: DuMont-Schauberg, 1907. 202 pp.
922. Zahn, Friedrich. "Deutschlands Volkswirtschaft beim Eintritt ins 20. Jahrhundert." Jahrbücher für Nationalökonomie und Statistik 76 (1901), 1-53.
923. Ziegenhagen, Norbert, ed. Wirtschaftsgeschichte 1870/71-1900. Berlin: VEB Deutscher Verlag der Wissenschaften, 1963. 54 pp.
924. Zilch, Reinhold. "Zur wirtschaftlichen Vorbereitung des deutschen Imperialismus auf den Ersten Weltkrieg." Zeitschrift für Geschichtswissenschaft 24 (1976), 202-15.
925. Zorn, Wolfgang. "Wirtschafts- und sozialgeschichtliche Zusammenhänge der deutschen Reichsgründungszeit, 1850-1879." Historische Zeitschrift 197 (1963), 318-42. (Also in H.-U. Wehler, ed. Moderne deutsche Sozialgeschichte. 5th ed. Cologne: Kiepenheuer & Witsch, 1966. pp. 254-70.)
926. Zumpe, Lotte, ed. Wirtschaft und Staat im Imperialismus. Beiträge zur Entwicklungsgeschichte des staatsmonopolistischen Kapitalismus. Berlin: Akademie, 1976. 312 pp.
927. Zunkel, Friedrich. "Die ausländischen Arbeiter in der deutschen Kriegswirtschaftspolitik des Ersten Weltkrieges." in G. A. Ritter, ed. Entstehung und Wandel der modernen Gesellschaft. Festschrift für H. Rosenberg. Berlin: de Gruyter, 1970. pp. 280-311.

SEE ALSO: 940, 950, 968, 971, 2288, 2347, 3503, 4071, 4813, 4867, 4869, 4941, 5002.

WEIMAR REPUBLIC--1919-1933

Bibliographic References

928. Brodnitz, Georg. "Bibliography: Recent Work in German Economic History (1900-1927)." Economic History Review (1927-28), 322-45.
929. Trumpp, Thomas and Renate Köhne, eds. Archivbestände zur Wirtschafts- und Sozialgeschichte der Weimarer Republik. Übersicht über Quellen in Archiven der Bundesrepublik Deutschland. Boppard am Rhein: Boldt, 1979. 380 pp.

WEIMAR REPUBLIC--1919-1933

930. Abraham, David. The Collapse of the Weimar Republic. Political Economy and Crisis. Princeton, NJ: Princeton University Press, 1981. 366 pp.
931. Becker, Walter et al. "Die Entwicklung der imperialistischen Wirtschaft in der Weimarer Republik." Wirtschaftwissenschaft 25 (1977), 1758-70.
932. Biechele, E. Der Kampf um die Gemeinwirtschaftskonzeption des Reichswirtschafts- ministeriums im Jahre 1919. Diss. Berlin, 1972. 264 pp.
933. Böhret, Carl. Aktionen gegen die "kalte Sozialisierung" 1926-1930. Ein Beitrag zum Wirken ökonomischer Einflussverbände in der Weimarer Republik. Berlin: Duncker & Humblot, 1966. 279 pp.
934. Borchardt, Knut. "Wirtschaftliche Ursachen des Scheiterns der Weimarer Republik." in Weimar. Selbstpreisgabe einer Demokratie. Eine Bilanz heute. Düsseldorf: Droste, 1980. pp. 211-49.
935. Buchta, Bruno. Die Junker und die Weimarer Republik. Charakter und Bedeutung der Osthilfe in den Jahren 1928-1933. Diss. Berlin, 1958. Berlin: Deutscher Verlag der Wissenschaften, 1959. 176 pp.
936. Costigliola, Frank C. "The United States and the Reconstruction of Germany in the 1920s." Business History Review 50 (1976), 477-502.
937. Davis, Joseph S. "Recent Economic and Financial Progress in Germany." Review of Economic Statistics 3 (1921), 141-65.
938. Dawes, Rufus C. The Dawes Plan in the Making. Indianapolis: Bobbs-Merrill, 1925. 525 pp. (German: Stuttgart, 1926)
939. Dobkowski, Michael N. and Isidor Wallimann. Toward the Holocaust: The Social and Economic Collapse of the Weimar Republic. Westport, CT: Greenwood Press, 1983. 422 pp.
940. Feldman, Gerald. Vom Weltkrieg zur Weltwirtschaftskrise: Studien zur deutschen Wirtschafts- und Sozialgeschichte 1914-1932. Göttingen: Vandenhoeck & Ruprecht, 1984. 272 pp.
941. Fischer, Harald. "Unternehmerverbände und Reichspolitik 1930-1932. Zum Verhältnis von ökonomischer und politischer Macht in der Endphase der Weimarer Republik." in Das Ende der Weimarer Republik. Hamburg: Focke & Jaffé, 1978. pp. 15-94.
942. Fischer, Wolfram. Deutsche Wirtschaftspolitik 1918 bis 1945. 3rd ed. Opladen: C. W. Leske, 1968. 125 pp.
943. Gebauer, Werner. "Wirtschaftspolitische Probleme der Weimarer Republik in neueren Darstellungen." Jahrbuch fur Sozialwissenschaft 2 (1951), 223-35.
944. Gossweiler, Kurt. Kapital, Reichswehr und NSDAP 1919-1924. Berlin: Akademie, 1982. 616 pp.
945. Grübler, Michael. Die Spitzenverbände der Wirtschaft und das erste Kabinett Brüning: vom Ende der grossen Koalition 1929/30 bis zum Vorabend der Bankenkrise 1931. Diss. Hamburg. Düsseldorf: Droste, 1982. 500 pp.
946. Hardach, Gerd. "Zur politischen Ökonomie der Weimarer Republik." in Die Zerstörung der Weimarer Republik. Cologne: Pahl-Rugenstein, 1977. pp. 14-37.
947. Henderson, William O. "The Economic Development of Germany 1918-39." in Economic Geography. Germany, 3. London: Naval Intelligence Division, 1944.
948. Hermant, Max. Les paradoxes économiques de l'Allemagne moderne, 1918-1931. Paris: Colin, 1931. 202 pp.

949. Hermens, Ferdinand A. and Theodor Schieder. Staat, Wirtschaft und Politik in der Weimarer Republik. Berlin: Duncker & Humblot, 1967. 507 pp.
950. Hesse, Friedrich. Die deutsche Wirtschaftslage von 1914 bis 1923. Krieg, Geldblähe und Wechsellagen. Jena: Fischer, 1938. 498 pp.
951. Hiden, John W. Germany and Europe, 1919-1939. London: Longman, 1977. 83 pp.
952. Hiden, John W. The Weimar Republic. London: Longman, 1974. 114 pp.
953. Holtfrerich, Carl-Ludwig. Alternativen zu Brünings Wirtschaftspolitik in der Weltwirtschafts- krise. Wiesbaden: Steiner, 1982. 25 pp.
954. Maier, Charles S. Recasting Bourgeois Europe. Stabilization in France, Germany and Italy in the Decade after World War I. Princeton: Princeton University Press, 1975. 650 pp.
955. Novy, Klaus. Strategien der Sozialisierung. Die Diskussion der Wirtschaftsreform in der Weimarer Republik. Frankfurt: Campus, 1978. 333 pp.
956. Nussbaum, Manfred. Wirtschaft und Staat in Deutschland während der Weimarer Republik. Berlin: Akademie, 1978. 423 pp.
957. Obermann, Karl. Die Beziehungen des amerikanischen Imperialismus zum deutschen Imperialis- mus in der Zeit der Weimarer Republik, 1918-1925. Berlin: Rütten & Loening, 1952. 167 pp.
958. Paduck, Arnold. Die Wandlung der kapitalistischen Wirtschaft nach dem ersten imperialistischen Krieg. Diss. Leipzig, 1947. 168 pp.
959. Petzina, Dietmar. Die deutsche Wirtschaft in der Zwischenkriegszeit. Wiesbaden: Steiner, 1977. 205 pp.
960. Petzina, Dietmar. "Grundriss der deutschen Wirtschaftsgeschichte, 1918-1945." in Deutsche Geschichte seit dem 1. Weltkrieg. Stuttgart: Deutsche Verlags-Anstalt, 1973. II, 665-784.
961. Petzina, Dietmar. "Hauptprobleme der deutschen Wirtschaftspolitik 1932-33." Vierteljahrs- hefte für Zeitgeschichte 15 (1967), 18-55.
962. Puchert, Berthold. Der Wirtschaftskrieg des deutschen Imperialismus gegen Polen 1925-1934. Berlin: Akademie, 1963. 210 pp.
963. Quigley, Hugh and Robert T. Clark. Republican Germany. A Political and Economic Study. London: Methuen, 1928. 318 pp.
964. Reinhold, Peter P. The Economic, Financial and Political State of Germany since the War. New Haven, CT: Yale University Press, 1928. 134 pp.
965. Ritter, Franz. Theorie und Praxis des demokratischen Sozialismus in der Weimarer Republik. Frankfurt a. M.: Campus, 1981. 320 pp.
966. Roll, Eric. Spotlight on Germany: A Survey of her Economic and Political Problems. London: Faber & Faber, 1933; rpt. New York: AMS Press, 1975. 302 pp.
967. Samhaber, Ernst. Die neuen Wirtschaftsformen 1914-1940. Diss. Kiel. Berlin: Neff, 1970. 364 pp.
968. Sartorius von Waltershausen, August. Die Umgestaltung der zwischenstaatlichen Wirtschaft. Ein geschichtlicher Rückblick 1914-1932. Jena: Fischer, 1935. 326 pp.
969. Scheele, Godfrey. The Weimar Republic. Overture to the Third Reich. London: Faber & Faber, 1946. 360 pp.
970. Singer, Kurt. Staat und Wirtschaft seit dem Waffenstillstand. Jena: Fischer, 1924. 233 pp.
971. Staudinger, Hans. Wirtschaftspolitik im Weimarer Staat: Lebenserinnerungen eines politischen Beamten im Reich und in Preussen 1889 bis 1934. Bonn: Verlag Neue Gesellschaft, 1982. 152 pp.
972. Thomas, Georg R. Geschichte der deutschen Wehr- und Rüstungswirtschaft 1918-1943/45. Boppard am Rhein: Boldt, 1966. 552 pp.
973. Treue, Wilhelm. "Germany between Capitalism and Socialism, 1918-19." in Proceedings of the Fifth International Economic History Conference, Leningrad, 1970. Paris: Mouton, 1979.
974. Vermeil, Edmond. L'Allemagne contemporaine (1919-1924). La structure et son évolution politique, économique et sociale. Paris: Alcan, 1925. 255 pp.
975. Winkel, Harald, ed. Finanz- und wirtschaftspolitischen Fragen der Zwischenkriegszeit. Berlin: Duncker & Humblot, 1973. 208 pp.
976. Wulf, Peter. Hugo Stinnes. Wirtschaft und Politik 1918-1924. Stuttgart: Klett-Cotta, 1979. 584 pp.

SEE ALSO: 1015, 4983, 5002, 5029, 5057, 5071.

THIRD REICH--1933-1945

Bibliographic Reference

977. Volkmann, Hans-Erich. Wirtschaft im Dritten Reich 1933-1939. Munich: Bernard & Graefe, 1980. 294 pp.

THIRD REICH--1933-1945

978. Barkai, Avraham. Das Wirtschaftssystem des Nationalsozialismus. Cologne: Verlag Wissenschaft & Politik, 1977. 214 pp.
979. Bartel, Walter. "Der Aufgabenbereich des Leiters des Amtes D IV des Wirtschaftsverwaltungs-hauptamtes der SS." Zeitschrift für Geschichtswissenschaft 14 (1966), 944-56.
980. Basch, Antonin. Germany's Economic Conquest of Czechoslovakia. Chicago: Czechoslovak National Council of America, 1939. 29 pp.
981. Beckenbach, Ralf. Der Staat im Faschismus. Ökonomie und Politik im Deutschen Reich 1920-1945. Berlin: Verlag für Studium der Arbeiterbewegung, 1974. 134 pp.
982. Bettelheim, Charles. L'économie allemande sous le nazisme. Munich: Trikont, 1974. 333 pp. (German: Munich, 1974)
983. Billig, Joseph. Centre de documentation juive contemporaine. Les Camps de concentration dans l'économie du Reich hitlérien. Paris: Presses universitaires de France, 1973. 348 pp.
984. Birkenfeld, Wolfgang. Der synthetische Treibstoff 1933-1945. Ein Beitrag zur national-sozialistischen Wirtschafts- und Rüstungspolitik. Göttingen: Musterschmidt, 1964. 279 pp.
985. Blaich, Fritz. Probleme der nationalsozialistischen Wirtschaftspolitik. Berlin: Duncker & Humblot, 1976. 174 pp.
986. Boelcke, Willi A. Die deutsche Wirtschaft 1930-1945. Düsseldorf: Droste, 1983. 389 pp.
987. Capelle, H. van. De Nazi-economie. Economie en buitenlandse handel in nationaal-socialistisch Duitsland. Assen: van Gorcum, 1978. 275 pp. (English and German summaries)
988. Carroll, Berenice A. Design for Total War. Arms and Economics in the Third Reich. The Hague: Mouton, 1968. 311 pp.
989. Cilek, Roman and Jan Ztehlik. Das Recht muss warten. Macht und Verbrechen. Vienna: Europa, 1968. 240 pp.
990. Dubail, René. Une expérience d'économie dirigée: l'Allemagne national socialiste. Paris: P. Dupont, 1962. 171 pp.
991. "The Economics of Fascism." in Economic History of Europe. New York: Harper & Row, 1968. pp. 265-95.
992. Eichholtz, Dietrich. Geschichte der deutschen Kriegswirtschaft, 1939-1945. 2 vols. Berlin: Akademie, 1968-85.
993. Erbe, René. Die nationalsozialistische Wirtschaftspolitik 1933-1939 im Lichte der modernen Theorie. Zurich: Polygraphischer Verlag, 1958. 197 pp.
994. Fischer, Conan. Stormtroopers. A Social, Economic and Ideological Analysis, 1929-35. London: Allen & Unwin, 1983. 239 pp.
995. Fischer, Wolfram. Die Wirtschaftspolitik des Nationalsozialismus. Lüneburg: Niedersächsische Landeszentrale für Politische Bildung, 1961. 64 pp.
996. Forstmeier, Friedrich and Hans-Erich Volkmann. Wirtschaft und Rüstung 1939-1945. Düsseldorf: Droste, 1977. 420 pp.
997. Guillebaud, Claude W. The Economic Recovery of Germany from 1933 to the Incorporation of Austria in March 1938. London: Macmillan, 1939. 303 pp.
998. Gurland, Arcadius R. L. et al. The Fate of Small Business in Nazi Germany. New York: H. Fertig, 1975. 152 pp.
999. Hennig, Eike. Thesen zur deutschen Sozial- und Wirtschaftsgeschichte 1933-1938. Frankfurt a. M.: Suhrkamp, 1973. 263 pp.
1000. Henning, Hansjoachim. "Kraftfahrzeugindustrie und Autobahnbau in der Wirtschaftspolitik des Nationalsozialismus 1933-1936. VSWG 65 (1978), 217-42.
1001. Herbst, Ludolf. Der totale Krieg und die Ordnung der Wirtschaft: die Kriegswirtschaft im Spannungsfeld von Politik, Ideologie und Propaganda 1939-1945. Stuttgart: Deutsche Verlags-Anstalt, 1982. 474 pp.

1002. Kannapin, Hans-Eckhardt. Wirtschaft unter Zwang. Cologne: Deutscher Industrieverlag, 1966. 334 pp.
1003. Kerner, Manfred. Staat, Krieg und Krise: die Varga-Diskussion und die Rolle des Zweiten Weltkriegs in der kapitalistischen Entwicklung. Cologne: Pahl-Rugenstein, 1981. 393 pp.
1004. Knauerhase, Ramon. An Introduction to National Socialism, 1920 to 1939. Columbus, OH: Merrill, 1972. 143 pp.
1005. Knorr, Klaus. The War Potential of Nations. Princeton, NJ: Princeton University Press, 1956. 310 pp.
1006. Küppers-Sonnenberg, G. A. "Produktion und Destruktion. Von der Kriegswirtschaft zum Wirt-schaftskrieg. Betrachtungen eines Wehrwirtschaftsstatistikers." Militärpolitisches Forum 3 (1954), 15-20.
1007. Mandelbaum, K. "An Experiment in Full Employment. Controls in the German Economy, 1933-1938." in F. A. Burchardt et al. The Economics of Full Employment. Oxford: Blackwell, 1944. pp. 181-209.
1008. Marcus, Alfred. "Zur wirtschaftlichen Lage und Haltung der deutschen Juden." Bulletin des Leo Baeck Instituts 18 (1979), 16-34.
1009. Milward, Alan S. The German Economy at War. London: Athlone Press, 1965. 214 pp. (German: Stuttgart, 1966)
1010. Nathan, Otto. The Nazi Economic System. Germany's Mobilization for War. Durham, NC: Duke University Press, 1944. 378 pp.
1011. Overy, Richard J. "Cars, Roads, and Economic Recovery in Germany, 1932-38." Economic History Review 28 (1975), 466-83.
1012. Overy, Richard J. "The German Motorisierung and Rearmament: A Reply." Economic History Review 32 (1979), 107-13.
1013. Overy, Richard J. "Hitler's War and the German Economy. A Reinterpretation." Economic History Review 35 (1982), 272-91.
1014. Overy, Richard J. The Nazi Economic Recovery 1932-1938. London: Macmillan, 1982. 76 pp.
1015. Peterson, Edward N. Hjalmar Schacht. For and Against Hitler. A Political-Economic Study of Germany, 1923-45. Boston: Christopher Publishing House, 1954. 416 pp.
1016. Schlick, Heinrich. Das Verhältnis von Staat und Wirtschaft im LIchte der neueren Wirtschafts-gesetzgebung. Würzburg: Triltsch, 1937. 60 pp.
1017. Schweitzer, Arthur. "Plans and Markets: Nazi Style." Kyklos 30 (1977), 88-115.
1018. Schweitzer, Arthur. "Die wirtschaftliche Wiederaufrüstung Deutschlands von 1934-1936." Zeitschrift für die gesamte Staatswissenschaft 114 (1958), 594-637.
1019. Shafferman, Ron. The Socio-Economic Ideology of National Socialism and its Realization in Corporate and Economic Policy. Diss. Basel, 1981. 285 pp.
1020. Simpson, Amos E. "The Struggle for Control of the German Economy, 1936-37." Journal of Modern History 31 (1959), 37-45.
1021. Sohn-Rethel, Alfred. Economy and Class Structure of German Fascism. London: CSE Books, 1978. 159 pp. (German: Frankfurt a. M., 1973)
1022. Spenceley, G. F. R. "R. J. Overy and the Motorisierung: A Comment." Economic History Review 32 (1979), 100-06.
1023. Steinhaus, Kurt. Auferstehung einer Grossmacht? Zum Problem der Kontinuität des "alten" und "neuen" deutschen Imperialismus. Cologne: Pahl-Rugenstein, 1980. 131 pp.
1024. Treue, Wilhelm. "Ein Fall von 'Arisierung' im Dritten Reich und heute. Dokumentation." Tradition 16 (1971), 288-301.
1025. Turner, Henry A., Jr. Faschismus und Kapitalismus in Deutschland. Studien zum Verhältnis zwischen Nationalsozialismus und Wirtschaft. 2nd ed. Göttingen: Vandenhoeck & Ruprecht, 1980. 185 pp.
1026. Zumpe, Lotte. Wirtschaft und Staat in Deutschland 1933 bis 1945. Berlin: Akademie, 1980. 552 pp.

SEE ALSO: 3751.

GERMANY REDIVIDED--1945-1975

Bibliographic References

1027. Bibliographie der Amtlichen Westdeutschen Statistik, 1945-1951. Munich: Deutsche Statistische Gesellschaft, 1952. 90 pp.
1028. Dapper, Karl-Peter and Gerhard Hahn, eds. Bibliographie zur Sozialen Marktwirtschaft. Die Wirtschafts- und Gesellschaftsordnung der Bundesrepublik Deutschland 1945/49-1981. Baden-Baden: Nomos, 1983. 269 pp.
1029. Germany (Democratic Republic, 1949 -). Zentralinstitut für Bibliothekswesen. Bibliographie zur Theorie und Praxis der Sozialistischen Wirtschaft. Leipzig: Verlag für Buch- und Bibliothekswesen, 1955. 104 pp.
1030. Milatz, Alfred and Thilo Vogelsang, eds. Hochschulschriften zur neueren Geschichte. Eine Bibliographie 1945-1955. Bonn: Kommission für Geschichte des Parlamentarismus und der Politischen Parteien, 1956. 142 pp.
1031. Sensing, Ekkehard, ed. Bibliographie der EG-Zeitschrift, 1952-1980. Kiel: Institut für Weltwirtschaft, 1981. 280 pp.
1032. Wittkowski, Adolf. Schriftum zum Marschallplan und zur wirtschaftlichen Integration Europas. Bad Godesberg: Bundesministerium für den Marschallplan, 1953. 382 pp.

GERMANY REDIVIDED--1945-1975

1033. Abelshauser, Werner. Wirtschaft in Westdeutschland 1945-1948. Rekonstruktion und Wachstumsbedingungen in der amerikanischen und britischen Zone. Diss. Bochum, 1972-73. Stuttgart: Deutsche Verlags-Anstalt, 1975. 177 pp.
1034. Abelshauser, Werner. Wirtschaftsgeschichte der Bundesrepublik Deutschland. Frankfurt a. M.: Suhrkamp, 1983. 187 pp.
1035. Adamsen, Heiner R. "Faktoren und Daten der wirtschaftlichen Entwicklung in der Frühphase der Bundesrepublik Deutschland 1948-1954." Archiv für Sozialgeschichte 18 (1978), 217-44.
1036. Ambrosius, Gerold. Die Durchsetzung der sozialen Marktwirtschaft in Westdeutschland. Beiträge zur Wirtschafts- und Sozialpolitik in Deutschland nach 1945. Stuttgart: Deutsche Verlags-Anstalt, 1977. 400 pp.
1037. Baar, Lothar et al., eds. Wirtschaftsgeschichte. Ein Leitfaden. Berlin: Verlag Die Wirtschaft, 1979. 278 pp.
1038. Barthel, Horst. Die wirtschaftlichen Ausgangsbedingungen der DDR. Zur Wirtschaftsentwicklung auf dem Gebiet der DDR, 1945-1949/50. Berlin: Akademie, 1979. 191 pp.
1039. Barthel, Horst. Zur Wirtschaftspolitik der SED. Vol. 1. Berlin: Dietz, 1984. 280 pp.
1040. Borchardt, Knut. "Die Teilung Deutschlands--Die Bundesrepublik--Im anderen Teil Deutschlands." in G. Stolper et al. Deutsche Wirtschaft seit 1870. 2nd ed. Tübingen: Mohr, 1966. pp. 203-360.
1041. Carden, Robert W. "Before Bizonia: Britain's Economic Dilemma in Germany." Journal of Contemporary History 14 (1979), 535-55.
1042. Cassel, Dieter et al., eds. 25 Jahre Marktwirtschaft in der Bundesrepublik Deutschland. Stuttgart: G. Fischer, 1972. 417 pp.
1043. Claude, Henri. Der Marshall-Plan. Münster: SZD-Verlag, 1979. 131 pp.
1044. Engels, Wolfram. "30 Jahre Bundesrepublik Deutschland. Die erfolgreichen Verlierer." Wirtschaftswoche 33- (1979).
1045. Ermrich, Roland, ed. Basisdaten. Zahlen zur sozialökonomischen Entwicklung der Bundesrepublik Deutschland. 2nd ed. Bonn: Neue Gesellschaft, 1974. 648 pp.
1046. Glastetter, Werner et al. Die wirtschaftliche Entwicklung in der Bundesrepublik Deutschland 1950-1980: Befunde, Aspekte, Hintergründe. Frankfurt a. M.: Campus, 1983. 614 pp.
1047. Gleitze, Bruno et al. Die Deutsche Demokratische Republik nach 25 Jahren. Berlin: Duncker & Humblot, 1975. 146 pp.
1048. Gohl, Dietmar. "Bevölkerungsverteilung und Struktur der Wirtschaftsräume der DDR. Veränderungen 1964-1974." Geographische Rundschau 29 (1977), 262-69. (English summary.)
1049. Grebing, Helga et al. Die Nachkriegsentwicklung in Westdeutschland 1945-1949. 2 vols. Stuttgart: Metzler, 1980.

44   HISTORY OF ECONOMIC CONDITIONS

1050. Gutmann, Gernot et al. Die Wirtschaftsverfassung der Bundesrepublik Deutschland. 2nd ed. Stuttgart: G. Fischer, 1979. 288 pp.
1051. Hartrich, Edwin. The Fourth and Richest Reich. New York: Macmillan, 1980. 302 pp.
1052. Jánossy, Ferenc. Das Ende der Wirtschaftswunder. Erscheinung und Wesen der wirtschaftlichen Entwicklung. Frankfurt a. M.: Neue Kritik, 1968. 274 pp.
1053. Jochimsen, Reimut. "Die gesamtwirtschaftliche Entwicklung in der DDR." Geschichte in Wissenschaft und Unterricht (1966), 713-29.
1054. Kellenbenz, Hermann. "Wirtschaftsgeschichte in der Bundesrepublik seit dem Zweiten Weltkrieg." in Tradition und Neubeginn. Internationale Forschungen zur deutschen Geschichte im 20. Jahrhundert. Cologne: Heymann, 1975. pp. 445-58.
1055. Kurlbaum, Georg and Uwe Jens, eds. Beiträge zur sozialdemokratischen Wirtschaftspolitik. Bonn: Verlag Neue Gesellschaft, 1983. 226 pp.
1056. Lamps, Maryse. "Vingt-cinquième anniversaire, dix années de reformes économiques en Republique Democratique Allemande." Revue d'Allemagne 6 (1972) 20-38.
1057. Lehmann, Karin and Heinzpeter Thümmler. "Forschungen zur Wirtschaftsgeschichte." in Historische Forschungen in der DDR 1960-1970. Berlin: Deutscher Verlag der Wissenschaften, 1970. pp. 95-120.
1058. Leptin, Gert. Deutsche Wirtschaft nach 1945. Ein Ost-West-Vergleich. Opladen: Leske & Budrich, 1980. 85 pp.
1059. Lieberman, Sima. "Economic Achievement in the German Democratic Republic, 1949-1969." SZVS 109 (1973), 555-78.
1060. Losser, Alphonse. "L'évolution économique de la Republique Democratique Allemande au cours des années 1970." Revue d'Allemagne 11 (1979), 517-53.
1061. Manz, Mathias. Stagnation und Aufschwung in der französischen Besatzungszone von 1945 bis 1948. Diss. Mannheim, 1968. 132 pp.
1062. Markovits, Andrei S., ed. The Political Economy of West Germany. Modell Deutschland. New York: Praeger, 1982. 238 pp.
1063. Meimberg, Rudolf. Die wirtschaftliche Entwicklung in Westberlin und in der Sowjetischen Zone. Berlin: Duncker & Humblot, 1951. 99 pp.
1064. Mendershausen, Horst. Two Postwar Recoveries of the German Economy. Amsterdam: North-Holland Publishing Co., 1955. 130 pp.
1065. Mitzscherling, Peter et al. DDR-Wirtschaft: eine Bestandsaufnahme. Frankfurt a. M.: Fischer, 1974. 464 pp.
1066. Müller, Georg. Die Grundlegung der westdeutschen Wirtschaftsordung im Frankfurter Wirtschaftsrat 1947-1949. Diss. Freiburg. Frankfurt a. M.: Haag + Herchen, 1982. 389 pp.
1067. Neelsen, Karl. Wirtschaftsgeschichte der BRD. Ein Grundriss. Berlin: Deutscher Verlag der Wissenschaften, 1971. 318 pp.
1068. Nöll von der Nahmer, Robert. Vom Werden des neuen Zeitalters. Heidelberg: Quelle & Meyer, 1957. 317 pp.
1069. Ortlieb, Heinz-Dietrich. "Der Weg der westdeutschen Wirtschaft. Zwischen Wohlstandserwartung und Leistungsüberdruss." in W. Scheel, ed. Nach dreissig Jahren. Die Bundesrepublik Deutschland. Vergangenheit, Gegenwart, Zukunft. Stuttgart: Klett-Cotta, 1979. pp. 92-114.
1070. Paul-Calm, Hanna. Ostpolitik und Wirtschaftsinteressen in der Ära Adenauer: 1955-1963. Frankfurt a. M.: Campus, 1981. 295 pp.
1071. Petzina, Dietmar and Walter Euchner, eds. Wirtschaftspolitik im Britischen Besatzungsgebiet 1945-1949. Düsseldorf: Schwann, 1984. 338 pp.
1072. Peuler, Wilhelm, ed. Der Wiederaufstieg der deutschen Wirtschaft. Cologne: Wort & Werk, 1953. 86 pp.
1073. Pfister, Bernhard. Aus Geschichte und Gegenwart. Betrachtungen eines Nationalökonomen. Berlin: Duncker & Humblot, 1977. 395 pp.
1074. Picht, Hartmut and Claus-Peter Matt. Staatsverwaltung und Wirtschaftswachstum. Eine empirische Untersuchung staatlicher Verdrängungseffekte für die Bundesrepublik Deutschland, 1960-1979. Speyer: Forschungsinstitut für öffentliche Verwaltung, 1981. 70 pp.
1075. Piettré, André. Economie Allemande Contemporaine: Allemagne Occidentale: 1945-52. Paris: M. T. Genin, 1952. 672 pp.
1076. Pines, Jerome M. United States Economic Policy Toward Germany, 1945-1949. Diss. Columbia University, 1958. 366 pp.

1077. Pünder, Tilmann. Das bizonale Interregnum. Die Geschichte des Vereinigten Wirtschafts-gebiets 1946-1949. Cologne-Spich: Grote, 1966. 404 pp.

1078. Redlich, Fritz. "Recent Developments in German Economic History." The Journal of Economic History 18 (1958), 516-36.

1079. Rendi, Giuliano. "L'économia tedesca del secondo dopoguerra." Cahiers Vilfredo Pareto 15 (1968), 51-92.

1080. Rosenberg, Hans. Machteliten und Wirtschaftskonjunkturen. Studien zur neueren deutschen Sozial- und Wirtschaftsgeschichte. Göttingen: Vandenhoeck & Ruprecht, 1978. 343 pp.

1081. Roskamp, Karl W. "Who did Better in the 1950's, East or West Germany?" Social Research. New School for Social Research 29 (1962), 221-25.

1082. Scharpf, Peter. Europäische Wirtschaftsgemeinschaft und Deutsche Demokratische Republik. Tübingen: Mohr, 1973. 194 pp.

1083. Schmiede, Rudi. "Das deutsche 'Wirtschaftswunder' 1945-1965." in B. Blanke et al., eds. Die Linke im Rechtsstaat. Berlin: Rotbuch-Verlag, 1976. I, 107-38.

1084. Schulz, Carola. Der gezähmte Konflikt. Zur Interessenverarbeitung durch Verbände und Parteien am Beispiel der Wirtschaftsentwicklung und Wirtschaftspolitik in der Bundesrepublik (1966-1976). Opladen: Westdeutscher Verlag, 1984. 406 pp.

1085. Schwartau, Cord. Von Plan zu Plan. 25 Jahre ökonomische Entwicklung in der DDR. Herford: Nicolai, 1974. 182 pp.

1086. Settel, Arthur, ed. Die deutsche Wirtschaft seit Potsdam. Oberursel (Taunus): Europa-Archiv, 1947. 72 pp.

1087. Simmert, Diethard B. Wirtschaft im Wandel. Vom Nachkriegsdeutschland bis heute. Stuttgart: Deutscher Sparkassenverlag, 1981. 109 pp.

1088. Smith, Eric O. The West German Economy. London: Croom Helm, 1983. 330 pp.

1089. Stolper, Wolfgang F. et al. "The Structure of the East German Economy." Social Research. New School for Social Research 28 (1961), 221-37.

1090. Tilly, Richard H. "Soll und Haben. Recent German Economic History and the Problem of Economic Development." The Journal of Economic History 29 (1969), 298-319.

1091. Tuchtfeldt, Egon. "The Development of the West German Economy since 1945." German Social Science Digest 1 (1955), 59-111.

1092. Uffelmann, Uwe. "Wirtschaft und Gesellschaft in der Gründungsphase der Bundesrepublik Deutschland. Eine Bestandsaufnahme in didaktischer Sicht." Aus Politik und Zeitgeschichte. Bundeszentrale für Politische Bildung (1982), 3-27.

1093. Vogt, Wilhelm A., ed. Germany 1945/1954. Schaan, Liechtenstein: Boas International, [after 1954]. 738 pp.

1094. Wallich, Henry C. Mainsprings of the German Revival. a Study of Post-War Germany's Economic Recovery. London: Oxford University Press, 1956. 424 pp.

1095. Wehler, Hans-Ulrich. Die moderne deutsche Geschichte in der internationalen Forschung 1945-1975. Göttingen: Vandenhoeck & Ruprecht, 1978. 286 pp.

1096. Wilkens, Herbert. "Un autre miracle économique allemand." Documents 28 (1973), 75-93.

1097. Winkel, Harald. Die deutsche Wirtschaft seit Kriegsende. Entwicklung und Probleme. Mainz: Institut für staatsbürgerliche Bildung in Rheinland-Pfalz, 1971. 199 pp.

1098. Winkel, Harald. Die Wirtschaft im geteilten Deutschland 1945-1970. Wiesbaden: F. Steiner, 1974. 217 pp.

1099. Wirtschaftlicher und sozialer Wandel in der Bundesrepublik Deutschland. Göttingen: O. Schwartz, 1977. 616 pp.

SEE ALSO: 3796, 3888, 3897, 5121, 5156.

GERMAN REGIONS

Alsace-Lorraine

1100. Bleicher, Albert. Elsass und Lothringen wirtschaftlich gesehen. Potsdam: Hayn's Erben, 1942. 332 pp.
1101. Hellwig, Fritz. "Elsass-Lothringen und seine Wirtschaft." Ruhr und Rhein. Wirtschaftszeitung 21 (1940), 293-94, 303-04, 315-16.
1102. Rossé, Joseph et al. Das Elsass von 1870-1932. 4 vols. Colmar: Alsatia, 1936-38.
1103. Schlenker, Max, ed. Die wirtschaftliche Entwicklung Elsass-Lothringens 1871 bis 1918. Frankfurt a. M.: Elsass-Lothringen-Institut, 1931-37. 652 pp.
1104. Silverman, Dan P. "The Economic Consequences of Annexation. Alsace-Lorraine and Imperial Germany, 1871-1918." Central European History 4 (1971), 34-53.
1105. Silverman, Dan P. Reluctant Union. Alsace-Lorraine and Imperial Germany 1871-1918. University Park: Pennsylvania State University Press, 1972. 262 pp.

Baden-Württemberg

1106. Aus Stadt- und Wirtschaftsgeschichte Südwestdeutschlands. Festschrift für Erich Maschke zum 75. Geburtstag. Stuttgart: Kohlhammer, 1975. 290 pp.
1107. Bartens, Albert. Die wirtschaftliche Entwicklung des Königreichs Württemberg. Frankfurt a. M.: E. Schnapper, 1901. 120 pp.
1108. Ehmer, Willi. Südwestdeutschland als Einheit und Wirtschaftsraum. Eine geschichtliche Wirtschaftskunde Südwestdeutschlands. Stuttgart: Kohlhammer, 1930. 223 pp.
1109. Fischer, Albert. Besiedlung. Wirtschaft und Volkstum des östlichen Heubergs. Ein Beitrag zur Kulturgeographie der Schwäbischen Alb. Freiburg i. B.: Poppen & Ortmann, 1939. 79 pp.
1110. Friz, Karl. Die Wirtschaftsgeschichte Riedlingens seit Beginn des 19. Jahrhunderts. Diss. Tübingen. Riedlingen: Ulrich, 1923. 115 pp.
1111. Gothein, Eberhard, ed. Wirtschaftsgeschichte des Schwarzwaldes und der angrenzenden Landschaften. 2 vols. Strassburg: Trübner, 1892; rpt. Ann Arbor, MI: 1980.
1112. Hecht, Moriz. "Wirtschaftskundliche Literatur über Baden." Deutsche Zeitschrift für Wirtschaftskunde 2 (1937), 276-82.
1113. Hentschel, Volker. "Prosperität und Krise in der württembergischen Wirtschaft 1871-1879. Methodische Überlegungen und diskriptive Untersuchung." VSWG 63 (1976), 339-89.
1114. Kistler, Franz. Die wirtschaftlichen und sozialen Verhältnisse in Baden 1849-1870. Freiburg i. B.: Albert, 1954. 249 pp.
1115. Köhrer, Erich, ed. Das Land Baden, seine Entwicklung und seine Zukunft. 2nd ed. Berlin: Deutsche Verlags-Anstalt, 1925. 296 pp.
1116. Köhrer, Erich, ed. Das Land Württemberg mit Hohenzollern, seine Entwicklung und seine Zukunft. Berlin: Deutsche Verlags-Anstalt, 1926. 304 pp.
1117. Krümmer, Heinz. Die Wirtschafts- und Sozialstruktur von Konstanz in der Zeit von 1806 bis 1850. Sigmaringen: Thorbecke, 1973. 162 pp.
1118. Kühne, Ingo. Der südöstliche Odenwald und das angrenzende Bauland. Die wirtschaftliche Entwicklung des badischen Hinterlandes um Mosbach seit der Mitte des 19. Jahrhunderts. Diss. Heidelberg, 1962. Heidelberg: Geographisches Institut, 1964. 364 pp.
1119. Riffel, Paul. Die wirtschaftliche Entwicklung der Stadt Bruchsal von 1690 bis zur Gegenwart. Diss. Frankfurt a. M. Bruchsal: Eisele & Wagner, 1930. 132 pp.
1120. Rosenberg, Douglas. Die Entwicklungsgrundlagen eines Weltbades. Ein Versuch zur Wirtschaftsgeschichte Baden-Badens im 19. Jahrhundert. Diss. Heidelberg, 1923. 146 pp.
1121. Schindler, Hermann. Die Reutlinger Wirtschaft von der Mitte des 19. Jahrhunderts bis zum Beginn des Ersten Weltkrieges. Tübingen: Mohr, 1969. 207 pp.
1122. Schliebe, Klaus. "Wirtschaftsentwicklung und Industrieansiedlungen in Baden-Württemberg von 1961-1970." Geographische Rundschau 28 (1976), 5-13.

1123. Schremmer, Eckart. "Zusammenhänge zwischen Katastersteuersystem, Wirtschaftwachstum und Wirtschaftsstruktur im 19. Jahrhundert. Das Beispiel Württemberg: 1821-1877-1903." in I. Bog et al., eds. Wirtschaft und Gesellschaft in der Zeit der Industrialisierung. Wirtschaftliche und soziale Strukturen im saekularen Wandel. Festschrift für Wilhelm Abel zum 70. Geburtstag, 3. Hannover: Schaper, 1974. pp. 679-706.
1124. Steimle, Theodor. Die wirtschaftliche und soziale Entwicklung der württembergischen Brüdergemeinden Korntal und Wilhelmsdorf. Diss. Frankfurt a. M., 1929. Korntal: Verlag der Brudergemeinde Korntal, 1929. 242 pp.
1125. Thoma, Hermann. Die wirtschaftliche Entwicklung der Stadt Reutlingen 1803-1914. Diss. Tübingen, 1929. 143 pp.
1126. Weber, Bernhard. Die wirtschaftliche Entwicklung Mannheims von 1870 bis 1900. Diss. Tübingen. Mannheim: J. Bensheimer, 1904. 103 pp.
1127. Weiss, Hans. Die Stellung der badischen Wirtschaft innerhalb der deutschen Volkswirtschaft. Ein Vergleich mit der Vorkriegszeit. Diss. Heidelberg, 1928. 223 pp.
1128. Wicki, Hans. Das Königreich Württemberg im ersten Weltkrieg. Seine wirtschaftliche, soziale, politische und kulturelle Lage. Bern: Lang, 1984. 239 pp.
1129. Wirtschaftswachstum, Wirtschaftskraft und Wirtschaftsstruktur im Rhein-Neckar-Raum in den Jahren 1957 bis 1964. Ludwigshafen: Amt für Stadtforschung, Statistik und Wahlen, 1966. 27 pp.
1130. Wybrecht, Günther. Die strukturellen Veränderungen der Mannheimer Wirtschaft von 1830-1914. Diss. Freiburg i. B., 1954. 160 pp.
1131. Zahlenbelege zur wirtschaftlichen Entwickelung und Bedeutung Mannheims. Dem Deutschen Handelstag gewidmet zu seinem 50jährigen Jubiläum von der Handelskammer für den Kreis Mannheim. Mannheim: Mannheimer Vereinsdruckerei, 1911. 63 pp.

SEE ALSO: 841, 1819, 3946, 5199.

Bavaria

Bibliographic References

1132. Grimm, Claus. Quellen zur Wirtschafts- und Sozialgeschichte Bayerns vom ausgehenden 18. Jahrhundert bis zur Mitte des 19. Jahrhunderts. Aufbruch ins Industrie-Zeitalter, 3. Munich: Oldenbourg, 1985.
1133. Schneider, Michael. Die bayerische Wirtschaft in der Fachliteratur von 1915-1946. Eine Sammlung von Büchern, Zeitschriften- und Zeitungsaufsätzen. Munich: Pflaum, 1947. 134 pp.
1134. Schultheiss, Werner et al. Bibliographie zur Nürnberger Wirtschaftsgeschichte. Nürnberg: Stadtarchiv, 1968.

Bavaria

1135. Beiträge zur Wirtschaftsgeschichte Nürnbergs. 2 vols. Nuremberg: Stadtarchiv Nürnberg, 1967.
1136. Blab, Wilhelm. "Wirtschaftliche Einteilung der Oberpfalz vor 100 Jahren." Die Oberpfalz 47 (1959).
1137. Bössenecker, Hermann. Bayern, Bosse und Bilanzen. Hinter den Kulissen der weiss-blauen Wirtschaft. Munich: Desch, 1972. 320 pp.
1138. Deininger, Heinz F. "Zur Augsburger Wirtschaftsgeschichte von der Fugger- bis zur Gründerzeit." Esslinger Studien 10 (1964).
1139. Doeberl, Michael. Bayern und die wirtschaftliche Einigung Deutschlands. Munich: Bayerische Akademie der Wissenschaften, 1915. 117 pp.
1140. Eberhardt, Hans. "Bevölkerungs- und Wirtschaftsgeschichte des Amtes Königsee in der ersten Hälfte des 19. Jahrhunderts." Rudolstädter Heimathefte 10 (1964), 18-31, 61-73.
1141. Flieger, Heinz, ed. Bayerns Wirtschaft. Vom Werden und Wirken eines weltoffenen Landes. Düsseldorf: Verlag für Deutsche Wirtschaftsbiographien, 1966. 485 pp.

1142. Gesch, Hans-Dieter. Die bayerische Wirtschaft in den ersten Jahren nach dem Zweiten Welt-krieg. Diss. Bern, 1968. 275 pp.
1143. Grimm, Claus, ed. Aufsätze zur Wirtschafts- und Sozialgeschichte Bayerns 1750-1850. Aufbruch ins Industrie-Zeitalter, 2. Munich: Oldenbourg, 1985.
1144. Hanny, H. "Ein Beitrag zur Entwicklung der Wirtschaft und des Handels in Ingolstadt in der ersten Hälfte des 19. Jahrhunderts." Ingolstädter Heimatblätter 26 (1963).
1145. Hoffmann, Ludwig. Ökonomische Geschichte Bayerns unter Montgelas. 1799-1817. 2 vols. Erlangen: Deichert, 1885.
1146. Jegel, August. Die wirtschaftliche Entwicklung von Nürnberg-Fürth, Stein und des Nürnberger Raumes seit 1806. Nürnberg: Spindler, 1952. 439 pp.
1147. Kellenbenz, Hermann. "Die Wirtschaft Mittelfrankens im 19. Jahrhundert." Fürther Heimat-blätter 9 (1959).
1148. Köhrer, Erich, ed. Alt-Bayern, seine Entwicklung und seine Zukunft. Berlin: Deutsche Verlag-Anstalt, 1927. 184 pp.
1149. Kuhnle, Robert R. Wirtschaftskräfte der Nordoberpfalz. Versuch einer Wirtschaftsgeschichte über 9 Jahrhunderte. Weiden: Heimatkundlicher Arbeitskreis im Oberpfälzer-Wald-Verein, 1964. 43 pp.
1150. Lee, W. Robert. Population Growth, Economic Development and Social Change in Bavaria, 1750-1850. New York: Arno Press, 1977. 462 pp.
1151. Lerner, Franz. Vor dem Wirtschaftswunder. Eine zeitgeschichtliche Quelle zur Soziographie, Wirtschaftsstruktur und Wirtschaftsplanung 3er oberfränkischer Gemeinden nach 1945. Kulmbach: Freunde der Plassenburg, 1965. 222 pp.
1152. Luebeck, Julius, ed. Die wirtschaftliche Entwicklung Bayerns und die Verwaltung von Handel, Industrie und Gewerbe. Denkschrift der Handelskammer München. Munich: Duncker & Humblot, 1919. 200 pp.
1153. Lütge, Friedrich. "Zur wirtschaftsgeschichtlichen Forschung in Bayern." Zeitschrift für Bayerische Landesgeschichte 15 (1949), 91-104.
1154. Mauersberg, Hans. Wirtschaft und Gesellschaft Fürth's in neuerer und neuester Zeit. Eine städtegeschichtliche Studie. Göttingen: Vandenhoeck & Ruprecht, 1974. 268 pp.
1155. Mück, Wolfgang. Die Aktienstallung in Neustadt an der Aisch. Ein Beitrag zur Wirtschafts- und Sozialgeschichte einer königlichen bayerischen Garnison im 19. Jahrhundert. Neustadt: Schmidt, 1984. 208 pp.
1156. Scherzer, Hans, ed. Gau Bayreuth. Land, Volk und Geschichte. Munich: Deutscher Volksverlag, 1943. 526 pp.
1157. Scherzer, Hans, ed. Gau Bayerische Ostmark. Land, Volk und Geschichte. Munich: Deutscher Volksverlag, 1940. 526 pp.
1158. Schremmer, Ekhart. Die Wirtschaft Bayerns vom hohen Mittelalter bis zum Beginn der Indust-rialisierung. Bergbau, Gewerbe, Handel. Munich: Beck, 1970. 804 pp.
1159. Schultheiss, Werner. Die wirtschaftliche Entwicklung Nürnbergs von 1040-1960. Nürnberg: Stadtsparkasse Nürnberg, 1961.
1160. Wächtler, Fritz, ed. Bayerische Ostmark. Vier Jahre nationalsozialistische Aufbauarbeit in einem deutschen Grenzgau. Bayreuth: Gauverlag Bayerische Ostmark, 1937. 158 pp.
1161. Wirtschaftsraum Mittelfranken. Gestern, heute, morgen. Eine Dokumentation der Industrie-und Handelskammer Nürnberg. Nuremberg: Industrie- und Handelskammer Nürnberg, 1965. 243 pp.
1162. Wolff, Hellmuth. Der Spessart. Sein Wirtschaftsleben. Aschaffenburg: Krebs, 1905. 482 pp.
1163. Zimmermann, Joseph. Die wirtschaftliche Entwicklung der Stadt Regensburg im 19. Jahrhundert und zu Beginn des 20. Jahrhunderts. Diss. Frankfurt a. M. Kallmünz: Lassleben, 1934. 133 pp.
1164. Zorn, Wolfgang. Kleine Wirtschafts- und Sozialgeschichte Bayerns 1806-1933. Munich-Pasing: Verlag Bayerische Heimatforschung, 1962. 98 pp.
1165. Zorn, Wolfgang. "Die wirtschaftliche Struktur Altbayerns im Vormärz (1815-1845)." Oberbayerisches Archiv 93 (1971).
1166. Zorn, Wolfgang and Leonhard Hillenbrand. Sechs Jahrhunderte schwäbische Wirtschaft. Beitrag zur Geschichte der Wirtschaft im bayerischen Regierungsbezirk Schwaben. 125 Jahre Industrie- und Handelskammer Augsburg. Augsburg: Industrie und Handelskammer Augsburg, 1969. 464 pp.

1167. Zugschwert, Hans. Die wirtschaftlichen Beziehungen der freien Reichsstadt Regensburg zum Herzogtum Bayern seit dem 14. Jahrhundert. Diss. Frankfurt a.M., 1931. Kallmünz: Lassleben, 1932. 168 pp.

Berlin

1168. Berlins Aufstieg zur Weltstadt. Ein Gedenkbuch. Berlin: Hobbing, 1929. 380 pp.
1169. Berlins Wirtschaft im Übergang. Die früheren Lebensgrundlagen. Der Weg seit dem Zusammenbruch. Berlins Zukunft. Berlin: Duncker & Humblot, 1947. 28 pp.
1170. Berlins Wirtschaft in der Blockade. Berlin: Duncker & Humblot, 1949. 138 pp.
1171. Büsch, Otto. Geschichte der Berliner Kommunalwirtschaft in der Weimarer Epoche. Berlin: de Gruyter, 1960. 230 pp.
1172. Döring, Walther. "Die Wirtschaft Westberlins 1950 bis 1953." Europa-Archiv 9 (1954), 6704-11.
1173. Grünig, Ferdinand. Analyse der Wirtschaftsentwicklung in Westberlin seit der Wähungsreform und Schlussfolgerungen für die Beseitigung der Arbeitslosigkeit. Referat über Sondersituation Berlin. Bonn: Arbeitsgemeinschaft Deutscher Wirtschaftswissenschaftlicher Forschungsinstitute, 1950. 8 pp.
1174. Grünig, Ferdinand and Rolf Krengel. Die Westberliner Wirtschaft 1949-1951. Berlin: Duncker & Humblot, 1951. 95 pp.
1175. Hantelmann, Klaus-Dietrich and Heinz Räntsch. "Die Wirtschaft Westberlins in den 70er Jahren" IPW-Forschungshefte 13 (1978), 49-79.
1176. Heller, Sigmund. Die Bundeshilfe an Berlin und seine Wirtschaft von 1949 bis 1959. Bonn: S. Heller, 1960. 169 pp.
1177. Meimberg, Rudolf. Die wirtschaftliche Entwicklung in Westberlin und in der Sowjetischen Zone. Berlin: Duncker & Humblot, 1951. 99 pp.
1178. Rachel, Hugo. Das Berliner Wirtschaftsleben im Zeitalter des Frühkapitalismus. Berlin: Rembrandt, 1931. 273 pp.
1179. Schmidt, Robert H. "Berlin zwischen Vergangenheit und Zukunft. Probleme seiner wirtschaftlichen Selbständigkeit." Frankfurter Hefte. Zeitschrift für Kultur und Politik 12 (1957), 31-37.
1180. "Vier Jahre Wiederaufbau in Westberlin, 1950-1953." Die Berliner Wirtschaft. Mitteilungen der Industrie- und Handelskammer zu Berlin 4 (1954), 863-92.

Brandenburg

1181. Lippert, Werner. Geschichte der 110 Bauerndörfer in der nördlichen Uckermark. Ein Beitrag zur Wirtschafts- und Sozialgeschichte der Mark Brandenburg. Ed. G. Heinrich. Cologne: Böhlau, 1968. 286 pp.

SEE ALSO: 1835.

Danzig

Bibliographic Reference

1182. Prinzhorn, Fritz, ed. Danzig-Polen Korridor und Grenzgebiete. Eine Bibliographie mit besonderer Berücksichtigung von Politik und Wirtschaft. Danzig: Langfuhr, 1932-36 (Vols. 1-4); Leipzig: Leipzig University Press, 1936-39 (Vols. 5-7).

East Prussia

1183. Gayl, Wilhelm von. Der politische und wirtschaftliche Kampf um Ostpreussen seit dem Ende des 19. Jahrhunderts. Leipzig: Quelle & Meyer, 1934. 30 pp.

1184. Heynicke, Hans. Entwicklung der ostpreussischen Städte. Eine wirtschaftshistorische Untersuchung. Königsberg: Gräfe und Unzer, 1931. 149 pp.
1185. Kohte, Wolfgang. "Volkstum und Wirtschaft des preussischen Ostens im 19. Jahrhundert." Deutsche Wissenschaftliche Zeitschrift für Polen 29 (1935), 231-59.
1186. Pape, Richard. Die Entwicklung des allgemeinen Wohlstandes in Ostpreussen seit dem Anfange des 19. Jahrhunderts nach deutschen, litauischen und slavischen Bezirken bzw. Kreisgruppen und im Vergleich zu anderen Provinzen der Monarchie betrachtet. Königsberg: Gräfe & Unzer, 1909. 94 pp.
1187. Wilder, Jan A. The Economic Decline of East Prussia. Gdynia: The Baltic Institute, 1937. 112 pp.
1188. Willoweit, Gerhard. Die Wirtschaftsgeschichte des Memelgebiets. 2 vols. Diss. Cologne, 1968. Marburg a. d. Lahn: Herder-Institut, 1969.
1189. Wyszomirski, Curt. "Wirtschaft und Verkehr in der Provinz Ostpreussen." Archiv für Eisenbahnwesen 74 (1964), 438-72.

Eastern Germany

1190. Aubin, Gustav. "Das Werden der ostdeutschen Wirtschaft." in K. C. Thalheim and A. H. Ziegfeld, eds. Der deutsche Osten, seine Geschichte, sein Wesen und seine Aufgabe. Berlin: Propyläen, 1936. pp. 425-43.
1191. Aubin, Hermann. "Die geschichtliche Stellung der ostdeutschen Wirtschaft." in H. Aubin, ed. Grundlagen und Perspektiven geschichtlicher Kulturraumforschung und Kulturmorphologie. Bonn: Röhrscheid, 1965. pp. 646-67.
1192. Bahr, Ernst, ed. Studien zur Geschichte des Preussenlandes. Festschrift für Erich Keyser zu seinem 70. Geburtstag. Marburg: Elwert, 1963. 517 pp.
1193. Dix, Arthur. "Die deutschen Ostseestädte und die Grundlagen ihrer wirthschaftlichen Entwicklung." Preussische Jahrbücher 101 (1900), 460-512.
1194. Gleitze, Bruno. "Die wirtschaftliche Entwicklung Ostdeutschlands im Industriezeitalter." in Das östliche Deutschland. Würzburg: Holzner, 1959. pp. 645-710.
1195. Hesse, Albert. Die Wirkungen des Friedens von Versailles auf die Wirtschaft des deutschen Ostens. Jena: Fischer, 1930. 62 pp.
1196. Hinkel, Heinz, "Sozial- und Wirtschaftsgeschichte Ost- und West-Preussens im Kartenbild." in Studien zur Geschichte des Preussenlandes. Festschrift für Erich Keyser zu seinem 70. Geburtstag. Marburg: N. G. Elwert, 1963. pp. 274-89.
1197. Kohte, Wolgang. "Wirtschaftsentwicklung und Volkstumskampf der neueren Zeit im deutsch-westslawischen Grenzraum." in Deutsche Ostforschung. Ergebnisse und Aufgaben seit dem ersten Weltkrieg. Leipzig: Hirzel, 1943. pp. 357-97.
1198. Mayer, Eduard W. Das Retablissement Ost- und Westpreussens. Jena: Fischer, 1916. 124 pp.
1199. Pacyna, Günther. "Die Auswirkungen der Kontinentalsperre auf die Wirtschaftsstruktur Ostdeutschlands." Alt-Preussische Forschungen 16 (1939), 77-110.
1200. Schultz, Eberhard G., ed. Leistung und Schicksal. Abhandlungen und Berichte über die Deutschen im Osten. Cologne: Böhlau, 1967. 414 pp.
1201. Seraphim, Peter-Heinz. Die Wirtschaft Ostdeutschlands vor und nach dem zweiten Weltkrieg. Stuttgart: Brentano, 1952. 110 pp.
1202. Seraphim, Peter-Heinz et al. Ostwärts der Oder und Neisse. Tatsachen aus Geschichte, Wirtschaft, Recht. Hannover: Wissenschaftliche Verlagsanstalt, 1949. 136 pp.
1203. Solta, Jan et al. Geschichte der Sorben. Von 1789-1917. Bautzen: VEB Domowina, 1974. 328 pp.

Hansa Cities

1204. Deissmann, Gerhard, ed. Wachsende Städte an der Unterweser. Bremen-Bremerhaven im Aufbau 1958 bis 1964. 2nd ed. Bremen: Bargmann, 1965. 243 pp.
1205. Gonsiorowski, Herbert. Die Berufe der Juden Hamburgs von der Einwanderung bis zur Emanzipation. Diss. Hamburg, 1927. Hamburg: Brünnler, 1927. 84 pp.

1206. Jacobs, Alfred. "Bremen im Wandel der Weltwirtschaft." Bremisches Jahrbuch 50 (1965), 361-73.
1207. Keibel, Rudolf. "Lübeck als Wirtschafts- und Kulturfaktor." Lübecker Bucht 1 (1926), 60-63.
1208. Willms, Manfred. Ökonomische Analyse der regionalen Entwicklung von Bevölkerung, Beschäftigten und Wirtschaft im Grossraum Hamburg. Kiel: Seminar für Wirtschaftspolitik und Strukturforschung der Universität Kiel, 1973. 136 pp.

Hesse

1209. Bausinger, Leopold, ed. Fünfundsiebzig Jahre Rheingaukreis. Rüdesheim: Kreisausschuss des Rheingaukreises, 1962. 333 pp.
1210. Bothe, Friedrich. Beiträge zur Wirtschafts- und Sozialgeschichte der Reichsstadt Frankfurt. Leipzig: Dunker & Humblot, 1906. 172 pp.
1211. Erb, Willi. Die Leitz-Werke, optische Werke Wetzlar. Ihre Geschichte und ihre Bedeutung für den Wetzlarer Raum. Diss. Marburg, 1955. Freiburg i. B.: Herder, 1956. 195 pp.
1212. Fuchs, Konrad. "Zur Bedeutung des Herzogtums Nassau als Wirtschaftsfaktor 1815-1866." Nassau Annales 78 (1967), 167-76.
1213. Goebel, Heinrich. Die wirtschaftliche Entwicklung des vorderen Odenwaldes, insbesondere des Gersprenztales von 1800-1925. Diss. Frankfurt a. M. Kallmünz: Lassleben, 1937. 143 pp.
1214. Hessen im Wandel der letzten hundert Jahre, 1860-1960. Wiesbaden: Hessisches statistisches Landesamt, 1960. 568 pp.
1215. Köhrer, Erich, ed. Das Land Hessen, seine Entwicklung und seine Zukunft. Berlin: Deutsche Verlags-Anstalt, 1927. 196 pp.
1216. Lerner, Franz. Wirtschafts- und Sozialgeschichte des Nassauer Raumes, 1816-1964. Wiesbaden: Nassauische Sparkasse, 1965. 382 pp.
1217. Mauersberg, Hans. Die Wirtschaft und Gesellschaft Fuldas in neuerer Zeit. Göttingen: Vandenhoeck & Ruprecht, 1969. 355 pp.
1218. Meissner, Maria. Die wirtschaftliche Entwicklung Offenbachs unter dem Hause Isenburg-Birstein. Offenbach a. M.: Offenbacher Geschichtsverein, 1972. 71 pp.
1219. Seidel, Friedrich. Die soziale Frage in der deutschen Geschichte. Mit besonderer Berücksichtigung des ehemaligen Fürstentums Waldeck-Pyrmont. Ein lehrgeschichtlicher Überblick. Wiesbaden: Steiner, 1964. 302 pp.
1220. Wagner, Erika. "Wirtschaftsgeschichte und heutige Wirtschaftslandschaft des Hohen Westerwaldes." Berichte zur Deutschen Landeskunde 20 (1958), 1-24.

SEE ALSO: 1870, 2529-30, 5281.

Lower Saxony

Bibliographic Reference

1221. Wilhelm, Otto. Bibliographie von Niedersachsen. Landeskunde und Landesentwicklung, Wirtschaft, Kultur, Staat. 2 vols. Hildesheim: Lax, 1964-68.

Lower Saxony

1222. Beyer, Hans. "Verwaltung, politisches Leben und Wirtschaft im Kreise Oldenburg 1867-1967." Jahrbuch für Heimatkunde im Kreise Oldenburg/Holstein (1967), 31-94.
1223. Brix, Ewald. Vom Markt zur Metropole. Werden und Wandlung in 7 Jahrhunderten stadt-hannoverscher Wirtschaftsentwicklung. Hannover: Schlüter, 1951. 214 pp.
1224. Eggeling, Hans-Hennig. Die wirtschaftliche Entwicklung der Stadt Northeim in Hannover vom Mittelalter bis zum Ersten Weltkrieg. Northeim: Hahnwald, 1960. 119 pp.
1225. Genau, Ewald. Die Wirtschaftsstruktur der Stadt und der Goldenen Mark Duderstadt in vergleichender Darstellung zu der Struktur der Städte und der Landkreise Göttingen und Northeim. Diss. Göttingen, 1961. 334 pp.

1226. Gerstenberg, Bruno. Die Hildesheimer Zeitungsunternehmen und die Spiegelung der städtischen Wirtschaft in den Zeitungen von 1705 bis 1866. Diss. Cologne, 1970. 284 pp.

1227. Horstmann, Kurt. "Bevölkerungs- und Wirtschaftsentwicklung in Minden-Ravensberg, Lippe und Osnabrück im ersten und zweiten Drittel des 19. Jahrhunderts." in Raumordnung im 19. Jahrhundert. Hannover: Akademie für Raumordnung und Landesplanung, 1965-67. I, 97-116.

1228. Hunke, Heinrich. 10 Jahre Wirtschaftsausbau in Niedersachsen im Spiegel der öffentlichen Haushalte. Bremen-Horn: Dorn, 1959. 48 pp.

1229. Kaufhold, Karl H. "Wirtschaft und Gesellschaft im südlichen Niedersachsen im 18. und frühen 19. Jahrhundert." in Weltwirtschaftliche und währungspolitische Probleme seit dem Ausgang des Mittelalters. Stuttgart: Gesellschaft für Sozial- und Wirtschaftsgeschichte, 1981. pp. 207-25.

1230. Kayser, Wilhelm. Die Lüneburger Heide. Landschaft, Bewohner, Geschichte, Wirtschaft. Hamburg: Matthiesen, 1955. 312 pp.

1231. Köhrer, Erich, ed. Niedersachsen, seine Entwicklung und seine Zukunft. Berlin: Deutsche Verlags-Anstalt, 1924. 325 pp.

1232. Kreis Herzogtum Lauenburg. Landschaft, Geschichte, Wirtschaft. Oldenburg: Stalling, 1959. 361 pp.

1233. Der Landkreis Friesland. Geschichte, Kultur, Landschaft, Wirtschaft. Oldenburg: Stalling, 1963. 379 pp.

1234. Der Landkreis Lüdinghausen. Geschichte, Kultur, Landschaft, Wirtschaft. Oldenburg: Stalling, 1963. 346 pp.

1235. Oberschelp, Reinhard. Niedersachsen 1760-1820. Wirtschaft, Gesellschaft, Kultur im Land Hannover und Nachbargebieten. 2 vols. Hildesheim: Lax, 1982.

1236. Schnell, Wilhelm. Der Altenauer Bergbaubezirk. Gangverhältnisse und Wirtschaftsgeschichte. Bremen-Horn: Dorn, 1954. 174 pp.

1237. Schulze, Heinz J. Oldenburgs Wirtschaft einst und jetzt. Eine Wirtschaftsgeschichte der Stadt Oldenburg vom Beginn des 19. Jahrhunderts bis zur Gegenwart. Oldenburg: Stalling, 1965. 239 pp.

1238. Tacke, Eberhard. Die Entwicklung der Landschaft im Solling. Ein Beitrag zur Wirtschaftsgeschichte und zur Geschichte der Siedlungsplanung in Niedersachsen. Oldenburg: Stalling, 1943. 213 pp.

1239. Treue, Wilhelm. Niedersachens Wirtschaft seit 1760. Von Agrar- zur Industriegesellschaft. Hannover: Niedersächsische Landeszentrale für politische Bildung, 1964. 75 pp.

1240. Wagner, Hermann. Die Lüneburger Heide. Landschaft und Wirtschaft im Wechsel der Zeit. Oldenburg: Stalling, 1937. 110 pp.

Mecklenburg

Bibliographic Reference

1241. Bezirk Rostock. 25 Jahre ökonomische Entwicklung. Eine Literaturzusammenstellung. Rostock: Willi-Bredel-Bibliothek, 1974. 55 pp.

Mecklenburg

1242. Hübner, Rudolf. "Die ordentliche Kontribution Mecklenburgs in ihrer geschichtlichen Entwicklung und rechtlichen Bedeutung." in Festschrift Otto Gierke. Weimar: Böhlau, 1911. pp. 1139-66.

1243. Schultz, Karl. Die Lewitz. Ihre Entstehung und Entwicklung zu einem intensiven Wirtschaftsgebiet. Schwerin: Druckerei Schweriner Volkszeitung, 1961. 150 pp.

North Rhine-Westphalia

Bibliographic Reference

1244. Ernst, Eckart et al., eds. Das Schrifttum über Wirtschaft und Verwaltung der Jahre 1968-1971. Bibliographie des Ruhrgebietes, 6. Baden-Baden: Nomos, 1980. 284 pp.

North Rhine-Westphalia

1245. Achter, Wilhelm, ed. Werden und Wachsen eines Wirtschaftsgebietes am Linken Niederrhein. Festschrift zur Feier ihres 100jährigen Bestehens. Mönchen-Gladbach: Industrie- und Handelskammer, 1937. 250 pp.
1246. Anker, Kurt, ed. Rhein, Ruhr, Saar in Geschichte, Kultur und Wirtschaft. Berlin: Aufklärungsdienst, 1923. 90 pp.
1247. Aubin, Hermann et al. Geschichte des Rheinlandes von der ältesten Zeit bis zur Gegenwart. 2 vols. Essen: Baedeker, 1922.
1248. Aus Vergangenheit und Gegenwart wirtschaftlichen Geschehens im Bezirk der Industrie- und Handelskammer für die Kreise Aachen-Land, Düren und Jülich zu Stolberg (Rheinland). Aachen: La Ruelle, 1925. 440 pp.
1249. Barkhausen, Max. Aus Territorial- und Wirtschaftsgeschichte. Ausgewählte Aufsätze. Krefeld: Stadt Krefeld, 1963. 314 pp.
1250. Beiträge zur Solinger Wirtschaftsgeschichte. Solingen: Industrie- und Handelskammer zu Solingen, 1927. 161 pp.
1251. Berg, Werner. Wirtschaft und Gesellschaft in Deutschland und Grossbritannien im Übergang zum "organisierten Kapitalismus": Unternehmer, Angestellte, Arbeiter und Staat im Steinkohlenbergbau des Ruhrgebietes und von Südwales, 1850-1914. Diss. Bielefeld, 1980. Berlin: Duncker & Humblot, 1984. 888 pp.
1252. Borscheid, Peter et al. Entwicklungsprobleme einer Region, das Beispiel Rheinland und Westfalen im 19. Jahrhundert. Ed. F. Blaich. Berlin: Duncker & Humblot, 1981. 276 pp.
1253. Brepohl, Wilhelm. Bevölkerung und Siedlung im Raum Wulfen. Entwicklung, Strukturen und Tendenzen 1824 bis 1961. Essen: Siedlungsverband Ruhrkohlenbezirk, 1967. 212 pp.
1254. Brinkmann, Carl. "Entwicklung und Gestaltung der rheinischen Wirtschaft." Schmoller 66 (1942), 297-324.
1255. Bruckner, Clemens. Zur Wirtschaftsgeschichte des Regierungsbezirks Aachen. Cologne: Rheinisch-Westfälisches Wirtschaftsarchiv, 1967. 563 pp.
1256. Burkhard, Wolfgang. Abriss einer Wirtschaftsgeschichte des Niederrheins. Strukturelle Wandlungen in Handel und Industrie in Duisburg und in den Kreisen Wesel und Kleve. Duisburg: Braun, 1977. 174 pp.
1257. Eichler, Hans and Richard Laufner. Hauptmarkt und Marktkreuz zu Trier. Eine kunst-, rechts- und wirtschaftsgeschichtliche Untersuchung. Trier: Linz, 1958. 140 pp.
1258. Die Eisenstadt. 650 Jahre Düsseldorf. Düsseldorf: Deutsche Bergwerks-Zeitung, 1938. 24 pp.
1259. Ernst, Ulrich. Die sozial- und wirtschaftsgeschichtliche Entwicklung des Kreises Warburg im 19. Jahrhundert. Paderborn: Bonifacius, 1980. 152 pp.
1260. Fuchs, Konrad. Die Erschliessung des Siegerlandes durch die Eisenbahn (1840-1917); ein Beitrag zur Verkehrs- und Wirtschaftsgeschichte Deutschlands. Wiesbaden: Steiner, 1974. 163 pp.
1261. Fuchs, Konrad. "Ursachen und Auswirkungen des wirtschaftlichen Strukturwandels im westlichen Siegerland in der zweiten Hälfte des 19. und im Anfang des 20. Jahrhunderts." Jahrbuch für Geschichte und Kunst des Mittelrheins 11 (1959), 34-41.
1262. Gieselmann, F. J. Nord-Westfalens Wirtschaft. Zum 100-jährigen Bestehen der Industrie- und Handelskammer Münster, Westfalen. Münster i. W.: Hansa-Druckerei, 1954. 25 pp.
1263. Glässer, Ewald. Ländliche Siedlung und Wirtschaft des Kreises Coesfeld in Vergangenheit und Gegenwart. Dülmen: Kreis Coesfeld, 1971. 112 pp.
1264. Haas, Ulrich. Wandlungen der wirtschafts- und sozialgeographischen Struktur des Siegerlandes im zweiten Viertel des 20. Jahrhunderts. Remagen: Bundesanstalt für Landeskunde, 1958. 85 pp.

1265. Haferkamp, Hanns. Die Walsum-Sterkrader Grossmark. Ein Beitrag zur Wirtschafts- und Siedlungsgeschichte des rechten Niederrheins. Diss. Münster, 1934. Bottrop i. W.: Postberg, 1934. 60 pp.
1266. Ham, Hermann van. Die Wirtschaftsnöte des Westens durch Kriegsausgang und Grenzziehung mit besonderer Berücksichtigung der Rheinprovinz. Berlin: Hobbing, 1928. 183 pp.
1267. Hammen, Oscar J. "Economic and Social Factors in the Prussian Rheineland in 1848." American Historical Review 54 (1949), 825-40.
1268. Hansen, Joseph, ed. Die Rheinprovinz 1815-1915. Hundert Jahre preussischer Herrschaft am Rhein. 2 vols. Bonn: Marcus & Weber, 1917.
1269. Hauser, Oswald. "Einige Grundzüge aus der Entwicklung des Ruhrgebiets." Geschichte in Wissenschaft und Unterricht 18 (1967), 449-56.
1270. Hellgreve, Henny. Dortmund als Industrie- und Arbeiterstadt. Eine Untersuchung der wirtschaftlichen und sozialen Entwicklung der Stadt. Dortmund: Ardey, 1951. 234 pp.
1271. Helmrich, Wilhelm. Das Ruhrgebiet. Wirtschaft und Verflechtung. 2nd ed. Münster i. W.: Aschendorff, 1949. 245 pp.
1272. Helmrich, Wilhelm. "Die wirtschaftliche Entwicklung Düsseldorfs." Atlantis 25 (1953), 265-77.
1273. Henning, Friedrich-Wilhelm. Düsseldorf und seine Wirtschaft. Zur Geschichte einer Region. 2 vols. Düsseldorf: Droste, 1981.
1274. Herberts, Hermann. Alles ist Kirche und Handel . . . Wirtschaft und Gesellschaft des Wuppertals im Vormärz und in der Revolution 1848/49. Neustadt a. d. Aisch: Schmidt, 1980. 277 pp.
1275. Hermanns, Heinz. Die Handelskammer für den Kreis Mülheim am Rhein (1871-1914) und die Wirtschaft des Köln-Mülheimer Raumes. Diss. Cologne, 1969. 427 pp.
1276. Hildenbrand, Hanswerner. Die strukturelle Entwicklung von Wirtschaft und Bevölkerung im Stadtkreis Hagen von 1945 bis 1967. Diss. Bochum. Hagen: Linnepe, 1970. 279 pp.
1277. Hilgermann, Bernhard. Der grosse Wandel. Erinnerungen aus den ersten Nachkriegsjahren. Kölns Wirtschaft unter der amerikanischen und britischen Militärregierung. Cologne: Bachem, 1961. 83 pp.
1278. Hömberg, Albert K. Wirtschaftsgeschichte Westfalens. Münster i. W.: Mehren & Hobbeling, 1968. 151 pp.
1279. Höroldt, Dietrich. "Die Wirtschaftsentwicklung der Stadt Bonn im Vormärz." in Festschrift für Edith Ennen. Bonn: Röhrscheid, 1972. pp. 816-45.
1280. Hoff, Hans V. von. Die Entwicklung der Wirtschafts- und Bevölkerungsstruktur in der kreisfreien Stadt Herne von 1950 bis 1970. Darstellung der strukturellen Entwicklung Hernes als einer typischen Stadt der Emscherzone des Ruhrgebiets. 2 vols. Bern: H. Lang, 1974.
1281. Holtfrerich, Carl-Ludwig. Quantitative Wirtschaftsgeschichte des Ruhrkohlenbergbaus im 19. Jahrhundert. Dortmund: Verlag der Gesellschaft für Westfälische Wirtschaftsgeschichte, 1973. 197 pp.
1282. Joest, Johannes J. Wirtschaftliche und soziale Entwicklung des Soester Raumes im 19. Jahrhundert und ihre Berücksichtigung in den Lokalzeitungen der Stadt. Diss. Ruhr-Universität Bochum, 1976. Soest: Mocker & Jahn, 1978. 384 pp.
1283. Jordan, Horst and Heinz Wolff, eds. Werden und Wachsen der Wuppertaler Wirtschaft. Von der Garnnahrung 1527 zur modernen Industrie. Wuppertal: Hammer, 1977. 155 pp.
1284. Kellenbenz, Hermann. "Wirtschafts- und Sozialentwicklung der nördlichen Rheinlande seit 1815." in Rheinische Geschichte. Düsseldorf: Schwann,1979. III, 1-192.
1285. Kellenbenz, Hermann, ed. Zwei Jahrtausende Kölner Wirtschaft. 2 vols. Cologne: Greven, 1975.
1286. Kettermann, Günter. Kleine Geschichte der Bielefelder Wirtschaft. Bielefeld: Pfeffer, 1985. 299 pp.
1287. Kittel, Erich. Geschichte des Landes Lippe. Heimatchronik der Kreise Detmold und Lemgo. Cologne: Archiv für Deutsche Heimatpflege, 1957. 440 pp.
1288. Köhrer, Erich, ed. Westfalen, seine Entwicklung und seine Zukunft. Berlin: Deutsche Verlags-Anstalt, 1925. 367 pp.
1289. Köllmann, Wolfgang. Die strukturelle Entwicklung des südwestfälischen Wirtschaftsraumes 1945-1967. Hagen: Linnepe-Verlag, 1969. 278 pp.
1290. Kohte, Wolfgang. Westfalen und der Emsmündungsraum. Dortmund: Ardey, 1960. 59 pp.

1291. Kuske, Bruno. Die Grossstadt Köln als wirtschaftlicher und sozialer Körper. Ein Beitrag zur allgemeinen Grossstadtforschung. Cologne: Oskar Müller, 1928. 239 pp.

1292. Kuske, Bruno. Grundlinien westfälischer Wirtschaftsgeschichte. Dortmund: Gesellschaft für westfälische Wirtschaftsgeschichte, 1955. 25 pp.

1293. Kuske, Bruno. "Die Grundzüge der Wirtschaftsentwicklung am Niederrhein vom Mittelalter bis zur Gegenwart." Annalen des Historischen Vereins fur den Niederrhein 115 (1929), 38-60.

1294. Kuske, Bruno. Köln, der Rhein und das Reich. Beiträge aus fünf Jahrzehnten wirtschafts-geschichtlicher Forschung. Cologne: Böhlau, 1956. 299 pp.

1295. Kuske, Bruno, ed. Wirtschaftskunde für Rheinland und Westfalen. Berlin: Hobbing, 1931. 229 pp.

1296. Landwehrmann, Friedrich. Europas Revier. Das Ruhrgebiet gestern, heute, morgen. Düsseldorf: Droste, 1980. 135 pp.

1297. Lehmkühler, Marlies. Die wirtschaftliche Entwicklung des Kreises Lüdinghausen seit 1800. Recklinghausen: Bitter, 1948. 143 pp.

1298. Mauersberg, Hans. "Wandlungen in der Wirtschafts- und Sozialverfassung Dortmunds von der Zeit Napoleons bis zum Beginn des 20. Jahrhunderts." Beitrag zur Geschichte Dortmunds und der Grafschaft Mark 59 (1962), 215-39.

1299. Mertes, Paul H. Das Werden der Dortmunder Wirtschaft. 2nd ed. Dortmund: Ruhfus, 1942. 274 pp.

1300. Milkereit, Gertrud. "Sozial- und Wirtschaftsentwicklung der südlichen Rheinlande seit 1815." in Rheinische Geschichte. Düsseldorf: Schwann, 1979. III, 193-327.

1301. Most, Otto. Handelskammer und Wirtschaft am Niederrhein. Zum hundertjährigen Bestehen der Niederrheinischen Industrie- und Handelskammer Duisburg-Wesel. Duisburg: "Rhein", 1931. 262 pp.

1302. Neuss in Geschichte und Wirtschaft. Angermund: Stadtverwaltung Neuss, 1947. 240 pp.

1303. Petri, Franz and Georg Droege, eds. Rheinische Geschichte. 3 vols. Düsseldorf: Schwann, 1979.

1304. Petri, Franz et al. Das Siegerland. Geschichte, Struktur und Funktionen. Münster: Aschendorff, 1955. 122 pp.

1305. Prahl, Anton. Die eigenwirtschaftliche Tätigkeit der Stadt Münster in Westfalen. Diss. Münster, 1936. 143 pp.

1306. Richartz, Erika. "Duisburg-Ruhrort in seiner wirtschafts- und sozialgeographischen Struktur." Duisburger Forschungen 4 (1961), 144-206.

1307. Ringel, Hermann. Bergische Wirtschaft zwischen 1790 und 1860. Probleme der Anpassung und Eingliederung einer frühindustriellen Landschaft. Remscheid: Bergische Industrie und Handelskammer zu Remscheid, 1966. 204 pp.

1308. Roderigo, Herbert. Die Neusser Wirtschaft unter dem Einfluss des 2. Weltkrieges. Diss. Cologne, 1960. 155 pp.

1309. Die Stadt Cöln im ersten Jahrhundert unter Preussischer Herrschaft, 1815 bis 1915. 2 vols. Cologne: P. Neubner, 1915-1916.

1310. Steinberg, Heinz G. "Die Entwicklung des Ruhrgebietes, 1840-1914." in Raumordnung im 19. Jahrhundert. Hannover: Akademie für Raumforschung und Landesplanung, 1965. I, 175-244.

1311. Steinkühler, Paul. Die Wandlungen in der wirtschaftlichen und sozialen Struktur des Lüden-scheider Wirtschaftsgebietes seit Beginn des 19. Jahrhunderts. Diss. Cologne, 1931. 96 pp.

1312. Stryk, Horst von. Auf ins dritte Jahrtausend! Das Ruhrgebiet gestern, heute, morgen. Cologne: Deutscher Industrieverlag, 1968. 166 pp.

1313. Thuiller, Guy. "Pour une histoire de l'économie rhénane de 1800 à 1830: les houillères de la Ruhr." Annales Economies. Sociétés, Civilisations 5 (1915), 882-97.

1314. Trende, Adolf. Aus der Werdezeit der Provinz Westfalen. Münster i. W.: Aschendorff, 1933. 454 pp.

1315. Treue, Wilhelm. "Die Juden in der Wirtschaftsgeschichte des rheinischen Raumes, 1648 bis 1945." in Monumenta Judaica-Handbuch. Cologne: Stadtmuseum, 1963. pp. 419-66.

1316. Wiel, Paul. "Die Entwicklung der Ruhrgebietswirtschaft nach dem Zweiten Weltkrieg." Geographische Rundschau 17 (1965), 138-46.

1317. Wiel, Paul. Das Ruhrgebiet in Vergangenheit und Gegenwart. Essen: Scharioth, 1963. 149 pp.

1318. Wiel, Paul. Wirtschaftsgeschichte des Ruhrgebietes. Tatsachen und Zahlen. Essen: Siedlungs-verband Ruhrkohlenbezirk, 1970. 416 pp.

1319. Wolfram, Kurt. Die wirtschaftsgeschichtliche Entwicklung der Stadt Neuwied. Versuch zur Begründung einer Wirtschaftsgeschichte der Stadt Neuwied. Diss. Cologne. Neuwied: P. Kehrein, 1927. 114 pp.
1320. Ziehen, Eduard. "Kurrheinische Wirtschaftspolitik und Reich Deutscher Nation." VSWG 34 (1941), 141-57.
1321. Zorn, Wolfgang. "Die historische Wirtschaftskarte der Rheinprovinz um 1820 vor der Fertigstellung." Rheinische Vierteljahrsblätter 32 (1968), 476-81.
1322. Zorn, Wolfgang. "Die Struktur der rheinischen Wirtschaft in der Neuzeit." Rheinische Vierteljahrsblätter 28 (1963), 37-61.
1323. Zorn, Wolfgang. "Die wirtschaftliche Struktur der Rheinprovinz um 1820." VSWG 54 (1967), 289-324, 477-80.

SEE ALSO: 2548, 2564, 2600.

Pomerania

1324. Hoppe, Hans A. Die wirtschaftlichen Unternehmungen der Stadt Stettin. Diss. Jena, 1930. Stettin: Pasenows, 1929. 121 pp.
1325. Köhrer, Erich, ed. Pommern, seine Entwicklung und seine Zukunft. Berlin-Charlottenburg: Lima, 1924. 292 pp.
1326. Köller, Bogislav von. Die wirtschaftliche Entwicklung des Kreises Cammin in Pommern. Diss. Würzburg, 1931. 224 pp.
1327. Peters, Jan. "Unter der schwedischen Krone. Zum 150. Jahrestag der Beendigung der Schwedenherrschaft in Pommern." Zeitschrift für Geschichtswissenschaft 14 (1966), 33-51.
1328. Schmidt, Erwin. Das Wirtschaftsgebären der Stadt Stolp. Greifswald: Bruncken, 1931. 83 pp.
1329. Wielopolski, Alfred. "The Economic Regression of Western Pomerania in the Era of Capitalism." Poland at the 14th International Congress of Historical Sciences in Stockholm. Wroclaw: Zaklad Narodowy im Ossolinakich, 1975. pp. 239-63.

Rhineland Palatinate

1330. Becker, Carl. Bevölkerung und Lebensraum des unteren Westerwaldes 1885-1925. (Eine Untersuchung der Zusammenhänge zwischen Bevölkerungsentwicklung und Erwerbsmöglichkeiten). Diss. Freiburg i. B., 1930. Bottrop i. W.: Postberg, 1933. 89 pp.
1331. Beiträge zur pfälzischen Wirtschaftsgeschichte. Speyer: Pfälzische Gesellschaft zur Förderung der Wissenschaften, 1968. 342 pp.
1332. Engels, Alfred. Die Zollgrenze in der Eifel. Eine wirtschaftsgeschichtliche Untersuchung für die Zeit von 1740 bis 1834. Diss. Cologne. Cologne: Rheinisch-Westfälisches Wirtschaftsarchiv, 1959. 127 pp.
1333. Gruber, Hansjörg. Die Entwicklung der pfälzischen Wirtschaft, 1816-1834 unter besonderer Berücksichtigung der Zollverhältnisse. Diss. Mannheim Wirtschaftshochschule. Saarbrücken: Institut für Landeskunde des Saarlandes, 1962. 178 pp.
1334. Köhrer, Erich and Franz Hartmann, eds. Die Pfalz, ihre Entwicklung und ihre Zukunft. Berlin: Deutsche Verlags-Anstalt, 1926. 283 pp.
1335. Nagel, Wolfgang A. Ludwigshafen an Rhein. Stadt der Chemie. 2nd ed. Hanau: Stadtverwaltung, 1963. 256 pp.
1336. Probst, Walter. Wirtschaftliche Schäden des Trierer Wirtschaftsraumes durch feindliche Massnahmen in der Nachkriegszeit. Diss. Cologne, 1933. Bottrop: Postberg, 1933. 83 pp.
1337. Weidmann, Werner. Streiflichter durch die Wirtschaftsgeschichte. Otterbach-Kaiserslautern: Arbogast, 1981. 120 pp.
1338. Winkel, Harald. Mittelrheinische Wirtschaft im Wandel der Zeit. Koblenz: Rhenania, 1983. 530 pp.
1339. Wysocki, Josef. "Von der Gründerzeit zu den zwanziger Jahren. Die wirtschaftliche Entwicklung der Pfalz in den Berichten der Ludwigshafener Handelskammer." Tradition 14 (1969), 65-88.

Saarland

1340. Keuth, Paul. Wirtschaft zwischen den Grenzen. 100 Jahre Industrie- und Handelskammer des Saarlandes. Saarbrücken: Funk, 1963. 289 pp.
1341. Overbeck, Hermann. "Die Saarwirtschaft." VSWG 27 (1934), 209-34.
1342. Remlinger, M. "L'évolution économique de la Sarre jusqu'à la République féderale (allemande)." Études et Conjoncture 15 (1960), 1060-1101.
1343. Scholl, Arnold. Die Entwicklung der wirtschaftlichen und sozialen Verhältnisse im Kreise Ottweiler (Saargebiet). Ein Beitrag zur Lehre über den wirtschaftlichen Liberalismus. Diss. Frankfurt a. M., 1927. Saarbrücken: Saarbrücker Druckerei, 1932. 218 pp.

Saxony

1344. Beck, Friedrich. Die wirtschaftliche Entwicklung der Stadt Greiz. Weimar: Böhlau, 1959. 250 pp.
1345. Beutler, Albert. Die Entwicklung der sozialen und wirtschaftlichen Lage der Weber im Sächsischen Vogtland. Greifswald: Abel, 1921. 134 pp.
1346. Engelmann, Hugo. Die wirtschaftliche Entwicklung des Kreises Worbis (Eichsfeld). Halle a. d. Saale: C. A. Kaemmerer, 1905. 223 pp.
1347. Freydank, Hanns. Die Hallesche Pfännerschaft 1500-1926. Halle a. d. Saale: A. Reichmann, 1930. 336 pp.
1348. Fünfzig Jahre sächsische Volkswirtschaft. Ed. Archiv des Bankhauses Gebr. Arnhold. Berlin: Eckstein, 1914. 103 pp.
1349. Gebauer, Heinrich. Die Volkswirtschaft im Königreiche Sachsen. Historisch, geographisch und statistisch dargestellt. 3 vols. Dresden: Baensch, 1893.
1350. Hundert Jahre Chemnitz und Mittelsachsen. Eine Chronik der Entwicklung. Eine Leistungsschau der Schaffenden. Chemnitz: J. C. F. Pickenhahn, 1938. 50 pp.
1351. Kötzschke, Rudolf and Hellmut Kretzschmar. Sächsische Geschichte. Werden und Wandlungen eines deutschen Stammes und seiner Heimat im Rahmen der deutschen Geschichte. Frankfurt a. M.: Weidlich, 1965. 453 pp.
1352. Magdeburgs Wirtschaftsleben in der Vergangenheit. 3 vols. Magdeburg: Industrie und Handelskammer zu Magdeburg, 1925-28.
1353. Pönicke, Herbert. "Zwei entscheidende Jahrzehnte sächsischer Wirtschaftsgeschichte, 1850-1870." in Hamburger mittel- und ostdeutsche Forschungen. Kulturelle und wirtschaftliche Studien in Beziehung zum gesamtdeutschen Raum. Hamburg: Ostdeutscher Kulturrat, 1957. I, 189-206.
1354. Schotte, Friedrich. Die Produktionsgrundlagen der Provinz Sachsen 1907-1927. Diss. Halle-Wittenberg, 1931. Halle a. d. Saale: Klinz, 1932. 173 pp.
1355. Selbmann, Fritz. "Erinnerungen: Anfänge der Wirtschaftsplanung in Sachsen." Beiträge zur Geschichte der Arbeiterbewegung 14 (1972), 76-82.
1356. Die wirtschaftliche Entwicklung Sachsens innerhalb der letzten fünf Jahrzehnte. Dresden: Sächsischer Handelskammer, 1912. 15 pp.
1357. Zander, Alfred. Die wirtschaftliche Entwicklung der Provinz Sachsen im 19. Jahrhundert. Halle: Akademischer Verlag, 1934. 235 pp.

SEE ALSO: 841, 5339.

Schleswig-Holstein

1358. Doose, Richard. Die Entwicklung der wirtschaftlichen Verhältnisse in der Probstei. Süderbarup: "Landpost", 1910. 130 pp.
1359. Hannsen, Georg. Historisch-statistische Darstellung der Insel Fehmarn. Ein Beitrag zur genauern Kunde des Herzogthums Schleswig. Altona: Hammerich, 1832. 352 pp.
1360. Iversen, Mads. "Den økonomiske Udvikling i Nordslesvig." Sønderjyllands Historie 5 (1933), 411-78.

1361. Koenenkamp, Wolf D. Wirtschaft, Gesellschaft und Kleidungsstil in den Vierlanden während des 18. und 19. Jahrhunderts. Zur Situation einer Tracht. Diss. Hamburg, 1975. Göttingen: Schwartz, 1978. 164 pp.
1362. Nernheim, Klaus. Der Eckernförder Wirtschaftsraum. Kiel: Geographisches Institut, 1958. 75 pp.
1363. Waschinski, Emil. "Zur Wirtschaftsgeschichte Schleswig-Holsteins." Zeitschrift der Gesellschaft für Schleswig-Holsteinische Geschichte 84 (1960), 93-120.
1364. Wenzel, Rüdiger. Bevölkerung, Wirtschaft und Politik im kaiserlichen Kiel zwischen 1870 und 1914. Diss. Kiel (Wirtschaftsstruktur und Bevölkerung der Stadt Kiel zwischen 1870 und 1914). Kiel: Gesellschaft für Kieler Stadtgeschichte, 1978. 291 pp.

Silesia

Bibliographic References

1365. Geldern-Crispendorf, Günther von, ed. "Die wichtigste Literatur über Oberschlesien." in Oberschlesien-Atlas. Geisler: Volk & Reich, 1938. pp. 33-40.
1366. Rister, Herbert, ed. Bibliographie zur Sozial- und Wirtschaftsgeschichte des gesamt-oberschlesischen Industriegebietes 1935-1951. Neumarkt: Verlag des Kulturwerks Schlesien, 1952. 32 pp.

Silesia

1367. Borcke, Hans-Otto von. Die Entwicklung der wirtschaftlichen und sozialen Verhältnisse in Westoberschlesien nach der Teilung. Berlin: Volk & Reich, 1937. 160 pp.
1368. Fuchs, Konrad. Vom Dirigismus zum Liberalismus. Die Entwicklung Oberschlesiens als Preussischer Berg- und Hüttenrevier. Ein Beitrag zur Wirtschaftsgeschichte Deutschlands im 18. und 19. Jahrhundert. Wiesbaden: F. Steiner, 1970. 314 pp.
1369. Fuchs, Konrad. "Wirtschaftliche Führungskräfte in Schlesien 1850-1914." Zeitschrift für Ostforschung 21 (1972), 264-88.
1370. Fuchs, Konrad. Wirtschaftsgeschichte Oberschlesiens 1871-1945. Aufsätze. Dortmund: Forschungsstelle Ostmitteleuropa, 1981. 260 pp.
1371. Fuchs, Konrad. "Zur Bedeutung Schlesiens als Wirtschaftsfaktor während des Zweiten Weltkriegs." Zeitschrift für Ostforschung 27 (1978), 337-52.
1372. Haines, Michael R. "Population and Economic Change in Nineteenth-Century Eastern Europe. Prussian Upper Silesia, 1840-1913." The Journal of Economic History 36 (1976), 334-58.
1373. Halbsguth, Johannes. Beiträge zur Sozial- und Wirtschaftsgeschichte der Stadt Jauer. Diss. Breslau, 1936. 216 pp.
1374. Hentschel, Volker. "Wirtschaftliche Entwicklung, soziale Mobilität und nationale Bewegung in Oberschlesien 1871-1914." in Modernisierung und nationale Gesellschaft im ausgehenden 18. und im 19. Jahrhundert. Berlin: Duncker & Humblot, 1979. pp. 231-73.
1375. Jecht, Richard. Die wirtschaftlichen Verhältnisse der Stadt Görlitz im ersten Drittel des 19. Jahrhunderts. Görlitz: Görlitzer Magistrat, 1916. 119 pp.
1376. Ohle, Karl. Der Kreis Waldenburg im niederschlesischen Industriegebiet in Vergangenheit und Gegenwart. Breslau: Korn, 1927. 142 pp.
1377. Popkiewicz, Józef. "Die Wirtschaft Schlesiens (Slask) unter der Herrschaft der deutschen Kapitalisten." Studia Historiae Oeconomicae 4 (1969), 81-98.
1378. Repetzki, Kurt. Oberschlesien. Industrie und Wirtschaft. 2nd ed. Bonn: Landmannschaft der Oberschlesier e.V., 1971. 113 pp.
1379. Roesler, Gerhard. "Wanderungen und Wirtschaftsentwicklung in Schlesien." Deutsche Zeitschrift für Wirtschaftskunde 4 (1939), 161-71, 255-65.
1380. Street, Cecil J. C. Upper Silesia. An Economic Tragedy. Redhill, England: Athenaeum Printing Works, 1924. 31 pp.
1381. Wendt, Heinrich. Historische Kommission für Schlesien. Ergebnisse der schlesischen Wirtschaftsgeschichte. Breslau: Nischkowsky, 1922. 32 pp.

1382. Zielinski, Henryk. "The Role of Silesia in Central Europe in the 19th and 20th Centuries." Acta Poloniae Historica 22 (1970), 108-22.

Thuringia

Bibliographic Reference

1383. Patze, Hans. Bibliographie zur thüringischen Geschichte. 2 vols. Cologne: Böhlau, 1965-66.

Thuringia

1384. Engel, Robert W. Wirtschaftliche und soziale Kämpfe vor dem Jahre 1848 in Thüringen (insonderheit im Herzogtum Meiningen). Diss. Marburg, 1926. Marburg: Fischer, 1927. 29 pp.
1385. John, Jürgen. "Wirtschafts- und Sozialgeschichte des 19. und 20. Jahrhunderts." Wissenschaftliche Zeitschrift der Friedrich-Schiller-Universität Jena 16 (1967), 245-58.
1386. Kühnert, Herbert. Quellenheft zur Wirtschaftsgeschichte von Grossthüringen. Jena: Jenaer Volksbuchhandlung, 1921. 72 pp.
1387. Rottstädt, Udo. Besiedelung und Wirtschaftsverfassung des Thüringer Waldes i. e., eine historisch-volkswirtschaftliche Studie. Munich: Duncker & Humblot, 1914. 100 pp.
1388. Thormann, Hanns and Erich Staab. Der mitteldeutsche Raum. Seine natürlichen, geschichtlichen und wirtschaftlichen Grenzen. Merseburg a. d. Saale: Stollberg, 1929. 168 pp.

SEE ALSO: 5371.

West Prussia

Bibliographic Reference

1389. Bahr, Ernst. "Neue polnische Veröffentlichungen zur Sozial- und Wirtschaftsgeschichte Westpreussens." Jahrbuch für die Geschichte Mittel- und Ostdeutschlands 13/14 (1965), 241-67.

West Prussia

1390. Aschkewitz, Max. "Der Anteil der Juden am wirtschaftlichen Leben Westpreussens um die Mitte des 19. Jahrhunderts." Zeitschrift für Ostforschung 11 (1962), 482-91.
1391. Vallentin, Wilhelm. Westpreussen seit den ersten Jahrzehnten dieses Jahrhunderts. Ein Beitrag zur Geschichte der Entwickelung des allgemeinen Wohlstandes in dieser Provinz und ihren einzelnen Teilen. Tübingen: Laupp, 1893. 225 pp.

2.
History of Agriculture

CENTRAL EUROPE

Bibliographic References

1392. Denman, Donald R. et al., eds. Bibliography of Rural Land Economy and Land Ownership, 1900-1957; a Full List of Works Relating to the British Isles and Selected Works from the United States and Western Europe. Cambridge: Cambridge University, 1958. 412 pp.

1393. International Bibliography of Agricultural Economics. 8 vols. Rome: International Institute of Agriculture, 1938-1946.

1394. Martin, Lee D., ed. A Survey of Agricultural Economics Literature. 3 vols. Minneapolis: University of Minnesota; Published for the American Agricultural Economics Association, 1977-1981.

1395. U.S. National Agricultural Library. Library List. Washington: U.S. National Agricultural Library, 1942- .

CENTRAL EUROPE

1396. Abel, Wilhelm. Agrarkrisen und Agrarkonjunktur. Eine Geschichte der Land- und Ernährungs- wirtschaft Mitteleuropas seit dem hohen Mittelalter. 3rd ed. Hamburg: Parey, 1978. 323 pp.

1397. Abel, Wilhelm. Agricultural Fluctuations in Europe from the Thirteenth to the Twentieth Centuries. New York: St. Martin's Press, 1980. 362 pp.

1398. Dovring, Folke. Land and Labour in Europe in the Twentieth Century. The Hague: Nijhoff, 1965. 511 pp.

1399. Dovring, Folke. "The Transformation of European Agriculture." in H. J. Habakkuk and M. M. Postan, eds. Cambridge Economic History of Europe. Cambridge: Cambridge University Press, 1965. VI, 603-72.

1400. Europäische Bauernparteien im 20. Jahrhundert. Stuttgart: Fischer, 1977. 702 pp.

1401. Finckenstein, Hans W. 130 Jahre Strukturwandel und Krisen der intensiven europäischen Landwirtschaft. Berlin: Weidmann, 1937. 45 pp.

1402. Frauendorfer, Sigmund von and Heinz Haushofer. Ideengeschichte der Agrarwirtschaft und Agrarpolitik im deutschen Sprachgebiet. 2 vols. Munich: Bayerischer Landwirtschaftsverlag, 1957-1958.

1403. Fussell, George E. The Classical Tradition in West European Farming. Rutherford, NJ: Fairleigh Dickinson University Press, 1972. 237 pp.

1404. Gollwitzer, Heinz. "Demokratische Agrarbewegungen als europäisches Phänomen im 20. Jahrhundert." Historische Zeitschrift 227 (1978), 529-51.

1405. Gras, Norman S. B. A History of Agriculture in Europe and America. New York: Crofts, 1925. 444 pp.
1406. Gunst, Peter and Tamos Hoffmann, eds. Large Estates and Small Holdings in Europe in the Middle Ages and Modern Times. National Reports. Budapest: Hungarian Academy of Sciences, 1982. 400 pp.
1407. Heckman, John and Anna Wheeler. Agricultural Cooperation in Western Europe. 3 sections. Washington: Government Printing Office, 1954-55.
1408. Huggett, Frank E. The Land Question and European Society. London: Thames & Hudson, 1975. 179 pp.
1409. Irvine, Helen D. The Making of Rural Europe. London: Allen & Unwin, 1923. 224 pp.
1410. Jones, Eric L. "Environment, Agriculture, and Industrialization in Europe." Agricultural History 51 (1977), 491-502.
1411. Jones, Eric L. and S. J. Woolf, eds. Agrarian Change and Economic Development. The Historical Problems. London: Methuen, 1969. 172 pp.
1412. Kuhn, G. "Der Bauer in Kultur und Geschichte des Abendlandes." Studium generale 11 (1958), 449-59.
1413. Löhr, Ludwig. Bergbauernwirtschaft im Alpenraum. Ein Beitrag zum Agrarproblem der Hang- und Berggebiete. Graz: Stocker, 1971. 296 pp.
1414. Mellor, John W. The Economics of Agricultural Development. Ithaca, NY: Cornell University Press, 1966. 403 pp.
1415. Parker, William N. and Eric L. Jones, eds. European Peasants and their Markets. Essays in Agrarian Economic History. Princeton, NJ: Princeton University Press, 1975. 366 pp.
1416. Priebe, Hermann. "The Changing Role of Agriculture, 1920-70." in C. W. Cipolla, ed. The Twentieth Century. Fontana Economic History of Europe. Glasgow: Fontana, 1976. V, 403-41.
1417. Sereni, Emilio et al. Agricultura e sviluppo del capitalismo. Rome: Istituto Gramsci, 1970. 723 pp.
1418. Thorner, Daniel. "Peasant Economy as a Category in Economic History." in Papers Presented to the Second International Economic History Conference. Aix-en-Provence. 1962. Paris: Mouton, 1965.
1419. Tracy, Michael. Agriculture in Western Europe: Challenge and Response. 1880-1980. 2nd ed. London: Granada, 1982. 419 pp.
1420. Trow-Smith, Robert. Life From the Land. The Growth of Farming in Western Europe. London: Longmans, 1967. 238 pp.
1421. Tuma, Elias H. Twenty-Six Centuries of Agrarian Reform. A Comparative Analysis. Berkeley: University of California Press, 1965. 309 pp.
1422. Warner, Charles K., ed. Agrarian Conditions in Modern European History. New York: Macmillan, 1966. 148 pp.
1423. Warriner, Doreen. Economics of Peasant Farming. London: Oxford University Press, 1939. 208 pp.
1424. Warriner, Doreen. "Some Controversial Issues in the History of Agrarian Europe." Slavonic and East European Review 32 (1953), 168-86.
1425. Yates, Paul L. Food. Land and Manpower in Western Europe. London: Macmillan, 1960. 294 pp.

SEE ALSO: 141, 1987, 2680.

CENTRAL EUROPE--1815-1918

1426. Bairoch, Paul. "Agriculture and the Industrial Revolution, 1700-1914." in C. M. Cipolla, ed. The Industrial Revolution. Fontana Economic History of Europe. Glasgow: Fontana, 1973. III, 452-506.
1427. Blum, Jerome. The End of the Old Order in Rural Europe. Princeton, NJ: Princeton University Press, 1978. 505 pp.
1428. Bog, Ingomar et al., eds. Agrarische Wirtschaft und Gesellschaft in vorindustrieller Zeit. Hannover: Schaper, 1974. 305 pp.
1429. Collins, Edward J. T. "Labour Supply and Demand in European Agriculture, 1800-1880." in E. L. Jones and S. J. Woolf, eds. Agrarian Change and Economic Development. London: Methuen, 1969. pp. 61-94.

62 HISTORY OF AGRICULTURE

1430. Conrad, J. "Agrarstatistische Untersuchungen." Jahrbücher für Nationalökonomie und Statistik 17 (1871), 225-97; 18 (1872), 377-416.
1431. Conze, Werner. "Agrarian Reform in Central Europe." in G. S. Metraux and F. Crouzet, eds. The Nineteenth Century World. New York: New American Library, 1963. pp. 86-103.
1432. Conze, Werner. "The Effects of Nineteenth Century Liberal Agrarian Reforms on Social Structure in Central Europe." in F. Crouzet et al. Essays in European Economic History. London: E. Arnold, 1969. pp. 53-81.
1433. Conze, Werner. "Die Wirkungen der liberalen Agrarreformen auf die Volksordnung in Mitteleuropa im 19. Jahrhundert." VSWG 38 (1949), 2-43.
1434. Diehl, Karl. "Der ältere Agrarsozialismus und die neuere Bodenreformbewegung in Amerika, England und Deutschland." Archiv für Geschichte des Sozialismus und der Arbeiterbewegung 1 (1910-11), 225-84.
1435. Goy, Joseph and E. LeRoy Ladurie. Tithe and Agrarian History from the Fourteenth to the Nineteenth Century. An Essay in Comparative History. Cambridge: Cambridge University Press, 1982. 206 pp.
1436. Gunst, Peter. The Comparative Impact of Industrialization on Western and Eastern European Agriculture in the Nineteenth and Early Twentieth Century." Agrartörteneti Szemle 18 (1976), supplement, 15-36.
1437. Hamerow, Theodore S. "The Transformation of Agriculture." in The Birth of a New Europe: State and Society in the Nineteen Century. Chapel Hill: University of North Carolina Press, 1983. pp. 32-58.
1438. Hauser, Albert. "Wechselbeziehungen zwischen der Schweizerischen und deutschen Landwirtschaft im 19. Jahrhundert." Schweizerische Zeitschrift für Geschichte 13 (1963), 206-14.
1439. Knapp, Georg F. "Die Bauernbefreiung in Österreich und in Preussen." Schmoller 18 (1894), 409-31.
1440. Kowalewsky, Maxime. Die ökonomische Entwicklung Europas bis zum Beginn der kapitalistischen Wirtschaftsform. 7 vols. Berlin: Prager, 1901-14.
1441. League of Nations. Agricultural Production in Continental Europe During the 1914-1918 War and the Reconstruction Period. Geneva: League of Nations, 1943. 122 pp.
1442. Sée, Henri. Esquisse d'une histoire du régime agraire en Europe aux 18. et 19. siècles. Paris: Girard, 1921. 276 pp.
1443. Slicher van Bath, Bernard H. The Agrarian History of Western Europe. A.D. 500-1850. New York: St. Martin's Press, 1963. 364 pp.
1444. Slicher van Bath, Bernard H. "Desarrollo agrícola en Europa entre 1800 y 1914." Jahrbuch für Geschichte von Staat, Wirtschaft und Gesellschaft Lateinamerikas 13 (1976), 20-30.
1445. Tracy, Michael. "Agriculture in Western Europe. The Great Depression 1880-1900." in Agrarian Conditions in Modern European History. New York: Macmillan, 1966. pp. 98-112.
1446. Wiatrowski, Leszek. "Modernised Agricultural Enterprise in Central and Eastern Europe in the Nineteenth and at the Beginning of the Twentieth Century." in Proceedings of the Seventh International Congress on Economic History, Edinburgh, 1978. Edinburgh: Edinburgh University Press, 1978.

SEE ALSO: 226, 1450, 2318.

CENTRAL EUROPE--1919-1975

1447. League of Nations. The Agricultural Crisis. 2 vols. Geneva: League of Nations, 1931.
1448. Morgan, Ora S., ed. Agricultural Systems of Middle Europe. London: Macmillan, 1933. 405 pp.
1449. Müller, Gerhard. "Die Entwicklung der Landwirtschaft in Westeuropa unter den Bedingungen der wissenschaftlich-technischen Revolution." Jahrbuch für Wirtschaftsgeschichte (1972), I, 277-89.
1450. Schloemer, Friedrich. Der Welthandel in Erzeugnissen der Landwirtschaft. Übersicht über seine Entwicklung 1842-1938. Rome: International Agricultural Institute, 1941. 96 pp.
1451. Timoshenko, Vladimir P. World Agriculture and the Depression. Ann Arbor: University of Michigan Press, 1933. 123 pp.

SEE ALSO: 1441.

AUSTRIA

1452. Bauer, Otto. <u>Der Kampf um Wald und Weide. Studien zur österreichischen Agrargeschichte und Agrarpolitik</u>. Vienna: Wiener Volksbuchhandlung, 1925. 244 pp.
1453. Bruckmüller, Ernst. "Die verzögerte Modernisierung. Mögliche Ursachen und Folgen des 'österreichischen Weges' im Wandel des Agrarbereiches." in <u>Wirtschafts- und sozialhistorische Beiträge. Festschrift für Alfred Hoffmann zum 75. Geburtstag</u>. Munich: Oldenbourg, 1979. pp. 289-307.
1454. Buchinger, Josef. <u>Der Bauer in der Kultur- und Wirtschaftsgeschichte Österreichs</u>. Vienna: Österreichischer Bundesverlag, 1952. 471 pp.
1455. Carlen, Louis and Fritz Steinegger, eds. <u>Festschrift Nikolaus Grass. Zum 60. Geburtstage</u>. 2 vols. Innsbruck: Wagner, 1974-1975.
1456. Kallbrunner, Hermann. <u>Der Väter Saat. Die österreichische Landwirtschaftgesellschaft von 1807-1938. Ein Beitrag zur Geschichte der österreichischen Landwirtschaft</u>. Vienna: Österreichischer Agrarverlag, 1963. 174 pp.
1457. Klein-Bruckschwaiger, Franz. <u>Beiträge zur österreichischen Agrargeschichte</u>. Vienna: Hochschülerschaft, 1979. 131 pp.
1458. Löhr, Ludwig. "Probleme der Bergbauernwirtschaft aus der Sicht der österreichischen Alpenländer. Historische Grundlagen, ökonomische Bedingungen und Leistungen der Bergbauern-bevölkerung." in <u>Berichte über Landwirtschaft</u>. Bonn: Bundesministerium für Ernährung, Landwirtschaft und Forste, 1960. pp. 161-87.
1459. Meihsl, Peter. "Die Landwirtschaft im Wandel der politischen und ökonomischen Faktoren." in Wilhelm Weber, ed. <u>Österreichs Wirtschaftsstruktur gestern, heute, morgen</u>. Berlin: Duncker & Humblot, 1961. II, 551, 837.

SEE ALSO: 297.

AUSTRIA-HUNGARY--1815-1918

Bibliographic Reference

1460. <u>Das Schrifttum der Bodenkultur</u>. 2 vols. Vienna: Österreichischer Fachzeitschriftenverlag, 1948-1950.

AUSTRIA-HUNGARY--1815-1918

1461. <u>Die Agrarfrage in der Österreichisch-Ungarischen Monarchie 1900-1918</u>. Bucharest: Akademie der Sozialistischen Republik Rumäniens, 1965. 308 pp.
1462. Blum, Jerome. "Land Tenure in the Austrian Monarchy before 1848." <u>Agricultural History</u> 19 (1945), 87-98.
1463. Blum, Jerome. <u>Noble Landowners and Agriculture in Austria 1815-1848. A Study in the Origins of the Peasant Emancipation of 1848</u>. Baltimore: Johns Hopkins University Press, 1948. 295 pp.
1464. Braf, Albin. "Der landwirtschaftliche Hypothekarkredit in Österreich während der letzten 50 Jahre." in <u>Geschichte der österreichischen Land- und Forstwirtschaft und ihrer Industrien 1848-1898</u>. Vienna: Perles, 1899-1901. I-II, 580-677.
1465. Bruckmüller, Ernst. "Wirtschaftsentwicklung und politisches Verhalten der agrarischen Bevölkerung in Österreich 1867-1914." <u>VSWG</u> 59 (1972), 489-529.
1466. Chambers, Jonathan D. and G. E. Mingay. <u>The Agricultural Revolution, 1750-1880</u>. London: Batsford, 1966. 222 pp.
1467. Czekner, John, Jr. "A Comparison of the Agricultural Systems of Austria and Hungary in the Two Decades before World War I." <u>East European Quarterly</u> 12 (1978), 461-73.
1468. Full, V. <u>Die Agrikultursocietäten und ihr Einfluss auf die Landwirtschaft der österreichisch-ungarischen Monarchie</u>. Diss. Vienna, 1937. 146 pp.

1469. Geschichte der österreichischen Land- und Forstwirtschaft und ihrer Industrien 1848-1898. Festschrift zur Feier der am 2. December 1898 erfolgten 50jährigen Wiederkehr der Thronbesteigung S. M. des Kaisers Joseph I. 5 vols. Vienna: Perles, 1899-1901.

1470. Grünberg, Karl. Studien zur österreichischen Agrargeschichte. Leipzig: Duncker & Humblot, 1901. 281 pp.

1471. Grünberg, Karl. "Studien zur österreichischen Agrargeschichte und Agrarpolitik." Schmoller 20 (1896), 23-88; 21 (1897), 135-99; 24 (1900), 1477-1556.

1472. Hoffmann, Alfred. "Das Kaisertum Österreich als Agrarstaat im Zeitalter des Neoabsolutismus (1849-1867)." in I. Bog and G. Franz, eds. Wirtschaftliche und soziale Strukturen im säkularen Wandel. Festschrift für Wilhelm Abel. Hannover: Schaper, 1974. III, 578-96.

1473. Hoffmann, Alfred, ed. Österreich-Ungarn als Agrarstaat. Wirtschaftliches Wachstum und Agrarverhältnisse in Österreich im 19. Jahrhundert. Vienna: Verlag für Geschichte und Politik, 1978. 274 pp.

1474. Kluge, Ulrich. "Agrarinterventionismus und Sozialprotektionismus in Österreich 1879 bis 1918. Politische, gesellschaftliche und wirtschaftliche Voraussetzungen der 'Bauerndemokratie' im 20 Jahrhundert." Zeitgeschichte 6 (1979), 199-222.

1475. Knapp, Georg F. "Die Bauernbefreiung in Österreich und in Preussen." Schmoller 18 (1894), 409-31.

1476. Komlos, John, Jr. "Austro-Hungarian Agricultural Development, 1827-1877." Journal of European Economic History 8 (1979), 37-60.

1477. Marchet, Gustav. 1848 bis 1888. Ein Rückblick auf die Entwicklung der österreichischen Agrarverwaltung. Vienna: Frick, 1889. 101 pp.

1478. Rozdolski, Roman. Die grosse Steuer- und Agrarreform Josefs II. Ein Kapitel zur österreichischen Wirtschaftsgeschichte. Warsaw: Panstwowe Wydawnictwo Naukowe, 1961. 197 pp.

1479. Sandgruber, Roman. Österreichische Agrarstatistik, 1750-1918. Munich: Oldenbourg, 1978. 265 pp.

1480. Schiff, Walter. "Geschichte der österreichischen Land- und Forstwirtschaft und ihrer Industrien 1848-1898." Jahrbücher für Nationalökonomie und Statistik 3 (1901), 375-412.

1481. Schiff, Walter. Österreichs Agrarpolitik seit der Grundentlastung. 2 vols. Tübingen: Laupp, 1898.

1482. Schreibers, Joseph R. Darstellung der Gründung und Entwickelung der k.k. Landwirthschafts-Gesellschaft in Wien, als Fest-Album bei Gelegenheit der 50jährigen Jubiläumsfeier der Gesellschaft. Vienna: K. K. Hof- und Staatsdruckerei, 1857. 336 pp.

1483. Sommeregger, Franz. Agrarverfassung der Landgemeinde und Landeskulturpolitik in Österreich seit der Grundentlastung. Diss. Berlin. Klagenfurt: St.-Josef, 1912. 123 pp.

1484. Sommeregger, Franz. Die Wege und Ziele der österreichischen Agrarpolitik seit der Grundentlastung. Vienna: Volksbund Verlag, 1912. 122 pp.

1485. Vilfan, Sergij. "Die Agrarsozialpolitik von Maria Theresia bis Kudlich." in Der Bauer Mittel- und Osteuropas im sozio-ökonomischen Wandel des 18. und 19. Jahrhunderts. Cologne: Böhlau, 1973. pp. 1-52.

SEE ALSO: 2967.

AUSTRIA--1919-1975

1486. Köttl, Hans. "Die Strukturänderung des agrarischen Aussenhandels in Österreich. Ein Vergleich der Jahre 1954-56 mit dem Zeitraum 1936-37." Die Bodenkultur 11 (1958), 19-42.

1487. Rumer, Willy. Die Agrarreformen der Donau-Staaten, 1917-1926. Innsbruck: W. Rumer, 1927. 170 pp.

1488. Zagorov, Slavcho D. et al. The Agricultural Economy of the Danubian Countries, 1935-45. Stanford, CA: Stanford University Press, 1955. 478 pp.

SEE ALSO: 395.

AUSTRIAN AND AUSTRO-HUNGARIAN REGIONS

Bohemia and Moravia

1489. Frommer, Rudolf. Einfluss des Weltkriegs auf die osteuropäische Forstwirtschaft unter besonderer Berücksichtigung der Karpathenforste. Diss. Freiburg i. B. Freiburg i. B.: Waibel, 1929. 70 pp.

1490. Grünberg, Karl. "Die Bauernbefreiung und die Auflösung des gutsherrlich-bäuerlichen Verhältnisses in Böhmen, Mähren und Schlesien." Archiv für Soziale Gesetzgebung und Statistik 7 (1894), 541-48.

1491. Heumos, Peter. Agrarische Interessen und nationale Politik in Böhmen 1848-1889. Wiesbaden: Steiner, 1979. 251 pp.

1492. Jelecek, Leos. "Ground Rent and Land Fund in Bohemia in the Second Half of the 19th Century." Hospodárské dejiny 2 (1978), 131-68.

1493. Klíma, Arnost. "Agrarian Class Structure and Economic Development in Pre-Industrial Bohemia." Past and Present 85 (1979), 49-67.

1494. Klíma, Arnost. "Ein Beitrag zur Agrarfrage in der Revolution von 1848 in Böhmen." in Studien zur Geschichte der Österreichisch-Ungarischen Monarchie. Graz: Böhlau, 1961. pp. 15-26.

1495. Lom, Frantisek. "Die Arbeitsproduktivität in der Geschichte der tschechoslowakischen Landwirtschaft." Zeitschrift für Agrargeschichte und Agrarsoziologie 19 (1971), 1-25.

1496. Spiesz, Anton. "Czechoslovakia's Place in the Agrarian Development of Middle and East Europe of Modern Times." Studia Historica Slovaca 6 (1969), 7-62.

1497. Stark, Werner. "Niedergang und Ende des landwirtschaftlichen Grossbetriebs in den böhmischen Ländern." Jahrbuch für Nationalökohomie und Statistik 146 (1937), 416-49.

1498. Stoklasa, Julius. "Die Entwicklung und der jetzige Stand der Landwirtschaft in Böhmen." in Das böhmische Volk. Prague: F. Rivnac, 1916. pp. 147-92.

Burgenland

1499. Kropf, Rudolf. "Agrargeschichte des Burgenlandes in der Neuzeit. Vom Beginn des 16. Jahrhunderts bis zur Aufhebung der Bruderherrschaft im Jahre 1848." Zeitschrift für Agrargeschichte und Agrarsoziologie 20 (1972), 3-22.

Carinthia

1500. Dinklage, Karl, ed. Geschichte der Kärntner Landwirtschaft. Klagenfurt: Heyn, 1966. 674 pp.

1501. Fresacher, Walther. Die Freisassen in Kärnten. Klagenfurt: Kärntner Landesarchiv, 1974. 195 pp.

1502. Neumann, Dieter. Das Kärntner Lesachtal. Werden und Wandlungen einer bergbäuerlichen Kultur- und Wirtschaftslandschaft. Klagenfurt: Kärtner Landesarchiv, 1977. 256 pp.

Hungary

1503. Csöppüs, Istvan. Die landwirtschaftliche Produktion in Ungarn zur Zeit des zweiten Weltkrieges. Cologne: Institute for Social Research, 1983. 69 pp.

1504. Dammang, Andreas. Die deutsche Landwirtschaft im Banat und in der Batschka. Munich: Reinhardt, 1931. 197 pp.

1505. Eddie, Scott M. "Agricultural Production and Output Per Worker in Hungary, 1870-1913." Journal of Economic History 28 (1968), 197-222.

1506. Eddie, Scott M. "The Changing Pattern of Land Ownership in Hungary, 1867-1914." Economic History Review 20 (1967), 293-310.

1507. Eddie, Scott M. "Farmers' Response to Price in Large Estate Agriculture. Hungary, 1870-1913." Economic History Review 24 (1971), 571-88.

1508. Eddie, Scott M. "Die Landwirtschaft als Quelle des Arbeitskraft-Angebots. Mutmassungen aus der Geschichte Ungarns, 1870-1913." VSWG 56 (1969), 215-32.

1509. Eddie, Scott M. "The Terms of Trade as a Tax on Agriculture. Hungary's Trade with Austria, 1883-1913." Journal of Economic History 32 (1972), 298-315.
1510. Gagyi, Jenö. La réforme agraire sur les territoires arrachés á la Hongrie. Budapest: Athenaeum, 1929. 50 pp.
1511. Held, Joseph, ed. The Modernization of Agriculture. Rural Transformation in Hungary, 1848-1975. Boulder, CO: East European Monographs, 1980. 508 pp.
1512. Komlos, John, Jr. "The Emancipation of the Hungarian Peasantry and Agricultural Development." in I. Völgyes, ed. The Peasantry of Eastern Europe. New York: Pergamon Press, 1949. I, 109-18.
1513. Mérèl, Gyula. "L'essor de l'agriculture capitaliste en Hongrie dans la première moitié du XIXe siècle." Revue d'Histoire Moderne 12 (1965), 51-64.
1514. Orosz, István. "Die landwirtschaftliche Produktion in Ungarn 1790-1849." Agrartörteneti Szemle 13 (1971), 1-24.
1515. Pach, Sigmond P. "Über einige charakteristische Züge des s. g. Preussischen Weges der Entwicklung der Landwirtschaft Ungarns in der 2. Hälfte des 19. Jahrhunderts." Zeitschrift für Geschichtswissenschaft 7 (1959), 1231-53.
1516. Puskás, Julianna. "Die Entwicklungstendenzen der landwirtschaftlichen Produktion in Ungarn von der zweiten Hälfte des 19. Jahrhunderts bis zum ersten Weltkrieg." Jahrbuch für Wirtschaftsgeschichte (1972), I, 229-260.
1517. Szabo, Ervin. "The Agrarian Question in Hungary (1908)." Peasant Studies 7 (1978), 28-37.
1518. Szuhay, Miklós. "Die kapitalistische Umgestaltung der Landwirtschaft in Ungarn zur Zeit des Habsburgschen Absolutismus, 1849-1867." in Einige Fragen der Wirtschaftstheorie und der Heranbildung von Volkswirtschaftlern. Budapest: Kossuth Könyvkiadó, 1969. pp. 93-111.
1519. Tóth, T. "Profitability and Cost-Efficiency in Hungarian Agriculture in the 1930s." Journal of European Economic History 11 (1982), 157-64.

Lower Austria

1520. Klein-Bruckschwaiger, Franz. "Dreifelderwirtschaft und Genossenschaft. Von der Markgemeinschaft zur Marktgemeinde St. Peter in der Au in Niederösterreich." in Festschrift Nikolaus Grass. Zum 60. Geburtstag dargebracht. Innsbruck: Wagner, 1974. I, 679-707.
1521. Lewis, Gavin. "The Peasantry. Rural Change and Conservative Agrarianism. Lower Austria at the Turn of the Century." Past and Present 81 (1978), 119-43.

SEE ALSO: 3013.

Rumania

1522. Evans, I. Leslie. The Agrarian Revolution in Roumania. Cambridge: Cambridge University Press, 1924. 197 pp.
1523. Mitrany, David. The Land and the Peasant in Rumania. The War and Agrarian Reform, 1917-21. New Haven, CT: Yale University Press, 1930. 627 pp.
1524. Moldoveanu, Constantin. Die grossen Agrarreformen seit dem Weltkriege. Bucharest: "Cartea de Aur", 1939. 127 pp.
1525. Stein, Thomas. "Zur Frage der rumänischen Landwirtschaft im Ersten Weltkrieg." Österreichische Osthefte 21 (1979), 115-24.

Styria

1526. Barth, Anna. Agrarpolitik im Vormärz. Die Steirische Landwirtschaftsgesellschaft unter Erzherzog Johann. Graz: Leykam, 1980. 141 pp.
1527. Lütge, Friedrich, "Die Grundentlastung (Bauernbefreiung) in der Steiermark." Zeitschrift für Agrargeschichte und Agrarsoziologie 16 (1968), 90-109.
1528. Posch, Fritz, ed. Das Bauerntum in der Steiermark. Ein geschichtlicher Überblick. Graz: Historischer Verein für Steiermark, 1963. 123 pp.

1529. Posch, Fritz. "Steirische Bauern- und Agrargeschichte." in Die Steiermark. Graz: Imago, 1971. pp. 945-57.
1530. Posch, Fritz. "Studien zur Dorf- und Flurgeschichte am Beispiel Safenau." in Festschrift für Otto Lamprecht. Graz: Historischer Verein für Steiermark, 1968. pp. 151-71.
1531. Schneiter, Fritz. Agrargeschichte der Brandwirtschaft. Graz: Selbstverlag der Historischen Landeskommission für Steiermark, 1970. 161 pp.

Tirol

1532. Dobler, Karl. Die Entwicklung der Landwirtschaft in Frastanz seit 1945. Innsbruck: Wagner, 1969. 81 pp.
1533. Gassner, Maria. Beiträge zur Siedelungs und Wirtschaftsgeschichte des innern Selraintales. Innsbruck: Museum Ferdinandeum, 1925. 79 pp.
1534. Grimm, Alois. Das landwirtschaftliche Genossenschaftswesen in Tirol, mit vergleichender Darstellung des landwirtschaftlichen Genossenschaftswesens in den angrenzenden österreichischen Alpenländern, sowie Bayern, Italien und der Schweiz. Diss. Zurich. Zurich: Aktien-Buchdruckerei, 1910. 81 pp.
1535. Moritz, Alois. Die Almwirtschaft im Stanzertal. Beiträge zur Wirtschaftsgeschichte und Volkskunde einer Hochgebirgstalschaft Tirols. Innsbruck: Wagner, 1956. 138 pp.
1536. Stolz, Otto. Die Schwaighöfe in Tirol. Ein Beitrag zur Siedlungs- und Wirtschaftsgeschichte der Hochalpentäler. Innsbuck: Deutscher und Österreichischer Alpenverein, 1930. 197 pp.
1537. Stolz, Otto. "Zur Geschichte der Landwirtschaft in Tirol." in Tirol. Tiroler Heimat NF 3 (1930).

SEE ALSO: 4423.

Transylvania

1538. Gyémánt, Ladislau. "L'intégration de la paysannerie dans le mouvement national roumain de Transylvanie durant la période 1790-1848." Revue Roumaine d'Histoire 20 (1981), 245-68.
1539. Kovács, Jósef. "Aus dem Kampf der siebenbürgischen Bauern gegen die lokalen Organe der Staatsmacht von Bürgertum und Grossgrundbesitz im Herbst des Jahres 1918." in Die Oktoberrevolution und Deutschland. Berlin: Kommission der Historiker der DDR und der UdSSR, 1958. pp. 465-74.
1540. Kovács, Jósef. "Zur Frage der siebenbürgischen Bauernbefreiung und der Entwicklung der kapitalistischen Landwirtschaft nach 1848." in Studien zur Geschichte der Österreichischen-Ungarischen Monarchie. Graz: H. Böhlaus Nachf., 1963. pp. 91-112.
1541. Móricz, Nicholas. The Fate of the Transylvanian Soil. A Brief Account of the Rumanian Land Reform of 1921. Budapest: Society of Transylvanian Emigrants, 1934. 204 pp.

Upper Austria

1542. Fuchs, Franz. "Ein Jahrhundert Landwirtschaft im oberen Mühlviertel. Jahrbuch des Bischoflichen Gymnnasiums Kollegium Petr., Linz/ Urfahr 49 (1952-53).
1543. Grüll, Georg. Bauer, Herr und Landesfürst. Sozialrevolutionäre Bestrebungen der oberösterreichischen Bauern von 1650 bis 1848. Graz: Böhlaus Nachfolger, 1963. 668 pp.
1544. Haslehner, Werner. Die Entwicklung der landwirtschaftlichen Genossenschaften in Oberösterreich. Vienna: Verlag Verband der Wissenschaftlichen Gesellschaften Österreichs, 1977. 207 pp.
1545. Hoffmann, Alfred, ed. Bauernland Oberösterreich. Entwicklungsgeschichte seiner Land- und Forstwirtschaft. Linz: Trauner, 1974. 784 pp.
1547. Die oberösterreichische Wirtschaft 1945-1949. Linz: Amt der oberösterreichischen Landesregierung, Abteilung Wirtschaft, Wirtschaftlicher Informationsdienst, 1950.

Vienna

1548. Brusatti, Alois. "Herrenland und Bauernland im Viertel unter dem Wienerwald." Unsere Heimat. Monatsblatt des Vereins für Landeskunde von Niederösterreich und Wien 28 (1957), 127-37.
1549. Schreibers, Joseph R. Darstellung der Gründung und Entwicklung der k. k. Landwirtschafts-Gesellschaft in Wien. Vienna: Gerald & Sohn, 1857. 337 pp.

SWITZERLAND

Reference

1550. Frei, Albert. Entwicklung und heutiger Stand der schweizerischen Agrarstatistik. Diss. Zurich, 1931. 183 pp.

SWITZERLAND

1551. 1863-1938. 75 Jahre Schweizerischer Alpwirtschaftlicher Verein. Langnau i. E.: Emmenthaler Blatt, 1939. 73 pp.
1552. Frei, Albert. Entwicklung und heutiger Stand der schweizerischen Agrarstatistik. Diss. Zurich, 1931. 183 pp.
1553. Herzig, Karl. Der Schweizerische Alpwirtschaftliche Verein. Rückblick und Ausblick. Langnau i. E.: Emmenthaler Blatt, 1942. 23 pp.
1554. Jaggi, Ernst. "Die Entwicklung der schweizerischen Landwirtschaft vom Ende des 19. Jahrhunderts bis zur Gegenwart." in H. Wahlen and E. Jaggi. Der schweizerische Bauernkrieg 1653 und die seitherige Entwicklung des Bauernstandes. Bern: Verbandsdruckerei, 1953. 198 pp.
1555. Kipfer, Werner. Die schweizerische Landwirtschaft. 3rd ed. Zollikofen: Ing.-Agronomen, 1982. 96 pp.
1556. Kupper, Walter. Die Zollpolitik der schweizerischen Landwirtschaft seit 1848. Bern: Stämpfli, 1929. 202 pp.
1557. Laur, Ernst F. Erinnerungen eines schweizerischen Bauernführers; ein Beitrag zur schweizerischen Wirtschaftsgeschichte. Bern: Verbandsdruckerei, 1943. 340 pp.
1558. Wahlen, Hermann. Baumeister unseres Bauernstandes. 14 Lebensbilder. Bern: Viktoria, 1966. 281 pp.

SEE ALSO: 2171, 3039, 3053-55, 4476.

SWITZERLAND--1815-1918

1559. Brugger, Hans. Die schweizerische Landwirtschaft. 1850-1914. Frauenfeld: Huber, 1979. 423 pp.
1560. Brugger, Hans. Die schweizerische Landwirtschaft in der ersten Hälfte des 19. Jahrhunderts. Frauenfeld: Huber, 1956. 270 pp.
1561. Chuard, Ernest. "Die Landwirtschaft." in P. Seippel, ed. Die Schweiz im 19. Jahrhundert. Bern: Schmid & Francke, 1900. III, 1-77.
1562. Hanssen, Georg. "Das Agrarwesen der deutschen Schweiz in seiner geschichtlichen Entwickelung. Nach v. Miaskowski's Untersuchungen." in Agrarhistorische Abhandlungen. Leipzig: Hirzel, 1880. I, 513-68.
1563. Hauser, Albert. "Zur Produktivität der schweizerischen Landwirtschaft im 19. Jahrhundert." in Festschrift Wilhelm Abel. Hannover: Schaper, 1964. pp. 597-616.
1564. Kraemer, Adolf. Die Entwicklung der Landwirtschaft in den letzten 100 Jahren. Basel: B. Schwabe, 1884. 50 pp.
1565. Kraemer, Adolf. Die Landwirtschaft im neunzehnten Jahrhundert. Frauenfeld: Huber, 1902. 105 pp.

1566. Miaskowski, August von. Die schweizerische Allmend in ihrer geschichtlichen Entwicklung von XIII. Jahrhundert bis zur Gegenwart. Leipzig: Duncker & Humblot, 1879. 245 pp.
1567. Miaskowski, August von. Die Verfassung der Land-, Alpen- und Forstwirtschaft der deutschen Schweiz in ihrer geschichtlichen Entwicklung. Basel: Georg, 1878. 131 pp.
1568. Schatzmann, Rudolf. Zwanzig Jahre schweizerische Alpwirtschaft. Aarau: J. J. Christen, 1880.
1569. Steiger, Thomas. Die Produktion von Milch und Fleisch in der schweizerischen Landwirtschaft des 19. Jahrhunderts als Gegenstand bäuerlicher Entscheidungen. Bern: Lang, 1982. 215 pp.
1570. Steiner, Max. Die Agrarpolitik in der Schweiz und Deutschland von 1833-1939. Diss. Basel, 1953. 209 pp.
1571. Wegener, Eduard. Die schweizerischen Bodenkreditinstitute 1846-1912. Munich: Duncker & Humblot, 1915. 316 pp.

SEE ALSO: 1438.

SWITZERLAND--1919-1975

1572. Bonorand, Jochen S. Verschiebungen der bergbäuerlichen wirtschaftlichen Existenzgrundlage in der Zwischenkriegszeit von 1920-1939. Diss. Bern. Rapperswil: Meyer, 1949. 125 pp.
1573. Hürlimann, Joseph. "Aufwands-, Ertrags- und Einkommensgestaltung der schweizerischen Landwirtschaft während des zweiten Weltkrieges." SZVS 82 (1946), 51-65.
1574. Jungo, Hubert. Sondermassnahmen des Bundes zugunsten der Berglandwirtschaft seit 1945. Bern: Abteilung für Landwirtschaft der Eidgenossenschaft, 1978. 119 pp.
1575. Pauli, Walter. "Beziehungen zwischen landwirtschaftlicher Produktion und Marktgestaltung während des Krieges." Agrarpolitische Revue 4 (1947-48), 121-43.

SWISS CANTONS

Aargau

1576. Brugger, Hans. Geschichte der aargauischen Landwirtschaft seit der Mitte des 19. Jahrhunderts. Brugg: Aargauische Landwirtschaftliche Gesellschaft, 1948.
1577. Howald, Oskar. Die Dreifelderwirtschaft im Kanton Aargau mit besonderer Berücksichtigung ihrer historischen Entwicklung und ihrer wirtschaftlichen und natürlichen Grundlagen. Diss. Zurich. Bern: Verbandsdruckerei, 1927. 236 pp.

Appenzell

1578. Grosser, Hermann. Die Geschäfte der Landsgemeinde von Appenzell i. Rh. der Jahre 1850-1967. Appenzell: s.n., 1967.
1579. Koller, Franz, Die appenzellische Land-, Milch- und Alpwirtschaft im Wandel der Zeiten. Appenzell: Genossenschafts-Buchdruckerei, 1964. 96 pp.

Basel

1580. Beiträge zur Entwicklungsgeschichte des Kantons Basel-Landschaft. Liestal: Basellandschaftliche Kantonalbank, 1964. 575 pp.
1581. Gutzwiller, Karl. Landwirtschaftliche Entwicklung und Wanderbewegung in Kanton Baselland im 19. Jahrhundert. Diss. Basel. Liestal: Lüdin, 1911. 93 pp.
1582. Weber, Karl. "Wirtschaft und Verkehr." in Geschichte der Landschaft Basel und des Kantons Basel-Landschaft. Liestal: Lüdin, 1932. II, 545-60.

Bern

1583. <u>Die Landwirtschaft im Kanton Bern</u>. Ed. Landwirtschaftsdirektion des Kantons Bern. Bern: Verbandsdruckerei Bern, 1978. 176 pp.
1584. Rubi, Christian. <u>Geschichte des Hofes Hertig im untern Frittenbach. Im Auftrag der Landwirtschaftsdirektion des Kantons Bern</u>. Bern: Haupt, 1941. 73 pp.

Glarus

1585. Hösli, Jost. <u>Glarner Land- und Alpwirtschaft in Vergangenheit und Gegenwart</u>. Diss. Zurich, 1948. 385 pp.

Lucerne

1586. Lemmenmeier, Max. <u>Luzerns Landwirtschaft im Umbruch. Wirtschaftlicher, sozialer und politischer Wandel in der Agrargesellschaft des 19. Jahrhunderts</u>. Luzern: Rex, 1983. 463 pp.

St. Gallen

1587. <u>Das Fünfziger Jubiläum der Landwirtschaftlichen Gesellschaft des Kantons St. Gallen</u>. St. Gallen: Landwirtschaftliche Gesellschaft, 1869.
1588. Gmür, Emil <u>Die Geschichte der Landwirtschaft im Kanton St. Gallen</u>. St. Gallen: Zollikofer, 1907. 38 pp.
1589. Gsell, Walter. "Die st. gallische Landwirtschaft in den Jahren 1888-1912." in <u>Statistik des Kantons St. Gallen</u> 31 (1913). 37 pp.
1590. Köppel, Josef. "Landwirtschaft, Handel, Gewerbe und Industrie." in <u>Aus der Geschichte der Gemeinde Au. Festschrift</u>. Au: s. n., 1955. pp. 89-94.

Schaffhausen

1591. Zimmermann, Walter. <u>Schaffhauser Ackerbau durch die Jahrhunderte</u>. Schaffhausen: P. Meili, 1974. 141 pp.

Solothurn

1592. <u>Hundert Jahre Landwirtschaftlicher Kantonalverein Solothurn 1845-1945</u>. Solothurn: Landwirtschaftlicher Kantonalverein Solothurn, 1945.

Thurgau

1593. Ausderau, Walter. <u>Betrachtungen über die Entwicklung, den Stand und die Tendenzen im thurgauischen landwirtschaftlichen Genossenschaftswesen</u>. Weinfelden: Neuenschwander, 1929. 221 pp.
1594. Brugger, Hans. <u>Geschichte der thurgauischen Landwirtschaft von 1835 bis 1935</u>. Frauenfeld: Huber, 1935. 221 pp.

Unterwalden

1595. Kiem, Martin. "Die Alpenwirtschaft und Agrikultur in Obwalden seit den ältesten Zeiten." <u>Geschichtsfreund</u> 21 (1866), 144-231.

Valais

1596. Hauser, Albert. "Land- und Forstwirtschaft im Wallis vor und nach der industriellen Revolution. Zur Agrarsoziologie einer Gebirgsregion." Agrarpolitische Revue 222 (1968), 422-29.

SEE ALSO: 2232.

Zug

1597. Die Landwirtschaft im Kanton Zug. Entwicklung, Stand, Ausblick. Zug: Volkswirtschafts-direktion, 1978. 160 pp.
1598. Der Zuger Bauer, ein Bild von der Entwicklung und dem heutigen Stand der zugerischen Land-wirtschaft. Baar: Landwirtschaftlicher Verein des Kantons Zug, 1851.

Zurich

1599. Honegger, Walter. Die wirtschaftliche Entwicklung der Landgemeinde Hinwil. Pfäffikon: Schellenberg, 1950. 181 pp.

LUXEMBURG

1600. Alsteen, P. "L'évolution agricole du Luxembourg belge depuis cent ans." A. Gembloux (1934), 285-313.
1601. 100 Joer Letzeburger Landwirtschaft 1848-1948. Letzeburg: Luja-Beffort, 1948. 85 pp.

GERMANY

Bibliographic References

1602. Ball, Joyce, ed. Foreign Statistical Documents: a Bibliography of German International Trade and Agricultural Statistics: Including Holdings of the Stanford University Libraries. Stanford, CA: Hoover Institution, 1967. 173 pp.
1603. Franz, Günther. Bücherkunde zur Geschichte des deutschen Bauerntums. Neudamm: Neumann, 1938. 97 pp.

GERMANY

1604. Abel, Wilhelm. Die drei Epochen der deutschen Agrargeschichte. Hannover: Schaper, 1962. 135 pp.
1605. Abel, Wilhelm. Kurze Geschichte der Agrarverfassung. Gross-Denkte/Wolfenbüttel: Rock, 1956. 54 pp.
1606. Bartels, Adolf. Der Bauer in der deutschen Vergangenheit. 2nd ed. Jena: Diederichs, 1934. 142 pp.
1607. Beckmann, Fritz. "Der Bauer im Zeitalter des Kapitalismus." Schmoller 50 (1926), 719-48; 51 (1927), 49-91.
1608. Berthold, Rudolf. "Bedeutung und Aufgaben der agraren Betriebsgeschichte." Jahrbuch für Wirtschaftsgeschichte (1966), II, 218-40.
1609. Bittermann, Eberhard. Die landwirtschaftliche Produktion in Deutschland, 1800-1950. Ein methodischer Beitrag zur Ermittlung der Veränderungen des Umfanges der landwirtschaftlichen Produktion und der Ertragssteigerung in den letzten 50 Jahren. Diss. Halle a. d. S. Halle a. d. S.: Kühn-Archiv, 1956. 149 pp.
1610. Blohm, Georg. "Die Entwicklung der Landwirtschaft." Berichte über Landwirtschaft 55 (1977), 1-18.
1611. Cecil, Robert. German Agriculture 1870-1970. London: University of London, 1979.
1612. Deck, Helmut. Die Entwicklung der Grundstückszusammmenlegung seit der Stein-Hardenberg'schen Reform. Diss. Breslau, 1940. Bleicherode a. H.: Nieft, 1939. 64 pp.
1613. Decken, Hans. Entwicklung der Selbstversorgung Deutschlands mit landwirtschaftlichen Erzeugnissen. Berlin: Parey, 1938. 152 pp.
1614. Deutsche Agrargeschichte. 3rd ed. Stuttgart: Ulmer, 1972. 327 pp.
1615. Dietze, Constantin. "Wege zur Agrarpolitik. Ein Stück Methodengeschichte der National-ökonomie in Deutschland von Moeser bis Roscher." Historisches Jahrbuch der Görres Gesellschaft 62/69 (1942/49), 491-538.
1616. Ekkehart, Klaus. Deutsche Bauerngeschichte. Gotha: Reissenweber, 1934. 125 pp.
1617. Ennen, Edith and Walter Janssen. Deutsche Agrargeschichte. Vom Neolithikum bis zur Schwelle des Industriezeitalters. Wiesbaden: Steiner, 1979. 273 pp.
1618. Finckenstein, Hans W. Die Entwicklung der Landwirtschaft in Preussen und Deutschland und in den alten preussischen Provinzen von 1800-1930. 3 vols. Bern: H. W. Finckenstein, 1959.
1619. Flemming, Jens. Landwirtschaftliche Interessen und Demokratie. Ländliche Gesellschaft, Agrarverbände und Staat 1890-1925. Bonn: Verlag Neue Gesellschaft, 1978. 366 pp.
1620. Franz, Günther, ed. Bauernschaft und Bauernstand 1500-1970. Limburg/Lahn: Starke, 1975. 358 pp.
1621. Franz, Günther, ed. Deutsches Bauerntum. 2 vols. Weimar: Böhlau, 1939.
1622. Franz, Günther. Kleine Geschichte des deutschen Bauerntums. Oldenburg: Stalling, 1953. 29 pp.
1623. Fuchs, Carl J. "Die Bedeutung der deutschen Agrargeschichte für die deutsche Volkswirt-schaftlehre." in Festgabe für Werner Sombart. Munich: Duncker & Humblot, 1933. pp. 113-19.
1624. Gerdes, Heinrich. Geschichte des deutschen Bauernstandes. Berlin: Teubner, 1928. 127 pp.
1625. Hanefeld, Kurt. Die Geschichte des deutschen landwirtschaftlichen Grundeigentums. Diss. Leipzig. Meissen: Nestler, 1929. 229 pp.
1626. Hanefeld, Kurt. Geschichte des deutschen Nährstandes. Leipzig: Franke, 1935. 514 pp.
1627. Haushofer, Heinz. Die deutsche Landwirtschaft im technischen Zeitalter. Stuttgart: Ulmer, 1963. 290 pp.

1628. Haushofer, Heinz. Die Furche der DLG, 1885 bis 1960. Frankfurt a. M.: DLG-Verlag, 1960. 238 pp.

1629. Haushofer, Heinz and Willi A. Boelcke, eds. Wege und Forschungen der Agrargeschichte. Festschrift zum 65. Geburtstag von Günther Franz. Frankfurt a. M.: DLG-Verlag, 1967. 364 pp.

1630. Henning, Friedrich-Wilhelm. Landwirtschaft und ländliche Gesellschaft in Deutschland. 2 vols. Paderborn: Schöningh, 1978-79.

1631. Hübner, Hans. "Der Kampf der deutschen Bauern und Landarbeiter um eine Bodenreform, 1848-1918-1945." in H.-J. Bartmuss et al. Die Volksmassen, Gestalter der Geschichte. Festgabe für Leo Stern zu seinem 60. Geburtstag. Berlin: Rütten & Loening, 1962. pp. 210-30.

1632. Huppertz, Barthel. Räume und Schichten bäuerlicher Kulturformen in Deutschland. Ein Beitrag zur deutschen Bauerngeschichte. Bonn: Röhrscheid, 1939. 315 pp.

1633. Jasny, Marie P. "Some Aspects of German Agricultural Settlement." Political Science Quarterly 52 (1937), 208-40.

1634. Kapitalismus und Überlieferung in der deutschen Landwirtschaft. Berlin: Engelmann, 1923. 44 pp.

1635. Kellenbenz, Hermann, ed. Agrarisches Nebengewerbe und Formen der Reagrarisierung im Spätmittelalter und 19./20. Jahrhundert. Stuttgart: Fischer, 1975. 237 pp.

1636. Klein, Ernst. Geschichte der deutschen Landwirtschaft. Ein Überblick. Stuttgart: Ulmer, 1969. 93 pp.

1637. Klein, Ernst. Geschichte der deutschen Landwirtschaft im Industriezeitalter. Wiesbaden: Steiner, 1973. 192 pp.

1638. Krzynowski, Richard. Geschichte der deutschen Landwirtschaft unter besonderer Berücksichtigung der technischen Entwicklung der Landwirtschaft bis zum Ausbruch des 2. Weltkrieges 1939. 3rd ed. Berlin: Duncker & Humblot, 1961. 441 pp.

1639. Landwirtschaft und ländliche Gesellschaft in Geschichte und Gegenwart. Festschrift Wilhelm Abel. Hannover: Schaper, 1964. 188 pp.

1640. Lapkès, Jacques. La main-d'oeuvre agricole en Allemagne, de la fin du XVIIIe siècle à 1926. Paris: Bureau d'éditions, de diffusion et de publicité, 1926. 166 pp.

1641. Leers, Johann von. Die bäuerliche Gemeindeverfassung in der deutschen Geschichte. Berlin: Spaeth & Linde, 1936. 82 pp.

1642. Leers, Johann von. Geschichte des deutschen Bauernrechts und des deutschen Bauerntums. 3rd ed. Leipzig: Kohlhammer, 1942. 72 pp.

1643. Lütge, Friedrich. "Die Ablösung der grundherrlichen Lasten in Mitteldeutschland." Jahrbücher für Nationalökonomie und Statistik 142 (1935), 282-304, 393-414.

1644. Lütge, Friedrich. Die Bauernbefreiung in der modernen Wirtschaftsgeschichte. Minden i. W.: Lutzeyer, 1948. 24 pp.

1645. Lütge, Friedrich. "Das Bauerntum im Wandel der Geschichte." Studium generale 11 (1958), 377-89.

1646. Lütge, Friedrich. "Die deutsche Grundherrschaft. Ein Forschungsbericht." Zeitschrift für Agrargeschichte und Agrarsoziologie 3 (1955), 129-37.

1647. Lütge, Friedrich. Geschichte der deutschen Agrarverfassung. 2nd ed. Stuttgart: Ulmer, 1967. 269 pp.

1648. Lütge, Friedrich. Die mitteldeutsche Grundherrschaft und ihre Auflösung. 2nd ed. Stuttgart: Fischer, 1957. 317 pp.

1649. Mayhew, Alan. Rural Settlement and Farming in Germany. New York: Barnes and Noble, 1963. 224 pp.

1650. Miller, Jakob. Deutsche Bauerngeschichte. Stuttgart: Ulmer, 1941. 330 pp.

1651. Mortensen, Hans. "Zur Entstehung der Gewannflur. Professor Dr. Hans Plischke zum 65. Geburtstag." Zeitschrift für Agrargeschichte und Agrarsoziologie 3 (1955), 30-48.

1652. Mullick, Mumammad A. H. Die Entwicklung des deutschen Agrarkreditsystems unter besonderer Berücksichtigung der allgemeinen Agrarverhältnisse und der Agrarpolitik. Diss. Bonn, 1967. 286 pp.

1653. Pfeffer, Karl H. Der Bauer. Leipzig: Schäfer, 1939. 155 pp.

1654. Puhle, Hans-Jürgen. Politische Agrarbewegungen in kapitalistischen Industriegesellschaften. Göttingen: Vandenhoeck & Ruprecht, 1975. 496 pp.

1655. Rühle, Otto. "Zur historischen Entwicklung der Landwirtschaft in Ost- und Westdeutschland." Zeitschrift für Geschichtswissenschaft 8 (1960), 599-628.

1656. Rumpf, Max. Deutsches Bauernleben. Stuttgart: Kohlhammer, 1936. 912 pp.

1657. Scheda, Karl, ed. Deutsches Bauerntum. Sein Werden. Niedergang und Aufstieg. Konstanz: F. Ehlers, 1935. 608 pp.
1658. Schindlmayr, Adalbert. Pioniere des Ackers. Eine Agrargeschichte in Lebensbildern. Munich: J. F. Lehmann, 1959. 162 pp.
1659. Schmidt, Klaus. Der Schicksalsweg des deutschen Bauerntums. Frankfurt a. M.: Diesterweg, 1943. 115 pp.
1660. Schreiner, G. "Die Entwicklung der deutschen Agrarstrukturpolitik von der Reichsgründung im Jahre 1871 bis zum Ende des zweiten Weltkrieges." Bericht über Landwirtschaft 53 (Oct. 1975), 291-317.
1661. Schröder-Lembke, Gertrud. Studien zur Agrargeschichte. Stuttgart: Fischer, 1978. 199 pp.
1662. Seraphim, Hans-Jürgen. Deutsche Bauern- und Landwirtschaftspolitik. Leipzig: Bibliographisches Institut, 1939. 151 pp.
1663. Timm, Albrecht. Studien zur Siedlungs- und Agrargeschichte Mitteldeutschlands. Cologne: Böhlau, 1956. 177 pp.
1664. Wege und Forschungen der Agrargeschichte. Frankfurt a. M.: DLG-Verlag, 1967. 364 pp.
1665. Wellmann, Imre. "Von der herkömmlichen Produktion zur landwirtschaftlichen Revolution der Neuzeit." Agrártörteneti Szemle 12 (1970), 1-66.
1666. White, Dan S. "The German Peasantry." Journal of Interdisciplinary History 1 (1970-71), 535-40.
1667. Wopfner, Hermann. "Bauerntum, Stadt und Staat." Historische Zeitschrift 164 (1941), 229-60, 472-95.
1668. Wunder, Heide. Die bäuerliche Gemeinde in Deutschland. Von der Herrschaft mit Bauern zur Herrschaft über Bauern. Göttingen: Vandenhoeck & Ruprecht, 1982. 110 pp.
1669. Wunderlich, Frieda. Farm Labor in Germany. 1810-1945: Its Historical Development Within the Framework of Agricultural and Social Policy. Princeton, NJ: Princeton University Press, 1961. 390 pp.

SEE ALSO: 2276, 3229, 3273, 3310, 3317-18, 3329.

GERMANY--1815-1918

1670. Abel, Wilhelm. Geschichte der deutschen Landwirtschaft vom frühen Mittelalter bis zum 19. Jahrhundert. 3rd ed. Stuttgart: Ulmer, 1978. 370 pp.
1671. Aereboe, Friedrich. Der Einfluss des Krieges auf die landwirtschaftliche Produktion in Deutschland. Stuttgart: Deutsche Verlags-Anstalt, 1927. 233 pp.
1672. Agrarische Wirtschaft und Gesellschaft in vorindustrieller Zeit. Hannover: Schaper, 1974. 305 pp.
1673. Bäuerliche Wirtschaft und landwirtschaftliche Produktion in Deutschland und Estland. 16. bis 19. Jahrhundert. Berlin: Akademie Verlag, 1982. 360 pp.
1674. Ballwanz, Ilona. "Der Zusammenhang zwischen der Produktionsentwicklung und der Betriebsgrösse in der deutschen Landwirtschaft von 1871 bis 1914." Jahrbuch für Wirtschaftsgeschichte (1978), III, 77-100.
1675. Barmeyer, Heide. Andreas Hermes und die Organisationen der Deutschen Landwirtschaft. Stuttgart: G. Fischer, 1971. 176 pp.
1676. Berdahl, Robert M. "Conservative Politics and Aristocratic Landholders in Bismarckian Germany." Journal of Modern History 44 (1972), 1-20.
1677. Berthold, Rudolf. "Zur Entwicklung der deutschen Agrarproduktion und der Ernährungswirtschaft zwischen 1907 und 1925." Jahrbuch für Wirtschaftsgeschichte (1974), IV, 83-111.
1678. Berthold, Rudolf and Wilfried Hombach. "Landwirtschaft und Agrarpolitik im imperialistischen Deutschland während des ersten Weltkrieges und der revolutionären Nachkriegskrise (1914-1923)." Wissenschaftliche Zeitschrift der Universität Rostock 23 (1974), 571-78; 613-31.
1679. Berthold, Rudolf et al. "Der preussische Weg der Landwirtschaft und neuere westdeutsche Forschungen." Jahrbuch für Wirtschaftsgeschichte (1970), IV, 259-89.
1680. Bischoff, Kurt. Die Kartoffel im Weltkrieg. Berlin: Unger, 1916. 23 pp.
1681. Bleiber, Helmut. "Zur Problematik des preussischen Weges der Entwicklung des Kapitalismus in der Landwirtschaft." Zeitschrift für Geschichtswissenschaft 13 (1965), 57-73.

1682. Borcke-Stargordt, Henning von. "Zur preussischen Agrargesetzgebung der Reformzeit." in Mensch und Staat in Recht und Geschichte. Festschrift für Herbert Kraus zur Vollendung seines 70. Lebensjahres. Kitzingen a. M.: Holzner, 1954. pp. 307-37.

1683. Brentano, Lujo. "Agrarian Reform in Prussia." Economic Journal 7 (1897), 1-20, 165-84.

1684. Cohnstaedt, Wilhelm. Die Agrarfrage in der deutschen Sozialdemokratie: von Karl Marx bis zum Breslauer Parteitag. Munich: Reinhardt, 1903. 248 pp.

1685. Conze, Werner. "Die Wirkungen der liberalen Agrarreform auf die Volksordnung in Mitteleuropa im 19. Jahrhundert." VSWG 38 (1949), 2-43.

1686. Croner, Johannes. Die Geschichte der agrarischen Bewegung in Deutschland. Berlin: G. Reimer, 1909. 269 pp.

1687. Dawson, William H. "Agricultural Co-operative Credit Associations." Economic Journal 12 (1902), 327-33.

1688. Dittmar, Gerhardt. "Zur praktischen Landagitation der deutschen Sozialdemokratie unter den deutschen Kleinbauern in den 90er Jahren des 19. Jahrhunderts." in Beiträge zur Geschichte der Deutschen Arbeiterbewegung. Berlin: Institut für Marxismus-Leninismus, 1968. X, 1091-1100.

1689. Elsner, Johann G. Die Fortschritte der deutschen Landwirthschaft vom letzten Jahrzehnt des vorigen Jahrhunderts an bis auf unsere Zeit. Stuttgart: Cotta, 1866. 134 pp.

1690. Die Entwicklung der preussichen Landwirtschaft 1888-1913. Festtagung des Königl. Preussischen Landes-Ökonomie-Kollegiums zur Feier des 25jährigen Regierungs-Jubiläums Sr. Maj. des Kaisers und Königs Wilhelm II. Berlin: Unger, 1913. 354 pp.

1691. Finckenstein, Hans W. Die Entwicklung der Landwirtschaft in Preussen und Deutschland. 1800-1930. Würzburg: Holzner, 1960. 392 pp.

1692. Franz, Günther. "Die agrarische Bewegung im Jahre 1848." Zeitschrift für Agrargeschichte 7 (1959), 176-93.

1693. Franz, Günther. Geschichte des deutschen Bauernstandes. 2nd ed. Stuttgart: Ulmer, 1976. 301 pp.

1694. Fuchs, Carl J. Deutsche Agrarpolitik vor und nach dem Kriege. Stuttgart: Kohlhammer, 1927. 106 pp.

1695. Fuchs, Carl J. Die Epochen der deutschen Agrargeschichte und Agrarpolitik. Jena: Fischer, 1898. 32 pp.

1696. Fuhrmann, Hans. Die Versorgung der deutschen Landwirtschaft mit Arbeitskräften im Weltkriege. Diss. Würzburg, 1937. 90 pp.

1697. Gagliardo, John G. From Pariah to Patriot. The Changing Image of the German Peasant. 1770-1840. Lexington: University of Kentucky Press, 1969. 338 pp.

1698. Ganghofer, Forstrath. "Der Wald im nationalen Wirthschaftsleben." Schmoller 4 (1880), 455-90.

1699. Gerd, Heinrich, ed. Die deutsche Landwirtschaft unter Kaiser Wilhelm II. Mutterland und Kolonien. Zum 25jährigen Regierungsjubiläum Seiner Majestät des Kaisers. Halle: Marhold, 1913. 703 pp.

1700. Gerschenkron, Alexander. Bread and Democracy in Germany. Berkeley: University of California Press, 1943. 238 pp.

1701. Gläsel, Ernst J. Die Entwicklung der Preise landwirtschaftlicher Produkte und Produktionsmittel während der letzten 50 Jahre. Berlin: P. Parey, 1917. 66 pp. [also in Landwirtschaftliche Jahrbücher (1917), 519-84.]

1702. Goltz, Theodor von der. Die Entwickelung der deutschen Landwirtschaft im 19. Jahrhundert. Bonn: Verlag der Landwirtschaftskammer für die Rheinprovinz, 1904; rpt. Aalen: 1963. 24 pp.

1703. Goltz, Theodor von der. Geschichte der deutschen Landwirtschaft. 2 vols. Stuttgart: Cotta, 1902-03.

1704. Grohmann, Heinrich. "Betrachtungen über die Wirtschaften der ländlichen Tagelöhner des deutschen Reichs." Schmoller 16 (1892) 855-910.

1705. Grünberg, Karl. "Agrargeschichte. (Die Hauptprobleme der deutschen Agrargeschichte.)" in Die Entwicklung der deutschen Volkswirtschaft in 19. Jahrhundert. Leipzig: Duncker & Humblot, 1908. 19 pp.

1706. Hardach, Karl W. "Die Haltung der deutschen Landwirtschaft in der Getreidezoll-Diskussion 1878-79." Zeitschrift für Agrargeschichte 15 (1967), 33-48.

1707. Heitz, Ernst. "Die Anbauverhältnisse in Deutschland, beschreibend und vergleichend dargestellt auf Grund der Erhebung von 1878." Schmoller 6 (1882), 859-943.

1708. Heitz, Gerhard. "Bauer und Gemeinde vor und zu Beginn der industriellen Revolution." Studia Historiae Oeconomicae 10 (1975), 45-54.
1709. Heitz, Gerhard. "Die Differenzierung der Agrarstruktur am Vorabend der bürgerlichen Agrarreformen." Zeitschrift für Geschichtswissenschaft 25 (1977), 910-27.
1710. Helling, Gertrud. "Berechnung eines Index der Agrarproduktion in Deutschland im 19. Jahrhundert." Jahrbuch für Wirtschaftgeschichte (1965), IV, 125-43.
1711. Helling, Gertrud. "Zur Entwicklung der Produktivität in der deutschen Landwirtschaft im 19. Jahrhundert." Jahrbuch für Wirtschaftsgeschichte (1966), I, 129-41.
1712. Hötzsch, Otto. "Der Bauernschutz in den deutschen Territorien vom 16. bis ins 19. Jahrhundert." Schmoller 26 (1902), 1137-69.
1713. Hunt, James C. "The 'Egalitarianism' of the Right. The Agrarian League in South-West Germany 1893-1914." Journal of Contemporary History 10 (1975), 513-30.
1714. Ipsen, Günther. "Die preussische Bauernbefreiung als Landesausbau." Zeitschrift für Agrargeschichte und Agrarsoziologie 2 (1954), 29-54.
1715. Judeich, Albert. Die Grundentlastung in Deutschland. Leipzig: Brockhaus, 1863. 230 pp.
1716. Kempter, Gerhard. Agrarprotektionismus: landwirtschaftliche Schutzzollpolitik im Deutschen Reich von 1879 bis 1914. Diss. Cologne. Frankfurt a. M.: Lang, 1985. 268 pp.
1717. Knapp, Georg F. Die Bauernbefreiung und der Ursprung der Landarbeiter in den älteren Teilen Preussens. 2 vols. Leipzig: Duncker & Humblot, 1927.
1718. Knapp, Georg F. "Die Erbunterthänigkeit und die kapitalistische Wirtschaft." Schmoller 15 (1891), 339-54.
1719. Knapp, Georg F. Die Landarbeiter in Knechtschaft und Freiheit. 2nd ed. Leipzig: Duncker & Humblot, 1909. 118 pp.
1720. Knapp, Georg F. "Zur Geschichte der Bauernbefreiung in den älteren Teilen Preussens." Forschungen zur Brandenburgischen und Preussischen Geschichte 1 (1888), 573-85.
1721. Knapp, Theodor. Gesammelte Beiträge zur Rechts- und Wirtschaftsgeschichte vornehmlich des deutschen Bauernstandes. Tübingen: Laupp, 1902. 485 pp.
1722. Kolossa, Tibor. "Der Zusammenhang einiger Probleme der Betriebsstruktur und der Produktion in der Landwirtschaft Ungarns und Deutschlands in der zweiten Hälfte des 19. und zu Beginn des 20. Jahrhunderts." Jahrbuch für Wirtschaftsgeschichte (1972), III, 179-96.
1723. Lambi, Ivo N. "The Agrarian Industrial Front in Bismarckian Politics, 1873-79." Journal of Central European Affairs 20 (1961), 378-96.
1724. Langethal, Chr. E. Geschichte der teutschen Landwirtschaft. 4 vols. Jena: Luden, 1847-56.
1725. Lenz, Friedrich. Agrarlehre und Agrarpolitik der deutschen Romantik. Berlin: P. Parey, 1912. 191 pp.
1726. Lette, Adolph. Die Vertheilung des Grundeigenthums im Zusammenhange mit der Geschichte, der Gesetzgebung und den Volkszuständen. Berlin: Duncker & Humblot, 1858. 202 pp.
1727. Lütge, Friedrich. Geschichte der deutschen Agrarverfassung vom frühen Mittelalter bis zum 19. Jahrhundert. 2nd ed. Stuttgart: Ulmer, 1967. 323 pp.
1728. Lütge, Friedrich. "Über die Auswirkungen der Bauernbefreiung in Deutschland." Jahrbücher für Nationalökonomie und Statistik 157 (1943), 353-404.
1729. Mauer, Hermann. "Die Verschuldungsgesetze für Bauerngüter in Preussen (1811-1843)." Archiv für Sozialwissenschaft und Sozialpolitik, 24 (1907), 547-57.
1730. Maurer, Georg L. von. Geschichte der Dorfverfassung in Deutschland. 2 vols. Erlangen: Enke, 1865-66.
1731. Maurer, Georg L. von. Geschichte der Fronhöfe, der Bauernhöfe und der Hofverfassung in Deutschland. 4 vols. Erlangen: Enke, 1862-63.
1732. Maurer, Georg L. von. Geschichte der Markenverfassung in Deutschland. Erlangen: Enke, 1856. 494 pp.
1733. Meyer, Hans. Die Entwicklung der Bodennutzungs- und Wirtschaftssysteme in der deutschen Landwirtschaft unter dem Einfluss verfassungsrechtlicher, sozialer und wirtschaftlicher Faktoren in der vorindustriellen Zeit. Diss. Kiel, 1968. 222 pp.
1734. Moeller, Robert G. "Peasants and Tariffs in the Kaiserreich. How Backwards were the Bauern?" Agricultural History 55 (1981), 370-84.
1735. Moll, Georg. "Kapitalistische Bauernbefreiung und industrielle Revolution. Zur Rolle des 'Loskaufs'." Jahrbuch für Wirtschaftsgeschichte (1972), I, 269-75.
1736. Moll, Georg. "Zum 'preussischen Weg' der Entwicklung des Kapitalismus in der deutschen Landwirtschaft." Zeitschrift für Geschichtswissenschaft 26 (1978), 52-62.

1737. Müller, Friedrich. Die geschichtliche Entwicklung des landwirtschaftlichen Genossenschafts-wesens in Deutschland von 1848/49 bis zur Gegenwart Leipzig: A. Deichert, 1901. 552 pp.
1738. Neumann, Anna. Die Bewegung der Löhne der ländlichen "freien" Arbeiter im Zusammenhang mit der gesamtwirtschaftlichen Entwicklung im Königreich Preussen gegenwärtigen Umfangs vom Ausgang des 18. Jahrhundert bis 1850. Berlin: Parey, 1911. 400 pp.
1739. Nichtweiss, Johannes. Die ausländischen Saisonarbeiter in der Landwirtschaft der östlichen und mittleren Gebiete des deutschen Reiches. Ein Beitrag zur Geschichte der preussisch-deutschen Politik von 1890-1914. Berlin: Rütten & Loening, 1959. 291 pp.
1740. Perkins, J. A. "The Agricultural Revolution in Germany, 1850-1914." Journal of European Economic History 10 (1981), 71-118.
1741. Petri, Georg W. C. Das landwirtschaftliche Genossenschaftswesen. Leipzig: H. Voigt, 1903. 69 pp.
1742. Die Provinz Preussen. Geschichte ihrer Cultur und Beschreibung ihrer land- und forstwirth-schaftlichen Verhältnisse. Berlin: Wiegandt & Hempel, 1864. 529 pp.
1743. Pruns, Herbert. Staat und Agrarwirtschaft 1800-1865: Subjekte und Mittel der Agrar-verfassung und Agrarverwaltung im Frühindustrialismus. Hamburg: Parey, 1979. 343 pp.
1744. Puhle, Hans-Jürgen. Von der Agrarkrise zum Präfaschismus. Thesen zum Stellenwert der agrarischen Interessenverbände in der deutschen Politik am Ende des 19. Jahrunderts. Wiebaden: Steiner, 1972. 60 pp.
1745. Rachfahl, Felix. "Zur Geschichte des Grundeigentums." Jahrbücher für Nationalökonomie und Statistik 3 (1900), 1-33, 161-216.
1746. Rybark, Joseph. Die Steigerung der Produktivität der deutschen Landwirtschaft im neun-zehnten Jahrhundert. Berlin: F. Stollberg, 1905. 55 pp.
1747. Schaaf, Fritz. Der Kampf der deutschen Arbeiterbewegung um die Landarbeiter und werk-tätigen Bauern 1848-1890. Berlin: Akademie, 1962. 371 pp.
1748. Schäffner, Rudolf. Zur Geschichte der Agrarkrisen im neunzehnten Jahrhundert. Diss. Heidelberg, 1933. 55 pp.
1749. Schissler, Hanna. Preussische Agrargesellschaft im Wandel. Wirtschaftliche, gesellschaft-liche und politische Transformationsprozesse von 1763 bis 1847. Göttingen: Vandenhoeck & Ruprecht, 1978. 285 pp.
1750. Schmoller, Gustav. "Der Kampf des preussichen Königthums um die Erhaltung des Bauernstandes." Schmoller 12 (1888), 645-55.
1751. Schreiber, Arno. Die Kriegsgeschichte der deutschen landwirtschaftlichen Genossenschaften 1914-1918. Berlin-Steglitz: Schreiber, 1934. 40 pp.
1752. Stolz, Otto. "Die Bauernbefreiung in Süddeutschland im Zusammenhang der Geschichte." VSWG 33 (1940), 1-68.
1753. Studien zu den Agrarreformen des 19. Jahrhunderts in Preussen und Russland. Berlin: Akademie, 1978. 353 pp.
1754. Teuteberg, Hans-Jürgen. Die deutsche Landwirtschaft beim Eintritt in die Phase der Hoch-industrialisierung. Cologne: Forschungsinstitut für Sozial- und Wirtschaftsgeschichte an der Universität, 1977. 92 pp.
1755. Tipton, Frank B., Jr. "Farm Labor and Power Politics in Germany, 1850-1914." Journal of Economic History 34 (1974), 951-79.
1756. Tirrell, Sarah R. German Agrarian Politics After Bismarck's Fall: the Formation of the Farmers League. London: Oxford University Press, 1951. 354 pp.
1757. Treue, Wolfgang. "Die preussische Agrarreform zwischen Rationalismus und Romantik." in G. Droege, ed. West-ostdeutsche Forschungsaufgaben. Die Wechselbeziehungen zwischen West- und Ostdeutschland als Forschungsaufgabe der geschichtlichen Landeskunde. Troisdorf: Wegweiser-verlag, 1955. pp. 55-58.
1758. Treue, Wolfgang. "Die preussische Agrarreform zwischen Romantik und Rationalismus." Rheinische Vierteljahrsblätter 20 (1955), 337-57.
1759. Ucke, Arnold. Die Agrarkrisis in Preussen während der zwanziger Jahre dieses Jahrhunderts. Halle: M. Niemeyer, 1888. 76 pp.
1760. Waltemath, Kuno. "Der deutsche Bauer." Preussische Jahrbücher 145 (1911), 193-222.
1761. Webb, Steven B. "Agricultural Protection in Wilhelminian Germany. Forging an Empire with Pork and Rye." Journal of Economic History 42 (1982), 309-26.
1762. Wittich, Werner. "Epochen der deutschen Agrargeschichte." in S. Altmann et al., eds. Grundriss der Sozialökonomik. Tübingen: Mohr, 1922. pp. 1-76.

1763. Wygodzinski, Wilhelm. "Raiffeisen Notizen zur Geschichte des Landwirtschaftlichen Genossenschaftswesen in Deutschland." Schmoller 23 (1899), 1071-86.

SEE ALSO: 1438, 2330, 2349-50, 2372, 2386, 3355, 3425, 3544, 3574, 3581, 3592, 3596.

WEIMAR REPUBLIC--1919-1933

1764. Beckmann, Fritz. Die weltwirtschaftlichen Beziehungen der deutschen Landwirtshaft und ihre wirtschaftliche Lage (1919-1926). 2nd ed. Berlin: Parey, 1926. 184 pp.
1765. Beyer, Hans. "Die Agrarkrise und das Ende der Weimarer Republik." Zeitschrift für Agrargeschichte und Agrarsoziologie 13 (1965), 62-92.
1766. Beyer, Hans. Die Agrarkrise und die Landvolksbewegung in den Jahren 1928-1932. Ein Beitrag zur Geschichte "revolutionärer" Bauernbewegungen zwischen den beiden Weltkriegen. Wedel b. Hamburg: Steinburg, 1962. 22 pp.
1767. Corni, Gustavo. "L'agricoltura nella repubblica di Weimar e l'avvento del nazional-socialismo." Rivista di storia contemporanea 5 (1976), 347-85.
1768. Gessner, Dieter. Agrardepression und Präsidialregierungen in Deutschland 1930 bis 1933. Probleme des Agrarprotektionismus am Ende der Weimarer Republik. Düsseldorf: Droste, 1977. 209 pp.
1769. Gessner, Dieter. "Agrarian Protectionism in the Weimar Republic." Journal of Contemporary History 12 (1977), 759-78.
1770. Gessner, Dieter. Agrarverbände in der Weimarer Republik. Wirtschaftliche und soziale Voraussetzungen agrarkonservativer Politik vor 1933. Düsseldorf: Droste, 1976. 304 pp.
1771. Lorz, Florian. Kriegsernährungswirtschaft und Nahrungsmittelversorgung vom Weltkrieg bis heute. Hannover: Schaper, 1938. 224 pp.
1772. Lüning, Hans-Ulrich. Die Ursachen der deutschen Agrarkrise der Nachkriegsjahre. Diss. Würzburg. Würzburg: Handelsdruck, 1929. 86 pp.
1773. Meyer, Lothar. Die deutsche Landwirtschaft während der Inflation und zu Beginn der Deflation. Tübingen: Mohr, 1924. 32 pp.
1774. Moeller, Robert G. "Winners as Losers in the German Inflation. Peasant Protest Over the Controlled Economy, 1920-23." in G. D. Feldman et al., eds. Die deutsche Inflation. Eine Zwischenbilanz. Berlin: de Gruyter, 1982. pp. 255-88.
1775. Müller, Klaus. "Agrarische Interessenverbände in der Weimarer Republik." Rheinisches Vierteljahrsblatt 38 (1974), 386-405.
1776. Osmond, Jonathan. "German Peasant Farmers in War and Inflation, 1914-1924. Stability or Stagnation?" in G. D. Feldman et al., eds. Die deutsche Inflation. Eine Zwischenbilanz. Berlin: de Gruyter, 1982. pp. 289-307.
1777. Roediger, Werner P. K. Die deutsche Agrarkrise der Nachkriegsjahre. Diss. Greifswald, 1926. Greifswald: Alder, 1927. 84 pp.
1778. Schiff, Walter. Die grossen Agrarreformen seit dem Kriege. Vienna: Wiener Volksbuchhandlung, 1926. 37 pp.
1779. Schumacher, Martin. Land und Politik. Eine Untersuchung über politische Parteien und agrarische Interessen 1914-1923. Düsseldorf: Droste, 1978. 589 pp.

SEE ALSO: 3709, 4070.

THIRD REICH--1933-1945

1780. Decken, S. Eberhard von der. Die Front gegen den Hunger. Ernährungskrieg 1939-43. Berlin: Engelhard, 1944. 175 pp.
1781. Farquharson, John E. The Plough and the Swastika. The NSDAP and Agriculture in Germany, 1928-1945. London: Sage Publications, 1976. 317 pp.
1782. Gies, Horst. "NSDAP und landwirtschaftliche Organisationen." Vierteljahrshefte für Zeitgeschichte 4 (1967), 341-76.
1783. Hanau, Arthur and Roderich Plate. Die deutsche landwirtschaftliche Preis- und Marktpolitik im Zweiten Weltkrieg. Stuttgart: Fischer, 1975. 126 pp.

1784. Hoeft, Klaus-Dieter. "Die Agrarpolitik des deutschen Faschismus als Mittel zur Vorbereitung des zweiten Weltkriegs." Zeitschrift für Geschichtswissenschaft 7 (1959), 1205-30.
1785. Lovin, Clifford R. "Agricultural Reorganization in the Third Reich. The Reich Food Corporation (Reichsnährstand), 1933-36." Agricultural History 43 (1969), 447-82.

SEE ALSO: 3791, 4070.

GERMANY REDIVIDED--1945-1975

1786. Baade, Fritz. Die deutsche Landwirtschaft im Gemeinsamen Markt. Revised ed. Baden-Baden: A. Lutzeyer, 1963. 197 pp.
1787. Bergmann, Theodor. "Die landwirtschaftlichen Genossenschaften in Ostdeutschland." Archiv für Öffentliche und Freigemeinwirtschaftliche Unternehmen 3 (1957), 361-79.
1788. Berthold, Rudolf et al. Von den bürgerlichen Agrarreformen zur sozialistischen Landwirtschaft in der DDR. Berlin: VEB Deutscher Landwirtschaftsverlag, 1978. 219 pp.
1789. Heitz, Gerhard. "Regionale Quellen und marxistisch-leninistische Agrargeschichte." Archivmitteilungen. Zeitschrift für Theorie und Praxis des Archivwesens 25 (1975), 138-44.
1790. Heitz, Gerhard et al. "Forschungen zur Agrargeschichte." in Historische Forschungen in der DDR 1960-1970. Berlin: Deutscher Verlag der Wissenschaften, 1970. pp. 121-46.
1791. Hermes, Peter. Die Christlich-Demokratische Union und die Bodenreform in der Sowjetischen Besatzungszone Deutschlands im Jahre 1945. Saarbrücken: Verlag der Saarbrücker Zeitung, 1963. 170 pp.
1792. Magura, Wilhelm. Chronik der Agrarpolitik und Agrarwirtschaft in der Bundesrepublik Deutschland von 1945-1967. Hamburg: Parey, 1979. 154 pp.
1793. Orgrissek, Rudi. Dorf und Flur in der Deutschen Demokratischen Republik. Kleine historische Siedlungskunde. Leipzig: VEB Verlag Enzyklopädie, 1961. 141 pp.
1794. Seidel, Gerhard. Die Entwicklung sozialistischer Produktionsverhältnisse in der Landwirtschaft der DDR. Berlin: VEB Deutscher Landwirtschaftverlag, 1960. 122 pp.
1795. Ulbricht, Walter. Über die landwirtschaftlichen Produktionsgenossenschaften. Aus dem Referat und Schlusswort und einem Diskussionsbeitrag auf der 2. Parteikonferenz der SED. Berlin: Dietz, 1952. 16 pp.
1796. Vogel, Georg, ed. Die sozialistische Umgestaltung der Landwirtschaft als Erfüllung des jahrhundertelangen Befreiungskampfes der deutschen Bauern. Berlin: Deutscher Landwirtschaftsverlag, 1962. 447 pp.
1797. Wachowitz, Heinz. Die Entwicklung der sozialistischen Produktionsverhältnisse in der Landwirtschaft der DDR. Berlin: Dietz, 1962. 102 pp.

SEE ALSO: 3799-3800, 3842, 3854, 3865, 3880, 3883, 3894, 3914.

GERMAN REGIONS

Baden Württemberg

1798. Bergdolt, Wilhelm. Badische Allmenden. Eine rechts- und wirtschaftsgeschichtliche Untersuchung über die Allmendverhältnisse der badischen Rheinhardt insbesonders der Dörfer Eggenstein. Liedolsheim und Russheim. Heidelberg: Hörning, 1926. 360 pp.
1799. Ehrler, Joseph. Agrargeschichte und Agrarwesen der Johannitenherrschaft Heitersheim. Ein Beitrag zur Wirtschaftsgeshichte des Breisgaus. Tübingen: Mohr, 1900. 77 pp.
1800. Ellering, Bernhard. Die Allmenden im Grossherzogtum Baden. Eine historische. statistische und wirtschaftliche Studie. Tübingen: Mohr, 1902. 99 pp.
1801. Facius, Friedrich. "Staat und Landwirtschaft in Württemberg 1780-1920. Zur Entstehung und Entwicklung der agrarischen Interessenvertretung. Berufsorganisation und Selbstverwaltung." in Festschrift Günther Franz. Sigmaringen: Thorbecke, 1982. pp. 288-313.
1802. Fleischmann, Sigmund. Die Agrarkrisis von 1845-1855 mit besonderer Berücksichtigung von Baden. Diss. Heidelberg, 1902. Heidelberg: Rössler, 1902. 108 pp.

1803. Franck, Fritz. Die Veränderung in den Betriebsgrössen und Anbauverhältnissen sowie in der Viehhaltung der württembergischen Landwirtschaft in der 2. Hälfte des 19. Jahrhunderts. Halle a. d. S: Pritschow, 1902. 100 pp.
1804. Häfner, Karl. Vom Schwäbischen Dorf um die Jahrhundertwende: Arbeits- und Lebensformen. Reutlingen: Knödler, 1981. 175 pp.
1805. Hippel, Wolfgang von. Die Bauernbefreiung im Königreich Württemberg. 2 vols. Boppard am Rhein: Boldt, 1977.
1806. Jungo, Hubert. Die Entwicklung der Freiburger Berg- und Tallandwirtschaft 1955-1980. Unter besonderer Berücksichtigung der Auswirkungen ausgewählter agrarpolitischer Massnahmen. Freiburg: Universitätsverlag, 1983. 311 pp.
1807. Kellner, Roman. Strukturänderungen in der württembergischen Landwirtschaft besonders seit dem Ausgang des 19. Jahrhunderts. Leipzig: Hirzel, 1941. 51 pp.
1808. Kleinboeck, Erwin. Die badische Landwirtschaft in der Nachkriegszeit. Diss. Giessen, 1926. Giessen: Giessener Studentenhilfe, 1927. 94 pp.
1809. Kopp, Adolf. Zehentwesen und Zehentablösung in Baden. Tübingen: Mohr, 1899. 151 pp.
1810. Kümmerlen, Julius. Zur Geschichte der Landwirtschaft auf der Leutkircher Heide. Diss. Tübingen. Stuttgart: Kohlhammer, 1905. 70 pp.
1811. Mangold, Josef. Untersuchungen über die Lage der Landwirtschaft im württembergischen Allgäu unter besonderer Berücksichtigung des Kriegs und seiner Einflüsse. Diss. Tübingen, 1923. 181 pp.
1812. Moll, Georg. "Bürgerliche Agrarreformen in spätbürgerlicher Sichtigung. Das Beispiel Württemburg und die Gesetzmässigkeit der Geschichte." Wissenschaftliche Zeitschrift der Wilhelm-Pieck-Universität Rostock 30 (1981), 3-12. (English summary)
1813. Monheim, Felix. "Fragen der Agrarlandschaftsentwicklung am Oberrhein, erläutert am Beispiel des Neckarschwemmkegels." Deutscher Geographentag Würzburg 31 (July-August 1957), 342-48.
1814. Moos, Hermann. Das landwirtschaftliche Kredit- und Einkaufsgenossenschaftswesen Württembergs im Kriege. Diss. Tübingen, 1923. 287 pp.
1815. Müller, Wolfgang, ed. Landschaft und Verfassung. Beiträge zur ländlichen Verfassungsgeschichte im deutschsprachigen Südwesten. Bühl: Konkordia, 1969. 434 pp.
1816. Reinhard, Otto. Die Grundentlastung in Württemberg. Tübingen: Laupp, 1910. 124 pp.
1817. Schremmer, Eckart. Die Bauernbefreiung in Hohenlohe. Stuttgart: Fischer, 1963. 207 pp.
1818. Stolz, Otto. "Die Bauernbefreiung in Süddeutschland im Zusammenhang der Geschichte." VSWG 33 (1940), 1-68.
1819. Winkel, Harald, ed. Geschichte und Naturwissenschaft in Hohenheim: Beiträge zur Natur-, Agrar-, Wirtschafts- und Sozialgeschichte Südwestdeutschlands; Festschrift für Günther Franz zum 80. Geburtstag. Sigmaringen: Thorbecke, 1982. 338 pp.

SEE ALSO: 3955.

Bavaria

References

1820. Haushofer, Heinz, ed. Bayerische Agrar-Bibliographie. München: Landwirtschaftsverlag, 1954. 480 pp.

Bavaria

1821. Blessing, Werner K. "Umwelt und Mentalität im ländlichen Bayern. Eine Skizze zum Alltagswandel im 19. Jahrhundert." Archiv für Sozialgeschichte, Friedrich-Ebert Stiftung 19 (1979), 1-42.
1822. Crailsheim, Franz von. Die Hofmarch Amerang. Ein Beitrag zur bayerischen Agrargeschichte. (Auf Grund archivalischer Quellen.) Berlin: Kohlhammer, 1913. 103 pp.
1823. Damianoff, Athanasius D. Die Zehentregulierung in Bayern. Stuttgart: Cotta, 1896. 56 pp.

1824. Demmel, Karl. Die Hofmark Maxlrain. Ihre rechtliche und wirtschaftliche Entwicklung. Hirschenhausen: J. Weber, 1941. 126 pp.
1825. Eheberg, Karl T. von. "Die Landwirtschaft in Bayern." Schmoller 14 (1890), 1121-41.
1826. Englert, Ferdinand. "Die landwirtschaftliche Verwaltung in Bayern 1890-1897." Schmoller 22 (1898), 411-39.
1827. Flaningam, Miletus L. "The Rural Economy of Northeastern France and the Bavarian Palatinate 1815 to 1830." Agriculture History 24 (1950), 166-70.
1828. Hausmann, Sebastian. Die Grund-Entlastung in Bayern. Wirthschaftsgeschichtlicher Versuch. Strassburg: Trübner, 1892. 164 pp.
1829. Raum, H. "Aus der bayerischen Landwirtschaft in der Mitte des 19. Jahrhunderts. (Eine literatur-historische Zusammenstellung.)" Bayerisches Landwirtschaftliches Jahrbuch 47 (1970), 860-96.
1830. Schlögl, Alois. Bayerische Agrargeschichte. Die Entwicklung der Land- und Forstwirtschaft seit Beginn des 19. Jahrhunderts. 2nd ed. Munich: Bayerischer Landwirtschaftsverlag, 1954. 916 pp.
1831. Schnorbus, Axel. "Die ländlichen Unterschichten in der bayerischen Gesellschaft am Ausgang des 19. Jahrhunderts." Zeitschrift für bayerische Landesgeschichte 30 (1967), 824-52.
1832. Sieveking, Heinrich. "Zur süddeutschen Agrarentwicklung." in Hauptprobleme der Soziologie. Munich: Duncker & Humblot, 1923. II, 317-38.
1833. Simon, Leonhard. "Die Landwirtschaft in der Umgebung von Ansbach vor 75 Jahren." Bayerisches Landwirtschaftliches Jahrbuch 53 (1967), 1002-21.
1834. Wismüller, Franz X. Geschichte der Teilung der Gemeindeländereien in Bayern. Stuttgart: Cotta, 1904. 253 pp.

SEE ALSO: 3971, 5233.

Brandenburg

1835. Brinkmann, Carl. Wustrau. Wirtschafts- und Verfassungsgeschichte eines brandenburgischen Ritterguts. Leipzig: Duncker & Humblot, 1911. 163 pp.
1836. Harnisch, Hartmut. Die Herrschaft Boitzenburg. Untersuchungen zur Entwicklung der sozial-ökonomischen Struktur ländlicher Gebiete in der Mark Brandenburg vom 14. bis zum 19. Jahrhundert. Weimar: Böhlau, 1968. 281 pp.
1837. Harnisch, Hartmut. Kapitalistische Agrarreform und industrielle Revolution. Weimar: H. Böhlaus Nachfolger, 1984. 368 pp.
1838. Lippert, Werner. Geschichte der 110 Bauerndörfer in der nördlichen Uckermark. Ein Beitrag zur Wirtschafts- und Sozialgeschichte der Mark Brandenburg. Gerd Heinrich, ed. Cologne: Böhlau, 1968. 286 pp.
1839. Schmidt, Georg. Die Wendelsteiner Holzmark. Ein Beitrag zu den Gemeinheitsteilungen im ehemaligen Fürstentum Brandenburg-Ansbach. Nürnberg: Krische, 1935. 73 pp.

SEE ALSO: 1181.

East Prussia

1840. Bartels, A. N. "Die durchschnittlichen Reinerträge des landwirtschaftlichen Grossbetriebes im Osten Preussens innerhalb der letzten Jahre und die Belastung der zugehörigen Flächen durch die Grundsteuer." Zeitschrift des Preussischen Statistischen Bureaus (1889), 243-77.
1841. Bilder zur Entwickelung und zeitigen Lage der ostpreussischen Landwirtschaft. Königsberg: Ostpreussische Druck und Verlags-Anstalt, 1925. 204 pp.
1842. Böhme, Karl. Gutsherrlich-bäuerliche Verhältnisse in Ostpreussen während der Reformzeit von 1770 bis 1830. Leipzig: Duncker & Humblot, 1902. 107 pp.
1843. Borcke-Starfordt, Henning von. "Grundherrschaft-Gutswirtschaft. Ein Beitrag zur Agrargeschichte." Jahrbuch der Albertus-Universität zu Königsberg 10 (1960), 176-212.
1844. Dickler, Robert A. Labor Market Pressure Aspects of Agricultural Growth in the Eastern Region of Prussia, 1840-1914. Diss. University of Pennsylvania, 1975. 547 pp.

1845. Dickler, Robert A. "Organisation and Change in Productivity in Eastern Prussia." in W. N. Parker and E. L. Jones, eds. European Peasants and their Markets. Princeton, NJ: Princeton University Press, 1975. pp. 269-72.

1846. Dimigen, Friedrich. "Die wirtschaftliche Entwicklung der ostpreussischen landwirtschaftlichen Betriebe seit dem ersten Weltkrieg." Berichte über Landwirtschaft 46 (1968), 518-68.

1847. Engelbrecht, Erwin. Die Agrarverfassung des Ermlandes und ihre historische Entwicklung. Munich: Duncker & Humblot, 1913. 256 pp.

1848. "Die Entwicklung der ostpreussischen Landwirtschaft im 19. Jahrhundert." Ostpreussenblatt 21 (1970), 10.

1849. Goltz, Theodor von der. "Die Entwickelung der ostpreussischen Landwirthschaft während der letzten 25 Jahre (1856-1881)." Schmoller 7 (1883), 809-65.

1850. Hansen, Johannes. Die Entwicklung der Landwirtschaft der Provinz Ostpreussen im Rahmen der deutschen Landwirtschaft im letzten Jahrhundert. Tübingen: Mohr, 1914. 27 pp.

1851. Hartmann, Ernst. Die Geschichte des Dorfes Ponarth bei Königsberg i. Pr. Marburg: Johann Gottfried Herder-Institut, 1963. 114 pp.

1852. Herrmann, Franz-Josef. Das Ermländliche Bauernvolk. Sein Erbe und sein Schicksal. Cologne: Bischof-Maxmilian-Kaller-Stiftung, 1962. 406 pp.

1853. Hertz-Eichenrode, Dieter. Politik und Landwirtschaft in Ostpreussen 1919-1930. Untersuchung eines Strukturproblems in der Weimarer Republik. Cologne: Westdeutscher Verlag, 1969. 352 pp.

1854. Hübner, Hans. "Die ostpreussischen Landarbeiter im Kampf gegen junkerliche Ausbeutung und Willkür (1848-1914)." Zeitschrift für Geschichtswissenschaft (1963), 552-69.

1855. Keil, Friedrich. Die Landgemeinde in den östlichen Provinzen Preussens und die Versuche, eine Landgemeindeordnung zu schaffen. Leipzig: Duncker & Humblot, 1890. 110 pp.

1856. Komatzki, Aloys. Das Kirchdorf Prossitten Kr. Rössel mit Begnitten, Fürstenau und Landau. Kisdorf: Heimatbund des Kreises Rössel, 1966. 230 pp.

Eastern Germany

1857. Bardroff, Karl. Liberales Bodenrecht und Bauernsiedlung. Zur Geschichte der bäuerlichen Siedlung im preussischen Osten in der Zeit von der Bauernbefreiung bis zum Weltkriege. Diss. Kiel, 1942. 31 pp.

1858. Boyens, Wilhelm F. Untergegangene Bauerndörfer auf ostdeutschem Boden. Berlin: Deutsche Landbuchhandlung, 1936. 107 pp.

1859. Fredrich-Freksa, Martin. Preussen und der Demiurg des Weltmarkts. Studie zur industriellen Revolution in Westeuropa und zu ihrer Wirkung auf die Agrarverhältnisse im östlichen Deutschland. Diss. Berlin, 1981. Freiburg: Hochschul-Verlag, 1982. 429 pp.

1860. Görlitz, Walter. Die Junker. Adel und Bauer im deutschen Osten. Geschichtliche Bilanz von 7 Jahrhunderten. Glücksburg an der Ostsee: Starke, 1956. 462 pp.

1861. Harnisch, Hartmut. "Die kapitalistischen Agrarreformen in den preussischen Ostprovinzen und die Entwicklung der Landwirtschaft in den Jahrzehnten vor 1848. Ein Beitrag zum Verhältnis zwischen kapitalistischer Agrarentwicklung und Industrieller Revolution." in Bäuerliche Wirtschaft und Landwirtschaftliche Produktion in Deutschland und Estland (16. bis 19. Jahrhundert.) Berlin: Akademie, 1982. pp. 135-53.

1862. Harnisch, Hartmut. "Statistische Untersuchungen zum Verlauf der kapitalistischen Agrarreformen in den preussischen Ostprovinzen (1811 bis 1865)." Jahrbuch für Wirtschaftsgeschichte (1974), IV, 149-82.

1863. Knapp, Georg F. "Über Leibeigenschaft in Russland und im Osten Deutschlands." Archiv für Soziale Gesetzgebung und Statistik 5 (1892), 471-74.

1864. Meyhöfer, Max. Die Landgemeinden des Kreises Lötzen. Ein Beitrag zur Besiedlung. Bevölkerungsentwicklung und Wirtschaftsgeschichte vom 14. Jahrhundert bis 1945. Würzburg: Holzner, 1966. 378 pp.

1865. Schmidt, Hermann. Die Landwirtschaft von Ostpreussen und Pommern. Geschichte, Leistung und Eigenart der Landwirtschaft in den ehemals ostdeutschen Landesteilen seit dem Kriege 1914-18 und bis Ende der dreissiger Jahre. Marburg: J. G. Herder-Institut, 1978. 118 pp.

1866. Spulber, Nikolas. "Eastern Europe: the Changes in Agriculture from Land Reforms to Collectivization." American Slavic and East European Review 13 (1954), 389-401.

1867. Treue, Wolfgang. "Der landwirtschaftliche Unternehmer in Ostdeutschland. Bemerkungen über einen vernachlässigten Bereich der Wirtschafts- und Sozialgeschichte." Tradition 3 (1958), 33-39.
1868. Zur ostdeutschen Agrargeschichte. Ein Kolloquium. Würzburg: Holzner, 1960. 104 pp.

SEE ALSO: 4010.

Hansa Cities

1869. Ackermann, Arthur. Die wirtschaftlichen und sozialen Verhältnisse des bremischen Bauerntums in der Zeit von 1870 bis 1930. Bremen: Geist, 1935. 158 pp.

Hesse

1870. Bog, Ingomar. "Die wirtschaftlichen Trends, der Staat und die Agrarverfassung in der Geschichte Hessens." Zeitschrift für Agrargeschichte und Agrarsoziologie 18 (1970), 185-96.
1871. Fleck, Peter. Agrarreformen in Hessen-Darmstadt. Agrarverfassung. Reformdiskussion und Grundlastenablösung (1770-1860). Darmstadt: Hessische Historische Kommission, 1982. 384 pp.
1872. Leithiger, Ernst L. Die Landwirtschaft im Grossherzogtum Hessen. Rückblick auf die Tätigkeit der landwirtschaftlichen Vereine von 1882-1906. Darmstadt: Verlag der Landwirtschafts-kammer, 1912. 688 pp.
1873. Muth, Heinrich. "Zur Geschichte des Hunsrücker Bauernvereins." Jahrbuch für Geschichte und Kunst des Mittelrheins 20/21 (1968/69), 178-219.
1874. Rudloff, Hans L. "Wirtschaftsergebnisse eines mittleren bäuerlichen Betriebes im hessischen Bergland (1888-1909)." Schmoller 35 (1911), 251-83.

SEE ALSO: 4053, 4063.

Lower Saxony

1875. Allmers, Robert. Die Unfreiheit der Friesen zwischen Weser und Jade. Eine wirtschafts-geschichtliche Studie. Stuttgart: Cotta, 1896. 132 pp.
1876. Bornstedt, Wilhelm. Geschichte des braunschweigischen Bauerntums. Ein Beitrag zur Rechts-, Sozial- und Kulturgeschichte der ländlichen Bevölkerung in Südostniedersachsen in der vorindustriellen Zeit. Braunschweig: Landkreisverwaltung, 1970. 183 pp.
1877. Conze, Werner. Die liberalen Agrarreformen Hannovers im 19. Jahrhundert. Hannover: Landbuch-Verlag, 1947. 18 pp.
1878. Deike, Ludwig. Die Entstehung der Grundherrschaft in den Hollerkolonien an der Niederweser. Diss. Hamburg, 1957. Bremen: Schünemann, 1959. 122 pp.
1879. Hesse, Richard. Entwicklung der agrar-rechtlichen Verhältnisse im Stifte, späterem Herzogtum Verden. Jena: Fischer, 1900. 244 pp.
1880. Hundert Jahre Verkoppelung. Flurbereinigung in Oldenburg. 1858-1958. Oldenburg: Kulturamt Oldenburg, 1958. 72 pp.
1881. Stöver, Werner. Die wirtschaftliche Entwicklung des Butjadinger Bauerntums. Gezeigt am Beispiel der Eckwarder Bauernhöfe. Oldenburg: G. Stalling, 1942. 136 pp.
1882. Ventker, August F. Stüve und die hannoversche Bauernbefreiung. Oldenburg: G. Stalling, 1935. 47 pp.
1883. Waltemath, Kuno. "Der Bund der Landwirte in Hannover." Preussische Jahrbücher 141 (1910), 61-77.
1884. "Wandlungen der niedersächsischen Agrarwirtschaft im 19. Jahrhundert." Niedersächsisches Jahrbuch für Landesgeschichte 50 (1978), 7-302.
1885. Wiarda, Diddo. Die geschichtliche Entwickelung der wirthschaftlichen Verhältnisse Ostfrieslands. Jena: Fischer, 1880. 87 pp.

84   HISTORY OF AGRICULTURE

1886. Wrase, Siegfried. Die Anfänge der Verkoppelungen im Gebiet des ehemaligen Königreichs Hannover. Diss. Göttingen, 1969. 151 pp.

SEE ALSO: 1239, 4075, 4079.

Mecklenburg

1887. Bentzien, Ulrich. Landbevölkerung und agrartechnischer Fortschritt in Mecklenburg vom Ende des 18. bis zum Ausgang des 20. Jahrhunderts. Berlin: Akademie, 1983. 200 pp.
1888. Brinker, Fritz. Die Entstehung der "ritterschaftlichen Bauernschaften" in Mecklenburg (Steder-Niendorf, Wendisch-Priborn, heute Freienhagen, Buchholz, Grabow, Zielow und Rossow). Diss. Rostock. Rostock: Hinstorff, 1940. 164 pp.
1889. Buddrus, Evelyn. "Die Durchführung der demokratischen Bodenreform im Kreis Bad Doberan und ihre historische Bedeutung." Wissenschaftliche Zeitschrift der Universität Rostock. Gesellschafts- und Sprachwissenschaftliche Reihe 10 (1961), 19-44.
1890. Gadow, Hans J. von. Ritter und Bauer in Mecklenburg. Berlin: Schlieffen, 1935. 51 pp.
1891. Ihle, W. "Hundert Jahre Bodenbearbeitung in Mecklenburg." in Festschrift zum 150. Geburtstag von Johann Heinrich von Thünen. Mecklenburg: Landwirtschaftskammer für Mecklenburg-Schwerin, 1933. pp. 51-69.
1892. Maybaum, Heinz. Die Entstehung der Gutsherrschaft im nordwestlichen Mecklenburg (Amt Gadebusch und Amt Grevesmühlen). Stuttgart: Kohlhammer, 1926. 269 pp.
1893. Mielck, O. "Die Entwicklung der mecklenburgischen Wirtschaftsweisen seit Thünens Zeiten." in Festschrift zum 150. Geburtstag von Johann Heinrich von Thünen. Mecklenburg: Landwirtschaftskammer für Mecklenburg-Schwerin, 1933. pp. 39-50.
1894. Moll, Georg. "Zum Verlauf des 'preussischen Weges' der Entwicklung des Kapitalismus in der Landwirtschaft Mecklenburgs." Wissenschaftliche Zeitschrift der Universität Rostock 13 (1964), 345-60.
1895. Tscharnke, Hans. "Mecklenburgs Bauerntum im 19. und 20. Jahrhundert." in R. Crull, ed. Mecklenburg, Werden und Sein eines Gaues. Bielefeld: Velhagen & Klasing, 1938. pp. 116-30.
1896. Werner, Lutz. "Johann Heinrich von Thünen, ein Exponent der Durchsetzung des Kapitalismus in der mecklenbugischen Landwirtschaft." Wissenschaftliche Zeitschrift der Wilhelm-Pieck-Universität Rostock 30 (1981), 13-19.
1897. Westphal, Hertha J. Die Agrarkrisis in Mecklenburg in den zwanziger Jahren des vorigen Jahrhunderts. Rostock: Hinstorff, 1925. 179 pp.

North Rhine-Westphalia

1898. Borchmeyer, Walther. Das Ende der sog. Leibeigenschaft im Veste Recklinghausen. Ein Beitrag zur vestischen Rechts- und Wirtschaftsgeschichte. Diss. Würzburg. Recklinghausen: Bauer, 1928. 86 pp.
1899. Closhen, Barbara. Die Entwicklung der mittelrheinischen Markgenossenschaft am Beispiel des Kreises Neuwied. Ein Beitrag zum Gesamtproblem der deutschen Markgenossenschaft. Diss. Bonn, 1970. 206 pp.
1900. Croon, Helmuth. "Die Versorgung der Grosstädte des Ruhrgebietes im 19. und 20. Jahrhundert." Jahrbücher für Nationalökonomie und Statistik 179 (1966), 356-68.
1901. Floer, Franz. Das Stift Borghorst und die Ostendorfer Mark. Grundherrschaft und Markgenossenschaft im Münsterland. Berlin: Kohlhammer, 1914. 157 pp.
1902. Goltz, Joachim von der. Auswirkungen der Stein-Hardenbergischen Agrarreform im Laufe des 19. Jahhunderts. Diss. Göttingen. Berlin: Deutsche Landbuchhandlung, 1936. 111 pp.
1903. Ipsen, Günther. "Landkreis im Sauerland. Meschede 1818-1915. Soziale Beharrung am Rande der grossen Industrie." Zeitschrift für Agrargeschichte und Agrarsoziologie 19 (1971),197-210.
1904. Kemper, Wilhelm. Studien zur lippischen Agrargeschichte. (Vom 18. zum 19. Jahrhundert.) Diss. Münster, 1926. Barmen: Montanus & Ehrenstein, 1926. 103 pp.
1905. Lappe, Josef. Ein Westfälischer Schulzenhof. (Der Hof zu Kump im Kreise Unna.) Ein Beitrag zur Sozial- und Wirtschaftsgeschichte des westfälischen Bauernstandes. Paderborn: Schöningh, 1935. 126 pp.

1906. Meyer, Wilhelm. "Guts- und Leibeigentum in Lippe seit Ausgang des Mittelalters." Jahrbücher für Nationalökonomie und Statistik 3 (1896), 801-37.
1907. Müller-Wille, Wilhelm. "Der Feldbau in Westfalen im 19. Jahrhundert." Westfälische Forschungen 1 (1939), 302-25.
1908. Müller-Wille, Wilhelm. "Feldsysteme in Westfalen um 1860." Deutsche geographische Blätter 42 (1939), 119-45.
1909. Panhuysen, Helene. Die Entwicklung der Agrarlandschaft im Raume Straelen seit 1800 unter besonderer Berücksichtung des Gemüse- und Blumenanbaus. Bonn: Dümmler, 1961. 107 pp.
1910. Teuteberg, Hans-Jürgen. "Der Einfluss der Agrarreformen auf die Betriebsorganisation und Produktion der bäuerlichen Wirtschaft Westfalens im 19. Jahrhundert." in Entwicklungsprobleme einer Region, das Beispiel Rheinland und Westfalen im 19. Jahrhundert. Berlin: Duncker & Humblot, 1981. pp. 167-276.

SEE ALSO: 2547.

Pomerania

1911. Benthien, Bruno. "Karten zur Entwicklungsgeschichte des vollgenossenschaftlichen Dorfes Stresow, Kreis Greifswald." Geographische Berichte 8 (1963), 1-9.
1912. Eggert, Oskar. Die Massnahmen der preussischen Regierung zur Bauernbefreiung in Pommern. Cologne: Böhlau, 1965. 268 pp.
1913. Fuchs, Carl J. Der Untergang des Bauernstandes und das Aufkommen der Gutsherrschaften. Nach archivalischen Quellen aus Neu-Vorpommern und Rügen. Strassburg: Trübner, 1888. 377 pp.
1914. Heitz, Gerhard, "Zu einer 'neuen Sicht' ostelbischer Agrargeschichte." Zeitschrift für Geschichtswissenschaft 9 (1961), 864-76.
1915. Livonius, Eberhard von. Die wirtschaftliche Entwicklung des Rittergutes Grumbkow in Pommern 1679-1926. Leipzig: Deichert, 1927. 95 pp.

SEE ALSO: 4131.

Rhineland Palatinate

1916. Antoni, Erhard. Studien zur Agrargeschichte von Kurtrier. Bonn: L. Röhrscheid, 1931. 81 pp.
1917. Müller, Adolf. Die Grundlagen der pfälzischen Landwirtschaft und die Entwicklung ihrer Produktion im 19. Jahrhundert bis zur Gegenwart. Leipzig: Deichert, 1912. 151 pp.
1918. Regula, Konrad. Die Allmenden der Pfalz in Vergangenheit und Gegenwart. Ein Beitrag zur Agrargeschichte Südwest-Deutschlands. Leipzig: Deichert, 1927. 133 pp.
1919. Winterwerber, Paul. Die geschichtliche Entwicklung der Flurverfassung und der Grundbesitz-verhältnisse im Kreis St. Goarshausen. Diss. Hohenheim, 1955. 136 pp.

Saarland

1920. Wizinger, Paul. Die Versorgung des Saargebietes mit landwirtschaftlichen Erzeugnissen vor und nach Errichtung der Zollgrenze. Diss. Heidelberg, 1929. 75 pp.

Saxony

1921. Bielefeldt, Karl. Das Eindringen des Kapitalismus in die Landwirtschaft unter besonderer Berücksichtigung Provinz Sachsen und der angrenzenden Gebiete. Diss. Berlin. Berlin: Unger, 1910. 154 pp.
1922. Dorno, Friedrich. Der Fläming und die Herrschaft Wiesenburg. Agrarhistorische Studien aus den nördlichen Ämtern des sächsischen Kurkreises. Munich: Duncker & Humblot, 1914. 111 pp.
1923. Gastmann, Alwin. "Die Geschichte des Dorfes Sommersdorf bei Magdeburg. Studien zur Entwicklung der deutschen Agrarverfassung." Kühn-Archiv 46 (1958), 1-123.

1924. Gross, Reiner. Die bürgerliche Agrarreform in Sachsen in der ersten Hälfte des 19. Jahrhunderts. Untersuchung zum Problem des Übergangs vom Feudalismus zum Kapitalismus in der Landwirtschaft. Weimar: Böhlaus Nachfolger, 1968. 245 pp.

1925. Hübner, Hans, ed. Bauern und Landarbeiter im Klassenkampf. Revolutionäre Traditionen der werktätigen Landbevölkerung im Bezirk Halle. Halle-Wittenberg: Martin-Luther-Universität, 1976. 152 pp.

1926. Kiesewetter, Hubert. "Agrarreform, landwirtschaftliche Produktion und Industrialisierung im Königreich Sachsen 1832-1861." in Entwicklungsprobleme einer Region, das Beispiel Rheinland und Westfalen im 19. Jahrhundert. Berlin: Verein für Socialpolitik, 1981. pp. 89-137.

1927. Kiesewetter, Hubert. "Bevölkerung, Erwerbstätige und Landwirtschaft im Königreich Sachsen 1815-1871." in Region und Industrialisierung. Studien zur Rolle der Region in der Wirtschaftsgeschichte der letzten zwei Jahrhunderte. Göttingen: Vandenhoeck & Ruprecht, 1980. pp. 89-106. (English summary.)

1928. Kraaz, Albert. Bauerngut und Frohndienste in Anhalt vom 16. bis zum 19. Jahrhundert. Jena: Fischer, 1898. 273 pp.

1929. Pohl, Elfe. Die Vogtleute. Diss. Münster. Düsseldorf: Nolte, 1934. 56 pp.

1930. Rach, Hans-Jürgen and Bernhard Weissel, eds. Bauer und Landarbeiter im Kapitalismus in der Magdeburger Börde. Zur Geschichte des dörflichen Alltags vom Ausgang des 18. Jahrhunderts bis zum Beginn des 20. Jahrhunderts. Berlin: Akademie, 1982. 438 pp.

1931. Rach, Hans-Jürgen and Bernhard Weissel, eds. Landwirtschaft und Kapitalismus. Zur Entwicklung der ökonomischen und sozialen Verhältnisse in der Magdeburger Börde vom Ausgang des 18. Jahrhunderts bis zum Ende des Ersten Weltkrieges. 2 vols. Berlin: Akademie, 1978-79.

1932. Reuning, Theodor. Die Entwicklung der sächsischen Landwirthschaft in den Jahren 1845-1854. Amtlicher Bericht an das Königlich Sächsische Ministerium des Innern. Dresden: Schönfeld, 1856. 220 pp.

1933. Schmidt, Otto. Die Entwicklung der Landwirtschaft der Stadt Anschersleben im XIX. Jahrhundert unter dem Einfluss des Samenbaues. Diss. Halle-Wittenberg. Halle: Kaemmerer, 1910. 114 pp.

1934. Schöne, Bruno. Die sächsische Landwirtschaft, ihre Entwicklung bis zum Jahre 1925 sowie Einrichtungen und Tätigkeit des Landeskulturrats Sachsen zu Dresden. Dresden: Landeskulturrat Sachsen, 1925. 517 pp.

1935. Volger, Wilhelm. Probleme des Klassenkampfes zwischen den Landarbeitern und Gutsbesitzern im Regierungsbezirk Merseburg (1918-1923). Diss. Halle, 1974. 523 pp.

1936. Ziegenhagen, Norbert. Die Entwicklung der Produktion und der Eigentumsverhältnisse in der Landwirtschaft der Provinz Sachsen von 1875 bis 1895. Diss. Leipzig, 1965. 273 pp.

SEE ALSO: 4148.

Schleswig-Holstein

1937. Beyer, Hans. "Zur Entwicklung des Bauernstandes in Schleswig-Holstein zwischen 1768 und 1848." Zeitschrift für Agrargeschichte und Agrarsoziologie 5 (1957), 50-69.

1938. Christiansen, Julius. Zur Agrargeschichte der Insel Sylt. Mannheim: Bensheimer, 1923. 49 pp.

1939. Hanssen, Georg. Agrarhistorische Abhandlungen. 2 vols. Leipzig: Hirzel, 1880.

1940. Mager, Friedrich. Entwicklungsgeschichte der Kulturlandschaft des Herzogtums Schleswig in historischer Zeit. 2 vols. Breslau: Hirt, 1930; Kiel: Heimat und Erbe, 1937.

1941. Sievers, Hinrich. Von der Hufenverfassung zum Erbhofgesetz. Ein Bild von den Wandlungen im Kultur- und Lebensstandard des holsteinischen Bauern, besonders seit dem Jahre 1760. Weimar: Böhlau, 1935. 91 pp.

1942. Volquardsen, J. Volkert. "Zur Agrarreform in Schleswig-Holstein nach 1945." Zeitschrift der Gesellschaft für Schleswig-Holsteinische-Geschichte 102-03 (1977/ 78), 187-344.

1943. Westphal, Günter. Vom Dorf zum Gut, vom Gut zum Dorf. Gereby-Carlsburg. Die Geschichte eines Gutes. Hamburg: Agricola, 1954. 72 pp.

SEE ALSO: 4166, 4170, 4179.

Silesia

1944. Bleiber, Helmut. _Zwischen Reform und Revolution. Lage und Kämpfe der schlesischen Bauern und Landarbeiter im Vormärz 1840-1847_. Berlin: Akademie, 1966. 245 pp.

1945. Boelcke, Willi A. _Bauer und Gutsherr in der Oberlausitz. Ein Beitrag zur Wirtschafts-, Sozial- und Rechtsgeschichte der ostelbischen Gutsherrschaft_. Bautzen: Domowina, 1957. 315 pp.

1946. Brössling, Fritz. _Die Lage der landwirtschaftlichen Arbeiter in Schlesien am Ende des 19. Jahrhunderts vom Standpunkte des Landwirtes aus_. Merseburg: F. Stollberg, 1900. 58 pp.

1947. Dessmann, Günter. _Geschichte der schlesischen Agrarverfassung_. Strassburg:Trübner, 1904. 261 pp.

1948. Frauenstädt, Paul. "Das schlesische Dreiding. Ein Beitrag zur Geschichte der gutsherrlich-bäuerlichen Verhältnisse." _Jahrbücher für Nationalökonomie und Statistik_ 3 (1895), 232-54.

1949. Haase, Alfons. _Schlesiens Landwirtschaft: ein Gang durch die Geschichte der schlesischen Landwirtschaft von den ersten Anfängen bis zum Leistungsstand bei Beginn des Zweiten Weltkrieges_. Wolfenbüttel: Grenzland-Verlag Rock, 1981. 397 pp.

1950. Haines, Michael R. "Agriculture and Development in Prussian Upper Silesia, 1846-1913." _Journal of Economic History_ 42 (1982), 355-84.

1951. Haines, Michael R. _Economic-Demographic Interrelations in Developing Agricultural Regions. A Case Study of Prussian Upper Silesia, 1840-1914_. Diss. Univ. of Pennsylvania, 1971. New York: Arno Press, 1977. 499 pp.

1952. Jacobi, Ludwig. _Der Grundbesitz und die landwirthschaftlichen Zustände der Preussischen Oberlausitz in ihrer Entwickelung und gegenwärtigen Gestaltung_. Görlitz: Heyn, 1860. 390 pp.

1953. Jacobi, Ludwig. _Ländliche Zustände in Schlesien während des vorigen Jahrhunderts_. H. Lange, ed. Breslau: W. G. Korn, 1884. 211 pp.

1954. Klein, Ernst. "Der Bauernaufstand in Schlesien im Februar." _Zeitschrift für Geschichts-wissenschaft_ 3 (1955), 29-45.

1955. Knapp, Georg F. and A. Kern. "Die ländliche Verfassung Niederschlesiens." _Schmoller_ 19 (1895), 69-93.

1956. "Landwirtschaft Schlesiens. Ein Culturbild der Provinz Schlesien im Hinblick auf ihre Land- und Forstwirthschaft." in _Festschrift für die XXVII. Versammlung deutscher Land- und Forstwirthe Breslau 1869_. Breslau: W. G. Korn, 1869. pp. 239-445.

1957. Magura, Wilhelm. _Oberschlesien und seine Landwirtschaft. Eine agrarhistorische Betrachtung von der Besiedlung bis zur Vertreibung_. Augsburg: Oberschlesien Heimatverlag, 1975. 134 pp.

1958. Meusel, Günter. "Zum Bodenreformversuch der Landarbeiter, Kleinbauern und Industrie-arbeiter von Weisskollm im März 1920." _Letopis. Jahrsschrift des Instituts für Sorbische Volksforschung_ 20 (1973), 1-13.

1959. Meyer, Waldtraut. _Gemeinde, Erbherrschaft und Staat im Rechtsleben des schlesischen Dorfes vom 16. bis 19. Jahrhundert_. Würzburg: Holzner Verlag, 1967. 196 pp.

1960. Musiat, Siegmund. _Zur Lebensweise des landwirtschaftlichen Gesindes in der Oberlausitz_. Bautzen: VEB Domowina, 1964. 180 pp.

1961. Reis, Karl. _Die Ursachen und ersten Äusserungen der schlesischen Agrarbewegung des Jahres 1848_. Diss. Heidelberg. Breslau: Nischkowsky, 1910. 33 pp.

1962. Seidler, Hanns F. _Die wirtschaftsgeschichtliche Entwicklung des Gutes Kohlo (Niederlausitz) seit 1825 mit besonderer Berücksichtigung der Arbeiter- und Lohnverhältnisse_. Diss. Halle-Wittenberg. Halle a. d. S.: Buchdruck der Hallischen Nachrichten, 1927. 118 pp.

1963. Solta, Jan. _Die Bauern der Lausitz. Eine Untersuchung des Differenzierungsprozesses der Bauernschaft im Kapitalismus_. Bautzen: Domowina, 1968. 269 pp.

1964. Solta, Jan. _Die Ertragsentwicklung in der Landwirtschaft des Klosters Marienstern. Zur Entwicklung der Getreideerträge unter den Bedingungen des preussischen Weges der bürgerlichen Agrarrevolution_. Bautzen: Domowina, 1958. 228 pp.

1965. Wiatrowski, Leszek. "Zur Entwicklung des schlesischen Dorfes in der ersten Hälfte des 19. Jahrhunderts." _Jahrbuch für Wirtschaftsgeschichte_ (1970), II, 253-68.

1966. Ziekursch, Johannes. _Hundert Jahre schlesischer Agrargeschichte. Vom Hubertusburger Frieden bis zum Abschluss der Bauernbefreiung_. 2nd ed. Breslau: Preuss & Jünger, 1927. Rpt. Aalen: Scientia, 1978. 442 pp.

1967. Zimmer, Norbert. _Entwickelung und Stand der oberschlesischen Landwirtschaft_. Diss. Erlangen. Brieg: Berger, 1927. 88 pp.

1968. Zwahr, Hartmut. Bauernwiderstand und sorbische Volksbewegung in der Oberlausitz (1900-1918). Bautzen: VEB Domowina, 1966. 295 pp.

West Prussia

1969. Karzel, Karl. Die deutsche Landwirtschaft in Posen in der Zeit zwischen den beiden Weltkriegen. Marburg a. d. L.: J.-G.-Herder-Institut, 1961. 205 pp.
1970. Kuss, Heinrich. "Die landwirtschaftliche Erzeugung in Westpreussen vor der Vertreibung." Westpreussen-Jahrbuch (1959), 83-87.

3.
History of Industry

CENTRAL EUROPE

Bibliographic References

1971. Alexander-Frutschi, Marian C. Stanford Research Institute. International Development Center. Small Industry: an International Annotated Bibliography. Glencoe, IL: Free Press, 1960. 218 pp.
1972. Treue, Wilhelm et al. Quellen zur Geschichte der industriellen Revolution. Göttingen: Musterschmidt, 1966. 285 pp.

CENTRAL EUROPE

1973. Adelman, Irma and Cynthia T. Morris. "Patterns of Industrialization in the Nineteenth and Early Twentieth Centuries." Research in Economic History 5 (1980), 1-84.
1974. Bärtschi, Hans-Peter. Industrialisierung, Eisenbahnschlachten und Städtebau. Basel: Birkhäuser, 1983.
1975. Bairoch, Paul. "International Industrialization Levels from 1750 to 1980." Journal of European Economic History 11 (1982), 269-333.
1976. Birnie, Arthur. "The Growth of Industry in Europe from the Later Middle Ages to the Present Day." in E. Eyre, ed. European Civilization, Its Origin and Development. New York: Oxford University Press, 1937. V, 252-325.
1977. Brown, Ernest H. P. A Century of Pay, The Course of Pay and Production in France, Germany, Sweden, the United Kingdom, and the United States of America, 1860-1960. London: Macmillan, 1968. 476 pp.
1978. Cameron, Rondo E. "The International Diffusion of Technology and Economic Development in the Modern Economic Epoch." in Papers Presented to the Sixth International Economic History Association Conference, Copenhagen, 1974. Copenhagen: Akademisk Forlag, 1978.
1979. Carlsson, Bo. "Structure and Performance in the West European Steel Industry. A Historical Perspective." in H. W. de Jong, ed. The Structure of European Industry. The Hague: M. Nijhoff, 1981. pp. 125-57.
1980. DeJong, H. W., ed. The Structure of European Industry. The Hague: M. Nijhoff. 1981. 322 pp.
1981. Fischer, Wolfram. "Rural Industrialization and Population Change." Comparative Studies in Society and History 15 (1973), 158-70.
1982. Freudenberger, Herman and Fritz Redlich. "The Industrial Development of Europe: Reality, Symbols, Images." Kyklos 17 (1964), 372-401.
1983. Habakkuk, H. John and Michael M. Postan, eds. The Industrial Revolutions and After, Incomes, Population and Technological Change. The Cambridge Economic History of Europe, 6. Cambridge: Cambridge University Press, 1965. 1040 pp.

1984. Hoffmann, Walther G. The Growth of Industrial Economies. Manchester: Manchester University Press, 1958. 183 pp.
1985. Hughes, Jonathan R. T. Industrialization and Economic History. Theses and Conjectures. New York: McGraw-Hill, 1970. 336 pp.
1986. Jewkes, John. "The Growth of World Industry." Oxford Economic Papers 3 (1951), 1-15.
1987. Jones, Eric L. "The Agricultural Origins of Industry." Past and Present 40 (1968), 58-71.
1988. Kaelble, Hartmut. "Educational Opportunities and Government Policies in the Period of Industrialization." in P. Flora and A. J. Heidenheimer, ed. The Development of Welfare States in Europe and America. New Brunswick, NJ: Transaction Books, 1981. pp. 239-68.
1989. Kemp, Tom. Historical Patterns of Industrialization. London: Longman, 1978. 183 pp.
1990. Kurth, James R. "The Political Consequences of the Product Cycle: Industrial History and Political Outcomes." International Organization 33 (1979), 1-34.
1991. Landes, David S. "Japan and Europe: Contrasts in Industrialization." in The State and Economic Enterprise in Japan. Princeton, NJ: Princeton University Press, 1965. pp. 93-182.
1992. Landes, David S. The Unbound Prometheus. Technological Change and Industrial Development in Western Europe from 1750 to the Present. Cambridge: Cambridge University Press, 1969. 566 pp. (German: Cologne, 1973.)
1993. Mathias, Peter. "Industrial Structure in the Twentieth Century. Economies Not Centrally Planned." in Papers Presented to the Fourth International Conference of Economic History. Bloomington. 1968. Paris: Mouton, 1973.
1994. Patel, Surendra J. "Rates of Industrial Growth in the Last Century, 1860-1958." Economic Development and Cultural Change 9 (1961), 316-30.
1995. Pollard, Sidney. "Industrialization and Integration of the European Economy." in O. Büsch et al., eds. Industrialisierung und "Europäische Wirtschaft". Berlin: de Gruyter, 1976. pp. 4-16.
1996. Pollard, Sidney. "Industrialization and the European Economy." The Economic History Review, ser. 2, 26 (1973), 636-48.
1997. Pollard, Sidney. Peaceful Conquest. The Industrialization of Europe 1760-1970. Oxford: Oxford University Press, 1981. 451 pp.
1998. Rimlinger, Gaston V. "Welfare Policy and Economic Development: A Comparative Historical Perspective." The Journal of Economic History 26 (1966), 556-71.
1999. Rosenberg, Nathan, ed. The Economics of Technological Change. Harmondsworth, England: Penguin, 1971. 509 pp.
2000. Wszelaki, Jan. "The Rise of Industrial Middle Europe." Foreign Affairs 30 (1951), 123-134.
2001. Zauberman, Alfred. Industrial Progress in Poland. Czechoslovakia. and East Germany 1937-1962. London: Oxford University Press, 1964. 338 pp.

SEE ALSO: 16, 116, 121, 130, 135, 142, 2693, 2718.

CENTRAL EUROPE--1815-1918

Reference

2002. Josephson, Aksel G. S., ed. A List of Books on the History of Industry and Industrial Arts. Chicago: John Crerar Library, 1915; rpt. Detroit: Gale Research Co., 1966. 486 pp.

CENTRAL EUROPE--1815-1918

2003. Bairoch, Paul. "Original Characteristics and Consequences of the Industrial Revolution." Diogenes 54 (1966), 47-58.
2004. Barbagallo, Corrado. "Le grandi cause del progresso dell'industria europea ed americana dal 1815 al 1850." Economia politica contemporanea 2 (1930), 233-56.
2005. Barnes, Thomas G. and Gerald D. Feldman, eds. Nationalism. Industrialization. and Democracy 1815-1914. Boston: Little, Brown, 1972. 317 pp.
2006. Berend, Iván T. and György Ranki. The European Periphery and Industrialization 1780-1914. Cambridge: Cambridge University Press, 1982. 180 pp.

2007. Berend, Iván T. and György Ranki. "Foreign Trade and the Industrialization of the European Periphery in the Nineteenth Century." Journal of European Economic History 9 (1980), 539-84.
2008. Büsch, Otto et al., eds. Industrialisierung und "Europäische Wirtschaft" im 19. Jahrhundert. Ein Tagungsbericht. Berlin: de Gruyter, 1976. 147 pp.
2009. Cipolla, Carlo M., ed. The Industrial Revolution. The Fontana Economic History of Europe, 3. London: Collins, 1973. 624 pp.
2010. Crouzet, François. "Western Europe and Great Britain 'Catching Up' in the First Half of the Nineteenth Century." in A. J. Youngson, ed. Economic Development in the Long Run. London: Allen & Unwin, 1972. pp. 98-125.
2011. Curtiss, George B. European Countries. The Industrial Development of Nations and a History of the Tariff Policies of the United States, and of Great Britain, Germany, France, Russia and Other European Countries, 1. Binghamton, NY: G. B. Curtiss, 1912. 640 pp.
2012. Dietz, Frederick C. The Industrial Revolution. New York: Holt, 1927. 111 pp.
2013. Doty, Stewart C., ed. The Industrial Revolution. New York: Holt, Rinehart & Winston, 1969. 135 pp.
2014. Fischer, Wolfram, ed. Wirtschafts- und sozialgeschichtliche Probleme der frühen Industrialisierung. Berlin: Colloquium, 1968. 542 pp.
2015. Freudenberger, Herman. The Industrialization of a Central European City. Edington: Pasold Research Fund Ltd., 1977. 220 pp.
2016. Gerschenkron, Alexander. "Die Vorbedingungen der Europäischen Industrialisierungen im 19. Jahrhundert." in W. Fischer, ed. Wirtschafts- und sozialgeschichtliche Probleme der frühen Industrialisierung. Berlin: Colloquium, 1968. pp. 21-28.
2017. Gille, Bertrand. Banking and Industrialisation in Europe, 1730-1914. London: Fontana, 1971. 49 pp. (German: Stuttgart, 1976)
2018. Hamerow, Theodore S. "The Rise of Industrialization." in The Birth of a New Europe. State and Society in the Nineteenth Century. Chapel Hill: University of North Carolina Press, 1983. pp. 3-31.
2019. Harder, Klaus P. "Major Factors in Business Formation and Development. Germany in the Early Industrialization Period." Nebraska Journal of Economics and Business 8 (1969), 72-81.
2020. Hartwell, Ronald M. The Industrial Revolution and Economic Growth. London: Methuen, 1971. 423 pp.
2021. Henderson, William O. Britain and Industrial Europe, 1750-1870. Studies in British Influence on the Industrial Revolution in Western Europe. 3rd ed. Leicester: Leicester University Press, 1972. 267 pp.
2023. Henderson, William O. The Industrialization of Europe, 1790-1914. New York: Harcourt, Brace & World, 1969. 215 pp.
2024. Horn, Norbert and Jürgen Kocka, eds. Recht und Entwicklung der Grossunternehmen im 19. und frühen 20. Jahrhundert. Göttingen: Vandenhoeck & Ruprecht, 1979. 685 pp.
2025. Kaelble, Hartmut. Industrialisierung und soziale Ungleichheit. Europa im 19. Jahrhundert. Göttingen: Vandenhoeck & Ruprecht, 1983. 237 pp.
2026. Kemp, Tom. Industrialization in Nineteenth-Century Europe. 2nd ed. London: Longman, 1973. 230 pp.
2027. Kenwood, A. G. and A. L. Lougheed. Technological Diffusion and Industrialisation Before 1914. London: Croom Helm, 1982. 216 pp.
2028. Kindleberger, Charles P. "Commercial Expansion and the Industrial Revolution." The Journal of European Economic History 4 (1975), 613-54.
2029. Koistinen, Paul A. C. "The 'Industrial-Military Complex' in Historical Perspective. World War I." Business History Review 41 (1967), 378-403.
2030. Kriedte, Peter et al. Industrialisation Before Industrialisation. Rural Industry in the Genesis of Capitalism. Cambridge: Cambridge University Press, 1981. 393 pp.
2031. Kuczynski, Jürgen. "Zum Problem der Industriellen Revolution." Zeitschrift für Geschichtswissenschaft 4 (1956), 501-24.
2032. Léon, Pierre et al., eds. L'industrialisation en Europe au XIX. siècle. Paris: Ed. du Centre National de la Recherche Scientifique, 1972. 619 pp.
2033. Lévy-Leboyer, Maurice. Les banques européennes et l'industrialisation internationale dans la première moitié du 19. siècle. Paris: Presses universitaires de France, 1964. 813 pp.
2034. Lieberman, Sima, ed. Europe and the Industrial Revolution. Cambridge, MA: Schenkman, 1972. 475 pp.

2035. Mathias, Peter. "Science and Technology in Processes of Industrialisation, 1700-1914." in Papers Presented to the Sixth International Economic History Association Conference. Copenhagen. 1974. Copenhagen: Akademisk Forlag, 1978.
2036. Mendels, Franklin F. "Proto-Industrialization. The First Phase of the Industrialization Process." The Journal of Economic History 32 (1972), 241-61.
2037. Mokyr, Joel. "Growing-up and the Industrial Revolution in Europe." Explorations in Economic History 13 (1976), 371-96.
2038. Nef, John U. "The Industrial Revolution Reconsidered." Journal of Economic History 3 (1943), 1-31.
2039. Pietrzak-Pawlowska, Irena. "Features of Industrialization of Agricultural Countries in Europe (up to 1918)." Studia Historiae Oeconomicae 9 (1974), 161-96.
2040. Pietrzak-Pawlowska, Irena. "Industrialisation des territoires européens arrières au XIX. siècle. Studia Historiae Oeconomicae 3 (1968), 181-200.
2041. Pollard, Sidney. Europa im Zeitalter der Industrialiserung. Eine Wirtschaftsgeschichte Europas 1750-1980. Göttingen: Vandenhoeck & Ruprecht, 1984. 170 pp.
2042. Pollard, Sidney and Lucian Holscher, eds. Region und Industrialisierung. Studien zur Rolle der Region in der Wirtschaftsgeschichte der letzten zwei Jahrhunderte. Göttingen: Vandenhoeck & Ruprecht, 1980. 300 pp.
2043. The Process of Industrialization 1750-1870. London: Arnold, 1968. 574 pp.
2044. Reeve, Robin. The Industrial Revolution. 1750-1850. London: London University Press, 1971. 272 pp.
2045. Rioux, Jean-Pierre. La révolution industrielle. 1780-1880. Paris: Éd. du Seuil, 1971. 252 pp.
2046. Sheehan, James J., ed. Industrialization and Industrial Labor in Nineteenth-Century Europe. New York: Wiley, 1973. 173 pp.
2047. Siegenthaler, Jürg K. "A Scale Analysis of Nineteenth-Century Industrialization." Explorations in Economic History 10 (1972-73), 75-107.
2048. Singer, Charles et al. The Industrial Revolution c. 1750-c. 1850. A History of Technology, 4. Oxford: Clarendon Press, 1958. 728 pp.
2049. Singer, Charles et al. The Late Nineteenth Century. c. 1850-c. 1900. A History of Technology, 5. Oxford: Clarendon Press, 1958. 888 pp.
2050. Supple, Barry E. The State and the Industrial Revolution. 1700-1914. London: Collins, 1971. 61 pp.
2051. Timm, Albrecht. "Zur Geschichte der Frühindustrialisierung in Mittel- und Osteuropa." Deutsche Studien. Vierteljahreshefte 34 (1971), 197-202.
2052. Trebilcock, Clive. "British Armaments and European Industrialization, 1890-1914." The Economic History Review, ser. 2, 26 (1973), 254-72.
2053. Trebilcock, Clive. The Industrialization of the Continental Powers 1780-1914. London: Longman, 1981. 495 pp.
2054. Wilson, G. B. L. "Technical Gains During the Nineteenth Century (1775-1905)." Cahiers d'histoire mondiale 6 (1960), 517-55.
2055. Wrigley, Edward A. Industrial Growth and Population Change. A Regional Study of the Coalfield Areas of North-West Europe in the Later 19th Century. London: Cambridge University Press, 1961. 193 pp.
2056. Zorn, Wolfgang. "Umrisse der frühen Industrialisierung Südosteuropas im 19. Jahrhundert." VSWG 57 (1970), 500-33.

SEE ALSO: 196, 200-201, 218, 224, 235, 1426, 1436, 1972, 2747.

CENTRAL EUROPE--1919-1975

2057. Artus, Jacques R. "Measures of Potential Output in Manufacturing for Eight Industrial Countries, 1955-78." International Monetary Fund 24 (1977), 1-35.
2058. Bannock, Girolamo. "Andamento della produttività nell'industria manifatturiera dagli anni dell'anteguerra al 1960." Revue de la mesure de la productivité (1963), 46-57.
2059. Boguszewski, Jan. "Growth and Productivity in Industry and its Principal Sectors in the FRG, Austria, Poland and Hungary." Eastern European Economics 18 (1979), 3-75.

2060. Boyer, Robert and Philippe Petit. Emploi et productivité dans six pays de la Communauté Européenne, 1960-1977. Paris: Centre d'Études Prospectives d'Économie Mathématique Appliquées à la Planification, 1979. 109 pp.
2061. "Changes in the Structure of West European Manufacturing Industry in the 1970s." Economic Survey of Europe 34 (1980), 186-243.
2062. Christensen, Laurits R. et al. "Relative Productivity Levels, 1947-1973. An International Comparison." European Economic Review 16 (1981), 61-94.
2063. Europa im Aufbau. Bericht über die Tätigkeit der Europäischen Produktivitäts-Zentrale von 1953 bis 1957. Berlin: Beuth, 1958. 33 pp.
2064. Henderson, William O. The Genesis of the Common Market. London: Cass, 1962. 201 pp.
2065. Jones, Dallas T. "Output, Employment and Labour Productivity in Europe since 1955." National Institute Economic Review 77 (1976), 72-85.
2066. Lamfalussy, Alexandre. The United Kingdom and the Six. An Essay on Economic Growth in Western Europe. London: Macmillan, 1963. 147 pp.
2067. Maier, Charles S. "Between Taylorism and Technocracy. European Ideologies and the Vision of Industrial Productivity in the 1920s." Journal of Contemporary History 5 (1970), 27-61.
2068. Schoetz, Robert F. "Le cout de la main-d'oeuvre et la productivité aux Etats-Unis et en Europe, 1955-1965." Revue de la Banque 31 (1967), 107-25.
2069. Stein, John P. and Allen Lee. Productivity Growth in Industrial Countries at the Sectoral Level, 1963-1974. Santa Monica, CA: Council on International Economic Policy, 1977. 107 pp.
2070. Varga, Werner. "Industrial Structure and Structural Change in the FRG, Austria, Poland, and Hungary and their Influence on Productivity, 1960-72." Eastern European Economics 18 (1980), 57-114.
2071. Wölfling, Manfred. Die Industriestruktur in Österreich und in der DDR. Eine komparativ-empirische Studie. Vienna: Wiener Institut für Internationale Wirtschaftsvergleiche, 1980. 31 pp.

AUSTRIA

2072. Koren, Stefan. "Die Industrialisierung Österreichs--vom Protektionismus zur Integration." in W. Weber, ed. Österreichs Wirtschaftsstruktur gestern-heute-morgen. Berlin: Dunker & Humblot, 1961. I, 223-549.
2073. Perspektiven der österreischischen Industrie. Vienna: Österreichischer Wirtschaftsverlag, 1982. 194 pp.
2074. Rudolph, Richard L. "Austrian Industrialisation. A Case Study in Leisurely Economic Growth." in Sozialismus. Geschichte und Wirtschaft. Festschrift für Eduard März. Vienna: Europa, 1973. pp. 249-62.
2075. Rudolph, Richard L. "The Pattern of Austrian Industrial Growth from the Eighteenth to the Early Twentieth Century." Austrian History Yearbook 11 (1975), 3-26.
2076. Werner, Karl H. "Österreichs Industrie- und Aussenhandelpolitik 1848-1948." in H. Mayer, ed. Hundert Jahre österreichischer Wirtschaftsentwickung, 1848-1948. Vienna: Springer, 1949. pp. 359-479.
2077. Wessely, Kurt. "Die Stellung Österreichs im Rahmen der Industrialisierung Europas." Österreichische Osthefte 14 (1972), 125-36.

SEE ALSO: 308, 2889.

AUSTRIA--1815-1975

Reference

2078. Gross, Nachum T. "Austrian Industrial Statistics 1880/85 and 1911/13." Zeitschrift für die gesamte Statswissenschaft 124 (1968), 35-69.

AUSTRIA--1815-1975

2079. Bachinger, Karl. "Zur Interdependenz von Verkehrsentwicklung und Industrialisierung (1830-1913)." in Bericht über den 11. österreichischen Historikertag in Innsbruck vom 4. bis 8. Oktober 1971. Vienna: Verband österreichischer Geschichtsvereine, 1972. pp. 212-23.
2080. Baltzarek, Franz. "Zu den regionalen Ansätzen der frühen Industrialisierung in Europa. Mit Überlegungen zum Stellenwert der frühen Industrialisierung im Habsburgerstaat des 18. und 19. Jahrhunderts." in Wirtschafts- und socialhistorische Beiträge. Festschrift für Alfred Hoffmann zum 75. Geburtstag. Munich: Oldenbourg, 1979. pp. 334-55.
2081. Berend, Iván T. "Besondere Charakterzüge der Industrierevolution in der Österreichisch-Ungarischen Monarchie. Zeitgeschichte 1 (1974), 229-38.
2082. Bermann, Moritz. Österreich-Ungarn im neunzehnten Jahrhundert. Vienna: H. Engel, 1884. 982 pp.
2083. Biberger, Rainer. Das österreichische Ertragsteuersystem und sein Einfluss auf die Industrialisierung im 19. Jahrhundert. Diss. Hohenheim, 1979. 270 pp.
2084. Blum, Jerome. "Transportation and Industry in Austria, 1815-1848." Journal of Modern History 15 (1943), 24-38.
2085. Brachelli, Hugo F. Österreichs commerzielle und industrielle Entwicklung in den letzten Jahrzehnten. Vienna: F. Mayer, 1873. 63 pp.
2086. Brusatti, Alois. "Österreich am Vorabend des industriellen Zeitalters." in Wirtschaftsgeschichte Österreichs. Vienna: Hirt, 1971. 223 pp.
2087. Exner, Wilhelm F., ed. Rohproduction und Industrie. Vienna: Braumüller, 1873. 558 pp.
2088. Gross, Nachum T. "Economic Growth and the Consumption of Coal in Austria and Hungary 1841-1913." Journal of Economic History 31 (1971), 898-916.
2089. Gross, Nachum T. "An Estimate of Industrial Production in Austria in 1841." Journal of Economic History 28 (1968), 80-101.
2090. Gross, Nachum T. "The Industrial Revolution in the Habsburg Monarchy 1750-1914." in The Fontana Economic History of Europe. Glasgow: Fontana Books, 1976. VI/I, 228-78. (German: London, 1973).
2091. Gross, Nachum T. Industrialization in Austria in the Nineteenth Century. Diss. University of California at Berkeley, 1966. 222 pp.
2092. Die Gross-Industrie Oesterreichs. Festgabe zum glorreichen 50jährigen Regierungsjubiläum seiner Majestät des Kaisers Josef I. Dargebracht von den Industriellen Oesterreichs. Vienna: Weiss, 1898. 348 pp.
2093. Hallwich, Hermann. Anfänge der Gross-Industrie in Österreich. Vienna: Weiss, 1898. 74 pp. (Offprint from Die Gross-Industrie Oesterreichs)
2094. Hertz, Friedrich O. Die Produktionsgrundlagen der österreichischen Industrie vor und nach dem Kriege. 2nd ed. Vienna: Verlag für Fachliteratur, 1917. 268 pp.
2095. Lampe, John R. "Varieties of Unsuccessful Industrialization: the Balkan States Before 1914." Journal of Economic History 35 (1975), 56-85.
2096. März, Eduard. Österreichs Industrie- und Bankpolitik in der Zeit Franz Joseph I. Vienna: Europa, 1968. 384 pp.
2097. Matis, Herbert. "Technik und Industrialisierung im österreichischen Vormärz." Technikgeschichte 36 (1969), 12-37.
2098. Matis, Herbert. "Zwei Jahrhunderte österreichischer Industriepolitik (1648-1848)." Österreich in Geschichte und Literatur 12 (1968), 197-206.
2099. Matis, Herbert and Karl Bachinger. "Österreichs industrielle Entwicklung." in A. Wandruszka, ed. Die Habsburgermonarchie 1848-1918. Vienna: Österreichische Akademie der Wissenschaften, 1973. I, 105-232.
2100. Merk, Grete. Zwei Pioniere der österreichischen Industrie. Alois Miesbach und Heinrich Drasche. Graz: Böhlaus Nachfolger, 1966. 112 pp.
2101. Mesch, Michael. Die Lohnentwicklung in Industrie und Gewerbe der österreichischen Alpenländer 1890-1914. Thesis: Vienna, 1980.
2102. Mosser, Alois. Die Industrieaktiengesellschaft in Osterreich 1880-1913: Versuch einer historischen Bilanz- und Betriebsanalyse. Vienna: Austrian Academy of Sciences, 1980. 338 pp.
2103. Mosser, Alois. "Konzentrationserscheinungen in der österreichischen Industrie bis 1914." in Bericht über den 11. österreichischen Historikertag. Vienna: Österreichischer Geschichtsverein, 1972. pp. 186-200.

2104. Mosser, Alois. "Raumabhängigkeit und Konzentrationsinteresse in der industriellen
       Entwicklung Österreichs bis 1914." Bohemia. Jahrbuch des Collegium Carolinum 17 (1976),
       136-92. (English and French summaries.)
2105. Otruba, Gustav. "Österreichs Industrie und Arbeiterschaft im Übergang von der Manufaktur
       zur Fabrikaturepoche (1790-1848)." Österreich in Geschichte und Literatur, 15 (1971),
       569-604.
2106. Otruba, Gustav. "Quantitative, strukturelle und regionale Dynamik des Industrialisierungs-
       prozesses in Österreich-Ungarn vom Ausgang des 18. Jahrhunderts bis zum Ausbruch des Ersten
       Weltkrieges." in Vom Kleingewerbe zur Grossindustrie. Berlin: Duncker & Humblot, 1975.
       pp. 105-63.
2107. Otruba, Gustav. "Zur Entstehung der "Industrie" in Österreich." Österreich in Geschichte und
       Literatur 11 (1967), 225-42.
2108. Poinstingl, Robert. Die Entwicklung der Industrie in der Zeit zwischen dem Ersten und Zweiten
       Weltkrieg in Österreich. Diss. Vienna, 1974. 89 pp.
2109. Riedl, Richard. Die Industrie Österreichs während des Krieges (1914-1918). Vienna: Hölder,
       Pichler, Tempsky, 1932. 374 pp.
2110. Rudolph, Richard L. "The Patterns of Austrian Industrial Growth From the 18th to the Early
       20th Century." Austrian History Yearbook 11 (1975), 3-43.
2111. Slokar, Johann. Geschichte der österreichischen Industrie und ihrer Förderung unter Kaiser
       Franz I. Vienna: F. Tempsky, 1914; Rpt. Graz: Akademische Druck- und Verlagsanstalt, 1975.
       674 pp.
2112. Wegs, James R. Austrian Economic Mobilization During World War I: With Particular
       Emphasis on Heavy Industry. Diss. Univ. of Illinois, 1970. 242 pp.

ADD: 337, 2059, 2141, 2980.

AUSTRIAN AND AUSTRO-HUNGARIAN REGIONS

Bohemia and Moravia

2113. Benedikt, Heinrich. "Die Anfänge der Industrie in Mähren." Der Donauraum 2 (1957), 39-51.
2114. Benedikt, Heinrich. "Die Anfänge der sudetendeutschen Industrie." Der Donauraum 5 (1960),
       107-11.
2115. Carter, F. W. "The Industrial Development of Prague, 1800-50." Slavonic and East European
       Review 51 (1973), 243-75.
2116. Faltus, Jozef. "Les industries des pays tchèques et de la Slovaquie héritées de la monarchie
       austro-hongroise." Studia Historica Slovaca 2 (1964), 190-211.
2117. Freudenberger, Herman. "Records of the Bohemian Iron Industry, l694-1875. The Basis for a
       Comprehensive Study of Modern Factories." Business History Review 43 (1969), 381-84.
2118. Freudenberger, Herman and Gerhard Mensch. Von der Provinzstadt zur Industrieregion
       (Brünn-Studie). Göttingen: Vandenhoeck & Ruprecht, 1975. 130 pp.
2119. Hassinger, Herbert. "Die Anfänge der Industrialisierung in den böhmischen Ländern."
       Bohemia. Jahrbuch des Collegium Carolinum 2 (1961), 164-81.
2120. Klíma, Arnóst. "The Beginning of the Machine-Building Industry in the Czech Lands in the First
       Half of the Nineteenth Century. A Study of the Influence of the English Industrial Revolution on
       the Continent." The Journal of European Economic History 4 (1975), 49-78.
2121. Klíma, Arnóst. "Industrial Growth and Entrepreneurship in the Early Stages of Industrialisa-
       tion in the Czech Lands." The Journal of European Economic History 6 (1977), 549-74.
2122. Komlos, John, Jr. et al. "Thoughts on the Transition From Proto-Industrialization to Modern
       Industrialization in Bohemia, 1795-1830." East Central Europe 7 (1980), 198-206.
2123. Otruba, Gustav. "Anfänge und Verbreitung der böhmischen Manufakturen bis zum Beginn des
       19. Jahrhunderts (1820)." Bohemia. Jahrbuch des Collegium Carolinum 6 (1965), 230-331.
2124. Otruba, Gustav. "Industrialisierung und Volkskultur im pannonischen Raum." in G. Károly, ed.
       Ethnographia Pannonica. Sozialhistorische und ethnologische Studien zum pannonischen Raum.
       Eisenstadt: Burgenländisches Landesarchiv, 1971. pp. 34-44.

2125. Otruba, Gustav and Rudolf Kropf. "Bergbau und Industrie Böhmens in der Epoche der Frühindustrialisierung (1820-1848)." Bohemia. Jahrbuch des Collegium Carolinum 12 (1971), 53-232. (English and French summaries)
2126. Paul, Ernst. "Industrialisierung und soziale Frage in den böhmischen Ländern." Bohemia. Jahrbuch des Collegium Carolinum 2 (1961), 182-92.
2127. Pryor, Frederick L. et al. "Czechoslovakia Aggregate Production in the Interwar Period." Review of Income and Wealth 17 (1971), 35-60.
2128. Purs, Jaroslav. "The Industrial Revolution in the Czech Lands." Historica 2 (1960), 183-272.
2129. Purs, Jaroslav. "The Situation of the Working Class in the Czech Lands in the Phase of the Expansion and Completion of the Industrial Revolution, 1849-1873." Historica 6 (1963), 145-237.
2130. Salz, Arthur. Geschichte der böhmischen Industrie in der Neuzeit. Munich: Duncker & Humblot, 1913. 628 pp.
2131. Eine Stimme aus Böhmen über die neuesten industriellen und merkantilischen Verhältnisse dieses Landes. Leipzig: Reclam, 1846. 200 pp.
2132. Teichova, Alice. "Industrial Structure in the Twentieth Century. Czechoslovakia." Papers Presented to the Fourth International Conference of Economic History, Bloomington, 1968. Paris: Mouton, 1973.

Burgenland

2133. Kacsich, Martin. Die Industrialisierung des Burgenlandes--Grundlagen, Entwicklung, Ausbau-möglichkeiten. Diss. Vienna Hochschule für Welthandel, 1960. 358 pp.
2134. Mayer, Karl. Die Entwicklung der burgenländischen Industrie (1921 bis 1938). Thesis Vienna Hochschule für Welthandel, 1972.

SEE ALSO: 3006.

Hungary

2135. Berend, Iván T. "Industrial Structure in the Twentieth Century. Hungary." Proceedings of the Fourth International Economic History Conference, Bloomington, 1968. Paris: Mouton, 1973.
2136. Berend, Iván T. and György Ránki. The Development of Manufacturing Industry in Hungary, 1900-44. Budapest: Hungarian Academy of Science, 1960. 169 pp.
2137. Berend, Iván T. and György Ránki. The Hungarian Manufacturing Industry, Its Place in Europe (1900-1938). Budapest: Hungarian Academy of Science, 1960. 37 pp.
2138. Berend, Iván T. and György Ránki. "Das Niveau der Industrie Ungarns zu Beginn des 20. Jahrhunderts im Vergleich zu dem Europas." in Studien zur Geschichte der Österreichisch-Ungarischen Monarchie. Budapest: Hungarian Academy of Science, 1961. pp. 267-97.
2139. Hollán, Alexandre de. "The Results of the Measures Taken in Hungary for the Development of Industry." Economic Journal 21 (1911), 37-52.
2140. Offergeld, W. Grundlagen und Ursachen der industriellen Entwicklung Ungarns. Jena: Lippert, 1914. 52 pp.
2141. Paulinyi, Akos. "Die Industriepolitik in Ungarn und in Oesterreich und das Problem der ökonomischen Integration (1880-1914)." Wirtschaft- und Sozialwissenschaften 2 (1977), 131-66.
2142. Ránki, György. "Problems of the Development of Hungarian Industry, 1900-1944." The Journal of Economic History 24 (1964), 204-28.
2143. Sándor, Vilmos. "Die grossindustrielle Entwicklung in Ungarn 1867-1900." Acta hist. Acad. Sci. hungaricae 3 (1956), 139-247.
2144. Sándor, Vilmos. "Die Hauptmerkmale der industriellen Entwicklung in Ungarn zur Zeit des Absolutismus (1849-1867)." in Etudes historiques publiées par la Commission Nationale des Historiens Hongrois. Budapest: Hungarian Academy of Science, 1960. II, 59-85.

SEE ALSO: 450, 457-58.

Lower Austria

2145. Benedikt, Heinrich. "Die Anfänge der Industrie in Niederösterreich." Der Donauraum 2 (1957), 200-11.
2146. Büttner, Rudolf. St. Pölten als Standort industrieller und grossgewerblicher Produktion seit 1850. St. Pölten: Magistrat der Stadt, 1972. 127 pp.
2147. Feigl, Helmuth and Andreas Kusternig, eds. Die Anfänge der Industrialisierung Niederösterreichs. Vienna: Niederösterreichischer Verein für Landeskunde, 1982. 469 pp.
2148. Nessl, Reinhard F. Die Entwicklung der Industrie in Wiener Neustadt 1945-1973 unter besonderer Berücksichtigung der Industriegebiete Nord, Süd und Ost. Thesis Vienna Wirtschaftsuniversität, 1977. 111 pp.
2149. Otruba, Gustav. "Die Anfänge und die Entwicklung der Industrie in Niederösterreich." Unsere Heimat 24 (1953), 73-85.
2150. Otruba, Gustav. "Die Quellenlage zur Frühgeschichte der Industrialisierung in Niederösterreich." Jahrbuch des Vereins für Landeskunde von Niederösterreich 33 (1957), 82-95.
2151. Wurm, Ernst and Erwin Stöckelmayer. Industrie im Raum Wiener Neustadt. Unternehmensschicksale in drei Jahrhunderten. Vienna: Handelskammer Niederösterreich, 1970. 61 pp.

Rumania

2152. Constantinescu, N. N. "The Problem of Industrial Revolution in Romania." Revue Romaine des Sciences Sociales: Série des Sciences Economiques 3 (1976), 209-33.
2153. Turnock, David. "The Industrial Development of Romania from the Unification of Principalities to the Second World War." in F. W. Carter, ed. An Historical Geography of the Balkans. London: Academic Press, 1977. pp. 319-368.

Salzburg

2154. Nawara, Alois. Die Entwicklung der Salzburger Industrie von 1930-1955. Thesis: Vienna Wirtschaftsuniversität, 1975. 111 pp.

Styria

2155. Chladek, Peter P. Geschichte und Probleme der Eisenindustrie in der Steiermark. Diss. Vienna, 1955. 186 pp.
2156. Haberleitner, Odilo. Handwerk in Steiermark und Kärnten vom Mittelalter bis 1850. Graz: Historische Landeskommision Steiermark, 1962. 179 pp.
2157. Pickl, Othmar, ed. Beiträge zur Geschichte der Industrialisierung des Südostalpenraumes im 19. Jahrhundert. Graz: Historische Landeskommission für Steiermark, 1970. 59 pp.
2158. Tremel, Ferdinand. "Die Rolle des Unternehmers in der industriellen Revolution am Beispiel der Steiermark." Tradition 15 (1970), 67-83.

Tirol

2159. Pixner, Albin. Die Industrie in Südtirol. Standorte und Entwicklung seit dem Zweiten Weltkrieg. Diss. Innsbruck, 1981. Innsbruck: Institut für Geographie, 1983. 132 pp.
2160. Zwanowetz, Georg. "Die Industrialisierung Tirols und Voralbergs bis etwa 1914." in Bericht über den 11. Österreichischen Historikertag. Vienna: Österreichischer Geschichtsverein, 1972. pp. 152-72.

Upper Austria

2161. Delena, W. Entwicklung und strukturelle Veränderungen in der oberösterreichischen Industrie während der Jahre 1938-1946. Vienna: University of Vienna, 1947. 225 pp.
2162. Knoblehar, Karl. Die oberösterreichische Industrie. Standort, Entwicklung und Leistung. Vienna: F. Berger, 1957. 56 pp.
2163. Kropf, Rudolf. "Die Entwicklung von Bergbau und Industrie in Oberösterreich. Oberösterreichs Industrie während der grossen Depression (1873-1895)." Oberösterreichische Heimatblätter 27 (1973), 170-252.
2164. Kropf, Rudolf. Oberösterreichs Industrie: (1873-1938). Ökonomisch-strukturelle Aspekte einer regionalen Industrieentwicklung. Linz: Trauner, 1981. 485 pp.
2165. Otruba, Gustav and Rudolf Kropf. "Die Entwicklung von Bergbau und Industrie in Oberösterreich. Die Gründerepoche bis zum Börsenkrach 1873." Oberösterreichische Heimatblätter 25 (1971), 50-97.
2166. Otruba, Gustav and Rudolf Kropf. "Die Entwicklung von Bergbau und Industrie in Oberösterreich. Von der Manufakturepoche bis zur Frühindustrialisierung." Oberösterreichische Heimatblätter 23 (1969), 3-19.

Vienna

2167. Banik-Schweizer, Renate and Gerhard Meissl. Industriestadt Wien. Vienna: Deuticke, 1983. 188 pp.
2168. Matis, Herbert. "Die industriellen Anfänge im Viertel unter dem Wienerwald." Unsere Heimat 37 (1966), 248-64.
2169. Meissl, Gerhard. "Industrie und Gewerbe in Wien 1835 bis 1845. Branchenmässige und regionale Strukturen und Entwicklungstendenzen im Spiegel der Gewerbeausstellungen von 1835, 1839 und 1845." in R. Banik-Schweitzer, ed. Wien im Vormärz. Vienna: Jugend & Volk, 1980. pp. 75-106.

SEE ALSO: 3033.

SWITZERLAND

2170. Bellaggio, Andrea, ed. Arbeitsalltag und Betriebsleben: zur Geschichte industrieller Arbeits- und Lebensverhältnisse in der Schweiz. Diessenhofen: Rüegger, 1981. 327 pp.
2171. Braun, Rudolf. "The Impact of Cottage Industry on an Agricultural Population." in D. S. Landes, ed. The Rise of Capitalism. New York: Macmillan, 1966. pp. 53-64.
2172. Grosjean, Georges. Die Schweiz: Industrie. 2nd ed. Bern: Geographisches Institut der Universität Bern, 1977. 74 pp.
2173. Hofmann, Emil. Die Schweiz als Industriestaat. Zurich: Schulthess, 1962. 132 pp.
2174. Hunold, Albert C. The Industrial Development of Switzerland. Zurich: Schweizerisches Institut für Auslandsforschung, 1954. 45 pp.
2175. Lehmann, Wolfgang. Die Entwicklung der Standorte der schweizerischen Industrien seit dem Ende des 19. Jahrhunderts. Diss. Zurich. Zurich: Juris, 1952. 167 pp.
2176. Masnata, Albert. Quelques traits généraux de l'histoire industrielle suisse. Lausanne: Office suisse d'expansion commerciale, 1963. 24 pp.
2177. Siegenthaler, Hansjörg. "Zur Geschichte der industriellen Unternehmung der Schweiz." Die Unternehmung 32 (1978), 85-100.
2178. Wehrli, Bernhard. "Entwicklungstendenzen der schweizerischen Industrie während der letzten 50 Jahre." in Das Esso-Buch. 2nd ed. Zurich: Esso Standard, 1951. pp. 63-70.

SEE ALSO: 539, 3080-81.

SWITZERLAND--1815-1975

Reference

2179. Wartmann, Hermann. Atlas über die Entwicklung von Industrie und Handel der Schweiz in dem Zeitraume vom Jahr 1770 bis zum Jahr 1870. Winterthur: Wurster & Randegger, 1873. 4 pp.

SWITZERLAND--1815-1975

2180. Bergier, Jean-François. "L'industrializzazione in un paese senza materie prime. Il caso della Svizzera, 1800-1850." Rassegna Economica 35 (1971), 1081-1100.
2181. Bergier, Jean-François. Naissance et croissance de la Suisse industrielle. Bern: Francke, 1974. 170 pp.
2182. Biucchi, Basilio M. "The Industrial Revolution in Switzerland." in C. M. Cipolla, ed. Fontana Economic History of Europe. London: Fontana, 1973. pp. 627-55.
2183. Biucchi, Basilio M. "Die Industrielle Revolution in der Schweiz 1700-1850." in Die Entwicklung der industriellen Gesellschaften. Europäische Wirtschaftgeschichte, 4. Stuttgart: Fischer, 1977. pp. 43-66.
2184. Büchler, Max. Die Anfänge der Entwicklung der Schweiz zum modernen Industriestaat. Basel: Monatsschrift für christliche Sozialreform, 1904. 60 pp.
2185. Casanova, Emilio. Die Entwicklung der schweizerischen Maschinenindustrie während des Weltkrieges und in der Nachkriegszeit, 1914-1931. Lugano: S. A. Tipográfia editrice, 1936. 303 pp.
2186. Fassbind, Rudolf. Die Schappe-Industrie in der Innerschweiz. Ein Beitrag zur schweizerischen Wirtschaftsgeschichte des 18. und 19. Jahrhunderts. Diss. Zurich, 1950. 137 pp.
2187. Fischer, Wolfram. "Drei Schweizer Pioniere der Industrie: Johann Conrad Fischer, 1773-1854, Johann Caspar Escher, 1775-1859, Johann Georg Bodmer, 1786-1864." Tradition 3 (1958), 215-30.
2188. Göldi, Hans. Der Export der schweizerischen Hauptindustrien während der Kriegszeit 1939-45. Zurich: Juris, 1949. 131 pp.
2189. Henderson, William O. "J. C. Fischer, a Swiss Industrial Pioneer." Zeitschrift für die gesamte Staatswissenschaft 119 (1963), 361-76.
2190. Hofmann, Hannes. Die Anfänge der Maschinenindustrie in der deutschen Schweiz 1800-1875. Zurich: University of Zurich--Historisches Seminar, 1962. 220 pp.
2191. Hottinger, Max. Geschichtliches aus der schweizerischen Metall und Maschinenindustrie. Frauenfeld: Huber, 1921. 188 pp.
2192. Kneschaurek, Francesco. "Wandlungen der schweizerischen Industriestruktur seit 1880." SZVS (1964), 133-66.
2193. Lechner Jean M. Le travail industriel de l'enfance en Suisse et sa protection légale jusqu'en 1874. Diss. Geneva. Geneva: Imprimerie du "Journal de Genève," 1942. 287 pp.
2194. Lincke, Bruno. Die schweizerische Maschinenindustrie und ihre Entwicklung in wirtschaftlicher Beziehung. Diss. Zurich, 1910. Frauenfeld: Huber, 1911. 218 pp.
2195. Müller, Klaus. Die Schweizer Industrie im Strukturwandel. Bern: NFP, 1983. 109 pp.
2196. Nobs, Ernst. Aus den Anfängen der industriellen Revolution in der Schweiz. Bern: Neues Leben, 1915.
2197. Rappard, William E. La révolution industrielle et les origines de la protection légale du travail en Suisse. Bern: Stämpfli, 1914. 343 pp.
2198. Schiff, Eric. Industrialization Without National Patents. The Netherlands 1869-1912. Switzerland, 1850-1907. Princeton, NJ: Princeton University Press, 1971. 137 pp.
2199. Veyrassat, Beatrice. "Les centres de gravité de l'industrialisation en Suisse au XIXe siècle (Aspects géographiques et sectoriels)." in L'industrialisation en Europe au XIXe siècle. Paris: Colloque international du C. N. R. S., 1970. pp. 483-86.
2200. Veyrassat, Beatrice. Negociants et fabricants dans l'industrie cotonnière suisse 1760-1840. Aux origines financieres de l'industrialisation. Lausanne: Payot, 1982. 385 pp.
2201. Wartmann, Hermann. Industrie und Handel der Schweiz im 19. Jahrhundert. Bern: A. Francke, 1902. 104 pp.

SEE ALSO: 3094, 3115, 3123, 3137.

SWISS CANTONS

Aargau

2202. Rey, Adolf. Die Entwicklung der Industrie im Kanton Aargau. Diss. Basel. Aarau: Buchdruck
E. Keller, 1937. 195 pp.

Bern

2203. Schwab, Fernand. Die industrielle Entwicklung der Stadt Biel. Biel: Buch und Kunstdruckerei
Andrew, 1918. 294 pp.
2204. Wegmüller, Walter. Die industrielle Entwicklung Langenthals. Diss. Bern. Langenthal:
Buchdruckerei Merkur, 1938. 323 pp.

SEE ALSO: 3172-73.

Fribourg

2205. Jedlicka, Georges. "Die Industrialisierung im Kanton Freiburg." Schweizer Jahrbuch für Bau
und Industrie 39 (1973), 55-56.
2206. Raemy de Bertigny, Héliodore. L'industrie à Fribourg au temps passé et de nos jours.
Fribourg: L. Fragnière, 1867.
2207. Walter, François. Le développement industriel de la ville de Fribourg entre 1847 et 1880.
Une tentative de 'démarrage' économique. Fribourg: Ed. Universitaires, 1974. 282 pp.

Glarus

2208. Bartel, Otto and Adolf Jenny, eds. Glarnerische Industrie. Glarus: Buchdruckerei Neue
Glarner Zeitung, 1936. 627 pp.
2209. Becker, Bernhard. Ein Wort über die Fabrikindustrie mit besonderer Hinsicht auf den Kanton
Glarus. Basel: Schwighausens, 1858. 118 pp.
2210. Winteler, Jakob. "Anfänge und Entwicklung der Glarner Industrie." in Die schweizerische
'Eternit'-Industrie. Zurich: s.n., 1953. pp. 5-7.

SEE ALSO: 602, 3177.

Lucerne

2211. Bernauer, Otto. Die Industrie des Kantons Luzern. Entstehung und Entwicklung, unter besonderer Berücksichtigung des industriellen Standortes. Diss. Bern. Luzern: Bucher-Räber, 1951.
181 pp.
2212. Dubler, Anne-Marie. Handwerk, Gewerbe und Zunft in Stadt und Landschaft Luzern. Lucerne:
Rex-Verlag, 1982. 480 pp.

St. Gallen

2213. Beerli, Hans. Industrie und Handel des Kantons St. Gallen 1901-1910. St. Gallen: Fehr, 1921.
322 pp.
2214. Hungerbühler, Johann M. Industriegeschichtliches über die Landschaft Toggenburg. St. Gallen:
Huber, 1852. 132 pp.
2215. Das industrielle Schaffen im Kanton St. Gallen. Eine Orientierung über die Entwicklung der St.
Gallischen Industrie seit 1800 anhand ihrer bedeutendsten Repräsentanten. St. Margarethen:
Huwile, 1954. 91 pp.

2216. Thalmann, Hanny. Die Industrie im Sarganserland. Entstehung, Entwicklung und Auswirkung mit Berücksichtigung des Standortes. Mels: Sarganserländische Buchdruckerei, 1943. 150 pp.
2217. Wartmann, Hermann. Industrie und Handel des Kantons St. Gallen auf Ende 1866. St. Gallen: Huber, 1870. 332 pp.
2218. Wartmann, Hermann. Industrie und Handel des Kantons St. Gallen 1867-1880. St. Gallen: Huber, 1887. 84 pp.
2219. Wartmann, Hermann. Industrie und Handel des Kantons St. Gallen 1867-1890. 3 vols. St. Gallen: Fehr, 1884-97.
2220. Wartmann, Hermann. Industrie und Handel des Kantons St. Gallen 1881-1890. St. Gallen: Ichrische Buchhandlung. 260 pp.
2221. Wartmann, Hermann. Industrie und Handel des Kantons St. Gallen 1891-1900. St. Gallen: Huber, 1913. 282 pp.

SEE ALSO: 1590, 3185-86.

Schaffhausen

2222. Traupel, Richard. Die industrielle Entwicklung des Kantons Schaffhausen (mit besonderer Berücksichtigung der allgemein-wirtschaftlichen Entwicklung des Kantons). Diss. Basel. Thayngen: Augustin, 1942. 246 pp.
2223. Winzeler, Johannes. Thayngen--vom Bauerndorf zum Industriedorf. Thayngen: Knorr Thayngen, 1957. 51 pp.

SEE ALSO: 619.

Solothurn

2224. Büchi, Hermann. Die industrielle Entwicklung des Kantons Solothurn. Solothurn: s.n, 1949.
2225. Flury, Werner. Die industrielle Entwicklung des Kantons Solothurn. Solothurn: Vogt & Schild, 1907. 92 pp.
2226. Meister, Paul. Die industrielle Entwicklung der Stadt Olten. Diss. Bern. Aarau: Fasler, 1953. 143 pp.
2227. Schwab, Fernand. Die industrielle Entwicklung des Kantons Solothurn und ihr Einfluss auf die Volkswirthschaft. Festschrift zum 50jährigen Bestehen des Solothurner Handels- und Industrievereins. 5 vols. Solothurn: Vogt & Schild, 1926-31.

Thurgau

2228. Isler, Egon. "Die Entwicklung der Industrie." in Thurgau gestern, heute, morgen. Frauenfeld: Huber, 1966. pp. 96-103.
2229. Isler, Egon. Industrie-Geschichte des Thurgaus. Chronik thurgauischer Firmen. Zurich: Brun, 1945. 444 pp.
2230. Wyler, Georg R. Die beruflichen Verbände in der thurgauischen Industrie vom Mittelalter bis zur Gegenwart. Diss. Zurich. Arbon: Genossenschaftsdruck, 1953. 211 pp.

SEE ALSO: 3192.

Unterwalden

2231. Flüeler, Karl. Rotzloch. Industrie seit 400 Jahren. Ein Beitrag zur Wirtschaftsgeschichte Nidwaldens mit genealogischen Notizen . . . und einem Bericht von Adalbert Vokinger über die Entwicklung der Industrie-Betriebe im Rotzloch in den letzten 50 Jahren. Stans: Historischer Verein Nidwalden, 1977. 268 pp.

Valais

2232. Kaufmann, Beat. Die Entwicklung des Wallis vom Agrar- zum Industriekanton. Diss. Basel, 1964. Winterthur: Keller, 1965. 173 pp.

Zug

2233. Bachmann, Hans et al. Aus den Anfängen der Schlierener Industrie. Schlieren: Maier, 1975. 30 pp.

Zurich

2234. Braun, Rudolf. "Early Industrialization and Demographic Change in the Canton of Zurich." in C. Tilly, ed. Historical Studies of Changing Fertility. Princeton, NJ: Princeton University Press, 1978. pp. 289-334.

2235. Braun, Rudolf. "The Rise of a Rural Class of Industrial Entrepreneurs [in Zurich Oberland]." Journal of World History 10 (1967), 551-66.

2236. Braun, Rudolf. Socialer und kultureller Wandel in einem ländlichen Industriegebiet (Zürcher Oberland) unter Einwirkung des Maschinen- und Fabrikwesens im 19. und 20. Jahrhundert. Erlenbach-Zurich: Rentsch, 1965. 368 pp.

2237. Bürkli-Meyer, Adolf. Der Wollenhof nach seiner 300jährigen Bedeutung für die Industrie Zürichs. Zurich: s.n., 1878.

2238. Denzler, Alice. "Die industrielle Entwicklung der Stadt Winterthur." Schweizer Verkehrs und Industrie-Revue 20 (1948), 22-31.

2239. Hummel, Oscar. Industrielle Entwicklung des Bauerndorfes Dietikon. Dietikon: Hummel, 1977. 40 pp.

2240. Kläui, Paul. Chronik Bezirk Horgen. Geschichte. Industrie. Handel. Gewerbe. Zurich: H. A. Bosch, 1945. 195 pp.

2241. Kläui, Paul. Chronik Bezirk Meilen. Geschichte. Industrie. Handel. Gewerbe. Zurich: H. A. Bosch, 1945. 191 pp.

2242. Kläui, Paul. Chronik Bezirk Uster. Geschichte. Industrie. Handel. Gewerbe. Zurich: H. A. Bosch, 1944. 187 pp.

2243. Mossdorf, Albert. Die Industrie in Bülach. Ihre Entwicklung. ihre Bedeutung. Bülach: Graf, 1942. 80 pp.

2244. Nabholz, Hans. Die Entwicklung der zürcherischen Industrie aus dem Gewerbe. Kriens: Buchdrückerei Kriens, 1945. 12 pp.

SEE ALSO: 634.

GERMANY

2245. Albrecht, Karl. Wirtschaftspraxis und Wirtschaftspolitik gestern, heute, morgen. Ed. W. Niermann. Düsseldorf: Econ-Verlag, 1964. 262 pp.
2246. Barkin, Kenneth D. "Adolf Wagner and the German Industrial Development." Journal of Modern History 41 (1969), 144-59.
2247. Bauert-Keetman, Ingrid. Deutsche Industriepioniere. Tübingen: R. Wunderlich, 1966. 327 pp.
2248. Blankertz, Herwig. Bildung im Zeitalter der grossen Industrie. Hannover: Schroedel, 1969. 168 pp.
2249. Brady, Robert A. The Rationalization Movement in German Industry. A Study in the Evolution of Economic Planning. Berkeley: University of California Press, 1933. 466 pp.
2250. Bry, Gerhard. Wages in Germany 1870-1945. Princeton, NJ: Princeton University Press, 1960. 486 pp.
2251. Chamberlin, Waldo, ed. Industrial Relations in Germany 1914-1939. Stanford, CA: Stanford University Press, 1942. 403 pp.
2252. Egle, Walter. "The Progress of Mass Production and the German Small-Scale Industries." Journal of Political Economy 46 (1938), 376-95.
2253. Feldman, Gerald D. and Ulrich Nocken. "Trade Associations and Economic Power: Interest Group Development in the German Iron and Steel and Machine Building Industries, 1900-1933." Business History Review 49 (1975), 413-45.
2254. Fischer, Wolfram and Peter Czada. "Industrial Structure in the Twentieth Century. Germany." Papers Presented to the Fourth International Conference of Economic History, Bloomington, 1968. Paris: Mouton, 1973.
2255. Fremdling, Rainer. "Railroads and German Economic Growth. A Leading Sector Analysis with a Comparison to the United States and Great Britain." Journal of Economic History 37 (1977), 583-604.
2256. Fuchs, Konrad. "Zur Rolle des deutsch-jüdischen Unternehmertums beim Industrialisierungsprozess im 19. und 20. Jahrhundert." Scripta Mercaturae 14 (1980), 71-90. (English and French summaries.)
2257. Geldern-Crispendorf, Günther von. Die deutschen Industriegebiete, ihr Werden und ihre Struktur. Karlsruhe: Moniger, 1933. 160 pp.
2258. Glaser, Hermann. Maschinenwelt und Alltagsleben: Industriekultur in Deutschland vom Biedermeier bis zur Weimarer Republik. Frankfurt a. M.: Krüger, 1981. 212 pp.
2259. Goebel, Joseph. Die Geschichte der Industriegegnerschaft. Unter besonderer Berücksichtigung der deutschen Literatur. Diss. Heidelberg. Mainz: Zaberndruck, 1936. 111 pp.
2260. Grumbach, Franz von and Heinz König. "Beschäftigung und Löhne der deutschen Industriewirtschaft 1888/1954." Weltwirtschaftliches Archiv 79 (1957), 125-55.
2261. Hallgarten, George W. F. and Joachim Radkau. Deutsche Industrie und Politik von Bismarck bis in die Gegenwart. Reinbek b. Hamburg: Rowohlt, 1981. 571 pp.
2262. Hardach, Karl W. Nationalismus: die deutsche Industrialisierungsideologie? Cologne: University of Cologne, 1976. 18 pp.
2263. Henderson, William O. "England und die Industrialisierung Deutschlands." Zeitschrift für die gesamte Staatswissenschaft 108 (1952), 264-94.
2264. Henning, Friedrich-Wilhelm. Das industrialisierte Deutschland 1914 bis 1976. 4th ed. Paderborn: F. Schöningh, 1978. 292 pp.
2265. Köllmann, Wolfgang. "The Process of Urbanization in Germany at the Height of the Industrialization Period." Journal of Contemporary History 4 (1969), 59-76.
2266. Krengel, Rolf. Anlagevermögen, Produktion und Beschäftigung der Industrie im Gebiet der Bundesrepublik von 1924-1956. Berlin: Duncker & Humblot, 1958. 107 pp.
2267. Lebovics, Herman. A Socialism for the German Middle Classes. The Social Conservative Response to Industrialism, 1900-1933. Diss. Yale University, 1965. 418 pp.
2268. Levy, Hermann. Industrial Germany. A Study of its Monopoly Organizations and their Control by the State. Cambridge: Cambridge University Press, 1935. 245 pp.
2269. Luebke, Anton. Das deutsche Rohstoffwunder. Wandlungen der deutschen Rohstoffwirtschaft. 2nd ed. Stuttgart: Verlag für Wirtschaft und Verkehr, 1938. 556 pp.
2270. Lündgreen, Peter. "Industrialization and the Educational Formation of Manpower in Germany." Journal of Social History 9 (1975), 64-80.

2271. Maschke, Erich. "Die Industrialisierung Deutschlands im Spiegel der Parlamentszusammen-
setzungen von 1848 bis heute." Tradition 10 (1965), 230-45.
2272. Maschke, Erich. "Industrialisierungsgeschichte und Landesgeschichte." Blätter für Deutsche
Landesgeschichte 10 (1967), 1-84.
2273. Mauersberg, Hans. Deutsche Industrien im Zeitgeschehen eines Jahrhunderts. Eine historische
Modelluntersuchung zum Entwicklungsprozess deutscher Unternehmen von ihren Anfängen bis zum
Stand von 1960. Stuttgart: G. Fischer, 1966. 584 pp.
2274. Müller, Johannes. Die Industrialisierung der deutschen Mittelgebirge. Eine wirtschaftskundliche Frage der Vergangenheit--ein wirtschaftspolitisches Problem der Gegenwart. Jena:
Fischer, 1938. 241 pp.
2275. Noll, Adolf. Sozio-ökonomischer Strukturwandel des Handwerks in der zweiten Phase der
Industrialisierung. Göttingen: Vandenhoeck & Ruprecht, 1975. 386 pp.
2276. Panzer, Arno. "Industrie und Landwirtschaft in Deutschland im Spiegel der Aussenwirtschaft
und Zollpolitik von 1870 bis heute." Zeitschrift für Agrargeschichte 23 (1975), 71-85.
2277. Parker, William N. "Entrepreneurship, Industrial Organization and Economic Growth. A
German Example." Journal of Economic History 14 (1954), 380-400.
2278. Pollard, Sidney and Lucian Hölscher, eds. Region und Industrialisierung. Studien zur Rolle der
Region in der Wirtschaftsgeschichte der letzten zwei Jahrhunderte. / Region and Industrialization. Studies on the Role of the Region in the Economic History of the Last Two Centuries.
Göttingen: Vandenhoeck & Ruprecht, 1980. 297 pp.
2279. Rübberdt, Rudolf. Geschichte der Industrialisierung. Wirtschaft und Gesellschaft auf dem Weg
in unsere Zeit. Munich: Beck, 1972. 407 pp.
2280. Ruppert, Wolfgang. Die Fabrik. Geschichte von Arbeit und Industrialisierung in Deutschland.
Munich: Beck, 1983. 311 pp.
2281. Schwerin von Krosigk, Lutz. Die grosse Zeit des Feuers. Der Weg der deutschen Industrie.
3 vols. Tübingen: Rainer Wunderlich Verlag Hermann Leins, 1957-59.
2282. Slotosch, Walter. "Das Industriepotential 1900-1950." Der Arbeitgeber 24 (1950), 2-8.
2283. Stearns, Peter N. "Adaptation to Industrialization: German Workers as a Test Case." Central
European History 3 (1970), 303-31.
2284. Vedder, Lothar. Die deutsche Industrie in den Jahren 1933 bis 1960. Krefeld: Industrie
Handelskammer, 1960. 140 pp.
2285. Zorn, Wolfgang. "Ein Jahrhundert deutscher Industrialisierungsgeschichte." Blätter für
Deutsche Landesgeschichte 108 (1972), 122-34.

SEE ALSO: 686, 722, 1977, 4674, 4680.

GERMANY--1815-1918

2286. Abelshauser, Werner. "Staat, Infrastruktur und regionaler Wohlstandsausgleich im Preussen
der Hochindustrialisierung." in F. Blaich, ed. Staatliche Umverteilungspolitik in historischer Perspektive. Beiträge zur Entwicklung des Staatsinterventionismus in Deutschland und Österreich.
Berlin: Duncker & Humblot, 1980. pp. 9-58.
2287. Armeson, Robert B. Total Warfare and Compulsory Labor. A Study of the Military-Industrial
Complex in Germany During World War I. The Hague: M. Nijhoff, 1964. 155 pp.
2288. Arndt, Paul. Wirthschaftliche Folgen der Entwicklung Deutschlands zum Industriestaat.
Berlin: Simion, 1899. 62 pp.
2289. Banfield, Thomas C. Industry of the Rhine. 2 vols. New York: Kelley, 1969.
2290. Barkin, Kenneth D. The Controversy Over German Industrialization 1890-1902. Chicago:
University of Chicago Press, 1970. 370 pp.
2291. Barth, Ernst. Entwicklungslinien der deutschen Maschinenbauindustrie von 1870-1914.
Berlin: Akademie, 1973. 212 pp.
2292. Benaerts, Pierre. Les origines de la grande industrie allemande. Paris: Turot, 1933. 688 pp.
2293. Blumberg, Horst. Die deutsche Textilindustrie in der industriellen Revolution. Berlin:
Akademie, 1965. 434 pp.
2294. Bog, Ingomar. "Wirtschaft und Gesellschaft im Zeitalter der industriellen Revolution."
Geschichte in Wissenschaft und Unterricht 20 (1969), 193-224.

2295. Bohse, Erich. Die Entstehung der industriellen Gewerbefreiheit in Preussen. Diss. Osnabrück, 1931. 78 pp.

2296. Borchardt, Knut. The Industrial Revolution in Germany, 1700-1914. The Fontana Economic History of Europe, 4. London: Fontana Books, 1972. 88 pp.

2297. Bowen, Ralph H. "The Roles of Government and Private Enterprise in German Industrial Growth, 1870-1914." Journal of Economic History Supp. 10 (1950), 68-81.

2298. Braun, Rudolf et al. Industrielle Revolution. Wirtschaftliche Aspekte. Cologne: Kiepenheuer & Witsch, 1972. 399 pp.

2299. Bueck, Henry A. Der Centralverband Deutscher Industrieller, 1876-1901. 3 vols. Berlin: Mitscher & Röstell (vol. 1); Guttentag (vols. 2-3), 1902-05.

2300. Bueck, Henry A. Der Centralverband Deutscher Industrieller und seine dreissigjährige Arbeit von 1876 bis 1906. Berlin: Guttentag, 1906. 88 pp.

2301. Cameron, Rondo E. "Some French Contributions to the Industrial Development of Germany, 1840-1970." The Journal of Economic History 16 (1956), 281-316.

2302. Clapham, Ronald. "Probleme der Übernahme und Verbreitung neuer Technologien im früh-industriellen Deutschland." Hamburger Jahrbuch für Wirtschafts- und Gesellschaftspolitik 21 (1976), 303-16. (English summary)

2303. Dahrendorf, Ralf. "Imperial Germany and the Industrial Revolution." in D. Schoonmaker, ed. German Politics. Lexington, MA: Heath, 1971. pp. 10-17.

2304. Dawson, William H. Industrial Germany. London: Collins, 1912. 264 pp.

2305. "Deutsche Frühindustrialisierung." Geschichte und Gesellschaft. Zeitschrift für historische Sozialwissenschaft 5 (1979), 173-250.

2306. Dreyfus, François G. "Révolution industrielle et villes allemandes." Annales Economies. Sociétés. Civilisations 17 (1962), 773-79.

2307. Dumke, Rolf H. "Anglo-deutscher Handel und Frühindustrialisierung in Deutschland 1822-1860." Geschichte und Gesellschaft. Zeitschrift für historische Sozialwissenschaft 5 (1979), 175-200.

2308. Fach, Wolfgang and Horst A. Wessel, eds. Hundert Thaler Preussisch Courant. Industrie-finanzierung in der Gründerzeit. Vienna: Molden, 1981. 223 pp.

2309. Feldman, Gerald D. Army. Industry and Labor in Germany 1914-1918. Princeton, NJ: Princeton University Press, 1966. 572 pp.

2310. Fichte, Richard. Die grosse Zeit im Deutschen Handwerk. Die Grundlage der gegenwärtigen Wirtschaftsorganisation des Deutschen Handwerks und seine Beteiligung an den Heereslieferungen im Weltkrieg. Berlin: Staatspolitischer Verlag, 1922. 148 pp.

2311. Fischer, Wolfram. "Das deutsche Handwerk in den Frühphasen der Industrialisierung." Zeitschrift für die gesamte Staatswissenschaft 120 (1964), 686-712.

2312. Fischer, Wolfram. "Government Activity and Industrialization in Germany 1815-70." in W. W. Rostow, ed. The Economics of Take-Off into Sustained Growth. London: Macmillan, 1963. pp. 83-94. (Also in Europe and the Industrial Revolution. Cambridge, MA: Schenkman, 1972. pp. 447-58.)

2313. Fischer, Wolfram. "Soziale Unterschichten im Zeitalter der Frühindustrialisierung." International Review of Social History 8 (1963), 415-35.

2314. Fischer, Wolfram. "Die Stellung der preussischen Bergrechtsreform von 1851-1865 in der Wirtschafts- und Sozialverfassung des 19. Jahrhunderts." Zeitschrift für die gesamte Staats-wissenschaft 117 (1961), 521-34.

2315. Forberger, Rudolf. "Zur Auseinandersetzung über das Problem des Übergangs von der Manufaktur zur Fabrik." in Beiträge zur deutschen Wirtschafts- und Sozialgeschichte des 18. und 19. Jahrhunderts. Berlin: Akademie, 1962. pp. 171-88.

2316. Fremdling, Rainer and Richard H. Tilly. Industrialisierung und Raum. Studien zur regionalen Differenzierung im Deutschland des 19. Jahrhunderts. Stuttgart: Klett-Cotta, 1979. 284 pp.

2317. Freudenberger, Hermann. "Zum Anfang der deutschen Firmengeschichte." Tradition 7 (1962), 55-58.

2318. Friedrich-Freska, Martin. Preussen und der Demiurg des Weltmarkts. Studie zur Industriellen Revolution in Westeuropa und zu ihrer Wirkung auf die Agrarverhältnisse. Freiburg i. B.: Hochschulverlag, 1982. 429 pp.

2319. Froriep, Otto. Zur Geschichte der Maschinenbau-Industrie und der Maschinenzölle im Deutschen Zollverein. Stuttgart: Kohlhammer, 1918. 117 pp.

2320. Hardach, Karl W. "Anglomanie und Anglophobie während der industriellen Revolution in Deutschland." Schmoller 91 (1971), 153-81. (English summary)
2321. Hauser, Henri. Economic Germany. German Industry Considered as a Factor Making for War. London: Nelson, 1915. 33 pp.
2322. Heggen, Alfred. Erfindungsschutz und Industrialisierung in Preussen. 1793-1877. Göttingen: Vandenhoeck & Ruprecht, 1975. 178 pp.
2323. Henderson, William O. The Industrial Revolution on the Continent. Germany. France. Russia. 1800-1914. London: Cass, 1961. 288 pp.
2324. Henderson, William O. "Peter Beuth and the Rise of Prussian Industry, 1810-1845." Economic History Review, ser. 2, 8 (1955), 113-20.
2325. Henderson, William O. The Rise of German Industrial Power. 1834-1914. London: Temple Smith, 1975. 264 pp.
2326. Henderson, William O. The State and the Industrial Revolution in Prussia. 1740-1870. Liverpool: Liverpool University Press, 1958. 232 pp.
2327. Henning, Friedrich-Wilhelm. "Humanisierung und Technisierung der Arbeitswelt. Über den Einfluss der Industrialisierung auf die Arbeitsbedingungen im 19. Jahrhundert." Archiv und Wirtschaft 9 (1976), 29-59.
2328. Henning, Friedrich-Wilhelm. Die Industrialisierung in Deutschland 1800 bis 1914. 4th ed. Paderborn: Schöningh, 1978. 304 pp.
2329. Henning, Hansjoachim. Das westdeutsche Bürgertum in der Epoche der Hochindustrialisierung 1760-1914. Wiesbaden: Steiner, 1972. 509 pp.
2330. Hoernecke, Wilhelm. Die Entwicklung Deutschlands vom Agrarstaat zum Industriestaat. Stuttgart: Berger, 1922. 126 pp.
2331. Horn, Norbert and Jürgen Kocka, eds. Law and the Formation of the Big Enterprise in the Nineteenth and Early Twentieth Centuries. Studies in the History of Industrialization in Germany. France. Great Britain and the United States. Göttingen: Vandenhoeck & Ruprecht, 1979. 685 pp. (German: Göttingen, 1979)
2332. Howard, Earl D. The Cause and Extent of the Recent Industrial Progress of Germany. London: Constable, 1907. 147 pp.
2333. Jahn, Georg. "Die Entstehung der Fabrik." Schmoller 69 (1949), 193-228.
2334. Kaelble, Hartmut. Industrielle Interessenpolitik in der wilhelminischen Gesellschaft. Centralverband deutscher Industrieller 1895-1914. Berlin: de Gruyter, 1967. 268 pp.
2335. Kaufhold, Karl H. "Das preussische Handwerk während der Frühindustrialisierung." in W. Fischer, ed. Beiträge zu Wirtschaftswachstum und Wirtschaftsstrucktur im 16. und 19. Jahrhundert. Berlin: Duncker & Humblot, 1971. pp. 169-93.
2336. Kiesewetter, Hubert. "Erklärungshypothesen zur regionalen Industrialisierung in Deutschland im 19. Jahrhundert." VSWG 67 (1980), 305-33.
2337. Kocka, Jürgen. "Capitalism and Bureaucracy in German Industrialization Before 1914." The Economic History Review, ser. 2, 34 (1981), 453-68.
2338. Kocka, Jürgen. "Family and Bureaucracy in German Industrial Management, 1850-1914." Business History Review, 45 (1971), 133-56.
2339. Kocka, Jürgen. "Industrielles Management: Konzeptionen und Modelle in Deutschland vor 1914." VSWG 56 (1969), 332-372.
2340. Kocka, Jürgen. Unternehmer in der deutschen Industrialisierung. Göttingen: Vandenhoeck & Ruprecht, 1975. 173 pp.
2341. Köllmann, Wolfgang. "Industrialisierung, Binnenwanderung und 'Soziale Frage.' Zur Entstehungsgeschichte der deutschen Industriegrosstadt im 19. Jahrhundert." VSWG 46 (1959), 45-70.
2342. Krämer, K., ed. Studien zur Geschichte der Produktivkräfte. Deutschland zur Zeit der Industriellen Revolution. Berlin: Akademie, 1979. 401 pp.
2343. Krüger, Horst. Zur Geschichte der Manufakturen und der Manufakturarbeiter in Preussen. Berlin: Rütten und Loenig, 1960. 796 pp.
2344. Kuczynski, Jürgen. "Einige Probleme der industriellen Revolution und der wissenschaftlich-technischen Revolution im Vergleich." in Festschrift Wilhelm Abel. Hannover: Schaper, 1964. pp. 667-78.
2345. Kulischer, Josef. "Die Ursachen des Übergangs von der Handarbeit zur maschinellen Betriebsweise um die Wende des 18. und in der ersten Hälfte des 19. Jahrhunderts." Schmoller 30 (1906), 31-79.

2346. Lambi, Ivo N. "The Protectionist Interests of the German Iron and Steel Industry, 1873-1879." Journal of Economic History 22 (1962), 59-70.
2347. Landes, David S. "Industrialization and Economic Development in Nineteenth-Century Germany." in International Conference of Economic History (1960), 83-86.
2348. Landgraf, Josef. "Industrielle Fachverbände, ihre Entstehung, ihre Aufgabe, ihre Erfolge." Jahrbücher für Nationalökonomie und Statistik 77 (1901), 343-65.
2349. Lebovics, Herman. "'Agrarians' versus 'Industrializers.' Social Conservative Resistance to Industrialism and Capitalism in Late Nineteenth Century Germany." International Review of Social History 12 (1967), 31-65.
2350. Linde, Hans. "Die Bedeutung der deutschen Agrarstruktur für die Anfänge der industriellen Entwicklung." Jahrbuch für Sozialwissenschaft 13 (1962), 179-95.
2351. Locke, Robert R. "Industrialisierung und Erziehungssystem in Frankreich und Deutschland vor dem 1. Weltkrieg." Historische Zeitschrift 225 (1977), 265-96.
2352. Lotz, Walther. "The Effect of Protection on Some German Industries." Economic Journal 14 (1904), 515-26.
2353. Lündgreen, Peter. Bildung und Wirtschaftswachstum im Industrialisierungsprozess des 19. Jahrhunderts. Berlin: Colloquium, 1973. 182 pp.
2354. Lündgreen, Peter. Techniker in Preussen während der frühen Industrialisierung. Berlin: Colloquium-Verlag, 1975. 307 pp.
2355. Machtan, Lothar. "Zum Innenleben deutscher Fabriken im 19. Jahrhundert." Archiv für Sozialgeschichte 21 (1981), 184-236.
2356. Matschoss, Conrad. Ein Jahrhundert deutscher Maschinenbau. Von der mechanischen Werkstätte bis zur Deutschen Maschinenfabrik 1819-1919. Berlin: Springer, 1919. 276 pp.
2357. Morrow, John H. "Industrial Mobilization in World War I." Journal of Economic History 37 (1977), 36-51.
2358. Mottek, Hans. "Einleitende Bemerkungen zum Verlauf und zu einigen Hauptproblemen der industriellen Revolution in Deutschland" in Studien zur Geschichte der industriellen Revolution in Deutschland. Berlin: Institut für Wirtschaftsgeschichte, 1960. pp. 11-63.
2359. Mottek, Hans et al. Studien zur Geschichte der industriellen Revolution in Deutschland. Berlin: Akademie, 1960. 240 pp.
2360. Müller-Link, Horst. Industrialisierung und Aussenpolitik. Preussen-Deutschland und das Zarenreich von 1860 bis 1890. Göttingen: Vandenhoeck & Ruprecht, 1977. 506 pp.
2361. Mummenhoff, Ernst. Der Handwerker in der deutschen Vergangenheit. 2nd ed. Jena: E. Diederichs, 1924. 142 pp.
2362. Ohno, Eiji. "The Historical Stage of German Capitalism. An Analysis of the Bismarck Regime." The Kyoto University Economic Review 40 (1970), 18-43.
2363. Peschke, Hans-Peter von. Elektroindustrie und Staatsverwaltung am Beispiel Siemens: 1847-1914. Frankfurt a. M.: Lang, 1981. 393 pp.
2364. Ponteil, Félix. "Le Zollverein et les débuts de la grande industrie allemande." Révue Hist. mod. 9 (1934), 48-54.
2365. Radtke, Wolfgang. Die preussische Seehandlung zwischen Staat und Wirtschaft in der Frühphase der Industrialisierung. Berlin: Colloquium, 1981. 432 pp.
2366. Reulecke, Jürgen. "Nachzügler und Pionier zugleich, das Bergische Land und der Beginn der Industrialisierung in Deutschland." in Region und Industrialisierung. Studien zur Rolle der Region in der Wirtschaftsgeschichte der letzten zwei Jahrhunderte. Göttingen: Vandenhoeck & Ruprecht, 1980. pp. 52-68.
2367. Ritter, Ulrich P. Die Rolle des Staates in den Frühstadien der Industrialisierung. Die preussische Industrieförderung in der ersten Hälfte des 19. Jahrhunderts. Berlin: Duncker & Humblot, 1961. 176 pp.
2368. Saul, Klaus. Staat, Industrie, Arbeiterbewegung im Kaiserreich. Düsseldorf: Bertelsmann, 1974. 620 pp.
2369. Schildt, Joachim. Auswirkungen der industriellen Revolution auf die deutsche Sprachentwicklung im 19. Jahrhundert. Berlin: Akademie, 1981. 480 pp.
2370. Schreiber, Erwin. Die Unternehmer-Organisationen der deutschen Industrie im Kriege. (Eine Untersuchung über ihre Betätigung und Bedeutung im Rahmen der deutschen Kriegswirtschaft.) Diss. Kiel. Berlin: Brönner, 1929. 157 pp.
2371. Schreiner, George A. The Iron Ration. The Economic and Social Effects of the Allied Blockade on Germany and the German People. London: Murray, 1918. 359 pp.

2372. Schremmer, Eckart. "Industrielle Rückständigkeit und strukturstabilisierender Fortschritt. Über den Einsatz von Produktionsfaktoren in der deutschen (Land-) Wirtschaft zwischen 1850 und 1913." in Wirtschaftliches Wachstum, Energie und Verkehr vom Mittelalter bis ins 19. Jahrhundert. Stuttgart: Akademie, 1978. pp. 205-33.
2373. Schremmer, Eckart. "Wie gross war der 'technische Fortschritt' während der Industriellen Revolution in Deutschland 1850-1913?" VSWG 60 (1973), 433-58.
2374. Schröter, Alfred and Walter Becker. Die deutsche Maschinenbauindustrie in der industriellen Revolution. Berlin: Akademie, 1962. 285 pp.
2375. Sedatis, Helmut. Liberalismus und Handwerk in Südwestdeutschland. Wirtschaft- und Gesellschaftskonzeption des Liberalismus und die Krise des Handwerks im 19. Jahrhundert. Stuttgart: Klett-Cotta, 1979. 243 pp.
2376. Simon, Manfred. Handwerk in Krise und Umbruch. Wirtschaftliche Forderungen und sozialpolitische Vorstellungen der Handwerksmeister im Revolutionsjahr 1848/49. Cologne: Böhlau, 1983. 652 pp.
2377. Sonnenmann, Rolf. Die Auswirkungen des Schutzzolls auf die Monopolisierung der deutschen Eisen- und Stahlindustrie 1879-1892. Berlin: Akademie Verlag, 1960. 114 pp.
2378. Spohn, Willfried. Weltmarktkonkurrenz und Industrialisierung Deutschlands 1870-1914. Eine Untersuchung zur nationalen und internationalen Geschichte der kapitalistischen Produktionsweise. Berlin: Olle & Wolter, 1977. 452 pp.
2379. Stern, Fritz R. Gold and Iron. Bismarck, Bleichröder and the Building of the German Empire. New York: Random House, 1979. 620 pp.
2380. Teuteberg, Hans-Jürgen. Geschichte der industriellen Mitbestimmung. Ursprung und Entwicklung ihrer Vorläufer im Denken und in der Wirklichkeit des 19. Jahrhunderts. Tübingen: Mohr, 1961. 587 pp.
2381. Tilly, Richard H. Kapital, Staat und sozialer Protest in der deutschen Industrialisierung. Göttingen: Vandenhoeck & Ruprecht, 1980. 320 pp.
2382. Ullmann, Hans-Peter. Der Bund der Industriellen. Organisation, Einfluss und Politik klein- und mittelbetrieblicher Industrieller im deutschen Kaiserreich 1895-1914. Göttingen: Vandenhoeck & Ruprecht, 1976. 464 pp.
2383. Veblen, Thorstein. Imperial Germany and the Industrial Revolution. 4th ed. New York: Viking Press, 1954. 343 pp.
2384. Wagenblass, Horst. Der Eisenbahnbau und das Wachstum der deutschen Eisen- und Maschinenbauindustrie 1835 bis 1860: ein Beitrag zur Geschichte der Industrialisierung Deutschlands. Stuttgart: Fischer, 1973. 334 pp.
2385. Wagenführ, Rolf. Die Industriewirtschaft. Entwicklungstendenzen der deutschen und internationalen Industrieproduktion 1860 bis 1932. Berlin: Reimar Hobbing, 1933. 69 pp.
2386. Walcker, Karl. Die Interessenkämpfe der Industrie, des Handels, der Landwirtschaft. Zittau: Pahl, 1897. 117 pp.
2387. Webb, Steven B. "Tariffs, Cartels, Technology and Growth in the German Steel Industry, 1879-1914." Journal of Economic History 40 (1980), 309-30.
2388. Weber, Wolfhard. "Industriespionage als technologischer Transfer in der Frühindustrialisierung Deutschlands." Technikgeschichte 42 (1975), 287-305.
2389. Wehler, Hans-Ulrich. "Industrial Growth and Early German Imperialism." in Studies in the Theory of Imperialism. London: Longman, 1972. pp. 71-92.
2390. Wehner, Heinz. "Deutschlands Weg zum Industriestaat. Einige Bemerkungen zu den Veröffentlichungen des Instituts für Wirtschaftsgeschichte der Hochschule für Ökonomie Berlin zu Fragen der industriellen Revolution in Deutschland." Jahrbuch für Wirtschaftsgeschichte (1969), I, 349-97.
2391. Williams, Ernest E. Made in Germany. London: Heinemann, 1896. 175 pp.
2392. Zunkel, Friedrich. Industrie- und Staatssozialismus. Der Kampf um die Wirtschaftsordnung in Deutschland 1914-1918. Düsseldorf: Droste, 1974. 227 pp.

SEE ALSO: 911, 1735, 1754, 2411, 3417, 3534, 4797, 4868, 4904, 4938, 4940, 4943-44, 4949.

WEIMAR REPUBLIC AND THIRD REICH--1919-1945

Bibliographic Reference

2393. Chamberlin, Waldo. Industrial Relations in Germany, 1914-1939. Annotated Bibliography of Materials in the Hoover Library on War, Revolution, and Peace and the Stanford University Library. Stanford, CA: Stanford University Press, 1942. 403 pp.

WEIMAR REPUBLIC AND THIRD REICH--1919-1945

2394. Block, Herbert. "Industrial Combination vs. Small Business. The Trend of Nazi Policy." Social Research 10 (1943), 175-99.
2395. Boelcke, Willi A. "Hitlers Befehle zur Zerstörung oder Lähmung des deutschen Industrie-potentials 1944-45." Tradition 13 (1968), 301-16.
2396. Brady, Robert A. "Modernized Cameralism in the Third Reich. The Case of the National Industry Group." Journal of Political Economy 50 (1942), 65-97.
2397. Czichon, Eberhard. "Der Primat der Industrie im Kartell der nationalsozialistischen Macht." Das Argument 10 (1968), 193-209.
2398. Czichon, Eberhard. Wer verhalf Hitler zur Macht?: zum Anteil der deutschen Industrie an der Zerstörung der Weimarer Republik. 4th ed. Cologne: Pahl-Rugenstein, 1976. 105 pp.
2399. Dawson, Philip. Germany's Industrial Revival. London: Williams and Norgate, 1926. 276 pp.
2400. Die deutsche Industrie im Kriege 1939-1945. Berlin: Duncker & Humblot, 1954. 216 pp.
2401. Eichholtz, Dietrich. "Das Minette-Revier und die deutsche Montanindustrie. Zur Kriegsziel-strategie der deutschen Monopole im Zweiten Weltkrieg, 1941-42." Zeitschrift für Geschichts-wissenschaft 25 (1977), 816-38.
2402. Emmendörfer, Hans G. Die geschäftlichen Beziehungen der deutschen Eisen- und Stahlindustrie zur eisenschaffenden Industrie in den besetzten Gebieten 1933-1945. Diss. Cologne, 1955. 246 pp.
2403. Feldman, Gerald D. "Aspekte deutscher Industriepolitik am Ende der Weimarer Republik 1930-1932." in K. Holl, ed. Wirtschaftskrise und liberale Demokratie. Göttingen: Vandenhoeck & Ruprecht, 1978. pp. 103-25.
2404. Feldman, Gerald D. Iron and Steel in the German Inflation, 1916-23. Princeton, NJ: Princeton University Press, 1977. 518 pp.
2405. Fritz, Martin. German Steel and Swedish Iron Ore, 1939-1945. Gothenburg, Sweden: Institute of Economic History, 1974. 136 pp.
2406. Hallgarten, George W. F. "Adolf Hitler and German Heavy Industry, 1931-1933." Journal of Economic History 12 (1952), 222-46.
2407. Homze, Edward L. Arming the Luftwaffe. The Reich Air Ministry and the German Aircraft Industry, 1919-1939. Lincoln: University of Nebraska Press, 1976. 296 pp.
2408. Liefmann, Robert. "German Industrial Organization since the World War." Quarterly Journal of Economics 40 (1926), 82-110.
2409. Liesebach, Ingolf. Der Wandel der politischen Führungsschicht der deutschen Industrie von 1918 bis 1945. Diss. Basel, 1957. 134 pp.
2410. Lochner, Louis P. Tycoons and Tyrant: German Industry From Hitler to Adenauer. Chicago: Henry Regnery, 1954. 304 pp. (German: Darmstadt, 1955)
2411. Maas, Walter. Methoden der deutschen und englischen Industriefinanzierung in der Periode von 1914-1939. Diss. Münster, 1947. 315 pp.
2412. Milward, Alan S. "Arbeitspolitik und Produktivität in der deutschen Kriegswirtschaft unter vergleichendem Aspekt." in Kriegswirtschaft und Rüstung 1939-1945. Düsseldorf: Militär-geschichtliches Forschungsamt, 1977. pp. 73-91.
2413. Mommsen, Hans et al. Industrielles System und politische Entwicklung in der Weimarer Republik. Düsseldorf: Droste, 1974. 1017 pp.
2414. Morgenstern, Claus. Gewerkschaftspolitik und Produktivität der Arbeit im Deutschland der Nachkriegszeit. Diss. Berlin. Berlin: Klokow, 1928. 45 pp.
2415. Neebe, Reinhard. Grossindustrie, Staat und NSDAP 1930-1933. Göttingen: Vandenhoeck & Ruprecht, 1981. 314 pp.

2416. Petzina, Dietmar. "Hitler und die deutsche Industrie." Geschichte in Wissenschaft und Unterricht (1966), 482-91.
2417. Raphael, Gaston. L'industrie allemande. Sa récente évolution. Paris: Flammarion, 1928. 318 pp.
2418. Reimann, G. Patents for Hitler. London: Gollancz, 1945. 160 pp.
2419. Rostas, Laszlo. "Industrial Production, Productivity and Distribution in Britain, Germany and the United States, 1935-37." Economic Journal 53 (1943), 39-54.
2420. Schröter, Verena. Die deutsche Industrie auf dem Weltmarkt 1929 bis 1933. Diss. Hamburg. Frankfurt a. M.: Lang, 1984. 581 pp.
2421. Stegmann, Dirk. "Zum Verhältnis von Grossindustrie und Nationalsozialismus 1930-1933. Ein Beitrag zur Geschichte der sogenannten Machtergreifung." Archiv für Sozialgeschichte 13 (1973), 399-482.
2422. Turner, Henry A., Jr. "Hitler's Secret Pamphlet for Industrialists, 1927." Journal of Modern History 40 (1968), 348-74.
2423. Turner, Henry A., Jr. "The Ruhrlade. Secret Cabinet of Heavy Industry in the Weimar Republic." Central European History 3 (1970), 195-228.
2424. Warriner, Doreen. Combines and Rationalisation in Germany, 1924-1928. London: P. S. King, 1931. 226 pp.
2425. Weisbrod, Bernd. "Economic Power and Political Stability Reconsidered. Heavy Industry in Weimar Germany." Social History 4 (1979).
2426. Weisbrod, Bernd. Schwerindustrie in der Weimarer Republik. Interessenpolitik zwischen Stabilisierung und Krise. Wuppertal: Hammer, 1978. 552 pp.
2427. Wolffsohn, Michael. "Grossunternehmer und Politik in Deutschland. Der Nutzen der Arbeits-beschaffung der Jahre 1932/33 für die Schwer- und Chemieindustrie." Zeitschrift für Unternehmensgeschichte 22 (1977), 109-33.
2428. Wrede, Klaus M. Produktivität und Distribution im Lichte der deutschen gewerkschaftlichen Lehrmeinungen der Weimarer Epoche. 1918-1933. Berlin: Duncker & Humblot, 1960. 195 pp.

SEE ALSO: 1000, 1006, 3673, 3722, 5011, 5082.

GERMANY REDIVIDED--1945-1975

Bibliographic References

2429. Deutsches Industrieninstitut, Cologne. Veröffentlichungen des Deutschen Industrieninstituts. 1951-1961. Cologne: Deutscher Industrie-Verlag, 1961. 65 pp.
2430. Fischer, Alfred and Hans Radandt, eds. "Bibliographie selbständiger Schriften zur Geschichte der Fabriken und Werke, die nach 1945 im Gebiet der Deutschen Demokratischen Republik erschienen sind." Jahrbuch für Wirtschaftsgeschichte (1960), II, 355-402; (1961), I, 363-71; (1968), IV, 403-23; (1969), IV, 271-83.
2431. Huffschmid, Jörg. Bibliographie Konzentration und Konzentrations-Politik. 1960-1966. Berlin: Duncker & Humblot, 1967. 284 pp.

GERMANY REDIVIDED--1945-1975

2432. Backs, Albert. "Lohn-, Preis-und Produktivitätsniveau in Westdeutschland seit 1949." Wirtschaftswissenschaftliche Mitteilungen 15 (1962), 17-20.
2433. Claassen, Rolf E. Analyse der industriellen Produktivitätsstruktur in der Bundesrepublik Deutschland 1950-1959. Diss. Basel, 1962. Seligenstadt: Sprey, 1963. 108 pp.
2434. Krengel, Rolf. Die Kapitalproductivität von 21 Industriezweigen im Gebiet der Bundesrepublik Deutschland von 1950 bis 1975. Brussels: Commission of the European Communities, 1968. 133 pp. (French: Brussels, 1968)
2435. Mann, Golo. Die Industrie in der Bundesrepublik Deutschland nach 1945. Eine historische Betrachtung. Cologne: Bundesverband der Deutschen Industrie, 1976. 34 pp.
2436. Markmann, Heinz. "Lohn- und Produktivitätsvergleiche in den Industriebereichen seit 1949." Wirtschaftswissenschaftliche Mitteilungen 15 (1962), 39-43.

2437. Mertens, Dieter. "Veränderungen der industriellen Branchenstruktur in der Bundesrepublik 1950-1960." in Wandlungen der Wirtschaftsstruktur in der Bundesrepublik Deutschland. Berlin: Duncker & Humblot, 1962. pp. 439-68.
2438. Nieth, Evelyn. Industriestruktur und regionale Entwicklung. Eine theoretische und empirische Untersuchung der Bundesrepublik 1960-1972. Berlin: Duncker & Humblot, 1980. 239 pp.
2439. Panić, M., ed. The United Kingdom and West German Manufacturing Industry 1954-72. A Comparison of Structure and Performance. 5th ed. London: National Economic Development Office, 1976. 151 pp.
2440. Radandt, Hans. "Der Stand der Geschichte der Fabriken und Werke in der Deutschen Demokratischen Republik. Jahrbuch für Wirtschaftsgeschichte (1960), II, 153-99.
2441. Roesler, Jörg. Produktionswachstum und Effektivität in Industriezweigen der DDR 1950-1970. Berlin: Akademie, 1983. 312 pp.
2442. Schulz, Hans-Jürgen. "Zur Entwicklung und historischen Rolle des Produktionsaufgebots in der Industrie der DDR." Unsere Zeit 2 (1962), 264-83.
2443. Seidl, Helmut. "Die Periodisierung einzelner Betriebsgeschichten auf Grund der nationalen Periodisierung für die Zeit ab 1945." Jahrbuch für Wirtschaftsgeschichte (1966), IV, 154-83.
2444. Simon, Claude. "Productivité et expansion de l'industrie allemande." Economie & Statistique 5 (1969), 29-42.
2445. Sternberg, Fritz. Die zweite industrielle Revolution. Frankfurt a. M.: Union-Druckerei, 1956. 50 pp.
2446. Uebe, Wolfgang. Industriestruktur und Standort. Regionale Wachstumsunterschiede der Industriebeschäftigung in der Bundesrepublik Deutschland 1950-1962. Stuttgart: Kohlhammer, 1967. 131 pp.
2447. Uebe, Wolfgang. Die regionale Verteilung des industriellen Wachstums in der Bundesrepublik Deutschland 1950-1962. Diss. Basel, 1965. 131 pp.

SEE ALSO: 2059, 2819, 2980, 3798, 3804, 3830-31, 3836, 3845, 3867, 3908, 3930, 5105.

GERMAN REGIONS

Alsace-Lorraine

2448. Bergeron, Louis. "Kapital und Industrialisierung in Lothringen vom Ende des 18. bis zum Beginn des 20. Jahrhunderts." in Region und Industrialisierung. Studien zur Rolle der Region in der Wirtschaftsgeschichte der letzten zwei Jahrhunderte. Göttingen: Vandenhoeck & Ruprecht, 1980. pp. 129-141. (English summary.)

Baden-Württemberg

2449. Bittmann, Karl. Hausindustrie und Heimarbeit im Grossherzogtum Baden zu Anfang des XX. Jahrhunderts. Karlsruhe: Macklot, 1907. 1207 pp.
2450. Borscheid, Peter. Textilarbeiterschaft in der Industrialisierung. Soziale Lage und Mobilität in Württemberg (19. Jahrhundert). Stuttgart: Klett-Cotta, 1978. 584 pp.
2451. Borst, Otto. "Staat und Unternehmer in der Frühzeit der württembergischen Industrie." Tradition 11 (1966), 105-26.
2452. Bundschuh, Hans. Lohn- und Lebensverhältnisse der Arbeiter in der Industrie des Neckartals mit Beschränkung auf die standörtlich gebundene Industrie. Diss. Heidelberg, 1923. 101 pp.
2453. Dessauer, Lothar. Die Industrialisierung von Gross-Stuttgart. Diss. Tübingen, 1916. 205 pp.
2454. Dietsche, Richard. Die industrielle Entwicklung des Wiesentales bis zum Jahre 1870. Diss. Basel. Schopfheim: Uehlin, 1937. 101 pp.
2455. Fischer, Wolfram. "Ansätze zur Industrialisierung in Baden 1770-1870." VSWG 47 (1960), 186-231.
2456. Fischer, Wolfram. Der Staat und die Anfänge der Industrialisierung in Baden 1800-1850. Berlin: Duncker & Humblot, 1962. 401 pp.

2457. Gutzler, Heinz. Das Rheinauer Industrie- und Hafengebiet von 1873 bis 1914. Ein Beitrag zur Geschichte der Industrie und der Schiffahrt am mittleren Oberrhein. Heidelberg: Winter, 1961. 120 pp.
2458. Häussler, Otto. Die Industrialisierung der Stadt Feuerbach. Diss. Tübingen. Stuttgart: Kohlhammer, 1932. 150 pp.
2459. Hippel, Wolfgang von. "Industrieller Wandel im ländlichen Raum. Untersuchungen im Gebiet des mittleren Neckar 1850-1914." Archiv für Sozialgeschichte 19 (1979), 43-122. (English and French summaries)
2460. Hirschmann, Rudolf. Die Industrieentwicklung in Ulm seit dem Mittelalter. Diss. Cologne. Cologne-Kalk: Welzel, 1926. 78 pp.
2461. Kaeser, Robert. Die Industrialisierung des Oberamts Esslingen. Diss. Heidelberg, 1925. 147 pp.
2462. Kaiser, Wilhelm. "Die Anfänge der fabrikmässig organisierten Industrie in Baden." Zeitschrift für die Geschichte des Oberrheins 85 (1932-33), 612-35.
2463. Keller, Ursula. Die Entwicklung der Industrie in Heidelberg im Rahmen ihrer geographischen und industriepolitischen Voraussetzungen. Diss. Basel. Heidelberg: A. Grosch, 1961. 177 pp.
2464. Klaiber, Bernhard. Die geschichtliche Entwickelung der produktiven Kräfte im Raum Reutlingen. Diss. Tübingen. Tübingen: Becht, 1938. 112 pp.
2465. Klein, Ernst. "Die Anfänge der Industrialisierung Württembergs in der ersten Hälfte des 19. Jahrhunderts." in Raumordnung im 19. Jahrhundert. Hannover: Akademie für Raumforschung und Landesplanung, 1967. II, 83-137.
2466. Laufer, Rudolf. Industrie und Energiewirtschaft im Land Baden 1945-1952. Diss. Freiburg i. B., 1977. Freiburg i. B.: Alber, 1979. 411 pp.
2467. Maschke, Erich and Jürgen Sydow, eds. Zur Geschichte der Industrialisierung in den südwestdeutschen Städten. Sigmaringen: Thorbecke, 1977. 176 pp.
2468. Megerle, Klaus. "Der Beitrag Württembergs zur Industrialisierung Deutschlands." Zeitschrift für württembergische Landesgeschichte 34/35 (1975/76), 324-57.
2469. Megerle, Klaus. Württemberg im Industrialisierungsprozess Deutschlands: ein Beitrag zur regionalen Differenzierung der Industrialisierung. Stuttgart: Klett-Cotta, 1981. 274 pp.
2470. Mehmke, Rolf L. "Entstehung der Industrie und Unternehmertum in Württemberg." Deutsche Zeitschrift für Wirtschaftskunde 4 (1939), 56-68, 113-31.
2471. Metz, Rudolf. "Die Bedeutung von Bergbau und Eisenhüttenwesen als Wegbereiter für die Industrialisierung im Schwarzwald." in Bausteine zur geschichtlichen Landeskunde von Baden-Württemberg. Stuttgart: Kommission für Geschichtliche Landeskunde in Baden-Württemberg, 1979. pp. 381-405.
2472. Petto, W. "Zur Geschichte der Eisenindustrie im Schwärzwalder Hochwald und ihrer Unternehmerfamilien von ihren Anfängen bis 1870." Zeitschrift für Geschichte der Saargegend 17-18 (1969-70), 112-70.
2473. Plumpe, Gottfried. Die württembergische Eisenindustrie im 19. Jahrhundert: eine Fallstudie zur Geschichte der industriellen Revolution in Deutschland. Wiesbaden: Steiner, 1982. 473 pp.
2474. Reitz, Adolf. Werke und Köpfe. Aufstieg und Bedeutung der südwestdeutschen Industrie. Leistung und Auftrag. Reutlingen: Oertel & Spörer, 1959. 346 pp.
2475. Rücklin, Rudolf, ed. Pforzheim und seine Industrie. 2nd ed. Frankfurt a. M.: Mushake, 1952. 100 pp.
2476. Schaeble, Otto E. Die industrielle Entwicklung der Stadt Esslingen a. N. Diss. Tübingen, 1931. Rottenburg: Rottenburger Zeitung, 1931. 109 pp.
2477. Schmid, Walter. Der Industriebezirk Reutlingen-Tübingen. Eine wirtschaftsgeographische Untersuchung. Tübingen: Hopfer-Verlag, 1960. 109 pp.
2478. Seybold, Gerhard. Württembergs Industrie und Aussenhandel vom Ende der Napoleonischen Kriege bis zum Deutschen Zollverein. Stuttgart: Kohlhammer, 1974. 177 pp.
2479. Steudel, Hans. Geschichtliche Entwicklung der Maschinenindustrie in Württemberg bis zum Weltkrieg. Diss. Tübingen, 1923. 207 pp.
2480. Vischer, L. Die industrielle Entwicklung im Königreich Württemberg und das Wirken der Centralstelle für Gewerbe und Handel in ihren ersten 25 Jahren. Stuttgart: C. Grüninger, 1875. 639 pp.
2481. Will, Werner. Wirtschaftsgeschichtliche Studien zur industriellen Entwicklung des Wiesentals 1870-1933. Diss. Basel. Lörrach: Schahl, 1938. 142 pp.

2482. Winkel, Harald. "Zur Rolle der Kaufleute als Kapitalgeber bei der Industrialisierung des Rhein-Neckar-Raumes." in Wirtschaftskräfte und Wirtschaftswege. Festschrift für Hermann Kellenbenz. 3rd ed. Stuttgart: Klett-Cotta, 1978. pp. 431-48.

SEE ALSO: 1122, 3936, 5192-94.

Bavaria

2483. Eckardt, Günther. Industrie und Politik in Bayern 1900-1919. Der Bayerische Industriellen-Verband als Modell des Einflusses von Wirtschaftsverbänden. Berlin: Duncker & Humblot, 1976. 201 pp.
2484. Eheberg, Karl T. von. Die industrielle Entwicklung Bayerns seit 1800. Erlangen: F. Junge, 1897. 36 pp.
2485. Fischer, Ilse. Industrialisierung, sozialer Konflikt und politische Willensbildung in der Stadtgemeinde. Ein Beitrag zur Sozialgeschichte Augsburgs. 1840-1914. Augsburg: Mühlberger, 1977. 413 pp.
2486. Geer, Johann S. "Die Industrialiserung des Nürnberger Raumes." Frankenland 12 (1960), 23-28.
2487. Glaser, Hermann et al. Industriekultur in Nürnberg. Munich: C. H. Beck, 1980. 375 pp.
2488. Grassmann, Josef. Die Entwicklung der Augsburger Industrie im 19. Jahrhundert. Augsburg: Gebrüder Reichel, 1894. 273 pp.
2489. Grimm, Claus, ed. Aufbruch ins Industrie-Zeitalter. 3 vols. Munich: Oldenbourg, 1985.
2490. Die Industrialisierungspolitik der Bayerischen Staatsregierung in den Jahren 1954-1970. Munich: Bayerisches Staatsministerium für Wirtschaft und Verkehr, 1973. 48 pp.
2491. Kuhlo, Alfred, ed. Geschichte der bayerischen Industrie. Munich: Bayerische Druck & Verlags-Anstalt, 1926. 527 pp.
2492. Osel, Heinrich. Zur Entwicklung von Bayerns Industrie und Handel. Munich: Huber, 1917. 94 pp.
2493. Paula, Herbert. "Zur Entwicklung der Beschäftigten und der Produktivität 1961 bis 1968." Bayern in Zahlen. Monatshefte des Bayerischen Statistischen Landesamts 25 (1971), 19-25.
2494. Pfarr, Karlheinz. Die industrielle Standortsdynamik im Raum von Nürnberg-Fürth-Erlangen nach dem Zweiten Weltkrieg. Diss. Nuremberg, 1956. 149 pp.
2495. Reismann, Otto. Der Bayerische Industriellenverband, seine Entwicklung und Wirtschaftspolitik. Diss. Erlangen, 1924. 170 pp.
2496. Schreyer, Klaus. Bayern, ein Industriestaat. Die importierte Industrialiserung. Das wirtschaftliche Wachstum nach 1945 als Ordnungs- und Strukturproblem. Diss. Erlangen-Nuremberg. Munich: Olzog, 1969. 404 pp.
2497. Schwarz, Gerard. "Nahrungsstand" und "erzwungener Gesellenstand." Mentalité und Strukturwandel des bayerischen Handwerks im Industrialisierungsprozess um 1860. Berlin: Duncker & Humblot, 1974. 266 pp.
2498. Slawinger, Gerhard. Die Manufaktur in Kurbayern. Die Anfänge der grossgewerblichen Entwicklung in der Übergangsepoche vom Merkantilismus zum Liberalismus 1740-1833. Stuttgart: Fischer, 1966. 359 pp.
2499. Wiessner, Paul. Die Anfänge der Nürnberger Fabrikindustrie. Diss. Frankfurt a. M., 1928. Langendreer: Pöppinghaus, 1929. 283 pp.
2500. Zorn, Wolfgang. "Probleme der Industrialisierung Oberfrankens im 19. Jahrhundert." Jahrbuch für fränkische Landesforschung 29 (1969), 295-310.
2501. Zorn, Wolfgang. "Zu den Anfängen der Industrialisierung Augsburgs im 19. Jahrhundert." VSWG 38 (1949), 155-68.

SEE ALSO: 1152, 1158, 3957, 3986, 3991.

Berlin

2502. Baar, Lothar. Die Berliner Industrie in der industriellen Revolution. Berlin: Akademie, 1966. 267 pp.

2503. Baar, Lothar. "Probleme der industriellen Revolution in grosstädtischen Industriezentren. Das Berliner Beispiel." in Wirtschafts- und sozialgeschichtliche Probleme der frühen Industrialisierung. Berlin: Friedrich-Meinecke-Institut der Freien Universität, 1968. pp. 529-42.

2504. Bergmann, Jürgen. Das Berliner Handwerk in den Frühphasen der Industrialisierung. Berlin: Colloquium, 1973. 401 pp.

2505. Borgmann, Maria. Betriebsführung, Arbeitsbedingungen und die soziale Frage. Eine Untersuchung zur Arbeiter- und Unternehmergeschichte in der Berliner Maschinenindustrie zwischen 1870 und 1914 unter besonderer Berücksichtigung der Grossbetriebe. Frankfurt a. M.: Lang, 1981. 324 pp.

2506. Büsch, Otto. "Festungsstadt und Industrie. Zur Geschichte von Spandau und Siemensstadt im Zeitalter der Industrialisierung." Jahrbuch für Geschichte Mittel- und Ostdeutschlands 20 (1971), 161-82.

2507. Büsch, Otto, ed. Untersuchungen zur Geschichte der frühen Industrialisierung im Wirtschaftsraum Berlin-Brandenburg. Berlin: Colloquium, 1971. 660 pp.

2508. Dietrich, Richard. "Probleme stadtgeschichtlicher Untersuchungen im Zeitalter der Industrialisierung am Beispiel Berlins." Jahrbuch für die Geschichte Mittel- und Ostdeutschlands 16/17 (1968), 169-209.

2509. Lündgreen, Peter. "Schulbildung und Frühindustrialisierung in Berlin/Preussen. Eine Einführung in den historischen und systematischen Zusammenhang von Schule und Wirtschaft." in O. Büsch, ed. Untersuchungen zur Geschichte der frühen Industrialisierung vornehmlich im Wirtschaftsraum Berlin/Brandenburg. Berlin: Brandenburg, 1971. pp. 562-610.

2510. Matschess, Conrad. Die Berliner Industrie, einst und jetzt. Eine Studie zur Berliner Industriegeschichte. Berlin: A. W. Schade, 1906. 29 pp.

2511. Schäfer, Hans-August. Die Entwicklung der Berliner Maschinenindustrie von ihren Anfängen bis zum Jahre 1879. Thesis Freie Universität Berlin, 1961.

2512. Thienel, Ingrid. Städtewachstum im Industrialisierungsprozess des 19. Jahrhunderts. Das Berliner Beispiel. Berlin: de Gruyter, 1973. 504 pp.

2513. Weiher, Sigfrid von. Berlins Weg zur Elektropolis. Technik- und Industriegeschichte an der Spree. Berlin: Stapp, 1974. 206 pp.

2514. Wiedfeldt, Otto. Statistische Studien zur Entwickelungsgeschichte der Berliner Industrie von 1720 bis 1890. Leipzig: Duncker & Humblot, 1898. 411 pp.

SEE ALSO: 2517.

Brandenburg

2515. Büsch, Otto. Industrialisierung und Gewerbe im Raum Berlin/Brandenburg. 2nd ed. 2 vols. Berlin: Colloquium, 1971-77.

2516. Koch, Käthe. Die Wandlungen der Wirtschaftsordunung im 18. und 19. Jahrhundert, dargestellt an der Industrialisierung von Luckenwalde. Diss. Freiburg i. B., 1943. 171 pp.

2517. Pfannschmidt, Martin. Die Industriesiedlung in Berlin und in der Mark Brandenburg. Ihre Entwicklung vom Absolutismus bis zur Gegenwart und ihre zukünftigen Entwicklungsmöglichkeiten. Stuttgart: Kohlhammer, 1937. 128 pp.

SEE ALSO: 1837.

East Prussia

2518. "Die Entwicklung der ostpreussischen Industrie bis zum 1. Weltkrieg." Der redliche Ostpreusse 17 (1966), 101-03.

2519. Henning, Friedrich-Wilhelm. "Mögliche Industrialisierungsansätze in Ostpreussen an der Schwelle zum Industrialisierungszeitalter." Preussenland 15 (1977), 38-44.

2520. Liedke, Fritz. Die Elbinger Industrie von 1772 bis zur Gründung der Schichauwerft im Jahre 1837. Diss. Konigsberg, 1931. Elbing: Wernich, 1932. 68 pp.

2521. Stattmiller, Siegfried. Fortschritte in der Industrialisierung Ostpreussens seit 1933. Diss. Cologne, 1941. Cologne: Orthen, 1941. 99 pp.

Eastern Germany

2522. Fuchs, Konrad. "Die industriellen Zusammenhänge der preussischen West- und Ostprovinzen im 18. und 19. Jahrhundert." Nassauische Annalen 77 (1966), 121-33.
2523. Zauberman, Alfred. Industrial Progress in Poland, Czechoslovakia and East Germany, 1937-1962. London: Oxford University Press, 1964. 352 pp.

SEE ALSO: 1859, 4006-07.

Hansa Cities

2524. Herms, Doris. Die Anfänge der bremischen Industrie. Vom 17. Jahrhundert bis zum Zollanschluss (1888). Bremen: C. Schünemann, 1952. 164 pp.
2525. Klinsmann, Luise. Die Industrialisierung Lübecks. Diss. Kiel, 1922; rpt. Lübeck: Schmidt-Römhild, 1984. 201 pp.

Hesse

2526. Lindenthal, Bernd K. Das Wetzlarer Gründungsjahrzehnt. Die Anfänge der Industrialisierung in Stadt und Kreis Wetzlar, 1870-1879. Zum 75-jährigen Jubiläum des Wetzlarer Geschichtsvereins. Wetzlar: Lindenthal, 1979. 124 pp.
2527. Möker, Ulrich. Nordhessen im Zeitalter der industriellen Revolution. Cologne: Böhlau, 1977. 268 pp.
2528. Petran, Helmut. Mühlen, Fabriken und Menschen am Ursebach: ein Beitrag zur Industrie- und Sozialgeschichte im Frankfurter Raum seit 1850. Frankfurt a. M.: Kramer, 1980. 308 pp.
2529. Sangmeister, Hartmut. Die wirtschaftliche Entwicklung eines Randgebietes im Zeitalter der Industrialisierung. (Dargestellt am Beispiel des südhessischen Odenwaldes 1871-1913.) Ein Beitrag zur Theorie und Praxis industrialisierungsgeschichtlicher Regionalforschung. Diss. Heidelberg, 1976. Wiesenbach: Volkmann, 1976. 305 pp.
2530. Schremmer, Eckart. "Der südhessische Odenwald. Ein Beispiel für ein wirtschaftliches Randgebiet während der Zeit der Industrialisierung, 1871-1913." Zeitschrift für Agrargeschichte und Agrarsoziologie 27 (1979), 1-18.
2531. Wulff, Fritz. Das untere und mittlere Lahngebiet. Strukturwandlungen seiner Industrie- und Bergwirtschaft seit dem Ausgang des Mittelalters. Diss. Bonn, 1962. 261 pp.

SEE ALSO: 4065, 5273-74.

Lower Saxony

2532. Aschenbrenner, Karl. Die Hannoversche Maschinenindustrie seit ihrer Entstehung im Anfang der 30er Jahre bis zum Jahre 1874. Diss. Göttingen, 1921. 60 pp.
2533. Buschmann, Walter. Linden. Geschichte einer Industriestadt im 19. Jahrhundert. Hildesheim: A. Lax, 1981. 600 pp.
2534. Stavenhagen, Gerhard and Karl-Heinz Schmidt. "Die Industrialisierung und ihre handwerksfördernden Kräfte in der zweiten Hälfte des 19. Jahrhunderts, dargestellt am Beispiel des Herzogtums Braunschweig." Neues Archiv für Niedersachsen 19- (1970).
2535. Wölbern, Hinrich. Das Land Oldenburg als Produktionsgebiet, unter Berücksichtigung seiner historischen Entwicklung. Diss. Cologne. Würzburg: Mayr, 1938. 97 pp.

SEE ALSO: 1239.

North Rhine-Westphalia

2536. Adelmann, Gerhard. "Die Beziehungen zwischen Arbeitgeber und Arbeitnehmer in der Ruhrindustrie vor 1914." Jahrbücher für Nationalökonomie und Statistik 175 (1963), 412-27.

2537. Adelmann, Gerhard. "Die Stadt Bielefeld als Zentrum fabrikindustrieller Gründungen nach 1850." in Festschrift Edith Ennen. Bonn: Röhrscheid, 1972. pp. 884-94.

2538. Beau, Horst. Das Leistungswissen des frühindustriellen Unternehmertums in Rheinland und Westfalen. Cologne: Rheinisch-westfälisches Wirtschaftsarchiv, 1959. 79 pp.

2539. Becker, Anton. Die Stolberger Messingindustrie und ihre Entwicklung. Munich: Duncker & Humblot, 1913. 83 pp.

2540. Becker, Heinrich. Rheine. Analyse einer Industriestadt des münsterländischen Textilgebietes. Diss. Münster, 1961. 146 pp.

2541. Beckers, Hubertus. Entwicklungsgeschichte der Industrieunternehmen in Düsseldorf, 1815-1914. Diss. Cologne,1958. 147 pp.

2542. Berg, Volker vom. Bildungsstruktur und industrieller Fortschritt. Essen (Ruhr) im 19. Jahrhundert. Stuttgart: Klett-Cotta, 1979. 244 pp.

2543. Beutin, Ludwig. Geschichte der südwestfälischen Industrie- und Handelskammer zu Hagen und ihrer Wirtschaftslandschaft. Hagen: Linnepe, 1955. 334 pp.

2544. Bochum, Ulrich. Industrie und Region: ökonomischer und sozialer Strukturwandel im Ruhrgebiet. Frankfurt a. M.: Lang, 1984. 340 pp.

2545. Bormann, Otto-Albert. Zur Entstehung und Entwicklung der metallverarbeitenden Industrie im Mönchen Gladbacher Industriebezirk. Ein Beitrag zur rheinischen Wirtschaftsgeschichte. Mönchen Gladbach: Boltze, 1925. 77 pp.

2546. Brepohl, Wilhelm. Bevölkerung und Siedlung im Raum Wulfen. Entwicklung. Strukturen und Tendenzen 1824 bis 1961. Essen: Siedlungsverband Ruhrkohlenbezirk, 1967. 212 pp.

2547. Brepohl, Wilhelm. Industrievolk im Wandel von der agraren zur industriellen Daseinsform dargestellt am Ruhrgebiet. Tübingen: Mohr, 1957. 400 pp.

2548. Bruckner, Clemens. Die wirtschaftsgeschichtlichen und standortstheoretischen Grundlagen der industriellen Tätigkeit innerhalb des Regierungsbezirks Aachen. Aachen: La Ruelle, 1924. 53 pp.

2549. Crew, David F. Industry and Community. The Social History of a German Town [Bochum]. 1860-1914. Diss. Cornell University, 1975. 425 pp.

2550. Croon, Helmuth. "Die Einwirkungen der Industrialisierung auf die gesellschaftliche Schichtung der Bevölkerung im rheinisch-westfälischen Industriegebiet." Rheinische Vierteljahrsblätter 20 (1955), 301-16.

2551. Dascher, Ottfried et al., eds. Der Raum Dortmund. Entwicklung einer Industrielandschaft. Eine Dokumentation. Dortmund: Stadtarchiv, 1971. 100 pp.

2552. Decker, Franz. Die betriebliche Sozialordnung der Dürener Industrie im 19. Jahrhundert. Diss. Cologne. Cologne: Rhein-Westfälisches Wirtschaftsarchiv, 1965. 245 pp.

2553. Dieterle, Paul. Städtische Industrien und Industriebevölkerung im Landkreise Bielefeld. Diss. Münster. Bielefeld: Siedhoff, 1913. 106 pp.

2554. Engels, Wilhelm and Paul Legers. Aus der Geschichte Remscheider und Bergischer Werkzeug- und Eisenindustrie. 2 vols. Remscheid: Bergischer Fabrikanten-Verein, 1928.

2555. Feldenkirchen, Wilfried. Die Eisen- und Stahlindustrie des Ruhrgebiets 1879-1914: Wachstum. Finanzierung und Struktur ihrer Grossunternehmen. Wiesbaden: Steiner, 1982. 610 pp.

2556. Fischer, Wolfram. Die Bedeutung der preussischen Bergrechtsreform (1851-1865) für den industriellen Ausbau des Ruhrgebiets. Dortmund: Ardey, 1961. 28 pp.

2557. Frie, Thea. Die Industrialisierung der Stadt Münster in Westfalen im 19. Jahrhundert. (Eine wirtschaftshistorische Studie.) Diss. Cologne, 1943. 173 pp.

2558. Gladen, Albin. Der Kreis Tecklenburg an der Schwelle des Zeitalters der Industrialisierung. Diss. Bochum, 1968. Münster i. W.: Aschendorff, 1970. 218 pp.

2559. Günther, Wilhelm. "Zur Geschichte der Eisenindustrie in der Nordeifel." Rheinische Vierteljahrsblätter 30 (1965), 309-33.

2560. Helmrich, Wilhelm, ed. Die Errichtung und Ansiedlung neuer Industriebetriebe im Lande Nordrhein-Westfalen, in der Zeit von Mitte 1945 bis Sommer 1948. Düsseldorf: Gesellschaft für Buchdruckerei und Verlag, 1949. 63 pp.

2561. Herker, Hellmuth, ed. Hundertfünfundzwanzig Jahre Niederrheinische Industrie- und Handelskammer Duisburg-Wesel. Duisburg-Ruhrort: Brendow, 1956. 210 pp.

2562. Herrmann, Walther. Die Industrialisierung des Verkehrs (dargestellt an der mittelrheinischen Wirtschaftsentfaltung). Jena: Fischer, 1940. 74 pp.
2563. Hinkers, Hans-Willi. Die geschichtliche Entwicklung der Dortmunder Schwerindustrie seit der Mitte des 19. Jahrhunderts. Diss. Cologne. Dortmund: Neumetzler, 1925. 78 pp.
2564. Hinz, Wolfgang. Die Veränderung der Sozialstruktur beim Übergang von der agraren zur industriellen Daseinsform, dargestellt am Beispiel der vestischen Gemeinde Gladbeck. Diss. Cologne, 1961. 158 pp.
2565. Hocker, Nicolaus. Die Grossindustrie Rheinlandes und Westfalens, ihre Geographie, Geschichte, Produktion und Statistik. Leipzig: Quandt & Händel, 1867. 466 pp.
2566. Hostert, Walter. Die Entwicklung der Lüdenscheider Industrie vornehmlich im 19. Jahrhundert. Vom Ende des 18. Jahrhunderts bis zum Ausbruch des 1. Weltkrieges. Lüdenscheid: Beucker, 1960. 204 pp.
2567. Hoth, Wolfgang. "Die ersten Dampfmaschinen im Bergischen Land. Ein Kapitel rheinischer Industriegeschichte." Scripta Mercaturae 11 (1977), 73-97. (English and French summaries)
2568. Hoth, Wolfgang. Die Industrialiserung einer rheinischen Gewerbestadt, dargestellt am Beispiel Wuppertal. Diss. Cologne. Cologne: Rheinisch-Westfälisches Wirtschaftsarchiv, 1975. 283 pp.
2569. Jankowski, Manfred D. Public Policy in Industrial Growth. The Case of Ruhr Mining Region, 1776-1865. New York: Arno Press, 1977. 300 pp.
2570. Kallen, Hermann-Josef. Die Neusser Industrien und ihre Unternehmer von der Mitte des 19. Jahrhunderts bis zum Beginn des Ersten Weltkrieges. Diss. Tübingen, 1973. 261 pp.
2571. Kelleter, Heinrich. Geschichte der Familie J. A. Henckels in Verbindung mit einer Geschichte der Solinger Industrie. Solingen: Henckels, 1924. 192 pp.
2572. Kermann, Joachim. Die Manufakturen im Rheinland 1750-1853. Diss. Bonn, 1969. Bonn: Röhrscheid, 1972. 745 pp.
2573. Kisch, Herbert. Die hausindustriellen Textilgewerbe am Niederrhein vor der industriellen Revolution: von der ursprünglichen zur kapitalistischen Akkumulation. Göttingen: Vandenhoeck & Ruprecht, 1981. 373 pp.
2574. Köllmann, Wolfgang, ed. Industrie- und Handelskammer Wuppertal. 1831-1956. Festschrift zum 125-jährigen Jubiläum am 17.1.1956. Wuppertal-Elberfeld: Lucas, 1956. 305 pp.
2575. Loose, Rainer. Eisengewinnung am Donnersberg: Studien zur Bevölkerung, Wirtschaft und Agrarsozialstruktur eines historischen Montanreviers 1800-1850. Winnweiler: Giloi, 1980. 105 pp.
2576. McCreary, Eugene C. Essen 1860-1914. A Case Study of the Impact of Industrialization on German Community Life. Diss. Yale University, 1964. 290 pp.
2577. Martin, Paul C. "Monetäre Probleme der Frühindustrialisierung am Beispiel der Rheinprovinz (1816-1848)." Jahrbücher für Nationalökonomie und Statistik 181 (1967), 117-50.
2578. Metzelder, Hans-Alwin. Der Wittener Steinkohlenbergbau im Umbruch zur Grossindustrie 1830-1860. Diss. Münster, 1964. 331 pp.
2579. Meyer, Friedrich A. Von der Ruhr über den Rhein. Rheinhausens Schwerindustrie. Rheinhausen: Schmidt, 1966. 370 pp.
2580. Muhlfriedel, Wolfgang. "Die rheinisch-westfälische Montanindustrie und Nationalgeschichte an der Wende vom 19. zum 20. Jahrhundert" in Beiträge zur Geschichte des Bergbaus, Hüttenwesens und der Montanwissenschaft. Leipzig: Deutscher Verlag für Grundstoffindustrie, 1964. pp. 55-72.
2581. Padberg, Ernst. Die industrielle Entwicklung der Stadt Hamm (Westfalen). Diss. Frankfurt a. M., 1929. Bochum-Langendreer: Poppinghaus, 1930. 97 pp.
2582. Pfläging, Kurt. Die Wiege des Ruhrkohlenbergbaus: die Geschichte der Zechen im südlichen Ruhrgebiet. Essen: Glückauf, 1980. 255 pp.
2583. Pierenkemper, Toni. "Regionale Differenzierung im östlichen Ruhrgebiet, 1850-1887, dargestellt am Beispiel der Einführung der Dampfkraft." in Industrialisierung und Raum. Studien zur regionalen Differenzierung im Deutschland des 19. Jahrhunderts. Stuttgart: Klett-Cotta, 1979. pp. 165-91. (English summary)
2584. Pierenkemper, Toni. Die westfälischen Schwerindustriellen 1852-1913. Soziale Merkmale und unternehmerischer Erfolg. Göttingen: Vandenhoeck & Ruprecht, 1979. 268 pp.
2585. Pietsch, Hartmut. Industrialisierung und soziale Frage in Duisburg. Duisburg: Braun, 1982. 92 pp.

2586. Pogge von Strandmann, Hartmut. "Entwicklungsstrukturen der Grossindustrie im Ruhrgebiet." in Politik und Gesellschaft im Ruhrgebiet. Beiträge zur regionalen Politikforschung. Königstein, Ts.: Hain/KNO, 1979. pp. 142-61.

2587. Rinne, Will. Ruhrgeist und Ruhrstahl. 125 Jahre eisenschaffendes Volk an Ruhr und Rhein. Berlin: Verlag für Sozialpolitik, Wirtschaft und Statistik, 1941. 244 pp.

2588. Röttgermann, Heinz. Die Entwicklung der Industrie im Wirtschaftsraum Menden (Sauerland) und ihre Probleme seit Beginn des 19. Jahrhunderts. Diss. Cologne. Menden: Riedel, 1939. 212 pp.

2589. Schaumann, Ralf. Technik und technischer Fortschritt im Industrialisierungsprozess. Bonn: Röhrscheid, 1977. 555 pp.

2590. Schmidt, Hermann T. "Belegschaftsbildung im Ruhrgebiet im Zeichen der Industrialisierung." Tradition 2 (1957), 265-73.

2591. Schmidt, Hermann T. Brühl. Eine wirtschafts- und sozialgeographische Untersuchung unter besonderer Berücksichtigung des Strukturwandels nach dem Erlöschen der Braunkohlenindustrie. 2nd ed. Diss. Cologne, 1962. Forsbach: H. Schmidt, 1963. 211 pp.

2592. Schneider, Wolf. Essen. Das Abenteuer einer Stadt. Düsseldorf: Econ-Verlag, 1963. 384 pp.

2593. Scholl, Lars U. Ingenieure in der Frühindustrialisierung. Staatliche und Private Techniker im Königreich Hannover und an der Ruhr (1815-1873). Göttingen: Vandenhoeck & Ruprecht, 1978. 482 pp.

2594. Schultz, Eduard. Die Aachener Maschinenindustrie in ihrer Entwicklung von der Gründung des Deutschen Reiches 1871 bis zum Ausbruch des Weltkrieges 1914. Diss. Cologne, 1924. 148 pp.

2595. Schumacher, Martin. "Zweckbau und Industrieschloss: Fabrikbauten der rheinisch-westfälischen Textilindustrie vor der Gründerzeit." Tradition 15 (1970), 1-48.

2596. Seeling, Hans. "Die belgischen Anfänge der Eisen- und Stahlindustrie in Düsseldorf zwischen 1850 und 1860. Eine industriegeschichtliche Studie." Düsseldorfer Jahrbuch 49 (1959), 210-40.

2597. Stein, Helmut. Die industrielle Entwicklung der Stadt Wermelskirchen seit Anfang des neunzehnten Jahrhunderts. Diss. Cologne. Düsseldorf: Nolte, 1939. 82 pp.

2598. Thun, Alphons. Die Industrie am Niederrhein und ihre Arbeiter. 2 vols. Leipzig: Duncker & Humblot, 1879.

2599. Tilly, Richard H. Die Industrialisierung des Ruhrgebiets und das Problem der Kapitalmobilisierung. Dortmund: Gesellschaft für westfälische Wirtschaftsgeschichte, 1969. 19 pp.

2600. Treue, Wilhelm. "Grundzüge einer Geschichte der wirtschaftlichen Entwicklung des Ruhrgebietes im Industriezeitalter." Tradition 13 (1968), 273-81.

2601. Troitzsch, Ulrich. "Belgien als Vermittler technischer Neuerungen beim Aufbau der eisenschaffenden Industrie im Ruhrgebiet um 1850." Technikgeschichte 39 (1972), 142-58.

2602. Watanabe, Hisashi. "From Werkstatt to Fabrik." The Kyoto University Economic Review 45 (1975), 23-42.

2603. Weber, Wolfhard. "Die Schiffbarmachung der Ruhr und die Industrialisierung im Ruhrgebiet." in Wirtschaftliches Wachstum. Energie und Verkehr vom Mittelalter bis ins 19. Jahrhundert. Bericht über die 6. Arbeitstagung der Gesellschaft für Sozial- und Wirtschaftsgeschichte. Stuttgart: Fischer, 1978. pp. 95-116.

2604. Weisbrod, Bernd. "'Wirtschaftsraum' und 'Geschichtslandschaft:' Ruhrgebiet und Schwerindustrie in den zwanziger Jahren." Rheinische Vierteljahrsblätter 45 (1981), 183-200.

2605. Wennig, Wolfgang. Geschichte der Hildener Industrie von den Anfängen gewerblicher Tätigkeit bis zum Jahre 1900. Hilden: Stadtarchiv, 1974. 287 pp.

2606. Wessel, Horst A. Die Entwicklung des elektrischen Nachrichtenwesens in Deutschland und die rheinische Industrie: von den Anfängen bis zum Ausbruch des Ersten Weltkrieges. Diss. Bonn. 1979. Wiesbaden: Steiner, 1983. 1097 pp.

2607. Wiel, Paul. Agglomerations-und Dezentralisationstendenzen der nordrhein-westfälischen Wirtschaft seit der Vorkriegszeit. Cologne: Westdeutscher Verlag, 1962. 72 pp.

2608. Zunkel, Friedrich. "Beamtenschaft und Unternehmertum beim Aufbau der Ruhrindustrie 1849-1880." Tradition 9 (1964), 261-77.

2609. Zunkel, Friedrich. "Die Rolle der Bergbaubürokratie beim industriellen Ausbau des Ruhrgebietes, 1815-1848." in J. A. Ritter, ed. Entstehung und Wandel der modernen Gesellschaft. Festschrift für Hans Rosenberg. Berlin: de Gruyter, 1970. pp. 130-47.

SEE ALSO: 1256, 1270, 1281, 1283, 2642, 2644-45, 4090, 4096, 4106, 4127, 5303, 5328.

Pomerania

2610. Langerstein, Julius. Die Entvölkerung des platten Landes in Pommern von 1890 bis 1905 und ihre Ursachen. Diss. Greifwald. Greifswald: Adler, 1912. 63 pp.

Rhineland Palatinate

2611. Eberhardt, Otto. Die industrielle Entwicklung der Stadt Worms. Diss. Heidelberg, 1922. 179 pp.
2612. Freitag, Willy. "Die Entwicklung der Kaiserslauterer Industrie von 1918-1956." Jahrbuch zur Geschichte von Stadt und Landkreis Kaiserslautern (1963-64), 83-121.
2613. Kube, Helga. Die Industrieansiedlung in Ludwigshafen am Rhein bis 1892. Stuttgart: P. Illg, 1962. 247 pp.
2614. Munzinger, Albert. Die Entwicklung der Industrie von Kaiserslautern. Kaiserslautern: Kayser, 1921. 120 pp.

Saarland

2615. Hasslacher, F. Anton, ed. Literatur über das Industriegebiet an der Saar. Im Auftrage der Königlichen Bergwerks-Direktion zu Saarbrücken. Saarbrücken: Klingsbeil, 1879. 176 pp.
2616. Kellenbenz, Hermann. "Der Staat als Unternehmer im saarländischen Steinkohlenbergbau 1750-1850." VSWG 57 (1970), 323-49.
2617. Latz, Rolf E. Die saarländische Schwerindustrie und ihre Nachbarreviere, 1878-1938. Saarbrücken: Saarbrücker Drucke, 1985. 253 pp.

Saxony

2618. Bein, Louis. Die Industrie des sächsischen Voigtlandes. Wirthschaftsgeschichtliche Studie. 2 vols. Leipzig: Duncker & Humblot, 1884.
2619. Blaschke, Karlheinz. "Industrialisierung und Bevölkerung in Sachsen im Zeitraum von 1850 bis 1890." in Raumordnung im 19. Jahrhundert. Hannover: Akademie für Raumforschung und Landesplanung, 1965. I, 69-95.
2620. Buttler, Alfred. Die Textilindustrie in Crimmitschau und die soziale Lage ihrer Arbeiter. Diss. Jena, 1921. 104 pp.
2621. Forberger, Rudolf. Die Industrielle Revolution in Sachsen, 1800-1861. 2 vols. Berlin: Akademie, 1982.
2622. Forberger, Rudolf. "Probleme der sächsischen Industrie- und Hüttengeschichte." Blätter für deutsche Landesgeschichte 101 (1965), 147-58.
2623. Forberger, Rudolf. "Zur Aufnahme der maschinellen Fertigung durch sächsische Manufakturen." Jahrbuch für Wirtschaftsgeschichte (1960), I, 225-98.
2624. Forberger, Rudolf. "Zur Wandlung der gewerblichen Betriebsweise Sachsens in der 1. Hälfte des 19. Jahrhunderts. Der Übergang von der Manufaktur zur Fabrik im Textilgewerbe." in Probleme der Ökonomie und Politik in den Beziehungen zwischen Ost- und Westeuropa vom 17. Jahrhundert bis zur Gegenwart. Berlin: Kommission der Historiker der DDR und CSR, 1960. pp. 125-37.
2625. Fuhlrott, Johannes. Die wirtschaftliche Entwicklung der Maschinenbauindustrie in Magdeburg unter besonder Berücksichtigung der Herkunft der Arbeiterschaft. Diss. Leipzig, 1923. 156 pp.
2626. Die Grossindustrie des Königreiches Sachsen im Wort und Bild. Eine Ehrengabe für Seine Majestät König Albert von Sachsen. 2 vols. Leipzig: Eckert & Pflug, 1892-93.
2627. Höhne, Ernst. Die Entwicklung der anhaltischen Maschinen-Industrie. (Eine wirtschafts-geschichtliche Monographie.) Diss. Rostock, 1927. Köthen-Anhalt: Greiner, 1928. 163 pp.
2628. März, Johannes. "Die Bedeutung des Unternehmerstandes für den industriellen Fortschritt in Sachsen. Ein Beitrag zur Geschichte der sächsischen Industrie." in Volkswirtschaftliche und wirtschaftsgeschichtliche Abhandlungen. Wilhelm Stieda als Festgruss zur 60sten Wiederkehr seines Geburtstages dargebracht. Leipzig: Veit, 1912. pp. 276-306.

2629. Miethke, Franz. Die Organisation der sächsischen Industrie in Vergangenheit und Gegenwart. Leipzig: Rossberg, 1919. 63 pp.
2630. Pönicke, Herbert. "Die Geschichte der Textilgewerbe der Stadt Reichenbach im Vogtland im Zeitalter der industriellen Revolution." Hamburger Mittel- und Ostdeutsche Forschung 4 (1963), 268-82.
2631. Pönicke, Herbert. Sachsens Entwicklung zum Industriestaate (1830-1871). Dresden: Volkmann, 1934. 97 pp.

SEE ALSO: 1354, 1926, 4142.

Schleswig-Holstein

2632. Haase, Nicolai. Das Aufkommen des gewerblichen Grossbetriebes in Schleswig-Holstein (bis zum Jahre 1845). Kiel: Gesellschaft für Schleswig-Holsteinische Geschichte, 1925. 328 pp.

Silesia

2633. Dlugoborski, Waclaw. "Industrialisierung und 'Nationale Frage' in Oberschlesien mit besonderer Berücksichtigung der Rolle der Migration von Arbeitskräften." in Modernisierung und nationale Gesellschaft im ausgehenden 18. und im 19. Jahrhundert. Berlin: Zentrum für Kontinentale Agrar- und Wirtschaftsforschung, 1979. pp. 193-230.
2634. Engelsing, Rolf. "Schlesische Leinenindustrie und Hanseatischer Überseehandel im 19. Jahrhundert." Jahrbuch der Schlesischen Friederich-Wilhelms-Universität zu Breslau 4 (1959), 207-27.
2635. Felsch, Gustav. Die Wirtschaftpolitik des Preussischen Staates bei der Gründung der oberschlesischen Kohlen- und Eisenindustrie (1741 bis 1871). Diss. Würzburg. Berlin: Ernst, 1919. 20 pp.
2636. Fuchs, Konrad. "Die Bismarckhütte in Oberschlesien. Ein Beitrag zur oberschlesischen Industriegeschichte in den achtziger Jahren des 19. Jahrhunderts." Tradition 15 (1970), 255-72.
2637. Fuchs, Konrad. Schlesiens Industrie. Eine historische Skizze. Munich: Delp, 1968. 61 pp.
2638. Fuchs, Konrad. "Wilhelm Kollemann und seine Bedeutung für die oberschlesische Eisen- und Blechindustrie 1870-1908." Zeitschrift für Ostforschung 25 (1976), 276-91.
2639. Fuchs, Konrad. "Zur Lage der Industrie West- und Ost-Oberschlesiens 1919-1939. Scripta Mercaturae 10 (1976), 53-74. (French and English summaries)
2640. Holtze, R. Die oberschlesische Industrie. Eine historisch-statistische Skizze. Beuthen: s.n., 1890.
2641. Hyckel, Georg. "Die Industrieanlagen der Herrschaft Ratibor (Nach dem Etat von 1823)." Jahrbuch der Schlesischen Friedrich-Wilhelms-Universität zu Breslau 10 (1965), 138-49.
2642. Kisch, Herbert. "The Textile Industries in Silesia and the Rhineland. A Comparative Study in Industrialisation." Journal of Economic History 19 (1959), 541-64.
2643. Pelick, Alfons. "Hegenscheidt und Caro. Zur Geschichte der beiden Unternehmergruppen im oberschlesischen Industrierevier." Tradition 8 (1963), 172-92.
2644. Pierenkemper, Toni. "Entrepreneurs in Heavy Industry. Upper Silesia and the Westphalian Ruhr Region, 1852-1913." Business History Review 53 (1979), 65-78.
2645. Pierenkemper, Toni. "Struktur und Entwicklung der Schwerindustrie in Oberschlesien und im westfälischen Ruhrgebiet 1852-1913." Zeitschrift für Unternehmensgeschichte 24 (1979), 1-28.
2646. Pounds, Norman J. G. The Upper Silesian Industrial Region. Bloomington: Indiana University Press, 1958. 242 pp.
2647. Schneider, Rudolf. "Die Entwickelung der Leinen-Industrie in Schlesien." in Festschrift zur XXIX. Hauptversammlung des Vereins Deutscher Ingenieure. Breslau: Verein Deutscher Ingenieure, 1888. pp. 114-75.
2648. Wolffsohn, Seew. Wirtschaftliche und soziale Entwicklungen in Brandenburg, Preussen, Schlesien und Oberschlesien in den Jahren 1640-1853. Frühindustrialisierung in Oberschlesien. Frankfurt a. M.: Lang, 1985. 183 pp.

SEE ALSO: 1366, 1368, 1376, 1378, 4176.

Thuringia

2649. Marquardt, Theodor. Der Einfluss der industriellen Entwicklung auf das Schuhmacher-Handwerk Erfurts. Diss. Frankfurt a. M. Borna-Leipzig: Noske, 1925. 74 pp.
2650. Sieber, Siegfried. Studien zur Industriegeschichte des Erzgebirges. Cologne: Böhlau, 1967. 152 pp.

SEE ALSO: 4183, 4185.

West Prussia

2651. Sommer, Edgar. Die Entwicklung der Industrie in Danzig und Westpreussen vom 19. Jahrhundert bis zur Gegenwart. Danzig: Käfemann, 1939. 8 pp.

4.
History of Business and Commerce

CENTRAL EUROPE

Bibliographic References

2652. Bibliographic Guide to Business and Economics. 2 vols. Boston: G. K. Hall, 1975.
2653. "Bibliographie." Konjunktur und Krise 10 (1966), 177-87.
2654. Business Periodicals Index. New York: H. W. Wilson, 1958- .
2655. Europäische Integration. Auswahlbibliographie. Bonn: E. G. Presse- und Informationsbüro, 1967. 76 pp.
2656. European Economic Integration. Paris: E. E. C., 1957. 104 pp.
2657. Guide to Foreign Trade Statistics. Washington: U. S. Bureau of the Census, 1969. 139 pp.
2658. The Harry W. Bass Collection in Business History: A Short Title Catalog. 6th ed. Norman: University of Oklahoma Libraries, 1977. 76 pp.
2659. Hamburg. Welt-Wirtschafts-Archiv. Verzeichnis der Fest- und Denkschriften von Unternehmungen und Organisationen der Wirtschaft. Hamburg: Welt-Wirtschafts-Archiv, 1961. 566 pp.
2660. Koster, Elisabeth Y. de. Bibliographie zur europäischen Integration. 2nd ed. Cologne: Europa-Union, 1965. 209 pp.
2661. Kujath, Karl. Bibliographie zur europäischen Integration. Bonn: Europa Union Verlag, 1977. 777 pp.
2662. Martinstetter, Hermann. Internationale Bibliographie des Zollwesens. Konstanz: C. Gehlsen, 1954. 189 pp.
2663. Neuman, Ina. "Bibliographie zur Firmengeschichte und Unternehmerbiographie." Tradition 12 (1967), 441-48, 545-52; 13 (1968), 48-56, 153-60, 265-72; 14 (1969), 57-64, 216-24, 339-46.
2664. Organization for Economic Cooperation and Development. Library. Bibliographie Spéciale Analytique. Paris: O. E. C. D., 1964. 84 pp.
2665. Prüfer, Walter. Methodologie zur Erforschung des Unternehmertums. Diss. Leipzig. Dresden: Risse, 1934. 73 pp.
2666. Schloss, Henry H. and William N. Breswick. A Selected and Annotated Bibliography of International Trade. Austin: University of Texas, Bureau of Business Research, 1951. 28 pp.
2667. Stewart, Charles and George B. Simmons. A Bibliography of International Business. New York: Columbia University Press, 1964. 603 pp.
2668. Wessel, Horst. "Bibliographie zur Unternehmensgeschichte und Unternehmerbiographie." Zeitschrift für Unternehmensgeschichte 25 (1980), 48-76.
2669. Wheeler, Lora J., ed. International Business and Foreign Trade. Detroit: Gale Research, 1966. 221 pp.

CENTRAL EUROPE

2670. Armstrong, John A. The European Administrative Elite. Princeton: Princeton University Press, 1973. 406 pp.
2671. Bairoch, Paul. "Geographical Structure and Trade Balance of European Foreign Trade from 1800 to 1970." The Journal of European Economic History 3 (1974), 557-608.
2672. Beard, Miriam. A History of Business. 2 vols. Ann Arbor: University of Michigan Press, 1962-63.
2673. Bosch, Margarete. Gelenkte Marktwirtschaft. Die geschichtliche Notwendigkeit einer Gestaltung der Wirtschaft. Stuttgart: Kohlhammer, 1939. 232 pp.
2674. Brähler, Rainer. Der Marshallplan: zur Strategie weltmarktorientierter Krisenvermeidung in der amerikanischen Westeuropapolitik 1933-1952. Diss. Cologne. Cologne: Pahl-Rugenstein, 1983. 311 pp.
2675. Cairncross, A. K. and J. Faaland. "Long-Term Trends in Europe's Trade." Economic Journal 62 (1952), 25-34.
2676. Chmelnizkaja, J. "Der westeuropäische Kapitalismus einst und jetzt." Sowjetwissenschaft. Gesellschaftswissenschaftliche Beiträge. Gesellschaft für Deutsch-Sowjetische Freundschaft 6 (1965), 582-94.
2677. Day, Clive. A History of Commerce. 4th ed. London: Longmans Green, 1938. 626 pp.
2678. Dupuigrenet-Desroussilles, Guy. Niveaux de vie et coopération économique dans l'Europe de l'Ouest. Paris: Presses Universitaires de France, 1962. 191 pp.
2679. Faust, Helmut. Geschichte der Genossenschaftsbewegung. Ursprung und Aufbruch der Genossenschaftsbewegung in England, Frankreich und Deutschland sowie ihre weitere Entwicklung im deutschen Sprachraum. 3rd ed. Frankfurt a. M.: Knapp, 1977. 782 pp.
2680. Fischer, H. "Entwicklungstendenzen landwirtschaftlicher Genossenschaften in einigen europäischen Ländern." Berichte über Landwirtschaft 31 (1953), 102-20.
2681. Flügge, Walter. "Stand, Entwicklung und Probleme der wirtschaftlichen Zusammenarbeit der Konsumgenossenschaft im europäischen Markt." Zeitschrift für das gesamte Genossenschaftswesen 20 (1970), 233-46. (English summary).
2682. Gibbins, Henry de Beltens. The History of Commerce in Europe. London: MacMillan, 1920. 243 pp.
2683. Huter, Franz and Georg Zwanowetz, eds. Erzeugung, Verkehr und Handel in der Geschichte der Alpenländer. Festschrift für Univ.-Prof. Dr. Herbert Hassinger. Innsbruck: Wagner, 1977. 475 pp.
2684. Kellenbenz, Hermann, ed. Wachstumsschwankungen: wirtschaftliche und soziale Auswirkungen (Spätmittelalter bis 20. Jahrhundert); Referate und Diskussionsbeiträge. Stuttgart: Klett-Cotta, 1981. 340 pp.
2685. Kindleberger, Charles P. Foreign Trade and the National Economy. New Haven, CT: Yale University Press, 1962. 265 pp.
2686. Kopecky, Kenneth J. Growth and Developed Economies. A Study of the OECD Countries. Diss. Brown University, 1970. 153 pp.
2687. Kravis, I. B. "Trade as a Handmaiden of Growth. Similarities Between the Nineteenth and Twentieth Centuries." Economic Journal 80 (1970), 850-72.
2688. Kruse, Alfred. Aussenwirtschaft. Die internationalen Wirtschaftbeziehungen. 2nd ed. Berlin: Duncker & Humblot, 1965. 660 pp.
2689. Kuczynski, Jürgen. "Zwei Studien über Handels- und Marktprobleme. 1. Die Entwicklung des Welthandels von Anbeginn bis zur Gegenwart. 2. Der nationale Markt." Jahrbuch für Wirtschaftsgeschichte (1960), II, 113-41.
2690. Kuske, Bruno. "Geschichte des Einzelhandels." in R. Seyffert, ed. Handbuch des Einzelhandels. Stuttgart: Poeschel, 1932. pp. 7-30.
2691. Lewis, W. Arthur. "World Production, Prices and Trade, 1870-1960." Manchester School 20 (1952), 105-38.
2692. Lundberg, Erik. Instability and Economic Growth. New Haven, CT: Yale University Press, 1968. 433 pp.
2693. Maizels, Alfred. Industrial Growth and World Trade. Cambridge: Cambridge University Press, 1963. 563 pp.
2694. Mandel, Ernest. Long Waves of Capitalist Development. The Marxist Interpretation. Cambridge: Cambridge University Press, 1981. 151 pp.

2695. Meier, Gerald M., ed. Leading Issues in Development Economics. New York: Oxford University Press, 1964. 572 pp.
2696. Meier, Gerald M. and Robert E. Baldwin. Economic Development. Theory, History, Policy. New York: J. Wiley, 1957. 588 pp.
2697. Meladim, Daniel et al. "Westeuropa. Grundprobleme seiner Entwicklung als imperialistisches Zentrum und Region der internationalen Beziehungen." IPW-Berichte 7 (1978), 1-11.
2698. Meyer, Henry C. Mitteleuropa in German Thought and Action 1815-1945. The Hague: Nijhoff, 1955. 378 pp.
2699. Neisser, Hans. Some International Aspects of the Business Cycle. Philadelphia: University of Pennsylvania Press, 1936. 176 pp.
2700. Okun, Bernard and Richard W. Richardson. Studies in Economic Development. New York: Holt Rinehart & Winston, 1965. 498 pp.
2701. Parker, William N. "Entrepreneurship, Industrial Organization and Economic Growth." Journal of Economic History 14 (1954), 380-400.
2702. Parker, William N. "Growth and Stagnation in the European Economy. A Summary and Critical Comments." in Warren Scoville and J. Clayburn La Force, eds. The Economic Development of Western Europe. Lexington, MA: Heath, 1970. V, 71-89.
2703. Raupach, Hans. "Strukurelle und institutionelle Auswirkungen der Weltwirtschaftskrise in Ost-Mitteleuropa." Vierteljahrshefte für Zeitgeschichte 24 (1976), 38-57.
2704. Reinhold, Otto. Die Wirtschaftskrisen. 2nd ed. Berlin: Dietz, 1977. 120 pp.
2705. Resnick, Stephen and Richard Wolff. "The Theory of Transitional Conjunctures and the Transition from Feudalism to Capitalism in Western Europe." The Review of Radical Political Economics 11 (1979), 3-22.
2706. Röpke, Wilhelm. Crises and Cycles. London: W. Hodge, 1936. 224 pp.
2707. Romano, Ruggiero. I prezzi in Europa dal XIII secolo a oggi. Torino: Einaudi, 1967. 590 pp.
2708. Rosenberg, Hans. Machteliten und Wirtschaftskonjunkturen. Göttingen: Vandenhoeck & Ruprecht, 1978. 343 pp.
2709. Rostow, Walt W. "The Beginnings of Modern Growth in Europe: an Essay in Synthesis." Journal of Economic History 33 (1973), 547-80.
2710. Salin, Edgar. "European Entrepreneurship." Journal of Economic History 12 (1952), 366-77.
2711. Schumpeter, J. A. Business Cycles. A Theoretical, Historical and Statistical Analysis of the Capitalist Process. 2 vols. New York: McGraw-Hill, 1939.
2712. Sieveking, Heinrich. Die Gestaltung der Handelspolitik in den wichtigsten Ländern. Berlin: de Gruyter, 1930. 128 pp.
2713. Sieveking, Heinrich. "Entstehung und Entwicklungstendenzen des Kapitalismus." in Reden zur Feier des Rektorwechsels Hamburg. Hamburg: C. Boysen, 1928. pp. 19-43.
2714. Singer, Hans W. International Development. Growth and Change. New York: McGraw-Hill, 1964. 295 pp.
2715. Staley, Eugene. World Economic Development. Effects on Advanced Industrial Countries. 2nd ed. Montreal: International Labour Office, 1945. 230 pp.
2716. Supple, Barry E., ed. The Experience of Economic Growth. Case Studies in Economic History. New York: Random House, 1963. 458 pp.
2717. Szapary, Georges. "Europe-Etats Unis 1899-1962." in Diffusion du progrés et convergence des prix. Etudes internationales. Louvain: Université Catholique de Louvain, 1966. II, 259-492.
2718. Vaizey, John. Capitalism and Socialism. A History of Industrial Growth. London: Wiedenfeld & Nicolson, 1980. 283 pp.
2719. Wee, Herman van der. "European Historical Statistics and Economic Growth." Explorations in Economic History 13 (1976), 347-51.
2720. Wirsching, Heinz A. Der Kampf um die handelspolitische Einigung Europas. Eine geschichtliche Darstellung des Gedankens der europäischen Zollunion. Diss. Erlangen. Feuchtwangen: Sommer & Schorr, 1928. 95 pp.
2721. Woytinsky, Wladimir. "Die Preisbewegung der Jahre 1901-1912 und 1925-1930." Weltwirtschaftliches Archiv 34 (1931), 491-524.
2722. Yates, Paul L. Forty Years of Foreign Trade. London: Allen & Unwin, 1959. 255 pp.

SEE ALSO: 16, 32, 40, 63, 123, 133-34, 144-45, 159-60, 178-79, 1396, 1401, 1450, 3320, 3469, 3561, 4211.

CENTRAL EUROPE--1815-1918

References

2723. Eulenburg, Franz. "Literatur über die wirtschaftliche Annäherung von Mitteleuropa." Weltwirtschaftliches Archiv 7 (1916), 397-420.
2724. Matlekovits, Alexander, ed. Bibliographie der mitteleuropäischen Zollunionsfrage. Budapest: s.n., 1917.
2725. Mulhall, Michael G. Progress of the World of Arts, Agriculture, Commerce, Manufactures, Instruction, Railways, and Public Wealth Since the Beginning of the Nineteenth Century. London: E. Stanford, 1880. 569 pp.
2726. Schilder, Sigmund. "Zur Literatur der mitteleuropäischen wirtschaftlichen Annäherung." Archiv fur Sozialwissenschaft und Sozialpolitik 44 (1917-18), 503-29.

CENTRAL EUROPE--1815-1918

2727. Bairoch, Paul. Commerce extérieur et développement économique de l'Europe au XIXe siècle. Paris: Mouton, 1976. 360 pp.
2728. Bairoch, Paul. "European Foreign Trade in the Nineteenth Century." Journal of European Economic History 2 (1973).
2729. Bairoch, Paul. "Free Trade and European Economic Development in the Nineteenth Century." European Economic Review 3 (1972), 211-45.
2730. Beer, Adolf. Geschichte des Welthandels im 19. Jahrhundert. 2 vols. Vienna: Braumüller, 1884.
2731. Cameron, Rondo E. "Economic Relations of France with Central and Eastern Europe, 1800-1914." Journal of European Economic History 10 (1981), 537-52.
2732. Clapham, John H. "Communication and Commerce in Western Europe Before the Railway Age." in Warren Scoville and J. Clayburn La Force, eds. The Economic Development of Western Europe. Lexington, MA: Heath, 1969. IV, 148-55.
2733. Daems, Herman and Herman van der Wee, eds. The Rise of Managerial Capitalism. The Hague: Nijhoff, 1974. 235 pp.
2734. Fesser, Gerd and Ursula Mader. "Mitteleuropakonzeptionen des deutschen Imperialismus." Zeitschrift für Geschichtswissenschaft 23 (1975), 430-32.
2735. Fischer, Gustav. "Ueber das Wesen und die Bedingungen eines Zollvereins." Jahrbuch für Nationalökonomie und Statistik 7 (1866), 225-304; 8 (1867), 252-350.
2736. Francke, Ernst. "Zollpolitische Einigungsbestrebungen in Mitteleuropa während des letzten Jahrzehnts." Schriften des Vereins für Sozialpolitik 1 (1900), 187-272.
2737. Gordon, Nancy M. "Britain and the Zollverein Iron Duties, 1842-45. Economic History Review 22 (1969), 75-87.
2738. Gourevitch, Peter A. "Étude comparative des réactions des grandes puissances face à la crise économique de 1873 à 1896." Études Internationales 6 (1975), 188-219.
2739. Gourevitch, Peter A. "International Trade, Domestic Coalitions and Liberty. Comparative Responses to the Crisis of 1873-96." Journal of Interdisciplinary History 8 (1977-78), 281-313.
2740. Green, Alan and M. C. Urquhardt. "Factor and Commodity Flows in the International Economy of 1870-1914. A Multi-Country View." The Journal of Economic History 36 (1976), 217-52.
2741. Grisebach, O. C. E. Zollverein, Souveränetät und ständische Rechte. 1844, 1862 und demnächst. Hannover: Hahn, 1862. 35 pp.
2742. Gruner, Erich. "Europa als Schöpfer und Zerstörer des Weltwirtschaftskreislaufes." Schweizerische Monatshefte für Politik 48 (1968-69), 258-72.
2743. Häpke, Rudolf. Der deutsche Kaufmann in den Niederlanden. Leipzig: Duncker & Humblot, 1911. 66 pp.
2744. Hahn, Max. "Deutscher Zollverein damals, Mitteleuropa heute. Zur hundertjährigen Wiederkehr des Gründungstages des Deutschen Zollvereins." Welt und Reich 10 (1934), 1-7.
2745. Henderson, William O. "A Nineteenth Century Approach to a West European Common Market." Kyklos, Internationale Zeitschrift für Sozialwissenschaften 10 (1957), 448-59.
2746. Henderson, William O. "Trade Cycles in the Nineteenth Century." History 18 (1933-34), 147-53.

2747. Hentschel, Volker. "Produktion, Wachstum und Produktivität in England, Frankreich und Deutschland von der Mitte des 19. Jahrhunderts bis zum Ersten Weltkrieg. Statistische Grenzen und Nöte beim internationalen wirtschaftshistorischen Vergleich." VSWG 68 (1981), 457-510.

2748. Hidy, Ralph W. "The Development of Business in England, Germany, and the United States of America during the Period of Early Industrialization. Inducements and Obstacles." Nebraska Journal of Economics and Business 8 (1969), 57-58.

2749. Holland, Bernard. The Fall of Protection 1840-1850. London: Arnold, 1913. 372 pp.

2750. Houth-Weber, F., ed. Der Zollverein seit seiner Erweiterung durch den Steuerverein. Eine Sammlung der betr. Zoll- und Steuer-Verträge. Hannover: Rümpler, 1861. 422 pp.

2751. Inama-Sternegg, Carl T. von. Beiträge zur Geschichte der Preise. Vienna: Hof- und Staatsdruckerei, 1873. 47 pp.

2752. Kellenbenz, Hermann, ed. Wirtschaftliches Wachstum, Energie und Verkehr vom Mittelalter bis ins 19. Jahrhundert. Bericht über die 6. Arbeitstagung der Gesellschaft für Sozial- und Wirtschaftsgeschichte. Stuttgart: Fischer, 1978. 248 pp.

2753. Kindleberger, Charles P. "The Rise of Free Trade in Western Europe, 1820-1875." Journal of Economic History 35 (1935), 20-55.

2754. Lang, Ludwig. Hundert Jahre Zollpolitik. Vienna: Fromme, 1906. 620 pp.

2755. Lavergne, Bernard. Les progrès de la coopération de consommation en Europe depuis dix ans (1900-1910). Paris: Recueil Sirey, 1911. 42 pp.

2756. Lis, Catharina and Hugo Soly. Poverty and Capitalism in Pre-Industrial Europe. Atlantic Highlands, NJ: Humanities Press, 1979. 267 pp.

2757. Milward, Alan S. "Cyclical Fluctuations and Economic Growth in Developed Europe, 1870-1913." in D. Petzina and G. van Roon, eds. Konjunktur, Krise und Gesellschaft. Wirtschaftliche Wechsellagen und soziale Entwicklung im 19. und 20. Jahrhundert. Stuttgart: Klett-Cotta, 1981. pp. 42-53. (English summary)

2758. Pályi, Eduard. Das mitteleuropäische Weltreichbündnis, gesehen von einem Nicht-Deutschen. Munich: Duncker & Humblot, 1916. 25 pp.

2759. Post, John D. "A Study in Meterological and Trade Cycle History. The Economic Crisis Following the Napoleonic Wars." Journal of Economic History 34 (1974), 315-49.

2760. Repertorium zu den Zollvereins-Verträgen und Verhandlungen aus dem Zeitraum von 1833 bis 1858. Berlin: Königliche Staatsdruckerei, 1858. 384 pp.

2761. Rosenberg, Hans. Grosse Depression und Bismarckzeit. Wirtschaftsablauf, Gesellschaft und Politik in Mitteleuropa. Berlin: de Gruyter, 1967. 301 pp.

2762. Rosenberg, Hans. Die Weltwirtschaftskrise 1857-1859. 2nd ed. Göttingen: Vandenhoeck & Ruprecht, 1974. 210 pp.

2763. Rosenberg, Hans. "Wirtschaftskonjunktur, Gesellschaft und Politik in Mitteleuropa, 1873-1896." in H.-U. Wehler, ed. Moderne deutsche Sozialgeschichte. Cologne: Kiepenheuer & Witsch, 1966. pp. 225-53.

2764. Rust, Bernhard. Über das Wesen und die Ursache unserer heutigen Wirtschaftskrisis. Jena: G. Fischer, 1905. 55 pp.

2765. Salin, Edgar. "Friedrich List und der europäische Zollverein." Mitteilungen der List Gesellschaft 2 (1959), 157-71.

2766. Scala, Otto E. von. "Die wirtschaftlichen Einigungsbestrebungen vom Wiener Kongress bis zum Zusammenbruch." in Die Anschlussfrage in ihrer kulturellen, politischen und wirtschaftlichen Bedeutung. Vienna: W. Braumüller, 1930. pp.19-35.

2767. Schilder, Sigmund. Mitteleuropäische Wirtschaftsvereine in Oesterreich. Mitteleuropa und die Handelspolitik der offenen Tür. Vienna: Fromme, 1918. 80 pp.

2768. Siegenthaler, Hansjörg. "Ansätze zu einer generalisierenden Interpretation langwelliger Wachstumsschwankungen und ihrer sozialen Implikationen im 19. und frühen 20. Jahrhundert." in Wachstumsschwankungen. Wirtschaftliche und soziale Auswirkungen (Spätmittelalter bis 20. Jahrhundert). Stuttgart: Klett-Cotta, 1981. pp. 1-45.

2769. Stein, Hans. Pauperismus und Assoziation. Soziale Tatsachen und Ideen auf dem westeuropäischen Kontinent vom Ende des 18. bis zur Mitte des 19. Jahrhunderts, unter besonderer Berücksichtigung des Rheingebiets. Leiden: Brill, 1936. 120 pp.

2770. Suter, Ernst. Die handelspolitische Kooperation des Deutschen Reiches und der Donaumonarchie 1890-94. Diss. Marburg, 1930. 114 pp.

2771. Tintner, Gerhard. "Die allgemeine Preisbildung 1890-1913." Schmoller 57 (1933), 253-64.

2772. Treue, Wilhelm. "Das österreichisch-mitteldeutsche und das norddeutsche staats- und privatwirtschaftliche Interesse am Bau des Suez-Kanals." VSWG 57 (1970), 534-55.
2773. Waller, Bruce. "Bismarck, the Dual Alliance and Economic Central Europe, 1877-1885." VSWG 63 (1976), 454-67.
2774. Wessely, Kurt. "Der osteuropäische Grosswirtschaftsraum und seine Vorgänger." Der Donauraum. Zeitschrift des Forschungsinstitutes für Fragen des Donauraumes 3 (1958), 1-25.
2775. "The Zollverein." History 19 (1934), 1-19.
2776. "Zollvereinswerk und Zollvereinsfeier." Mitteilungen der Friedrich List-Gesellschaft 25 (1934), 481-503.

SEE ALSO: 214, 229, 234, 2007, 2028, 2865, 3470, 3553.

CENTRAL EUROPE--1919-1945

2777. Brunner, Karl, ed. The Great Depression Revisited. Boston: M. Nijhoff, 1981. 360 pp.
2778. Delle Donne, Ottavio. European Tariff Policies Since the World War. New York: Adelphi, 1928. 288 pp.
2779. "The Depression." in Economic History of Europe. Twentieth Century. New York: Harper, 1968. pp. 213-63.
2780. Donaldson, John. International Economic Relations. A Treatise on World Economy and World Politics. London: Longmans Green, 1928. 674 pp.
2781. Enderle, Georges. Die Auswirkungen der Weltwirtschaftskrise der Dreissiger Jahre auf die personelle Einkommens- und Vermögensverteilung: methodische und theoretische Probleme. Diss. Fribourg. Fribourg: Fribourg University Press, 1982. 302 pp.
2782. Fearon, Peter. The Origins and Nature of the Great Slump 1929-1932. London: Macmillan, 1979. 69 pp.
2783. Fossati, Eraldo. "Tendenzen und Entwicklung des Weltaussenhandels von der Depression von 1932 bis zum Kriegsbeginn." Weltwirtschaftliches Archiv 57 (1943), 584-611.
2784. Hodson, Henry V. Slump and Recovery, 1929-1937. A Survey of World Economic Affairs. London: Oxford University Press, 1938; rpt. New York: Garland, 1983. 484 pp.
2785. Jent, Viktor. Die handelspolitischen Bestrebungen des Völkerbundes. Zurich: Gutzmiller, 1926. 109 pp.
2786. Kindleberger, Charles P. The Terms of Trade. A European Case Study. London: Chapman & Hall, 1956. 382 pp.
2787. Lewis, Cleona. Nazi Europe and World Trade. Washington, D. C.: Brookings Institution, 1941. 200 pp.
2788. Pilisi, Paul. "Le projet de la 'Communauté Economique de l'Europe Centrale' de E. Hantos, 1923-1933. Une idée de l'integration fonctionnelle en Europe centrale et orientale entre les deux Guerres Mondiales." Südost-Forschungen 38 (1979), 206-12.
2789. Rees, Goronwy. The Great Slump. Capitalism in Crisis, 1929-33. London: Weidenfeld & Nicolson, 1970. 310 pp.
2790. Riedel, Richard. Kollektiver Zollabbau und Europäisches Wirtschaftsbündnis. Anträge der österreichischen Gruppe der Internationalen Handelskammer zu den Beschlüssen der 10. Völkerbundsversammlung. Berlin: Springer, 1929. 24 pp.
2791. Robbins, Lionel. The Great Depression. London: Macmillan, 1934. 238 pp.
2792. Salter, Arthur et al. The World's Economic Crisis. New York: Kennikat Press, 1932. 194 pp.
2793. Teichova, Alice and Philip L. Cottrell, eds. International Business and Central Europe, 1918-1939. New York: St. Martin's Press, 1983. 459 pp.
2794. Wee, Herman van der, ed. The Great Depression Revisited. Essays on the Economics of the Thirties. The Hague: Nijhoff, 1973. 290 pp.
2795. Wendt, Bernd-Jürgen. Appeasement 1938. Wirtschaftliche Rezession und Mitteleuropa. Frankfurt a. M.: Europäische Verlagsanstalt, 1966. 151 pp.

SEE ALSO: 249, 256-58, 262, 1447, 1451, 2862, 4276, 4308.

CENTRAL EUROPE--1945-1975

Bibliographic References

2796. "Bibliographie commentée et documentation de la C. E. E." Les Problèmes de l'Europe (1958-).
2797. Der Gemeinsame Markt. Bibliographie. 3 vols. Luxemburg: European Economic Community, 1957-59.
2798. Morris, Brian et al. The European Community. A Guide for Business and Government. Bloomington: University of Indiana Press, 1981. 303 pp.
2799. Wild, J. E. The European Common Market and European Free Trade Association. 3rd ed. London: Library Association, 1962. 62 pp.

CENTRAL EUROPE--1945-1975

2800. Abelshauser, Werner. "Wiederaufbau vor dem Marshall-Plan. Westeuropas Wachstumschancen und die Wirtschaftsordnungspolitik in der zweiten Hälfte der vierziger Jahre." Vierteljahrshefte für Zeitgeschichte 29 (1981), 545-78.
2801. Albrecht-Carrié, Réné. The Unity of Europe: An Historical Survey. London: Secker & Warburg, 1966. 346 pp.
2802. Alting von Gensau, Frans A. M., ed. The Lorné Convention and a New International Economic Order. Leyden: A. W. Sijthoff, 1972. 249 pp.
2803. Die Auswirkungen der EFTA und der EWG auf den Handel 1959-1967. Geneva: EFTA, 1972. 177 pp.
2804. Blacksell, Mark. Post-war Europe. A Political Geography. Boulder, CO: Westview Press, 1978. 205 pp.
2805. Böhi, Hans. "Die europäische Nachkriegskonjunktur." Aussenwirtschaft 10 (1955), 91-107.
2806. Boguszewski, Jan. Wachstum und Produktivität in der Industrie und ihren Hauptbereichen in der BRD, Österreich, Polen und Ungarn im Zeitraum 1960-1972. Vienna: Österreichisches Institut für Wirtschaftsforschung, 1979. 71 pp.
2807. Boltho, Andrea, ed. The European Economy. Growth and Crisis. Oxford: Oxford University Press, 1982. 668 pp.
2808. Bonvoisin, Pierre. "Background of the Common Market." in H. V. Prochnow, ed. World Economic Problems and Policies. New York: Harper & Row, 1965. pp. 350-69.
2809. Bourguignon, Pierre. "De l'entrée en vigueur du Traité de Paris à celle des Traités de Rome." Studia Diplomatica 34 (1981), 293-325.
2810. Brugmans, Hendrick. L'Idee Européenne 1920-1970. Bruges: de Tempel, 1970. 405 pp.
2811. Cairncross, Alexander K. and J. Faaland. Long-Term Trends in Europe's Trade (Over the Past 40 Years)." Economic Journal 62 (1962), 25-34.
2812. Christiansen, Ragnvald. "Die Europäische Zollunion, Erreichtes und Erstrebtes." Zeitschrift für Zölle und Verbrauchssteuern 54 (1978), 354-58.
2813. Cleveland, Harold van Buren. "The Common Market after de Gaulle." Foreign Affairs. Council on Foreign Relations 47 (1969), 697-710.
2814. Cornwall, John. "Postwar Growth in Western Europe. A Re-Evaluation." The Review of Economics and Statistics 50 (1968), 361-68.
2815. Cripps, T. F. and R. J. Tarling. Growth in Advanced Capitalist Economies, 1950-1970. London: Cambridge University Press, 1973. 58 pp.
2816. Dankert, Jochen et al. Politik in Westeuropa. Integrationsprozesse vom Ende des Zweiten Weltkrieges bis zur Gegenwart. Berlin: VEB Deutscher Verlag der Wissenschaften, 1975. 480 pp.
2817. Denil, Bernard. "Intégration des marchés régionaux dans la Communauté des Six 1958-1970." Revue Economique du Sud-Ouest 25 (1976), 277-88. (English and Spanish summaries)
2818. Denison, Edward F. Why Growth Rates Differ. Postwar Experience in Nine Western Countries. Washington D.C.: The Brookings Institution, 1967. 494 pp.
2819. Die deutsche Industrie im Gemeinsamen Markt. Bericht über die bisherigen Auswirkungen der Europäischen Wirtschaftsgemeinschaft, 1958 bis 1963. Cologne: Bundesverband der deutschen Industrie, 1964. 88 pp.
2820. Diebold, William, Jr. The Schuman Plan. A Study in Economic Cooperation, 1950-1959. New York: Praeger, 1959. 750 pp.

2821. EFTA Secretariat. Building EFTA. A Free Trade Area in Europe. Geneva: EFTA, 1966. 145 pp.
2822. Ellis, Harry B. The Common Market. Cleveland: World Publishing, 1965. 204 pp.
2823. Etappen nach Europa. Chronik der Europäischen Gemeinschaft. Luxembourg: European Community, 1981. 70 pp.
2824. The European Communities: Establishment and Growth. New York: C. Scribner's, 1975. 208 pp.
2825. Farnsworth, Clyde H. Out of this Nettle. A History of Postwar Europe. New York: Day, 1973. 209 pp.
2826. Fischer, Wolfram. "Some Recent Developments of Business History in Germany, Austria, and Switzerland." Business History Review 37 (1963), 416-36.
2827. Foyer, H. and H. Krijnse Locker. "Les exportations de biens d'équipement de la Communauté. Analyse historique et prévisions jusqu'à 1970." in Statistische Information. Brussels: Statistics Office of the European Communities, 1967. I, 69-79.
2828. Franko, Lawrence G. The European Multinationals. New York: Harper & Row, 1976. 276 pp.
2829. Groeben, Hans von der. Aufbaujahre der europäischen Gemeinschaft. Das Ringen um den gemeinsamen Markt und die politische Union (1958-1966). Baden-Baden: Nomos, 1982. 404 pp.
2830. Groeben, Hans von der. "Zum 25. Jahrestag der Unterzeichung der Rom-Verträge." Aus Politik und Zeitgeschichte 12 (1982), 3-16.
2831. Gustavson, Carl G. Europe in the World Community since 1939. Boston: Allyn & Bacon, 1971. 548 pp.
2832. Haak, Ernst. Die wachsende Ungleichmässigkeit der Entwicklung des Kapitalismus nach dem zweiten Weltkrieg. Berlin: Dietz, 1965. 111 pp.
2833. Haesele, Kurt W. Europas letzter Weg. Montan-Union und EWG. Frankfurt a. M.: Knapp, 1958. 352 pp.
2834. Hay, Laszlo. "Il declino del 'miracolo economico' in Europa." in Tendenze del capitalismo europeo. Rome: Editori Riuniti, 1966. pp. 401-10.
2835. Heinrich, Walter. "Die Rekonstruktion des Welthandels nach dem zweiten Weltkrieg." Universitas 8 (1953), 131-38.
2836. Holtrop, Marius W. "The Economic and Financial Recovery of Europe and its Effect on the United States." De Economist. Orgaan van de Stichting "Het Nederlandsch Economisch Instituut" 108 (1960), 1-12.
2837. Ioannides, Yannis M. Migration and Economic Growth. Towards an Understanding of the Post-war European Experience. Berlin: International Institute of Management, 1976. 12 pp.
2838. Jansen, Max. History of European Integration 1945-1975. Amsterdam: Europa Instituut, 1975. 132 pp.
2839. Kasten, Hans. Die europäische Wirtschaftsintegration. Grundlagen. Munich: Fink, 1978. 120 pp.
2840. Kirchner, Emil. "The European Community and the Economic Recession 1973-79." in A. Cox, ed. Politics, Policy and the European Recession. London: Macmillan, 1982. pp. 218-54.
2841. Kramer, Hans-R. "EWG und EFTA. Ein Vergleich der Verträge zur Gründung der Europäischen Wirtschaftsgemeinschaft (EWG) und zur Errichtung der Europäischen Freihandelsassoziation EFTA." Jahrbuch für Internationales Recht 10 (1961), 49-88.
2842. Kuntze, Oskar-Erich. "Kontinentaleuropa im Zeichen der Nachwehen des Booms." Wirtschaftskonjunktur. Vierteljahresberichte des Ifo-Instituts für Wirtschaftsforschung (1971), 14-18.
2843. Kuntze, Oscar-Erich. "Verflechtung des "Intra-EFTA-Handels 1960/69." Ifo-Schnelldienst. Ifo-Institut fur Wirtschaftsforschung 23 (1970), 15-19.
2844. Lamote, L. "Union tarifaire douanière de la C.E.E. (1958-1970). Bulletin de Documentation 12 (1965), 5-24.
2845. Laubereau, Horst. "Rechte und Pflichten der Mitgliedstaaten bei der Herstellung des Gemein-samen Marktes, am Beispiel der Zollunion." in Zur Stellung der Mitgliedstaaten im Europarecht. Berlin: Duncker & Humblot, 1967. pp. 60-79.
2846. Lecerf, Jean. La communauté en péril. Histoire de l'Unité Européenne, 2. Paris: Gallimard, 1975. 404 pp.
2847. Licari, Joseph A. and Mark Gilbert. "Is There a Postwar Growth Cycle?" Kyklos 27 (1974), 511-20.
2848. Lieberman, Sima. The Growth of European Mixed Economies, 1945-1970. A Concise Study of the Economic Evolution of Six Countries. New York: Schenkman, 1977. 347 pp.

2849. Lindberg, Leon N. and Stuart A. Scheingold. Europe's Would-Be Polity. Patterns of Change in the European Community. Englewood Cliffs, NJ: Prentice-Hall, 1970. 314 pp.
2850. Littmann, Ernst-Ludwig. "Zur Entwicklung des Handels mit landwirtschaftlichen Produkten zwischen Ost- und Westeuropa seit Beginn der fünfziger Jahre." in Berichte über Landwirtschaft. Hamburg: Parey, 1972. pp. 900-24.
2851. Maier, Lutz. "Besonderheiten der Entwicklung Westeuropas zu einem imperialistischen Zentrum." IPW-Berichte. Institut für Internationale Politik und Wirtschaft 6 (1977), 10-23.
2852. Marczewski, Jan. L'Europe dans la conjoncture mondiale. Esquisse d'une théorie des fluctuations et de la croissance. Paris: I. S. E. A., 1963. 314 pp.
2853. Mayne, Richard. The Recovery of Europe. From Devastation to Unity. New York: Harper & Row, 1970. 375 pp.
2854. Mockers, Jean-Pierre. Croissances économiques comparées. Allemagne. France. Royaume-Uni 1950-1967. Paris: Dunod, 1969. 273 pp.
2855. Monaco, Riccardo. "Cenni storici." in L'integrazione economica europea all'inizio della seconda tappa. Rome: Istituto per l'Economia Europea, 1962. pp. 17-37.
2856. Müller, Lothar. "Die Auswirkungen des europäischen Niederlassungsabkommens vom 13. Dezember 1955 auf das Gewerberecht." Gewerbearchiv. Zeitschrift für Verwaltungs-. Gewerbe- und Handwerksrecht 12 (1966), 49-53.
2857. Negotiations for a European Free Trade Area 1956-1958. Stockholm: Norstedt, 1959. 79 pp. (Swedish: Stockholm, 1959.)
2858. Ouin, Marc. "The Establishment of the Customs Unions." in American Enterprise in the European Common Market. Ann Arbor: University of Michigan Press, 1962. I, 101-88.
2859. Paretti, Vittorio and Gilbert Bloch. Energie und wirtschaftliches Wachstum. Entwicklung 1950-61 im Gebiet der europäischen Gemeinschaften und Vorausschätzungen für die Jahre 1965 und 1970. Freiburg i. B.: Haufe, 1964. 248 pp.
2860. Parker, Florence E. Cooperatives in Postwar Europe. Survey of Developments in Scandinavian Countries and Eastern. Central. and Western Europe. Washington: Government Printing Office, 1948. 22 pp.
2861. Paxton, John. The Developing Common Market. The Structure of the EEC in Theory and in Practice. Boulder, CO: Westview Press, 1976. 240 pp.
2862. Petzina, Dietmar. Krisen gestern und heute--die Rezension von 1974/75 und die Erfahrungen der Weltwirtschaftskrise. Dortmund: Gesellschaft für westfälische Wirtschaftsgeschichte, 1977. 35 pp.
2863. Pinder, John H. M. and Roy Pryce. Europe after De Gaulle. Toward the United States of Europe. Baltimore: Penguin, 1969. 191 pp.
2864. Ploeg, Stephen S. van der. Customs Union Theory. Collective Preferences, and Protectionism. Analysis and Historical Perspective. Diss. Duke University, 1976. 178 pp.
2865. Röpke, Wilhelm. "Le Zollverein et le Marché Commun Européen." in Mélanges d'histoire économique et sociale. En hommage au Antony Babel à l'occasion de son 75. anniversaire. Geneva: s.n., 1963. II, 449-57.
2866. Sadzikowski, Wieslaw. "The 1974-1975 Economic Crisis. Its Impact on the Condition of Working People in Western Europe." Oeconomica Polonica 3 (1976), 351-62.
2867. Salin, Edgar. "Kerneuropa und die Freihandelszone." in Kerneuropa und die Freihandelszone. Zwei Reden zur europäischen Politik. Tübingen: Mohr, 1960. pp. 24-53.
2868. Salvadori, Massimo. "Capitalism in Postwar Europe." in J. F. Dewhurst et al., eds. Europe's Needs and Resources: Trends and Prospects in Eighteen Countries. New York: Twentieth Century Fund, 1961. pp. 737-58.
2869. Savage, Katherine. The Story of the Common Market. New York: Walck, 1970. 192 pp.
2870. Siegler, Heinrich von. Dokumentation der europäischen Integration. 2 vols. Bonn: Siegler, 1961-64.
2871. Spitäller, Erich. "The 1961 Revaluations and Exports of Manufactures." International Monetary Fund 17 (1970) 110-26.
2872. Strauss, Erich. Common Sense About the Common Market. Germany and Britain in Post-War Europe. London: Allen & Unwin, 1958. 168 pp.
2873. Strauss, Franz J. "25 Jahre Europäische Gemeinschaft." Politische Studien. Hanns-Seidel-Stiftung 33 (1982), 235-42.
2874. Swanepoel, J. Europese ekonomiese samewerking sedert die 2. Wêreldoorlog. Pretoria: University of South Africa, 1959. 48 pp.

2875. Tinbergen, Jan. "Croissance et emploi en Europe. Leçons de vingt dernières années." in Emploi et chomage en Europe. Fondation Européenne de la Culture. Paris: Economica, 1981. pp. 51-76.
2876. Triantalfillou, Panagiotis. Ökonomische Ursachen und Wirkungen der regionalen Bevölkerungsbewegungen in Europa nach dem 2. Weltkrieg. Diss. Frankfurt a. M., 1978. 327 pp.
2877. Tsoukalis, Loukas. The European Community. Past, Present and Future. Oxford: B. Blackwell, 1983. 244 pp.
2878. Ulmer, Ferdinand. "Die wirtschaftliche Integration Westeuropas." in Die Bedeutung der Wirtschaftspolitik in der Auseinandersetzung zwischen Ost und West. Bad Nauheim: Gesellschaft für burschenschaftliche Geschichtsforschung, 1960. pp. 77-90.
2879. Vaciago, Giacomo. "Rendimenti crescenti e 'residuo' nello sviluppo europeo, 1950-1970." Moneta e Credito. Banca Nazionale del Lavoro 27 (1974), 395-420.
2880. Vernon, Raymond, ed. Big Business and the State. Changing Relations in Western Europe. London: Macmillan, 1974. 310 pp.
2881. Ways, Max. "The Postwar Advance of the Five Hundred Million." Fortune 70 (August 1964), 104-09.
2882. Westhof, Jacques. "L'Union de l'Europe Occidentale avant et après l'élargissement des Communautés Européenes." Annuaire Européen 23 (1977), 94-123.
2883. Wilken, Paul H. Entrepreneurship. A Comparative and Historical Study. Norwood, NJ: Ablex, 1979. 306 pp.
2884. Willis, Frank R. France, Germany, and the new Europe 1945-1967. Stanford, CA: Stanford University Press, 1968. 431 pp.
2885. Yannopoulos, George N. "Migrant Labour and Economic Growth. The Post-War Experience of the EEC Countries." in The EEC and the Mediterranean Countries. Cambridge: Cambridge University Press, 1976. pp. 99-138.
2886. Zeller, Willy. "Die Europäischen Gemeinschaften an der Schwelle zur Zollunion. Erreichtes und Erstrebtes." Europa-Archiv 23 (1968), 415-22.

SEE ALSO: 273, 1032, 2066, 3147.

AUSTRIA

Reference

2887. Karner, Wolfgang A. and H. M. Mayrzedt. Österreich in der europäischen Integration. Bibliographie. Innsbruck: Akadmische Vereinigung für Aussenpolitik, 1964. 189 pp.

AUSTRIA

2888. Csató, Tamás. "The Development of Internal Trade in East Central and South-East Europe." Acta Historica 23 (1977), 397-440.
2889. Dobretsberger, Josef. Konkurrenz und Monopol in der gegenwärtigen Wirtschaft mit besonderer Berücksichtigung der österreichischen Industrie. Vienna: Deuticke, 1929. 149 pp.
2890. Ellegast, Franz. Erinnerungen eines alten Kaufmannes. Vienna: Eigenverlag der Handelskammer Niederösterreich, 1967. 54 pp.
2891. Feil, Erich et al. Die Gesellschaft mbH & Co., Kommanditgesellschaft. im österreichischen Handels-, Steuer-und Bilanzrecht. Eisenstadt: Prugg, 1968. 93 pp.
2892. Fluss, Max. Donaufahren und Donauhandel im Mittelalter und in neueren Zeiten. Prague: Haase, 1920. 78 pp.
2893. Garhofer, Emil "Hundert Jahre österreichische Gewerbepolitik." in H. Mayer, ed. Hundert Jahre österreichische Wirtschaftsentwicklung. Vienna: Springer, 1949. pp. 480-517.
2894. Haberl, Fred. Weg einer Idee. 125 Jahre Konsumgenossenschaften in Österreich. Vienna: Verlag Urac, 1981. 199 pp.
2895. Hoffmann, Alfred. "Die Donau und Österreich." Südosteuropa-Jahrbuch 5 (1961), 28-44, 166.

2896. Korntheuer, Hermann. Zoll- und Wirtschaftsgeschichte Österreichs. Vienna: Waldheim-Eberle, 1933. 191 pp.
2897. März, Eduard and Maria Szecsi. "Stagnation und Expansion. Eine vergleichende Analyse der wirtschaftlichen Entwicklung in der Ersten und Zweiten Republik." Wirtschaft und Gesellschaft 8 (1982), 321-40.
2898. Oebser, Arno. Das deutsche Genossenschaftswesen in den Gebieten der ehemaligen Tschecko-slowakei, in Rumänien, Südslawien und Ungarn. Diss. Halle-Wittenberg. Stuttgart: Kohlhammer, 1940. 258 pp.
2899. Pollan, Wolfgang. "Die langfristige Entwicklung der Preise und Einkommen in Österreich." Creditanstalt-Bankverein. Wirtschaftsberichte 12 (1977), 20-30.
2900. Preise und Austauschrelationen im österreichischen Aussenhandel 1924-1955. Vienna: Österreichisches Institut für Wirtschaftsforschung, 1956. 36 pp.
2901. Pribram, Alfred F. Materialien zur Geschichte der Preise und Löhne in Österreich. Vienna: Ueberreuter, 1938. 879 pp.
2902. Rothschild, Kurt W. "Austria and Switzerland." in Is the Business Cycle Obsolete? New York: Wiley-Interscience, 1969. pp. 225-50.
2903. Rothschild, Kurt W. "Zyklisches Verhalten und Niveau der österreichischen Arbeitslosigkeit." Zeitschrift für Nationalökonomie 37 (1977), 183-96.
2904. Schmidt, Franz R. Triumph einer Idee. 100 Jahre Konsumgenossenschaften in Österreich. Vienna: Regenbogenverlag, 1956. 56 pp.
2905. Seibert, Franz. Die Konsumgenossenschaften in Österreich. Geschichte und Funktion. Vienna: Europaverlag, 1978. 198 pp.
2906. Swoboda, Hannes. "Sozialstaat und kapitalistische Entwicklung in Österreich." Österreichische Zeitschrift für Politikwissenschaft 2 (1973), 333-53.
2907. Vukovich, Andreas. Die österreichische Konsumgenossenschaftsbewegung. Entwicklung, Probleme, Aufgaben. Vienna: Regenbogenverlag, 1957. 11 pp.
2908. Wagner, Josef. Handels- und Wechselrecht. 6th ed. Vienna: Österreichischer Gewerbeverlag, 1963. 103 pp.
2909. "Was war die Krone wert? Preisvergleich 1914-1951. Der Lebensstandard in der 'guten alten Zeit'". Der Österreichische Volkswirt 37 (1951), 4-6.

SEE ALSO: 297, 2076, 3274, 3286, 3328, 3980.

AUSTRIA-HUNGARY--1815-1918

2910. Bazant, J. Die Handelspolitik Österreich-Ungarns 1845 bis 1892 in ihrem Verhältnisse zum Deutschen Reiche und zum westlichen Europa. Leipzig: Duncker & Humblot, 1894. 193 pp.
2911. Becher, Siegfried. Statistische Uebersicht des Handels der Österreichischen Monarchie mit dem Auslande während der Jahre 1829 bis 1838. Stuttgart: Cotta, 1841. 347 pp.
2912. Beer, Adolf. Die österreichische Handelspolitik im 19. Jahrhundert. Vienna: Manz, 1891. 618 pp.
2913. Bortoli, G. de et al. "Il movimento dei prezzi in Austria dal 1800 al 1900." Giornale degli Economisti e Annali di Economia, N.S. 23 (1964), 589-600.
2914. Brezigar, Emil. "Die wirtschaftlichen Konjunktur- und Depressionswellen in Österreich seit dem Jahre 1896." Zeitschrift für Volkswirtschaft, Sozialpolitik und Verwaltung 23 (1914), 1-39.
2915. Burgstaller, Wolf-Dieter. Das österreichische Handelsministerium unter Karl Ludwig Freiherr von Bruck und der Kampf um die politische und wirtschaftliche Vormachtstellung im deutschen Raum. Diss. Graz, 1971. 197 pp.
2917. Diamant, Alfred. Austrian Catholics and the First Republic. Democracy, Capitalism, and the Social Order, 1918-1934. Princeton, NJ: Princeton University Press, 1960. 325 pp.
2918. Don, Yehuda. "Comparability of International Trade Statistics. Great Britain and Austria-Hungary Before World War I." Economic History Review 21 (1968), 78-92.
2919. Eddie, Scott M. et al. "Austria in the Dual Monarchy. Her Trade, Within and Without the Customs Union." East Central Europe 7 (1980), 225-47.
2920. Engel-Janosi, Friedrich. "Die Krise des Jahres 1864 in Österreich." in Historische Studien. Vienna: Steyermühl, 1929. pp. 141-95.

2921. Erceg, Ivan. "Aussenhandel der Nordadriatischen Seestädte als Faktor im Entstehen der kapitalistischen Beziehungen in Österreich im 18. und 19. Jahrhundert." VSWG 55 (1969), 464-80.

2922. Exner, Wilhelm F. Beiträge zur Geschichte der Gewerbe und Erfindungen Oesterreichs von der Mitte des 18. Jahrhunderts bis zur Gegenwart. 2 vols. Vienna: Braumüller, 1873.

2923. Die Export-Enquête des Oesterreichisch-ungarischen Export-Vereines 14. und 15. April 1898. Vienna: Export-Verein, 1898. 325 pp.

2924. Fink, Krisztina M. Die österreichisch-ungarische Monarchie als Wirtschaftsgemeinschaft. Ein historischer Beitrag zu aktuellen Integrationsproblemen. Munich: Trofenik, 1968. 87 pp.

2925. Gaertner, Alfred. Der Kampf um den Zollverein zwischen Österreich und Preussen von 1849 bis 1853. Strassburg i. E.: Herder, 1911. 346 pp.

2926. Görlich, Ernst J. "Wirtschaftliche Tendenzen in der mitteleuropäischen Idee in Österreich, 1848-1859." VSWG 35 (1942), 58-65.

2927. Good, David F. "Economic Integration and Regional Development in Austria-Hungary, 1867-1913." in P. Bairoch and M. Lévy-Leboyer, eds. Disparities in Economic Development since the Industrial Revolution. London: Macmillan, 1981.

2928. Good, David F. "The Great Depression and Austrian Growth after 1873." Economic History Review 31 (1978), 290-94.

2929. Good, David F. "Stagnation and 'Take-Off' in Austria, 1873-1913." The Economic History Review 27 (1974), 72-87.

2930. Good, David F. et al. "Modern Economic Growth in the Habsburg Monarchy." East Central Europe 7 (1980), 247-68.

2931. Grunzel, Josef. Handelspolitik und Ausgleich in Österreich-Ungarn. Vienna: Hölder, 1912. 253 pp.

2932. Helleiner, Karl F. Free Trade and Frustration. Anglo-Austrian Negotiations. 1860-70. Toronto: University of Toronto Press, 1973. 152 pp.

2933. Hudsczek, Karl. Österreichische Handelspolitik im Vormärz 1815-1848. Vienna: Konegen, 1918. 154 pp.

2934. Ihde, Wilhelm. Karl Ludwig von Bruck. Der österreichische Minister aus Preussen und sein grosseuropäischer Wirtschaftsgedanke. Leipzig: Lühe, 1943. 57 pp.

2935. Irresberger, Carl. Das deutsch-österreichisch-ungarische Wirtschafts- und Zollbündnis. Eine Studie mit besonderer Berücksichtigung des österreichisch-ungarischen Standpunktes. Berlin: Springer, 1916. 39 pp.

2936. Kaizl, Josef. "Die Reform des Gewerberechts in Österreich vom Jahre 1883." Jahrbücher für Nationalökonomie und Statistik 8 (1884), 593-605.

2937. Kann, Robert A. The Habsburg Empire. New York: Praeger, 1957. 227 pp. (German: Graz, 1962.)

2938. Kassowitz, Antonie. Die neueren handelspolitischen Beziehungen zwischen Österreich-Ungarn und den Balkanländern bis zum Ausbruch des Weltkrieges. Diss. Berlin. Berlin: Scholem, 1917. 61 pp.

2939. Kerekes, Lajos. "Der Anschluss und die 'Alternative' der Donaukonföderation in der Aussenpolitik Otto Bauers in den Jahren 1918-1919." Acta Historica Academiae Scientiarum Hungaricae 19 (1973), 335-64.

2940. König, Wilhelm. Die Schwierigkeiten einer Zoll-Union. Persönliche Erinnerungen an den Ausgleich zwischen Österreich und Ungarn vom Jahre 1907. Vienna: Ployer, 1953. 24 pp.

2941. Komlos, John, Jr. The Habsburg Monarchy as a Customs Union. Princeton, NJ: Princeton University Press, 1983. 347 pp.

2942. Lang, Lajos. Hundert Jahre Zollpolitik. Vienna: C. Fromme, 1906. 620 pp.

2943. Long, Dwight C. "The Austro-French Commercial Treaty of 1866." American Historical Review 41 (1935-36), 474-91.

2944. Long, Dwight C. "Efforts to Secure an Austro-German Customs Union in the Nineteenth Century." in A. E. R. Boak, ed. University of Michigan Historical Essays. Ann Arbor: University of Michigan Press, 1937.

2945. Lorenz, Reinhold. "Der erste österreichisch-japanische Freundschafts- und Handelsvertrag (Okt. 1869)." in Japan und Mitteleuropa. Brno: R. M. Rohrer, 1944. pp. 118-40.

2946. Mamroth, Karl. Die Entwicklung der österreichisch-deutschen Handelsbeziehungen 1849-1865. Berlin: Carl Heymanns, 1887. 195 pp.

2947. Matis, Herbert. "Industrielles Wachsen und konjunkturelle Dynamik in der Franz-Joseph-Zeit." Bericht über den 11. österreichischen Historikertag in Innsbruck 11 (1972), 200-12.

2948. Matis, Herbert. "Der österreichische Unternehmer." in K.-H. Manegold, ed. Wissenschaft, Wirtschaft und Technik. Studien zur Geschichte. Wilhelm Treue zum 60. Geburtstag. Munich: Bruckmann, 1969. pp. 286-98.

2949. Matlekovits, Alexander. Die Zollpolitik der oesterreichisch-ungarischen Monarchie von 1850 bis zur Gegenwart. Budapest: Franklin-Verein, 1877. 230 pp.

2950. Mentschl, Josef. "Das österreichische Unternehmertum." in Die Habsburgermonarchie 1848-1918. Vienna: Österreichische Akademie der Wissenschaften, 1973. I, 250-77.

2951. Mises, Ludwig von. "Die Störungen im Wirtschaftsleben der österreichisch-ungarischen Monarchie während der Jahre 1912-1913." Archiv für Sozialwissenschaft und Sozialpolitik 39 (1914-15), 174-86.

2952. Mühlpeck, Vera et al. "Index der Verbraucherpreise 1800-1914. Eine Rückberechnung für Wien und den Gebietsstand des heutigen Österreichs." in Geschichte und Ergebnisse der zentralen amtlichen Statistik in Österreich 1829-1977. Vienna: Staatsdruckerei, 1979. 720 pp.

2953. Neumann, Franz. Oesterreich und der Zollverein in den letzten fünfundzwanzig Jahren. Vienna: Seidel, 1864. 35 pp.

2954. Neumann, Franz. Österreichs Handelspolitik in der Vergangenheit. Gegenwart und Zukunft. Vienna: C. Gerold's Sohn, 1864. 111 pp.

2955. Op de Hipt, Joseph. Tendenzen des österreichisch-ungarischen Aussenhandels seit den siebziger Jahren. Diss. Cologne, 1925. Kempen: Thomas, 1926. 99 pp.

2956. Pavelka, H. Englisch-österreichische Wirtschaftsbeziehungen in der ersten Hälfte des 19. Jahrhunderts. Graz: Böhlau, 1968. 192 pp.

2957. Peez, Alexander. "Die österreichische Handelspolitik der letzten fünfundzwanzig Jahre." Schriften des Vereins für Sozialpolitik 49 (1892), 167-93.

2958. Philippovich, Eugen von. "Austrian-Hungarian Trade Policy." Economic Journal 12 (1902), 177-81.

2959. Pickl, Othmar. "Das Wirtschaftswachstum der Habsburger Monarchie und ihre Verflechtung in den internationalen Handel im 19. Jahrhundert." in Wirtschaftliches Wachstum. Energie und Verkehr vom Mittelalter bis ins 19. Jahrhundert. Stuttgart: Fischer, 1978. pp. 183-203.

2960. Pribram, Karl. Geschichte der österreichischen Gewerbepolitik von 1740 bis 1860. Auf Grund der Akten. 3 vols. Leipzig: Duncker & Humblot, 1907.

2961. Ránki, György. "Einige Probleme der wirtschaftlichen Entwicklung in der Österreichisch-Ungarischen Monarchie." in Der österreichisch-ungarische Ausgleich 1867. Bratislava: Verlag der Slowakischen Akademie der Wissenschaften, 1971. pp. 394-411.

2962. Ránki, György and Iván T. Berend. "Prejudice and Reality. Economic Development in the Dual Monarchy." The New Hungarian Quarterly 40 (1970), 129-37.

2963. Sandgruber, Roman. Die Anfänge der Konsumgesellschaft. Konsumgüterverbrauch. Lebensstandard und Alltagskultur in Österreich im 18. und 19. Jahrhundert. Vienna: Verlag für Geschichte und Politik, 1982. 468 pp.

2964. Sandgruber, Roman. "Wirtschaftswachstum, Energie und Verkehr in Österreich 1840-1913." in Wirtschaftliches Wachstum. Energie und Verkehr vom Mittelalter bis ins 19. Jahrhundert. Bericht über die 6. Arbeitstagung der Gesellschaft für Sozial- und Wirtschaftsgeschichte. Stuttgart: Fischer, 1978. pp. 67-93.

2965. Schäffle, Albert E. F. "Der grosse Börsenkrach des Jahres 1873." in Gesammelte Aufsätze und Mittheilungen aus dem Börsenblatt für den deutschen Buchhandel. Leipzig: Börsenblatt für den deutschen Buchhandel, 1886. II, 67-136.

2966. Schielin, Ulrike. Aussenhandel des österreichischen Zollgebiets 1815-1838. Diss. Vienna, 1968. 347 pp.

2967. Schneller, Maria. Wachstumsprobleme der Ackerbauproduktion in der österreichischen Reichshälfte der Donaumonarchie von 1848 bis 1913. Diss. Vienna, 1974. 246 pp.

2968. Sieghart, Rudolf. Zolltrennung und Zolleinheit. Die Geschichte der österreichisch-ungarischen Zwischenzoll-Linie. Vienna: Manz, 1915. 413 pp.

2969. Smolensky, Max. Oesterreich-Ungarns wirtschaftliche Beziehungen zur Schweiz. Vienna: Manz, 1918. 76 pp.

2970. Die Störung im deutschen Wirtschaftsleben während der Jahre 1900 ff. in ihren Rückwirkungen auf die industriellen Effekten- und Geldmarktsverhältnisse Österreichs. Ed. Verein für Socialpolitik. Leipzig: Duncker & Humblot, 1903. 261 pp.

2971. Tremel, Ferdinand. "Wirtschaftliche Führungskräfte in Österreich 1850-1914." in Führungskräfte der Wirtschaft im neunzehnten Jahrhundert 1790-1914. Limburg: C. A. Starke, 1977.
II, 145-75.
2972. Wirth, Max. Oesterreichs Wiedergeburt aus den Nachwehen der Krisis. Vienna: Manz, 1876.
522 pp.
2973. Worliczek, Ernst. Aussenhandel des österreichischen Zollgebietes 1839-1850. Diss. Vienna,
1970. 339 pp.

SEE ALSO: 337-38, 369-70, 2085, 2101, 2141, 2767, 3021, 3354, 3358, 3507.

AUSTRIA--1919-1975

2974. Bonner, Josef. Strukturwandlungen und Nachkriegsprobleme der Wirtschaft Österreichs.
Kiel: Institut für Weltwirtschaft, 1950. 64 pp.
2975. Breuss, Fritz. Österreichs Aussenwirtschaft 1945-1982. Vienna: Signum-Verlag, 1983.
700 pp.
2976. Bruckmüller, Ernst. "Österreich, die Tschechoslowakei und Frankreich in der Zwischenkriegszeit: Politisch-wirtschaftliche Beziehungen." Österreich in Geschichte und Literatur 16 (1972),
417-31.
2977. Curtius, Julius. Bemühung um Oesterreich. Das Scheitern des Zollunionsplans von 1931.
Heidelberg: Winter, 1947. 106 pp.
2978. Hassinger, Herbert. "Forschungen über Firmen und Unternehmer in Österreich seit 1945."
Tradition 2 (1957), 172-184.
2979. Hoffmann, Robert. "Die wirtschaftlichen Grundlagen der britischen Österreichpolitik 1919."
Mitteilungen des Österreichischen Staatsarchivs 30 (1977), 251-87.
2980. Kager, Marianne. Entwicklung der Industriestruktur in Österreich und der BRD, 1960-1975.
Vienna: Orac, 1979. 246 pp.
2981. Katzenstein, Peter J. "Trends and Oscillations in Austrian Integration Policy since 1955.
Alternative Explanations." Journal of Common Market Studies 14 (1975), 171-97.
2982. Marton, Adám. Consumer Prices in Austria and Hungary 1945-1972. Some Aspects of Price
Formation. Price Development and Price Patterns. Vienna: Verein Wiener Institut für Internationale Wirtschaftsvergleiche, 1974. 174 pp.
2983. Neiss, Hubert and Hans Seidel. "Der Zusammenhang zwischen der österreichischen und der
internationalen Konjunktur 1950 bis 1964." Österreichisches Institut für Wirtschaftsforschung.
Monatsberichte 39 (1966), 7-13.
2984. Pollan, Wolfgang. "Vielfältige Bewegungen der Verbraucherpreise seit 1967." Österreichisches Institut für Wirtschaftsforschung 53 (1980), 179-93.
2985. Richter, Josef. "Exportleistungen kleiner und mittlerer Unternehmen." Wirtschaftspolitische
Blätter 28 (1981), 79-87.
2986. Seidel, Hans. "Die Grundlagen der wirtschaftlichen Entwicklung seit dem Zweiten Weltkrieg."
in Die Rezession 1974-75, ein Wendepunkt der längerfristigen Wirtschaftsentwicklung?
Stuttgart: G. Fischer, 1977. pp. 7-17.
2987. Skarke, Anna Maria and Peter Skarke. Wachstumsunterschiede der österreichischen Bundes-
länder 1964-7l. Eine Anwendung der Shift and Share Analysis. Vienna: Institut für Höhere
Studien, 1974. 30 pp.
2988. Slavik, G. Der Aussenhandel und die Handelspolitik Österreichs 1918-1926. Klagenfurt:
Kleinmayr, 1928. 83 pp.
2989. Stankovsky, Jan. "Die Ausfuhr industrieller Fertigwaren in die Oststaaten 1961 bis 1967."
Österreichisches Institut für Wirtschaftsforschung. Monatsberichte 42 (1969), 54-65.
2990. Stiefel, Dieter. Konjunkturelle Entwicklung und struktureller Wandel der österreichischen
Wirtschaft in der Zwischenkriegszeit. Vienna: Institut für Höhere Studien, 1978. 92 pp.
2991. Strasser, Hellmuth. Der Weg Österreichs zu den Verträgen mit Brüssel. Vienna:
Österreichische Gesellschaft für Aussenpolitik und Internationale Beziehungen, 1972. 87 pp.
2992. Suppanz, Christian. Die österreichische Inflation, 1918-1922. Vienna: Institut für Höhere
Studien, 1976. 196 pp.
2993. Tichy, Gunther. "Die Beschleunigung des Wirtschaftswachstums im Aufschwung 1967 bis
1971." Österreichisches Institut für Wirtschaftsforschung. Monatsberichte 45 (1972), 148-60.

2994. Tichy, Gunther. Indikatoren der österreichischen Konjunktur 1950 bis 1970. Vienna: Österreichisches Institut für Wirtschaftsforschung, 1972. 94 pp.
2995. Weber, Wilhelm and K. Socher. "Inflation und Inflationsbekämpfung in Österreich seit 1945." in G. Bombach, ed. Stabile Preise in wachsender Wirtschaft. Das Inflationsproblem. Tübingen: Mohr, 1960.
2996. Zehn Jahre österreichische Integrationspolitik. 1956-1966. Eine Dokumentation des Bundesministeriums für Handel und Wiederaufbau. Vienna: Österreichische Staatsdruckerei, 1966. 318 pp.

SEE ALSO: 413, 1486, 2917, 3488, 3654, 3675, 3679, 3686, 3702, 3704, 3711, 3713, 3715, 3723, 3733, 3742, 3758, 3773.

AUSTRIAN AND AUSTRO-HUNGARIAN REGIONS

Bohemia and Moravia

2997. Gajan, Koloman. "Die Rolle der Tschechoslowakei in Mitteleuropa 1918-1945." Österreichische Osthefte 8 (1966), 185-91.
2998. Kellenbenz, Hermann. "Die wirtschaftlichen Beziehungen zwischen Westdeutschland und Böhmen-Mähren im Zeitalter der Industrialisierung." Bohemia. Jahrbuch des Collegium Carolinum 3 (1962), 239-59.
2999. Klíma, Arnóst. "Verhandlungen über den Beitritt Böhmens zum deutschen Zollverein 1848." in H. Knittler, ed. Wirtschafts- und sozialhistorische Beiträge. Munich: Oldenbourg, 1979. pp. 308-20.
3000. Pribram, Alfred F. Das Böhmische Commerzcollegium und seine Thätigkeit. Prague: Verlag des Vereins für Geschichte der Deutschen in Böhmen, 1898. 278 pp.
3001. Schwarz, E. F. 20 Jahre Leistungskampf sudetendeutscher Genossenschaften "Schulze-Delitzsch" (1918-1938). Aussig: Sudetendeutscher Genossenschafts-Verband, 1938. 289 pp.

SEE ALSO: 426, 2121, 2976.

Burgenland

3002. Bachinger, Karl. Geschichte der gewerblichen Wirtschaft des Burgenlandes. Eisenstadt: Kammer der Gewerblichen Wirtschaft für Burgenland, 1973. 364 pp.
3003. Grohotolsky, Rudolf. "Der burgenländische Handel in den letzten fünfzig Jahren." in 50 Jahre Wirtschaft im Burgenland. Eisenstadt: Burgenländisches Landesarchiv, 1971.
3004. Kühnelt, Victor. "Die gewerbliche Organisation im Burgenland." in 10 Jahre Burgenland. seine politische, kulturelle und wirtschaftliche Entwicklung in den Jahren 1921-1931. Vienna: Amt der burgenländischen Landesregierung, 1931.
3005. Rottensteiner, Anton. "Das burgenländische Gewerbe." in 50 Jahre Wirtschaft im Burgenland. Eisenstadt: Burgenländisches Landesarchiv, 1971.
3006. Wagner, Johann. "Handel, Gewerbe und Industrie im Burgenland." in 25 Jahre Burgenland. Eine Rückschau auf seine politische, kulturelle und wirtschaftliche Entwicklung. Vienna: Amt der Burgenländischen Landesregierung, 1946.
3007. Zirkovits, Ernst. Burgenlands Handel einst und jetzt. Vienna: Österreichischer Wirtschaftsverlag, 1973. 119 pp.

SEE ALSO: 432.

Carinthia: SEE 435.

Hungary

3008. Eddie, Scott M. "The Terms and Patterns of Hungarian Foreign Trade, 1882-1913." Journal of Economic History 37 (1977), 329-58.
3009. Fabinyi, Thomas de. 15 années de relations économiques hungar-suisse (1931-1945). Zurich: Fluntern, 1948. 232 pp.
3010. Mérei, György. Der Aussenhandel des Königreichs Ungarn, 1790-1848. Budapest: Hungarian Academy of Science, 1980. 33 pp.
3011. Zorn, Wolfgang. "Das Unternehmertum in Ungarn im 19. Jahrhundert. Fritz Redlich zum 80. Geburtstag gewidmet." Tradition 17 (1972), 1-7.

SEE ALSO: 2141, 2958, 3762.

Lower Austria

3012. Danninger, Gerhard. Das Linzer Handwerk und Gewerbe von Verfall der Zunfthoheit über die Gewerbefreiheit bis zum Innungszwang. Linz: Trauner, 1981. 232 pp.
3013. Fünfzig Jahre landwirtschaftliches Genossenschaftswesen in Niederösterreich. Vienna: Niederösterreichische Landwirtschaftliche Genossenschafts-Zentralkasse, 1936. 377 pp.
3014. Holzmann, Gustav. Unternehmensgeschichte in Niederösterreich. Struktur, Funktion, Bibliographie. Vienna: Eigenverlag der Handelskammer Niederösterreich, 1972. 44 pp.
3015. Nemschak, Franz. 60 Jahre Niederösterreichische Genossenschafts-Zentralkasse, 1898-1958. Vienna: Niederösterreichische Genossenschafts-Zentralkasse, 1958. 99 pp.
3016. Niederösterreich an der Arbeit. Entwicklung und Leistung der gewerblichen Wirtschaft des Landes. Horn: F. Berger, 1948.
3017. Otruba, Gustav. Der Aussenhandel Österreichs unter besonderer Berücksichtigung Niederösterreichs nach der älteren amtlichen Handelsstatistik. Vienna: Kammer für Arbeiter und Angestellte in Niederösterreich, 1950. Vol. I.

Romania

3018. Gheorghiu, Panait R. The Foreign Trade of Roumania from the Treaty of Adrianople (1829) up to the Great Depression (1929). Bucarest: Vacarescu, 1936. 240 pp.
3019. Stanciu, I. "Considérations sur l'évolution des rapports commerciaux entre la Roumanie et les États-Unis d'Amérique jusqu'en 1914." Révue Roumaine d'Histoire 11 (1972), 603-30.
3020. Tonch, Hans. Wirtschaft und Politik auf dem Balkan. Untersuchung zu den deutsch-rumänischen Beziehungen in der Weimarer Republik. Frankfurt a. M.: Lang, 1984. 250 pp.
3021. Zane, Gheorge. "Die österreichischen und die deutschen Wirtschaftsbeziehungen zu den rumänischen Fürstentümern 1774-1874." Weltwirtschaftliches Archiv 26 (1927), 30-47, 262-81.

SEE ALSO: 2898, 3614, 3783.

Salzburg

3022. Klein, Herbert. "Salzburgs Handel im Wandel der Zeiten." in Festschrift zum 65. Geburtstag von Herbert Klein. Salzburg: Gesellschaft für Salzburger Landeskunde, 1965. pp. 559-74.
3023. Martin, Franz. "Industrie, Gewerbe und Kunst in Salzburg 1819." Mitteilungen der Gesellschaft für Salzburger Landeskunde 81 (1941), 145-60.
3024. Wysocki, Josef. "Die gewerbliche Wirtschaft Salzburgs von 1816 bis 1860." Zeitschrift für Unternehmensgeschichte 24 (1979), 150-79.

Styria

3025. Mensi, Franz. "Zur Geschichte der Preise und Löhne in Steiermark." in Festschrift Mell. Graz: Historischer Verein für Steiermark, 1935. pp. 103-06.
3026. Popelka, Fritz. Geschichte der Grazer Messen. Graz: Deutsche Vereinsdruckerei, 1921. 59 pp.
3027. Tremel, Ferdinand, ed. Steirische Unternehmer des 19. und 20. Jahrhunderts. Eine Sammlung von Lebensbildern. Graz: Historischer Verlag für Steiermark, 1965. 110 pp.

SEE ALSO: 2158.

Tirol

3028. Santner, Egon. Handwerk und Gewerbe in Innsbruck in der ersten Hälfte des 19. Jahrhunderts. Diss. Innsbruck, 1976. 300 pp.
3029. Stolz, Otto. Geschichte des Zollwesens, Verkehrs und Handels in Tirol und Vorarlberg von den Anfängen bis ins 20. Jahrhundert. Innsbruck: Universität-Verlag, 1953. 315 pp.

SEE ALSO: 493, 497, 1534.

Upper Austria

3030. Molterer, Hermann. Beiträge zur Preis- und Lohngeschichte der Stadt Wels in Oberösterreich. 3 vols. Diss. Innsbruck, 1933.
3031. Pisecky, Franz. "Das oberösterreichische Gewerbe in historischer Sicht." Oberösterreich 23 (1973), 16-24.
3032. Prummer, Ulrike. Die Auswirkungen der Welser Messe auf die Stadt Wels und die wirtschaftliche Entwicklung von Wels. Thesis Vienna Economics University, 1973. 106 pp.

SEE ALSO: 1544.

Vienna

3033. Bandion, Erwin. Das Wiener Gewerbe und die Wiener Industrie im Rahmen der österreichischen Monarchie in der ersten Hälfte des neunzehnten Jahrhunderts. Diss. Vienna, 1949. 1234 pp.
3034. Jubiläumsbericht 1910-1935. 25 Jahre Gewerbeförderung in Wien und Niederösterreich. Vienna: Gewerbeförderungsinstitut der Kammer für Handel, Gewerbe und Industrie in Wien, 1935. 167 pp.
3035. Peyfuss, Max D. "Balkanorthodoxe Kaufleute in Wien." Österreichisches Ost- und Südosteuropa-Institut 17 (1975), 258-68.
3036. Rondorf, Richard and Richard Till. Geschichte des Wiener Marktwesens. Vienna: Geitner, 1939. 61 pp.
3037. Zatschek, Heinz. Handwerk und Gewerbe in Wien. Von den Anfängen bis zur Erteilung der Gewerbefreiheit im Jahre 1859. Vienna: Österreichischer Gewerbeverlag, 1949. 272 pp.

SEE ALSO: 519, 2169, 2952.

Vorarlberg: SEE 497, 525, 3029.

SWITZERLAND

Reference

3038. Handbuch der schweizerischen Volkswirtschaft. 2 vols. Bern: Schweizerische Gesellschaft für Statistik und Volkswirtschaft, 1939.

SWITZERLAND

3039. Abt, Roman. Beiträge zur Geschichte der Entwicklung des landwirthschaftlichen Genossenschaftswesens in der Schweiz. Brugg: Epprecht & Keller, 1910. 135 pp.

3040. Bairoch, Paul. "Le volume des exportations de la Suisse de 1851 à 1975." Manuscript. S.l.: s.n., 1977.

3041. Barth, Alfred. Die wirtschaftliche Verflechtung der Schweiz mit dem Ausland. Winterthur: Keller, 1966. 184 pp.

3042. Baumgartner, Jean-Pierre. Le trafic des moyens de transport et la conjuncture économique en Suisse de 1901 à 1944. Diss. Bern. Bern: Staempfli, 1947. 124 pp.

3043. Berwert, Peter. Export und Wirtschaftswachstum. Der Fall der Schweiz. Bern: Lang, 1977. 229 pp.

3044. Bleuler, Werner. Studien über Aussenhandel und Handelspolitik der Schweiz. Zurich: Schulthess, 1929. 170 pp.

3045. Böhi, Hans. "Hauptzüge einer schweizerischen Konjunkturgeschichte." SZVS 100 (1964), 71-105.

3046. Boson, Marcel. Co-op in der Schweiz. Betrachtungen zu den Anfängen und zur Entwicklung der Co-op Genossenschaften. Basel: Buchdruck VSK, 1965. 562 pp. (Original: French, 1965)

3047. Bosshardt, Alfred. "Die langfristigen Auswirkungen der europäischen Integration auf die schweizerische Volkswirtschaft." in Aussenhandels-, Integrations- und Währungspolitik aus schweizerischer Sicht. Zurich: Schweizerisches Institut für Aussenwirtschafts- und Marktforschung, 1970. pp. 84-104.

3048. Bosshardt, Alfred and A. Nydegger. "Die schweizerische Aussenwirtschaft im Wandel der Zeiten." SZVS 100 (1964), 302-27.

3049. Boveri, Walter. Unsere wirtschaftliche Krisis. Aarau: Sauerländer, 1921. 26 pp.

3050. Curti, Giuseppe. Les relations économiques entre la Suisse et l'Italie de 1871 à nos jours. Geneva: Bellinzona & Grassi, 1949. 484 pp.

3051. Dérobert, Eugène. La politique douanière de la confédération suisse. Étude sur la politique douanière suisse, depuis la constitution de l'Etat fédéral jusqu'à douanier actuel. Geneva: Jent, 1926. 448 pp.

3052. Ducommun, Charles F. Essai sur la théorie des crises économiques et les positions du syndicalisme suisse. Diss. Lausanne. Lausanne: F. Roth, 1941. 344 pp.

3053. Durtschi, Ernst. "Entwicklung und Bedeutung der genossenschaftlichen Selbsthilfe in der schweizerischen Landwirtschaft." Schweizerische Landwirtschaftliche Monatshefte 35 (1957), 150-56.

3054. Durtschi, Ernst. "Die landwirtschaftlichen Genossenschaften in der Schweiz." Zeitschrift für das gesamte Genossenschaftswesen 3 (1953), 314-22.

3055. Durtschi, Ernst. "Die landwirtschaftlichen Genossenschaften in der Schweiz." Zeitschrift für das gesamte Genossenschaftswesen 12 (1962), 231-38.

3056. Erdman, Paul. Swiss-American Economic Relations. Their Evolution in an Era of Crises. Basel: Kyklos-Verlag, 1959. 173 pp.

3057. Faucherre, Henry. Umrisse einer genossenschaftlichen Ideengeschichte. Basel: Verband Schweizerische Konsumvereine, 1925-28. 224 pp.

3058. Fischer, Otto. "30 Jahre schweizerische Gewerbepolitik." Unternehmungsführung im Gewerbe 12 (1980), 37-40.

3059. Fischer, Otto. "Gewerbe und Wirtschaftspolitik." in Schweizerische Wirtschaftspolitik zwischen gestern und morgen. Festgabe zum 65. Geburtstag von Hugo Sieber. Bern: P. Haupt, 1976. pp. 407-15.

3060. Das Gewerbe in der Schweiz. 100 Jahre Schweizerischer Gewerbeverband 1879-1979. Bern: Schweizerischer Gewerbeverband, 1979. 300 pp.

3061. Gutersohn, Alfred. Das Gewerbe in der schweizerischen Wirtschaftspolitik. Der Schweizerische Gewerbeverband. 1879-1954. Zurich: Schweizerischer Gewerbeverband, 1954. 328 pp.

3062. Heuberger, Max. Die Strukturwandlungen des schweizerischen Aussenhandels in den Jahren 1938-1949. Diss. Basel, 1955. 119 pp.

3063. His, Eduard. "Wandlungen der Handels- und Gewerbefreiheit in der Schweiz." in Beiträge zum Handelsrecht. Festgabe . . . Carl Wieland. Basel: Helbing & Lichtenhahn, 1934. pp. 241-60.

3064. "Integrationspolitik der Schweiz und Österreichs. Bisherige Erfahrungen und Zukunftsperspektiven." Aussenwirtchaft 29 (1974), 49-62.

3065. Kupper, Walter. Die Zollpolitik der schweizerischen Landwirtschaft seit 1848. Diss. Zurich. Zurich: Stämpfli, 1929. 201 pp.

3066. Lang, Alexander V. Bevölkerungsstruktur. Wirtschaftswachstum und Produktivitätsentwicklung. dargestellt am Beispiel der Schweiz. Diss. Basel, 1964. 110 pp.

3067. Lüthy, Herbert. "Wandlungen des schweizerischen Handels in der Neuzeit." in Der schweizerische Grosshandel in Geschichte und Gegenwart. Basel: Delegation des Handels, 1944. pp. 47-135.

3068. Mühlemann, Hans E. Anfänge der schweizerischen Konsumgenossenschaftsbewegung. Diss. Bern, 1939. Affoltern am Albis: Weiss, 1940. 137 pp.

3069. Munz, Hans. Das Phänomen Migros. Die Geschichte der Migros-Gemeinschaft. Zurich: Verlag Ex Libris, 1973. 420 pp.

3070. Napolski, Friedrich von. Der Weg zum ersten Handelsvertrag zwischen der Schweiz und Deutschland. Bergisch Gladbach: Heider, 1961. 78 pp.

3071. Reichesberg, Naum. Betrachtungen über die schweizerische Handelspolitik in Vergangenheit und Zukunft. Bern: Francke, 1918. 77 pp.

3072. Rutz, Wilfried. Die schweizerische Volkswirtschaft zwischen Währungs- und Beschäftigungspolitik in der Weltwirtschaftskrise: wirtschaftspolitische Analyse der Bewältigung eines Zielkonflikts. Diss. St. Gallen, 1969. Zurich: Polygraphischer Verlag, 1970. 300 pp.

3073. Der schweizerische Grosshandel in Geschichte und Gegenwart. Basel: Delegation des Handels, 1943. 184 pp.

3074. Das schweizerische Zollwesen. Bern: Eidgenössische Oberzolldirektion, 1948. 222 pp.

3075. Steiger, Kurt von. Die schweizerische Zollpolitik von 1900 bis 1930. Diss. Bern. Bern: Schenk, 1933. 281 pp.

3076. Verband schweizerischer Produktivgenossenschaften 1932-1982: 50 Jahre Verband schweizerischer Produktivgenossenschaften. Zurich: Verband schweizerischer Produktivgenossenschaften, 1982. 45 pp.

3077. Vogel, René M. W. Politique commerciale suisse. Montreux: Ed. Léman, 1966. 498 pp.

3078. Vogler, Albert. Die schweizerischen Militärausgaben von 1850-1963 und ihre Auswirkungen auf die wirtschaftliche Entwicklung der Schweiz. Diss. Fribourg, 1965. 169 pp.

3079. Wagner, Julius, ed. Fünfundzwanzig Jahre Schweizer Mustermesse. Zurich: Verkehrsverlag, 1942. 275 pp.

3080. Wehrli, Bernhard. Aus der Geschichte des schweizerischen Handels- und Industrievereins 1870-1970. Erlenbach-Zurich: Eugen Rentsch, 1970. 319 pp.

3081. Weisz, Leo. Studien zur Handels- und Industriegeschichte der Schweiz. 2 vols. Zurich: Verlag der Neuen Zürcher Zeitung, 1938-1940.

3082. Wittmann, Walter. "Wachstum, Konjunktur und Preisniveau der schweizerischen Volkswirtschaft." Zeitschrift für die gesamte Staatswissenschaft 118 (1962), 426-41.

3083. Würgler, H. "Perspektiven der schweizerischen Wirtschaft." Gewerbliche Rundschau 20 (1975), 79-92.

3084. Wunderle, Karl. Der Detailhandel mit Lebensmitteln und die Konsumgenossenschaften. Historische Darstellung und kritische Würdigung der schweizerischen Entwicklung. Diss. Basel. Basel: Buchdruck VSK, 1957. 170 pp.

3085. Wyss, Annemarie. Die konsumgenossenschaftlichen Grundsätze in der Schweiz von den Anfängen bis zur Gegenwart. Diss. Zurich. Basel: Buchdruck VSK, 1949. 132 pp.

SEE ALSO: 1556, 3009, 3582.

SWITZERLAND--1815-1918

3086. Balmer, Hans. Messung interregionaler Wohlstandesunterschiede. Ein Vergleich Schweiz-Österreich. Bern: Lang, 1981. 252 pp.

3087. Bauer, Hans. Von der Zunftverfassung zur Gewerbefreiheit in der Schweiz. 1798 bis 1874. Basel: Nationalzeitung, 1929. 263 pp.

3088. Beck, Bernhard. Lange Wellen wirtschaftlichen Wachstums in der Schweiz 1814-1913. Eine Untersuchung der Hochbauinvestitionen und ihrer Bestimmungsgründe. Bern: Haupt, 1983. 175 pp.

3089. Binswanger, Hans C. "Europaische Zollunionspläne in der Schweiz vor dem Ersten Weltkrieg." Aussenwirtschaft 13 (1958), 89-95.

3090. Brand, Urs. Die schweizerisch-französischen Unterhandlungen über einen Handelsvertrag und der Abschluss des Vertragswerkes von 1865. Ein Beitrag zur Geschichte der schweizerischen Wirtschaft und Diplomatie. Diss. Bern. Bern: Lang, 1968. 323 pp.

3091. Dietschi, Erich. "Die Handelsverträge der Schweiz mit den süddeutschen Staaten 1824-1828." Zeitschrift für die gesamte Staatswissenschaft 83 (1930-31), 55-100.

3092. Dietschi, Erich. "Die Schweiz und der entstehende deutsche Zollverein 1828-1835." Zeitschrift für die Geschichte des Oberrheins 44 (1930), 287-344.

3093. Dietschi, Erich. Die Schweiz und Deutschland in ihren handelspolitischen Beziehungen in der Zeit der Entstehung des deutschen Zollvereins 1815-1835. Diss. Basel, 1927. 162 pp.

3094. Geering, Traugott. Handel und Industrie der Schweiz unter dem Einfluss des Weltkriegs. Basel: B. Schwabe, 1928. 851 pp.

3095. Gozenbach, August von. Über die Handelsverhältnisse zwischen der Schweiz und den deutschen Zollvereinsstaaten während des Jahres 1840. Lucerne: s.n., 1845.

3096. Gruner, Erich. "Die Handels- und Gewerbefreiheit und die Staatsordnung von 1874-1914." Wirtschaft und Recht 12 (1960), 149-55.

3097. Gruner, Erich. "Werden und Wachsen der schweizerischen Wirtschaftsverbände im 19. Jahrhundert. Der Einfluss der schweizerischen Wirtschaftsverbände auf das Gefüge des liberalen Staates." Schweizerische Zeitschrift für Geschichte 6 (1956), 33-101, 315-368.

3098. Hauser, Albert. "Die Schweiz und der Deutsche Zollverein." SZVS 94 (1958), 732-94.

3099. Hauser, Albert. Schweizerische Unternehmergestalten aus früheren Jahrhunderten. Zurich: Rügg, 1953. 59 pp.

3100. Hauser, Albert. "Die wirtschaftlichen Beziehungen der Schweiz zu Deutschland in der ersten Hälfte des 19. Jahrhunderts." Schweizerische Zeitschrift für Geschichte 8 (1958), 355-82.

3101. Heussler, Heinz. Die Auseinandersetzungen über den Beitritt der Schweiz zum Deutschen Zollverein und ihre Auswirkungen auf die Entstehung des schweizerischen Bundesstaates. Diss. Zurich, 1969. Zurich: Juris Druck und Verlag, 1971. 136 pp.

3102. Hilfiker, Otto. Krisen und Konjunkturen in der Schweiz zur Zeit der 80er Jahre des neunzehnten Jahrhunderts. Studien zur schweizerischen Wirtschaftsgeschichte. Diss. Bern. Lungern: Burch, 1944. 148 pp.

3103. Huber, Albert. Die Entwicklung des eidgenössischen Zollwesens vom Beginn der ersten Tarife bis zur Bundesverfassung des Jahres 1848. Bern: Stämpfli, 1890. 243 pp.

3104. Hunziker, O. Geschichte der Schweizerischen Gemeinnützigen Gesellschaft. 2nd ed. Zurich: Zürcher & Furrer, 1910. 259 pp.

3105. Iff, Werner. Der Einfluss des Zolltarifs von 1902 und der Handelsverträge von 1904/06 auf die Gestaltung der wirtschaftlichen Verhältnisse der Schweiz bis zum Ausbruch des Weltkrieges. Aarau: Sauerländer, 1923. 159 pp.

3106. Iff, Werner. Unsere Exportindustrie und die schweizerische Zoll- und Wirtschaftspolitik. Aarau: Sauerländer, 1925. 259 pp.

3107. Lorenz, Jacob. Die Detailpreise der schweizerischen Konsumvereine 1912-1918. 20 vols. Basel: Buchdruck VSK, 1919.

3108. Miller, Hans. Die schweizerischen Konsumgenossenschaften. ihre Entwicklung und ihre Resultate. Basel: Verlag des Verbands Schweizerischer Konsumvereine, 1896. 455 pp.

3109. Pfenninger, Rudolf. Die Handelsbeziehungen zwischen der Schweiz und Deutschland während des Krieges 1914-1918. Diss. Zurich, 1927. Zurich: Gutzwiller, 1928. 138 pp.

3110. Rupli, Walther. Zollreform und Bundesreform in der Schweiz 1815-48: die Bemühungen um die wirtschaftliche Einigung der Schweiz und ihr Einfluss auf die Gründung des Bundesstaates von 1848. Zurich: Europa, 1949. 267 pp.

3111. Tschumi, Hans. Der schweizerische Gewerbeverband 1879-1929. Bern: Schweizerischer Gewerbeverband, 1929. 720 pp.
3112. Untersuchungen über Preisbildung. Vol. 5. Leipzig: Duncker & Humblot, 1928. 303 pp.
3113. Verband Landwirtschaftlicher Genossenschaften der Nordwestschweiz. Denkschrift für Fünfundvierzig Jahre genossenschaftlicher Arbeit. 1880 bis 1925. Zur Eröffnung des neuen Verbandslagerhauses in Solothurn. Solothurn: Vogt-Schild, 1925. 64 pp.
3114. Wehrli, Bernhard. Le Vorort, mythe ou réalité de l'Union suisse du commerce et de l'industrie, 1870-1970. Neuchâtel: Baconnière, 1972. 345 pp.
3115. Welche Einflüsse hatte der deutsch-französische Krieg 1870-71 auf schweizerischen Handel und Industrie? Basel: s.n., 1872.
3116. Zwingli, Ulrich and Edgar Ducret. "Das Sozialprodukt als Wertmesser des langfristigen Wirtschaftswachstums. Das schweizerische Sozialproduckt 1910 und in früheren Jahren." SZVS 100 (1964), 328-68.

SEE ALSO: 2179, 2198, 2969, 3595.

SWITZERLAND--1919-1945

3117. Baumgartner, Otto. Die schweizerische Aussenhandelspolitik von 1930 bis 1936. Diss. Zurich. Zurich: E. Lang, 1943. 138 pp.
3118. Billaud, Félix. Essai sur le régime des limitations à l'importation en Suisse au cours de la période 1931-1939. Geneva: s.n., 1942. 131 pp.
3119. Bosshardt, Alfred. "Die schweizerische Aussenhandelspolitik in den dreissiger Jahren." SZVS 81 (1945), 65- .
3120. Comtesse, Jean-Laurent. La crise de 1929 et l'industrie horlogère suisse. Diss. Neuchâtel. Lausanne: Impr. Héliographia, 1952. 189 pp.
3121. Dickenmann, Heinz. Das Bundespersonal in der Wirtschaftskrise 1931-1939. Diss. Zurich, 1983. 436 pp.
3122. Frei, Gerhard. Kontingentierung und Einfuhrbeschränkung als Mittel der schweizerischen Aussenhandelspolitik (1931-1936). Diss. Bern, 1941. Lucerne: Keller, 1941. 70 pp.
3123. Haab, Robert and Carl Koechlin. Handel, Industrie und Verkehr der Schweiz im Kampf um ihre Existenz. Gläubiger und Schuldner in der Krise. 2 vols. Basel: Helbing & Lichtenhahn, 1934.
3124. Hellinger, Kurt. Die Aussenhandelspolitik der Schweiz in der Weltwirtschaftskrise. Diss. Heidelberg. Coburg: Tageblatt-Haus, 1938. 61 pp.
3125. Homberger, Heinrich. Schweizerische Handelspolitik im Zweiten Weltkrieg. Ein Überblick auf Grund persönlicher Erlebnisse. Erlenbach-Zurich: Rentsch, 1970. 131 pp.
3126. Hotz, J. "Zur schweizerischen Zollpolitik der Nachkriegszeit." in Festgabe für . . . Edmund Schulthess. Zurich: Polygraphischer Verlag, 1938. pp. 183-200.
3127. Huber, Johannes. Die wirtschaftliche Rettung der Schweiz aus der heranrückenden grossen Wirtschaftskrise. Basel: S. Huber, 1920. 47 pp.
3128. Jenny, Hans. "Kriegs- und Nachkriegsprobleme des schweizerischen Grosshandels." SZVS 81 (1945), 79-94.
3129. Kneschaurek, Francesco. Der schweizerische Konjunkturverlauf und seine Bestimmungsfaktoren. Dargestellt auf Grund der Periode 1929 bis 1939. Zurich: Polygraphischer Verlag, 1952. 256 pp.
3130. Leuthäusel, Josef. Der Ausbau der Wirtschaftsbeziehungen zwischen der Schweiz und Sowjetrussland. Basel: Verlag von Frobenius, 1932. 41 pp.
3131. Masnata, Albert. "Les rapports réciproques entre l'émigration industrielle et l'exportation suisse sous l'action de la politique douanière étrangère (1925-1939)." in Schweizerische Wirtschaftsfragen. Festgabe für Fritz Mangold. Basel: Helbing & Lichtenhahn, 1941. pp. 170-78.
3132. Petitat, Paul. La gestation des chemins de fer fédéraux sous l'influence de la crise (1930-39). Diss. Geneva. Aarau: A. Trüb, 1940. 312 pp.
3133. Schaffner, Hans. "Gedanken zur Aussenhandelspolitik der Schweiz in zweiten Weltkrieg." in Festgabe für. . . Konrad Ilg . . . . Bern: Schweizerischer Metall-Uhrenarbeiterverband, 1947. pp. 109-29.
3134. "Der schweizerische Aussenhandel unter den Einwirkungen des Krieges 1939-1946." Die Volkswirtschaft 19 (1946), 2-24.

3135. Schweizerische Export-Probleme der Kriegs- und Nachkriegszeit. Zurich: Börzig, 1941. 90 pp.
3136. Siegenthaler, Hansjörg. "Grosse Depression und erfinderische Aktivität in der Schweiz." in
        H. Winkel, ed. Finanz- und wirtschaftspolitische Fragen der Zwischenkriegszeit. Berlin: Duncker
        & Humblot, 1973. pp. 175-208.
3137. Stebler, Alexander. Der industrielle Konjunkturverlauf in der Schweiz 1919-1939. Diss.
        Basel, 1943. Immensee: Calendaria, 1946. 117 pp.
3138. Steiner, Max. Die Verschiebungen in der schweizerischen Aussenhandelsstruktur während des
        zweiten Weltkrieges. Diss. Bern. Zurich: Juris, 1950. 147 pp.
3139. Stucki, Walter. "25 Jahre schweizerische Aussenhandelspolitik." in Festgabe für. . . Edmund
        Schulthess. . .. Zurich: Polygraphischer Verlag, 1938. pp. 123-43.
3140. Vaudaux, Adolphe. Blockade und Gegenblockade. Handelspolitische Sicherung der schweize-
        rischen Ein- und Ausfuhr im zweiten Weltkrieg. Diss. Basel. Zurich: Polygraphischer Verlag,
        1948. 128 pp.

SEE ALSO: 577, 579, 1575, 3156, 4530, 4544, 4546-47.

SWITZERLAND--1945-1975

3141. Allenspach, Heinz. "25 Jahre Wirtschaftswachstum. Nur eine negative Bilanz?" Schweizer
        Monatshefte 57 (1977), 23-29.
3142. Cordey, Franklin. La Suisse face à l'intégration européenne. Diss. Lausanne, 1971. 401 pp.
3143. Gloor, Gérard R. Die wirtschaftlichen Beziehungen zwischen der Schweiz und der Südafrikani-
        schen Union seit dem 2. Weltkrieg. Winterthur: Keller, 1959. 200 pp.
3144. Ins, German von. Das Problem der Überbeschäftigung in der Nachkriegszeit. Diss. Basel.
        Grosshöchstetten: Jakob, 1956. 111 pp.
3145. Kamber, Markus. "Die Entwicklung und die Probleme des Gewerbes in der Schweiz 1959-
        1979." IHA/GfM Nachrichten 2 (1979), 8-10.
3146. Kneschaurek, Francesco. Der "Trendbruch" der siebziger Jahre und seine wirtschaftlichen
        Konsequenzen. Diessenhofen: Rüegger, 1980. 85 pp.
3147. Monney, André. Les échanges de marchandises entre la Suisse et le Marché commun.
        Fribourg: Estavoyer-le-Lac, 1965. 216 pp.
3148. Pfister, Max. Die Sonderstellung der Schweiz in der internationalen Wirtschaftspolitik.
        Aussenwirtschaftspolitik 1945-1959. Winterthur: Keller, 1961. 294 pp.
3149. Roethlisberger, Eric. La Suisse dans l'AELE 1960-1966. Sept ans d'intégration économique
        dans un cadre européen restreint. Neuchâtel: Baconnière, 1969. 309 pp.
3150. Scherer, Theodor. Die Importfunktion der Schweiz. Eine empirische Untersuchung für das
        Dezennium 1961-1970. Zurich: Juris-Verlag, 1974. 201 pp.
3151. Schmid, Erich. Die schweizerische Zollpolitik von 1945 bis 1960. Diss. Zurich, 1964. 108 pp.
3152. Seidlitz, Henri de. L'inflation en Suisse de 1950 à 1963 et ses relations avec le crédit.
        Lausanne: Payot, 1964. 254 pp.
3153. Semadeni, O. Die schweizerische Nachkriegsinflation 1945-1948. Diss. St. Gallen. St. Gallen:
        W. Weinhold, 1954. 245 pp.
3154. Sommaruga, Cornelio. "La Suisse et l'intégration économique européenne, hier, aujourd'hui,
        demain." in L'organisation de l'économie internationale au seuil des années 1980. Fribourg:
        Institute for Economic & Social Sciences, 1981. pp. 57-68.
3155. Spahni, Walter. Der Ausbruch der Schweiz aus der Isolation nach dem Zweiten Weltkrieg.
        Frauenfeld: Huber, 1977. 304 pp.
3156. Steiner, M. Die Verschiebungen in der schweizerischen Aussenhandelsstruktur während des
        zweiten Weltkrieges. Bern: Juris, 1950. 147 pp.
3157. Veyrassat, Paul. La Suisse et la création de l' AELE. 1958-1960. Diss. Geneva, 1968.
        Neuchâtel: Baconnière, 1969. 238 pp.
3158. Vogel, René M. W. Politique commerciale suisse. Montreux: Ed. Léman, 1966. 498 pp.

SEE ALSO: 4541, 4555.

SWISS CANTONS

Aargau

3159. Dubler, Anne-Marie and Jean J. Siegrist. Wohlen. Geschichte von Recht, Wirtschaft und Bevölkerung. Aargau: Sauerländer, 1975. 712 pp.

Basel

3160. Angst, Emil. Zum 75jährigen Jubiläum des Allgemeinen Consumvereins beider Basel. Basel: ACV beider Basel, 1940. 182 pp.
3161. Bürgin, Alfred. Geschichte des Geigy-Unternehmens von 1758 bis 1939. Ein Beitrag zur Basler Unternehmer- und Wirtschaftsgeschichte. Basel: Birkhäuser, 1958. 325 pp.
3162. Egloff, Robert. Basels Handel und Handelspolitik von 18l5-1835. Diss. Basel. Mulhouse: Impr. centr., 1930. 115 pp.
3163. Frey, Adalbert. Gewerbeverband und Gewerbepolitik im Kanton Basel-Stadt seit 1918. Bern: Francke, 1949. 223 pp.
3164. Hahn, Eduard. Die Auswirkung der Zollpolitik des Auslandes auf die drei Basler Haupt-industrien: Seidenband-, Schappe- und Teerfarbenfabrikation seit der Freihandelsära der 1860er Jahre. Diss. Basel. Osterode am Harz: Giebel & Oehlschlägel, 1934. 105 pp.
3165. His, Eduard. Basler Handelsherren des 19. Jahrhunderts. Basel: Schwabe, 1929. 194 pp.
3166. Jastrow, Ignaz. Alt-Basel: eine deutsche Fabrik- und Handelsstadt in ihrer Geschichte und Geschichtsschreibung. Basel: Handel und Industrie der Stadt Basel, 1886.
3167. Joneli, Hans. Die ersten Konsumvereine in Basel. Basel: G. Krebs, 1907. 23 pp.
3168. Mangold, Walter. Die Entstehung und Entwicklung der Basler Exportindustrie mit besonderer Berücksichtigung ihres Standortes. Basel: Philographischer Verlag, 1935. 123 pp.
3169. Notz, Emil. Die säkulare Entwicklung der Kaufkraft des Geldes für Basel in den Perioden 1800-1833 und 1892-1923. Jena: G. Fischer, 1925. 283 pp.
3170. Wanner, Gustav A. Das Basler Gewerbe an der Arbeit, 1834-1984. Basel: Basel-Stadt, 1984. 163 pp.

SEE ALSO: 4563.

Bern

3171. Baumann, H. "12 Jahre bernische Gewerbepolitik. Referat gehalten an der Delegierten-versammlung des Kantonal-Bernischen Gewerbeverbandes vom 28. April 1965 in Thun." Gewerbliche Rundschau 10 (1965), 56-62.
3172. Geiser, Karl. Handel, Gewerbe und Industrie im Kanton Bern bis zum Jahr 1860. Bern: Neukomm & Zimmermann, 1910. 50 pp.
3173. Geiser, Karl and Adolf Buri. Bernischer Verein für Handel und Industrie. Denkschrift zur Feier des 50jährigen Bestehens 1860-1910. Bern: Neukomm & Zimmermann, 1910. 102 pp.
3174. Müller, Hans. "Das bernische Gewerbe gestern, heute und morgen." Handwerk und Gewerbe 18 (1948), 26-34.
3175. Stauffer, Hans. Geschichte der Konsumgenossenschaften des deutschen Sprachgebietes der Kantone Bern und Freiburg (Kreis IIIa des VSK). Diss. Bern. Basel: Buchdruckerei VSK, 1957. 88 pp.
3176. Über Preise und Teuerung auf Grund der Lebensmittelpreisstatistik und weiterer Unter-suchungen von 1912/13-1921 im Kanton Bern. Bern: Francke, 1922. 136 pp.

SEE ALSO: 599.

Glarus

3177. Jenny-Trümpy, Adolf. Handel und Industrie des Kantons Glarus. 2 vols. Glarus: Aktienbuchdruckerei Glarus, 1898-1900.

Lucerne

3178. Blaser, Robert and Fritz Blaser. Geschichte der Gemeinnützigen Gesellschaft der Stadt Luzern 1812-1960. Luzern: Gemeinnützige Gesellschaft Luzern, 1962. 126 pp.
3179. Gmür, Leonhard. Die Entwicklung der Gewerbefreiheit im Kanton Luzern von der Helvetik bis zur Bundesverfassung von 1874. Diss. Bern, 1924. 104 pp.
3180. Der Kampf für gewerbliche Selbständigkeit. Festschrift zum 60jährigen Bestande des Gewerbeverbandes der Stadt Luzern. Luzern: Bucher, 1935. 257 pp.
3181. Schwendimann, Johannes. Luzernische Handels- und Gewerbepolitik vom Mittelalter bis zur Gegenwart. Ein Beitrag zur Geschichte des schweizerischen Mittelstandes. Luzern: Räber, 1918. 390 pp.
3182. Schwendimann, Johannes. Luzerns Handelsstand ehemals und heute. Festschrift zum 25-jährigen Jubiläum des Rabattsparvereins Luzern. Luzern: Räber, 1928. 118 pp.

SEE ALSO: 2212.

St. Gallen

3183. Bodmer, Albert. Die Gesellschaft zum Notenstein und das Kaufmännische Directorium. Ein Beitrag zur Sozial- und Wirtschaftsgeschichte der alten Stadtrepublik St. Gallen. St. Gallen: Fehr, 1962. 76 pp.
3184. Bürgi, Paul. 150 Jahre st. gallisches Gewerbe. St. Gallen: Gewerbeverbände St. Gallen-Appenzell, 1953. 24 pp.
3185. Handel und Industrie im Kanton St. Gallen. Denkschrift zum 75jährigen Bestehen des Handels- und Industrievereins St. Gallen, 1875-1950. St. Gallen: Zollikofer, 1950. 159 pp.
3186. Wartmann, Hermann. "Handel und Industrie des Kantons St. Gallen 1803-1903." in Der Kanton St. Gallen 1803-1903. St. Gallen: Zollikofer, 1903. pp. 215- .

SEE ALSO: 1590, 2213, 2217-21.

Schaffhausen

3187. Pfaff, Robert. "Schaffhausen und die Entstehung des deutschen Zollvereins." Schaffhauser Beiträge zur vaterländischen Geschichte 44 (1967), 7-41.
3188. Steinegger, Albert. "Schaffhausens Handel und Verkehr nach der Westschweiz und Lyon." Schaffhauser Beiträge zur vaterländischen Geschichte 12 (1939), 5-46.

Solothurn

3189. Berger, Hermann. Festschrift zum 100-Jahr-Jubiläum des Consumvereins Olten, 1862-1962. Olten: Consumverein, 1962. 100 pp.
3190. Zimmermann, Hans. Das solothurnische Zollwesen von der Helvetik bis zur Ablösung durch die Bundesverfassung von 1848. Diss. Bern. Affoltern a. A.: Weiss, 1940. 114 pp.

Thurgau

3191. Beuttner, Paul, ed. 1892-1942. 50 Jahre Thurgauische Gewerbepolitik. Frauenfeld: Huber, 1942. 83 pp.

3192. Helg, Robert. 100 Jahre Thurgauischer Handels- und Industrieverein 1870-1970. Kurzer Abriss der Vereinsgeschichte, aufgezeichnet nach den Protokollen und Jahresberichten. Kreuzlingen: Thurgauischer Handels- und Industrieverein, 1970. 92 pp.

SEE ALSO: 1593.

Unterwalden: SEE 627.

Zurich

3193. Grossmann, Marcel. Das Kaufmännische Direktorium in Zürich, 1662-1834. Diss. Zurich, 1927. 91 pp.
3194. Heeb, Friedrich. Hundert Jahre Konsumgenossenschaften in den Kantonen Zürich und Schaffhausen. Basel: Verband schweizerischer Konsumvereine, 1952. 255 pp.
3195. Peyer, Hans C. Von Handel und Bank im alten Zürich. Zurich: Berichthaus, 1968. 323 pp.
3196. Richard, Emil. Kaufmännische Gesellschaft Zürich und Zürcher Handelskammer 1873-1923. 2 vols. Zurich: Zürcher Handelskammer, 1924.
3197. Ruckstuhl, Hans. Die Ausbildung der zürcherischen Handels- und Gewerbefreiheit in den 1830er Jahren. Diss. Zurich. Zurich: Leemann, 1914. 95 pp.
3198. Salzmann, Martin. Die Wirtschaftskrise im Kanton Zürich, 1845-1848. Ihre Stellung und Wertung im Rahmen der wirtschaftlich-sozialen Entwicklung in der ersten Hälfte des 19. Jahrhunderts. Bern: Lang, 1978. 399 pp.
3199. Sieveking, Heinrich. "Zur zürcherischen Handelsgeschichte." Jahrbuch für Schweizer Geschichte 35 (1910), 69*-130*.
3200. Weisz, Leo. Die zürcherische Exportindustrie. Ihre Entstehung und Entwicklung. Wirtschaftsgeschichtliche Untersuchungen. 2nd ed. Zurich: Neue Zürcher Zeitung, 1937. 237 pp.
3201. Widmer, Hans. Die Stadt Winterthur in der Krise 1930-34. Winterthur: Buchdruck Winterthur, 1936. 112 pp.

SEE ALSO: 641, 2235, 2240-42.

GERMANY

References

3202. Arbeitsgegenstand und ökonomisches Wachstum. Bibliographie. 3 vols. Berlin: Deutsche Akademie der Wissenschaften, 1971-72.
3203. Bibliographie des Einzelhandels, 1883-1933. Stuttgart: Foeschel, 1935. 375 pp.
3204. Bibliographie selbständiger Schriften zur Betriebsgeschichte. Berlin: Deutsche Akademie der Wissenschaften, 1964. 45 pp.
3205. Eyll, Klara van et al., eds. Deutsche Wirtschaftsarchive. Nachweis historischer Quellen in Unternehmen, Kammern und Verbänden der Bundesrepublik Deutschland. 2 vols. Wiesbaden: Steiner, 1978-82.
3206. Fischer, Alfred. "Bibliographie von Veröffentlichungen zur Geschichte der Kapitalistischen Unternehmen, die nach 1945 in Westdeutschland und Westberlin erschienen sind." Jahrbuch für Wirtschaftsgeschichte (1960), II, 355-402; (1962), III, 207-72; (1968), II, 407-23.
3207. Humpert, Magdalene. Bibliographie der Kameral Wissenschaften. Cologne: Schroeder, 1937. 1184 pp.
3208. Meier, P. J. "The Work of the Hamburg Research Center in Entrepreneurial History." Journal of Economic History 21 (1961), 364-76.
3209. Neumann, Ina. "Bibliographie zur Firmengeschichte und Unternehmerbiographie." Tradition 12 (1967), 545-52.
3210. Neuss, Erich. "Werkegeschichte und Unternehmerbiographie in Mitteldeutschland." Tradition 5 (1960), 217-30.

3211. Redlich, Fritz. "Research on German Entrepeneurship." Explorations in Economic History 2 (1949-50), 100-02; 4 (1951-52), 38-43.

GERMANY

3212. Abelshauser, Werner and Dietmar Petzina. "Krise und Rekonstruktion. Zur Interpretation der gesamtwirtschaftlichen Entwicklung Deutschlands im 20. Jahrhundert." in Historische Konjunkturforschung. Stuttgart: Klett-Cotta, 1981. pp. 75-114.
3213. Ambrosius, Gerold et al. Die Rolle des Staates für die wirtschaftliche Entwicklung. 2 vols. Stuttgart: Klett, 1976.
3214. Ashley, Percy. Modern Tariff History. Germany, United States, France. 3rd ed. London: Murray, 1926. 365 pp.
3215. Aubin, Hermann. "Wirtschaftsgeschichte und Konjunkturtheorie." in Der Stand und die nächste Zukunft der Konjunkturforschung. Festschrift für Arthur Spielhoff. Munich: Duncker & Humblot, 1933. pp. 22-23.
3216. Baudis, Dieter et al. "Der Unternehmer in der Sicht der Westdeutschen Firmen und Wirtschaftsgeschichte." Zeitschrift für Geschichtswissenschaft 11 (1963), 78-103.
3217. Bechtel, Heinrich. Der Wirtschaftstil des deutschen Unternehmers in der Vergangenheit. Dortmund: Gesellschaft für westfälische Wirtschaftsgeschichte, 1955. 27 pp.
3218. Berding, Helmut. "Die Entstehung des deutschen Zollvereins als Problem historischer Forschung." in Vom Staat des Ancien Régime zum modernen Parteienstaat. (Festschrift für Theodor Schieder.) Munich: Oldenbourg, 1978. pp. 225-37.
3219. Bernholz, Peter. Aussenpolitik und internationale Wirtschaftsbeziehungen. Frankfurt a. M.: Klostermann, 1967. 202 pp.
3220. Blesius, N. Zur Entstehungsgeschichte des neuzeitlichen ländlichen Genossenschaftswesens. Berlin: Commerz, 1929. 38 pp.
3221. Bohner, Theodor. Der ehrbare Kaufmann. Vom Werden und Wirken deutscher Wirtschaft. Hamburg: Meiner, 1956. 552 pp.
3222. Bohner, Theodor. Der offene Laden. Aus der Chronik des Einzelhandels. 2nd ed. Frankfurt a. M.: Verlag für Wirtschaftspraxis, 1958. 296 pp.
3223. Bondi, Gerhard. "Die erste Etappe der Entwicklung eines nationalen Marktes in Deutschland." Wirtschaftswissenschaft 3 (1955), 247-60.
3224. Bondi, Gerhard. "Zu einigen Fragen der Entwicklung des nationalen Marktes." in Forschen und Wirken. Festschrift zur 150. Jahr-Feier der Humboldt-Universität zu Berlin, 1810-1960. Berlin: Deutscher Verlag der Wissenschaft, 1960. pp. 521-36.
3225. Bonn, Moritz J. Das Schicksal des deutschen Kapitalismus. Berlin: S. Fischer, 1926. 62 pp.
3226. Borchardt, Knut. Wachstum, Krisen, Handlungspielräume der Wirtschaftspolitik: Studien zur Wirtschaftsgeschichte des 19. und 20. Jahrhunderts. Göttingen: Vandenhoeck & Ruprecht, 1982. 302 pp.
3227. Born, Karl E. "Die Weltwirtschaftskrise als zeitgeschichtlicher Hintergrund der Einführung der gesetzlichen Pflichtprüfung." in V. Muthesius, ed. 75 Jahre Deutsche Treuhand-Gesellschaft, 1890-1965. Frankfurt a. M.: Deutsche Treuhand-Gesellschaft, 1965. pp. 53-97.
3228. Bredeck, Heinz. Entwicklungstendenzen in den genossenschaftlichen Selbsthilfebestrebungen des mittelständischen Lebensmitteleinzelhandels--von ihrem Beginn bis zur Gegenwart. Diss. Cologne. Munich: Fotodruck Mikrokopie, 1957. 162 pp.
3229. Brenning, Heinz. Entwicklung und Aufbau der Bezirksorganisationen im deutschen ländlichen Genossenschaftswesen. Diss. Göttingen. Bückeburg: Grimme, 1928. 179 pp.
3230. Brinkmann, Carl. Zur Wirtschaftsgeschichte der deutschen Unternehmung. Berlin: Duncker & Humblot, 1942. 97 pp.
3231. Broesicke, Marianne H. Der deutsche Grosskaufmann in seiner Entwicklung. Diss. Berlin, 1941. Würzburg: K. Triltsch, 1941. 136 pp.
3232. Brusatti, Alois. Der Unternehmerbegriff. Vienna: Verein der wissenschaftlichen Forschung auf dem Gebiete der Unternehmerbiographie und Firmengeschichte, 1974. 45 pp.
3233. Christiansen, Ragnvald. Vom deutschen Zollverein zur Europäischen Zollunion. Bonn: Stollfuss, 1978. 47 pp.
3234. Clausnitzer, Martin. Deutsche Zollgeschichte von Ursprung der Zölle bis zur Gründung der Reichsfinanzverwaltung. Leipzig: Gnauck, 1933. 103 pp.

3235. Curtius, Julius. "Die deutsch-österreichische Zollunionsaktion." in Curtius: Sechs Jahre Minister der Deutschen Republik. Heidelberg: Winter, 1948. pp. 188-212.

3236. Dessauer, Marianne. Entwicklungstendenzen der betrieblichen Exportwirtschaft in Deutschland seit der Mitte des 19. Jahrhunderts: unter besonderer Berücksichtigung der Exportorganisation. Munich: Florentz, 1982. 260 pp.

3237. Dietrich, Hugo. Der deutsche Export von Gebrauchswaren nach China, Britisch Indien, Niederländisch Indien. Diss. Cologne. Emsdetten: Lechte, 1935. 94 pp.

3238. Dietze, Hugo. Geschichte des deutschen Handels. Leipzig: Gloeckner, 1923. 144 pp.

3239. Dollinger, Philippe. The German Hansa. Stanford, CA: Stanford University Press, 1970. 474 pp.

3240. Elsas, Moritz J. "Zur Methode der Preisgeschichte." Zeitschrift für die gesamte Staatswissenschaft 94 (1933), 213-31.

3241. Faust, Helmut. Genossenschaftswesen. Stuttgart: Schwann, 1969. 192 pp.

3242. Faust, Helmut. Schulze-Delitzsch und sein genossenschaftliches Werk. Marburg: Simon, 1949. 71 pp.

3243. Finckh, Ellen. Einkommens- und Verbrauchsgestaltung in Deutschland von 1899-1913 und 1924-1927. Ein statistischer Beitrag zur Konjunkturanalyse. Diss. Kiel. Wiesbaden: Ritter, 1931. 51 pp.

3244. Fischer, Curt E. "Die Geschichte der deutschen Versuche zur Lösung des Kartell- und Monopolproblems." Zeitschrift für die gesamte Staatswissenschaft 110 (1954), 425-56.

3245. Fischer, Wolfram. "Der Deutsche Zollverein, die Europäische Wirtschaftsgemeinschaft und die Freihandelszone." Europa-Archiv 16 (1961), 105-14.

3246. Franz, Günther. "Die Entstehung des Landwarenhandels." Tradition 5 (1960), 65-82.

3247. Freudenberger, Herman. "Fashion, Sumptuary Laws, and Business. Business History Review 37 (1963), 37-48.

3248. Fritzsching, Leonhard. "Der Mittelstand als Klasse. Zur Wirtschaftsethik des nicht-kapitalistischen Unternehmers." Schmoller 54 (1930), 109-130.

3249. Fünfzig Jahre Raiffeisen 1877-1927. Neuwied: Deutsche Raiffeisenbank, 1927. 211 pp.

3250. Gartmayr, Eduard. Nicht für den Gewinn allein. Die Geschichte des deutschen Einzelhandels. Frankfurt a. M.: Verlag für Wirtschaftspraxis, 1964. 182 pp.

3251. Gellately, Robert. "Zur Entstehungsgeschichte der Massenkonsumgesellschaft Deutschlands." in Tradition und Neubeginn. Internationale Forschungen zur deutschen Geschichte im 20. Jahrhundert. Cologne: Heymann, 1975. pp. 467-80.

3252. Glismann, Hans H. and Horst Rodemer. Der wirtschaftliche Niedergang in der Bundesrepublik Deutschland und in der Weimarer Republik. Kiel: Institut für Weltwirtschaft, 1982. 18 pp.

3253. Goldsmith, Raymond W. "The National Balance Sheet of Germany, 1850-1972." Konjunkturpolitik 22 (1976), 153-72.

3254. Gugumus, Jakob. Konjunktur und Eheschliessung im Deutschen Reich seit 1820. Diss. Cologne. Cologne: Orthen, 1940. 132 pp.

3255. Hahn, L. Albert. Fünfzig Jahre zwischen Inflation und Deflation (1912-1962). Tübingen: Mohr, 1963. 247 pp.

3256. Hahn, Max. "Deutscher Zollverein damals, Mitteleuropa heute. Zur hundertjährigen Wiederkehr des Gründungstages des Deutschen Zollvereins." Volk und Reich 30 (1931), 1-7.

3257. Hasselmann, Erwin. Geschichte der deutschen Konsumgenossenschaften. Frankfurt a. M.: Knapp, 1971. 740 pp.

3258. Hasselmann, Erwin. Im Strom der Zeit. 60 Jahre Zentralverband Deutscher Konsumgenossenschaften. Hamburg: Verlagsgesellschaft Deutscher Konsumgenossenschaften, 1963. 55 pp.

3259. Henderson, William O. "Prince Smith and Free Trade in Germany." Economic History Review 2 (1949-50), 295-302.

3260. Hieke, Ernst. Zur Geschichte des deutschen Handels mit Ostafrika. 2 vols. Hamburg: Christians, 1939.

3261. Hoffmann, Walther G. "Das Wachstum der Wirtschaft Schwedens und Deutschlands 1861 bis 1968. Ein statistischer Vergleich." in Analyse und Prognose in der quantitativen Wirtschaftsforschung. Festgabe für Ingeborg Esenwein-Rothe zum 60. Geburtstag. Berlin: Duncker & Humblot, 1971. pp. 208-38.

3262. Hoffmann, Walther G. "Wachstumsschwankungen in der deutschen Wirtschaft 1850-1967." in W. G. Hoffmann, ed. Untersuchungen zum Wachstum der deutschen Wirtschaft. Tübingen: Mohr, 1971. pp. 77-92.

3263. Hoffmann, Walther G., ed. Untersuchungen zum Wachstum der deutschen Wirtschaft. Tübingen: Mohr, 1971. 302 pp.

3264. Hoffmann, Walther G. and J. Heinz Müller, eds. Das deutsche Volkseinkommen 1851-1957. Tübingen: Mohr, 1959. 162 pp.

3265. Jacobs, Alfred and Hans Richter. Die Grosshandelspreise in Deutschland von 1792-1934. Berlin: Hanseatische Verlagsanstalt, 1935. 111 pp.

3266. Kammler, Hans. Das Problem einer deutsch-polnischen Zollunion. Diss. Greifswald. Danzig: Käfemann, 1933. 55 pp.

3267. Kaufmann, Heinrich. Ein konsumgenossenschaftlicher Blick in die Zukunft. Vergangenheit, Gegenwart und Zukunft des konsumgenossenschaftlichen Grosseinkaufs. Hamburg: Grosseinkaufs-Gesellschaft Deutscher Consumvereine, 1921. 40 pp.

3268. Kehrein, Paul. Konjunktureinflüsse in der Grosseisenindustrie. Eine Untersuchung der Bilanzen von 9 Unternehmungen der Grosseisenindustrie von 1880-1914 unter dem Einfluss der Schein-gewinnwirkung. Diss. Frankfurt a. M., 1928. Gelnhausen: Kalbfleisch, 1930. 238 pp.

3269. Kellenbenz, Hermann. "Handelshochschulen--Betriebswirtschaft--Wirtschaftsarchive." Tradition 10 (1965), 301-09.

3270. Kellenbenz, Hermann, ed. Wachstumsschwankungen. Wirtschaftliche und soziale Aus-wirkungen (Spätmittelalter bis 20. Jahrhundert). 8. Arbeitstagung der Gesellschaft für Sozial- und Wirtschaftsgeschichte. Stuttgart: Klett-Cotta, 1981. 340 pp.

3271. Kellenbenz, Hermann, ed. Wirtschaftliches Wachstum im Spiegel der Wirtschaftsgeschichte. Darmstadt: Wissenschaftliche Buchgesellschaft, 1978. 475 pp.

3272. Klein, Fritz. Selbsthilfe aus christlicher Verantwortung. Die Geschichte der christlichen Konsumvereine. Recklinghausen: Kommunal, 1967. 208 pp.

3273. Klusak, Gustav. "Entwicklung und Aufgaben der Spitzenorganisation des deutschen ländlichen Genossenschaftswesens." in Festschrift für Andreas Hermes zum 80. Geburtstag. Neuwied: Verlag Raiffeisendruckerei, 1958. pp. 197-212.

3274. Kniesche, Herbert. Die grossdeutsche Wirtschaftseinheit. Geschichte und Gegenwartsprobleme der österreichisch-deutschen Wirtschaftsverflechtung. Leipzig: Hofstetter, 1929. 195 pp.

3275. Knorring, Ekkehard von. "Strukturwandlungen des privaten Konsums im Wachstumsprozess der deutschen Wirtschaft seit der Mitte des 19. Jahrhunderts." in W. G. Hoffmann, ed. Untersuchungen zum Wachstum der deutschen Wirtschaft. Tübingen: Mohr, 1971. pp. 167-91.

3276. König, Erika. Die deutsche Sozialdemokratie und die aufkommenden Wirtschaftsmonopole. Berlin: Dietz, 1958. 282 pp.

3277. König, Paul. "Edeka und Raiffeisen." in Festschrift für Andreas Hermes zum 80. Geburtstag. Neuwied: Verlag Raiffeisendruckerei, 1958. pp. 213-26.

3278. Koepsel, Kurt. Die Entwicklung des japanischen Aussenhandels. Kassel: Kasseler Post, 1929. 96 pp.

3279. Kraus, Otto. Inflation, Deflation. Hamburg: Hanseatische Verlagsanstalt, 1956. 94 pp.

3280. Kroll, Gerhard. "Die deutsche Wirtschaftspolitik in der Weltwirtschaftskrise." in K. E. Born, ed. Moderne deutsche Wirtschaftsgeschichte. Cologne: Kiepenheuer & Witsch, 1966. pp. 398-409.

3281. Kroll, Gerhard. Von der Weltwirtschaftskrise zur Staatskonjunktur. Berlin: Duncker & Humblot, 1958. 743 pp.

3282. Kruedener, Jürgen. "Die Jahresberichte der Preussischen Bank (1847-1975) als Quelle zur Konjunkturgeschichte." VSWG 62 (1975), 465-99.

3283. Kuczynski, Jürgen. Löhne and Konjunktur in Deutschland 1887-1932. Berlin: Finanzpolitische Korrespondenz, 1933. 39 pp.

3284. Kuczynski, Jürgen. Studien zur Geschichte der zyklischen Überproduktionskrisen in Deutschland, 1918 bis 1945. Berlin: Akademie, 1963. 200 pp.

3285. Kuczynski, Jürgen. Studien zur Geschichte des staatsmonopolistischen Kapitalismus in Deutschland 1918-1945. Berlin: Akademie, 1963. 287 pp.

3286. Kühl, Joachim. "Die europäische Bedeutung des deutsch-österreichischen Zollunionsplans." in Föderationspläne im Donauraum und in Ostmitteleuropa. Munich: Oldenbourg, 1958. pp. 75-84.

3287. Kuske, Bruno. "Der Einsatz des Genossenschaftsgedankens in der Entwicklung der deutschen Wirtschaft." in Karl Arnold Festschrift. Cologne: Arbeitsgemeinschaft für Forschung des Landes Nordrhein-Westfalen, 1955. pp. 493-504.

3288. Lange, Hellmut. Die Stellung des deutschen Unternehmers zum Kartell. Ein Beitrag zur Geistes-geschichte des modernen Unternehmertums. Diss. Berlin. Berlin: C. Heymann, 1937. 69 pp.

3289. Lederer, Emil. Kapitalismus, Klassenstruktur und Probleme der Demokratie in Deutschland 1910-1940. Göttingen: Vandenhoeck & Ruprecht, 1979. 310 pp.
3290. Lerner, Franz. Kaufmannstum und Handelsstätten. Bielefeld: A. Oetker Nährmittelfabrik, 1960. 28 pp.
3291. Lerner, Franz. "Neue Beiträge zur Geschichte der Preise und Löhne in Deutschland, Holland und Italien." VSWG 39 (1952), 251-65.
3292. Lüke, Rolf E. Von der Stabilisierung zur Krise. Zurich: Polygraphischer Verlag, 1958. 363 pp.
3293. Mehlan, Arno. "Historischer Überblick über die deutsch-bulgarischen Wirtschaftsbeziehungen." Schmoller 61 (1937), 425-44.
3294. Meyer, Paul W. "Gedanken über die Entfaltung der Handelssysteme und der Handlungsformen seit 1844." in Handelsforschung heute. Festschrift zum 50jährigen Bestehen der Forschungsstelle für den Handel. Berlin: Duncker & Humblot, 1979. pp. 59-68.
3295. Möller, Hans. Aussenwirtschaftspolitik. Wiesbaden: Gabler, 1961. 147 pp.
3296. Niemann, Hans-Werner. Das Bild des industriellen Unternehmers in deutschen Romanen der Jahre 1890 bis 1945. Berlin: Colloquium, 1982. 336 pp.
3297. Nölting, Erik. Wirtschaftsformen gestern, heute und morgen. Hamburg: Verlag des Zentralverbandes Deutscher Konsumgenossenschaften, 1949. 19 pp.
3298. Nussbaum, Helga. Unternehmer gegen Monopole. Über Struktur und Aktionen antimonopolistischer bürgerlicher Gruppen zu Beginn des 20. Jahrhunderts. Berlin: Akademie, 1966. 254 pp.
3299. Oppen, Dietrich von. Verbraucher und Genossenschaft. Zur Soziologie und Sozialgeschichte der deutschen Konsumgenossenschaften. Cologne: Westdeutscher Verlag, 1959. 111 pp.
3300. Papritz, Johannes. "Stand und Aufgaben der Forschung zur deutschen Handelsgeschichte in Ostmitteleuropa." in Hermann Aubin et al. Deutsche Ostforschung. Ergebnisse und Aufgaben seit dem ersten Weltkrieg. Leipzig: S. Hirzel, 1943. pp. 596-642.
3301. Petzina, Dietmar and Ger van Roon, eds. Konjunktur, Krise, Gesellschaft. Wirtschaftliche Wechsellagen und soziale Entwicklungen im 19. und 20. Jahrhundert. Stuttgart: Klett-Cotta, 1981. 350 pp.
3302. Philippi, Georg. "Preise, Löhne und Produktivität in Deutschland von 1500 bis zur Gegenwart." Konjunkturpolitik 12 (1966), 305-35.
3303. Pichler, Michael. Die süddeutschen Konsumgenossenschaften und ihre Verbände im Wandel der Zeit. Hamburg: Verlagsgesellschaft Deutscher Konsumgenossenschaften, 1952. 76 pp.
3304. Pohl, Hans. Absatzstrategien deutscher Unternehmen gestern-heute-morgen: am 13. Mai 1981 in Fürth. Wiesbaden: Steiner, 1982. 93 pp.
3305. Pohl, Hans, and Wilhelm Treue, eds. Die Konzentration in der deutschen Wirtschaft seit dem 19. Jahrhundert. Wiesbaden: Steiner, 1978. 87 pp.
3306. Pohl, Hans and Wilhelm Treue, eds. Stiftung und Unternehmung. Erfahrungen und Zukunftsperspektiven. Wiesbaden: Steiner, 1979. 62 pp.
3307. Postelt, Walter. Werden und Ringen der Konsumgenossenschaft "Produktion". Zum 50jährigen Jubiläum. 1899-1949. Hamburg: "Freie Gewerkschaft," 1949. 31 pp.
3308. Predöhl, A. Aussenwirtschaft. Weltwirtschaft, Handelspolitik und Währungspolitik. Göttingen: Vandenhoeck & Ruprecht, 1949. 354 pp.
3309. Quark, Max. Die Entwicklung des Handels, Transports und Verkehrs in Deutschland. Berlin: Courier, 1929. 279 pp.
3310. Raiffeisen in unserer Zeit. Zum hundertjährigen Bestehen der ländichen Genossenschaften. Bonn: Deutscher Raiffeisenverband, 1949. 271 pp.
3311. Redlich, Fritz. The Beginnings and Development of German Business History. Boston: Business Historical Society, 1952. 82 pp. (German: Baden-Baden, 1959)
3312. Rieker, Karlheinrich. "Die Konzentrationsentwicklung in der gewerblichen Wirtschaft. Eine Auswertung der deutschen Betriebszählungen von 1870 bis 1950." Tradition 5 (1960), 116-31.
3313. Rittershausen, Heinrich. "Die deutsche Aussenhandelspolitik von 1879 bis 1948. Eine Auseinandersetzung zwischen monopolistischen Interessen und sich anbahnender Wettbewerbsordnung in der Welt." Zeitschrift für die gesamte Staatswissenschaft 105 (1948), 126-68.
3314. Rosenberg, Hans. Machteliten und Wirtschaftskonjunkturen. Studien zur neueren deutschen Sozial- und Wirtschaftsgeschichte. Göttingen: Vandenhoeck & Ruprecht, 1978. 343 pp.
3315. Sachtler, Heinz. Wandlungen des industriellen Unternehmers in Deutschland seit Beginn des 19. Jahrhunderts. Ein Versuch zur Typologie des Unternehmers. Diss. Halle-Wittenberg. Berlin: Maetze, 1936. 69 pp.
3316. Samhaber, Ernst. Die neuen Wirtschaftsformen 1914-1940. Berlin: Neff, 1940. 364 pp.

3317. Schack, Gerhard. Raiffeisen in Deutschland. Idee. Organisation und gegenwärtiger Stand des ländlichen Genossenschaftswesens im Bundesgebiet. 3rd ed. Neuwied: Verlag der Raiffeisendruckerei, 1961. 67 pp.

3318. Schneider, Ernst. Beiträge zur Kenntnis der Entwicklung der landwirtschaftlichen Bezugs- und Absatzgenossenschaften. Diss. Berlin. Charlottenburg: Hoffmann, 1928. 89 pp.

3319. Schröder, Wilhelm H. and Reinhard Spree, eds. Historische Konjunkturforschung. Stuttgart: Klett-Cotta, 1981. 419 pp.

3320. Schücking, Walther. Die Versuche zur Schaffung eines gesamtdeutschen Wirtschaftsraums seit Friedrich List. Diss. Giessen. Giessen: Noske, 1939. 84 pp.

3321. Schultz, Reinhard. Genossenschaftswesen. Berlin: de Gruyter, 1970. 219 pp.

3322. Schumpeter, J. A. Konjunkturzyklen. Eine theoretische, historische und statistische Analyse des kapitalistischen Prozesses. 2 vols. Göttingen: Vandenhoeck & Ruprecht, 1961.

3323. Schwarz, Günter R. Die Entwicklung des Bezugs- und Absatzgeschäftes der deutschen ländlichen Genossenschaften und deren Einfluss auf die Verminderung der Preisspanne zwischen Erzeuger- und Verbraucherpreis. Diss. Rostock. Berlin: s.n., 1927. 120 pp.

3324. Schwerin von Krosigk, Lutz Graf. Alles auf Wagnis. Der Kaufmann gestern, heute und morgen. Tübingen: Wunderlich, 1963. 607 pp.

3325. Sombart, Werner. "Emporkommen, Entfaltung und Auswirkung des Kapitalismus in Deutschland." Volk und Reich der Deutschen 1 (1929), 199-219.

3326. Sombart, Werner. Liebe. Luxus und Kapitalismus: über die Entstehung der modernen Welt aus dem Geist der Verschwendung. Berlin: Wagenbach, 1983. 202 pp.

3327. Strauss, Walter. "Gewerbefreiheit und Vertragsfreiheit. Eine rechtsgeschichtliche Erinnerung." in Wirtschaftsordnung und Staatsverfassung. Festschrift für Franz Böhm zum 80. Geburtstag. Tübingen: Mohr, 1975. pp. 603-14.

3328. Sussitz, Hermann. Ökonomische Integrationsbestrebungen zwischen Österreich und Deutschland 1815-1931. Diss. Vienna Hochschule für Welthandel, 1975. 232 pp.

3329. Tausend Jahre Kampf der deutschen Bauern um ihre Freiheit. Der Weg der deutschen Bauern von der Marktgenossenschaft zur landwirtschaftlichen Produktionsgenossenschaft. Berlin: Dietz, 1961. 176 pp.

3330. Taxacher, H. Entwicklungsgeschichte der deutsch-westindischen Wirtschaftsbeziehungen. Diss. Cologne, 1929. 117 pp.

3331. Teschemacher, Hans. Der deutsche Staat und der Kapitalismus. Stuttgart: Kohlhammer, 1933. 45 pp.

3332. Tilly, Richard H. "The Growth of Large-Scale Enterprise in Germany since the Middle of the Nineteenth Century." in The Rise of Managerial Capitalism. Louvain: Université Catholique de Louvain, 1974. pp. 145-69.

3333. Tilly, Richard H. "Renaissance der Konjunkturgeschichte?" Geschichte und Gesellschaft. Zeitschrift für historische Sozialwissenschaft 6 (1980), 243-62.

3334. Treue, Wilhelm. "Die Bedeutung der Firmengeschichte für die Wirtschafts- und für die Allgemeine Geschichte." VSWG 41(1954), 42-65.

3335. Voigt, Manfred. "Grundzüge des Handels und der Handelspolitik des deutschen Imperialismus gegenüber Ägypten von Beginn des 20. Jahrhunderts bis zur Gegenwart." Jahrbuch für Wirtschaftsgeschichte (1967), II, 187-234.

3336. Wagenführ, Horst. Schöpferische Wirtschaft. Pionier-Leistungen deutscher Erfinder und Unternehmer. Heidelberg: Werkschrift, 1954. 320 pp.

3337. Weber, Max. Wirtschaft und Gesellschaft: Grundriss der verstehenden Soziologie. Tübingen: Mohr, 1980. 945 pp.

3338. Westenberger, Hans. "Die handelspolitischen und wirtschaftlichen Beziehungen Deutschlands und Lettlands bis zum Abschluss des deutsch-lettländischen Vertrages vom 28. Juni 1926." Ost-Europa 1 (1926), 656-67.

3339. Weuster, Arnulf. Theorie der Konsumgenossenschaftsentwicklung. Die deutschen Konsumgenossenschaften bis zum Ende der Weimarer Zeit. Berlin: Duncker & Humblot, 1980. 700 pp.

3340. Wiedenfeld, Kurt. "Süddeutsche Aspeckte der räumlichen Ordnung des Zollvereins." in Raumordnung im 19. Jahrhundert. Hannover: Akademie für Raumforschung und Landesplanung, 1967. pp. 151-78.

3341. Wilken, Paul H. "Prussia-Germany." in Entrepreneurship. A Comparative and Historical Study. Norwood, NJ: Ablex, 1979. pp. 13- .

3342. Witt, Henry. Die Triebkräfte des industriellen Unternehmertums vor 100 Jahren und heute. Diss. Hamburg. Hamburg: Günther, 1929. 229 pp.
3343. Zippe, Herbert. Grosse Unternehmer. Lebensbilder aus fünf Jahrhunderten. Thansau-Rosenheim: Fachverlag H. Riedler, 1954. 272 pp.
3344. Zorn, Wolfgang. "Das deutsche Unternehmerporträt in sozialgeschichtlicher Betrachtung." Tradition 7 (1962), 79-92.
3345. Zorn, Wolfgang. "Typen und Entwicklungskräfte deutschen Unternehmertums." in K. E. Born, ed. Moderne deutsche Wirtschaftsgeschichte. Cologne: Kiepenheuer & Witsch, 1966. pp. 25-41.
3346. Zorn, Wolfgang. "Unternehmer und Aristokratie in Deutschland. Ein Beitrag zur Geschichte des sozialen Stils und Selbstbewusstseins in der Neuzeit." Tradition 8 (1963), 241-54.

SEE ALSO: 114, 531, 680, 686, 694, 725, 739, 1602, 2253, 2256, 2277, 2998, 3070.

GERMANY--1815-1918

Bibliographic References

3347. Buck, Herbert, ed. Zur Geschichte der Produktivkräfte und Produktionsverhältnisse in Preussen 1810-1933 (Spezialinventar des Bestandes des Preussischen Ministeriums für Handel und Gewerbe). 3 vols. Berlin & Weimar: Rütten & Loening, 1960-1970.
3348. Sachse, Wieland. Bibliographie zur preussischen Gewerbestatistik 1750-1850. Göttingen: O. Schwartz, 1981. 392 pp.

GERMANY--1815-1918

3349. Adler, A. Die Entwicklungsgeschichte des deutschen Zollvereins. Leipzig: Gebhardt, 1872. 24 pp.
3350. Aegidi, Ludwig K. Aus der Vorzeit des Zollvereins. Beitrag zur deutschen Geschichte. Hamburg: Boyes & Geisler, 1888. 132 pp.
3351. "Die Ära der wirthschaftlichen Kartelle." Preussische Jahrbücher 89 (1897), 309-25.
3352. Arup, Erik. Studier i engelsk og tysk handels historie. Copenhagen: Gyldendal, 1907. 515 pp.
3353. Aufsass, Otto von. Die Zölle und Steuern sowie die vertragsmässigen auswärtigen Handelsbeziehungen des Deutschen Reiches. 5th ed. Munich: Hirth, 1900. 430 pp.
3354. Battaglia, Roger Freiherr von. Ein Zoll- und Wirtschaftsbündnis zwischen Österreich-Ungarn und Deutschland. (Geschichte, Konstruktion, Einwendungen.) Vienna: Braumüller, 1917. 803 pp.
3355. Bauert-Keetman, Ingrid. Raiffeisen. Verwicklichung einer Idee. Tübingen: Wunderlich, 1970. 163 pp.
3356. Benedikt, Heinrich. "Der deutsche Zollverein und Österreich." Der Donauraum. Zeitschrift des Forschungsinstitutes für den Donauraum 6 (1961), 25-34.
3357. Bergmann, Jürgen. "Ökonomische Voraussetzungen der Revolution von 1848. Zur Krise von 1845 bis 1848 in Deutschland." in Geschichte als politische Wissenschaft. Sozialökonomische Ansätze. Analyse politikhistorischer Phänomene. politologische Fragestellungen in der Geschichte. Stuttgart: Klett-Cotta, 1979. pp. 24-54.
3358. Bertrand, Adrien. La conquête de l'Autriche-Hongrie par l'Allemagne. Une nouvelle forme du pangermanisme, le "Zollverein". Paris: Berger-Levrault, 1916. 58 pp.
3359. Best, Heinrich. Interessenpolitik und nationale Integration 1848/49. Handelspolitische Konflikte im frühindustriellen Deutschland. Diss. Cologne. Göttingen: Vandenhoeck & Ruprecht, 1980. 433 pp.
3360. Beyerndorff, R. Die Geschichte der Reichsgewerbeordnung. Eine Einführung in das deutsche Gewerberecht für Beamte. Studien. Industrielle. Leipzig: Hirschfeld, 1907. 89 pp.
3361. Bieber, León E. Las relaciones economicas de Bolivia con Alemania 1880-1920. Berlin: Colloquium, 1984. 134 pp.
3362. Bienengräber, A. Statistik des Verkehrs und Verbrauchs im Zollvereine für die Jahre 1842-1864. 2 vols. Berlin: A. Duncker, 1868.
3363. Bissing, Wilhelm M. "Der Deutsche Zollverein und die monetären Probleme." Schmoller 79 (1959), 199-214.

3364. Bittel, Karl. Eduard Pfeiffer und die deutsche Konsumgenossenschaftsbewegung. Munich: Duncker & Humblot, 1915. 171 pp.
3365. Blaich, Fritz. "Die Anfänge der deutschen Antikartellpolitik zwischen 1897 und 1914." Jahrbuch für Sozialwissenschaft 21 (1970), 127-50.
3366. Blaich, Fritz. "Der Einfluss der Kartellierung der deutschen Grundstoffindustrie auf den Konjunkturablauf zwischen 1900 und 1914." Scripta Mercaturae 10 (1976), 5-22.
3367. Blaich, Fritz. Kartell- und Monopolpolitik im Kaiserlichen Deutschland. Das Problem der Marktmacht im deutschen Reichstag zwischen 1879 und 1914. Düsseldorf: Droste, 1973. 329 pp.
3368. Blaich, Fritz. "Die Kartellenquête (1902-1905)." in Festschrift Wilhelm Abel. Hannover: Schaper, 1974. pp. 775-86.
3369. Blaich, Fritz. "Der 'Standard-Oil-Fall' vor dem Reichstag. Ein Beitrag zur deutschen Monopolpolitik vor 1914." Zeitschrift für die gesamte Staatswissenschaft 126 (1970), 663-82.
3370. Böhme, Helmut. "Big Business Pressure Groups and Bismarck's Turn to Protectionism, 1873-79." Historical Journal 10 (1967), 218-36.
3371. Böhtlingk, Arthur. Carl Friedrich Nebenius. Der deutsche Zollverein, das Karlsruher Polytechnik und die erste Stadtbahn in Deutschland. Karlsruhe: Gutsch, 1899. 119 pp.
3372. Bondi, Gerhard. Deutschlands Aussenhandel 1815-1870. Berlin: Akademie, 1958. 156 pp.
3373. Bondi, Gerhard. "Zur Vorgeschichte der 'Kleindeutschen Lösung' 1866-1871. Eine wirtschaftshistorische Betrachtung." Jahrbuch für Wirtschaftsgeschichte (1966), II, 11-33.
3374. Borchardt, Knut. "Regionale Wachstumsdifferenzierung in Deutschland im 19. Jahrhundert unter besonderer Berücksichtigung des West-Ost-Gefälles." in Wirtschaft, Geschichte und Wirtschaftsgeschichte. Stuttgart: G. Fisher, 1966. pp. 325-39.
3375. Borckenhagen, Fritze. National- und handelspolitische Bestrebungen in Deutschland (1815-1822) und die Anfänge Friedrich Lists. Berlin: Rothschild, 1915. 83 pp.
3376. Bosc, L. Zollalliancen und Zollunionen in ihrer Bedeutung für die Handelspolitik der Vergangenheit und Zukunft. Berlin: E. Staude, 1907. 365 pp.
3377. Bouniatian, Mentor. Wirtschaftskrisen und Überkapitalisation. Eine Untersuchung über die Erscheinungsformen und Ursachen der periodischen Wirtschaftskrisen. Munich: E. Reinhardt, 1908: rpt. Leipzig, 1976. 188 pp.
3378. Bowring, John. Report on the Prussian Commercial Union, addressed to the Right Honorable Lord Viscount Palmerston, Her Majesty's Secretary of State for Foreign Affaires. London: Clowes, 1840. 287 pp.
3379. Braun, Karl. Die Männer des Zollvereins. Berlin: Simion, 1881. 68 pp.
3380. Breger, Monika. Die Haltung der industriellen Unternehmer zur staatlichen Sozialpolitik in den Jahren 1878-1891. Frankfurt a. M.: Haag + Herchen, 1982. 289 pp.
3381. Bretano, Lujo. "Die Arbeiter und die Produktionskrisen." Schmoller 2 (1878), 565-632.
3382. Brinkmann, Carl. Die Preussische Handelspolitik vor dem Zollverein und der Wiederaufbau vor 100 Jahren. Berlin: De Gruyter, 1922. 242 pp.
3383. Brockhage, Bernhard. Zur Entwicklung des preussisch-deutschen Kapitalexports. Leipzig: Duncker & Humblot, 1910. 217 pp.
3384. Buchheim, C. "Aspects of Nineteenth Century Anglo-German Trade Rivalry Reconsidered." Journal of European Economic History 10 (1981), 273-89.
3385. Busche, Manfred. "Zur Gründungsgeschichte der preussischen Zentralgenossenschaftskasse." Tradition 13 (1969), 81-89.
3386. Canis, Konrad. "Wirtschafts- und handelspolitische Aspekte der deutschen Aussenpolitik zu Beginn der 80er Jahre des 19. Jahrhunderts." Jahrbuch für Geschichte 16 (1977), 139-80.
3387. Champier, Laurent. "Die Wirtschaft der Länder des Zollvereins nach der französischen Untersuchung von 1867. A. Univ. saravensis R. Philos. 10 (1961), 51-82.
3388. Cohn, Arthur. Verbände, Kartelle und Syndikate im Grosshandel. Berlin: Hobbing, 1919. 23 pp.
3389. Corsten, Hermann, ed. Alfred Krupp, der Treuhänder eines deutschen Familienunternehmens. Ein Beitrag zu westdeutscher Wirtschaftsgeschichte im 19. Jahrhundert. Düsseldorf: Bagel, 1937. 304 pp.
3390. Dane, Hendrik. Die wirtschaftlichen Beziehungen Deutschlands zu Mexiko und Mittelamerika im 19. Jahrhundert. Cologne: Böhlau, 1971. 265 pp.
3391. Darius, Rudolf. Die Entwicklung der deutsch-mexikanischen Handelsbeziehungen von 1870-1914. Diss. Cologne, 1927. 79 pp.
3392. Dawson, William H. "The Genesis of the German Tariff." Economic Journal 14 (1904), 11-23.

3393. Dawson, William H. "The New German Tariff." Economic Journal 12 (1902), 15-23.
3394. Dawson, William H. Protection in Germany. A History of German Fiscal Policy During the Nineteenth Century. London: King, 1904. 259 pp.
3395. Der Deutsche Handelstag 1861-1911. 2 vols. Berlin: Heymann, 1911-13.
3396. Dieterici, Carl F. W. Statistische Übersicht der wichtigsten Gegenstände des Verkehrs und Verbrauchs im Preussischen Staate und im deutschen Zollverbande in dem Zeitraume von 1831-1836. 6 vols. Berlin: E. S. Mittler, 1838.
3397. Dietrich, Richard. "Die wirtschaftlichen Führungsschichten in Mitteldeutschland von 1850 bis zum Ersten Weltkrieg." in Führungskräfte der Wirtschaft im neunzehnten Jahrhundert 1790-1914. Limburg: C. A. Starke, 1977. II, 109-43.
3398. Dietzel, H. "The German Tariff Controversy." Quarterly Journal of Economics 17 (1903), 365-416.
3399. Domeratsky, L. Tariff Relations between Germany and Russia (1890-1914). Washington, D. C.: Government Printing Office, 1918. 23 pp.
3400. Dumke, Rolf H. "Intra-German Trade in 1837 and Regional Economic Development." VSWG 64 (1977), 468-96.
3401. Dumke, Rolf H. The Political Economy of Integration. The Case of the German Zollverein of 1834. Kingston, Ontario: Institute for Economic Research, 1974. 94 pp.
3402. Dumke, Rolf H. The Political Economy of German Economic Unification. Tariffs. Trade and Politics of the Zollverein Era. Diss. Univ. of Wisconsin, 1976. 394 pp.
3403. Eagly, Robert V. "Business Cycle Trends in France and Germany, 1869-79: A New Appraisal." Weltwirtschaftliches Archiv 99 (1967), 90-106.
3404. Eckert, Christian. "Zur Vorgeschichte des deutschen Zollvereins." Schmoller 26 (1902), 505-56.
3405. Edwards, W. H. Englische Expansion und deutsche Durchdringung als Faktoren im Welthandel. Jena: Fischer, 1916. 89 pp.
3406. Ehm, Hans O. Die deutsch-belgischen Handelsbeziehungen von 1871 bis 1914. Diss. Cologne, 1936. Cologne: Orthen, 1937. 57 pp.
3407. Eisenhart, Wilfried et al. Vorgeschichte und Begründung des Deutschen Zollvereins 1815-1834. Akten der Staaten des Deutschen Bundes und der europäischen Mächte. 3 vols. Berlin: Hobbing, 1934.
3408. Eistert, Ekkehard. Die Beeinflussung des Wirtschaftswachstums in Deutschland von 1883 bis 1913 durch das Bankensystem. Eine theoretisch-empirische Untersuchung. Berlin: Duncker & Humblot, 1970. 189 pp.
3409. Elsässer, Markus. Die Rochdaler Pioniere: religiöse Einflüsse in ihrer Bedeutung für die Entstehung der Rochdaler Pioniergenossenschaft von 1844. Berlin: Duncker & Humblot, 1982. 129 pp.
3410. Emminghaus, Arwed. Entwicklung. Krisis und Zukunft des deutschen Zollvereins. Leipzig: Wigand, 1863. 110 pp.
3411. Endemann, W. "Das Genossenschaftswesen nach dem Bundesgesetz vom 4. Juli 1868." Preussische Jahrbücher 25 (1870), 1-32.
3412. Engelsing, Rolf. "Die wirtschaftliche und soziale Differenzierung der deutschen kaufmännischen Angestellten 1690-1900." Zeitschrift für die gesamte Staatswissenschaft 123 (1967), 347-80, 482-514.
3413. Ermel, Horst. Der Übergang vom Kapitalismus der freien Konkurrenz zum Imperialismus in Deutschland. Cologne: Pahl-Rugenstein, 1974. 48 pp.
3414. Esslen, Joseph. Konjunktur und Geldmarkt 1902-1908. Eine Untersuchung der Wechselwirkung beider in Deutschland. Stuttgart: Cotta, 1909. 320 pp.
3415. Eude, Michel. "Les Relations économiques et financières entre la France et l'Allemagne de 1898 à 1914." Revue d'histoire des doctrines économiques et sociales 49 (1971), 129-34.
3416. Eulenburg, Franz. "Ideen und Probleme in der deutschen Handelsgeschichtsforschung." in Die Entwickung der deutschen Volkswirtschaftslehre im neunzehnten Jahrhundert. Leipzig: Duncker & Humblot, 1908. II, 49.
3417. Eulenburg, Franz. Die Stellung der deutschen Industrie zum wirtschaftlichen Zweibund. Munich: Duncker & Humblot, 1916. 127 pp.
3418. Falke, Johannes. Die Geschichte des deutschen Handels. 2 vols. Leipzig: Mayer, 1859-60.
3419. Falke, Johannes. Die Geschichte des deutschen Zollwesens. Leipzig: Veit, 1869; rpt. Frankfurt a. M., 1968. 426 pp.

3420. Feig, Johannes. "Deutschlands gewerbliche Entwickelung seit dem Jahre 1882." Zeitschrift für die gesamte Staatswissenschaft 56 (1900), 658-95.

3421. Feiler, Arthur. Die Konjunktur-Periode 1907-1913 in Deutschland. Jena: Fischer, 1914. 204 pp.

3422. Féltoronyi, Nicolas B. "Allemagne-Angleterre 1792-1913." in Diffusion du progrés et convergence des Prix. Etudes internationales. Louvain: Université Catholique de Louvain, 1966. pp. 41-258.

3423. Festenberg-Packisch, Hermann. Geschichte des Zollvereins mit besonderer Berücksichtigung der staatlichen Entwickelung Deutschlands. Leipzig: Brockhaus, 1869. 457 pp.

3424. Field, Alexander J. "The Relative Stability of German and American Industrial Growth, 1880-1913." in Historische Konjunkturforschung. Stuttgart: Klett-Cotta, 1981. pp. 208-33.

3425. Finis, Beate. Wirtschaftliche und ausserwirtschaftliche Beweggründe mittelständischer Genossenschaftspioniere des landwirtschaftlichen Bereichs am Beispiel F. W. Raiffeisen und W. Haas. Zur Integration der Beweggründe in eine empirische Genossenschaftstheorie und in Theorien der Sozial- und Wirtschaftspolitik. Berlin: Duncker & Humblot, 1980. 326 pp.

3426. Fischer, Gustav. "Prüfung zweier Ansichten über die intellectuelle Urheberschaft des deutschen Zollvereins." Jahrbücher für Nationalökonomie und Statistik 4 (1865), 486-91.

3427. Fischer, Gustav. "Über das Wesen und die Bedingungen eines Zollvereins." Jahrbücher für Nationalökonomie und Statistik 2 (1864), 317-85; 397-432; 7 (1866), 225-304; 8 (1867), 252-350.

3428. Fischer, Wolfram, ed. Beiträge zu Wirtschaftswachstum und Wirtschaftsstruktur im 16. und 19. Jahrhundert. Berlin: Duncker & Humblot, 1971. 279 pp.

3429. Fischer, Wolfram. "The German Zollverein. A Case Study in Customs Unions." Kyklos. Internationale Zeitschrift für Sozialwissenschaften 13 (1960), 65-89.

3430. Fischer, Wolfram. "Die Rolle des Kleingewerbes im wirtschaftlichen Wachstumsprozess in Deutschland 1850-1914." in Wirtschaftliche und soziale Probleme der gewerblichen Entwicklung im 15.-16. und 19. Jahrhundert. Stuttgart: G. Fischer, 1968. pp. 131-42.

3431. Fischer, Wolfram. Unternehmerschaft, Selbstverwaltung und Staat. Die Handelskammern in der deutschen Wirtschafts- und Staatsverfassung des 19. Jahrhunderts. Berlin: Duncker & Humblot, 1964. 122 pp.

3432. Flaningam, Miletus L. "German Eastward Expansion, Fact and Fiction: a Study in German-Ottoman Trade Relations, 1890-1914." Journal of Central European Affairs 14 (1955), 319-33.

3433. Flaningham, Miletus L. "German Economic Controls in Bulgaria, 1894-1914." Slavic Review 20 (1961), 99-108.

3434. Flux, A. W. "British Trade and German Competition." Economic Journal 7 (1897), 34-45.

3435. Forbes, Ian L. D. "German Informal Imperialism in South America before 1914." Economic History Review 31 (1978), 384-98.

3436. Franck, Hans-Peter. Zunftwesen und Gewerbefreiheit. Zeitschriftenstimmen zur Frage der Gewerbeverfassung im Deutschland der ersten Hälfte des 19. Jahrhunderts. Diss. Hamburg, 1969. Bamberg: Bamberger Fotodruck R. Rodenbusch, 1971. 326 pp.

3437. Franz, Eugen. "Ein Weg zum Reich. Die Entstehung des Deutschen Zollvereins." VSWG 27 (1934), 105-36.

3438. Franz, Eugen. "Ludwig Freiherrn von der Pfordtens Kampf gegen den preussisch-französischen Handelsvertrag vom 29. März 1862." Forschungen zur Brandenburgischen und Preussischen Geschichte 44 (1932), 130-55.

3439. Franz, Eugen. "Preussens Kampf mit Hannover um die Anerkennung des preussisch-französischen Handelsvertrag von 1862." Historische Vierteljahrschrift 26 (1931), 787-839.

3440. Fremdling, Rainer. Eisenbahnen und deutsches Wirtschaftswachstum 1840-1879. Ein Beitrag zur Entwicklungstheorie und zur Theorie der Infrastruktur. Dortmund: Gesellschaft für Westfälische Wirtschaftsgeschichte, 1975. 217 pp.

3441. Freymark, Hermann. Die Reform der preussischen Handels- und Zollpolitik von 1800-1821 und ihre Bedeutung. Jena: Fischer, 1898. 103 pp.

3442. Fuchs, Johann L. Konjunktur und Bilanz in der deutschen Braunkohlenindustrie in den Jahren 1895-1913. Diss. Frankfurt a. M. Gleiwitz: Neumann, 1934. 143 pp.

3443. Fuchs, Konrad. "Die Bedeutung des Deutschen Zollvereins als Institution zur Austragung des preussisch-österreichischen Gegensatzes 1834-1866." Nassauer Annalen 78 (1967), 208-15.

3444. Gahlen, Bernhard and Helmut Hesse. "Das Wachstum des Nettoinland-Produkts in Deutschland 1850-1913." Zeitschrift für die gesamte Staatswissenschaft 121 (1965), 452-97.

3445. Gast, Georg. "Der preussiche Partikularismus und sein Zollverein." Finanzarchiv, N.F. 27 (1968), 291-317.
3446. Gedenkschrift zum hundertsten Jahrestag der Errichtung des Deutschen Zollvereins. Berlin: Reichsdruckerei, 1934. 83 pp.
3447. Geiss, Immanuel. "The German Empire and Imperialism, 1871-1918." Australian Journal of Politics and History 20 (1974), 11-21.
3448. Gessner, Dieter. "Wachstumszyklen und staatliche Gewerbepolitik im Zeitalter der Früh-industrialisierung. Konjunkturelle und strukturelle Probleme des Bijouteriegewerbes am Unter-main und Mittelrhein 1790-1865." Scripta Mercaturae 15 (1981), 37-58.
3449. Goeken, Ferdinand. Die Entwicklung des Gewerbes in Münster in Westfalen während des 19. Jahrhunderts. Diss. Münster, 1924. 174 pp.
3450. Görlich, Ernst J. "Zur Geschichte eines europäischen Zollvereines. Ein unbekanntes Kapitel der Geschichte der europäischen Einigungsbestrebungen." Österreichische Osthefte 11 (1969), 321-34.
3451. Gordon, Nancy M. "Britain and the Zollverein Duties, 1842-45." Economic History Review 22 (1969), 75-87.
3452. Grossmann, Hermann. Der Handelsboykott gegen Deutschland in französischer Beurteilung. Berlin: Hobbing, 1918. 44 pp.
3453. Guber, Christian. Der deutsche Kaufmann. Leipzig: Teubner, 1905. 704 pp.
3454. Halle, Ernst von. "The Rise and Tendencies of German Transatlantic Enterprise." Economic Journal 17 (1907), 490-503. (also published in London: King, 1908. 16 pp.)
3455. Hammerbacher, John. Die Konjunkturen in der deutschen Eisen- und Maschinen-Grossindustrie. Ein Beitrag zur Theorie und Praxis der Konjunkturen unter hauptsächlicher Berücksichtigung der Zeit von 1892 bis 1911. Munich: Oldenbourg, 1914. 120 pp.
3456. Hampke, Thilo. "Der Verband Deutscher Gewerbevereine, seine Entstehung, Organisation und bisherige Wirksamkeit." Schmoller 17 (1893), 1141-73.
3457. Hansen, Alvin H. Cycles of Prosperity and Depression in the United States, Great Britain and Germany. A Study of Monthly Data 1902-1908. Madison: University of Wisconsin, 1921. 112 pp.
3458. Hantos, Elemér. Europäischer Zollverein und mitteleuropäische Wirtschaftsgemeinschaft. Berlin: Organisation, 1928. 66 pp.
3459. Hardach, Karl W. "Beschäftigungspolitische Aspekte in der deutschen Aussenhandelspolitik ausgangs der 1870er Jahre." Schmoller 86 (1966), 641-54.
3460. Hartmann, Stefan. Als die Schranken fielen: der Deutsche Zollverein. Mainz: von Hase & Koehler, 1984. 148 pp.
3461. Hasselmann, Erwin. "Welchen Einfluss hatten Owens Ideen auf die sozialen und genossen-schaftlichen Strömungen des 19. Jahrhunderts in Deutschland? Zur 200. Wiederkehr des Geburts-tages von Robert Owen." Zeitschrift für das gesamte Genossenschaftswesen 21 (1971), 128-47. (English Summary)
3462. Henderson, William O. "British Economic Activity in the German Colonies, 1884-1914." Economic History Review 15 (1945), 56-66.
3463. Henderson, William O. "Economic Aspects of German Imperial Colonisation." Scottish Geographical Magazine 54 (1938).
3464. Henderson, William O. "The German Colonial Empire, 1884-1918." History 20 (1935), 151-58.
3465. Henderson, William O. "German Colonisation." German Life & Letters 1 (1937), 241-54.
3466. Henderson, William O. "German Economic Penetration in The Middle East 1870-1914." Economic History Review 18 (1948), 54-64.
3467. Henderson, William O. "Germany and Mitteleuropa." German Life & Letters 2 (1938), 161-74.
3468. Henderson, William O. "Germany's Trade with her Colonies, 1884-1914." Economic History Review 9 (1938-39), 1-16.
3469. Henderson, William O. "Mitteleuropäische Zollvereinspläne, 1840-1940." Zeitschrift für die gesamte Staatswissenschaft 122 (1966), 130-62.
3470. Henderson, William O. "A Nineteenth Century Approach to a West European Common Market." Kyklos 10 (1957), 448-59.
3471. Henderson, William O. "The Pan-German Movement." History 26 (1941), 188-98.
3472. Henderson, William O. Studies in German Colonial History. London: F. Cass, 1962. 150 pp.
3473. Henderson, William O. "The War Economy of German East Africa, 1914-1917." Economic History Review 13 (1943), 104-10.

3474. Henderson, William O. "The Zollverein." History 19 (1934), 1-19.
3475. Henderson, William O. The Zollverein. Cambridge: Cambridge University Press, 1939. 375 pp.
3476. Henning, Friedrich-Wilhelm. "Die Einführung der Gewerbefreiheit und ihre Auswirkungen auf das Handwerk in Deutschland." in Handwerksgeschichte in neuer Sicht. Göttingen: O. Schwartz, 1978. pp. 147-77.
3477. Henning, Hansjoachim. "Bismarcks Kolonialpolitik. Export einer Krise?" in Gegenwarts-probleme der Wirtschaft und der Wirtschaftswissenschaft. Tübingen: Mohr, 1978. pp. 53-83.
3478. Hentschel, Volker. Die deutschen Freihändler und der Volkswirtschaftliche Kongress 1858 bis 1885. Diss. Heidelberg, 1974. Stuttgart: Klett, 1975. 308 pp.
3479. Hesse, Helmut. "Die Entwicklung der regionalen Einkommensdifferenzen im Wachstumsprozess der deutschen Wirtschaft vor 1913." in W. Fischer, ed. Beiträge zu Wirtschaftswachstum und Wirtschaftsstruktur im 16. und 19. Jahrhundert. Berlin: Duncker & Humblot, 1971. pp. 261-79.
3480. Hieke, Ernst. "Aus der Frühzeit des deutschen Handels mit China." Ostasiatische Rundschau 20 (1939), 93-97.
3481. Hilbert, Lothar W. Deutscher Zollverein, historisches Vorbild für EWG oder EFTA? Ziele, Wirkungsweise, Bedeutung. Luxembourg: Faculté Internationale de Droit Comparé, 1962. 26 pp.
3482. Hoefer, Hellmut. Der Kompensationsverkehr als internationale Güterverkehrsform während des Weltkrieges und in der Übergangszeit mit besonderer Berücksichtigung Deutschlands. Diss. Erlangen. Coburg: Tageblatt-Haas, 1929. 91 pp.
3483. Hoffman, Ross. Great Britain and the German Trade Rivalry 1875-1914. Philadelphia: University of Pennsylvania Press, 1933. 363 pp.
3484. Hoffmann, Walther G. "Die unverteilten Gewinne der Kapitalgesellschaften in Deutschland 1871-1957." Zeitschrift für die gesamte Staatswissenschaft 115 (1959), 271-91.
3485. Hohorst, Gerd. Wirtschaftswachstum und Bevölkerungsentwicklung in Preussen. 1816 bis 1914. Diss. Münster, 1975. 467 pp.
3486. Hollaender, Albert. Die Einwirkung des Krieges auf überseeische vor dem Kriege geschlossene Abladegeschäfte. Hamburg: Westermann, 1918. 128 pp.
3487. Holthaus, Ewald. Die Entwicklung der Produktivkräfte in Deutschland nach der Reichsgründung bis zur Jahrhundertwende. Diss. Münster, 1978. Frankfurt a. M.: Haag + Herchen, 1980. 380 pp.
3488. Horn, Hugo. Die Wirtschaftsbeziehungen des Deutschen Reiches zu Oesterreich in den letzten 15 Jahren. Diss. Vienna, 1937. 32 pp.
3489. Hundt, Wolfgang J. Die Wandlung im deutschen Messe- und Ausstellungswesen im 19. Jahr-hundert und seine Weiterentwicklung bis zum Jahre 1933 unter besonderer Berücksichtigung der Messen in Frankfurt am Main und Leipzig. Diss. Frankfurt a. M., 1957. 188 pp.
3490. Hunt, James C. "Peasants, Grain Tariffs, and Meat Quotas. Imperial German Protectionism Re-examined." Central European History 7 (1974), 311-31.
3491. Ihde, Wilhelm, ed. Los von England. Der deutsche Abwehrkampf gegen Englands wirtschaft-liche Weltmachtstellung in der ersten Hälfte des 19. Jahrhunderts. 2nd ed. Leipzig: Lühe-Verlag, 1940. 242 pp.
3492. Jacobi, Johannes, Jr. "Die Innungsbewegung in Deutschland und die Novelle zur Reichs-Gewerbeordnung vom 18. Juli 1881." Schmoller 7 (1883), 1197-1233.
3493. Jaeger, Hans. Unternehmer in der deutschen Politik (1890-1918). Bonn: Röhrscheid, 1967. 383 pp.
3494. Jaeger, Hans. "Unternehmer und Politik im wilhelminischen Deutschland." Tradition 13 (1968), 1-21.
3495. Jaschinski, Heinrich. Zur Organisationsform einiger Staatsunternehmungen im Zeitalter des Frükapitalismus. Diss. Marburg. Bochum-Langendreer: Pöppinghaus, 1936. 70 pp.
3496. Jerussalimski, A. S. Die Aussenpolitik und die Diplomatie des deutschen Imperialismus Ende des 19. Jahrhunderts. Berlin: Dietz, 1954. 847 pp.
3497. Jerussalimski, A. S. "Das Eindringen der deutschen Monopole in China an der Wende vom 19. zum 20. Jahrhundert." Zeitschrift für Geschichtswissenschaft 8 (1960), 1832-61.
3498. Johnston, Charles. "The Russo-German Tariff War." Economic Journal 4 (1894), 136-39.
3499. Kampffmeyer, Paul. Zur Entwicklungsgeschichte des Kapitalismus in Deutschland. Berlin: Verlag der Berlinischen Arbeit.-Bibliothek, 1890. 84 pp.
3500. Kathgen, Karl. "Deutschland und England auf dem Weltmarkt." Schmoller 37 (1913), 1-14.
3501. Kaufhold, Karl H. "Die Auswirkungen der Einschränkung der Gewerbefreiheit in Preussen durch die Verordnung vom 9.2.1849 auf das Handwerk." in Vom Kleingewerbe zur Grossindustrie. Berlin: Verein für Sozialpolitik, 1975. pp. 165-88.

3502. Kaufhold, Karl H. "Inhalt und Probleme einer preussischen Gewerbestatistik vor 1860." in Festschrift für Wilhelm Abel. Hannover: Schaper, 1974. pp. 707-19.

3503. Kaufhold, Karl H. "Wirtschaft und Gewerbe in Preussen 1817. Ein Überblick nach einem Bericht von G. J. Ch. Kunth." in Wirtschaftskräfte und Wirtschaftswege. Festschrift für Hermann Kellenbenz. Stuttgart: Klett-Cotta, 1978. III, 265-79.

3504. Kaufmann, Heinrich. Die Konsumgenossenschaftsbewegung. Vortrag über Ursprung, Entwicklung und Grundsätze der Konsumgenossenschaftsbewegung unter besonderer Berücksichtigung des heutigen Standes des deutschen Konsumvereinswesens. Hamburg: Zentralverband deutscher Konsumvereine, 1904. 40 pp.

3505. Kellenbenz, Hermann, ed. Wirtschaftliche Wachstumsschwankungen. Stuttgart: Fischer, 1978. 248 pp.

3506. Kennedy, Paul M. The Rise of the Anglo-German Antagonism, 1860-1914. London: Allen & Unwin, 1980. 604 pp.

3507. Kernbauer, Hans and Eduard März. "Das Wirtschaftswachstum in Deutschland und Österreich von der Mitte des 19. Jahrhunderts bis zum Ersten Weltkrieg, eine vergleichende Darstellung." in Historische Konjunkturforschung. Stuttgart: Klett-Cotta, 1981. pp. 47-59. (English summary)

3508. Kiel, Erich. Die handelspolitischen Beziehungen zwischen Deutschland und Japan in der Nachkriegszeit. Diss. Münster, 1933. 107 pp.

3509. Kirchner, Walther. "Russian Tariffs and Foreign Industries Before 1914. The German Entrepreneur's Perspective." Journal of Economic History 41 (1981), 361-79.

3510. Kocka, Jürgen. "Familie, Unternehmer und Kapitalismus. An Beispielen aus der frühen deutschen Industrialisierung." Zeitschrift für Unternehmensgeschichte 24 (1979), 99-135.

3511. Kocka, Jürgen. "Organisierter Kapitalismus im Kaiserreich?" Historische Zeitschrift 230 (1980), 613-31.

3512. Kocka, Jürgen. Unternehmensverwaltung und Angestelltenschaft am Beispiel Siemens 1847-1914. Stuttgart: Klett, 1969. 639 pp.

3513. König, Alfred. Das sozialreformatorische Genossenschaftswesen der neunziger Jahre. Ein Beitrag zur Geschichte des Genossenschaftswesens und des Konservativismus. Diss. Halle-Wittenberg. Halle a. d. S.: s.n., 1926. 83 pp.

3514. Kössler, Armin. Aktionsfeld Osmanisches Reich: die Wirtschaftsinteressen des Deutschen Kaiserreiches in der Türkei 1871-1908. Diss. Freiburg i. B., 1978. 429 pp.

3515. Kollmann, Paul. "Die deutsche Gewerbe-Aufnahme vom 1. Dezember 1875 in ihren Hauptergebnissen." Schmoller 6 (1882), 443-562.

3516. Krafft, Eberhard. Die Haltung des wirtschaftenden Bürgertums im 19. Jahrhundert, dargestellt an Handwerker, Kaufmann und Unternehmer. Halle a. d. S.: Akademie, 1941. 91 pp.

3517. Kraft, Heinz. "Die Entwicklung des Zunftwesens und die geistesgeschichtlichen Grundlagen der Gewerbefreiheit." Zeitschrift für die gesamte Staatswissenschaft 106 (1950), 54-86.

3518. Krahl, Elisabeth. Die Entstehung der Gewerbeordnung von 1869. Diss. Berlin. Jena: Neuenhahn, 1937. 96 pp.

3519. Kubitschek, Helmut. "Zu Tendenzen des staatsmonopolistischen Kapitalismus in Deutschland vor dem ersten Weltkrieg." Jahrbuch für Wirtschaftsgeschichte (1963), II, 103-42.

3520. Kuczynski, Jürgen. "Studien zur Frühgeschichte des Kapitalismus." Jahrbuch für Wirtschaftsgeschichte (1962), IV, 89-111.

3521. Kuczynski, Jürgen. Studien zur Geschichte der zyklischen Überproduktionskrisen in Deutschland 1873 bis 1914. Berlin: Akademie, 1961. 210 pp.

3522. Kuczynski, Jürgen. "Zur Geschichte der bürgerlichen Krisentheorie." Jahrbuch für Wirtschaftsgeschichte (1960), I, 29-52.

3523. Kuhlo, Karl C. "Zur Wachstumsanalyse der deutschen Wirtschaft (1850-1913)." Ifo-Studien, Zeitschrift des Ifo-Instituts für Wirtschaftsforschung 12 (1966), 121-45.

3524. Kutz, Martin. "Die deutsch-britischen Handelsbeziehungen von 1790 bis zur Gründung des Zollvereins." VSWG 56 (1969), 178-214.

3525. Kutz, Martin. Deutschlands Aussenhandel von der Französischen Revolution bis zur Gründung des Zollvereins. Wiesbaden: Steiner, 1974. 395 pp.

3526. Lambi, Ivo N. Free Trade and Protection in Germany, 1868-1879. Wiesbaden: Steiner, 1963. 267 pp.

3527. Landes, David S. "The Structure of Enterprise in the Nineteenth Century. The Cases of Britain and Germany." in Extraits des Rapports du XI. Congrès International des Sciences Historiques. Stockholm, 1960. Berkeley: University of California, 1960. pp. 107-28.

3528. Langenbeck, Wilhelm. Geschichte des deutschen Handels seit dem Ausgange des Mittelalters. 2nd ed. Leipzig: Teubner, 1918. 141 pp.

3529. Laues, Theodor. "Die deutsche Waaren-Ein- und Ausfuhr und die Durchfuhr durch das Deutsche Reich von 1880 bis 1882." Schmoller 8 (1884), 1189-1213.

3530. Lemcke, Ernst. Die Entwicklung der Raiffeisen-Organisation in der Neuzeit. Ein Beitrag zur Geschichte des deutschen Genossenschaftswesens. Karlsruhe: Braun, 1913. 139 pp.

3531. Lenz, Friedrich. "Wesen und Struktur des deutschen Kapitalexports vor 1914. Weltwirtschaftliches Archiv 18 (1922), 42-54.

3532. Liefmann, Robert. Die Kartelle in und nach dem Kriege. Berlin: D. Reimer, 1918. 40 pp.

3533. Lindecke, Otto. Das Genossenschaftswesen in Deutschland. Leipzig: G. J. Göschen, 1908. 144 pp.

3534. Loehnis, Hermann. Der Marasmus in Handel und Industrie 1877. London: Trübner, 1877. 56 pp.

3535. Lorscheider, Horst M. "The Commercial Treaty between Germany and Serbia of 1904." Central European History 9 (1976), 129-45.

3536. Lotsch, Fritz. Beiträge zur Entwicklung des deutschen Aussenhandels in der Zeit von 1800-1834. Diss. Kiel, 1920. 170 pp.

3537. Lütge, Friedrich, ed. Wirtschaftliche und soziale Probleme der gewerblichen Entwicklung im 15.-16. und 19. Jahrhundert. Stuttgart: Fischer, 1968. 155 pp.

3538. MacGregor, D. H. "The Development and Control of German Syndicates." Economic Journal 24 (1914), 24-32.

3539. Mascher, H. A. Das deutsche Gewerbewesen von der frühesten Zeit bis auf die Gegenwart. Nach Geschichte, Recht, Nationalökonomie und Statistik. Potsdam: Döring, 1866. 797 pp.

3540. Maschke, Erich. "Deutsche Kartelle im späten Mittelalter und im 19. Jahrhundert vor 1870." in F. Lütge, ed. Wirtschaftliche und soziale Probleme der gewerblichen Entwicklung im 15.-16 und 19. Jahrhundert. Stuttgart: Fischer, 1968.

3541. Maschke, Erich. Grundzüge der deutschen Kartellgeschichte bis 1914. Dortmund: Gesellschaft für westfälische Wirtschaftsgeschichte, 1964. 65 pp.

3542. Matschoss, Conrad. Preussens Gewerbeförderung und ihre grossen Männer. Dargestellt im Rahmen der Geschichte des Vereins zur Beförderung des Gewerbefleisses 1821-1921. Berlin: Verlag des Vereines deutscher Ingenieure, 1921.

3543. Merritt, H. P. "Bismarck and the German Interest in East Africa, 1884-85." Historical Journal 21 (1978), 97-116.

3544. Metz, Rainer. "Agrarpreiszyklen und Wirtschaftskonjunktur, Spektralanalytische Untersuchungen zu Kölner Agrarpreisreihen des 19. Jahrhunderts." in Historische Konjunkturforschung. Stuttgart: Klett-Cotta, 1981. pp. 255-88.

3545. Metz, Rainer and Reinhard Spree. "Kuznets-Zyklen im Wachstum der deutschen Wirtschaft während des 19. und frühen 20. Jahrhunderts." in Konjunktur, Krise und Gesellschaft. Wirtschaftliche Wechsellagen und soziale Entwicklung im 19. und 20. Jahrhundert. Stuttgart: Klett-Cotta, 1981. pp. 343-76.

3546. Meyer, Henry C. "German Economic Relations with Southeastern Europe, 1870-1914." American Historical Review 57 (1951-52), 77-90.

3547. Michaelis, Otto. Volkswirthschaftliche Schriften. 2 vols. Berlin: Herbig, 1873.

3548. Mieck, Ilja. Preussische Gewerbepolitik in Berlin 1806-1844. Staaatshilfe und Privatinitiative zwischen Merkantilismus und Liberalismus. Berlin: Historische Kommission beim Friedrich-Meinecke-Institut, 1965. 276 pp.

3549. Milkereit, Gertrud. Das Unternehmerbild im zeitkritischen Roman des Vormärz. Cologne: Forschungsinstitut für Sozial- und Wirtschaftsgeschichte an der Universität, 1970. 32 pp.

3550. Molodowsky, N. "Germany's Foreign Trade Terms in 1899-1913." Quarterly Journal of Economics 27 (1941), 664-83.

3551. Mottek, Hans. "Die Gründerkrise. Produktionsbewegung, Wirkungen, theoretische Problematik." Jahrbuch für Wirtschaftsgeschichte (1966), I, 51-128.

3552. Mühlpfordt, Günter. "Der Übergang vom Feudalismus zum Kapitalismus auf dem 'preussischen Weg'. Eine Gemeinsamkeit der russischen, polnischen und deutschen Geschichte." Jahrbuch für Geschichte der deutsch-slawischen Beziehungen 1 (1956), 135-70.

3553. Müller, Julius O. Voraussetzungen und Verfahrensweisen bei der Errichtung von Genossenschaften in Europa vor 1900. Göttingen: Vandenhoeck & Ruprecht, 1976. 262 pp.

3554. Münsterberg, Otto. Wandlungen im Handel. Lissa i. P.: Eulitz, 1914. 34 pp.

3555. Munjal, Singh. Wirtschaftswachstumsprozess. Ein Vergleich zwischen Deutschland (im 19. Jahrhundert) und Indien (im 20. Jahrhundert). Diss. Mannheim, 1964. 110 pp.
3556. Neuburger, Hugh M. and Houston H. Stokes. "The Anglo-German Trade Rivalry, 1897-1913. A Counterfactual Outcome and its Implications." Social Science History 3 (1979), 187-201.
3557. Nipp, Luitgard. Kapitalausstattung im ländlichen Kleingewerbe in der 2. Hälfte des 19. Jahrhunderts. New York: Arno Press, 1981. 255 pp.
3558. Obermann, Karl. "Zur Frage der unbedingten Übereinstimmung der Produktionsverhältnisse mit dem Charakter der Produtivkräfte in Deutschland im 19. Jahrhundert." Zeitschrift für Geschichtswissenschaft 1 (1953), 737-54.
3559. O'Farrell, Horace H. "British and German Export Trade Before the War." Economic Journal 26 (1916), 161-67.
3560. Ogger, Günter. Die Gründerjahre: als der Kapitalismus jung und verwegen war. Zurich: Droemer Knaur, 1982. 384 pp.
3561. Patijn, S. Landmarks in European Unity. Leiden: Sijthoff, 1970. 223 pp.
3562. Pesmazoglu, J. S. "Some International Aspects of German Cyclical Fluctuations, 1880-1913." Weltwirtschaftliches Archiv 64 (1950), 77-107.
3563. Philippi, F. E. F. Beiträge zur Geschichte und Statistik der deutschen Messen. Frankfurt a. d. O.: Harnecker, 1857. 112 pp.
3564. Pierard, Richard V. "A Case Study in German Economic Imperialism. The Colonial Economic Committee, 1896-1914." Scandinavian Economic History Review 16 (1968), 155-67.
3565. Plum, Werner. German Trade Promotion in the First Half of the Nineteenth Century. Bonn-Bad Godesberg: Friedrich-Ebert-Stiftung, 1974. 155 pp. (German: Bonn-Bad Godesberg, 1972)
3566. Pogge von Strandmann, Hartmut. "Domestic Origins of Germany's Colonial Expansion Under Bismarck." Past and Present 42 (1969), 140-59.
3567. Poidevin, Raymond. Les relations économiques et financières entre la France et l'Allemagne, de 1898 à 1914. Paris: A. Colin, 1969. 929 pp.
3568. Prager, Ludwig. Die Handelsbeziehungen des Deutschen Reiches mit den Vereinigten Staaten von Amerika bis zum Ausbruch des Weltkrieges im Jahre 1914. Weimar: Böhlau, 1926. 161 pp.
3569. Preuss, Georg F. " Helmar Gerkens. Ein Beitrag zur deutschen Zollgeschichte." in Hermann Grauert . . . gewidmet . . . Festgabe. Freiburg i. B.: Herder, 1910. pp. 284-318.
3570. Price, Arnold H. The Evolution of the Zollverein. Ann Arbor: University of Michigan Press, 1949. 298 pp.
3571. Rachel, Hugo. Die Handels-, Zoll- und Akzisepolitik Preussens. Berlin: Parey, 1928. 812 pp.
3572. Rathgen, Karl. Die Ansichten über Freihandel und Schutzzoll in der deutschen Staatspraxis des neunzehnten Jahrhunderts. Leipzig: s.n., 1908. 54 pp.
3573. Raubaum, Jörg. "Die deutsche Arbeiterklasse und die Konsumgenossenschaften bis zum ersten Weltkrieg." Zeitschrift für Geschichtswissenschaft 16 (1968), 54-67.
3574. Richter, Heinrich. Friedrich Wilhelm Raiffeisen und die Entwicklung seiner Genossenschaftsidee. Diss. Erlangen, 1965. 207 pp.
3575. Richter, Siegfried. "Die Struktur des deutschen Aussenhandels von 1872 bis 1892. Ein Beitrag zur Geschichte des deutschen Imperialismus." Wissenschaftliche Zeitschrift der Martin-Luther-Universität Halle-Wittenberg 11 (1962), 901-04.
3576. Roehl, Hugo. Beiträge zur preussischen Handwerkerpolitik vom Allgemeinen Landrecht bis zur Allgemeinen Gewerbeordung von 1845. Leipzig: Duncker & Humblot, 1900. 276 pp.
3577. Rohrscheidt, Kurt von. "Geschichte der Polizeitaxen in Deutschland und Preussen und ihre Stellung in der Reichsgewerbeordnung." Jahrbücher für Nationalökonomie und Statistik 17 (1889), 353-408.
3578. Rohrscheidt, Kurt von. Vom Zunftzwange zur Gewerbefreiheit. Eine Studie nach den Quellen. Berlin: Heymann, 1898. 668 pp.
3579. Rohrscheidt, Kurt von. "Vor- und Rückblicke auf Zunftzwang und Gewerbefreiheit." Jahrbücher für Nationalökonomie und Statistik 3 (1894), 1-55, 481-535.
3580. Rosch, Karl. Kreditinflation und Wirtschaftskrisen unter besonderer Berücksichtigung der Konjunkturentwicklung Deutschlands vor dem Krieg. Jena: Fischer, 1927. 194 pp.
3581. Rothkegel, Walter. "Die Bewegung der Kaufpreise für ländliche Besitzungen und die Entwicklung der Getreidepreise im Königreich Preussen von 1895 bis 1909." Schmoller 34 (1910), 1689-1747.

3582. Rückert, Franz. Die Handelsbeziehungen zwischen Deutschland und der Schweiz, mit besonderer Berücksichtigung der Gestaltung der handelspolitischen Verhältnisse seit dem Beginn des 19. Jahrhunderts. Leipzig: A. Deichert, 1926. 237 pp.

3583. Ruhmer, Otto. Entstehungsgeschichte des deutschen Genossenschaftswesens. Die ersten deutschen Genossenschaften. Hamburg-Blankensee: Kröger, 1937. 294 pp.

3584. Sayous, André E. La crise allemande de 1900-1902. Paris: Sirey, 1903. 377 pp.

3585. Scherner, Karl O. and Dietmar Willoweit. Vom Gewerbe zum Unternehmen: Studien zum Recht der gewerblichen Wirtschaft im 18. und 19. Jahrhundert. Darmstadt: Wissenschaftliche Buchgesellschaft, 1982. 304 pp.

3586. Schieck, Hans. Der Kampf um die deutsche Wirtschaftspolitik nach dem Novemberumsturz 1918. Diss. Heidelberg, 1958. 268 pp.

3587. Schmidt, Karl-Heinz. "Die Rolle des Kleingewerbes in regionalen Wachstumsprozessen in der zweiten Hälfte des 19. Jahrhunderts." in Wirtschaftliche und soziale Strukturen im saekularen Wandel. Festschrift für Wilhelm Abel zum 70. Geburtstag. Hannover: G. Fischer, 1974. III, 720-52.

3588. Schmitz, Otto. Die Bewegung der Warenpreise in Deutschland von 1851 bis 1902 nebst 2 Ergänzungen: Bankdiskont, Goldproduktion und Warenpreisstand, der Weizenpreis von 400 vor Christus bis 1900. Berlin: Siemenroth, 1903. 443 pp.

3589. Schoer, Karl. "Origins of Junker Capitalism in Germany." Social Scientist, Indian School of Social Sciences 53 (1976), 33-46.

3590. Schramm, Percy E. "Deutschland und Übersee: der deutsche Handel mit den anderen Kontinenten, insbesondere Afrika, von Karl V. bis zu Bismarck." American Historical Review 57 (1951), 157-58.

3591. Schramm, Percy E. "Überseekaufleute im 19. Jahrhundert." Tradition 7 (1962), 93-107.

3592. Schreiber, Arno. Die Kriegsgeschichte der deutschen landwirtschaftlichen Genossenschaften 1914-1918. Berlin: A. Schreiber, 1934. 40 pp.

3593. Schröter, Alfred. Krieg-Staat-Monopole, 1914-1918. Berlin: Akademie, 1965. 172 pp.

3594. Schuchardt, Jürgen. "Die Wirtschaftskrise vom Jahre 1866 in Deutschland." Jahrbuch für Wirtschaftsgeschichte (1962), II, 91-141.

3595. Schwabach, Alexander. "Die Einwirkungen des Weltkrieges auf die deutsch-schweizerischen Handelsbeziehungen." Weltwirtschaftliches Archiv 14 (1919), 108-22.

3596. Seelmann-Eggebert, Erich L. Friedrich Wilhelm Raiffeisen. Sein Lebensgang und sein genossenschaftliches Werk. Stuttgart: Kohlhammer, 1928. 491 pp.

3597. Simon, Oskar. Die Fachbildung des preussischen Gewerbe- und Handelsstandes im 18. und 19. Jahrhundert nach den Bestimmungen des Gewerberechts und der Verfassung des gewerblichen Unterrichtswesens. Berlin: J. J. Heine, 1902. 928 pp.

3598. Smith, Woodruff D. The German Colonial Empire. Chapel Hill: University of North Carolina Press, 1978. 274 pp.

3599. Smith, Woodruff D. "The Ideology of German Colonialism, 1840-1906." Journal of Modern History 46 (1974), 641-62.

3600. Soetbeer, Adolf. "Das Niveau der Warenpreise in den Jahren 1886-1890." Jahrbücher für Nationalökonomie und Statistik N. F., 23 (1892), 588-96.

3601. Soetbeer, Adolf. "Veränderungen im Niveau der allgemeinen Warenpreise in den Jahren 1881-1889." Jahrbücher für Nationalökonomie und Statistik N.F., 21 (1890), 412-22.

3602. Sombart, Werner. Gewerbewesen. 2nd ed. 2 vols. Berlin: de Gruyter, 1929.

3603. Sonnemann, Rolf and Siegfried Richter. "Zur Rolle des Staates beim Übergang vom vormonopolistischen Kapitalismus zum Imperialismus in Deutschland." Jahrbuch für Wirtschaftsgeschichte (1964), II/III, 240-55.

3604. Sourab, Siawusch. Die deutsch-persischen Wirtschaftsbeziehungen vor dem 1. Weltkrieg. Frankfurt a. M.: Lang, 1976. 514 pp.

3605. Spencer, Elaine G. West German Coal, Iron and Steel Industrialists as Employers, 1896-1914. Diss. Univ. of California Berkeley, 1969. 280 pp.

3606. Spree, Reinhard. Die Wachstumszyklen der deutschen Wirtschaft von 1840 bis 1880. Mit einem konjunkturstatistischen Anhang. Berlin: Duncker & Humblot, 1977. 577 pp.

3607. Stein, Walter. Handels- und Verkehrsgeschichte der deutschen Kaiserzeit. Berlin: K. Curtius, 1922. 383 pp.

3608. Stieda, Wilhelm. "Ältere deutsche Kartelle." Schmoller 37 (1913), 725-55.

3609. Stoecker, Helmuth. Deutschland und China im 19. Jahrhundert. Das Eindringen des deutschen Kapitalismus. Berlin: Rütten und Loening, 1958. 307 pp.

3610. Die Störungen im deutschen Wirtschaftsleben während der Jahre 1900 ff. 8 vols. Leipzig: Duncker & Humblot, 1903.

3611. Straube, Hans J. Die Gewerbeförderung Preussens in der ersten Hälfte des 19. Jahrhunderts mit besonderer Berücksichtigung der Regierungsmassnahmen zur Förderung der Industrie durch Erziehung und Fortbildung. Diss. Berlin. Berlin: V. D. I., 1933. 75 pp.

3612. Strauss, Rudolph. "Löhne und Preise in Deutschland 1750 bis 1850." Jahrbuch für Wirtschaftsgeschichte (1963) I, 189-219; II, 212-29, 230-36; IV, 257-80; (1964), I, 270-80; IV, 307-17; (1965), I, 233-49; II, 185-92; III, 211-19; IV, 266-80.

3613. Stresemann, Gustav. Englands Wirtschaftskrieg gegen Deutschland. Stuttgart: Deutsche Verlags-Anstalt, 1915. 40 pp.

3614. Ströll, Moriz. "Über die wirtschaftpolitischen Beziehungen Deutschlands zu Rumänien." Schmoller 19 (1895), 1143-63.

3615. Teuteberg, Hans-Jürgen. "Zum Problem von Staat und Wirtschaft in Preussen am Beginn der Industrialisierung. Bemerkungen zu einer Untersuchung von Ilja Mieck." Jahrbuch für Nationalökonomie und Statistik 181 (1967), I, 51-60. (Review of Mieck above.)

3616. Thiedig, Werner. Englands Übergang zum Freihandel und die deutsche Handelspolitik. 1840-1846. Diss. Giessen. Berlin: Spengler, 1927. 38 pp.

3617. Thiess, Karl. "Die Konsumvereine und die neueste deutsche Wirtschaftspolitik." Archiv für Sozialwissenschaft und Sozialpolitik 10 (1897), 49-82.

3618. Thorwart, Friedrich. Hermann Schulze-Delitzsch. Leben und Wirken. Berlin: Guttentag, 1913. 359 pp.

3619. Tipton, Frank B. Jr. "National Growth Cycles and Regional Economic Structures in Nineteenth Century Germany." in Historische Konjunkturforschung. Stuttgart: Klett-Cotta, 1981. pp. 29-46.

3620. Tipton, Frank B. Jr. Regional Variations in the Economic Development of Germany During the Nineteenth Century. Middletown, CT: Wesleyan University Press, 1976. 270 pp.

3621. Townsend, Mary E. "The Economic Impact of Imperial Germany. Commercial and Colonial Policies." Journal of Economic History, Supplement, 3 (1943), 124-34.

3622. Treitschke, Heinrich G. von. Die Gründung des Deutschen Zollvereins. Leipzig: R. Voigtländer, 1913. 213 pp.

3623. Treue, Wilhelm. "Deutsch-portugiesische Wirtschaftsbeziehungen im 19. und 20. Jahrhundert. VSWG 50 (1963), 25-56.

3624. Treue, Wilhelm. "Der Unternehmer und die Differenzierung der deutschen Gesellschaft im 19. Jahrhundert. Ein erster Versuch." Zeitschrift für Unternehmensgeschichte 22 (1977), 9-25.

3625. Treue, Wilhelm. "Wirtschafts- und Aussenpolitik. Zu dem Problem der deutschen Weltmachtstellung, 1900-1914." Tradition 9 (1964), 193-218.

3626. Urbs, Rudolf. Der Kapitalismus im Weltkrieg. Ein offenes Wort an die Staatsmänner der alliierten Mächte. Prague: Rivnàc, 1920. 175 pp.

3627. Wätjen, Hermann. "Die Anfänge des deutsch-japanischen Handelsverkehrs im 19. Jahrhundert. Zeitschrift des Vereins für hamburgische Geschichte 35 (1956), 1-21.

3628. Walter, Rolf. Venezuela und Deutschland 1815-1870. Wiesbaden: Steiner, 1983. 420 pp.

3629. Weiss, Erich. Die wirtschaftspolitischen Strömungen in Deutschland von 1879 bis zur Jahrhundertwende. Diss. Frankfurt a. M., 1926. 76 pp.

3630. Wendel, Hugo C. M. The Evolution of Industrial Freedom in Prussia. 1845-1849. Freeport, NY: Books for Libraries Press, 1970. 114 pp.

3631. Weyh, Gerhard. Der Typ des deutschen Unternehmers des neunzehnten Jahrhunderts. Diss. Breslau, 1931. Breslau: Mevius, 1930. 64 pp.

3632. Wiedemann, Ernst. Die Entwicklung der deutsch-dänischen Handelsbeziehungen in den letzten 30 Jahren. Braunschweig: F. Vieweg, 1911. 294 pp.

3633. Wiedenfeld, Kurt. "Die Organisation des deutschen Getreidehandels und die Getreidepreisbildung im 19. Jahrhundert." Schmoller 24 (1900), 623-61.

3634. Wieske, Alfred. Der Elbhandel und die Elbhandelspolitik bis zum Beginn des 19. Jahrhunderts. Halberstadt: Meyer, 1927. 198 pp.

3635. Willaume, Juliusz. "Die wirtschaftlichen Beziehungen zwischen Preussen und dem Herzogtum Warschau." Wissenschaftliche Zeitschrift der Universität Berlin 10 (1961), 29-36.

3636. Wirth, Max. Geschichte der Handelskrisen. 4th ed. Frankfurt a. M.: 1890; rpt. Leipzig: 1975. 660 pp.

3637. Wirth, Max. Die Reform der Umlaufsmittel im Deutschen Reiche. Ein Nachtrag zur "Geschichte der Handelskrisen". Frankfurt a. M.: Sauerländer, 1875. 70 pp.
3638. Wuttig, Martin. Versicherungs- und Genossenschaftswesen als wechselseitige Hilfsorganisationen. Eine geschichtliche Studie. Berlin: Generalverband Ländlicher Genossenschaften für Deutschland, 1914. 168 pp.
3639. Wutzmer, Heinz. "Die Herkunft der industriellen Bourgeoisie Preussens in den vierziger Jahren des 19. Jahrhunderts." in Studien zur Geschichte der industriellen Revolution in Deutschland. Berlin: Akademie, 1960. pp. 145-63.
3640. Wygodzinski, Wilhelm. Das Genossenschaftswesen in Deutschland. 2nd ed. Leipzig: B. G. Teubner, 1929. 287 pp.
3641. Wygodzinski, Wilhelm. Die neuere Entwicklung des landwirtschaftlichen Genossenschaftswesens. Hannover: Helwing, 1913. 86 pp.
3642. Zimmermann, Alfred. "Die russisch-preussischen Handelsbeziehungen, 1814-1833." Schmoller 16 (1892), 333-79.
3643. Zimmermann, F. W. R. "Die deutsche Handelstatistik in ihrer geschichtlichen Entwicklung und ihrem derzeitigen Stand." Jahrbücher für Nationalökonomie und Statistik 90 (1908), 289-324; 433-73.
3644. Zorn, Wolfgang. "Typen und Entwicklungskräfte deutschen Unternehmertums im 19. Jahrhundert." VSWG 44 (1957), 57-77.
3645. Zorn, Wolfgang. "Eine Wirtschaftskarte Deutschlands um 1820 als Spiegel der gewerblichen Entwicklung." Jahrbücher für Nationalökonomie und Statistik 179 (1966), 344-55.
3646. "Zur Statistik der Preise. Grosshandelspreise wichtiger Waren an deutschen Plätzen im Jahre 1902 und in den 20 Jahren 1883-1902. Vierteljahrshefte zur Statistik des Deutschen Reiches (1903), 9-42.
3647. Zwiedineck-Südenhorst, O. von. "Zur Entstehungsgeschichte des Deutschen Zollvereins." Jahrbuch für Nationalökonomie und Statistik, 142 (July 1935), 25-34.

SEE ALSO: 805, 873-74, 876, 950, 1706, 1716, 1736-37, 1741, 1748, 1751, 1759, 2019, 2307, 2340, 2346, 2352-53, 2377-78, 2386-87, 2925, 2935, 2944, 2946, 3021, 3091, 3093, 3095, 3098, 3100-01, 3109, 3115, 4762, 4783-84, 4792, 4859.

WEIMAR REPUBLIC--1919-1933

3648. Abraham, Erich W. Konzernkrach. Hintergründe. Entwicklung und Folgen der deutschen Konzernkrisen. Berlin: Stilke, 1933. 199 pp.
3649. Aldcroft, Derek H. From Versailles to Wall Street 1919-1929. London: Allen Lane, 1977. 372 pp.
3650. Alexandrowitz, Rafael. Der Arbeitsmarkt in der deutschen Konjunkturbewegung der Jahre 1924-1928. Diss. Bern. Berlin: Ebering, 1929. 77 pp.
3651. Auf dem Marsch zum Führer: Unternehmer zwischen Brüning und Hitler. Hamburg: Focke & Jaffé, 1979. 98 pp.
3652. Beitel, Werner. Deutsch-sowjetische Wirtschaftsbeziehungen in der Zeit der Weimarer Republik: eine Bilanz im Hinblick auf gegenwärtige Probleme. Baden-Baden: Nomos, 1979. 273 pp.
3653. Bennett, Edward W. Germany and the Diplomacy of the Financial Crisis, 1931. Cambridge, MA: Harvard University Press, 1962. 342 pp.
3654. Berndt, Roswitha. Die wirtschaftlichen Beziehungen des deutschen Imperialismus zu Österreich in der Zeit der Weltwirtschaftskrise 1929-31. 2 vols. Diss. Halle-Wittenberg, 1965.
3655. Biber, Erich. Die Entwicklung der Handelsbeziehungen Deutschlands zu den Vereinigten Staaten von Amerika nach dem Kriege. Diss. Frankfurt a. M. Stuttgart: Zuffenhausener, 1928. 126 pp.
3656. Blaich, Fritz. Der Schwarze Freitag: Inflation und Wirtschaftskrise. Munich: Deutscher Taschenbuch Verlag, 1985. 172 pp.
3657. Blaich, Fritz. Die Wirtschaftskrise 1925/26 und die Reichsregierung. Kallmünz/Opf.: Lassleben, 1977. 196 pp.
3658. Böhme, Klaus-Richard. "Die deutsch-polnischen Handelsbeziehungen 1923-1933." Zeitschrift für Ostforschung 12 (1963), 500-18.

3659. Böhmer, Walther. Mit Gott für Trust und Dividende. Pietätlose Schilderung selbsterlebter Tatsachen und zwangsläufiger Konsequenzen aus dem Welt-Wirtschaftskrieg 1919-27. Zurich: Viktoria, 1928. 213 pp.

3660. Born, Karl E. "The German Inflation After the First World War." The Journal of European Economic History 6 (1977), 109-16.

3661. Brooks, Sidney. America & Germany 1918-1925. New York: Macmillan, 1927. 167 pp.

3662. Büsch, Otto and Gerald D. Feldman. Historische Prozesse der deutschen Inflation. 1914 bis 1924. Berlin: Colloquium, 1978. 466 pp.

3663. Campus, Eliza. "La position de la Petite Entente devant le plan Austro-Allemand d'Union Douanière de 1931." in Nouvelles études d'histoire. Bucharest: Comité National des Historiens de la République Socialiste de Roumanie, 1965. pp. 363-74.

3664. Capelle, H. van. "Het wonder van Schacht. De duitse super-hyperinflatie van de jaren twintig; oorzaken, gevolgen, oplossing." ESB 65 (1980), 168-75.

3665. Capelle, H. van. "Waardeloos geld. De duitse superhyperinflatie van de jaren twintig: oorzaken, gevolgen en oplossing." Intermediair 13 (1977), 1-6.

3666. Clausing, Gustav. Die wirtschaftlichen Wechsellagen von 1919 bis 1932. Jena: Fischer, 1933. 146 pp.

3667. Dietzel, Hans. Konjunkturbewegungen des letzten Jahrzehnts im deutschen privaten Kredit-bank-Gewerbe (1914-1924). Stuttgart: Poeschel, 1925. 94 pp.

3668. Eschenbach, Anne-Marie. Strukturwandlungen in der deutschen Aussenwirtschaft und die Wirtschaftsentwicklung seit dem Kriege. Diss. Berlin. Berlin: Elsner, 1939. 211 pp.

3669. Fack, Fritz U. Die deutschen Stahlkartelle in der Weltwirtschaftskrise. Untersuchung über den ökonomisch-politischen Einfluss ihres Verhaltens und ihrer Marktmacht auf den Verlauf der grossen deutschen Staats- und Wirtschaftskrise. Diss. Berlin, 1957. 210 pp.

3670. Falkus, Malcolm E. "The German Business Cycle in the 1920's." The Economic History Review Ser. 2, 28 (1975), 451-65.

3671. Feldman, Gerald D., ed. Die deutsche Inflation: eine Zwischenbilanz. Berlin: de Gruyter, 1982. 431 pp.

3672. Feldman, Gerald D. "German Business Between War and Revolution. The Origins of the Stinnes-Legien-Agreement." in G. A. Ritter, ed. Entstehung und Wandel der modernen Gesell-schaft. Festschrift für Hans Rosenberg. Berlin: de Gruyter, 1970. pp. 312-41.

3673. Feldman, Gerald D. and Heidrun Homburg. Industrie und Inflation. Studien und Dokumente zur Politik der deutschen Unternehmer 1916-1923. Hamburg: Hoffmann & Campe, 1977. 421 pp.

3674. Fried, Ferdinand. Das Ende des Kapitalismus. Jena: Diederichs, 1931. 264 pp.

3675. Geigenmüller, Ernst. "Botschafter von Hoesch und der deutsch-österreichische Zollunionsplan von 1931." Historische Zeitschrift 195 (1962), 581-95.

3676. "The German Inflation of 1923." Midland Bank Review (1975), 20-29.

3677. Giustiniani, Gaston. Le commerce et l'industrie devant la dépreciation et la stabilisation monétaire. L'experience allemande. Paris: F. Alcan, 1927. 211 pp.

3678. Glücks, Willy. Die Handels- und Verkehrsbedeutung des Suezkanals für die deutsche Volkswirt-schaft nach dem Weltkrieg. Mönchen-Gladbach: J. Rixen, 1929. 132 pp.

3679. Goldinger, Walter. "Das Projekt einer deutsch-österreichischen Zollunion von 1931." in Österreich und Europa. Vienna: Institut für österreichische Geschichtsforschung, 1965. pp. 527-46.

3680. Gossweiler, Kurt. "Der Übergang von der Weltwirtschaftskrise zur Rüstungskonjunktur in Deutschland 1933-1934." Jahrbuch für Wirtschaftsgeschichte (1968), II, 55-116.

3681. Graham, Frank D. Exchange. Prices. and Production in Hyper-Inflation: Germany. 1920-1923. Princeton, NJ: Princeton Univ. Press, 1930; rpt. New York: Russell and Russell, 1967. 362 pp.

3682. Grotkopp, Wilhelm. Die grosse Krise (1929-32). Lehren aus der Überwindung der Wirtschafts-krise 1929/32. Düsseldorf: Econ-Verlag, 1954. 408 pp.

3683. Haberland, Günther. Elf Jahre staatlicher Regelung der Ein- und Ausfuhr. Eine systematische Darstellung der deutschen Aussenhandelsregelung in den Jahren 1914-1925. Leipzig: Noske, 1927. 134 pp.

3684. Härig, Hermann. Die deutsch-schwedischen Handelsbeziehungen seit der Jahrhundertwende mit besonderer Berücksichtigung der Nachkriegszeit. Diss. Cologne, 1930. 159 pp.

3685. Hardach, Gerd. Weltmarktorientierung und relative Stagnation. Währungspolitik in Deutschland 1924-1931. Berlin: Duncker & Humblot, 1976. 182 pp.

3686. Hauser, Oswald. "Der Plan einer deutsch-österreichischen Zollunion von 1931 und die europäische Föderation." Historische Zeitschrift 179 (1955), 45-92.
3687. Hermens, Ferdinand A. "Das Kabinett Brüning und die Depression." in Staat, Wirtschaft und Politik in der Weimarer Republik. Berlin: Duncker & Humblot, 1967. pp. 287-310.
3688. Hertz-Eichenrode, Dieter. Wirtschaftskrise und Arbeitsbeschaffung: Konjunkturpolitik 1925/26 und die Grundlagen der Krisenpolitik Brünings. Frankfurt a. M.: Campus, 1982. 317 pp.
3689. Hill, Lewis E. et al. "Inflation and the Destruction of Democracy. The Case of the Weimar Republic." Journal of Economic Issues 11 (1977), 299-317.
3690. Hillmeister, Leo. Russischer Aussenhandel in der Nachkriegszeit unter besonderer Berücksichtigung zu Deutschland. Mönchen-Gladbach: Volksverein, 1928. 122 pp.
3691. Himmer, Robert. "Rathenau, Russia and Rapallo." Central European History 9 (1976), 146-83.
3692. Holl, Karl, ed. Wirtschaftskrise und liberale Demokratie. Das Ende der Weimarer Republik und die gegenwärtige Situation. Göttingen: Vandenhoeck & Ruprecht, 1978. 152 pp.
3693. Holtfrerich, Carl-Ludwig. "Amerikanischer Kapitalexport und Wiederaufbau der deutschen Wirtschaft 1919-23 im Vergleich zu 1924-29." VSWG 64 (1977), 497-529.
3694. Holtfrerich, Carl-Ludwig. Die deutsche Inflation 1914-1923: Ursachen und Folgen in internationaler Perspektive. Berlin: de Gruyter, 1980. 360 pp.
3695. Holtfrerich, Carl-Ludwig. "Internationale Verteilungsfolgen der deutschen Inflation 1918-1923." Kyklos 30 (1977), 271-92.
3696. Hupka, Benno. Der mittelbare Protektionismus in der Handelspolitik der Nachkriegszeit. Diss. Göttingen, 1931. Breslau: Schatzky, 1932. 191 pp.
3697. Jacobs, Rodney L. The Dynamics of Hyperinflation. Diss. Stanford University, 1975. 95 pp.
3698. Jostock, Paul. Der deutsche Katholizismus und die Überwindung des Kapitalismus. Eine ideengeschichtliche Skizze. Regensburg: Pustet, 1932. 213 pp.
3699. Kindleberger, Charles P. The World in Depression 1929-1939. Rev. ed. Berkeley: University of California Press, 1986. 355 pp.
3700. Koerner, V. "Die deutschen Handelsverträge seit dem Kriege." Nord und Süd 51 (1928), 43-50.
3701. Kortmann, Emil. "Wer zeigte der deutschen Arbeiterklasse den Ausweg aus der Wirtschaftskrise 1929 bis 1932?" Wirtschaftswissenschaft 11 (1963), 925-33.
3702. Krulis-Randa, Jan. Das deutsch-österreichische Zollunionsproject von 1931. Die Bemühungen um eine wirtschaftliche Annährung zwischen Deutschland und Österreich. Diss. Zurich. Zurich: Europa-Verlag, 1955. 214 pp.
3703. Kul'baken, V. D. "Economic Relations with the Soviet Union and the Stand Taken by the Social Forces of Germany, 1929-32." Voprosy Istorii 5 (1977), 63-76.
3704. Langsam, Walter C. "United States and British Press Opinion of the Proposed Austro-German Customs Union of 1931." Journal of Central European Affairs 2 (1942-43), 377-85.
3705. Laursen, Karsten, and Jørgen Pedersen. The German Inflation 1918-1923. Amsterdam: North-Holland, 1964. 140 pp.
3706. Lewinsohn, Richard. Histoire de l'inflation. Paris: Payot, 1926. 416 pp.
3707. Marcus, Alfred. Die wirtschaftliche Krise des deutschen Juden. Eine soziologische Untersuchung. Berlin: Stilke, 1931. 184 pp.
3708. Megerle, Klaus. "Weltwirtschaftskrise und Aussenpolitik. Zum Problem der Kontinuität der deutschen Politik in der Endphase der Weimarer Republik." in Geschichte als politische Wissenschaft. Sozialökonomische Ansätze. Analyse Politik-historischer Phänomene. politologische Fragestellungen in der Geschichte. Stuttgart: Klett-Cotta, 1979. pp. 116-140.
3709. Michel, Felix. Das deutsche landwirtschaftliche Genossenschaftswesen in der Inflationszeit und nach der Währungstabilisierung. Diss. Berlin. Charlottenburg: Hoffmann, 1928. 75 pp.
3710. Muranjan, Sumant K. Shadows of Hyper-Inflation. Bombay: Hind Kitabs, 1949. 59 pp.
3711. Newman, M. D. "Britain and the German-Austrian Customs Union Proposal of 1931." European Studies Review 6 (1976), 449-72.
3712. Nezihi, Hasen. Die Gestaltung der deutsch-türkischen Handelsbeziehungen seit dem Lausanner Friedensvertrag (1923) und die Möglichkeiten ihrer rationelleren Gestaltung in der Zukunft. Cologne: Orthen, 1972. 72 pp.
3713. Orde, Anne. "The Origins of the German-Austrian Customs Union Affair of 1931." Central European History 13 (1980), 34-59.
3714. Orlean, A. "Une nouvelle interpretation de l'hyperinflation allemande." Revue Economique 30 (1979), 518-39.

3715. Papousek, Jaroslav. Politischer Hintergrund der deutsch-österreichischen Zollunion. Prague: "Orbis", 1931. 59 pp.
3716. Perels, Joachim. Kapitalismus und politische Demokratie. Privatrechtsystem und Gesellschaftsstruktur in der Weimarer Republik. Frankfurt a. M.: Europäische Verlags-Anstalt, 1973. 88 pp.
3717. Petzina, Dietmar. "Germany and the Great Depression." Journal of Contemporary History 4 (1969), 59-74.
3718. Pohl, Karl H. "Die Finanzkrise bei Krupp und die Sicherheitspolitik Stresemanns. Ein Beitrag zum Verhältnis von Wirtschaft und Aussenpolitik in der Weimarer Republik." VSWG 61 (1974), 505-25.
3719. Puchert, Berthold. "Die Entwicklung der deutsch-sowjetischen Handelsbeziehungen von 1918 bis 1939." Jahrbuch für Wirtschaftsgeschichte (1973), IV, 11-36.
3720. Respondek, Erwin. Wirtschaftliche Zusammenarbeit zwischen Deutschland und Frankreich. Berlin: Heymann, 1929. 222 pp.
3721. Ringer, Fritz K. The German Inflation of 1923. London: Oxford University Press, 1969. 228 pp.
3722. Robinson, Nehemiah. "German Foreign Trade and Industry After the First World War." Quarterly Journal of Economics 58 (1944), 615-36.
3723. Rochebrochard, Guy de la. L'Union douanière austro-allemande. Paris: Pédone, 1934. 225 pp.
3724. Roedler, Carl L. Grundzüge der deutschen Konjunkturbewegung 1920-1925 unter besonderer Berücksichtigung der chemischen Industrie. Diss. Frankfurt a. M. Frankfurt a. M.: Maubach, 1926. 180 pp.
3725. Röseler, Klaus. "Unternehmer in der Weimarer Republik." Tradition 13 (1968), 217-40.
3726. Rüstow, H.-J. "The Economic Crisis of the Weimar Republic and How It Was Overcome. A Comparison With the Present Recession." Cambridge Journal of Economics 2 (1978), 409-21.
3727. Schaefer, Hans. Die deutsch-kanadischen Wirtschaftsbeziehungen seit Beendigung des Weltkrieges unter besonderer Berücksichtigung der kanadischen Wirtschaftsentwicklung. Cologne: Doepgen, 1934. 188 pp.
3728. Schmidt, Carl T. German Business Cycles, 1924-1933. London: Macmillan, 1934. 283 pp.
3729. Schumann, Wolfgang. "Das Scheitern einer Zoll- und Währungsunion zwischen dem faschistischen Deutschland und Dänemark 1940." Jahrbuch für Geschichte 9 (1973), 515-66.
3730. Siebold, Hermann. Die handelspolitischen Beziehungen Deutschlands zu Spanien seit dem Weltkrieg. Diss. Munich, 1938. 58 pp.
3731. Sievers, Wilm. Die Widerstände der fremden Mächte gegen die Zollunion des Deutschen Reiches mit Österreich vom Jahre 1931. Diss. Erlangen. Zeulenroda: Sporn, 1934. 83 pp.
3732. Sprecht, Agnete von. Politische und wirtschaftliche Hintergründe der deutschen Inflation 1918-1923. Diss. Konstanz, 1978. Frankfurt a. M.: Lang, 1982. 157 pp.
3733. Stambrook, F. G. "The German-Austrian Customs Union Project of 1931: A Study of German Methods and Motives." Journal of Central European Affairs 21 (1961), 15-44.
3734. Sternberg, Fritz. Der Niedergang des deutschen Kapitalismus. Berlin: Rowohlt, 1932. 400 pp.
3735. Strücker, Edmund. Die deutsch-französischen Handelsvertragsverhandlungen von staatlicher und privater Seite von 1918 bis Juni 1927. Diss. Cologne, 1927. 100 pp.
3736. Temin, Peter. "The Beginning of the Depression in Germany." Economic History Review 24 (1971), 240-48.
3737. Treue, Wilhelm. "Der deutsche Unternehmer in der Weltwirtschaftskrise 1928 bis 1933." in Die Staats- und Wirtschaftskrise des Deutschen Reichs 1929/33. Stuttgart: Klett, 1967. pp. 82-125.
3738. Treue, Wilhelm, ed. Deutschland in der Weltwirtschaftskrise in Augenzeugenberichten (1929-1933). Düsseldorf: K. Rauch, 1967. 439 pp.
3739. Trummel, Hans J. Die Entwicklung der deutsch-argentinischen Handelsbeziehungen im Wandel der letzten 25 Jahre (1913-1937). Diss. Cologne. Würzburg: Mayr, 1938. 189 pp.
3740. Turner, Henry A., Jr. "Grossunternehmertum und Nationalsozialismus 1930-1933. Kritisches und Ergänzendes zu zwei neuen Forschungsbeiträgen." Historische Zeitschrift 221 (1975), 18-68.
3741. Vierhaus, Rudolf. "Auswirkungen der Krise um 1930 in Deutschland. Beiträge zu einer historisch-psychologischen Analyse." in Die Staats- und Wirtschaftskrise des Deutschen Reichs 1929/33. Stuttgart: Klett, 1967. pp. 155-75.

3742. Wedel, Otto. Der deutsch-österreichische Zollunionsplan im Spiegel der reichsdeutschen Presse. Diss. Heidelberg, 1936. Würzburg: Mayr, 1937. 99 pp.
3743. Welter, Erich. Der Krach von 1931. Frankfurt a. M.: Societäts-Verlag, 1932. 55 pp.
3744. Wiedenfeld, Kurt. Die Gegenwartsaufgaben deutscher Handelspolitik und der deutsche Zollverein. Leipzig: Quelle & Meyer, 1934. 22 pp.
3745. Winkler, Hans-Joachim. Preussen als Unternehmer 1923-1932. Staatliche Erwerbsunternehmen im Spannungsfeld der Politik am Beispiel der Preussag, Hibernia und VEBA. Berlin: de Gruyter, 1965. 223 pp.
3746. Zirwas, Reinhold. Die Entwicklung der deutschen Verbrauchergenossenschaften in den Jahren 1924 bis 1935. Hamburg: Deutsche Grosseinkaufs-Gesellschaft, 1936. 230 pp.

SEE ALSO: 950, 1765-66, 1768-69, 1772-74, 1776-77, 2404, 3020, 3488, 5033, 5053, 5060, 5065.

THIRD REICH--1933-1945

3747. Bay, Achim. Der nationalsozialistische Gedanke der Grossraumwirtschaft und seine ideologischen Grundlagen. Diss. Nürnberg. Cologne: University of Cologne, 1962. 207 pp.
3748. Bengtson, John R. Nazi War Aims. The Plans for the Thousand Year Reich. Rock Island, IL: Augustana College, 1962. 155 pp.
3749. Blaich, Fritz. "Die wirtschaftliche Entwicklung Deutschlands 1933 bis 1939 als Problem der Betriebs- und Firmengeschichte." Archiv und Wirtschaft 12 (1979), 73-82.
3750. Bludau, Kuno. Nationalsozialismus und Genossenschaften. Diss. Basel. Hannover: Verlag für Literatur und Zeitgeschehen, 1968. 240 pp.
3751. Bonnell, Allen T. German Control Over International Economic Relations. 1930-40. Urbana: University of Illinois Studies in Social Sciences, 1940. 167 pp.
3752. Carr, William. Arms, Autarchy and Aggression. A Study in German Foreign Policy. 1933-39. London: Arnold, 1972. 136 pp.
3753. Czollek, Roswitha and Dietrich Eichholtz. "Die deutschen Monopole und der 22. Juni 1941. Dokumente zu Kriegszielen und Kriegsplanung führender Konzerne beim Überfall auf die Sowjetunion." Zeitschrift für Geschichtswissenschaft 15 (1967), 64-76.
3754. Diehl, Alfred. Der grossdeutsche Wirtschaftsraum unter geschichtlich-politischen und wehrwirtschaftlichen Gesichtspunkten. Diss. Giessen. Giessen: Schaidt, 1939. 73 pp.
3755. Duff, Katharine. "Economic Relations between Germany and Italy, 1940-43." in A. Toynbee, ed. Hitler's Europe. London: Oxford University Press, 1954. pp. 317-23.
3756. Duisberg, Curt. "Die Einstellung der deutschen Unternehmer zur Wirtschaftspolitik des 'Dritten Reiches'." Tradition 13 (1968), 243-49.
3757. Einhorn, Marion. "Les monopoles allemands en Espagne en 1938-1939." in 1938-1941. Le monde prend feu. Paris: s.n., 1961. pp. 88-112.
3758. Einzig, Paul. Bloodless Invasion. German Economic Penetration into the Danubian State and the Balkans. London: Duckworth, 1938. 126 pp.
3759. Enderle, Georges. Die Auswirkungen der Weltwirtschaftskrise der Dreissiger Jahre auf die apersonelle Einkommens- und Vermögensverteilung: methodische und theoretische Probleme. Diss. Fribourg. Fribourg: Fribourg University Press, 1982. 302 pp.
3760. Esenwein-Rothe, Ingeborg. Die Wirtschaftsverbände von 1933-1945. Berlin: Duncker & Humblot, 1965. 209 pp.
3761. Foster, Edwin D. "The Trend of Soviet-German Commercial Relations and its Significance." Harvard Business Review 11 (1932), 376-85.
3762. Friedman, Philip. "The Welfare Costs of Bilateralism. German-Hungarian Trade, 1933-38." Explorations in Economic History 13 (1976), 113-26.
3763. Harper, Glenn T. German Economic Policy in Spain During the Spanish Civil War. 1936-39. Paris: Mouton, 1967. 152 pp.
3764. Hillmann, H. C. "Analysis of Germany's Foreign Trade and the War." Economica 7 (1940), 66-88.
3765. Höffding, W. "German Trade with the Soviet Union." Slavonic and East European Review 14 (1936), 473-94.
3766. Jacobs, Alfred. Die Grosshandelspreise in Deutschland 1934-1944. S.l.: Kopft, 1945. 18 pp.

3767. Kaiser, Peter M. "Monopolprofit und Massenmord im Faschismus und Vernichtungslager im faschistischen Deutschland." Blätter für Deutsche und Internationale Politik 20 (1975), 552-77.
3768. Kesel, Gerhard. Die Abwicklung von Vorkriegsverträgen der deutschen Wirtschaft mit dem Ausland. Zugleich ein Beitrag zum Problem der Geschäftsgrundlage. Tübingen: Mohr, 1948. 18 pp.
3769. Köhler, Bernhard. Das dritte Reich und der Kapitalismus. Frankfurt a. M.: National-sozialistische Arbeitergemeinschaft für Ständische Wirtschaftsgestaltung, 1934. 30 pp.
3770. Kolko, Gabriel. "American Business and Germany, 1930-1941." The Western Political Quarterly 15 (1962), 713-28.
3771. Laser, Kurt. "Die Auswirkungen der Machtübertragung an die Nazipartei auf die deutsch-sowjetischen Wirtschaftsbeziehungen. " Jahrbuch für Wirtschaftsgeschichte (1974), IV, 57-74.
3772. Look, Hans-Dietrich. "Zur 'Grossgermanischen Politik' des 3. Reiches." Vierteljahrshefte für Zeitgeschichte 8 (1960), 37-63.
3773. Luza, Radomir. Austro-German Relations in the Anschluss Era. Princeton, NJ: Princeton University Press, 1975. 438 pp.
3774. Mahrad, Ahmad. Die Wirtschafts- und Handelsbeziehungen zwischen Iran und dem National-sozialistischen Deutschen Reich. 2nd ed. Frankfurt a. M.: P. Lang, 1982. 319 pp.
3775. Maltitiz, Horst von. The Evolution of Hitler's Germany. The Ideology, the Personality, the Moment. New York: McGraw-Hill, 1973. 479 pp.
3776. Neal, Larry. "The Economics and Finance of Bilateral Clearing Agreements. Germany, 1934-38." Economic History Review 32 (1979), 391-404.
3777. "Die Preise in Deutschland in zehn Jahren nationalsozialistischer Wirtschaftsführung." Wirtschaft und Statistik 23 (1943), 19-21.
3778. Pribilla, Max. "Das Verhalten der Unternehmer im Dritten Reich. Moraltheologisches Gut-achten." Stimmen der Zeit. Monatschrift für das Geistesleben der Gegenwart 74 (1948-49), 171-85.
3779. Roesler, Hans. Die weltanschauliche Entwicklung der gewerblichen Kreditgenossenschaften und der Konsumvereine Deutschlands (unter Berücksichtigung ihrer wirtschaftlichen Bedeutung und der Stellung zum Nationalsozialismus.) Diss. Berlin. Oelde i. W.: Holterdorf, 1936. 119 pp.
3780. Schloesser, Robert and Otto Ruhmer. Die ersten Haushalt- (Konsum-) Genossenschaften Gross-Deutschlands, ihre Leiden und Kämpfe. Hamburg: Herrmann & Kröger, 1939. 196 pp.
3781. Schweitzer, Arthur. Big Business in the Third Reich. Bloomington, IL: Indiana University Press, 1965. 739 pp.
3782. Schweitzer, Arthur. "Der organisierte Kapitalismus. Die Wirtschaftsordnung in der ersten Periode der nationalsocialistischen Herrschaft." Hamburger Jahrbuch für Wirtschafts- und Gesellschaftspolitik 7 (1962), 32-47.
3783. Steica-Olteanu, Mihai S. Die deutsch-rumänischen Wirtschaftsbeziehungen nach 1933. Diss. Berlin. Berlin: Pfau, 1941. 96 pp.
3784. Swatek, Dieter. Unternehmenskonzentration als Ergebnis und Mittel nationalsozialistischer Wirtschaftspolitik. Berlin: Duncker & Humblot, 1972. 172 pp.
3785. Troemel, Constantin. Die Entwicklung der deutsch-sowjetrussischen Handelsbeziehungen seit 1928 unter besonderer Berücksichtigung ihrer handelsverträglichen Grundlagen. Leipzig: Moltzen, 1939. 118 pp.
3786. Übersicht über die Entwicklung der deutschen Verbrauchergenossenschaften (ohne die auf Grund des Gesetzes v. 21. Mai 1935 liquid. Genossenschaften.) in den Jahren 1934 bis 1938. Hamburg: Deutsche Grosseinkaufs-Gesellschaft, 1938.
3787. Wagenführ, Horst. "Ein Index der staatlich geregelten Preise für industrielle Erzeugnisse 1934-1938." Kartell-Rundschau. Monatsschrift für Recht und Wirtschaft im Kartell- und Konzernwesen 39 (1941), 145-51.
3788. Wandlungen in der wirtschaftlichen Dynamik seit 1933. Zur Wirtschaftslage im Frühsommer 1938. Berlin: Arbeitswissenschaftliches Institut der Deutschen Arbeitsfront, 1938. 43 pp.
3789. Wendt, Bernd-Jürgen. Economic Appeasement: Handel and Finanz in der britischen Deutsch-land-Politik 1933-1939. Düsseldorf: Bertelsmann, 1971. 695 pp.
3790. Wittmann, K. Schwedens Wirtschaftsbeziehungen zum Deutschen Reich 1933-1945. Vienna: Oldenbourg, 1978. 479 pp.
3791. Zaruba, Hans. Die landwirtschaftlichen Genossenschaften im nationalsozialistischen Deutsch-land. Diss. Vienna. 1941. 97 pp.

SEE ALSO: 471, 987, 998, 1783, 2394, 2427, 3488, 3729.

GERMANY REDIVIDED--1945-1975

Bibliographic Reference

3792. Maur, Hans, ed. "Auswahlbibliographie zur Methodik und zur Methodologie der Marxistischen Betriebsgeschichtsforschung. Veröffentlichungen der Jahre 1945 bis 1970." Jahresschrift des Instituts für Sorbische Volksforschung 20 (1973), 120-28.

GERMANY REDIVIDED--1945-1975

3793. Ahrens, Hanns D. Demontage: Nachkriegspolitik der Alliierten. Munich: Universitas, 1982. 295 pp.
3794. Albrecht, Gerhard. Die soziale Funktion des Genossenschaftswesens. Abhandlungen und Vorträge. Berlin: Duncker & Humblot, 1965. 402 pp.
3795. Altvater, Elmar et al. "Entwicklungsphasen und -tendenzen des Kapitalismus in Westdeutschland." Probleme des Klassenkampfs. Zeitschrift für politische Ökonomie und sozialistische Politik 13 (1974), 101-32; 16 (1974), 55-149.
3796. Altvater, Elmar et al. Vom Wirtschaftswunder zur Wirtschaftskrise. Ökonomie und Politik in der Bundesrepublik. 2 vols. Berlin: Olle & Wolter, 1980.
3797. Andersch-Niestedt, Heidrun. Betriebliche Führung im Vergleich. Bundesrepublik Deutschland-Deutsche Demokratische Republik. Berlin: Spiess, 1981. 177 pp.
3798. Artus, Jacques R. "Measures of Potential Output in Manufacturing for Eight Industrial Countries, 1955-78." International Monetary Fund 24 (1977), 1-35.
3799. Barthelmann, Robert. "Die revolutionär-demokratische Umwandlung der landwirtschaftlichen Genossenschaften des Kapitalismus und ihre Mitwirkung bei der Entwicklung des sozialistischen Genossenschaftsgedankens in der Landwirtschaft der DDR." Wissenschaftliche Zeitschrift der Friedrich-Schiller-Universität Jena 12 (1963), 117-28.
3800. Barthelmann, Robert. "Über die Rolle der bäuerlichen Genossenschaften im Gebiet der DDR in den Etappen der revolutionären Umwälzung." Wissenschaftliche Zeitschrift der Friedrich-Schiller-Universität Jena 11 (1962), 333-37.
3801. Beaud, Michel. La croissance de l'Allemagne de l'Ouest. (1949-1962). Suivi d'une note sur la situation économique de l'Allemagne de l'Ouest en 1965. Paris: Cujas, 1966. 338 pp.
3802. Böhme, Hans. "Die wirtschaftliche Entwicklung in beiden Teilen Deutschlands zwischen 1945 und 1949." Aus Politik und Zeitgeschichte (1969), 35-54.
3803. Boris, Dieter. "Geschichte und Struktur der Aussenwirtschaftsbeziehungen der Bundesrepublik." in Beiträge zu einer Geschichte der Bundesrepublik Deutschland. Cologne: Pahl-Rugenstein, 1979. pp. 155-200.
3804. Brulin, Monique. "La réduction de la durée du travail et la croissance de l'industrie allemande 1954-1967." Economies et Sociétés 3 (1969), 2141-80.
3805. Busche, Manfred. "Über die Entwicklung der Konsumgenossenschaften Mitteldeutschlands sowjetische Besatzungszone auf dem flachen Lande." Zeitschrift für das gesamte Genossenschaftswesen 8 (1958), 293-99.
3806. Cellier, François. "Déformations sectorielles et évolution économique de la République Féderale d'Allemagne, 1950-1975." Statistiques & Etudes Financières 35 (1978), 39-68.
3807. Cox, Ingrid. Lohn- und Preisbewegungen in der Bundesrepublik Deutschland von 1968 bis 1979: eine Analyse mit Hilfe des Box-Jenkins-Verfahrens. Diss. Cologne, 1982. Krefeld: Marchal & Matzenbacher, 1983. 242 pp.
3808. Dahrendorf, Gustav. Der Mensch, das Mass aller Dinge. Reden und Schriften zur deutschen Politik 1945-1954. Hamburg: Verlagsgesellschaft Deutscher Konsumgenossenschaften, 1955. 293 pp.
3809. Domar, Evsey D. et al. "Economic Growth and Productivity in the United States, Canada, United Kingdom, Germany and Japan in the Post-War Period." The Review of Economics and Statistics 46 (1964), 33-40.
3810. Domdey, Karl-Heinz. "Zur Krise der aggressiven Bonner Integrationspolitik (1958-1959)." in Krisenerscheinungen in der kapitalistischen Wirtschaft 1957-1959. Berlin: Die Wirtschaft, 1960. pp. 83-148.
3811. Dow, J. C. R. "Cyclical Developments in France, Germany, and Italy Since the Early 1950's." in Is the Business Cycle Obsolete? New York: Wiley-Interscience, 1969. pp. 140-96.

3812. Eberspächer, Helmut. Unternehmertum in der Tradition. Vortrag. Bonn-Bad Godesberg 1978. Herford: Maximilian, 1979. 27 pp.

3813. Eglau, Hans O. Die Kasse muss stimmen. So hatten sie Erfolg im Handel. Von der Kleider-dynastie Brenninkmeyer über die Discountbrüder Albrecht bis zur Sexversenderin Beate Uhse. Düsseldorf: Econ Verlag, 1972. 260 pp.

3814. Einige Probleme des staatsmonopolistischen Kapitalismus in Westdeutschland. Berlin: Institut für Gesellschaftswissenschaften beim ZK der SED, 1962. 141 pp.

3815. Emmerich, Klaus. "Am Ende des Konjunktur-Lateins. Die Krise. Von der hausgemachten Infla-tion zum ungewollten Wachstumsverfall." Die Aussprache. Arbeitsgemeinschaft Selbständiger Unternehmer 21 (1971), X, 3-6.

3816. Feld, Werner. West Germany and the European Community. New York: Praeger, 1981. 151 pp.

3817. Fels, Gerhard and Klaus-Dieter Schmidt. Die deutsche Wirtschaft im Strukturwandel. Tübingen: Mohr, 1980. 368 pp.

3818. Flemig, G. et al. "Die Wirtschaft der Bundesrepublik Deutschland nach dem Boom." Die Weltwirtschaft (1970), II, 1-18.

3819. Flender, Alfred. "Zwanzig Jahre danach. Die Verantwortung des Unternehmers." Die Aussprache. Arbeitsgemeinschaft Selbständiger Unternehmer 16 (1966), 73-76.

3820. Freund, Elmar. "Wissenschaft und Wirtschaftswachstum." in Offene Welt 95/96 (1967), 30-43.

3821. Friedrich, Klaus. "West Germany's Trade Policies." Current History 54 (1968), 288-92.

3822. Gatz, Werner. Die Bestimmungsfaktoren der westdeutschen Fertigwareneinfuhr. 1950-1958. Kiel: Institut für Weltwirtschaft an der Universität Kiel, 1959. 47 pp.

3823. Giersch, Herbert. Growth. Cycles and Exchange Rates: The Experience of West Germany. Stockholm: Almqvist & Wiksell, 1970. 39 pp.

3824. Glastetter, Werner. "Die wirtschaftliche Entwicklung der Bundesrepublik Deutschland im Zeitraum 1950 bis 1975. Ein empirischer Befund." in Krise und Reform in der Industriegesell-schaft. Frankfurt a. M.: Europäische Verlagsanstalt, 1976. pp. 22-151.

3825. Glismann, Hans H. and Horst Rodemer. Der wirtschaftliche Niedergang in der Bundesrepublik Deutschland und in der Weimarer Republik. Kiel: Institut für Weltwirtschaft an der Universität Kiel, 1982. 18 pp.

3826. Goldberg, Jörg and Heinz Jung, ed. Die Wirtschaftskrise 1974-1976 in der Bundesrepublik Deutschland. Frankfurt a. M.: Marxistische Blätter, 1976. 92 pp.

3827. Grevsmähl, Johannes. "Branchenstruktur, Wirtschaftswachstum und Beschäftigung in der Bundesrepublik Deutschland 1960 bis 1966." WWI Mitteilungen. Wirtschaftswissenschaftliches Institut der Gewerkschaften 21 (1968), 263-69.

3828. Grube, Frank. Die Schwarzmarktzeit: Deutschland zwischen 1945 und 1948. Hamburg: Hoffmann & Campe, 1979. 187 pp.

3829. Gschwendtner, Helmut. "Wirkungen von Konjunktur und Wachstum auf die Inflation in der Bundesrepublik Deutschland 1953-1974." Jahrbücher für Nationalökonomie und Statistik 192 (1977), 114-26. (English Summary.)

3830. Gündel, Rudi. "Zum relativ hohen Wachstumstempo der westdeutschen Industrieproduktion im Verlauf der Aufschwungsphase von 1950-1957." Probleme der politischen Ökonomie 3 (1960), 261-308.

3831. Gündel, Rudi. "Zur Entwicklung des Widerspruches zwischen Produktion und Konsumtion im Verlauf der Aufschwungsphase des westdeutschen Nachkriegszyklus." Konjunktur und Krise 2 (1958), 16-33.

3832. Haak, Ernst. "Die wichtigsten Ursachen der verstärkten ungleichmässigen Entwicklung West-deutschlands und Grossbritanniens nach dem zweiten Weltkrieg." in K. H. Domdey et al. Neueste Probleme des Imperialismus. Berlin: Verlag "Die Wirtschaft", 1963. pp. 83-133, 261-308.

3833. Hanhardt, Arthur M., Jr. The German Democratic Republic. Baltimore: Johns Hopkins University Press, 1968. 126 pp.

3834. Hanke, Manfred. Als unsere Marktwirtschaft laufen lernte: eine Wirtschaftsbericht aus dem Jahre 1950. Cologne: Informedia, 1980. 93 pp.

3835. Hansen, Gerd. Ein ökonometrisches Modell für die Bundesrepublik 1951-1964. Versuch der Erklärung von Wachstum und Konjunktur. Göttingen: Vandenhoeck & Ruprecht, 1967. 144 pp.

3836. Hartig, Günter. "Industrie der DDR 1950 bis 1966. Untersuchungen über das Wachstum der Produktion und einiger Wachstumsfaktoren." Statistische Praxis. Staatliche Zentralverwaltung für Statistik 23 (1968), 133-40.

3837. Hartmann, Heinz and Ulrich Hornung. "Die westdeutschen Unternehmerinnen, 1950-1961." Jahrbücher für Nationalökonomie und Statistik 178 (1965), 316-34.
3838. Hegemann, Margot and Günter Möschner. "Die DDR als Wirtschaftspartner der sozialistischen Staaten in den ersten Jahren des RGW." Jahrbuch für Geschichte 12 (1974), 245-79.
3839. Hein, John. "Revisited. Germany's 'Economic Miracle'." Across the Board 17 (1980), 47-56.
3840. Heininger, Horst. Der Nachkriegszyklus der westdeutschen Wirtschaft. 1945-1950. Berlin: Verlag "Die Wirtschaft", 1959. 279 pp.
3841. Heininger, Horst. "Zur zyklischen Wirtschaftsentwicklung in Westdeutschland. Zu einigen Problemen der ersten beiden Entwicklungsphasen in der Zeit von 1945 bis 1950." Probleme der politischen Ökonomie 1 (1957), 120-68.
3842. Herker, Paul. Die landwirtschaftlichen Genossenschaften in der antifaschistisch-demokratischen Ordnung. Berlin: Deutscher Bauernverlag, 1949. 40 pp.
3843. Hermann, Walther. "Konjunkturforschung und Konjunkturberichterstattung nach dem Kriege." Zeitschrift für handelswissenschaftliche Forschung N.F., 4 (1952), 49-70.
3844. Hoffmann, Walther G. "The Take-off in Germany." in W. W. Rostow, ed. The Economics of Take-Off into Sustained Growth. London: Macmillan, 1963. pp. 95-118.
3845. Hofmann, Rolf. "Wachstumstendenzen in der Industrie von 1960 bis 1980, unter besonderer Berücksichtigung der Chemie." Der Betrieb 29 (1976), 1-8, 61-65.
3846. Honecker, Erich. "Der Siegeszug des Sozialismus auf deutschem Boden." Einheit. Zentralkomitee der Sozialistischen Einheitspartei Deutschlands 34 (1979), 899-907.
3847. Hopp, Rüdiger. "Initialzündungen und konjunkturelle Aufschwungswirkungen in den drei Wachstumszyklen seit 1954." Konjunkturpolitik 14 (1968), 135-56.
3848. Hopp, Rüdiger. Schwankungen des wirtschaftlichen Wachstums in Westdeutschland 1954-1967. Meisenheim/Glan: Hain, 1969. 136 pp.
3849. Hoth, Werner. Die Bedeutung und Stellung der Konsumgenossenschaften in Deutschland nach 1945. Diss. Graz, 1968. Vienna: Notring, 1971. 244 pp.
3850. Huffschmid, Jörg and Herbert Schui, eds. Gesellschaft im Konkurs?: Handbuch zur Wirtschaftskrise 1973-76 in der BRD. 2nd ed. Cologne: Pahl-Rugenstein, 1977. 538 pp.
3851. Jaeger, Hans. "Business History in Germany. A Survey of Recent Developments." Business History Review 48 (1974), 28-48.
3852. Jensen, Wiebke. Die gegenseitigen Beeinflussungen von Binnenkonjunktur und aussenwirtschaftlichen Leistungsströmen. dargestellt am Beispiel der Bundesrepublik Deutschland 1958 bis 1967. Diss. Hamburg. Hamburg: Weltwirtschaftsarchiv, 1969. 157 pp.
3853. Kahn, Siegbert. "Zur zyklischen Entwicklung in Westdeutschland seit dem Ende des Zweiten Weltkrieges." Jahrbuch für Wirtschaftsgeschichte (1969), III, 127-33.
3854. Kathe, Rainer. Entwicklung. Stand. Probleme und Möglichkeiten des ländlichen genossenschaftlichen Bildungswesens in der Bundesrepublik Deutschland. Münster i. W.: Fotodruck Max Kramer, 1962. 154 pp.
3855. Keinath, Karl. Regionale Konjunkturschwankungen. Eine empirische Analyse der Bundesrepublik Deutschland 1950-1974. Tübingen: Mohr, 1978. 335 pp.
3856. Kleffel, Andreas. "Unternehmer gestern, heute, morgen." in Für Erich Selbach. zum 70. Geburtstag. 25.7.1975. Krefeld: Vorstand der Girmes-Werke Aktiengesellschaft und vom Präsidium der Industrie- und Handelskammer, 1975. pp. 173-82.
3857. Klein, Philip A. "Postwar Growth Cycles in the German Economy." in Historische Konjunkturforschung. Stuttgart: Klett-Cotta, 1981. pp. 115-40.
3858. Knapp, Manfred. Von der Bizonengründung zur ökonomisch-politischen Westintegration. Studien zum Verhältnis zwischen Aussenpolitik und Aussenwirtschaftsbeziehung in der Entstehungsphase der Bundesrepublik Deutschland. Frankfurt a. M.: Haag + Herchen, 1984. 311 pp.
3859. Köhler, Heinz. Economic Integration in the Soviet Bloc. With an East German Case Study. New York: Praeger, 1965. 402 pp.
3860. Köhler, Heinz. "On East Germany's Foreign Economic Relations." Social Research. New York School for Social Reseach 29 (1962), 221-25.
3861. Kohl, Horst. "On the Impact of Socialist Economic Integration on the Spatial Structure of Industry in the GDR." Geographia Polonica 36 (1977), 127-32.
3862. Kohlmey, Gunther. RGW. DDR. 25 Jahre Zusammenarbeit. Berlin: Akademie, 1974. 223 pp.
3863. Kokot, Józef. "The Economic Aspects of the Resettlement of German Population after the Second World War." Polish Western Affairs 5 (1964), 92-119.

3864. Die Konsumgenossenschaften in der Deutschen Demokratischen Republik. Berlin: Verband Deutscher Konsumgenossenschaften, 1965. 63 pp.
3865. Krebs, Christian. "Die Entwicklung der ländlichen Genossenschaften in der DDR." in Mitgliederversammlung des Bundesverbandes der Raiffeisen-Warengenossenschaften. Berlin: Bundesverband der Raiffeisen-Warengenossenschaften, 1975. pp. 59-71.
3866. Krengel, Rolf. "Ähnlichkeiten zwischen der sowjetischen und der westdeutschen Wirtschaftsentwicklung nach dem Kriege." in Bericht über den wissenschaftlichen Teil der 24. Mitgliederversammlung der Arbeitsgemeinschaft Deutscher Wirtschaftswissenschaftlicher Forschungsinstitute am 2. und 3. Juni 1961. Berlin: Duncker & Humblot, 1961. pp. 28-50.
3867. Krengel, Rolf. "Produktionskapazitäten, Kapitalintensität und Kapazitätsausnutzung der westdeutschen Industrie. Ein Überblick über die Jahre 1950 bis 1960." Vierteljahrshefte zur Wirtschaftsforschung (1962), 45-62.
3868. Kroczeck, Heinz. Seite an Seite in RGW. 30 Jahre Befreiung von Faschismus. Eine Bilanz. Leipzig: VEB Fachbuchverlag, 1975. 239 pp.
3869. Krumholz, Karin. "Beschäftigungsstruktur und Wirtschaftswachstum 1960 bis 1965." Vierteljahrshefte zur Wirtschaftsforschung (1966), 58-70.
3870. Letsch, Kurt. Sozialistische ökonomische Integration. Der Rat für Gegenseitige Wirtschaftshilfe. RGW. Bernau: s.n., 1971. 57 pp.
3871. Loesch, Dieter. "The Economic Present and the Future of West Germany." Giornale degli Economisti e Annali di Economia 40 (1981), 287-99.
3872. Losser, Alphonse. "Bilan économique de la République Fédérale d'Allemagne 1948-1968." Revue d'Allemagne (1969), 32-77.
3873. Mante, Helmut. "Die Konjunkturschwankungen und Krisenerscheinungen in Westdeutschland 1952 bis 1954." Konjunktur und Krise 3 (1959), 238-50.
3874. Maurischat, Gerd. "Die Konjunkturbewegung in Westdeutschland in der Nachkriegszeit." Wirtschaftswissenschaft 13 (1965), 1323-40.
3875. Menges, Günter and J. Gossmann. Ökonometrische Untersuchungen der Preisentwicklung in der Bundesrepublik Deutschland. Düsseldorf: Stahleisen, 1968. 179 pp.
3876. Merx, Volker. "Die vier Wachstumszyklen in der Wirtschaftsentwicklung der Bundesrepublik Deutschland." Berichte des Deutschen Industrieinstituts zur Wirtschaftspolitik 1 (1967), 1-45.
3877. Meyer, Fritz. "Der Aussenhandel der westlichen Besatzungszonen Deutschlands und der Bundesrepublik, 1945-1952." in L. Einaudi et al. Wirtschaft ohne Wunder. Zurich-Erlenbach: E. Rentsch, 1953. 359 pp.
3878. Miller, Norman C. "Offset and Growth Coefficients for Five Industrial Countries, 1960-1970." The Review of Economics and Statistics 62 (1980), 319-38.
3879. Mintz, Ilse. Dating Postwar Business Cycles. Methods and their Application to Western Germany, 1950-67. New York: Columbia University Press, 1969. 111 pp.
3880. Möbes, Karl. Das landwirtschaftliche Genossenschaftswesen gestern und heute. Berlin: Deutscher Bauernverlag, 1949. 147 pp.
3881. Molsberger, Josef. "Hat die deutsche Aufwertung von 1969 den Export gebremst? Ausfuhrpreise und Auftragseingänge in wichtigen deutschen Exportindustrien nach der DM-Aufwertung von 1969." Wirtschaftspolitische Chronik 2 (1971), 23-43.
3882. Mussler, Werner. Der kapitalistische Sektor der Industrie als Problem der Übergangsperiode zum Sozialismus in der Deutschen Demokratischen Republik. Berlin: Verlag Die Wirtschaft, 1959. 190 pp.
3883. Neide, K. von der. Raiffeisens Ende in der Sowjetischen Besatzungszone. Bonn: Deutscher Bundes-Verlag, 1952. 55 pp.
3884. Neumann, Gerd. "Die Entwicklung der Ost-West-Beziehungen." Jahrbuch für Wirtschaftsgeschichte (1976), III, 11-29.
3885. Neuner, Friederike. Die Bedeutung der Gastarbeiterwanderungen für das wirtschaftliche Wachstum der europäischen Industrienationen am Beispiel der BRD. Thesis Vienna Hochschule für Welthandel, 1974. 120 pp.
3886. Petzina, Dietmar. Krisen gestern und heute. Die Rezession von 1974-75 und die Erfahrungen der Weltwirtschaftskrise. Dortmund: Gesellschaft für Westfälische Wirtschaftsgeschichte, 1977. 35 pp.
3887. Pohl, Hans. "Unternehmensgeschichte in der Bundesrepublik Deutschland. Stand der Forschung und Forschungsaufgaben für die Zukunft." Zeitschrift für Unternehmensgeschichte 22 (1977), 26-41.

3888. Preiser, Erich and Wilhelm Krelle. "Analysis of Economic Developments in Western Germany since the Currency Reform of 1948." in E. Lundberg, ed. The Business Cycle in the Post-War World. London: International Economic Association, 1955. pp. 122-54.

3889. Radandt, Hans. "Forschungen zur Betriebsgeschichte." in Historische Forschungen in der DDR 1960-1970. Berlin: Deutscher Verlag der Wissenschaften, 1970.

3890. Rakowski, Horst. "Die Entwicklung der wirtschaftlichen sozialistischen Integration zwischen der DDR und der UdSSR (Juni 1964 bis Dezember 1968)." Jahrbuch für Geschichte 6 (1972), 417-47.

3891. Rattinger, Hans. "Die 'Tradition' 1956 bis 1971. Themen und Trends in Firmengeschichte und Unternehmerbiographie." Tradition 18 (1973), 4-17.

3892. Reissig, Karl. "Der Weg in die Gemeinschaft freier Völker. Zur Geschichte der internationalen Wirtschaftspolitik der SED (1945-1955)." Zeitschrift für Geschichtswissenschaft 12 (1964), 1138-57.

3893. Roesch, Hans. Das dritte Talent. Die Leistung der Frau als Unternehmerin gestern, heute, morgen. Berlin: Ullstein, 1970. 240 pp.

3894. Rosenbrock, E. Der Deutsche Raiffeisenverband in der Wirtschafts- und Agrarpolitik, 1945-1971. Wiesbaden: Deutscher Genossenschafts-Verlag, 1976. 559 pp.

3895. Roskamp, Karl W. Economic Growth, Capital Formation, and Public Policy in West Germany 1948 to 1957. Diss. University of Michigan, 1959. 433 pp.

3896. Roskamp, Karl W. "Note on Income Distribution, Structure of Production and Fiscal Policy in Early West German Economic Growth." Weltwirtschaftliches Archiv 102 (1969), 278-81.

3897. Rüstow, H.-J. "Die Nachkriegsentwicklung der deutschen Wirtschaft." Ifo-Studien. Zeitschrift des Ifo-Instituts für Wirtschaftsforschung 18 (1972), 253-73.

3898. Scharf, Claus and Hans-Jürgen Schröder, eds. Politische und ökonomische Stabilisierung Westdeutschlands 1945-1949. Fünf Beiträge zur Deutschlandpolitik der westlichen Alliierten. Wiesbaden: Steiner, 1978. 93 pp.

3899. Scharpf, Peter. Europäische Wirtschaftsgemeinschaft und Deutsche Demokratische Republik. Die Entwicklung ihrer Rechtsbeziehungen seit 1948 unter besonderer Berücksichtigung des innerdeutschen Handels. Diss. Tübingen. Tübingen: Mohr, 1973. 194 pp.

3900. Schatz, Klaus-Werner. Wachstum und Strukturwandel der westdeutschen Wirtschaft im internationalen Vergleich. Tübingen: Mohr, 1974. 266 pp.

3901. Schlecht, Otto. Erfahrungen und Lehren aus dem jüngsten Konjunkturzyklus. Tübingen: Mohr, 1972. 67 pp.

3902. Schmidt, Helmut. "Zuversicht und Vertrauen in die gesamtwirtschaftliche Entwicklung." in Presse- und Informationsamt der Bundesregierung, (1975), 1109-15.

3903. Schmidt, Ute and Tilman Fichter. Der erzwungene Kapitalismus. Klassenkämpfe in den Westzonen 1945-48. Berlin: Wagenbach, 1971. 177 pp.

3904. Schmitt, Hans O. "The West German 'Miracle' Reconsidered." Challenge. Institute of Economic Affairs 13 (1964/65), 4-6.

3905. Schroeder, Klaus. Der Weg in die Stagnation. Eine empirische Studie zur Konjunkturentwicklung und Konjunkturpolitik in der Bundesrepublik von 1967-1982. Opladen: Westdeutscher Verlag, 1984. 345 pp.

3906. Schulte, Matthias. Anmerkungen zur Genese der Konsumgenossenschaften in Deutschland. Arbeitsgruppe für Verbraucherforschung und Verbraucherpolitik. Wuppertal: Gesamthochschule Wuppertal, 1980. 245 pp.

3907. Schwanse, Peter. Beschäftigungsstruktur und Wirtschaftswachstum in der Bundesrepublik Deutschland 1950 bis 1963. Berlin: Duncker & Humblot, 1965. 115 pp.

3908. Seiler, Volkmar. Technischer Fortschritt und Branchenwachstum in der Industrie der Bundesrepublik Deutschland 1950-1966. Diss. Fribourg, 1971. 247 pp.

3909. Siebert, Georg. "Das sozialökonomische Wachstum der letzten zwanzig Jahre. Erfahrungen, Aufgaben und Möglichkeiten." Offene Welt 95/96 (1967), 21-29.

3910. Siemens, Peter von. "Unternehmensführung und Geschichtsbewusstsein." Zeitschrift für Unternehmensgeschichte 22 (1977), 3-8.

3911. Smulders, A. A. J. "De conjunctuurontwikkeling van West Duitsland in de periode 1954-1958." Maandschrift 'Economie' 23 (1959), 545-54.

3912. Snell, Edwin M. and Marilyn Harper. "Postwar Economic Growth in East Germany. A Comparison with West Germany." in Economic Developments in Countries of Eastern Europe. Washington, D. C.: Subcommittee on Foreign Economic Policy-Joint Economic Committee, 1970. pp. 558-607.

3913. Sohmen, Egon. "Competition and Growth: the Lesson of West Germany." The American Economic Review 49 (1959), 986-1003.
3914. Sommer, Josef. "Die Entwicklung der landwirtschaftlichen Produktionsgenossenschaften von 1952 bis 1960." Wissenschaftliche Zeitschrift der Hochschule für Landwirtschaftliche Produktionsgenossenschaften. Meissen 5 (1962), 229-67.
3915. Spröte, Wolfgang. "15 Jahre DDR im Rat für Gegenseitige Wirtschaftshilfe." Deutsche Aussenpolitik 10 (1965), 1099-1107.
3916. Staatsmonopolistischer Kapitalismus der Bundesrepublik Deutschland in Daten und Fakten. Frankfurt a. M.: IMSF, 1981. 425 pp.
3917. Stent, Angela. From Embargo to Ostpolitik. The Political Economy of West German-Soviet Relations. 1955-1980. Cambridge: Cambridge University Press, 1981. 328 pp.
3918. Stiemerling, Karl-Heinz. "30 Jahre DDR. Steigende Leistungskraft, Grundlage des steigenden Lebensniveaus." Wirtschaftswissenschaft 27 (1979), 1025-41. (English summary)
3919. Störmer, Karl-Heinz. Öffentliche Investitionen in das Sozialkapital und Wirtschaftswachstum in der Bundesrepublik Deutschland von 1950-1964. Diss. Fribourg, 1967. 177 pp.
3920. Thomas, Rainer. Auswirkungen von Variationen der Körperschaftsteuerbelastung auf das wirtschaftliche Wachstum. dargestellt am Beispiel der Bundesrepublik Deutschland seit 1950. Diss. Hamburg. Hamburg: HWWA-Institut für Wirtschaftsforschung, 1970. 229 pp.
3921. Tipton, Frank B., Jr. "Government Policy and Economic Development in Germany and Japan. A Skeptical Reevaluation." The Journal of Economic History 41 (1981), 139-50.
3922. Tschapek, Walter. "Die Entwicklung des genossenschaftlichen Eigentums." Wissenschaftliche Zeitschrift der Martin-Luther-Universität Halle-Wittenberg 10 (1961), 359-67.
3923. Tscheprakow, W. Über die Verschärfung der allgemeinen Krise des Kapitalismus nach dem zweiten Weltkrieg. Berlin: Dietz, 1952. 167 pp.
3924. Vajna, Thomas G. "Der Konjunkturzyklus 1967/71 im Lichte der Prognosen und Zielprojektionen." Berichte des Deutschen Industrieinstituts zur Wirtschaftspolitik 6 (1972), 1-41.
3925. Vingt ans de réussite allemande. Une enquête du Monde. Paris: Economica, 1979. 127 pp.
3926. Vogt, Winfried. Die Wachstumszyklen der westdeutschen Wirtschaft von 1950 bis 1965 und ihre theoretische Erklärung. Tübingen: Mohr, 1968. 78 pp.
3927. Wagner, Adolf. Die Wachstumszyklen in der Bundesrepublik Deutschland. Eine komparativ-dynamische Komponentenanalyse für die Jahre 1951-1970. Tübingen: Mohr, 1972. 435 pp.
3928. Weathers, Milledge W. Die Entwicklung des deutschen Aussenhandels in bezug auf den Dollarraum mit besonderer Berücksichtigung der Terms of Trade nach der Währungsreform von 1948. Diss. Munich. Munich: UNI-Druck, 1961. 122 pp.
3929. Wegner, Klaus. Im Blickpunkt. Sachverständigenrat und Konjunktur- und Wachstumspolitik der Bundesregierung seit 1964. Frankfurt a. M.: R. G. Fischer, 1981. 350 pp.
3930. Willmann, Helga. Analyse der konjunkturellen Entwicklung in der Bundesrepublik Deutschland von 1950 bis 1974 unter besonderer Berücksichtigung des aus dem industriellen Produktionsprozess abgeleiteten endogen bedingten konjunkturellen Zyklenablaufs und seiner exogenen Beeinflussung durch Faktoren des gesamtwirtschaftlichen Systems. Diss. Bonn, 1976. 573 pp.
3931. Winkler, Heinrich A. Politische Weichenstellungen im Nachkriegsdeutschland. Göttingen: Vandenhoeck & Ruprecht, 1979. 297 pp.
3932. Zweig, Konrad. Germany Through Inflation and Recession. an Object Lesson in Economic Management. 1973-1976. London: Centre for Policy Studies, 1976. 52 pp.

SEE ALSO: 1061, 1064, 1787, 1795, 3206, 5106, 5129, 5135, 5143-44.

GERMAN REGIONS

Baden-Württemberg

3933. Beck, Joseph. Carl Friedrich Nebenius. Ein Lebensbild eines deutschen Staatsmannes und Gelehrten. Zugleich ein Beitrag zur Geschichte Badens und des deutschen Zollvereins. Mannheim: Schneider, 1866. 128 pp.
3934. Bergheimer, Siegfried. Die gewerbliche Entwicklung Breisachs. Diss. Freiburg i. B., 1924. 112 pp.

3935. Eberle, Rudolf. "Wirtschaftsförderung in Baden-Württemberg in Vergangenheit und Zukunft." Rationalisierung. Rationalisierungs-Kuratorium der Deutschen Wirtschaft 28 (1977), 175-77.
3936. Gessner, Dieter. "Grosshandel und Industrialisierung am Mittelrhein und Untermain (1780-1856)." Scripta Mercaturae 12 (1978), 21-48.
3937. Gothein, Eberhard. Pforzheims Vergangenheit. Ein Beitrag zur deutschen Städte- und Gewerbegeschichte. Leipzig: Duncker & Humblot, 1889. 85 pp.
3938. Hasselmann, Erwin. Und trug hundertfältige Frucht. Ein Jahrhundert konsumgenossenschaftlicher Selbsthilfe in Stuttgart. Stuttgart: Konsumgenossenschaft Stuttgart, 1964. 174 pp.
3939. Haverkamp, Frank. Staatliche Gewerbeförderung im Grossherzogtum Baden. Unter besonderer Berücksichtigung der Entwicklung des gewerblichen Bildungswesens im 19. Jahrhundert. Diss. Freiburg i. B., 1978. Freiburg i. B.: Alber, 1979. 496 pp.
3940. Heyd, Wilhelm. Beiträge zur Geschichte des deutschen Handels. Die grosse Ravensburger Gesellschaft. Stuttgart: Cotta Nachf., 1890. 86 pp.
3941. Huss, Hans-Peter. Gründung und Entwicklung der Württembergischen Konsumvereine bis zum Jahre 1871. Eine Untersuchung unter besonderer Berücksichtigung des Einflusses der Arbeiterbewegung. Diss. Tübingen, 1977. 418 pp.
3942. Kellenbenz, Hermann. "Unternehmertum in Südwestdeutschland." Tradition 10 (1965), 163-88.
3943. Köhler, Ludwig. Das württembergische Gewerbe-Recht von 1805 bis 1870. Tübingen: Laupp, 1891. 292 pp.
3944. Körting, Johannes. Geschichte der Gewerbeförderung in Baden. Karlsruhe: C.F. Müller, 1965. 207 pp.
3945. Körting, Johannes. Geschichte der Gewerbeförderung in Baden bis 1933. Karlsruhe: Berenz, 1965. 344 pp.
3946. Loreth, Hans. Das Wachstum der württembergischen Wirtschaft von 1818 bis 1918. Stuttgart: s.n., 1974.
3947. Merker, Otto. Handel und Verkehr in Ravensburg vom Übergang der Stadt an die Krone Württembergs bis zur Gründung des Deutschen Reiches 1810-1871. Diss. Tübingen, 1959. 313 pp.
3948. Meuth, H. 90 Jahre staatliche Gewerbeförderung in Württemberg. Stuttgart: Württembergisches Landesgewerbeamt, 1938. 7 pp.
3949. Müller, Hans P. Das Grossherzogtum Baden und die Deutsche Zolleinigung. 1819-1835/36. Diss. Frankfurt. Frankfurt a. M.: Lang, 1984. 363 pp.
3950. Önsoy, Rifat. Die Handelsbeziehungen zwischen den süddeutschen Staaten und dem Osmanischen Reich von 1815-1871. Diss. Würzburg, 1972. 214 pp.
3951. Osswald, Joseph. Mannheims Umschlagsverkehr von 1879 bis 1908. Diss. Heidelberg, 1908. Heidelberg: Zöller, 1910. 131 pp.
3952. Schäfer, Hermann. "Konjunkturdifferenzierung mit Hilfe quantitativer und qualitativer Indikatoren. Das Beispiel Baden 1900-1914/18." in Industrialisierung und Raum. Studien zur regionalen Differenzierung in Deutschland des 19. Jahrhunderts. Stuttgart: Klett-Cotta, 1979. pp. 132-64. (English Summary.)
3953. Schübelin, Walter. Das Zollparlament und die Politik von Baden, Bayern und Württemberg 1866-1870. Berlin: Ebering, 1935. 142 pp.
3954. Schumacher, Carl. 100 Jahre Stuttgart. Zur Frühgeschichte der Konsumgenossenschaften. Hamburg: Verlagsgesellschaft Deutscher Konsumgenossenschaften, 1965. 20 pp.
3955. Stockmann, Günther. "Das Werden der Verbindung von Landwirtschaft und Gewerbe in Württemberg (verglichen mit Niedersachsen und anderen Teilen des Reichs)." Schmoller 58 (1934), 551-68, 675-708.
3956. Uhland, Robert. "Gewerbeförderung in Baden und Württemberg im 19. Jahrhundert und die Entstehung staatlicher Zentralstellen." in Bausteine zur geschichtlichen Landeskunde von Baden-Württemberg. Stuttgart: Kohlhammer, 1979. pp. 435-67.

SEE ALSO: 841, 1802, 2470, 2478, 2480, 5194.

Bavaria

Bibliographic Reference

3957. Hilsenbeck, Adolf. Bayerns Handel, Gewerbe und Industrie. Verzeichnis der wichtigsten Bücher und Zeitschriftenaufsätze. Seit 1870. Munich: Staatsbibliothek, 1922. 300 pp.

Bavaria

3958. Anegg, Ernst. Zur Gewerbestruktur und Gewerbepolitik Bayerns während der Regierung Montgelas. Diss. Munich, 1965. 227 pp.
3959. Bergschmidt, Hans H. Das Wachstum der bayrischen Wirtschaft seit 1950 im Vergleich zum Wirtschaftswachstum in der Bundesrepublik Deutschland. Diss. Munich, 1964. 168 pp.
3960. Brandl, August. Geschichte der Konsumgenossenschaften in Bayern. Diss. Erlangen. Kallmünz: Lassleben, 1930. 134 pp.
3961. Dirr, Pius. Der Handelsvorstand Nürnberg. 1560-1910. Nuremberg: Fehrle & Sippel, 1910. 116 pp.
3962. Eibert, Georg. Unternehmenspolitik Nürnberger Maschinenbauer (1835-1914). Stuttgart: Klett-Cotta, 1979. 421 pp.
3963. "Einzelhandelspreise wichtiger Waren in 9 bayerischen Gemeinden 1937 bis 1941." Zeitschrift des Bayerischen Statistischen Landesamts 75 (1943), 52-54.
3964. Gömmel, Rainer. "Die Bedeutung des Unternehmers in Franken während der Industrialiserung und Ursachen seines Auftretens." Wirtschaftskräfte und Wirtschaftswege. Festschrift für Hermann Kellenbenz. Stuttgart: Klett-Cotta, 1978. III, 341-85.
3965. Gömmel, Rainer. Wachstum und Konjunktur der Nürnberger Wirtschaft. 1815-1914. Diss. Erlangen-Nuremberg, 1977. Stuttgart: Klett-Cotta, 1978. 242 pp.
3966. "Grosshandelspreise wichtiger Waren in Bayern 1937 bis 1941." Zeitschrift des Bayerischen Statistischen Landesamts 75 (1943), 42-45.
3967. Haushalter, -- . "Die Anfänge der modernen Zollverwaltung Bayerns." Forschungen zur Geschichte Bayerns 16 (1908), 177-205.
3968. Held, Max. Das Arbeitsverhältnis im Nürnberger Handwerk von der Einverleibung der Stadt in Bayern bis zur Einführung der Gewerbefreiheit. Stuttgart: Cotta, 1909. 100 pp.
3969. Herwig, Christoph J. Beiträge zur Geschichte des bayerischen Zollwesens. Bamberg: s.n., 1861.
3970. Höfle, Anton. Die Gewerbeordnung der Pfalz seit der französischen Revolution bis 1868. Diss. Erlangen, 1907. Munich: Schweitzer, 1908. 43 pp.
3971. Hohenegg, Ernst. Raiffeisen in Bayern 1893-1968. 75 Jahre Bayerischer Raiffeisenverband. Bayerische Raiffeisen-Zentralkasse. Munich: Bayerischer Raiffeisenverband, 1968. 326 pp.
3972. Kaizl, Josepf. Der Kampf um Gewerbereform und Gewerbefreiheit in Bayern von 1799-1868. Nebst einem einleitenden Überblick über die Entwicklung des Zunftwesens und der Gewerbefreiheit in Deutschland. Leipzig: Duncker & Humblot, 1879. 174 pp.
3973. Klaus, Karl. Die Entwicklung des mittelfränkischen Handwerks von 1945-1960 unter besonderer Berücksichtigung der Gewerbefreiheit. Diss. Erlangen, 1963. 172 pp.
3974. Mauerer, Roman. Entwicklung und Funktionswandel der Märkte in Altbayern seit 1800. Munich: Wölfle, 1971. 177 pp.
3975. Mayer, Manfred. Bayerns Handel im Mittelalter und in der Neuzeit. Munich: Pohl, 1892. 100 pp.
3976. Paulus, Robert H. Strukturwandlungen der gewerblichen Wirtschaft Erlangens vom Spätmittelalter bis zum Ende des 19. Jahrhunderts. Diss. Erlangen, 1963. 350 pp.
3977. Pfeiffer, Gerhard. "400 Jahre Handelsvorstand Nürnberg, 1560-1960." Mitteilungsblatt der Industrie- und Handelskammer Nürnberg. Special issue (1960).
3978. Popp, August. Die Entstehung der Gewerbefreiheit in Bayern. Leipzig: Noske, 1928. 185 pp.
3979. Rohmeder, A. F. München als Handelsstadt in Vergangenheit, Neuzeit und Gegenwart. 2nd ed. Munich: Kellerer, 1905. 220 pp.
3980. Sackmann, Franz. "Entwicklung der wirtschaftlichen Beziehungen zwischen Bayern und den Donaustaaten." Donauraum 17 (1972), 129-42.

3981. Schertel, L. W. Über den Zustand der Bayerischen Gewerbeindustrie insbesondere seit dem segensreichen Regierungs-Antritte Sr. Majest. Ludwig I. Munich: Franz, 1836. 15 pp.

3982. Schmidt, Jochen. Bayern und das Zollparlament. Politik und Wirtschaft in den letzten Jahren vor der Reichsgründung (1866/67-1870). Munich: Wölfle, 1973. 442 pp.

3983. Schröder, Peter. Die Entwicklung des Nürnberger Grossgewerbes 1806-1970. Nuremberg: Stadtarchiv Nürnberg, 1971. 262 pp.

3984. Schwarzwälder, Wilhelm. Die Entwicklung des Nürnberg-Fürther Exportes nach den Vereinigten Staaten von Nordamerika von seinen Anfängen an bis zur Gegenwart. Nuremberg: Hilz, 1912. 143 pp.

3985. Seiffert, Karl. "Beitrag zur Geschichte der Zölle und indirekten Steuern in Bayern." Jahrbücher für Nationalökonomie und Statistik 2 (1891), 426-35.

3986. Sprekelsen, Wolfgang. Die Bedeutung des Handels und der Industrie im Verfassungsleben Bayerns im Zeitraum von 1808-1951. Diss. Munich, 1951. 249 pp.

3987. Strieder, Jakob. Zur Genesis des modernen Kapitalismus. Forschungen zur Entstehung der grossen bürgerlichen Kapitalvermögen am Ausgange des Mittelalters und zu Beginn der Neuzeit, zunächst in Augsburg. Munich: Duncker & Humblot, 1935. 232 pp.

3988. Veit, Ludwig. Handel und Wandel mit aller Welt. Aus Nürnbergs grosser Zeit. Aus Anlass des 400jährigen Bestehens des Handelsvorstandes Nürnberg. Munich: Prestel, 1960. 51 pp.

3989. Wenz, Edgar M. Die Entwicklung der Gewerbefreiheit in Bayern. Diss. Erlangen, 1951. 237 pp.

3990. Wiest, Helga. Die Entwicklung des Gewerbes des rechtsrheinischen Bayern in der Frühzeit der deutschen Zolleinigung. Diss. Munich, 1970. 409 pp.

3991. Zorn, Wolfgang. Handels- und Industriegeschichte Bayerisch-Schwabens 1648-1870. Wirtschafts-, Sozial- und Kulturgeschichte des schwäbischen Unternehmertums. Augsburg: Verlag der Schwäbischen Forschungsgemeinschaft, 1961. 375 pp.

3992. Zorn, Wolfgang. "Unternehmer und Unternehmensverflechtung in Bayern im 20. Jahrhundert." Zeitschrift für Unternehmensgeschichte 24 (1979), III, 180-88.

3993. Zorn, Wolfgang. "Zur Nürnberger Handels- und Unternehmergeschichte des 19. Jahrhunderts." in Beiträge zur Wirtschaftsgeschichte Nürnbergs. Nuremberg: Stadtrat, 1968. pp. 851-64.

SEE ALSO: 1137, 1144, 1152, 1158, 2492, 3953.

Berlin

3994. Beiträge zur Geschichte des Berliner Handels und Gewerbefleisses aus der ältesten Zeit bis auf unsere Tage. Festschrift zur Feier des 50jährigen Bestehens der Korporation der Berliner Kaufmannschaft am 2. 3. 1870. Berlin: Unger, 1870. 116 pp.

3995. Kaelble, Hartmut. Berliner Unternehmer während der frühen Industrialisierung. Herkunft, sozialer Status und politischer Einfluss. Berlin: de Gruyter, 1972. 302 pp.

3996. Die Korporation der Kaufmannschaft von Berlin. Festschrift zum hundertjährigen Jubiläum am 2. März 1920. Berlin: Mittler, 1920. 690 pp.

3997. Lüke, Rolf E. Die Berliner Handels-Gesellschaft in einem Jahrhundert deutscher Wirtschaft 1856-1956. Berlin: Hartmann, 1956. 275 pp.

3998. Rachel, Hugo et al. Berliner Grosskaufleute und Kapitalisten. 3 vols. Berlin: Gsellius, 1934-39.

3999. Schmieder, Eberhard. "Die wirtschaftliche Führungsschicht in Berlin 1790-1850." in Führungskräfte der Wirtschaft im neunzehnten Jahrhundert 1790-1914. Limburg: C. A. Starke, 1977. II, 1-58.

SEE ALSO: 2505.

Brandenburg: SEE 2515.

Danzig

4000. Becker, Hans et al. Danzigs Handel in Vergangenheit und Gegenwart. Danzig: Käfemann, 1925. 185 pp.
4001. Funk, Jakob. Die Danzig-polnische Zollunion. Der bisherige und der künftige Zollverteilungsschlüssel. Jena: Fischer, 1926. 189 pp.

East Prussia

4002. Denkschrift über Memels Seehandel, den Minge-Schmeltelle-Canal und die Zweigbahn Insterburg-Tilsit-Memel. Memel: Mangelsdorf, 1862. 124 pp.
4003. Mischke, Alfred. Die Entwicklung des modernen Genossenschaftswesens in Ostpreussen von seinen ersten Anfängen bis zur Gegenwart. Königsberg: Gräfe und Unzer, 1933. 142 pp.
4004. Sembritzki, Johannes. Geschichte der königlich Preussischen See- und Handelsstadt Memel. Memel: Siebert, 1900. 334 pp.
4005. Zum fünfzigjährigen Jubiläum der Korporation der Kaufmannschaft von Königsberg. Königsberg: Hartung, 1873. 103 pp.

Eastern Germany

4006. Aubin, Hermann. Die volkspolitische Bedeutung von Gewerbe und Industrie in Ostdeutschland. Breslau: Schlesien-Verlag, 1941. 45 pp.
4007. Böhm, Bruno, ed. Industrie und Gewerbe in Bromberg. Eine Darstellung der industriellen Entwickelung Brombergs vom technisch-wirtschaftlichen Standpunkte unter besonderer Berücksichtigung der letzten 50 Jahre. Bromberg: Dittmann, 1907. 378 pp.
4008. Crüger, Hans. Die Schulze-Delitzschen Genossenschaften in Posen als ein Bollwerk des Deutschtums." Schmoller 37 (1913), 813-24.
4009. Laubert, Manfred. Die Befreiung von Handel und Gewerbe in der Provinz Posen durch die 3 Maigesetze von 1833. Leipzig: Hirzel, 1941. 192 pp.
4010. Messerschmidt, F. Die landwirtschaftlichen Genossenschaften in der Provinz Grenzmark Posen-Westpreussen. Entwicklungsgeschichte des Verbandes der vereinigten landwirtschaftlichen und Raiffeisen-Genossenschaften der Grenzmark Posen-Westpreussen. Schneidemühl: Verband der vereinigten landwirtschaftlichen und Raiffeisen-Genossenschaften der Grenzmark Posen-Westpreussen, 1936. 112 pp.
4011. Ein Rückblick auf Thorn als Handelsplatz. Festschrift zur Feier des 25jährigen Bestehens der Handelskammer. Thorn: Rathsbuchdruckerei, 1877. 64 pp.
4012. Die Wandlungen des Thorner Handels. Festschrift der Handelskammer zu Thorn aus Anlass ihres 50jährigen Bestehens. Thorn: Thorner Ostdeutsche Zeitung, 1902. 63 pp.

Hansa Cities

4013. Ahrens, Gerhard. "'Es sind wahrhaft amerikanische Zustände!' Aus dem Briefwechsel der Juristenfamilie Voigt über die hamburgische Wirtschaftskrise von 1857." Scripta Mercaturae 13 (1979), 97-132. (English and French summaries.)
4014. Baasch, Ernst. "Die Anfänge des modernen Verkehrs Hamburgs mit Vorderindien und Ostasien." Mitteilungen der Geographischen Gesellschaft in Hamburg 13 (1897), 92-130.
4015. Baasch, Ernst. "Beiträge zur Geschichte der Handelsbeziehungen zwischen Hamburg und Amerika." in Hamburgerische Festschrift zur Erinnerung an die Entdeckung Amerika's. Hamburg: Wissenschaftlicher Ausschuss des Komités für die Amerika-Feier, 1892. I, 256.
4016. Baasch, Ernst. Forschungen zur Hamburgischen Handelsgeschichte. 3 vols. Hamburg: Herold'sche Buchhandlung, 1889-1902.
4017. Beutin, Ludwig. Bremen und Amerika. Zur Geschichte der Weltwirtschaft und der Beziehungen Deutschlands zu den Vereinigten Staaten. Bremen: Schünemann, 1953. 356 pp.

4018. Böhme, Helmut. "Wirtschaftskrise, Merchant Bankers und Verfassungsreform. Zur Bedeutung der Weltwirtschaftskrise von 1857 in Hamburg." Zeitschrift des Vereins fur hamburgische Geschichte 54 (1968), 77-127.

4019. Brandt, Ahasver von. Das alte Lübecker Kaufmannshaus in Wirtschaft und Gesellschaft. Skizzen aus der Vergangenheit von Schabbelhaus und Kaufmannschaft zu Lübeck. 2nd ed. Lübeck: Matthiesen, 1964. 32 pp.

4020. Büttner, Ursula. Hamburg in der Staats- und Wirtschaftskrise 1928-1931. Hamburg: Christians, 1982. 748 pp.

4021. Engelsing, Rolf. "Bremisches Unternehmertum. Sozialgeschichte 1780-1870." Jahrbuch der Wittheit zu Bremen 2 (1958), 7-112.

4022. Entholt, Hermann and Ludwig Beutin. Bremen und Nordeuropa. Weimar: Böhlau, 1937. 113 pp.

4023. Entholt, Hermann and Ludwig Beutin. Quellen und Forschungen zur bremischen Handels-geschichte. 2 vols. Weimar: Böhlau, 1937.

4024. Fischer, Wilhelm. Sechzig Jahre GEG, 1894-1954. 60 Jahre Dienst am Verbraucher. Gross-einkaufs-Gesellschaft Deutscher Konsumgenossenschaften mit beschränkter Haftung. Hamburg: GEG, 1954. 242 pp.

4025. "Hamburg und die Handelskrisis." Preussische Jahrbücher 1 (1858), 275-92.

4026. Hansen, Johannes. Beiträge zur Geschichte des Getreidehandels und der Getreidepolitik Lübecks. Lübeck: Schmidt, 1912. 39 pp.

4027. Jochmann, Werner. "Hamburgisch-schlesische Handelsbeziehungen. Ein Beitrag zur abendländischen Wirtschaftsgeschichte." in Geschichtliche Landeskunde und Universalgeschichte. Festgabe für Hermann Aubin zum 23. Dezember 1950. Hamburg: "Wihag", 1950. pp. 217-28.

4028. Kellenbenz, Hermann. "Der Bremer Kaufmann. Versuch einer sozialgeschichtlichen Deutung." Bremisches Jahrbuch 51 (1969), 19-49.

4029. Kerst, Georg. "Die Bedeutung Bremens für die frühen deutsch-japanischen Beziehungen." Bremisches Jahrbuch 50 (1965), 303-23.

4030. Krawehl, Otto-Ernst. Hamburgs Schiffs- und Warenverkehr mit England und den englischen Kolonien 1814-1860. Diss. Cologne, 1975. Cologne: Böhlau, 1977. 536 pp.

4031. Laspeyres, E. "Hamburger Waarenpreise 1851-1863 und die californisch-australischen Gold-entdeckungen seit 1848." Jahrbücher für Nationalökonomie und Statistik 3 (1864), 81-118, 209-36.

4032. Lehe, Erich von. Die Märkte Hamburgs von den Anfängen bis in die Neuzeit. Wiesbaden: Steiner, 1966. 97 pp.

4033. Lührs, Wilhelm. Die Freie Hansestadt Bremen und England in der Zeit des Deutschen Bundes (1815-1867). Bremen: W. Dorn, 1958. 178 pp.

4034. Oppel, A. "Hamburgs und Bremens Stellung im internationalen Warenhandel." Weltwirtschaft-liches Archiv 1 (1913), 361-76.

4035. Peters, Fritz. "Über bremische Firmengründungen in der ersten Hälfte des 19. Jahrhunderts (1814-1847). Bremisches Jahrbuch 36 (1936), 306-61.

4036. Prüser, Friedrich. "Bremer Kaufleute als Wegbereiter Deutschlands in Übersee." Koloniale Rundschau 33 (1942-43), 71-91.

4037. Prüser, Friedrich. "Bremische Firmengeschichte." Bremisches Jahrbuch 46 (1959), 319-35.

4038. Prüser, Jürgen. Die Handelsverträge der Hansestädte Lübeck, Bremen und Hamburg mit über-seeischen Staaten im 19. Jahrhundert. Bremen: Schünemann, 1962. 159 pp.

4039. Rassmussen, Nora. Handel und Handelspolitik Lübecks vom Ende der Franzosenherrschaft (1813) bis zum Anschluss an den Zollverein (1868). Diss. Kiel, 1924. 134 pp.

4040. Rauers, Friedrich. Bremer Handelsgeschichte im 19. Jahrhundert. Bremer Handelsstatistik vor dem Beginn der öffentlichen administrativen Statistik. Bremen: Leuwer, 1913. 126 pp.

4041. Rauers, Friedrich. Geschichte des Bremer Binnenhandels im 19. Jahrhundert namentlich unter den alten Verkehrsformen und im Übergang. Bremen: Leuwer, 1913. 282 pp.

4042. Reincke, Heinrich. Hamburgs Weg zum Reich und in die Welt. Urkunden zur 750-Jahr-Feier des Hamburger Hafens. Hamburg: Petermann, 1939. 321 pp.

4043. Schäffle, Albert E. F. "Die Handelskrisis von 1857 in Hamburg, mit besonderer Berücksichti-gung auf das Bankwesen." in A. E. F. Schäffle. Gesammelte Aufsätze. Tübingen: Laupp, 1886. pp. 32-66.

4044. Schramm, Percy E. "Die deutschen Überseekaufleute im Rahmen der Sozialgeschichte." Bremisches Jahrbuch 49 (1964), 31-54.

4045. Schramm, Percy E. "Kaufleute während Besatzung, Krieg und Belagerung (1817-1915). Der Hamburger Handel in der Franzosenzeit." Tradition 4 (1959), 88-114.
4046. Schramm, Percy E. Kaufleute zu Haus und über See. Hamburgische Zeugnisse des 17., 18. und 19. Jahrhunderts. Hamburg: Hoffmann & Campe, 1949. 596 pp.
4047. Schweer, Walther. "Hamburg-New York. Handels- und Schiffahrtsbeziehungen einst und jetzt." Hamburg. Übersee-Jahrbuch (1928), 17-40.
4048. Vieth, Ferdinand. Die Entwicklung der Konsumvereinsbewegung in Hamburg (1852 bis 1930). Hamburg: Verlag Gesellschaft Deutscher Konsumvereine, 1931. 54 pp.
4049. Wätjen, Hermann. "Die Hansestädte und Brasilien 1820 bis 1870." Weltwirtschaftliches Archiv 22 (1925), 33-56, 221-50.
4050. Wiskemann, Erwin. Hamburg und die Welthandelspolitik von den Anfängen bis zur Gegenwart. Hamburg: Friederichsen & de Gruyter, 1929. 373 pp.

Hesse

4051. "Beiträge zur Geschichte der Preise und des Tagelohns in Hessen." Jahrbücher für Nationalökonomie und Statistik 19 (1872), 145-67.
4052. Böhme, Helmut. "Stadtregiment, Repräsentativverfassung und Wirtschaftskonjunktur in Frankfurt am Main und Hamburg im 19. Jahrhundert." Esslinger Studien 15 (1969).
4053. Cordes, Hans. Gründung und Entwicklung der Raiffeisengenossenschaften und des Kurhessischen Landesbundes im Regierungsbezirk Kassel, der beiden grössten freien landwirtschaftlichen Berufsorganisationen Kurhessens. Diss. Göttingen, 1928. Göttingen: Kurhessischer Landbund, 1929. 124 pp.
4054. Dietz, Alexander. Frankfurter Handelsgeschichte. 4 vols. Frankfurt a. M.: Minjon, 1910-25.
4055. Entwicklung der Verbraucherpreise in Hessen 1970 bis 1980. Wiesbaden: Hessisches Statistisches Landesamt, 1981. 25 pp.
4056. Frank, Walter. "Volumens- und Preisentwicklung in der hessischen Wirtschaft." Staat und Wirtschaft in Hessen. Hessisches Statistisches Landesamt 20 (1965), 113-17.
4057. Franz, H. J. "Wirtschaftsleistung und Produktivität in Hessen 1961 bis 1968." Staat und Wirtschaft in Hessen 25 (1970), 229-31.
4058. Fuchs, Konrad. Siegerländer Unternehmer des 19. Jahrhunderts und ihr Werk. Wiesbaden: Steiner, 1979. 235 pp.
4059. Geisthardt, Fritz. Wiesbaden und seine Kaufleute. Wiesbaden: Wirtschaftsverlag, 1980. 298 pp.
4060. Haver, Ursula. Am Strassenkreuz Europas. Frankfurter Messen und Ausstellungen in Vergangenheit und Gegenwart. Festschrift zum 50-jährigen Bestehen der Messe- und Ausstellungs-Gesellschaft. Frankfurt a. M.: Messe- und Ausstellungs-Gesellschaft, 1957. 163 pp.
4061. Kanter, Hugo. Die Entwicklung des Handels mit gebrauchsfertigen Waren von der Mitte des 18. Jahrhunderts bis 1866 zu Frankfurt a. M. Tübingen: Mohr, 1902. 143 pp.
4062. Köhler, Walter. Der landwirtschaftliche Genossenschaftskredit und das ländliche Kreditgenossenschaftswesen in Hessen seit der Währungsstabilisierung. Diss. Giessen. Giessen: Schneider, 1932. 96 pp.
4063. Maxeiner, Rudolf. Über Zeit und Raum. Die Geschichte des Raiffeisenverbandes Rhein-Main, 1873-1973. Frankfurt a. M.: Raiffeisenverband Rhein-Main, 1973. 207 pp.
4064. Modlinger, J. Neue Mustermessen. Aus der Geschichte der ersten Jahre der wiedererstandenen Frankfurter Messen. Frankfurt a. M.: Messamt für die Frankfurter Internationalen-Messen, 1924. 24 pp.
4065. Pudill, -- . "Der Export der hessichen Industrie 1950 bis 1960." Staat und Wirtschaft in Hessen. Statistische Mitteilungen 16 (1961), 145-50.
4066. Rohde, Karl H. Die deutsche Gewerbereform im 19. Jahrhundert unter besonderer Berücksichtigung des Grossherzogtums Hessen bis zum Erlass der Gewerbeordnung von 21. Juni 1869. Diss. Giessen. Giessen: Uhde, 1930. 78 pp.
4067. Ullmann, Wilhelm. Die hessische Gewerbepolitik von der Zeit des Rheinbundes bis zur Einführung der Gewerbefreiheit im Jahre 1866, insbesondere das Handwerk und das Hausiergewerbe. Diss. Heidelberg. Darmstadt: Herbert, 1903. 96 pp.
4068. Die Verbraucherpreise 1960 bis 1965. Wiesbaden: Hessisches Statistisches Landesamt, 1967. 303 pp.

4069. Von der alten Reichs- und Messestadt Frankfurt am Main. Eine Sammlung von Aufsätzen. Frankfurt a. M.: Messamt für die Frankfurter Internationalen-Messen, 1922. 77 pp.

Lower Saxony

4070. Beukweing, Cornelius H. J. van. Der deutsch-niederländische Handel und die deutsche Agrareinfuhr in den Jahren 1920-1940. Diss. Mainz, 1953. 214 pp.

4071. Bläsing, Joachim F. E. Das goldene Delta und sein eisernes Hinterland. 1815-1851. Von niederländisch-preussischen zu deutsch-niederländischen Wirtschaftsbeziehungen. Leiden: Kroese, 1973. 276 pp.

4072. "Durchschnittspreise verschiedener Produkte und Nährungsmittel in den Jahren 1859 bis 1870." Statistische Nachrichten über das Grossherzogthum Oldenburg 13 (1872), 129-68.

4073. Franz, Eugen. "Preussens Kampf mit Hannover um die Anerkennung des preussisch-französischen Handelsvertrags von 1862." Historische Vierteljahrschrift 26 (1931), 787-839.

4074. Gebauer, Johannes H. Geschichte des Handels und des Kaufmannstandes in der Stadt Hildesheim. Bremen-Horn: Dorn, 1950. 142 pp.

4075. Hering, Gerhard. Die Entwicklung des landwirtschaftlichen Genossenschaftswesens in Ostfriesland von seinen Anfängen bis zur Gegenwart. Diss. Frankfurt a. M. Grimmen i. P.: Grimmer Kreis-Zeitung, 1930. 136 pp.

4076. Jeschke, Jörg. Gewerberecht und Handwerkswirtschaft des Königreichs Hannover im Übergang 1815-1866. Eine Quellenstudie. Göttingen: Schwartz, 1977. 530 pp.

4077. Lemelsen, Joachim. "Das Bruttoinlandsprodukt ausgewählter Förderungsgebiete Niedersachsens. (1957 bis 1966)." Neues Archiv für Niedersachsen 18 (1969), 135-138.

4078. Luntowski, Gustav. "Lüneburgs Unternehmer im 19. Jahrhundert. Zur neueren Wirtschafts- und Sozialgeschichte einer Mittelstadt." Tradition 11 (1966), 201-17.

4079. Meyerholz, Robert. 65 Jahre ländliche Genossenschaftsarbeit in Hannover-Braunschweig. Erinnerungsschrift zum 65jährigen Bestehen des Verbandes Ländlicher Genossenschaften Hannover-Braunschweig. Hannover: Verband Ländlicher Genossenschaften, 1954. 236 pp.

4080. Schmidt, Karl-Heinz. "Das Wachstum des Bruttoinlandsprodukts im niedersächsischen Zonengrenzgebiet von 1957 bis 1966." Neues Archiv für Niedersachsen 18 (1969), 128-34.

4081. Struve, Walter. Die Republik Texas. Bremen und das Hildesheimische. Hildesheim: Lax, 1983. 195 pp.

Mecklenburg

4082. Luck, Herbert. Zur Entstehung der kapitalistischen Junkerwirtschaft in Mecklenburg. Berlin: "Die Wirtschaft", 1956. 184 pp .

SEE ALSO: 1897.

North Rhine-Westphalia

Reference

4083. Die Wirtschaft Westfalens und des Ruhrgebiets in Firmen-Festschriften. Dortmund: Westfälisches Wirtschaftsarchiv, 1952. 79 pp.

North Rhine-Westphalia

4084. Adelmann, Gerhard. "Führende Unternehmer im Rheinland und in Westfalen 1850-1914." Rheinische Vierteljahrsblätter 35 (1971), 335-52.

4085. Beau, Horst. Das Leistungswissen des frühindustriellen Unternehmertums in Rheinland und Westfalen. Diss. Cologne. Cologne: Rheinisch-Westfälisches Wirtschaftsarchiv, 1959. 79 pp.

4086. Croon, Helmuth. "Die wirtschaftliche Führungsschicht des Ruhrgebietes 1850-1914." in Führungskräfte der Wirtschaft im neunzehnten Jahrhundert 1790-1914. Limburg: C. A. Starke, 1977. II, 201-344.

4087. Diefendorf, Jeffery M. Businessmen and Politics in the Rhineland, 1789-1834. Princeton, NJ: Princeton University Press, 1980. 401 pp.

4088. Einkommen, Preise und Konsumverhalten 1960-1966. Düsseldorf: Statistisches Landesamt Nordrhein-Westfalen, 1967. 119 pp.

4089. Fischer, Wolfram. "Konjunkturen und Krisen im Ruhrgebiet seit 1840 und die wirtschafts-politische Willensbildung der Unternehmer." Westfälische Forschungen 21 (1968), 42-53.

4090. Frommhold, Gerhard, ed. Die gesamtwirtschaftliche und industriestrukturelle Entwicklung Wittens von 1957 bis 1964 im Vergleich zu den übrigen kreisfreien Städten des Ruhrgebietes, dem Ballungszentrum des Ruhrgebietes, dem Land Nordrhein-Westfalen und der Bundesrepublik Deutschland. Witten: Hauptamt, 1967. 11 pp.

4091. Hartsough, Mildred L. "Business Leaders in Cologne in the Nineteenth Century." Journal of Economics and Business History 2 (1930), 332-52.

4092. Helmrich, Wilhelm. "Beziehungen zwischen Wirtschaftsstruktur und Krisenfestigkeit. Darge-legt am Beispiel rheinisch-westfälischer Städte." Deutsche Zeitschrift für Wirtschaftskunde 5 (1940/41), 189-99.

4093. Henning, Hansjoachim. "Soziale Verflechtungen der Unternehmer in Westfalen 1860-1914. Ein Beitrag zur Diskussion um die Stellung der Unternehmer in der Gesellschaft des deutschen Kaiserreiches." Zeitschrift für Unternehmensgeschichte 23 (1978), 1-30.

4094. Hentschel, Volker. Die deutschen Freihändler und der volkswirtschaftliche Kongress 1858 bis 1885. Stuttgart: Klett, 1975. 308 pp.

4095. Hilse, Gotthard. Geschäfts- und Investitionsentwicklung bei der rheinischen Warenzentrale, Hauptgenossenschaft Landwirtschaflicher Genossenschaften eGmbH. Köln von 1953 bis 1963. Diss. Bonn, 1966. 113 pp.

4096. Hogaust, Walter. Die Konjunkturentwicklung im rheinisch-westfälischen Industriebezirk seit der Währungsstabilisierung. Diss. Cologne, 1942. 351 pp.

4097. Huck, Gerhard. "Arbeiterkonsumverein und Verbraucherorganisation. Die Entwicklung der Konsumgenossenschaften im Ruhrgebiet 1860-1914." in Fabrik, Familie, Feierabend. Beiträge zur Sozialgeschichte des Alltags im Industriezeitalter. Wuppertal: Hammer, 1978. pp. 215-45.

4098. Jarecki, Christel. Die neuzeitliche Strukturwandel an der Ruhr. Marburg: Geographisches Institut der Universität, 1967. 247 pp.

4099. Kellenbenz, Hermann and Klara van Eyll. Die Geschichte der unternehmerischen Selbstver-waltung in Köln 1797-1914. Cologne: Rheinisch-Westfälisches Wirtschaftsarchiv, 1972. 34 pp.

4100. Kocks, Werner. Verhaltensweise und geistige Einstellung niederbergischer Unternehmer der frühindustriellen Zeit. Diss. Cologne, 1956. 97 pp.

4101. Köllmann, Wolfgang. "Frühe Unternehmer." in Ruhrgebiet und neues Land. Cologne: Grote, 1968. pp. 9-46.

4102. Köllmann, Wolfgang. Struktur und Wachstum der Wirtschaft des bergisch-märkischen Raumes. Bochum: Berg-Verlag, 1971. 94 pp.

4103. Lange, Gisela. Das ländliche Gewerbe in der Grafschaft Hark am Vorabend der Industrialisie-rung. Cologne: Rheinisch-Westfälisches Wirtschaftsarchiv, 1976. 255 pp.

4104. Laumanns, Carl. Handel und Wandel in Alt-Lippstadt. Ein Beitrag zur Wirtschaftsgeschichte Westfalens. Lippstadt: C. Laumanns, 1944. 72 pp.

4105. Lehmann, Herbert. Duisburgs Grosshandel und Spedition vom Ende des 18. Jahrhunderts bis 1905. Duisburg: Renckhoff, 1958. 294 pp.

4106. Linder, Wilhelm E. Das Zollgesetz von 1818 und Handel und Industrie am Niederrhein. Diss. Bonn. Trier: Lintz, 1911. 112 pp.

4107. Löhne, Preise und Verbrauch, 1971-1976. Düsseldorf: Landesamt für Datenverarbeitung und Statistik, Nordrhein-Westfalen, 1977. 151 pp.

4108. Milz, Herbert. Das Kölner Grossgewerbe von 1750 bis 1835. Cologne: Rheinland-westfäli-sches Wirtschaftsarchiv, 1962. 144 pp.

4109. Novy, Klaus, ed. Anders leben: Geschichte und Zukunft der Genossenschaftskultur. Beispiele aus Nordrhein-Westfalen. Berlin: Dietz, 1985. 231 pp.

4110. Das östliche Ruhrgebiet 1960 bis 1970. Ein Vergleich der wirtschaftlichen Entwicklung mit der im Gebiet der "Rheinschiene", im mittleren Ruhrgebiet und in den übrigen Gebieten des Landes Nordrhein-Westfalen. Dortmund: Industrie- und Handelskammer, 1971. 51 pp.

4111. Philipps, Wilhelm. Der Unternehmer in der Solinger Stahlwarenindustrie im 19. Jahrhundert. Ein Beitrag zur Geschichte der sozialen Verhältnisse der Unternehmer im 19. Jahrhundert. Diss. Cologne. Braunschweig: Dissertationsverlag Pöhling, 1956. 108 pp.

4112. Potthoff, Heinz. "Geschichte von Gewerbe und Handel (von Minden-Ravensberg)." in Minden-Ravensberg unter die Herrschaft der Hohenzollern. Bielefeld: Belhagen & Klasing, 1909.

4113. Reitz, Fritz J. Entwicklung und Wesen der Konsumgenossenschaften des Siegerlandes. Diss. Giessen, 1928. 51 pp.

4114. Renard, Georg. Struktur- und Konjunkturtendenzen im Düsseldorfer Wirtschaftsraum. Diss. Cologne. Essen: Essner Verlags-Anstalt, 1936. 231 pp.

4115. Rickelmann, Hubert. Die Tüötten in ihrem Handel und Wandel und die Wolle- und Leinen-erzeugung im Tecklenburger Land: ein Beitrag zur Wirtschafts-. und Sozial- und Familien-geschichte in der ehem. Obergrafschaft Lingen, der Grafschaft Tecklenburg und den benachbarten Gegenden. 3rd ed. Paderborn: Schöningh, 1983. 522 pp.

4116. Schröder, Ernst. Die Entwicklung der Kruppschen Konsumanstalt. Ein Beitrag zur Essener Sozial- und Wirtschaftsgeschichte. Essen: s.n., 1977. 96 pp.

4117. Schumacher, Martin. Auslandsreisen deutscher Unternehmer 1750-1851 unter besonderer Berücksichtigung von Rheinland und Westfalen. Diss. Bonn. Cologne: Rheinisch-Westfälisches Wirtschaftsarchiv, 1968. 393 pp.

4118. Spencer, Elaine G. "Rulers of the Ruhr: Leadership and Authority in German Big Business Before 1914." Business History Review 53 (1979), 40-64.

4119. Stock, Adolf. Handel und Verkehr im Dortmunder Raum seit Beginn des 19. Jahrhunderts. Diss. Cologne, 1949. 382 pp.

4120. Thom, Reinhard. Bergische Unternehmer in der Selbstverwaltung. Zu ihrem 125jährigen Jubiläum. Remscheid: Bergische Industrie- und Handelskammer, 1965. 121 pp.

4121. Tiemann, Richard. Das lippische Gewerbe im Lichte der Gewerbepolitik des 19. Jahrunderts. Ein Beitrag zur lippischen Wirtschaftspolitik. Diss. Cologne. Detmold: Meyer, 1929. 119 pp.

4122. Tigges, Wilhelm. Konsumvereine in Westfalen 1844-1867. Ein Beitrag zur Frühgeschichte der Genossenschaftsbewegung. Diss. Cologne. Witten-Ruhr: Pott, 1929. 82 pp.

4123. Vier Jahre Wirtschaftsaufstieg im rheinisch-westfälischen Industriebezirk. Zahlen und Kurven. Hamburg: Hanseatische Verlagsanstalt, 1937. 72 pp.

4124. Wiel, Paul. "Gross- und Einzelhandel im Ruhrgebiet 1938 bis 1960." Rheinisch-westfälisches Institut für Wirtschaftsforschung. Essen 13 (1962), 239-54.

4125. Wilhelms, Carl. Die Übererzeugung im Ruhrkohlenbergbau 1913-1932. Diss. Bonn. Jena: Fischer, 1938. 276 pp.

4126. Winterfeld, Luise von. Handel, Kapital und Patriziat der Stadt Köln und ihre Auswirkungen in der Vergangenheit und Gegenwart. Lübeck: Hänsischer Geschichtsverein, 1925. 83 pp.

4127. Zerres, Michael P. Handel und Industrie des Bergischen Landes im 19. Jahrhundert. Ein Bei-trag zur Wirtschaftsgeschichte Deutschlands. Zurich: Deutsch, 1978. 223 pp.

4128. Zunkel, Friedrich. "Köln während der Weltwirtschaftskrise 1929-1933." Zeitschrift für Unternehmensgeschichte 26 (1981), 104-28. (English summary.)

4129. Zunkel, Friedrich. Der rheinisch-westfälische Unternehmer 1834-1879. Ein Beitrag zur Ge-schichte des deutschen Bürgertums im 19. Jahrhundert. Cologne: Westdeutscher Verlag, 1962. 284 pp.

4130. Zunkel, Friedrich. "Das rheinisch-westfälische Unternehmertum 1834-1878." in Probleme der Reichsgründungszeit 1848-1879. Cologne: Kiepenheuer & Witsch, 1968. pp. 104-13.

SEE ALSO: 1251, 1256-57, 1275, 1301, 2543, 2561, 2574.

Pomerania

4131. Hoffmann, Hans. Karl Sparr, 1860-1932. Wanderlehrer der ländlichen Genossenschaften Pommerns. Stettin: Sauniers, 1939. 16 pp.

4132. Hoppe, Hans A. Die wirtschaftlichen Unternehmungen der Stadt Stettin. Stettin: Paschow, 1929. 121 pp.

4133. Rudorff, Eberhard. Entwicklung und Aussichten des Stettiner Handels (1886-1912). Berlin: Puttkammer & Mühlbrecht, 1914. 64 pp.

4134. Schmidt, Th. Zur Geschichte des Handels und der Schifffahrt Stettins von 1786-1840. Stettin: Gesellschaft für Pomm. Geschichte und Alterthumskunde, 1875. 160 pp.
4135. Schoene, Elmar. "Der Stettiner Seehandel nach 1813." Baltische Studien 55 (1969), 75-110.

SEE ALSO: 1329.

Rhineland-Palatinate: SEE 1332-33.

Saarland

4136. Müller, Hermann. Die Übererzeugung im Saarländer Hüttengewerbe von 1856 bis 1913. Jena: Fischer, 1935. 137 pp.

Saxony

4137. Bauer, Hans. Die Welt in einer Nuss. Literarische Zeugnisse über die Reichsmesse Leipzig aus 3 Jahrhunderten. Leipzig: Reichsmesseamt, Pressedienst, 1941. 39 pp.
4138. Beck, Friedrich. "Die Anfänge der Kaufmannschaft in der Stadt Greiz." in Forschungen zur Thüringischen Landesgeschichte. Weimar: Böhlau, 1958. pp. 273-94.
4139. Beiträge zur 800-Jahrfeier der Leipziger Messe. Leipzig: Leipziger Messeamt, 1964. 25 pp.
4140. Dankelmann, Otfried. "Die Handelsbeziehungen Deutschlands zur Sowjetunion während der Jahre der Weltwirtschftskrise (1929-1932) am Beispiel einer Halleschen Maschinenfabrik." Wissenschaftliche Zeitschrift der Martin-Luther-Universität Halle-Wittenberg 10 (1961), 741-55.
4141. Donndorf, Günter. Die Leipziger Messe und das Verkehrsgewerbe Leipzigs in der Zeit von 1800-1920. Leipzig: Leipziger Messeamt, 1964. 35 pp.
4142. Haake, Heinrich. Handel und Industrie der Provinz Sachsen 1889-1899 unter dem Einfluss der deutschen Handelspolitik. Stuttgart: Cotta, 1901. 152 pp.
4143. Haase, Ernst. Geschichte der Leipziger Messen. Leipzig: Jablonowski'sche Gesellschaft, 1885; rpt. Leipzig: 1963. 516 pp.
4144. Helbig, Herbert. Die Vertrauten: 1680-1980. Eine Vereinigung Leipziger Kaufleute. Beitrag zur Sozialfürsorge und zum bürgerlichen Gemeinsinn einer kaufmännischen Führungsschicht. Stuttgart: Hiersemann, 1980. 181 pp.
4145. Heubner, Paul L. "100 Jahre Wandel und Wachstum der Leipziger Messen." Schmoller 61 (1937), 589-606.
4146. Horster, Paul. Die Entwicklung der sächsischen Gewerbeverfassung (1780-1861). Diss. Heidelberg. Crefeld: Greven, 1908. 170 pp.
4147. Kirsch, Hermann. Vom Jahrmarkt zur Weltmesse. Ein Streifzug durch die Geschichte der Leipziger Messe. Leipzig: Urania, 1958. 250 pp.
4148. Kretzschmar, Herbert. Das ländliche Genossenschaftswesen in Königreich Sachsen. Eine kritische Untersuchung zwanzigjähriger genossenschaftlicher Entwicklung. Berlin: Kohlhammer, 1914. 501 pp.
4149. Kroker, Ernst. Handelsgeschichte der Stadt Leipzig. Die Entwicklung des Leipziger Handels und der Leipziger Messen von der Gründung der Stadt bis auf die Gegenwart. Leipzig: Bielefeld, 1925. 339 pp.
4150. Kunze, Arno. Der Frühkapitalismus in Chemnitz. Forschungsergebnisse aus dem Stadtarchiv Karl-Marx-Stadt und anderen deutschen Archiven. Karl-Marx-Stadt: Stadtarchiv, 1958. 178 pp.
4151. Die Leipziger Messe. Die Entwicklung der Leipziger Messe zum Weltmarkt von Industrieprodukten. Leipzig: Leipziger Messamt, 1936. 32 pp.
4152. Die Leipziger Messe (im Wandel von 7 Jahrhunderten). Leipzig: Leipziger Messamt, 1934. 11 pp.
4153. Die Leipziger Messe seit 800 Jahren. Leipzig: Leipziger Messamt, 1963. 37 pp.
4154. Misselwitz, Alfred. Die Entwicklung des Gewerbes in Halle a.S. während des 19. Jahrhunderts. Jena: Fischer, 1913. 125 pp.

4155. Moltke, Siegfried. Die Leipziger Messen im Kriege einst und jetzt. Leipzig: Messamt für die Mustermessen, 1917. 55 pp.
4156. Moltke, Siegfried. "Zwei Kapitel aus Leipzigs Handels- und Verkehrsgeschichte." in Volkswirtschaftliche und wirtschaftsgeschichtliche Abhandlungen. Wilhelm Stieda als Festgruss zum 60sten Wiederkehr seines Geburtstages dargebracht. Leipzig: Veit, 1912. pp. 1-19.
4157. Müller, Kurt. Siebenhundert Jahre Messen in Leipzig. Ein Abriss der Geschichte der gegenwärtigen Bedeutung und ihrer Aufgaben. Leipzig: Messamt, 1939. 20 pp.
4158. Netta, Gheron. Die Handelsbeziehungen zwischen Leipzig und Ost- und Südosteuropa bis zum Verfall der Warenmessen. Diss. Zurich, 1920. Zurich: Leemann, 1920. 149 pp.
4159. Pönicke, Herbert. Wirtschaftskrise in Sachsen vor hundert Jahren. Ein Beitrag zur sächsischen Wirtschaftsgeschichte. Herrnhut: Winter, 1933. 46 pp.
4160. Rothe, Edith. Die Leipziger Messe. Leipzig: Verlag für Buch- und Bibliothekswesen, 1957. 213 pp.
4161. Schiffel, Walther. Sachsens Kaufleute und Handwerker auf der Leipziger Messe. Ein Beitrag zur Geschichte der Reichsmesse Leipzig im 18. und 19. Jahrhundert. Diss. Leipzig, 1942. 263 pp.
4162. Schulze, Willi. "Löhne und Preise 1800 bis 1850 nach den Akten und Rechnungsbelegen des Stadtarchivs Quedlinburg." Jahrbuch für Wirtschaftsgeschichte (1967), I, 301-40.
4163. Settecent'anni di Fiere a Lipsia. Un compendio di storia, importanza e funzione attuale. Leipzig: Reichsmesseamt, 1940. 20 pp.
4164. Voss, Paul. Die Leipziger Messe einst, heute und morgen. Ein Gang durch ihre Geschichte in Wort und Bild. Leipzig: Leipziger Buchdruckerei, 1947. 15 pp.

SEE ALSO: 841.

Schleswig-Holstein

4165. Ehlers, Franz, ed. Zoll- und Steuergeschichte Schleswig-Holsteins. Kiel: Oberfinanzdirektion Kiel, 1967. 549 pp.
4166. Fünfundsiebzig Jahre Schleswig-Holsteinische Landwirtschaftliche Hauptgenossenschaft, 1899-1973. Lebendige Tradition, zukunftsgewandter Fortschritt. Kiel: Schleswig-Holsteinische Landwirtschaftliche Hauptgenossenschaft, 1973. 106 pp.
4167. Haas, Walter. Bestrebungen und Massnahmen zur Förderung des Kieler Handels in Vergangenheit und Gegenwart (1242-1914). Diss. Kiel. Kiel: Lüdtke, 1922. 224 pp.
4168. Hoffmann, Friedrich. "Die Stellung der Kieler Universitätswissenschaft zu Schleswig-Holsteins Beitritt zum Deutschen Zollverein." Zeitschrift der Gesellschaft für Schleswig-holsteinische Geschichte 77 (1953), 167-83.
4169. Kall, Peter. Das Zollwesen in Flensburg und im deutsch-dänischen Grenzgebiet. Flensburg: Gesellschaft für Flensburger Stadtgeschichte, 1978. 212 pp.
4170. Lüthje, Albert. 75 Jahre landwirtschaftliches Genossenschaftswesen in Schleswig-Holstein. Kiel: Schmidt & Klaunig, 1959. 85 pp.
4171. Lüthje, Albert. Landwirtschaftliches Genossenschaftswesen in Schleswig-Holstein, 70 Jahre. (Verband der Schleswig-holsteinischen Landwirtschaftlichen Genossenschaften 1884-1954.) Kiel: Schmidt & Klaunig, 1954. 66 pp.
4172. Lüthje, Albert. Vier Ökonomieräte. Pioniere des landwirtschaftlichen Genossenschaftswesens in Schleswig-Holstein und Hamburg. Kiel: Raiffeisenverband Schleswig-Holstein und Hamburg, 1981. 63 pp.
4173. Schlüter, G. A. "Die Erzeuger- und Grosshandelspreise seit 1950." Statistische Monatshefte Schleswig-Holstein 9 (1957), 250-56.

Silesia

4174. Cauer, E. "Zur Geschichte der Breslauer Messe." Zeitschrift für die Geschichte Schlesiens 5 (1863), 63-80, 222-50.
4175. Fuchs, Konrad. "Wirtschaftliche Führungskräfte in Schlesien vom ausgehenden 18. Jahrhundert bis zum Beginn des Ersten Weltkrieges." in Führungskräfte der Wirtschaft im neunzehnten Jahrhundert 1790-1914. Limburg: C. A. Starke, 1977. II, 59-108.

4176. "Handel und Industrie Schlesiens." Provinz-Blätter 88 (1828), 136-50.
4177. Kredel, Otto. "Schlesiens Handel nach dem Südosten (seit 1742)." Archiv für Politik und Geschichte 6 (1928), 375-81.
4178. Neugebauer, Julius. "Die frühere Bedeutung Breslaus, dessen Gassen und Handelsstrassen, sowie die Gefahren im Handelsverkehr." Bericht des Kaufmännischen Vereins (1868), 8-14.
4179. Schlegel, Fritz. Entwicklung der deutschen landwirtschaftlichen Genossenschaften seit der Inflation bis 1932, unter besonderer Berücksichtigung der schlesischen Verhältnisse. Diss. Breslau. Breslau: Nischkowsky, 1937. 150 pp.
4180. Weber, Friedrich B. Über den Handel Breslaus in neuster Zeit im Vergleich gegen den in den letzten Jahren vor 1806. Jena: s.n., 1836.
4181. Wende, Ernst A. Tariflohn und Konjunktur. Betrachtungen zur Lohngestaltung der niederschlesischen Grossindustrie 1924-1928. Diss. Breslau. Ohlau: Eschenhagen, 1929. 60 pp.
4182. Wendt, Heinrich. Schlesien und der Orient. Ein geschichtlicher Rückblick. Breslau: Hirt, 1916. 244 pp.

SEE ALSO: 4027.

Thuringia

4183. Dressel, Hans. Die Entwicklung von Handel und Industrie in Sonneberg. Gotha: F. A. Perthes, 1909. 137 pp.
4184. Huschke, Wolfgang. Forschungen über die Herkunft der thüringischen Unternehmerschicht des 19. Jahrhunderts. Baden-Baden: Lutzeyer, 1962. 69 pp.
4185. Kühnert, Herbert. Über die Standorte älterer Ilmenauer Gewerbe- und Industriebetriebe. Aufsätze mit ausführlichen Quellen- und Literatur-Hinweisen. Ilmenau: Kulturbund, 1959. 71 pp.
4186. Nordhoff, Fritz. Die Entwicklung der Raiffeisen-Organisation in Thüringen nach dem Kriege. Diss. Jena. Stadtroda: Richter, 1928. 58 pp.
4187. Wegemann-Kiel, Georg. Beitrag zur Geschichte des Erfurter Handels. Kiel: Mühlau, 1941. 23 pp.

5.
History of Finance

CENTRAL EUROPE

Bibliographic Reference

4188. Dillen, J. G. van, ed. History of the Principal Public Banks Accompanied by Extensive Bibliographies of the History of Banking and Credit in Eleven European Countries. The Hague: Nijhoff, 1934. 480 pp.

CENTRAL EUROPE

4189. Ames, Edward and Richard T. Rapp. "The Birth and Death of Taxes." The Journal of Economic History 37 (1977), 161-78.

4190. Basler, Werner. "Die USA und die europäischen Mächte in den zwanziger Jahren." in Die USA und Europa 1917-1945. Berlin: Akademie, 1975. pp. 87-128.

4191. Berend, Iván T. "Investment Strategies in East Central Europe in the Nineteenth and Twentieth Centuries." in Proceedings of the Sixth International Congress on Economic History, Copenhagen, 1974. Copenhagen: University of Copenhagen Institute of Economic History, 1974.

4192. Bloch, Marc. Esquisse d'une histoire monétaire de l'Europe. Paris: Colin, 1954. 96 pp.

4193. Cameron, Rondo E. Banking and Economic Development. Some Lessons of History. London: Oxford University Press, 1972. 267 pp.

4194. Cameron, Rondo E. "The Crédit Mobilier and the Economic Development of Europe." Journal of Political Economy 61 (1953), 461-88.

4195. Coffey, Peter. The European Monetary System--Past, Present and Future. Dordrecht: Nijhoff, 1984. 150 pp.

4196. Crowley, Ronald W. "Long Swings in the Role of Government. An Analysis of Wars and Government Expenditures in Western Europe Since the Eleventh Century." Public Finance 26 (1971), 27-43.

4197. Ellis, Howard S. Exchange Control in Central Europe. Cambridge, MA: Harvard University Press, 1941. 413 pp.

4198. Emden, Paul H. Money Powers of Europe in the Nineteenth and Twentieth Centuries. London: Appleton-Century, 1938; rpt. New York, 1983. 428 pp.

4199. Hirsch, Fred and Peter Oppenheimer. "The Trial of Managed Money. Currency, Credit and Prices, 1920-1970." in C. M. Cipolla, ed. The Twentieth Century. Fontana Economic History of Europe, vol. 5, pt. 2. Glasgow: Collins/Fontana, 1976. pp. 603-97.

4200. Hobsbawn, Eric J. The Age of Capital, 1848-1975. New York: Scribner, 1975. 354 pp.

4201. Jens, Albers. Vom Armenhaus zum Wohlfahrtsstaat: Analysen zur Entwicklung der Sozialversicherung in Westeuropa. Frankfurt a. M.: Campus Verlag, 1982. 280 pp.

4202. Kellenbenz, Hermann, ed. Weltwirtschaftliche und währungspolitische Probleme seit dem Ausgang des Mittelalters. Stuttgart: Fischer, 1981. 241 pp.
4203. Kindleberger, Charles P. A Financial History of Western Europe. London: Allen & Unwin, 1984. 525 pp.
4204. Kindleberger, Charles P. The Formation of Financial Centers. A Study in Comparative Economic History. Princeton. NJ: International Finance Section, Dept. of Economics, Princeton University, 1974. 82 pp.
4205. Kindleberger, Charles P. International Short-Term Capital Movements. New York: Columbia University Press, 1937. 262 pp.
4206. Kindleberger, Charles P. and Jean-Pierre Laffargue, eds. Financial Crises. Theory. History and Policy. Cambridge: Cambridge University Press, 1982. 301 pp.
4207. Köhler, Peter A. and Hans F. Zacher, eds. Ein Jahrhundert Sozialversicherung in der Bundesrepublik Deutschland. Frankreich. Grossbritannien. Österreich und der Schweiz. Berlin: Duncker & Humblot, 1981. 871 pp.
4208. Köllner, Lutz. Von der preussischen Staatsbank zum europäischen Währungssystem: 100 Jahre Währung und Politik in Deutschland und Europa. Frankfurt a. M.: Lang, 1981. 102 pp.
4209. Kuznets, Simon. "Quantitative Aspects of the Economic Growth of Nations. The Long Term Trends in Capital Formation Proportions." Economic Development and Cultural Change 7-11 (1959-1963).
4210. Lange, Ernst. Die Goldbewegungen in England. Frankreich. Russland. den Vereinigten Staaten von Amerika und Deutschland vom Kriegsausbruch bis zum Ende des Jahres 1927. Leipzig: Noske, 1930. 78 pp.
4211. Morgenstern, Oskar. International Financial Transactions and Business Cycles. Princeton, NJ: Princeton University Press, 1959. 591 pp.
4212. Paulat, Vladislav J. "Investment Policy and the Standard of Living in East Mid-European Countries." Journal of Central European Affairs 14 (1954), 38-64.
4213. Peláez, Carlos M. "A Comparison of Long-Term Monetary Behaviour and Institutions in Brazil, Europe and the United States." Journal of European Economic History 5 (1976), 439-50.
4214. Schmidt, Gerhard. "Jewish Money in History." Rivista Internazionale di Scienze Economiche e Commerciali 24 (1977), 248-59.
4215. Schwinger, Aribert. Vom nationalen zum internationalen und übernationalen Recht der Sozialversicherung. Diss. Mainz, 1963. 260 pp.
4216. Triffin, Robert. The Evolution of the International Monetary System. Historical Reappraisal and Future Perspectives. Princeton, NJ: Princeton University Press, 1964. 87 pp.
4217. Triffin, Robert. Our International Monetary System. Yesterday. Today and Tomorrow. New York: Random House, 1968. 206 pp.
4218. Wechsberg, Joseph. The Merchant Bankers. London: Weidenfeld & Nicolson, 1967. 365 pp.
4219. Welfling, Weldon. Mutual Savings Banks. The Evolution of a Financial Intermediary. Cleveland, OH: Case Western Reserve University, 1968. 307 pp.
4220. Wysocki, Josef. "Machtgegensätze in einer Währungsunion. Ein historisches Fallbeispiel." Kredit und Kapital 6 (1973), 295-321. (English Summary).
4221. Yeager, Leland B. International Monetary Relations. Theory. History and Policy. 2nd ed. New York: Harper & Row, 1976. 667 pp.
4222. Zöllner, Detlev. "Vergleich von Sozialversicherungssystemen verschiedener Länder in ihrer geschichtlichen Entwicklung." Zeitschrift für die gesamte Versicherungswirtschaft 69 (1980), 215-24.
4223. Zur Geschichte des Kreditgeschäftes: Notizen zu Finanzierungsproblemen vom 18. bis zum 20. Jahrhundert. Frankfurt a. M.: Knapp, 1982. 87 pp.

SEE ALSO: 16, 124.

CENTRAL EUROPE--1815-1918

4224. Aghevli, Bijan B. "The Balance of Payments and the Money Supply Under the Gold Standard Regime, 1879-1914." American Economic Review 65 (1975), 40-58.
4225. Bloomfield, Arthur I. Monetary Policy Under the International Gold Standard. 1880-1914. New York: Federal Reserve Bank of New York, 1959; rpt. New York, 1979. 62 pp.

4226. Bloomfield, Arthur I. Patterns of Fluctuation in International Investment Before 1914. Princeton, NJ: Princeton University Press, 1968. 55 pp.
4227. Bloomfield, Arthur I. Short Term Capital Movements Under the pre-1914 Gold Standard. Princeton, NJ: Princeton University Press, 1963. 104 pp.
4228. Cameron, Rondo E. Banking in the Early Stages of Industrialization. New York: Oxford University Press, 1967. 349 pp.
4229. Cameron, Rondo E. "Banking in the Early Stages of Industrialization. A Preliminary Survey." The Scandinavian Economic History Review 11 (1963), 117-34.
4230. Cameron, Rondo E. "Theoretical Bases of a Comparative Study of the Role of Financial Institutions in the Early Stages of Industrialization." in Papers Presented to the Second International Conference of Economic History, Aix-en-Provence, 1962. Paris: Mouton, 1965.
4231. Creanga, George D. Die direkte Besteuerung in Preussen und Rumänien. Darstellung der Reformen der direkten Besteuerung in Preussen (von 1810 bis zur Gegenwart) und die relative Anwendung derselben auf das rumänische Steuerwesen. Berlin: Ebering, 1900. 237 pp.
4232. Crouzet, François, ed. Capital Formation in the Industrial Revolution. London: Methuen, 1972. 261 pp.
4233. Davis, Joseph S. "World Currency Expansion During the War and in 1919." Review of Economic Statistics 2 (1920), 8-20.
4234. DeCecco, Marcello. Money and Empire. The International Gold Standard, 1890-1914. London: Blackwell, 1974. 254 pp.
4235. La dette publique aux 18, et 19, siècles, son développement sur le plan local, régional et national. Brussels: Crédit Communal de Belgique, 1980. 323 pp.
4236. Feis, Herbert. Europe, the World's Banker 1870-1914. An Account of European Foreign Investment and the Connection of World Finance with Diplomacy Before the War. New Haven, CT: Yale University Press, 1931. 469 pp.
4237. Friedman, Elisha M. International Finance and its Reorganization. New York: E. P. Dutton, 1922. 702 pp.
4238. Funck, Walter. Die Notmünzen der deutschen (und österreichisch-ungarischen) Kriegsgefangenenlager 1914-1918. 2 vols. Neuenburg: W. Funck, 1962-64.
4239. Gerloff, Wilhelm. Die Entstehung des Geldes und die Anfänge des Geldwesens. Frankfurt a. M.: Klostermann, 1947. 260 pp.
4240. Good, David F. "Backwardness and the Role of Banking in Nineteenth-Century European Industrialization." The Journal of Economic History 33 (1973), 845-50.
4241. Helfferich, Karl T. Die Folgen des Deutsch-Österreichischen Münzvereins von 1857. Ein Beitrag zur Geld- und Währungs-Theorie. Strassburg: Trübner, 1894. 134 pp.
4242. Helfferich, Karl T. "Die geschichtliche Entwickelung der Münzsysteme." Jahrbücher für Nationalökonomie und Statistik 3 (1895), 801-28.
4243. Henry, James A. "Banking and the Industrial Breakthrough." The South African Bankers' Journal 64 (1967), 399-406.
4244. Hildreth, Richard. The History of Banks, to which is Added a Demonstration of the Advantages and Necessity of Free Competition in the Business of Banking. Boston: Hilliard, Gray, 1837; rpt. New York: Kelley, 1968. 142 pp.
4245. A History of Banking in All the Leading Nations. 4 vols. New York: Journal of Commerce and Commercial Bulletin, 1896; rpt. New York, 1971.
4246. Jakob, Ludwig H. von. Die Staatsfinanzwissenschaft. Theoretisch und praktisch dargestellt und durch Beispiele aus der neuern Finanzgeschichte europäischer Staaten erläutert. 2nd ed. Halle: Schwetschke, 1837. 911 pp.
4247. Landes, David S. "The Old Bank and the New. The Financial Revolution of the Nineteenth Century." in F. Crouzet, ed. Essays in European Economic History 1789-1914. New York: St. Martin's Press, 1969. pp. 112-27.
4248. Liefmann, Robert. Die Geldvermehrung im Weltkriege und die Beseitigung ihrer Folgen. Stuttgart: Deutsche Verlags-Anstalt, 1918. 199 pp.
4249. Lindert, Peter H. Key Currencies and Gold, 1900-13. Princeton, NJ: Princeton University Press, 1969. 85 pp.
4250. Martin, David A. "The Impact of Mid-Nineteenth Century Gold Depreciation Upon Western Monetary Standards." Journal of European Economic History 6 (1977), 641-58.
4251. Nugent, Jeffrey B. "Exchange Rate Movements and Economic Development in the Late Nineteenth Century." Journal of Political Economy 81 (1973), 1110-35.

4252. Popovics, Alexander. Das Geldwesen im Kriege. Vienna: Hölder-Pichler-Tempsky, 1925. 185 pp.

4253. Poschinger, Heinrich von. Die Banken im deutschen Reiche, Oesterreich und der Schweiz. 2 vols. Erlangen: H. Dufft, 1876-77.

4254. Ramstein, Adolf. Das Verhältnis der Notenbanken zur Kriegsfinanzierung in England, Frankreich, Deutschland und der Schweiz. Bern: Haupt, 1923. 101 pp.

4255. Redlich, Fritz. "Payments Between Nations in the Eighteenth and Early Nineteenth Centuries." Quarterly Journal of Economics 50 (1936), 694-705.

4256. Redlich, Fritz."Two Nineteenth-Century Financiers and Autobiographers. A Comparative Study in Creative Destructiveness and Business Failure." Economy and History 10 (1967), 37-128.

4257. Schmoller, Gustav. "Historische Betrachtung über Staatenbildung und Finanzentwicklung." Schmoller 33 (1909), 1-64.

4258. Schmoller, Gustav. Skizze einer Finanzgeschichte von Frankreich, Österreich, England und Preussen (1500-1900). Historische Betrachtungen über Staatenbildung und Finanzentwicklung. Leipzig: Duncker & Humblot, 1909. 64 pp.

4259. Schönborn, Theodor. "Ursprung und geschichtliche Entwickelung des Sparkassenwesens in Europa." Schmoller 8 (1884), 157-84.

4260. Shaw, William A. The History of Currency, 1251 to 1894, Being an Account of the Gold and Silver Moneys and Monetary Standards of Europe and America, Together With an Examination of the Effects of Currency and Exchange Phenomena on Commercial and National Progress and Well-Being. 3rd ed. New York: Putnam's Sons, 1896. 437 pp.

4261. Sumner, Michael T. and George Zis, eds. European Monetary Union, Progress and Prospects. New York: St. Martin's Press, 1982. 284 pp.

4262. Trende, Adolf et al. Frühgeschichte des europäischen Sparkassenwesens. Vienna: Sparkassenverlag, 1969. 94 pp.

4263. Vilar, Pierre. A History of Gold and Money, 1450-1920. London: New Left Books, 1976. 36 pp.

4264. Willis, Henry P. A History of the Latin Monetary Union, A Study of International Monetary Action. Chicago: University of Chicago Press, 1901. 332 pp.

4265. Wysocki, Josef. "Machtgegensätze in einer Währungsunion. Ein historisches Fallbeispiel." Kredit und Kapital 6 (1973), 295-321. (English and French summaries)

CENTRAL EUROPE--1919-1975

4266. Albergo, Ernesto d' La Politica finanziaria dei grandi stati dal dopoguerra ad oggi. Milano: Istituto per gli studi di politica internazionale, 1939. 276 pp.

4267. Alessio, Domenico. "L'evoluzione della sicurezza sociale e suo costo nei paesi della C.E.E." I Problemi della Sicurezza Sociale 29 (1974), 101-16. (English Summary)

4268. Aliber, Robert Z. "Speculation in the Foreign Exchanges. The European Experience, 1919-26." Yale Economic Essays 2 (1962), 171-245.

4269. Antonucci, Alceste. La liquidation financière de la guerre et la reconstruction en Europe centrale. Paris: Giard, 1933. 463 pp.

4270. Bandera, V. N. Foreign Capital as an Instrument of National Economic Policy. A Study Based on the Experience of East European Countries Between the World Wars. The Hague: Nijhoff, 1964. 155 pp.

4271. Bell, Edward P. Europe's Economic Sunrise. Chicago: Chicago Daily News, 1927. 217 pp.

4272. Brown, William A. The International Gold Standard Reinterpreted, 1914-34. 2 vols. New York: National Bureau of Economic Research, 1940.

4273. Cassel, Gustav. The Crisis in the World's Monetary System. Oxford: Oxford University Press, 1932. 117 pp.

4274. Cassel, Gustav. The Downfall of the Gold Standard. London: Oxford University Press, 1936. 262 pp.

4275. Cassel, Gustav. Post-War Monetary Stabilization. New York: Columbia University Press, 1928. 109 pp.

4276. Choudhri, E. U. and L. A. Kochin. "The Exchange Rate and the International Transmission of Business Cycle Disturbances. Some Evidence from the Great Depression." Journal of Money, Credit and Banking 12 (1980), 565-74.

4277. Clarke, Stephen V. O. Central Bank Co-Operation, 1924-31. New York: Federal Reserve Bank of New York, 1967. 234 pp.
4278. Clarke, Stephen V. O. The Reconstruction of the International Monetary System. The Attempts of 1922 and 1933. Princeton, NJ: Princeton University Department of Economics, 1973. 48 pp.
4279. Costigliola, Frank C. The Politics of Financial Stabilization. American Reconstruction Policy in Europe 1924-30. Diss. Cornell, 1973. 529 pp.
4280. Einzig, Paul. World Finance 1914-1935. New York: Macmillan, 1935. 382 pp.
4281. Frenkel, Jacob A. "Exchange Rates, Prices and Money. Lessons from the 1920s." American Economic Review 70 (1980), 235-42.
4282. Frenkel, Jacob A. and Kenneth W. Clements. "Exchange Rates in the 1920s. A Monetary Approach." in M. J. Flanders and A. Razin, eds. Development in an Inflationary World. New York: Academic Press, 1981. pp. 283-318.
4283. German. Austrian and Middle Eastern Questions. 1929-1930. London: Statistics Office, 1975. 852 pp.
4284. Gibbons, Herbert A. Europe Since 1918. London: Cape, 1923. 622 pp.
4285. Glasgow, George. From Dawes to Locarno. Being a Critical Record of an Important Achievement in European Diplomacy 1924-1925. London: Benn, 1925. 185 pp.
4286. Grotius, Fritz. "Die europäischen Geldreformen nach dem zweiten Weltkrieg." Weltwirtschaftliches Archiv 63 (1949), 106-52; 276-325.
4287. Harris, Seymour E. Exchange Depreciation. Its Theory and History. 1931-35. With Some Consideration of Related Domestic Policies. Cambridge, MA: Harvard University Press, 1936; rpt. New York, 1979. 516 pp.
4288. Hill, Robert L. "The Role of Rigidity in the Failure of the Gold Standard." Weltwirtschaftliches Archiv 77 (1956), 85-106.
4289. Horsefield, John K. "Currency Devaluation and Public Finance, 1929-37." Economica 6 (1939), 322-44.
4290. Jack, Daniel T. The Restoration of European Currencies. London: P. S. King, 1927. 218 pp.
4291. Kane, Daniel R. The Eurodollar Market and the Years of Crisis. New York: St. Martin's Press, 1982. 189 pp.
4292. Köllner, Lutz. Der internationale Kapitalverkehr seit dem letzten Kriege 1945-60. Frankfurt a. M.: Knapp, 1963. 314 pp.
4293. Kriz, Miroslav A. Postwar International Lending. Princeton, NJ: Princeton University Press, 1947. 29 pp.
4294. League of Nations. International Currency Experience. Lessons of the Inter-War Period. Geneva: League of Nations, 1944; rpt. New York, 1979. 249 pp.
4295. Lehfeldt, Robert A. Restoration of the World's Currencies. London: P. S. King, 1923. 146 pp.
4296. Little, Jane S. Euro-Dollars. The Money-Market Gypsies. New York: Harper & Row, 1975. 301 pp.
4297. Meyer, Richard H. Bankers' Diplomacy. Monetary Stabilisation in the Twenties. New York: Columbia University Press, 1970. 170 pp.
4298. Moggridge, Donald E. "Financial Crises and Lenders of Last Resort. Policy in the Crises of 1920 and 1929." Journal of European Economic History 10 (1981), 47-69.
4299. Morsel, Henri. "La position financière et économique de l'Europe au lendemain de la Première Guerre Mondiale." Relations Internationales 8 (1976), 313-22.
4300. Nötel, Rudolf. "International Capital Movements and Finance in Eastern Europe, 1919-49." VSWG 61 (1974), 65-112.
4301. Palyi, Melchior. The Twilight of Gold. 1914-36. Myths and Realities. Chicago: H. Regnery, 1972. 365 pp.
4302. Polak, Jacques J. "European Exchange Depreciation in the early Twenties." Econometrica 2 (1943), 151-62.
4303. Rowland, Benjamin M., ed. Balance of Power or Hegemony. The Interwar Monetary System. New York: New York University Press, 1976. 266 pp.
4304. Schwarz, Otto. Die Weltfinanzlage bei Kriegsbeginn und die Entwicklung der Weltfinanzen seit Ausgang des Weltkriegs. Stuttgart: Kohlhammer, 1940. 46 pp.
4305. Stern, Siegfried. Fourteen Years of European Investments. 1914-28. New York: Bankers Publishing Company, 1929. 279 pp.
4306. Strandh, Johannes. "Some Notes on the History of International Capital Movements, 1930-32." Economy and History 5 (1962), 46-80.

4307. Teichova, Alice. "Versailles and the Expansion of the Bank of England into Central Europe." in N. Horn and J. Kocka, eds. Recht und Entwicklung der Grossunternehmen im 19. und frühen 20. Jahrhundert. Göttingen: Vandenhoeck & Ruprecht, 1979.
4308. Temin, Peter. Did Monetary Forces Cause the Great Depression? New York: W. W. Norton, 1976. 210 pp.
4309. Thomas, Lloyd B. "Some Evidence on International Currency Experience, 1919-25." Nebraska Journal of Economics and Business 11 (1972), 145-55.
4310. Trachtenberg, Marc. Reparation in World Politics. France and European Economic Diplomacy. 1916-1923. New York: Columbia University Press, 1980. 423 pp.
4311. Traynor, Dean E. International Monetary and Financial Conferences in the Interwar Period. Washington, D. C.: Catholic University of America Press, 1949. 196 pp.
4312. Tsiang, Sho-Chieh. "Fluctuating Exchange Rates in Countries with Relatively Stable Economies. Some European Experiences After World War I." International Monetary Fund Staff Papers 7 (1959-60), 244-73.
4313. United Nations. International Capital Movements During the Inter-War Period. New York: United Nations, 1949; rpt. New York, 1979. 70 pp.
4314. United Nations. Public Debt. 1914-46. New York: United Nations, 1946. 159 pp.
4315. White, David. European Investment Bank: 25 Years: 1958-1983. Saarbrücken: Saarbrücker Zeitung, 1983. 116 pp.
4316. Williams, David. "The 1931 Financial Crisis." Yorkshire Bulletin of Economic and Social Research 15 (1963), 92-110.

SEE ALSO: 189, 259, 263.

AUSTRIA

4317. Bachinger, Karl and Herbert Matis. Der österreichische Schilling. Geschichte einer Währung. Graz: Verlag Styria, 1974. 326 pp.
4318. Bachmayer, Othmar. Die Geschichte der österreichischen Währungspolitik. Vienna: Manz, 1960. 154 pp.
4319. Brusatti, Alois et al. Wien. am Graben 21. 150 Jahre Erste Österreichische Spar-Casse. 1819-1969. 150 Jahre österreichische Geschichte. Vienna: Die Erste Österreichische Spar-Casse, 1969. 272 pp.
4320. Gratz, Alois. "Die österreichische Finanzpolitik von 1848 bis 1948." in H. Meyer, ed. Hundert Jahre österreichischer Wirtschaftsentwicklung. Vienna: Springer, 1949. pp. 222-309.
4321. Hoffmann, Alfred, ed. 150 Jahre Sparkassen in Österreich. 5 vols. Vienna: Hauptverband der Österreichischen Sparkassen, 1972.
4322. Ein Jahrhundert Creditanstalt-Bankverein. (1855-1955). Vienna: Creditanstalt-Bankverein, 1957. 391 pp.
4323. Kamitz, Reinhard. "Geldpolitik und Bankwesen in Österreich." Österreichisches Bank-Archiv 4 (1956), 2-8.
4324. Kamitz, Reinhard. "Die österreichische Geld- und Währungspolitik von 1848 bis 1948." in H. Mayer, ed. Hundert Jahre österreichischer Wirtschaftsentwicklung. Vienna: Springer, 1949. pp. 127-221.
4325. Klauhs, Hellmuth, ed. Hundertfünfzig Jahre Raiffeisen. Die Raiffeisen-Geldorganisation in Österreich. Vienna: Manz, 1969. 110 pp.
4326. Köfer, Rupert. Die Entwicklung der österreichischen Sparkassen. (Eine betriebswirtschaftliche Untersuchung.) Diss. Vienna University for World Trade, 1938. 194 pp.
4327. Linhardt, Hanns. "Die österreichische Bankwirtschaft vom Wiener Kongress bis zur Gegenwart. Vergleiche mit Europa und Übersee." in Das Kreditwesen in Österreich. Vienna: Österreichische Bankwissenschaftliche Gesellschaft, 1968. pp. 30-44.
4328. Loehr, August von. Österreichische Geldgeschichte. Vienna: Universum, 1946. 89 pp.
4329. März, Eduard. "Die historischen Voraussetzungen des Credit-Mobilier-Bankwesens in Österreich." Schmoller 79 (1959), 573-87.

4330. Pausch, Alfons. "Internationale Steuergeschichte im Aufwind. Neue Ausstellung der Bundes-finanzakademie in Wien." Deutsche Steuer-Zeitung, 67 (1979), 386-96.
4331. Pressburger, Siegfried. Das österreichische Noteninstitut 1816-1966. 7 vols. Vienna: Österreichische Nationalbank, 1969-76.
4332. Radner, Alfred. "Die historisch-soziologischen Grundlagen der Sozialversicherung." Die Versicherungsrundschau 35 (1980), 354-74.
4333. Scheffer, Egon. Das Bankwesen in Österreich. Entstehung. Entwicklung. Bedeutung für Wirtschaft und Geist. Vienna: Burgverlag, 1924. 408 pp.
4334. Schinnerer, Erich. "Ein Beitrag zur österreichischen Bankgeschichte." Österreichisches Bank-Archiv 17 (1969), 226-35.
4335. Thausing, Friedrich. Hundert Jahre Sparkasse. Vienna: Selbstverlag der Ersten Österreichi-schen Sparkassen, 1919. 589 pp.
4336. Walré de Bordes, J. van. The Austrian Crown. London: P. S. King, 1924; rpt. New York: Garland, 1983. 252 pp.
4337. Wirth, Max. "A History of Banking in Austria-Hungary." in A History of Banking in All the Leading Nations. New York: Journal of Commerce & Commercial Bulletin; rpt. New York: A. M. Kelly, 1971. IV, 69-187.

SEE ALSO: 308.

IMPERIAL AUSTRIA-HUNGARY AND WORLD WAR ONE--1815-1918

4338. Amery, Leopold S. "Austro-Hungarian Financial Relations." Economic Journal 8 (1898), 314-24.
4339. Ausch, Karl. Als die Banken fielen. Zur Soziologie der politischen Korruption. Vienna: Europa Verlag, 1968. 439 pp.
4340. Bechler, Siegfried. Das österreichische Münzwesen vom Jahre 1524 bis 1838 in histori-scher, statistischer und legislativer Hinsicht. 2 vols. Vienna: Mösle & Braumüller, 1838.
4341. Beer, Adolf. Die Finanzen Oesterreichs im XIX. Jahrhundert. Prague: Tempsky, 1877. 458 pp.
4342. Beer, Adolf. Finanzgeschichtliche Studien. Vienna: Kaiserliche Akademie der Wissenschaften, 1903. 72 pp.
4343. Beer, Adolf. Der Staatshaushalt Oesterreich-Ungarns seit 1868. Prague: F. Tempsky, 1881. 524 pp.
4344. Brandt, Harm-Hinrich. Der österreichische Neoabsolutismus. Staatsfinanzen und Politik 1848-1860. 2 vols. Göttingen: Vandenhoeck & Ruprecht, 1978.
4345. Brauneis, Viktor. Die Entstehung der Oesterreichischen Nationalbank--Memorandum verfasst zur Information der Delegierten des Völkerbundes. Vienna: Österreichische Nationalbank, 1924.
4346. Brusatti, Alois. "Unternehmensfinanzierung und Privatkredit im österreichischen Vormärz. Mitteilungen des Österreichischen Staatsarchivs 13 (1960), 331-79.
4347. Cottrell, Philip L. "London Financiers and Austria, 1863-75. The Anglo-Austrian Bank." Business History 11 (1969), 106-19.
4348. Denkschrift über den Gang der Währungsfrage seit dem Jahre 1867. Vienna: Finanz-Ministe-rium, 1892. 18 pp.
4349. Ellis, Howard S. "Exchange Control in Austria and Hungary." Quarterly Journal of Economics 54 (1939), 1-188.
4350. Engländer, Oskar. "Die österreichischen Salinenscheine 1848-1899 als Vorläufer der Politik des offenen Marktes." in Festschrift für Otto Peterka. Brno: R. M. Rohrer, 1936. pp. 1-11.
4351. Fischer, Erich. "Der Staatsbankerott von 1816 und die Sanierung der österreichischen Finanzen nach den napoleonischen Kriegen. in Zeitschrift für Volkswirtschaft und Sozialpolitik, N. F. 4 (1924), 252-317.
4352. Die Frage des Finanzkapitals in der Österreichisch-Ungarischen Monarchie 1900-1918. Mit-teilungen auf der Konferenz der Geschichtswissenschaftler. Bucharest: Academy of the Socialist Republic of Rumania, 1965. 85 pp.
4353. Globocnik, Alexander. Geschichte der deutschen Bank- und Münzgesetzgebung seit der ersten Erneuerung des Reichsbankprivilegs. Berlin: Puttkammer & Mühlbrecht, 1913. 187 pp.
4354. Good, David F. "Financial Integration in Late Nineteenth Century Austria." Journal of Economic History 37 (1977), 890-910.

4355. Good, David F. "National Bias in the Austrian Capital Market Before World War I." Explorations in Economic History 14 (1977), 141-66.
4356. Grunwald, Max. Samuel Oppenheimer und sein Kreis. (Ein Kapitel aus der Finanzgeschichte Österreichs). Vienna: Braumüller, 1913. 358 pp.
4357. Hauer, Josef Ritter von. Beiträge zur Geschichte der österreichischen Finanzen. Vienna: Wallishausser, 1848. 255 pp.
4358. Hönig, Fritz. Österreichs Finanzpolitik im Kriege von 1866. Vienna: Steinmann, 1937. 30 pp.
4359. Industriefinanzierung in Österreich. Vienna: Sparkassenverlag, 1975. 151 pp.
4360. Kalkmann, Philipp. Die Entwertung der österreichischen Valuta im Jahre 1893 und ihre Ursachen. Freiburg i. B: J. C. B. Mohr, 1899. 73 pp.
4361. Keller, Arnold. Die Abstempelungen der österreichisch-ungarischen Banknoten 1918-1920. Berlin: A. Keller, 1962. 143 pp.
4362. Kleinwächter, Friedrich. Die Entwicklung des Geld- und Währungswesens in Oesterreich-Ungarn unter der Regierung des Kaisers Franz Joseph I. Czernowitz: University of Czernowitz, 1896. 58 pp.
4363. Komlos, John, Jr. "Discrimination in the Austrian Capital Market?" Explorations in Economic History 17 (1980), 431-33.
4364. Kramár, Karel. Das Papiergeld in Österreich seit 1848. Leipzig: Duncker & Humblot, 1886. 122 pp.
4365. Leiter, Friedrich. Die Entwicklungstendenz des österreichischen Staatshaushaltes. Vienna: Dorn, 1909. 63 pp.
4366. Leonhardt, Gustav. Die Verwaltung der Oesterreichisch-Ungarischen Bank 1878-1885. Vienna: A. Hölder, 1886. 315 pp.
4367. März, Eduard. "Die Entwicklung des Bankwesens in den letzten Jahrzehnten der Österreich-Ungarischen Monarchie." in Die Frage des Finanzkapitals in der Österreichisch-Ungarischen Monarchie 1900-1918. Mitteilungen auf der Konferenz der Geschichtswissenschaftler. Bucharest: Academy of the Socialist Republic of Rumania, 1965. pp. 67-85.
4368. März, Eduard. Oesterreichische Bankpolitik in der Zeit der grossen Wende 1913-1923: am Beispiel der Creditanstalt für Handel und Gewerbe. Munich: Oldenbourg, 1981. 608 pp.
4369. Mayer, Karl von. Die Münzreform in Oesterreich. Vienna: J. Ludwig, 1856. 38 pp.
4370. Mikoletzky, Hanns L. "Schweizer Händler und Bankiers in Österreich (vom 17. bis zur Mitte des 19. Jahrhunderts)." in Österreich und Europa. Festgabe für Hugo Hantsch. Zum 70. Geburtstag. Graz: Styria, 1965. pp. 149-81.
4371. Mises, Ludwig von. "The Foreign Exchange Policy of the Austro-Hungarian Bank." Economic Journal 19 (1909), 201-11.
4372. Müller, Stefan. Die finanzielle Mobilmachung Österreichs und ihr Ausbau bis 1918. Berlin: L. Weiss, 1918. 175 pp.
4373. Petrisch, L. "The Fiscal Question and the Experience of the Austro-Hungarian Empire." Economic Journal 14 (1904), 24-28.
4374. Probszt, Günther. Österreichische Münz- und Geldgeschichte. Von den Anfängen bis 1918. 2nd ed. Vienna: Böhlau, 1983. 684 pp.
4375. Probszt, Günther. Quellenkunde der Münz- und Geldgeschichte der ehemaligen österreichisch-ungarischen Monarchie. Graz: Akademische Druck- und Verlags-Anstalt, 1954. 134 pp.
4376. Püregger, J. "50 Jahre Staatsschuld 1862-1912. Wien 1912; Die Entwicklung der österreichischen Staatsschuld seit Beginn der Verfassung." Jahrbuch der Gesellschaft österreichischer Volkswirte (1912).
4377. Reinitz, Max. Das österreichische Staatsschuldenwesen von seinen Anfängen bis zur Jetztzeit. Munich: Duncker & Humblot, 1913. 182 pp.
4378. Rudolph, Richard L. "Austria, 1800-1914." in R. E. Cameron, ed. Banking and Economic Development. Some Lessons of History. New York: Oxford University Press, 1972. pp. 26-57.
4379. Rumpler, Helmut. "Der Kampf um die Kontrolle der österreichischen Staatsfinanzen 1859/60." in G. Ritter, ed. Gesellschaft, Parlament und Regierung. Zur Geschichte des Parlamentarismus in Deutschland. Düsseldorf: Droste, 1974. pp. 165-88.
4380. Schlesinger, Karl. "The Disintegration of the Austro-Hungarian Currency." Economic Journal 30 (1920), 26-38.
4381. Schreder, Evelyne. "Die Steuerverfassung Österreichs im 18. und 19. Jahrhundert." Institut für Volkswirtschaftslehre und Weltwirtschaftslehre an der Hochschule für Welthandel in Wien (1959), 22-31.

4382. Schwabe von Waisenfreund, Carl. Versuch einer Geschichte des österreichischen Staats-. Credits- und Schuldwesens. 2 vols. Vienna: Gerold, 1860-66.
4383. Schwarzer, Ernst von. Geld und Gut in Neu-Oesterreich. Vienna: Wallishausser, 1857. 208 pp.
4384. Sieghart, Rudolf. "Das österreichische Budget in den letzten 30 Jahren." Finanzarchiv 19 (1902), 173-82.
4385. Sieghart, Rudolf. "The Reform of Direct Taxation in Austria." Economic Journal 8 (1898), 173-82.
4386. Steefel, L. D. "The Rothschilds and the Austrian Loan of 1865." Journal of Modern History 8 (1936), 27-39.
4387. Stein, Lorenz J. von. Die neue Gestaltung der Geld- und Credit-Verhältnisse in Österreich. Vienna: W. Braumüller, 1855. 54 pp.
4388. Steiner, Fritz G. Die Entwicklung des Mobilbankwesens in Oesterreich. Von den Anfängen bis zur Krise von 1873. Vienna: Konegen, 1913. 271 pp.
4389. Tebeldi, Albrecht. Die Geldangelegenheiten Oesterreichs. Leipzig: Barth, 1847. 393 pp.
4390. Winkler, Wilhelm. Die Einkommensverschiebungen in Österreich während des Weltkrieges. Vienna: Hölder-Pichler-Tempsky, 1930. 278 pp.
4391. Wysocki, Josef. "Einige Verteilungsprobleme des österreichiscen Staatshaushalts von 1870 bis 1900." in F. Blaich, ed. Staatliche Umverteilungspolitik in historischer Perspektive. Berlin: Duncker & Humblot, 1980. pp. 225-50.
4392. Wysocki, Josef. Infrastruktur und wachsende Staatsausgaben. Das Fallbeispiel Österreich 1868-1913. Stuttgart: G. Fischer, 1975. 257 pp.
4393. Wysocki, Josef. "Die österreichische Finanzpolitik." in A. Wandruszka and P. Urbanitsch, eds. Die Habsburgermonarchie 1848-1918. Vienna: Austrian Academy of Sciences, 1973. I, 68-104.
4394. Yeager, Leland B. "Fluctuating Exchange Rates in the Nineteenth Century. The Experience of Austria and Russia." in R. A. Mundell and A. K. Swoboda, eds. Monetary Problems of the International Economy. Chicago: University of Chicago Press, 1969.

SEE ALSO: 1464, 2083, 2096, 4238, 4241, 4253, 4258.

AUSTRIA--1919-1975

4395. Berger, Peter-Robert. Der Donauraum im wirtschaftlichen Umbruch nach dem Ersten Weltkrieg: Währung und Finanzen in den Nachfolgestaaten Österreich, Ungarn und Tschechoslowakei 1918-1929. Diss. Vienna University of Economics, 1979. 2 vols. Vienna: VWGÖ, 1982.
4396. Decoudu, Jean. Le partage des dettes publiques autrichiennes et hongroises. 1918-1926. Paris: Société anonyme de publications périodiques, 1926. 159 pp.
4397. Fibich, Alexander. Die Entwicklung der österreichischen Bundesausgaben in der Ersten Republik 1919-1938. Diss. Vienna, 1977. 214 pp.
4398. Fritz, Hedwig. "Neue Wege der Unternehmensforschung am Beispiel des österreichischen Sparkassenwesens." Tradition 16 (1971), 123-39.
4399. Grebler, Leo and Wilhelm Winkler. The Cost of the War to Germany and Austria-Hungary. New Haven, CT: Yale University Press, 1940. 192 pp.
4400. Kinnen, René J. B. Die Entwicklung der Banken in Österreich von 1919 bis 1929. Diss. Vienna University of Economics, 1979. 128 pp.
4401. League of Nations. The Financial Reconstruction of Austria. 42 vols. Geneva: League of Nations, 1923-1926.
4402. Melas, Reinhold. "Die österreichische Sozialversicherung seit 1945." Soziale Sicherheit 4 (1951), 222-29.
4403. Pressburger, Fritz G. "Die Krise der österreichischen Creditanstalt." Revue Internationale d'Histoire de la Banque 2 (1969), 83-118.
4404. Reisch, Richard. "Aufgaben und Entwicklung der Oesterreichischen Nationalbank in den Jahren 1923 bis 1928." in W. Exner, ed. 10 Jahre Wiederaufbau. Vienna: Wirtschaftszeitungs-Verlag, 1928.
4405. Scharnagl, Johann. "Die Entwicklung des Sozialversicherungsrechts in Österreich seit 1945." Die Öffentliche Fürsorge (1950), 1-33.
4406. Schwarz, Robert. L'Autriche de 1919-1924. Aperçu économique et financier. Diss. Paris. Paris: A. Pédone, 1925. 149 pp.

4407. Smekal, Christian. "Die Entwicklung der Sozialversicherung in Österreich 1955-1979." Das Öffentliche Haushaltswesen in Österreich 22 (1981), 190-206.
4408. Walch, Dietmar. Die jüdischen Bemühungen um die materielle Wiedergutmachung durch die Republik Österreich. Diss. Salzburg, 1969. Vienna: Geyer, 1969. 233 pp.

AUSTRIAN AND AUSTRO-HUNGARIAN REGIONS

Bohemia and Moravia

4409. Pryor, Zora P. "Czechoslovak Fiscal Policies in the Great Depression." Economic History Review 32 (1979), 228-40.
4410. Rasína, Aloise. Les finances de la Tchécoslovaquie jusqu'à la fin de 1921. Paris: Bossard, 1923. 237 pp.
4411. Rasína, Aloise. Financial Policy of Czechoslovakia during the First Year of its History. London: Clarendon, 1923. 160 pp.
4412. Rudolph, Richard L. Banking and Industrialization in Austria-Hungary. The Role of Banks in the Industrialization of the Czech Crownlands. 1873-1914. Cambridge: Cambridge University Press, 1976. 291 pp.
4413. Rudolph, Richard L. The Role of Financial Institutions in the Industrialization of the Czech Crownlands 1880-1914. Diss. Wisconsin, 1968. 552 pp.

SEE ALSO: 4395.

Burgenland

4414. Streeruwitz, Ernst. "Die burgenländische Landes-Hypothekenanstalt." in 10 Jahre Burgenland. ...1921-1931. Vienna: Amt der burgenländischen Landesregierung, 1931.

Carinthia

4415. Trende, Adolf. "Zur Geschichte der Sparkassen Kärntens." Carinthia 153 (1963), 676-702.

Hungary

4416. Deutsch, Anton. 25 Jahre ungarischer Finanz- und Volkswirtschaft (1867-1892). Berlin: Puttkammer & Mühlbrecht, 1892. 95 pp.
4417. Ecker, Lowell L. "The Hungarian Thrift Crown." American Economic Review 23 (1933), 471-74.

SEE ALSO: 457, 4395.

Lower Austria

4418. Kühnel, Harry. 125 Jahre Sparkasse in Krems. Krems: Sparkasse in Krems, 1981. 80 pp.

Rumania

4419. Baicoianu, Constantin J. La Banque nationale de Roumanie pendant l'occupation. novembre 1916--novembre 1918. Paris: Sirey, 1921. 163 pp.
4420. Mann, Fritz K. "Das Geldproblem in der rumänischen Besatzungswirtschaft." Weltwirtschaftliches Archiv 14 (1919), 1-30.

SEE ALSO: 4231.

Salzburg

4421. Landauer, Robert. Geld im alten Salzburg. Salzburg: Kiesel, 1940. 21 pp.

SEE ALSO: 4429.

Styria

4422. Fritsch, Wilhelm von. "Die Entwicklung des Geld- und Münzwesens in der Steiermark." in B. Sutter, ed. Die Steiermark. Graz: Imago, 1971. pp. 862-66.

Tirol

4423. Fischer, August. Dreimal Raiffeisen in Tirol. Inzing: F. August, 1969. 47 pp.
4424. Huter, Franz. Geschichte der Sparkasse der Stadt Innsbruck. Das erste heimische Geldinstitut Tirols im Spiegel der politischen und wirtschaftlichen Entwicklung. 1822-1958. Innsbruck: Wagner, 1962. 359 pp.
4425. Martin, Manfred. Das Bankwesen in Tirol bis 1945. Innsbruck: Wagner, 1970. 171 pp.
4426. Schlegel, Herbert. Die Tiroler Landes-Hypothekenanstalt. Innsbruck: Wagner, 1966. 144 pp.

Transylvania

4427. Deutsch, E. et al. "Über die Vorherrschaft des Finanzkapitals in Transsilvanien in den ersten Jahrzehnten des 20. Jahrhunderts." in Die Frage des Finanzkapitals in der Österreichisch-Ungarischen Monarchie 1900-1918. Bucharest: Academy of the Socialist Republic of Rumania, 1965. pp. 53-65
4428. Steiner, Edgar. Die Finanzen der Selbstverwaltungskörper Siebenbürgens einst und jetzt. Diss. Erlangen, 1933. 101 pp.

Upper Austria

4429. Pröschl, S. Entwicklungsgeschichte und Bedeutung einer Kommerzbank als Beitrag zur Wirtschafts- und Finanzgeschichte des oberösterreichischen und salzburg. Raumes. Diss. Linz, 1972.

Vienna

4430. Baltzarek, Franz. "Finanzplatz Wien. Die innerstaatliche und internationale Stellung in historischer Perspektive." Girozentrale und Bank der Österreichischen Sparkassen Aktiengesellschaft 15 (1980), 11-63.
4431. Baltzarek, Franz. Die Geschichte der Wiener Börse. Vienna: Kommission für Wirtschafts-, Sozial- und Stadtgeschichte, 1973. 173 pp.
4432. Bidermann, Ignaz. "Die Wiener Stadt-Bank. Ihre Entstehung, ihre Einteilung und Wirksamkeit, ihre Schicksale." Archiv für Kunde österreichischer Geschichtsquellen 20 (1958), 341-446.
4433. Morawitz, Karl. 50 Jahre Geschichte einer Wiener Bank. Vienna: J. N. Vernay, 1913. 78 pp.
4434. Morgenstern, Oskar. "Kapital- und Kursveränderungen der an der Wiener Börse notierten österreichischen Aktiengesellschaften 1913-1930." Zeitschrift für Nationalökonomie (1932), 251-55.
4435. Schalk, Karl. Wiens Geldwesen seit Ottokar (als König von Böhmen II.) 1251 bis zur Einführung der Kronenwährung 1892. Vienna: s. n., 1894. 95 pp.

SWITZERLAND

Bibliographic Reference

4436. "Schweizerische Bibliographie über das Bank- und Kreditwesen (1893 bis 1951)." in In der
Schweiz veröffentlichte Arbeiten über ausländische Banken." Zurich: Schweizerische Nationalbank, 1951. 202 pp.

SWITZERLAND

4437. Allizé, Fabrice. L'organisation des banques en Suisse. Paris: Payot, 1923. 250 pp.
4438. Ammann, J. "Rückblick auf sieben Jahrzehnte schweizerischer Goldpolitik." Wirtschaft und
Recht 30 (1978), 54-66.
4439. Bär, Hans J. The Banking System of Switzerland. 3rd ed. Zurich: Schulthess, 1964. 84 pp.
4440. Banken und Bankgeschäfte in der Schweiz. Bern: Haupt, 1969. 428 pp.
4441. Baschy, René. Börsengeschichtliche Betrachtungen. Zurich: Lienberger, 1952. 28 pp.
4442. Bauer, Hans. Schweizerischer Bankverein 1872-1972. Basel: Schweizerischer Bankverein,
1972. 555 pp.
4443. Beuret, Henry. Studien über die Entwicklung und die Bedeutung der schweizerischen Bank-
publizistik. Weinfelden: Neuenschwander, 1942. 216 pp.
4444. Beuttner, Paul. Die Finanzgebarung der Genossenschaften, mit besonderer Berücksichtigung
der schweizerischen Bank- und Konsumgenossenschaften. Diss. Geneva, 1925. 398 pp.
4445. Bickel, Wilhelm. "Die öffentlichen Finanzen." Schweizerische Zeitschrift für Volkswirtschaft
und Statistik 100 (1964), 273-301.
4446. Bodmer, Max E. Zur Tätigkeit und Stellung der Privatbankiers in der Schweiz. Zurich: Schulthess, 1934. 119 pp.
4447. Bohren, Arnold. "Das Werden unserer Sozialversicherung." in G. Bernasconi, ed. Die Schweiz
der Arbeit, 1848-1948. La Suisse du travail. Zurich: Schweizerischer Gewerkschaftsbund,
1948. pp. 63-76.
4448. Brestel, Heinz et al. Ein Konto in der Schweiz. Niederglatt: Heidelberger, 1976. 277 pp.
4449. Coraggioni, Leodegar. Münzgeschichte der Schweiz. Geneva, 1896; rpt. Bologna: Forni, 1896.
196 pp.
4450. Essars, Pierre des. "Banking in Switzerland." in A History of Banking in All the Leading
Nations. New York: Journal of Commerce and Commercial Bulletin; rpt. New York: A. M. Kelly,
1971. III, 287-305.
4451. Fehrenbach, Theodore R. The Gnomes of Zurich. London: Frewin, 1974. 303 pp.
4452. Grüebler, Christoph. Die Geldmenge der Schweiz 1907-1954. Zurich: Polygraphischer Verlag,
1958. 134 pp.
4453. Hagenbach, Paul. Die Entwicklung zur Goldwährung in der Schweiz. Weinfelden: Neuenschwander, 1929. 137 pp.
4454. Handbuch der Aktiengesellschaften und Geldinstitute der Schweiz. Zurich: O. Füssli, 1896.
581 pp.
4455. Hartmann, Alfred. Der Konkurrenzkampf zwischen den schweizerischen Grossbanken und
Kantonalbanken. Diss. Zurich. Zurich: Kommerzdruck, 1947. 239 pp.
4456. Heizmann-Hauser, Fritz. Banken und Konjunktur mit besonderer Berücksichtigung der schweizerischen Volkswirtschaft. St. Gallen: F. Heizmann-Hauser, 1931. 93 pp.
4457. Herold, Hans. "Voraussetzungen und Ursprünge der Sozialversicherung." Schweizerische
Zeitschrift für Sozialversicherung 9 (1965), 98-126.
4458. Iklé, Max. Die Schweiz als internationaler Bank- und Finanzplatz. Zurich: O. Füssli, 1970.
187 pp.
4459. Jöhr, Walter A. Schweizerische Kreditanstalt, 1856-1956. 100 Jahre im Dienste der
schweizerischen Volkswirtschaft. Zurich: O. Füssli, 1956. 564 pp.
4460. Jöhr, Walter A. Die schweizerischen Grossbanken und Privatbankiers. Zurich: Polygraphischer Verlag, 1940. 91 pp.
4461. Kleinewefers, Henner. Das Auslandsgeschäft der Schweizer Banken. Zurich: Schulthess,
1972. 247 pp.

4462. Knüsel, René and Félix Zurita. Assurances sociales, une sécurité pour qui? La Loi Forrer et les origines de l'état social en Suisse. Lausanne: Institut de science politique, 1979. 396 pp.
4463. Kurz, Hermann and Glieb Bachmann. Die schweizerischen Grossbanken. Zurich: O. Füssli, 1928. 324 pp.
4464. Linder, Albert. Die schweizerischen Grossbanken. Bern: Stämpfli, 1927. 242 pp.
4465. Matter, Albert. Denkschrift zum 50-jährigen Jubiläum des Verbandes Schweizerischer Kantonalbanken, 1907-1957. Basel: Verband Schweizerischer Kantonalbanken, 1957. 250 pp.
4466. Meier, Paul. Der Währungswirrwarr von der Helvetik bis zur Bundesverfassung. Diss. Bern. Bern: Arnaud, 1951. 148 pp.
4467. Oechslin, Hanspeter. Die Entwicklung des Bundessteuersystems der Schweiz von 1848 bis 1966. Diss. Fribourg. Einsiedeln: Etzel-Druck, 1967. 240 pp.
4468. Petrzilka, Willy. Die Wirkungen des Kriegsausbruchs auf das Geld- und Kreditwesen in der Schweiz 1914 und 1939/40. Diss. Zurich. Zurich: Lang, 1943. 123 pp.
4469. Püntener, August. Das schweizerische Bankwesen: Geschichte und Struktur. Bern: Haupt, 1977. 72 pp.
4470. Ritzmann, Franz. "Die Entwicklung des schweizerischen Geld- und Kreditsystems." SZVS 100 (1964), 235-72.
4471. Ritzmann, Franz. Die Schweizer Banken. Geschichte. Theorie. Statistik. Bern: Haupt, 1973. 387 pp.
4472. Rosen, Josef. "L'arbre généalogique de nos monnaies." Revue Internationale d'Histoire de la Banque, 17 (1978), 157-71.
4473. Schelhammer, Carlo. Die Banken in der Schweiz. Zurich: Zürcher Kantonalbank, 1981. 92 pp.
4474. Schmid, Werner. Die Geschichte des Schweizer Frankens. 2nd ed. Bern: Verlag Evolution, 1969. 191 pp.
4475. Schwarz, Fritz. 50 Jahre Schweizerische Nationalbank. Bern: Liberalsozialistische Partei, 1957. 32 pp.
4476. Schweizer Verband der Raiffeisenkassen. 75 Jahre Raiffeisen. Festschrift zum 75-jährigen Bestehen des Schweizer Verbandes der Raiffeisenkassen. St. Gallen: Schweizer Verband der Raiffeisenkassen, 1977. 140 pp.
4477. Schweizerische Nationalbank 1907-1957. Zurich: Nationalbank, 1957.
4478. Soldan, Bernhard. Die Entwicklung des Hartgeldes während der letzten hundert Jahre 1850-1949, unter besonderer Berücksichtigung der Schweiz, ihrer Nachbarländer, Englands und der Vereinigten Staaten von Nordamerika. Diss. Bern. Bern: Polygraphische Gesellschaft, 1953. 181 pp.
4479. Stauffer, Peter and Urs Emch. Das schweizerische Bankgeschäft. Thun: Ott, 1972. 494 pp.
4480. Tschudi, Hans P. "25 Jahre Ausgleichskassen. Zur Geschichte der schweizerischen Sozialversicherung." Schweizerische Zeitschrift für Sozialversicherung, 9 (1965), 89-97.
4481. Ungerer, Martin. Finanzplatz Schweiz. Seine Geschichte, Bedeutung und Zukunft. Vienna: Econ Verlag, 1979. 184 pp.
4482. Vicker, Ray. Those Swiss Money Men. New York: Scribner, 1973. 340 pp.
4483. Waller, Leslie. The Swiss Bank Connection. New York: New American Library, 1972. 192 pp.
4484. Weber, Max. Geschichte der schweizerischen Bundesfinanzen. Bern: Haupt, 1969. 55 pp.
4485. Weissenrieder, Franz X. 100 Jahre schweizerisches Münzwesen, 1850-1950. Ein Querschnitt durch ein Jahrhundert eidgenössischer Münzgeschichte und Währungspolitik. St. Gallen: Thur, 1950. 101 pp.
4486. Weisskopf, Erich. Das schweizerische Münzwesen von seinen Anfängen bis zur Gegenwart. Diss. Bern. Bern: Werder, 1948. 224 pp.
4487. Wenzel, Edmond. Die deutschen Stillhalteabkommen und ihre Auswirkungen auf die schweizerischen Banken. Diss. Geneva. Bern: Büchler, 1940. 189 pp.
4488. Winter, André. Die Entwicklung der Finanzplanung des Bundes. Diessenhofen: Rüegger, 1978. 194 pp.
4489. Wittmann, Walter. Die Finanzgesinnung des Bundes im Lichte der parlamentarischen Beratungen: von der Weltwirtschaftskrise bis zur Gegenwart. Zurich: Polygraphischer Verlag, 1969. 115 pp.
4490. Woernle, Günter. Die Privatbankiers in der Schweiz. Bastion der Vermögensverwaltung. Geneva: Wernlinia, 1978. 143 pp.
4491. Yaux, Francis. L'évolution de la banque commerciale dans le cadre du système bancaire suisse. Lausanne: Impr. Réunies, 1949. 231 pp.

SWITZERLAND--1815-1918

4492. Blaum, Kurt. Das Geldwesen der Schweiz seit 1798. Strassburg: Trübner, 1908. 176 pp.
4493. Burckhardt, Carl F. W. Zur Geschichte der Privatbankiers in der Schweiz. Diss. Zurich. Zurich: O. Füssli, 1914. 110 pp.
4494. Burckhardt Bischoff, Adolf. "Das schweizerische Münzwesen und der Pariser Münzvertrag vom 5. 11. 1878." Jahrbücher für Nationalökonomie und Statistik 32 (1879), 371-409.
4495. Godet, Marcel. Das Problem der Zentralisation des schweizerischen Banknotenwesens. Leipzig: Duncker & Humblot, 1902. 86 pp.
4496. Greulich, Karl-Hans. Die Verlagerung der Aufgaben und finanziellen Lasten von den Kantonen auf den Bund in der Zeit von 1848 bis 1912. Diss. Bern, 1965. Zurich: Keller, 1966. 94 pp.
4497. Haegglund, John. Statsfinanserna i Danmark, Norge, Holland och Schweiz under Krigsåren 1914-1918. Stockholm: A.B. Nordiska Bokhandel, 1918. 92 pp.
4498. Huber, Samuel. Die schweizerischen Gemeindebanken. Diss. Zurich. Elberfeld: Köhler, 1920. 110 pp.
4499. Just, Robert. Die Geldinflation mit besonderer Berücksichtigung der Geldpolitik der Schweiz während des Weltkrieges. Jena: G. Fischer, 1921. 114 pp.
4500. Kurz, Hermann. Die Grossbanken im schweizerischen Wirtschaftsleben. Zurich: O. Füssli, 1922. 324 pp.
4501. Landmann, Julius. The Swiss Banking Law. Study and Criticism of the Swiss Legislation Respecting Banks of Issue, and especially of the Federal Act of Oct. 6, 1905, Concerning the Swiss National Bank. Washington, D. C.: National Monetary Commission, 1910. 269 pp.
4502. Luterbacher, Walter. Zur Krise des Schweizer Hypothekar-Kredites während des Krieges und in der Übergangszeit. Zurich: O. Füssli, 1922. 151 pp.
4503. Perrelet, Bernard. La Banque nationale suisse. Essai historique et juridique. Diss. Geneva. Geneva: Chaulmontet, 1907. 192 pp.
4504. Pfau, J. J. Das Bankwesen der Schweiz und des Auslandes. Zurich: O. Füssli, 1875. 78 pp.
4505. Pfister, Bruno. Beiträge zur Entwicklung der schweizerischen Klein- und Mittelbanken. Diss. Zurich. Zurich: O. Füssli, 1916. 182 pp.
4506. Plucer-Sarna, Nussen. Die Konzentration im schweizer Bankwesen. Zurich: Speidel & Wurzel, 1911. 207 pp.
4507. Roeder, Adolf. Die Entwickelung des schweizerischen Notenbankwesens unter näherer Berücksichtigung der Epoche 1881-1906. Diss. Erlangen. Meiningen: Keysener, 1906. 90 pp.
4508. Schanz, Georg. Die Steuern der Schweiz in ihrer Entwicklung seit Beginn des 19. Jahrhunderts. 5 vols. Stuttgart: Cotta, 1890.
4509. Schlesinger, William. Das Geldproblem in der öffentlichen Meinung der Schweiz, 1803-1850. St. Gallen: Fehr, 1936. 135 pp.
4510. Schüepp, J. Neue Beiträge zur Schweizerischen Münz- und Währungsgeschichte 1850-1918. Frauenfeld: Huber, 1919. 82 pp.
4511. Schwarz, Jutta. Bruttoanlageinvestitionen in der Schweiz von 1850 bis 1914. Eine empirische Untersuchung zur Kapitalbildung. Diss. Bern. Bern: Haupt, 1981. 487 pp.
4512. Das schweizerische Bankwesen in den Jahren 1906/13, 1914/15, 1917, 1918, 1919. 5 vols. Bern: Schweizerische Nationalbank, 1915-1921.
4513. Siegenthaler, Hansjörg. "Kapitalbildung und sozialer Wandel in der Schweiz 1850 bis 1914." Jahrbücher für Nationalökonomie und Statistik 193 (1978), 1-29.
4514. Über Banken und deren Anwendung in der Schweiz. Zurich: O. Füssli, 1835.
4515. Über die Einführung von Banken in der Schweiz. Zurich: O. Füssli, 1836.
4516. Wegener, Eduard. Die schweizerischen Bodenkreditinstitute 1846-1912. Diss. Basel, 1926. Munich: Duncker & Humblot, 1925. 316 pp.
4517. Wetter, Ernst. Bankkrisen und Bankkatastrophen der letzten Jahre in der Schweiz. Zurich: O. Füssli, 1918. 331 pp.
4518. Wetter, Ernst. Die Lokal- und Mittelbanken der Schweiz. Zurich: O. Füssli, 1914. 114 pp.

SEE ALSO: 4253-54.

SWITZERLAND 1919-1975

4519. Aeppli, Roland et al. Schweizerische Nationalbank. 75 Jahre Schweizerische Nationalbank: die Zeit von 1957 bis 1982. Zurich: Neue Zürcher Zeitung, 1982. 538 pp.

4520. Andermatt, Richard. Restriktive Kreditpolitik als Mittel zur Wirtschaftsstabilisierung. Unter besonderer Berücksichtigung der schweizerischen Verhältnisse 1950-1958. Diss. Fribourg. Winterthur: Keller, 1962. 133 pp.

4521. Bachmann, Glieb. "The Return to the Gold Standard in Switzerland." American Economic Review 19 (1929), 198-205.

4522. Baer, Ulrich. Der Kapitalverkehr in der schweizerischen Zahlungsbilanz von 1957-1964. Diss. Basel. Zurich: Polygraphischer Verlag, 1967. 106 pp.

4523. Bodmer, Daniel. L'intervention de la Confédération dans l'économie bancaire suisse (notamment durant la période de 1929 à 1936. Diss. Geneva. Basel: National-Zeitung, 1948. 219 pp.

4524. Bouvier, Jean. Histoire économique et histoire sociale. Recherches sur le capitalisme contemporain. Geneva: Droz, 1968. 281 pp.

4525. Burkhalter, Jakob. Der schweizerische Effektenmarkt 1922-32. Diss. Zurich. Affoltern am Albis: J. Weiss, 1938. 95 pp.

4526. Cruchon, Amédée. Le franc suisse pendant et après la guerre. 1914-1930. Diss. Lausanne. Lausanne: Payot, 1932. 241 pp.

4527. Duft, Emil O. Der schweizerische Geld- und Kapitalmarkt und die Wirtschaftskrise 1920-21. Diss. Zurich. Affoltern am Albis: J. Weiss, 1931. 137 pp.

4528. Durrer, Marco. Die schweizerisch-amerikanischen Finanzbeziehungen im Zweiten Weltkrieg. Diss. Geneva. Bern: Haupt, 1984. 348 pp.

4529. Erb, Rudolf. Die Stellungnahme der schweizerischen Grossbanken zu den bank- und währungs- politischen Problemen der Kriegs- und Nachkriegszeit. Diss. Zurich. Zurich: Leemann, 1931. 155 pp.

4530. Göttisheim, Ernst. Der Einfluss der Wirtschaftskonjunktur auf den schweizerischen Bundes- haushalt in den Jahren 1924-1933. Diss. Basel. Cologne: K. Schroeder, 1925. 112 pp.

4531. Grimm, Robert. Zur Wirtschafts- und Kreditkrise der Schweiz. (Deflation und Abwertung). Bern: Sozialdemokratische Partei des Kantons Bern, 1936. 60 pp.

4532. Gygax, Paul. "Schweizerische Kreditprobleme, 1930-1948." in Probleme der öffentlichen Finanzen. Festgabe für Eugen Grossmann. Zurich: Polygraphischer Verlag, 1949. pp. 242-57.

4533. Hagenbach, Paul. Die Entwicklung zur Goldwährung in der Schweiz. Weinfelden: Neuen- schwander, 1929. 137 pp.

4534. Heeb, Walter. Die Geldvermehrung in der Schweiz. 1938-1950. Eine Analyse an Hand der Ausweise und Bilanzen der Notenbank und der Kreditbanken. Diss. Basel. Grosshöchstetten: Buchdruck Jakob, 1956. 151 pp.

4535. Hess, Mario W. Strukturwandlungen im schweizerischen Bankwesen von der Schaffung des Bankengesetzes (1935) bis 1958. Diss. Bern. Winterthur: P. G. Keller, 1963. 124 pp.

4536. Hurni, Walter. Entwicklung, Gestaltung und Auswirkungen des gebundenen Zahlungsverkehrs in der schweizerischen Volkswirtschaft in den Jahren 1945 bis 1955. Diss. Fribourg, 1960. 92 pp.

4537. Hurst, Willard. "Holland, Switzerland and Belgium and the English Gold Crisis of 1932." Journal of Political Economy 40 (1932), 638-60.

4538. Jaberg, Paul. Die schweizerischen Banken in der Wirtschaftskrise. Bern: Schweizerische Bankgesellschaft, 1934. 23 pp.

4539. Kellenberger, Eduard. "Die schweizerische Münzpolitik im Kriege." in Geld- und Kredit- system der Schweiz: Festgabe für Gottlieb Bachmann. 2nd ed. Zurich: Schulthess, 1944. pp. 159-76.

4540. Kellenberger, Eduard. Theorie und Praxis des schweizerischen Geld-, Bank-, und Börsen- wesens seit Ausbruch des Weltkrieges (1914-1930). 4 vols. Bern: A. Francke, 1930-42.

4541. Künzle, Robert. Hochkonjunktur und Stabilisierung der Kaufkraft des Schweizerfrankens. 1954-1957. Winterthur: Keller, 1965. 151 pp.

4542. Lehmann, Ernst. Das Sparkassenwesen der Schweiz seit Ausbruch des Weltkrieges. Bern: P. Haupt, 1926. 96 pp.

4543. Pestalozzi, Antonio. Die Frage der Liquidität unter besonderer Berücksichtigung der schweize- rischen Banken. 1935-40. Zurich: Schulthess, 1943. 145 pp.

4544. Reinger, Edwin. Der flukturierende Wechselkurs des Schweizerfrankens von 1914-1924. Winterthur: Keller, 1957. 123 pp.
4545. Die Rentabilitätsverhältnisse der Schweizer Grossbanken im Laufe der vier Kriegsjahre. Zurich: City-Druck, 1943.
4546. Schenkel, Fritz. Der Einfluss der Wirtschaftskrise 1930-36 auf den Finanzhaushalt der Schweiz und die Folgen und Perspektiven für das Verhältnis von Fiskus und Wirtschaft. Weinfelden: Neuenschwander, 1940. 87 pp.
4547. Scherrer, Hans R. Die Steuerpolitik des Bundes während der Wirtschaftsdepression der dreissiger Jahre (1930-38). Diss. Zurich. Zurich: Juris, 1949. 159 pp.
4548. Schneider, Ernst. Die schweizerischen Grossbanken im zweiten Weltkrieg 1939-1945. Diss. Zurich. Zurich: Brunner & Bodmer, 1951. 293 pp.
4549. Schweizerische Nationalbank. 75 Jahre Schweizerische Nationalbank: die Zeit von 1957 bis 1982. Zurich: Schweizerische Nationalbank, 1982. 538 pp.
4550. Specker, Max. Die Konzentrationsbewegung im schweizerischen Bankgewerbe in den Jahren 1918-1938. Diss. Bern, 1948. 707 pp.
4551. Stucki, Walter. Die schweizerischen Effektenbörsen während und nach dem Weltkrieg 1914-1921. Zurich: Rascher, 1924. 165 pp.
4552. Tschudi, Hans P. "Die Entwicklung der schweizerischen Sozialversicherung seit dem Zweiten Weltkrieg." SZVS 112 (1976), 311-28.
4553. Urech, Willy. Die staatliche Beaufsichtigung der Banken in der Schweiz nach dem Bundesgesetz über die Banken und Sparkassen vom 8. Nov. 1934. Diss Zurich, 1944. 111 pp.
4554. Vontobel, Hans. Dreissig Jahre Börsenberichte: '49-'79. Zurich: Neue Zürcher Zeitung, 1980. 281 pp.
4555. Wagner, Antonin. "Die Auswirkung der öffentlichen Haushalte auf den Konjunkturverlauf in der Schweiz, 1955-1970." SZVS 109 (1973), 17-57.
4556. Wegmann, Jakob. Die Genossenschaft als Bankbetriebsform unter Zugrundlegung der genossenschaftlichen Kreditinstitute der Schweiz. Diss. Zurich. Zurich: Langen, 1921. 140 pp.

SWISS CANTONS

Aargau

4557. Bieri, Markus. Geschichte der aargauischen Steuern von 1803-1968, insbesondere der direkten Staatssteuer. Aarau: Keller, 1972. 388 pp.
4558. Obrist, Karl. 50 Jahre Verband aargauischer Lokalbanken und Sparkassen 1913-1963. Entstehung und Entwicklung des aargauischen Bankwesens 1812-1962. Baden: Verband aargauischer Lokalbanken und Sparkassen, 1963. 76 pp.
4559. Roesle, Alphonse E. Das Münzrecht im Kanton Aargau. Beitrag zur Geschichte des schweizerischen Münzrechtes. Schwarzenburg: Gerber, 1946. 127 pp.

SEE ALSO: 581.

Appenzell

4560. Alder, Hans. Appenzell-Ausserrhodische Kantonalbank. Die geschichtliche Entwicklung. Herisau: Appenzell-Ausserrhodische Kantonalbank, 1977. 182 pp.
4561. Senn, Niklaus. Denkschrift zum 50jährigen Jubiläum der Appenzell-Innerrhodischen Kantonalbank. Appenzell: Appenzell-Innerrhodische Kantonalbank, 1950.

Basel

4562. Festschrift zum 50jährigen Jubiläum 1862-1912. Basel: Basler Handelsbank, 1910.
4563. Fischer, Boris. Die Einwirkungen der Wirtschaftskonjunktur auf den Staatshaushalt des Kantons Basel-Stadt in den Jahren 1923-1934. Diss. Basel. Cologne: Schroeder, 1937. 92 pp.

4564. Grieder, Willy. Der Staatshaushalt des Kantons Baselland 1833-1923. Diss. Zurich. Liesthal: Buchdruck zum Landschaftler, 1926. 218 pp.
4565. Kinkelin, Hermann. Geschichte der Handwerkerbank Basel 1860-1910. Basel: s.n., 1910.
4566. Ludwig, Alfred. Die Finanzpolitik der Basler Konservativen von 1833 bis 1914. Diss. Basel. Weinfelden: Neuenschwander, 1946. 246 pp.
4567. Mangold, Friedrich. Die Bank in Basel 1844-1907 und die Entwicklung des Konkordats der schweizerischen Emissionsbanken. Basel: Kreis, 1909. 365 pp.
4568. Renz, Jean. La Bourse des valeurs mobilières à Bâle. Etude historique et économique. Diss. Neuchâtel. Strasbourg: Heitz, 1933. 107 pp.
4569. Scherrer, Werner. Die Basler Kantonalbank. 1899-1949. Denkschrift zum 50jährigen Geschäftsjubiläum. Basel: Basel Kantonbank, 1949. 248 pp.

Bern

4570. Das Bernische Finanzwesen von 1803-1848. Rückblicke und Aussichten. Bern: s.n., 1849.
4571. Burkhard, Erwin et al. 100 Jahre Bank in Langenthal. 1867-1967. Langenthal: Die Bank, 1967. 119 pp.
4572. Egger, Walter. Kantonalbank von Bern. 1834-1934. Bern: Hallwag, 1934. 252 pp.
4573. Geiser, Karl. Die Gründung der Ersparniskasse für den Amtsbezirk Aarwangen im Jahre 1823 und ihre Entwicklung bis 1923. Bern: Büchler, 1923. 372 pp.
4574. Geschichte des bernischen Bankwesens und Entwicklung des Schweizerischen Bankvereins. Bern: Schweizerischer Bankverein, 1960. 31 pp.
4575. Kummer, Fritz. Geschichte des Kreditwesens im Berner Jura. Diss. Bern. Bern: Marti, 1953. 116 pp.
4576. Leuenberger, Paul F. Geschichte der Kantonalbank von Bern. Diss. Zurich. Bern: Horst, 1912. 164 pp.
4577. Reichenau, Willi. Der Finanzhaushalt des Kantons Bern. 1916-1936. Bern: Francke, 1945. 140 pp.
4578. Richli, Julius. Der Zusammenbruch der Diskonto- und Lombardbank A. G. Bern. Ein Beitrag zur Geschichte der Institute des gewerbsmässigen Handels mit Prämienobligationen und des Animierbankwesens der Schweiz. Diss. Bern, 1931. 133 pp.
4579. Schaufelberger, Albert. Die Geschichte des bernischen Bankwesens. Diss. Zurich. Thun: Ott, 1948. 143 pp.
4580. Tavel, Rudolf. Die Deposito-Cassa der Stadt Bern. . .1825-1925. Bern: Büchler, 1925. 114 pp.

Fribourg

4581. Wysocki, Josef. Waisch, wo der Weg zuem gulden isch? Jubiläumsschrift zum 150-jährigen Bestehen der öffentlichen Sparkasse Freiburg. Fribourg: ÖSF, 1976. 240 pp.

Graubünden

4582. Capaul, Duri. Graubündner Kantonalbank. 1930-1970. 40 Jahre im Dienste der Bündner Volkswirtschaft. Chur: Graubündner Kantonalbank, 1974. 252 pp.
4583. Denoth, Caspar. Die bündnerischen Zölle und Gefälle von der Mediation bis zu ihrer Ablösung. Ein Beitrag zur Geschichte der Finanzen des Kantons Graubünden. Diss. Zurich. Lachen: "Gutenberg", 1930. 147 pp.
4584. Gieré, Otto. Der Staatshaushalt des Kantons Graubünden seit der Einführung der direkten Steuern bis heute (1856-1914). Bern: Stämpfli, 1916. 211 pp.
4585. Tscharner, Johann F. von. Die Staatssteuern des Kantons Graubünden in neuer und neuester Zeit (1838-1913). Diss. Munich, 1914. Stuttgart: Union Deutsche Verlagsgesellschaft, 1915. 223 pp.

SEE ALSO: 605.

Lucerne

4586. Blankart, Charles. Bank in Luzern 1856-1906. Lucerne: C. J. Bucher, 1906. 43 pp.
4587. Blum, Fred. Die Luzerner Kantonalbank. 1850-1932. Diss. Bern, 1937. 205 pp.
4588. Brunner, Franz. Die Entwicklung der Landbanken des Kantons Luzern. Arlesheim: Buchdruck Arlesheim, 1949. 81 pp.
4589. Hug, J. F. Zur Frage des Zusammenhangs zwischen Wirtschaftsstruktur und Steuersystem (Dargestellt an der Entwicklung im Kanton Luzern). Diss. Jena. Weinfelden: Neuenschwander, 1934. 103 pp.
4590. Ruckli, Max. Geschichte des Bankwesens im Kanton Luzern. Diss. Bern. Lucerne: Räber, 1939. 156 pp.
4591. Wielandt, Friedrich. Münz- und Geldgeschichte des Standes Luzern. Schweizerischer Bankverein. Lucerne: Bucher, 1969. 176 pp.
4592. Zust-Schmid, Heinrich. Die Luzerner Kantonalbank. 1850-1950. Überblick über ihre Geschichte. Organisation und Entwicklung. Lucerne: Räber, 1950. 232 pp.

St. Gallen

4593. Allenspach, Alex. Die Organisation der Steuerveranlagung und des Steuerbezugs im Kanton St. Gallen. Diss. Zurich. Winterthur: Schellenberg, 1961. 139 pp.
4594. Elser, Alfred. Die St. Gallische Kantonalbank. 1868-1942. Diss. Zurich. Zurich: Meyerhans Erben, 1943. 237 pp.
4595. Gmür, Hans. "Der St.-Gallische Staatshaushalt Anno 1803 und seine Entwicklung in 150 Jahren." Verwaltungs-Praxis 7 (1952/53), 224-31.
4596. Gygax, Paul. Bank in St. Gallen 1837-1907. Die Geschichte einer schweizerischen Notenbank. St. Gallen: Zollikofer & Cie, 1907. 398 pp.
4597. Stampfli, Franz. Die Steuern des Kantons St. Gallen 1890-1922. Diss. Fribourg. Uznach: Oberholzer, 1929. 176 pp.
4598. Walder, Emil. Die Geschichte des Handelsbankwesens in St. Gallen. Beitrag zur praktischen Bankpolitik. St. Gallen: Fehr, 1913. 260 pp.
4599. Walder, Emil. Die Toggenburger Bank. 1863-1912. St. Gallen: Zollikofer, 1914. 136 pp.

Schaffhausen

4600. Böhme, Helmut. "Gründung und Anfänge des Schaffhausenschen Bankvereins, der Bank des Berliner Kassenvereins, der Direktion der Disconto-Gesellschaft und der Darmstädter Bank für Handel und Industrie. Ein Beitrag zur preussischen Bankpolitik von 1848-1853." Tradition 10 (1965), 189-212; 11 (1966), 34-56.
4601. Braumandl, Martin. Zur Geschichte des Bank- und Kreditwesens im Kanton Schaffhausen. Diss. Zurich. Wädenswil: Villiger, 1946. 294 pp.
4602. Fünzig Jahre Schaffhauser Kantonalbank. 1883-1932. Schaffhausen: Schaffhauser Kantonalbank, 1933. 25 pp.

Schwyz

4603. Reichlin, Josef. Denkschrift zum 50jährigen Geschäftsjubiläum der Kantonalbank Schwyz. 1890-1940. Einsiedeln: Benziger, 1940. 118 pp.
4604. Reichlin, Josef. Die Kantonalbank Schwyz 1890-1924. Schwyz: J. Reichlin, 1924. 232 pp.
4605. Wielandt, Friedrich. Münz- und Geldgeschichte des Standes Schwyz. Schwyz: Kantonalbank Schwyz, 1964. 122 pp.

Solothurn

4606. Ackermann, Franz. Der Finanzhaushalt des Kantons Solothurn seit Einführung der direkten Staatssteuer. Diss. Bern. Solothurn: A. Bachtler, 1929. 253 pp.
4607. Ackermann, Franz. Solothurner Handelsbank. 1847-1947. Solothurn: Buch- and Kunstdruckerei Union, 1948.
4608. Stampfli, Arthur. Die Solothurner Kantonalbank 1886-1910. Diss. Solothurn. Solothurn: Zepfil, 1911. 99 pp.
4609. Weber, Max. Die neuere Entwicklung der Staats-Steuern des Kantons Solothurn. Diss. Zurich. Zurich: Leemann, 1926. 102 pp.

Thurgau

4610. Goldinger, Heinrich. Die Staatssteuern des Kantons Thurgau 1890-1938. Diss. Zurich. Sulgen: Bircher, 1941. 126 pp.
4611. Häberlin, Heinz. Der Finanzhaushalt des Kantons Thurgau in den Jahren 1900-1923. Diss. Bern. Frauenfeld: Huber, 1924. 157 pp.

Unterwalden

4612. Stober, Carl. Fünfzig Jahre Nidwaldner Kantonalbank. 1879-1929. Diss. Fribourg. Zurich: Leemann, 1932. 140 pp.

SEE ALSO: 626.

Uri

4613. 50 Jahre Urner Kantonalbank. 1879-1929. Diss. Fribourg. Zurich: Leemann, 1932. 140 pp.

Zug

4614. Denkschrift zum fünfzigjährigen Jubiläum. 1891-1941 der Zuger Kantonalbank. Zug: Zuger Kantonalbank, 1941.
4615. Lusser, Augustin. Jubiläumsfeier 75 Jahre Zuger Kantonalbank. Zug: Zuger Kantonalbank, 1967. 31 pp.
4616. Lusser, Werner. Die Einwohnergemeinde-Finanzen im Kanton Zug 1950 bis 1965: unter besonderer Berücksichtigung von Wirtschaft. Bevölkerung und Recht. Diss. Fribourg, 1979. Bern: Lang, 1982. 729 pp.

Zurich

4617. Bleuler, Werner. Bank in Zürich 1836-1906. Zurich: Schweizer Kreditanstalt, 1913. 336 pp.
4618. Bucher, O. Der Zusammenbruch der Leih- und Sparkassen Aadorf und Eschlikon. Zurich: O. Füssli, 1918. 127 pp.
4619. Die Finanzen der Stadt Zürich. 1893-1952. Zurich: Statistisches Amt, 1955. 158 pp.
4620. Fischer, Georges, ed. Wachstum. Währung und Wohlstand 1956-1965. Aus den Wochenberichten einer Zürcher Privatbank. Zurich: Polygraphischer Verlag, 1965. 310 pp.
4621. Ganz, Heinrich. Das Bankwesen und die wirtschaftliche Entwicklung unserer Stadt in den letzten 40 Jahren. Winterthur: Buchdruck Winterthur, 1949.
4622. Gross, T. Die Entwicklung der öffentlichen Ausgaben in der Schweiz mit besonderer Berücksichtigung des Kantons Zürich 1860-1910. Bern: Lang, 1980. 133 pp.
4623. Kägi, Erich. Der Finanzhaushalt des Kantons Zürich in der Regenerationszeit. Zurich: Europa Verlag, 1954. 200 pp.

4624. Peyer, Hans C. Von Handel und Bank im alten Zürich. Zurich: Verlag Berichthaus, 1968. 323 pp.
4625. Rathgeb, Hans, ed. Zwischen Zürichsee und Walensee. Jubiläumsgabe zum 125-jährigen Bestehen der Bank vom Linthgebiet. Uznach: Bank vom Linthgebiet, 1974. 162 pp.
4626. Schmid, Hans R. 100 Jahre Bank Wädenswil. Wädenswil: Stutz, 1964. 95 pp.
4627. Schmid, Hans R. and Richard T. Meier. Die Geschichte der Zürcher Börse. Zum hundertjährigen Bestehen der Zürcher Börse. Zurich: Effecktenbörsenverein, 1977. 355 pp.
4628. Sommer, Ernst. Die Finanzen der Stadt Winterthur 1910-1920. Diss. Zurich. Leipzig: Nemnich, 1922. 89 pp.
4629. Sulzer, Claus. Der Finanzhaushalt des Kantons Zürich. 1848-1900. Diss. Zurich, 1954. 159 pp.
4630. Uebersicht der Staatsrechnungen des Kantons Zürich von 1803 bis 1837 sowie Uebersicht des Staatsvermögens von 1830 bis Ende 1835. Zurich: O. Füssli, 1837.
4631. Weisz, Leo. "Der organisierte Kredit in Zürich von der Reformation bis zum Jahre 1835." in Geld- und Kreditsystem der Schweiz. Festgabe für Gottlieb Bachmann. 2nd ed. Zurich: Schulthess, 1944. pp. 135-56.
4632. Wetter, Ernst. Die Bank in Winterthur 1862-1912. Winterthur: G. Binkert, 1914. 172 pp.
4633. Zahner, Max. Die Gewerbebank Zürich. 1868-1935. Diss. Zurich. Affoltern: J. Weiss, 1937. 146 pp.
4634. Die zürcherischen Creditinstitute in den Jahren 1902-1930. Sparkassenstatistik. Gewinn- und Verlustrechnungen und Bilanzen. 15 vols. Zurich: Zurcher Kantonalbank, 1906-32.

SEE ALSO: 3195.

LIECHTENSTEIN

4635. Batliner, Emil H. Das Geld- und Kreditwesen des Fürstentums Liechtenstein in Vergangenheit und Gegenwart. Winterthur: Keller, 1959. 171 pp.
4636. Rittmann, Herbert. Kleine Münz- und Geldgeschichte von Liechtenstein Bank in Liechtenstein Aktiengesellschaft. Hilterfingen: Helvetische Münzenzeitung, 1977. 77 pp.

LUXEMBURG

4637. Braun, Michael. "Die Sozialversicherung in Luxemburg 1897-1940. Gesetzgebung und soziale Wirklichkeit." Zeitschrift für die Gesamte Versicherungswissenschaft 69 (1980), 643-69.
4638. Calmès, Albert. "Das Geldsystem des Grossherzogtums Luxemburg." Schmoller 31 (1907), 635-99.
4639. Jaans-Hoche, Jutta. Banque Nationale du Grand-Duché de Luxembourg 1873-1881. Eine Episode in der luxemburgischen Währungsgeschichte. Luxemburg: Saint-Paul, 1981. 237 pp.
4640. Neuman, Henri. Les communes, leur administration, leurs finances et leurs domaines. 1840 à 1891. Luxemburg: Bück, 1894. 288 pp.
4641. Runge, Hans-Joachim. "Historischer Überblick über die Entwicklung des Luxemburgischen Kreditwesens." Bankhistorisches Archiv 2 (1976), 49-60.
4642. Treue, Wilhelm. "Die Gründung der Internationalen Bank in Luxemburg vor 125 Jahren." Bankhistorisches Archiv 7 (1981), 3-15. (English and French summaries)
4643. Zehn Jahre Spar- und Darlehnskassen (System Raiffeisen) in Luxemburg. Luxemburg: Verlag der Raiffeisenzentrale des Grossherzogtums Luxemburg, 1936. 224 pp.

GERMANY

References

4644. Cassier, Siegfried C. Biographie einer Unternehmerbank. Der Weg der Industriebank (Industriekreditbank AG-Deutsche Industriebank) und der langfristige Industriekredit in Deutschland. Frankfurt a. M.: Knapp, 1977. 223 pp.
4645. Hänel, Wolfgang. Bibliographie des periodischen Schrifttums in der Sozialen Sicherheit. 2nd ed. Bonn-Bad Godesberg: Asgard, 1976. 76 pp.
4646. Jantz, Kurt and Eberhart Finke. Studienwerk der Sozialversicherung, Sozialhilfe und Versorgung. Bibliographie. Wiesbaden: Gabler, 1968. 60 pp.
4647. Reparationen und Demontagen. Eine Zusammenstellung der wichtigen Texte, Dokumente, Anweisungen und Verordnungen sowie der einschlägigen Literatur des In- und Auslandes. Oberursel: Europa-Archiv, 1949. 21 pp.
4648. Sichtermann, Siegfried. Schrifttum des Bank- und Kreditwesens von 1920-1960 nach Stichworten geordnet. Frankfurt a. M.: Knapp, 1963-64. 305 pp.

GERMANY

4649. Achterberg, Erich. Schwarz auf Weiss. Meine vierzig Lehrjahre. Bankhistorische und geldpolitische Essays. Frankfurt a. M.: Knapp, 1960. 244 pp.
4650. Achterberg, Erich and Maximilian Müller-Jabusch. Lebensbilder deutscher Bankiers aus 5 Jahrhunderten. Frankfurt a. M.: Knapp, 1963. 271 pp.
4651. Andic, Stephan and Jindrich Veverka. "The Growth of Government Expenditure in Germany Since the Unification." Finanzarchiv 23 (1963/64), 169-278.
4652. Baker, James C. The German Stock Market. Its Operations, Problems, and Prospects. New York: Praeger, 1970. 204 pp.
4653. Bauriedl, Ulrich. "100 Jahre Deutsche Sozialversicherung. Rückblick auf ein Jahrhundert Sozialer Sicherheit durch Selbstverwaltung." Internationale Revue für Soziale Sicherheit 34 (1981), 443-49.
4654. Beckerath, Erwin. "Die neuere Geschichte der deutschen Finanzwissenschaft (seit 1800)." in W. Gerloff and F. Neumark, eds. Handbuch der Finanzwissenschaft. 2nd ed. Tübingen: Mohr, 1952-1965. I, 416-69.
4655. Bennathan, Esra. "German National Income, 1850-1960." Business History 5 (1962), 45-53.
4656. Bernstein, Daniel. "Finanzwesen." in S. Kaznelson, ed. Juden im deutschen Kulturbereich. Ein Sammelwerk. 2nd ed. Berlin: Jüdischer Verlag, 1959. pp. 720-59.
4657. Boesler, Felix. "Stand und Aufgaben der Finanzgeschichtsforschung." Schmoller 65 (1941), 137-65.
4658. Born, Karl E. Geld und Banken im 19. und 20. Jahrhundert. Stuttgart: Kröner, 1977. 663 pp.
4659. Brinkmann, Carl. "Zukunftsprobleme der Finanzgeschichte." Finanzarchiv, N. F. 1 (1932-33), 46-63.
4660. Castillon, Richard. Les réparations allemandes. Deux expériences: 1919-1932, 1945-1952. Paris: Presses universitaires de France, 1953. 197 pp.
4661. Cherubini, Arnaldo. "Note sulle origini delle assicurazioni sociali in Germania." Revisita degli Infortuni e delle Malattie Professionali 50 (1963), 180-215, 447-500, 701-98.
4662. Deutsche Bankengeschichte. 3 vols. Frankfurt a. M.: Knapp, 1982- .
4663. Deutsche Bundesbank. Währung und Wirtschaft in Deutschland 1876-1975. Frankfurt a. M.: Knapp, 1976. 796 pp.
4664. Deutsches Geld- und Bankwesen in Zahlen, 1876-1975. Frankfurt a. M.: Knapp, 1976. 364 pp.
4665. Dieckmann, Jens. Der Einfluss der deutschen Sparkassenorganisation auf die staatliche Wirtschaftspolitik in der historischen Entwicklung. Frankfurt a. M.: R. G. Fischer, 1981. 226 pp.
4666. Eckerlin, Friedrich. Kriseninstitute in Deutschland und Italien. Ein Beitrag zur Geschichte des Bankwesens und der staatlichen Kreditpolitik. Diss. Berlin, 1943. 212 pp.
4667. Ehrlicher, Werner. Die deutsche Finanzpolitik seit 1924. Bonn: Inst. Finanzen und Steuern, 1961. 26 pp.
4668. Emminger, Otmar. Währungspolitik im Wandel der Zeit. Frankfurt a. M.: Knapp, 1966. 264 pp.

4669. Engberg, Holger L. Mixed Banking and Economic Growth in Germany, 1850-1931. Diss. Columbia University; rpt. New York: Arno Press, 1981. 251 pp.
4670. Faingar, Isakhar M. Die Entwicklung des deutschen Monopolkapitals. Grundriss. Berlin: Verlag Die Wirtschaft, 1959. 340 pp.
4671. Franzke, Hans-Ulrich. Geldhoheit und Währungssteuerung. Frankfurt a. M.: Knapp, 1964. 183 pp.
4672. Fremdling, Rainer and Richard H. Tilly. "German Banks, German Growth and Econometric History." Journal of Economic History 36 (1976), 416-24.
4673. Fricke, Rolf. "Finanzwirtschaft und Geschichte." Finanzarchiv, N. F. 4 (1936), 361-402.
4674. Gehr, Martin. Das Verhältnis zwischen Banken und Industrie in Deutschland seit der Mitte des 19. Jahrhunderts bis zur Bankenkrise von 1931 unter besonderer Berücksichtigung des industriellen Grosskredits. Diss. Tübingen, 1960. 150 pp.
4675. Grasser, Walter. Deutsche Münzgesetze 1871-1971. Munich: Battenberg, 1971. 431 pp.
4676. Grossfeld, Bernhard. Die Einkommensteuer. Geschichtliche Grundlage und rechtsvergleichender Ansatz. Tübingen: Mohr, 1981. 53 pp.
4677. Henning, Friedrich-Wilhelm. "Fünfzig Jahrgänge Steuer und Wirtschaft. Probleme und Wirtschaft. Probleme des Steuerwesens vor dem realgeschichtlichen Hintergrund." Steuer und Wirtschaft. Zeitschrift für die gesamte Steuerwissenschaft 50 (1973), 288-305.
4678. Herrmann, Arthur R. Zweihundert Jahre öffentliches Bankwesen. Berlin: Heymann, 1935. 157 pp.
4679. Hielscher, Erwin. Das Jahrhundert der Inflationen in Deutschland. Munich: Olzog, 1968. 159 pp.
4680. Hoffmann, Walther G. "Die Entwicklung der Sparkassen im Rahmen des Wachstums der deutschen Wirtschaft (1850-1967). Zeitschrift für die Gesamte Staatswissenschaft 125 (1969), 561-605. (English summary)
4681. Hotzel, Kurt. Geld macht Geschichte. Das Werk politischer Bankiers. Berlin: Verlag "Das Reich", 1933. 105 pp.
4682. Hundert Jahre Sozialversicherung. Von der Kaiserlichen Botschaft zum Recht auf soziale Sicherheit." Bundesarbeitsblatt (1981), 5-57.
4683. Innovation, Know How, Rationalization and Investment in the German and Japanese Economies: 1868/1871-1930/80. Wiesbaden: Steiner, 1982. 287 pp.
4684. Jaeger, Kurt. Die deutschen Reichsmünzen seit 1871. 4th ed. Basel: Münzen & Medaillen A. G., 1965. 195 pp.
4685. Kimmel, Christian. Die wirtschaftlichen Folgen der Reparationszahlungen Deutschlands nach den Weltkriegen. Diss. Munich, 1973. 194 pp.
4686. Kirberger, W. Staatsentlastung durch private Verbände: die finanzpolitische Bedeutung der Mitwirkung privater Verbände bei der Erfüllung öffentlicher Aufgaben. Baden-Baden: Nomos, 1978. 393 pp.
4687. Kleeis, Friedrich. Die Geschichte der sozialen Versicherung in Deutschland. Berlin: Verlag der Arbeiter-Versorgung, 1928; rpt. Bonn: Dietz, 1981. 297 pp.
4688. Koch, Arwed. Banken und Bankgeschäfte unter besonderer Berücksichtigung der Rechtsverhältnisse. Jena: Fischer, 1931. 329 pp.
4689. Köllner, Lutz. Militär und Finanzen: zur Finanzgeschichte und Finanzsoziologie von Militärausgaben in Deutschland. Munich: Bernard & Graefe, 1982. 320 pp.
4690. Köster, Thomas. Die Entwicklung kommunaler Finanzsysteme am Beispiel Grossbritanniens, Frankreichs und Deutschlands 1790-1980. Diss. Cologne, 1983. Berlin: Duncker & Humblot, 1984. 422 pp.
4691. Komlos, John, Jr. "The Kreditbanken and German Growth." Journal of Economic History 38 (1978), 476-79, 483-86.
4692. Krull, Christian. "Die deutsche Kaufmannschaft und das Problem der Münz- und Währungseinheit, 1765-1865-1962." Finanzarchiv, N.F. 23 (1963), 124-31.
4693. Kruse, Heinrich W. "Fünfzig Jahrgänge Steuer und Wirtschaft. Ein Ausschnitt aus der Geschichte des Steuerrechts." Steuer und Wirtschaft. Zeitschrift für die gesamte Steuerwissenschaft 50 (1973), 273-87.
4694. Kuske, Bruno. "Die Entstehung der Kreditwirtschaft und des Kapitalverkehrs." in B. Kuske. Köln, der Rhein und das Reich. Beiträge aus fünf Jahrzehnten wirtschaftsgeschichtlicher Forschung. Cologne: Böhlau, 1956. pp. 48-137.

4695. Lanter, Max. Die Finanzierung des Krieges. Quellen, Methoden und Lösungen seit dem Mittelalter bis Ende des 2. Weltkrieges 1939-1945. Diss. Zurich. Luzern: Haag, 1950. 217 pp.

4696. Lege, Klaus-Wilhelm. "Die Geschäftspolitik der deutschen Sparkassen im Wandel der Zeit." Archiv für das Spar-, Giro- und Kreditwesen 6 (1968), 3-26.

4697. Lernen und Entscheiden. Festschrift zum 50jährigen Bestehen des Lehrinstituts für das Kommunale Sparkassen- und Kreditwesen, 1928-1978. Stuttgart: Deutscher Sparkassenverlag, 1978. 491 pp.

4698. Leverkuehn, Paul, ed. Wirtschaftliche Bestimmungen in Friedensverträgen. Hamburg: Rechts- und Staatswissenschaftlicher Verlag, 1948. 303 pp.

4699. Lütge, Friedrich. "Die deutsche Kriegsfinanzierung im ersten und zweiten Weltkrieg." in Beiträge zur Finanzwirtschaft und zur Geldtheorie. Festschrift für Rudolf Stucken. Göttingen: Vandenhoeck & Ruprecht, 1953.

4700. Mackenzie, Kenneth. The Banking Systems of Great Britain, France, Germany and the United States of America. 3rd ed. London: Macmillan, 1945. 284 pp.

4701. Menzel, Peter. Deutsche Notmünzen und sonstige Geldersatzmarken, 1873-1932. Berlin: Transpress, 1982. 648 pp.

4702. Möller, Hans, ed. Zur Vorgeschichte der deutschen Mark. Basel: Kyklos, 1961. 534 pp.

4703. Müller, J. Heinz. "Die deutsche Sozialversicherung. Ihre Entwicklung und aktuellen Probleme." in T. Dams, ed. Aktuelle Probleme der Sozialpolitik in Japan und in der Bundesrepublik Deutschland. Berlin: Duncker & Humblot, 1982. pp. 87-100.

4704. Neuburger, Hugh M. and Houston H. Stokes. "German Banking and Japanese Banking. A Comparative Analysis." The Journal of Economic History 35 (1975), 238-52.

4705. Newcomer, Mabel. Central and Local Finance in Germany and England. New York: Columbia University Press, 1937. 381 pp.

4706. Orsagh, Thomas L. "The Probable Geographical Distribution of German Income, 1882-1962." Zeitschrift für die gesamte Staatswissenschaft 124 (1968), 280-311.

4707. Penzkofer, Peter. "Wirtschaftliche und gesellschaftliche Einflüsse auf die Entstehung und Entwicklung der privaten Geschäftsbanken Ende des 19. und im 20. Jahrhundert." in Wirtschaft, Gesellschaft, Geschichte. Stuttgart: Metzler, 1974. pp. 43-201.

4708. Peschke, Paul. Geschichte der deutschen Sozialversicherung. Der Kampf der unterdrückten Klassen um soziale Sicherung. Berlin: Tribüne, 1962. 501 pp.

4709. Peters, Horst. Die Geschichte der sozialen Versicherung. 3rd ed. Sankt Augustin: Asgard-Verlag, 1978. 240 pp.

4710. Pirnat, Karl. Dämon Steuer. Ein Leidensweg der Menschheit. Vienna: Fromme, 1956. 253 pp.

4711. Pohl, Manfred. Einführung in die deutsche Bankengeschichte. Die Entwicklung des gesamten deutschen Kreditwesens. Frankfurt a. M.: Knapp, 1976. 154 pp.

4712. Pohl, Manfred. "Die Geschichte der Nationalbank für Deutschland." Bankhistorisches Archiv 7 (1981), 16-49.

4713. Pohl, Manfred. "Konzentration und Krisen im deutschen Bankwesen zwischen 1848 und 1937." in H. Kellenbenz, ed. Wachstumsschwankungen. Wirtschaftliche und soziale Auswirkungen (Spätmittelalter bis 20. Jahrhundert). Stuttgart: Klett, 1981. pp. 237-72.

4714. Quante, Peter. "Die neuere Entwicklung der deutschen Sozialversicherung und ihre Reform." Schmoller 74 (1954), 681-716.

4715. Rabe, Harry. Geschichte, Aufgaben und volkswirtschaftliche Bedeutung der privaten Sparkassen Deutschlands. Leipzig: Deichert, 1940. 123 pp.

4716. Radandt, Hans. "100 Jahre Deutsche Bank." Jahrbuch für Wirtschaftsgeschichte (1972), III, 37-62.

4717. Rath, Wilhelm. Stadt und Kreis. Ein Beitrag zur Geschichte und Theorie der Steuerverfassung der preussischen Landkreise und ihrer Städte. Berlin-Friedenau: Deutscher Kommunal-Verlag, 1928. 139 pp.

4718. Ritter, Erich. Die Stellungnahme der Gewerkschaften zu den Problemen der Sozialversicherung in Deutschland. Diss. Frankfurt, 1932. Wertheim a. M.: Bechstein, 1933. 70 pp.

4719. Rosen, Antonius V. Geschichte und heutige Bedeutung der freigemeinwirtschaftlichen Sparkassen. Diss. Cologne, 1965. 223 pp.

4720. Sarnat, Marshall and A. Engelhardt. "Nominal and Real Rates of Return on Common Stock in Germany 1871-1976." Konjunkturpolitik. Zeitschrift für angewandte Konjunkturforschung 26 (1980), 277-92.

4721. Schäfer, Walther. Die Steuervereinheitlichung in der deutschen Steuergesetzgebung von der Gründung des Norddeutschen Bundes bis zur Gegenwart. Diss. Frankfurt a. M., 1938. Bückeburg: Prinz, 1938. 250 pp.

4722. Schewe, Dieter. "Die Geschichte der Sozialversicherung" als Legitimation für die Gegenwart. Zugleich eine Auseinandersetzung mit neuen Schriften." Sozialer Fortschritt (1977), 241-44.

4723. Schwalm, Carl. Die Grundsätze der Steuerpolitik im Wechsel der staats- und wirtschaftspolitischen Anschauungen vom Zeitalter des Kameralismus bis zur Gegenwart. Diss. Frankfurt a. M. Frankfurt a. M.: Baum, 1936. 115 pp.

4724. Siebeck, Theo. Die Entwicklung der Sozialversicherung. Voraussetzungen und Reformen. Essen: C. W. Haarfeld, 1967. 49 pp.

4725. "Siebzig Jahre Sozialversicherungsrecht." Bundesarbeitsblatt (1953), 752-84.

4726. Sommer, Albrecht. Geistesgeschichte der deutschen Sparkassen. Berlin: Heymann, 1935. 85 pp.

4727. Standfest, Erich. "Hundert Jahre 'Kaiserliche Botschaft'. Bemerkungen zur Ermittlung der Sozialversicherung." Soziale Sicherheit 30 (1981), 321-25.

4728. Stolleis, Michael. "Rechtsgeschichtliche Entwicklung. Hundert Jahre Sozialversicherung in Deutschland." Zeitschrift für die Gesamte Versicherungswissenschaft 69 (1980), 155-75.

4729. Stucken, Rudolf. Deutsche Geld- und Kreditpolitik 1914-1963. 3rd ed. Tübingen: Mohr, 1964. 341 pp.

4730. Terhalle, Fritz. "Geschichte der deutschen öffentlichen Finanzwirtschaft vom Beginn des 19. Jahrhunderts bis zum Schluss des 2. Weltkrieges." in W. Gerloff and F. Neumark, eds. Handbuch der Finanzwissenschaft. 2nd ed. Tübingen: Mohr, 1952-1965. I, 273-326.

4731. Thude, Günther. "Über die Sozialversicherung in Deutschland, früher und heute." Die Arbeit 7 (1953), 860-68.

4732. Trende, Adolf. "Beiträge zur Geschichte der deutschen Sparkassen." Tradition 3 (1958), 120-27.

4733. Trende, Adolf. Geschichte der deutschen Sparkassen. Stuttgart: Deutscher Sparkassen-verlag, 1957. 610 pp.

4734. Tucker, Donald S. The Evolution of People's Banks. New York: AMS Press, 1967. 272 pp.

4735. Währung und Wirtschaft in Deutschland 1876-1975. Frankfurt a. M.: Knapp, 1976. 796 pp.

4736. Wagner, Kurt. Stationen deutscher Bankgeschichte. 75 Jahre Bankenverband. Cologne: Bank-Verlag, 1976. 140 pp.

4737. Waldheim, Harald von. Zeitgemässe Reformen der deutschen Sozialversicherung in historischer und wirtschaftlicher Beleuchtung. Diss. Berlin, 1929. Berlin: Heymann, 1930. 175 pp.

4738. Whale, Philip B. Joint Stock Banking in Germany. A Study of the German Credit Banks Before and After the War. London: Macmillan, 1930. 369 pp.

4739. Wilde, Klaus. "Hundert Jahre Sozialversicherung in Deutschland." Aus Politik und Zeitgeschichte (1981), 3-20.

4740. Winkel, Harald. "Kapitalquellen und Kapitalverwendung am Vorabend des industriellen Aufschwungs in Deutschland." Schmoller 90 (1970), 275-301.

4741. Wirth, Max. "A History of Banking in Germany." in A History of Banking in All the Leading Nations. New York: Journal of Commerce and Commercial Bulletin, 1896; rpt. New York, 1971. IV, 1-68.

4742. Wolff, Hertha. Die Stellung der Sozialdemokratie zur deutschen Arbeiterversicherungsgesetzgebung von ihrer Entstehung an bis zur Reichsversicherungsordnung. Diss. Freiburg i. B., 1926. Berlin: Michel, 1933. 93 pp.

4743. Zahn, Friedrich. "50 Jahre deutsche Sozialversicherung. Rückblick und Ausblick." Allgemeines Statistisches Archiv 22 (1932), 1-17.

4744. Zahn, Johannes C. D. Der Privatbankier. Frankfurt a. M.: Knapp, 1963. 122 pp.

4745. Zeiger, Philipp. Das deutsche Geldwesen. Leipzig: G. A. Gloeckner, 1925. 119 pp.

4746. Zorn, Wolfgang. "Staatliche Wirtschafts- und Sozialpolitik und öffentliche Finanzen 1800-1970." in H. Aubin and W. Zorn, eds. Handbuch der deutschen Wirtschafts- und Sozialgeschichte. Stuttgart: Klett-Cotta, 1976. II, 148-97.

4747. Zur Geschichte des Kreditgeschäftes: Notizen zu Finanzierungsproblemen vom 18. bis zum 20. Jahrhundert. Frankfurt a. M.: Knapp, 1982. 87 pp.

SEE ALSO: 1652, 3308.

GERMANY--1815-1918

Bibliographic Reference

4748. Frankenstein, Kuno. Bibliographie des Arbeiterversicherungswesens im Deutschen Reiche. Leipzig: Hirschfeld, 1895. 42 pp.

GERMANY--1815-1918

4749. Achterberg, Erich. Öffentliche Banken vor hundert Jahren. Stuttgart: Deutscher Sparkassenverlag, 1963. 55 pp.
4750. Arps, Ludwig. "Bismarck rechnete bis zum Jahre 1969. Ein Rückblick auf die ersten Jahrzehnte der deutschen Sozialversicherung." Arbeit und Sozialpolitik 19 (1965), 143-47.
4751. Augspurg, G. Diedrich. Zur deutschen Münzfrage. 9 vols. Bremen: Geisler, 1868-1874.
4752. Bach, Heinrich. Reichsbank und Reichsfinanzen in den Jahren 1876-1923 (unter Mitberücksichtigung der preussischen Finanzen). Diss. Leipzig. Leipzig: Schwarzenberg & Schumann, 1930. 96 pp.
4753. Bark, Thomas. Vertragsfreiheit und Staat im Kapitalismus. Ökonomische und politische Grundlagen der Wucher- und Zinsgesetzgebung in Preussen-Deutschland 1850-1900. Diss. Frankfurt a. M., 1977. Berlin: Guhl, 1978. 225 pp.
4754. Bendicente, Francisco C. "Consecuencias de la guerra mundial sobre las monedas de Alemania, Inglaterra y Estados Unidos de Norteamerica." Revista de la Facultad de ciencias económicas, comerciales y políticas, Universidad nacionál del litoral 8 (1939), 25-63.
4755. Benöhr, Hans-Peter. "Wirtschaft und Sozialversicherung vor hundert Jahren." Zeitschrift für Arbeitsrecht 13 (1982), 19-48.
4756. Bettges, Addy. Die Meinungen über die Münz- und Zettelbankreform von 1857 bis zu den Gesetzentwürfen von 1871 bezw. 1874. Diss. Cologne. Barmen: Dahmann, 1926. 87 pp.
4757. Blaich, Fritz. "Zinsfreiheit als Problem der deutschen Wirtschaftspolitik zwischen 1857 und 1871." Schmoller 91 (1971), 269-306.
4758. Bloch, David W. Die Entwertung der deutschen Valuta im Weltkrieg unter besonderer Berücksichtigung der Inflation. Basel: Finckh, 1918. 79 pp.
4759. Böhmert, Wilhelm. "Die mittleren Klassen der Einkommensteuer in einigen deutschen Grossstädten in den Jahren 1880-1895." Schmoller 20 (1896), 1227-53.
4760. Bösselmann, Kurt. Die Entwicklung des deutschen Aktienwesens im 19. Jahrhundert. Berlin: de Gruyter, 1939. 208 pp.
4761. Böttcher, Alexander. Die Auswirkung der Realsteuerreform auf den preusssischen Finanzausgleich unter besonderer Berücksichtigung der geschichtlichen Entwicklung. Diss. Marburg. Marburg: Koch, 1938. 50 pp.
4762. Bonus, Heinz. "Konjunktur und Haushalt. Die preussischen Kommunalfinanzen der Vorkriegszeit." Finanzarchiv, N. F. 4 (1936), 170-81.
4763. Bopp, Karl R. "Die Tätigkeit der Reichsbank von 1876 bis 1914." Weltwirtschaftliches Archiv 72 (1954), 34-59, 179-224.
4764. Borchard, Karl. Staatsverbrauch und öffentliche Investitionen in Deutschland 1780-1850. Diss. Göttingen, 1968. 335 pp.
4765. Borchardt, Julian. Das Papiergeld in der Revolution 1797-1920. Berlin: Der Firn, 1921. 30 pp.
4766. Borchardt, Knut. "Zum Problem der Erziehungs- und Ausbildunginvestitionen im 19. Jahrhundert." in H. Aubin et al. Beiträge zur Wirtschafts- und Stadtgeschichte. Wiesbaden: Steiner, 1965. pp. 380-92.
4767. Borchardt, Knut. "Zur Frage des Kapitalmangels in der ersten Hälfte des 19. Jahrhunderts in Deutschland." Jahrbücher für Nationalökonomie und Statistik 173 (1961), 401-21.
4768. Borght, Richard van der. Die Entwicklung der Reichsfinanzen. Leipzig: Göschen, 1908. 170 pp.
4769. Brasilianische Bank für Deutschland, Hamburg-Brasilien 1887-1912. Hamburg: Lütcke & Wulff, 1912. 39 pp.
4770. Breslauer, Berthold. "Brief Sketch of the History of Savings Banks in Germany." in Miscellaneous Articles on German Banking. Washington: National Monetary Commission, 1910. pp. 405-16.

4771. Clemen, Reinhard. Die Finanzwirtschaft der kleineren preussischen Städte und ihre Entwicklung seit 1871. Diss. Halle-Wittenberg. Jena: G. Fischer, 1911. 348 pp.
4772. Cohn, Gustav. "German Experiments in Fiscal Legislation." Economic Journal 23 (1913), 537-46.
4773. Cohn, Samuel. Die Finanzen des Deutschen Reiches seit seiner Begründung. Berlin: Guttentag, 1899. 209 pp.
4774. Coing, Helmut and Walter Wilhelm, eds. Geld und Banken. Wissenschaft und Kodification des Privatsrechts im 19. Jahrhundert, 5. Frankfurt a. M.: Klostermann, 1980. 168 pp.
4775. Collani, Hans-Joachim von. Die Finanzgebarung des Preussischen Staates zur Zeit des Verfassungskonfliktes 1862-1866. Düsseldorf: Nolte, 1939. 57 pp.
4776. Costas, Ilse. Auswirkungen der Konzentration des Kapitals auf die Arbeiterklasse in Deutschland (1880-1914). Frankfurt a. M.: Campus, 1981. 445 pp.
4777. Crämer, Rudolf. "Bismarcks Erbe in der Sozialversicherung." Jahrbuch. Arbeitswissenschaftliches Institut der Deutschen Arbeitsfront 1 (1940-41), 125-48.
4778. Croner, Johannes. "Die Entwicklung der deutschen Börsen von 1870-1914." Preussische Jahrbücher 192 (1923), 343-56; 193 (1923), 304-14.
4779. Daniels, Emil. "Zur Genesis der 'Deutschen Bank'." Preussische Jahrbucher 188 (1922), 129-45.
4780. Deutsches Papiergeld 1772-1870. Frankfurt a. M.: Deutsche Bundesbank, 1964. 52 pp.
4781. Diehl, Karl. Über Fragen des Geldwesens und der Valuta während des Krieges und nach dem Kriege. Jena: Fischer, 1918. 140 pp.
4782. Dieterici, Carl F. W. Zur Geschichte der Steuer-Reform in Preussen von 1810 bis 1820. Berlin: G. Reimer, 1875. 442 pp.
4783. Düring, Siegfried. Der deutsche Geld- und Kapitalmarkt als Erreger der Konjunkturbewegung in den Jahren 1900-1913. Diss. Giessen. Berlin: Litfass, 1928. 97 pp.
4784. Eistert, Ekkehard and Johannes Ringel. "Die Finanzierung des wirtschaftlichen Wachstums durch die Banken. Eine quantitativ-empirische Untersuchung für Deutschland 1850-1913." in Untersuchungen zum Wachstum der deutschen Wirtschaft. Tübingen: Mohr, 1971. pp. 93-165.
4785. Ekvall, Waldemar. Det inre kreditväsendets organsation i Tyskland och Holland under kriget. Stockholm: Norstedt, 1918. 92 pp.
4786. Esser, Wilfried. Die Entwicklung des Sparkassenwesens in Preussen bis zum Beginn des 20. Jahrhunderts. Königswinter: Gesellschaft für Wirtschafts- und Verkehrswissenschaftliche Forschung, 1979. 122 pp.
4787. Farny, Dieter et al., eds. Entwicklung und Aufgaben von Versicherungen und Banken in der Industrialisierung. Berlin: Duncker & Humblot, 1980. 295 pp.
4788. Fay, Sidney B. "State Ownership in Germany." Current History 18 (1950), 129-33.
4789. Fechter, Ursula. Schutzzoll und Goldstandard im Deutschen Reich (1879-1914). Der Einfluss der Schutzzollpolitik auf das internationale Goldwährungsmechnismus. Cologne: Böhlau, 1974. 172 pp.
4790. Fischer, Wolfram. "The Strategy of Public Investment in Nineteenth Century Germany." Journal of European Economic History 6 (1977), 431-42.
4791. Geld im Kriege. 3 vols. Hamburg: Hanseatische Verlagsanstalt, 1938.
4792. Gerloff, Wilhelm. Die Finanz- und Zollpolitik des Deutschen Reiches nebst ihren Beziehungen zu Landes- und Gemeindefinanzen von der Gründung des Norddeutschen Bundes bis zur Gegenwart. Jena: Fischer, 1913. 553 pp.
4793. Gerloff, Wilhelm. "Zur Geschichte der Entwicklung der Personalbesteuerung in Preussen." Zeitschrift für die gesamte Staatswissenschaft 82 (1927), 384-93.
4794. German, Peter. Die Geschichte der Börsenkrisen. Vienna: Verlag "Die Börse," 1921. 46 pp.
4795. Geschichte und Wirkungskreis des Reichs-Versicherungsamts. Leipzig: Breitkopf & Härtel, 1911. 334 pp.
4796. Goldberg, Martin. Geschichte der deutschen Bank- und Münzgesetzgebung seit der ersten Erneuerung des Reichsbankprivilegs. Berlin: Puttkammer & Mühlbrecht, 1913. 187 pp.
4797. Goldscheid, Rudolf. "The Political Economy of Public Finance and the Industrialization of Prussia, 1815-1866." Journal of Economic History 26 (1966), 484-97.
4798. Grabower, Rolf. "Bismarck und die Steuern. Zugleich ein Beitrag zur Lehre von der Tradition im Steuerwesen." Finanzarchiv 22 (1963), 377-461.
4799. Grabower, Rolf. Preussens Steuern vor und nach den Befreiungskriegen. Berlin: Liebmann, 1932. 688 pp.

4800. Graeff, Friedrich. Die Fortbildung der Erbschaftssteuer in Deutschland, England, Frankreich und Belgien seit dem Weltkriege. Diss. Zurich. Charlottenburg: Hoffmann, 1925. 52 pp.
4801. Grice, James W. National and Local Finance. A Review of the Relations Between the Central and Local Authorities in England, France, Belgium and Prussia During the Nineteenth Century. London: P. S. King, 1910. 404 pp.
4802. Grunwald, Kurt. "Pénétration pacifique. The Financial Vehicles of Germany's 'Drang nach dem Osten.'" Jahrbuch des Instituts für Deutsche Geschichte (1975), 85-103.
4803. Grunwald, Kurt. "Three Chapters of German-Jewish Banking History." Leo Baeck Institute Yearbook 22 (1977), 191-208.
4804. Gutsche, Willibald. "Probleme des Verhältnisses zwischen Monopolkapital und Staat in Deutschland vom Ende des 19. Jahrhunderts bis zum Vorabend des Ersten Weltkrieges." in Studien zum deutschen Imperialismus vor 1914. Berlin: Zentralinstitut für Geschichte, 1976. pp. 33-84.
4805. Gutsche, Willibald. "Zum Funktionsmechanismus zwischen Staat und Monopolkapital in Deutschland in den ersten Monaten des Ersten Weltkrieges, 1914-1915." Jahrbuch für Wirtschaftsgeschichte (1973), I, 63-98.
4806. Helfferich, Karl T. Die Reform des deutschen Geldwesens nach der Gründung des Reiches. 2 vols. Leipzig: Duncker & Humblot, 1898.
4807. Hertner, Peter. "Das Vorbild deutscher Universalbanken bei der Gründung und Entwicklung italienischer Geschäftsbanken neuen Typs 1894-1914." in Entwicklung und Aufgaben von Versicherungen und Banken in der Industrialisierung. Berlin: Duncker & Humblot, 1980. pp. 195-282.
4808. Heuer, Gerd F. "Wege und Möglichkeiten der Kriegsfinanzierung. Ein finanzwirtschaftlicher Rückblick auf den Weltkrieg." Wissen und Wehr (1941), 420-28.
4809. Holden, Edward. Cost of the War to America, Britain & Germany, The Reichsbank's Predicament. London: The Statist, 1919. 11 pp.
4810. Holtfort, Hans-Günther. Bismarks finanz- und steuerpolitische Auffassung im Lichte der heutigen Finanzwissenschaft. Diss. Bonn. Würzburg: Triltsch, 1937. 49 pp.
4811. Holzhauer, Georg. "Das deutsche Kriegsnotgeld 1914. (Ein Beitrag zum Notgeldproblem der Kriegs- und Nachkriegszeit.)" Wissen und Wehr 19 (1938), 485-91.
4812. Hoppe, Ernst. Der Krieg und die deutsche Geldwirtschaft. Essen: Baedeker, 1919. 70 pp.
4813. Ibbeken, Rudolf. Das aussenpolitische Problem Staat und Wirtschaft in der deutschen Reichspolitik 1880-1914. Schleswig: J. Ibbeken, 1928. 285 pp.
4814. Ilgen, Theodor et al. Sphragistik, Heraldik, Deutsche Münzgeschichte. 2nd ed. Leipzig: Teubner, 1912. 132 pp.
4815. Jaeger, Kurt. Die deutschen Banknoten seit 1871. Engelberg: Speidel-Nübling, 1963. 171 pp.
4816. Jastrow, Ignaz. "Die preussische Steuerreform. Ihre Stellung in der allgemeinen Verwaltungs- und Sozialpolitik." Archiv für Sozialwissenschaft und Sozialpolitik 7 (1894), 103-65.
4817. Joseph, Leopold. The Evolution of German Banking. London: Layton, 1913. 124 pp.
4818. Jürgens, Ulrich. Selbstregulierung des Kapitals. Erfahrungen aus der Kartellbewegung in Deutschland um die Jahrhundertwende. Zum Verhältnis von Politik und Ökonomie. Frankfurt a. M.: Campus, 1980. 233 pp.
4819. Julius, Gustav. Die Bankbewegungen in Deutschland. Fortsetzung der Flugschrift: Spuk des Bankgespenstes. 2 vols. Leipzig: Fernbach, 1846.
4820. Kabisch, Thomas R. Deutsches Kapital in den USA. Von der Reichsgründung bis zur Sequestrierung (1917) und Freigabe. Stuttgart: Klett-Cotta, 1982. 413 pp.
4821. Kahl, Hans-Dietrich. Hauptlinien der deutschen Münzgeschichte vom Ende des 18. Jahrhunderts bis 1878. Frankfurt a. M.: Peus Nachfolger, 1972. 89 pp.
4822. Kahn, Julius. Geschichte des Zinsfusses in Deutschland seit 1815 und die Ursachen seiner Veränderung. Stuttgart: J. G. Cotta, 1884. 247 pp.
4823. Kalle, Fritz. "Zur Staats- und Communalsteuerreform in Preussen." Preussische Jahrbücher 50 (1882), 439-63.
4824. Kamlah, Irmgard. Karl Georg Maassen und die preussische Finanzreform von 1816-1822. Diss. Halle a. d. S. Särchen b. Eisleben: Klöppel, 1934. 64 pp.
4825. Kellenbenz, Hermann. "Die öffentlichen Finanzen im Reich von der Mitte des 17. Jahrhunderts bis ins 19. Jahrhundert." in Finances publiques d'ancien régime. Brussels: Crédit communal de Belgique, 1972. pp. 133-57.
4826. Kellenbenz, Hermann. "Verkehrs- und Nachrichtenwesen, Handel, Geld-, Kredit- und Versicherungswesen 1800-1850." in H. Aubin and W. Zorn, eds. Handbuch der deutschen Wirtschafts- und Sozialgeschichte. Stuttgart: Klett-Cotta, 1976. I, 369-425.

4827. Keller, Arnold. Das Papiergeld der deutschen Kolonien. 3rd ed. Berlin: A. Keller, 1962. 83 pp.
4828. Keller, Arnold. Das Papiergeld des Deutschen Reiches seit 1874. 3rd ed. Berlin: A. Keller, 1929. 19 pp.
4829. Keller, Arnold et al. Das deutsche Notgeld 1914-1922. 5 vols. Frankfurt a. M.: Cahn, 1914-22.
4830. Klein, Ernst. Geschichte der öffentlichen Finanzen in Deutschland (1500-1870). Wiesbaden: Steiner, 1974. 145 pp.
4831. Klein, Ernst. "Das Südamerika-Geschäft der Deutschen Bank vor dem Ersten Weltkrieg." Beiträge zu Wirtschafts- und Währungsfragen und zur Bankgeschichte 16 (1978), 11-23.
4832. Klein, Ernst. Von der Reform zur Restauration. Finanzpolitik und Reformgesetzgebung des preussischen Staatskanzlers Karl August von Hardenberg. Berlin: de Gruyter, 1965. 352 pp.
4833. Kleine-Natrop, Heinrich. Verfassung und Geschichte der Maklerbanken. Munich: Duncker & Humblot, 1913. 112 pp.
4834. Knauerhase, Ramon. "Some Observations on the Institutional Development of the Reichsbank, 1875-1910." International Review of the History of Banking 8 (1974).
4835. Knauss, Robert. Die deutsche, englische und französische Kriegsfinanzierung. Berlin: de Gruyter, 1923. 194 pp.
4836. Kronenberger, Fritz. Die Preisbewegung der Effekten in Deutschland während des Krieges. Berlin: Ebering, 1920; rpt. Frankfurt a. M.: Keip, 1980. 45 pp.
4837. Krug, Leopold. Geschichte der preussischen Staatsschulden. Breslau: Bergius, 1861; rpt. Vaduz: Topos, 1977. 356 pp.
4838. Kümmel, H. "Die Aufgaben der Sparkassen in Deutschland als Lebensversicherungsinstitute für die unteren Volksklassen." Schmoller 27 (1903), 99-141.
4839. Kurzer Abriss aus der deutschen Münzgeschichte, oder historische Darstellung des mit dem Jahr 536 in Deutschland begonnenen Münzwesens, und dessen vielfältigen Gestaltungen, Veränderungen und Schicksale bis auf unsere Zeiten. Nördlingen: Beck, 1837. 88 pp.
4840. Lansburgh, Alfred. Das deutsche Bankwesen. Berlin-Charlottenburg: Bank-Verlag, 1909. 64 pp.
4841. Lansburgh, Alfred. Die deutschen Banken von 1907/8 bis 1912/13. Berlin-Charlottenburg: Bank-Verlag, 1913. 28 pp.
4842. Laves, Walter H. C. "German Governmental Influence on Foreign Investments 1871-1915." Political Science Quarterly 43 (1928), 498-519.
4843. Lee, W. R. "Tax Structure and Economic Growth in Germany, 1750-1850." The Journal of European Economic History 4 (1975), 153-78.
4844. Lehmann, Max. "Der Ursprung der preussischen Einkommensteuer." Preussische Jahrbücher 103 (1901), 1-37.
4845. Leitzmann, Johann J. Wegweiser auf dem Gebiete der deutschen Münzkunde oder geschichtliche Nachrichten über das Münzwesen Deutschlands. Weissensee: G. F. Grossmann, 1869. 782 pp.
4846. Lewy, Max. Die Nationalbank für Deutschland zu Berlin 1881-1909. Berlin: K. Curtius, 1912. 104 pp.
4847. Lexis, Wilhelm. "Bemerkungen über Parallelwährung und Sortengeld." Jahrbücher für Nationalökonomie und Statistik 3 (1895), 829-36.
4848. Lexis, Wilhelm. "The German Bank Commission 1908-09." Economic Journal 20 (1910), 211-21.
4849. Linzbach, Peter. Der Werdegang der preussischen Einkommensteuer unter besonderer Berücksichtigung ihrer kausalen Entwicklungsfaktoren: ein Beitrag zur Theorie der Durchsetzbarkeit der Einkommensteuer. Diss. Cologne. Frankfurt a. M.: Lang, 1984. 259 pp.
4850. Lotz, Walther. Die deutsche Staatsfinanzwirtschaft im Kriege. Stuttgart: Deutsche Verlags-Anstalt, 1927. 151 pp.
4851. Lotz, Walther. Geschichte der deutschen Notenbanken bis zum Jahre 1857. Diss. Strassburg. Leipzig: Duncker & Humblot, 1888. 81 pp.
4852. Loveday, Alexander. "German War Finance in 1914." Economic Journal 26 (1916), 44-56.
4853. Luczak, Czeslaw. "Le rôle du capital bancaire dans la germanisation de la Grande Pologne dans les années 1870-1914." Studia Historiae Oeconomicae 1 (1966), 123-34.
4854. Malou, Jules E. X. Notice historique sur la réforme monétaire en Allemagne. Brussels: s. n., 1879. 27 pp.
4855. Martin, Paul C. "Die Entstehung des preussischen Aktiengesetzes von 1843." VSWG 56 (1969), 499-542.

4856. Martin, Paul C. "Rahmenordnung und Geldwirtschaft der frühen Industrialisierung." in H. Kellenbenz, ed. Öffentliche Finanzen und privates Kapital im späten Mittelalter und in der ersten Hälfte des 19. Jahrhunderts. Stuttgart: G. Fischer, 1971. pp. 87-117.
4857. Mauer, Hermann. Das landwirtschaftliche Kreditwesen Preussens. Strassburg: K. J. Trübner, 1907. 48 pp.
4858. Mauz, Fritz. Geschichte der preussischen Einkommensteuer bis zu ihrer Reform im Jahre 1891. Diss. Tübingen, 1936. Göppingen: Illig, 1935. 203 pp.
4859. Mellin, Ignaz von. Die Schutzzölle und ihr Einfluss auf die deutschen Reichsfinanzen (von 1892-1912). Munich: Reichhardt, 1918. 60 pp.
4860. Metzler, Ludwig. Studien zur Geschichte des deutschen Effektenbankwesens vom ausgehenden Mittelalter bis zur Jetztzeit. Leipzig: Poeschel, 1911. 155 pp.
4861. Miaskowski, August von. "Zur Geschichte und Literatur des Arbeiterversicherungswesens in Deutschland." Schmoller, N. F., 4 (1882), 474-96.
4862. Müller, Willi. Die Entwicklung des Zinsfusses in Deutschland, England und Nordamerika 1914-1926. Diss. Frankfurt a. M., 1928. 87 pp.
4863. Nasse, Erwin. "Die deutschen Zettelbanken während der Krisis von 1866." Jahrbücher für Nationalökonomie und Statistik 11 (1868), 1-23.
4864. Nasse, Erwin. "Die Währungsfrage in Deutschland." Preussische Jahrbücher 55 (1885), 295-345.
4865. National Monetary Commission. The Reichsbank 1876-1900. Washington, D. C.: Government Printing Office, 1910. 362 pp.
4866. Neidlinger, Karl. Studien zur Geschichte der deutschen Effektenspekulation von ihren Anfängen bis zum Beginn der Eisenbahnaktienspekulation. Jena: Fischer, 1930. 94 pp.
4867. Neuburger, Hugh M. German Banks and German Economic Growth from Unification to World War I. Diss. Univ. of Chicago, 1974. New York: Arno Press, 1977. 135 pp.
4868. Neuburger, Hugh M. "The Industrial Politics of the Kreditbanken , 1880-1914." Business History Review 51 (1977), 190-207.
4869. Neuburger, Hugh M. and Houston H. Stokes. "German Banks and German Growth, 1883-1913. An Empirical View." The Journal of Economic History 34 (1974), 710-31.
4870. Neustaetter, Eugen. Deutsches Kriegsnotgeld. Ein Verzeichnis der während des Krieges verwendeten Notgeldscheine und Münzen. Munich: E. Neustaetter, 1919. 223 pp.
4871. Niebuhr, Barthold G. "Das Projekt einer Preussischen Landesbank in den Jahren 1824 und 1825." in A. Trende, ed. Barthold Georg Niebuhr als Finanz- und Bankmann. Berlin: Berliner Kommissionsbuchhandlung, 1929. pp. 205-61.
4872. Obermann, Karl. "Die Rolle der ersten deutschen Aktienbanken in den Jahren 1848 bis 1856." Jahrbuch für Wirtschaftsgeschichte (1960), II, 47-75.
4873. O'Farrell, Horace H. The Franco-German War Indemnity and its Economic Results. London: Harrison, 1913. 80 pp.
4874. Ohnishi, Takeo. "Die Entstehung des ersten preussischen Staatshaushaltets im Jahre 1821." in J. Schneider, ed. Wirtschaftskräfte und Wirtschaftswege. Festschrift für Hermann Kellenbenz. Stuttgart: Klett-Cotta, 1978. III, 281-95.
4875. Ohnishi, Takeo. "Die preussische Steuerreform nach dem Wiener Kongress." in B. Vogel, ed. Preussische Reformen 1807-1820. Königstein: Athenäum, 1980. pp. 266-84.
4876. Pallain, André. La Caisse centrale prussienne des associations coopératives. Paris: J. B. Baillière, 1902. 178 pp.
4877. Pfeifer, Kurt. Die Einwirkung des Weltkriegs und der Nachkriegszeit auf die deutsche Effektenbörse. Diss. Bern. Landau: Kaussler, 1926. 71 pp.
4878. Pielmann, Ernst. Die Finanzpolitik des Zentrums unter der Kanzlerschaft Bismarcks. Diss. Heidelberg. Heidelberg: Pfeffer, 1928. 118 pp.
4879. Plenge, Johann. Von der Diskontpolitik zur Herrschaft über den Geldmarkt. Berlin: J. Springer, 1913. 431 pp.
4880. Pohl, Hans et al. Das deutsche Bankwesen (1806-1848). Die Entwicklung des deutschen Bankwesens zwischen 1848 und 1870. Frankfurt a. M.: Knapp, 1982. 371 pp.
4881. Pohl, Manfred. Konzentration im deutschen Bankwesen, 1848-1980. Frankfurt a. M.: Knapp, 1982. 812 pp.
4882. Poidevin, Raymond. "Les intérêts financiers français et allemands en Serbie de 1895 à 1914." Revue Historique 232 (1964), 49-66.

4883. Poschinger, Heinrich von. Bankwesen und Bankpolitik in Preussen. Nach amtlichen Quellen. 3 vols. Berlin: Springer, 1878-79.
4884. Prange, Gustav. Das deutsche Kriegsnotgeld. Eine kulturgeschichtliche Beschreibung. 2 vols. Görlitz: Görlitzer Nachrichten und Anzeiger, 1921-22.
4885. Quartier, Walter. "Die Rede vor dem Reichstag war der Beginn. Gedanken zur kaiserlichen Botschaft vom 17. 11. 1881." Die Angestellten-Versicherung, 28 (1981), 433-44.
4886. Redlich, Fritz. "Two Nineteenth Century Financiers and Autobiographers. A Comparative Study in Creative Destructiveness and Business Failure." Economy and History 10 (1967), 37-128.
4888. Die Reichsbank, 1876-1900. Jena: Fischer, 1900. 485 pp.
4889. Die Reichsbank, 1876 bis 1910. Berlin: Reichsdruckerei, 1912. 251 pp.
4890. Reuter, Hans-Georg. "Verteilungs- und Umverteilungseffekte der Sozialversicherungsgesetz-gebung im Kaiserreich." in F. Blaich, ed. Staatliche Umverteilungspolitik in historischer Perspektive. Beiträge zur Entwicklung des Staatsinterventionismus in Deutschland und Österreich. Berlin: Duncker & Humblot, 1980. pp. 107-63.
4891. Ries, Hans. Die Devisen-Gesetzgebung des Deutschen Reiches als kriegswirtschaftliche Massnahme. Göttingen: Schönhütte, 1928. 117 pp.
4892. Riesser, Jacob. Die deutschen Grossbanken und ihre Konzentration im Zusammenhang mit der Entwicklung der Gesamtwirtschaft in Deutschland. 4th ed. Jena: G. Fischer, 1912. 768 pp.
4893. Riesser, Jacob. The German Great Banks and Their Concentration. in Connection with the Economic Development of Germany. 3rd ed. Washington D. C.: National Monetary Connission, 1911. 1042 pp.
4894. Riesser, Jacob. Von 1848 bis heute. Jena: G. Fischer, 1912. 141 pp.
4895. Riesser, Jacob. Zur Entwicklungsgeschichte der deutschen Grossbanken mit besonderer Rücksicht auf die Konzentrationsbestrebungen. Jena: G. Fischer, 1906. 284 pp.
4896. Rist, Charles. Les finances de guerre de l'Allemagne. Paris: Payot, 1921. 294 pp.
4897. Rittmann, Herbert. Auf Heller und Pfennig. Die faszinierende Geschichte des Geldes und der wirtschaftlichen Entwicklung in Deutschland. Munich: Battenberg, 1976. 132 pp.
4898. Rittmann, Herbert. Deutsche Geldgeschichte 1484-1914. Munich: Battenberg, 1975. 1067 pp.
4899. Roettinger, Bruno. Das deutsche Gefangenenlagergeld sowie Gruben- und Zechengeld 1914-1918. Frankfurt a. M.: Cahn, 1922. 42 pp.
4900. Rosenberg, Harry. Die Banknoten des Deutschen Reiches ab 1871. 5th ed. Braunschweig: Borek, 1979. 157 pp.
4901. Rosendorff, Richard. "Die deutschen Banken im überseeischen Verkehr." Schmoller 29 (1904), 1245-86.
4902. Row-Fogo, J. "Local Taxation in Germany." Economic Journal 11 (1901), 354-78.
4903. Ruedorffer, Robert A. von. Reichsbank und Darlehnskassen in der Kriegsfinanzierung 1914-18. Cologne: Institut für Bankwirtschaft und Bankrecht, 1968. 176 pp.
4904. Saul, Klaus. "Wirtschafts- und sozialpolitische Grundlagen. Industrialisierung, Systemstabilisierung und Sozialversicherung. Zur Entstehung, politischen Funktion und sozialen Realität der Sozialversicherung des kaiserlichen Deutschlands." Zeitschrift für die Gesamte Versicherungswissenschaft 69 (1980), 177-98.
4905. Schär, Johann F. Umgestaltung der Geld- und Währungsverhältnisse, des zwischenstaatlichen Zahlungsverkehrs und der Wechselkurse durch den Krieg. Berlin: Simon, 1920. 42 pp.
4906. Schissler, Hanna. "Preussische Finanzpolitik nach 1807. Die Bedeutung der Staatsverschuldung als Faktor der Modernisierung des preussischen Finanzsystems." Geschichte und Gesellschaft 8 (1982), 367-85.
4907. Schmalz, Erwin. Die deutsche Sozialversicherung während des Weltkrieges. Diss. Erlangen, 1927. Erlangen: Höfer & Limmert, 1930. 108 pp.
4908. Schmidt, Fritz. "Die Wechselkurse und ihre Beherrschung während des Weltkriegs und der Übergangszeit." Weltwirtschaftliches Archiv 14 (1919), 210-74.
4909. Schmitt-Lermann, Hans. "Bismarcks Stellung zum Versicherungswesen." Zeitschrift für die Gesamte Versicherungswissenschaft 54 (1965), 51-79.
4910. Schmoller, Gustav. "Die Epochen der preussischen Finanzpolitik." Schmoller 1 (1877), 33-114.
4911. Schmoller, Gustav. "Historische Betrachtung über Staatenbildung und Finanzentwicklung." Schmoller 33 (1909), 1-64.
4912. Schmoller, Gustav. Preussische Verfassungs-, Verwaltungs- und Finanzgeschichte. Berlin: Verlag der Täglichen Rundschau, 1921. 236 pp.

4913. Schmoller, Gustav. "Über die Ausbildung einer richtigen Scheidemünzpolitik vom 14. bis 19. Jahrhundert. Schmoller 24 (1900), 1247-74.

4914. Schonbeck, Otto. "Die Einkommensteuer unter den Nachfolgern Steins. Ein Beitrag zur Geschichte des Ministeriums Altenstein-Dohna." Forschungen zur Brandenburgischen und Preussischen Geschichte 25 (1913), 117-77.

4915. Schramm, Albert. Deutsches Notgeld 1914-1919. 2 vols. Leipzig: Deutscher Verein für Buch- und Schriftwesen, 1918-1920.

4916. Schrötter, Friedrich von. Das preussische Münzwesen 1806-1873. 3 vols. Berlin: Parey, 1925-26.

4917. Schultz, Bruno. Kleine deutsche Geldgeschichte des 19. und 20. Jahrhunderts. Berlin: Duncker & Humblot, 1976. 294 pp.

4918. Schumacher, Hermann A. "The Concentration of German Banking." Political Science Quarterly 22 (1907), 83-104.

4919. Schumacher, Hermann A. "Geschichte der deutschen Bankliteratur im 19. Jahrhundert." in Die Entwicklung der deutschen Volkswirtschaftslehre im neunzehnten Jahrhundert. Leipzig: Duncker & Humblot, 1908. 39 pp.

4920. Schumacher, Hermann A. "Die Ursachen und Wirkungen der Konzentration im deutschen Bankwesen." Schmoller 30 (1906), 883-925.

4921. Schumann, Friedrich. Die vier letzten Privatnotenbanken. Ein Beitrag zur Geschichte des Bankwesens. Gautzsch b. Leipzig: Dietrich, 1910. 13 pp.

4922. Schweyer, Franz. Die Bankdepotgeschäfte in geschichtlicher, wirtschaftlicher und rechtlicher Beziehung. Munich: J. Schweitzer, 1899. 171 pp.

4923. Seeger, Manfred. Die Politik der Reichsbank von 1876 bis 1914 im Lichte der Spielregeln der Goldwährung. Berlin: Duncker & Humblot, 1968. 161 pp.

4924. Seidel, Max. "The German Savings Banks." Zeitschrift für die gesamte Staatswissenschaft (1908), 58-107, 341-403.

4925. Seidenzahl, Fritz. "Eine Denkschrift David Hansemanns vom Jahre 1856. Ein Beitrag zur Entstehungsgeschichte der deutschen Aktienbanken." in K. E. Born, ed. Moderne deutsche Wirtschaftsgeschichte. Cologne: Kiepenheuer & Witsch, 1966. pp. 214-25. [first appeared in Tradition 5 (1960), 83-94.]

4926. Seidenzahl, Fritz. "Das Spannungsfeld zwischen Staat und Bankier im Wilhelminischen Zeitalter." Tradition 13 (1968), 142-50.

4927. Siebert, Albert. "Die Entwicklung der direkten Besteuerung in den süddeutschen Bundesstaaten im letzten Jahrhundert." Zeitschrift für die gesamte Staatswissenschaft 68 (1912), 1-52.

4928. Soetbeer, Adolf. Beiträge zur Geschichte des Geld- und Münzwesens in Deutschland. Göttingen: Dieterich, 1861-64.

4929. Soetbeer, Adolf. Denkschrift betreffend die Einführung der Goldwährung in Deutschland. Hamburg: H. G. Voigt, 1856. 32 pp.

4930. Soetbeer, Adolf. "Volkseinkommen im preussischen Staate 1876 und 1888." Jahrbücher für Nationalökonomie und Statistik 52 (1889), 414-27.

4931. Spittel, Oskar. Die deutschen Sparcassen, deren Entstehung, Einrichtung, Aufgaben und Ziele. Gotha: Thienemann, 1880; rpt. Frankfurt a. M.: 1970. 58 pp.

4932. Sprenger, Bernd. Geldmengenänderungen in Deutschland im Zeitalter der Industrialisierung (1835-1913). Diss. Cologne. Cologne: Forschungsinstitut für Sozial- und Wirtschaftsgeschichte, 1982. 201 pp.

4933. Sprenger, Bernd. Währungswesen und Währungspolitik in Deutschland von 1834 bis 1875. Cologne: Forschungsinstitut für Sozial- und Wirtschaftsgeschichte, 1981. 147 pp.

4934. Steitz, Walter. "Zur Etablierung der Realbesteuerung in den süddeutschen Staaten im Rahmen der sich auflösenden Feudalstrukturen 1806-1850." VSWG 63 (1976), 145-79.

4935. Der Streit um die Verstaatlichung der Reichsbank. Berlin: Norddeutsche Buchdruckerei und Verlagsanstalt, 1889. 159 pp.

4936. Thorwart, Friedrich. "Die Entwicklung des Banknotenumlaufs in Deutschland von 1851-1880." Jahrbücher für Nationalökonomie und Statistik 41 (1883), 193-250.

4937. Tille, Armin. "Getreide als Geld." Jahrbücher für Nationalökonomie und Statistik 20 (1900), 721-54.

4938. Tilly, Richard H. "Banken und Industrialisierung in Deutschland, Quantifizierungsversuche." in Entwicklung und Aufgaben von Versicherungen und Banken in der Industrialisierung. Berlin: Duncker & Humblot, 1980. pp.165-93.

4939. Tilly, Richard H. "Capital Formation in Germany in the Nineteenth Century." in P. Mathias and M. M. Postan, eds. Cambridge Economic History of Europe. vol. 7, pt. 1. Cambridge: Cambridge University Press, 1978. pp. 382-441.

4940. Tilly, Richard H. "Finanzielle Aspekte der preussischen Industrialisierung, 1815-1870." in W. Fischer, ed. Wirtschafts- und sozialgeschichtliche Probleme der frühren Industrialisierung. Berlin: Colloquium, 1968. pp. 477-91.

4941. Tilly, Richard H. "Fiscal Policy and Prussian Economic Development, 1815-1866." Journal of Economic History 26 (1966), 484-97; 27 (1967), 391.

4942. Tilly, Richard H. "Germany, 1815-70." in R. E. Cameron, ed. Banking in the Early Stages of Industrialisation. New York: Oxford University Press, 1967. pp. 151-82.

4943. Tilly, Richard H. "The Political Economy of Public Finance and Industrialization of Prussia, 1815-1866." Journal of Economic History 26 (1966), 484-97.

4944. Tilly, Richard H. "Zur Entwicklung des Kapitalmarktes und Industrialisierung im 19. Jahrhundert unter besonderer Berücksichtigung Deutschlands." VSWG 60 (1973), 145-65.

4945. Trende, Adolf. Geschichte der deutschen Sparkassen bis zum Anfang des 20. Jahrhunderts. Stuttgart: Deutscher Sparkassenverlag, 1957. 610 pp.

4946. Treue, Wilhelm. "Der Privatbankier an der Wende vom 19. zum 20. Jahrhundert. Dem Privatbankier Friedrich Carl Freiherrn von Oppenheim zum 70. Geburtstag." Tradition 15 (1970), 225-38.

4947. Treue, Wilhelm. "Das Privatbankwesen im 19. Jahrhundert." in H. Coing, ed. Wissenschaft und Kodifikation des Privatrechts im 19. Jahrhundert. Frankfurt a. M.: Klostermann, 1980. V, 94-127.

4948. Ullmann, Hans-Peter. "Deutsche Unternehmer und Bismarcks Sozialversicherungssystem." in Die Entstehung des Wohlfahrtsstaates in Grossbritannien und Deutschland 1850-1950. Stuttgart: Deutsches Historisches Institut London, 1982. pp. 142-58.

4949. Ullmann, Hans-Peter. "Industrielle Interessen und die Entstehung der deutschen Sozialversicherung 1880-1889." Historische Zeitschrift 229 (1979), 574-610.

4950. Vagts, Alfred. "The Golden Chains. The Jew and Wilhelminic Imperialism." Maryland Historian 4 (1973), 47-58.

4951. Vogel, Walter. Bismarcks Arbeiterversicherung, ihre Entstehung im Kräftespiel der Zeit. Braunschweig: Westermann, 1951. 192 pp.

4952. Von der königlichen Bank zur Deutschen Reichsbank. Berlin: Reichsbank, 1940. 69 pp.

4953. Waldecker, Ludwig. Reichseinheit und Reichsfinanzen. Nachdenkliche Kapitel für Juristen und Nichtjuristen über ein Problem deutscher Vergangenheit, Gegenwart und Zukunft. Tübingen: Mohr, 1916. 205 pp.

4954. Wallich, Hermann. "Aus der Frühgeschichte der Deutschen Bank. Aufzeichnungen." in Beiträge zu Wirtschafts- und Währungsfragen und zur Bankgeschichte. Frankfurt a. M.: Deutsche Bank, 1976. pp. 27-43.

4955. Warnack, Max. Die Entwicklung des deutschen Banknotenwesens. Berlin: E. Ebering, 1905. 236 pp.

4956. Wassermann, Sigmund. Das Sortengeschäft in Deutschland in seiner geschichtlichen Entwicklung. Diss. Erlangen. Bamberg: W. Gärtner, 1912. 266 pp.

4957. Weibezahn, Hermann. "Deutschland's Uebergang zur Goldwährung vermöge der französischen Kriegsentschädigung." Jahrbücher für Nationalökonomie und Statistik 15 (1870), 145-81.

4958. Wielandt, Friedrich. "Die Frankfurter Bundesversammlung und die Frage der deutschen Münzeinheit." Blätter für Münzfreunde und Münzforschung 80 (1956), 483-501.

4959. Wilcke, Julius. Daler, Mark og Kroner 1481-1914. Copenhagen: Gad, 1931. 206 pp.

4960. Wintzingerode, Graf von. "Ein Beitrag zur Grundsteuerfrage in Preussen." Preussische Jahrbücher 30 (1872), 572-90.

4961. Wirth, Max. Die Münzkrisis und die Notenbank-Reform im Deutschen Reiche. Cologne: DuMont-Schauberg, 1874. 118 pp.

4962. Witt, Peter-Christian. Die Finanzpolitik des Deutschen Reiches von 1903-1913. Eine Studie zur Innenpolitik des Wilhelminischen Deutschland. Lübeck: Matthiesen, 1970. 421 pp.

4963. Witte, Klaus. Bismarcks Sozialversicherungen und die Entwicklung eines marxistischen Reformverständnisses in der deutschen Sozialdemokratie. Cologne: Pahl-Rugenstein, 1980. 144 pp.

4964. Woeniger, August T. Die Preussische Bank. Ein geschichtlich-kritischer Beitrag zur Beurtheilung der neuesten Bankreform. Berlin: Cohn, 1846. 164 pp.

4965. Wurm, Emanuel. Die Finanzgeschichte des Deutschen Reiches. Hamburg: Dubber, 1910. 272 pp.
4966. Wysocki, Josef. "Fragen örtlicher Kapitalbildung in der deutschen Sparkassengeschichte des 19. Jahrhunderts." Sparkasse. Zeitschrift des Deutschen Sparkassen- und Giroverbandes 92 (1975), 158-62.
4967. Wysocki, Josef. Untersuchungen zur Wirtschafts- und Sozialgeschichte der deutschen Sparkassen im 19. Jahrhundert. Stuttgart: Deutscher Sparkassenverlag, 1980. 233 pp.
4968. Zahlen zur Geldentwertung in Deutschland 1914 bis 1923. Berlin: Hobbing, 1925. 54 pp.
4969. Zedlitz und Neukirch, Octavio W. F. O. K. von. "Die directen Steuern in Preussen." Preussische Jahrbücher 44 (1879), 115-51.
4970. Zuchardt, Karl. Die Finanzpolitik Bismarcks und der Parteien im norddeutschen Bunde. Diss. Leipzig, 1909. Leipzig: Quelle & Meyer, 1910. 8 pp.

SEE ALSO: 885, 897, 950, 1687, 2308, 2411, 3408, 3414-15, 3667, 4231, 4238, 4241, 4253-54, 4258.

WEIMAR REPUBLIC--1919-1933

Bibliographic Reference

4971. Curth, Hermann. "Bibliographie zum wirtschaftlichen Problem der deutschen Reparationen." Weltwirtschaftliches Archiv 22 (1926), 124-75; 23 (1926), 25-65.

WEIMAR REPUBLIC--1919-1933

4972. Abel, Andrew et al. "Money Demand During Hyperinflation." Journal of Monetary Economics 5 (1979), 97-104.
4973. Baruch, Bernard M. The Making of the Reparation and Economic Sections of the Treaty. New York: Harper, 1920; rpt. New York, 1970. 352 pp.
4974. Bennett, Edward W. Germany and the Diplomacy of the Financial Crisis, 1931. Cambridge, MA: Harvard University Press, 1962. 342 pp.
4975. Berber, Fritz. Das Diktat von Versailles. Entstehung. Inhalt. Zerfall. Eine Darstellung in Dokumenten. Essen: Essener Verlagsanstalt, 1939. 1672 pp.
4976. Bergmann, Carl. "Die Geschichte des Reparationsproblems. Vorwort eines Buches." in Der Eiserne Steg. Jahrbuch. Frankfurt a. M.: Frankfurter Societäts-Druckerei, 1926. pp. 111-15.
4977. Bernard, Francis. Les finances de la France, de l'Angleterre, de l'Allemagne et de la Roumanie 1914-1925. Paris: Librairie de jurisprudence, 1925. 190 pp.
4978. Bogs, Walter. Die Sozialversicherung in der Weimarer Demokratie. Munich: Schweitzer, 1981. 137 pp.
4979. Bonn, Moritz J. Stabilization of the Mark. Chicago: First National Bank of Chicago, 1922. 56 pp.
4980. Borsky, G. The Greatest Swindle in the World. The Story of German Reparations. London: New Europe, 1942. 78 pp.
4981. Brentano, Lujo. "Was Deutschland gezahlt hat. Die bisherigen deutschen Leistungen auf Grund des Vertrages von Versailles." Weltwirtschaftliches Archiv 20 (1924), 235-51.
4982. Bresciani-Turroni, Costantino. The Economics of Inflation. A Study of Currency Devaluation in Post-War Germany. London: Allen & Unwin, 1937. 464 pp.
4983. Bücher, Hermann. Finanz- und Wirtschaftsentwicklung Deutschlands in den Jahren 1921 bis 1925. Berlin: Heymann, 1925. 190 pp.
4984. Bunselmeyer, Robert E. The Cost of the War, 1914-1919. British Economic War Aims and the Origins of Reparation. Hamden, CT: Archon Books, 1975. 249 pp.
4985. Callot, Maurice. Le mark allemand depuis 1924. Diss. Paris. Paris: Rousseau, 1934. 178 pp.
4986. Cassel, Gustav. Das Geldwesen nach 1914. Leipzig: G. A. Gloeckner, 1925. 220 pp.
4987. Comstock, Alzada P. "Reparation Payments in Perspective." American Economic Review 20 (1930), 199-209.
4988. Crook, James W. The Reparations Problem and the Dawes Report. Amherst, MA: Amherst College, 1924. 47 pp.

4989. D'Abernon, Edgar V. "German Currency, its Collapse and Recovery, 1920-26." Journal of Royal Statistical Society 90 (1927), 1-40.
4990. Die deutsche Sozialversicherung seit 1914. Essen-Ruhr: Baedeker, 1929. 158 pp.
4991. Elster, Karl. Von der Mark zur Reichsmark. Die Geschichte der deutschen Währung in den Jahren 1914 bis 1924. Jena: Fischer, 1928. 480 pp.
4992. Eynern, Gert von. Die Reichsbank. Probleme des deutschen Zentralnoteninstituts in geschichtlicher Darstellung. Jena: Fischer, 1928. 144 pp.
4993. Felix, David. "Reparations With a Vengeance." Central European History 4 (1971), 171-79.
4994. Felix, David. Walther Rathenau and the Weimar Republic. The Politics of Reparations. Baltimore: Johns Hopkins Press, 1971. 210 pp.
4995. Fergusson, Adam. When Money Dies. The Nightmare of the Weimar Collapse. London: W. Kimber, 1975. 256 pp.
4996. Flink, Salomon J. The German Reichsbank and Economic Germany. A Study of the Policies of the Reichsbank in Their Relation to the Economic Development of Germany, with Special Reference to the Period after 1923. New York: Harper, 1930. 267 pp.
4997. Fourgeaud, André. La dépréciation et la revalorisation du mark allemand et les enseignements de l'expérience monétaire allemande. Paris: Payot, 1926. 284 pp.
4998. Frenkel, Jacob A. "The Forward Exchange Rate, Expectations and the Demand for Money. The German Hyperinflation." American Economic Review 67 (1977), 653-70.
4999. Frenkel, Jacob A. "Further Evidence on Expectations and the Demand for Money During the German Hyperinflation." Journal of Monetary Economics 5 (1979), 81-96.
5000. "German Reaction to the Economic Demands of the Treaty." in S. B. Clough, ed. Economic History of Europe. New York: Harper & Row, 1968. pp. 87-89.
5001. German Reparation and Allied Military Control 1923. London: Stat. Office, 1978. 1027 pp.
5002. Gossweiler, Kurt. Grossbanken, Industriemonopole, Staat. Ökonomie und Politik des staatsmonopolistischen Kapitalismus in Deutschland 1914-1932. Berlin: Deutscher Verlag der Wissenschaften, 1971. 423 pp.
5003. Gradl, Baptist. Geschichte der Reparations-Sachleistungen. Berlin: "Germania", 1933. 150 pp.
5004. Habedank, Heinz. Die Reichsbank in der Weimarer Republik. Zur Rolle der Zentralbank in der Politik des deutschen Imperialismus. 1919-1933. Berlin: Akademie, 1981. 257 pp.
5005. Harris, Charles R. S. Germany's Foreign Indebtedness. London: Oxford University Press, 1935; rpt. New York, 1979. 124 pp.
5006. Heitger, Anneliese. Die konjunkturelle Bewegung der ordentlichen Reichseinnahmen seit 1924 und ihre finanzwirtschaftlichen Probleme. Diss. Cologne. Cologne: Orthen, 1939. 111 pp.
5007. Helbich, Wolfgang J. "Die Bedeutung der Reparationsfrage für die Wirtschaftspolitik der Regierung Brüning." in G. Jasper, ed. Von Weimar zu Hitler 1930-1933. Cologne: Kiepenheuer & Witsch, 1968. pp. 72-98.
5008. Helbich, Wolfgang J. Die Reparationen in der Ära Brüning. Zur Bedeutung des Young-Plans für die deutsche Politik 1930 bis 1932. Berlin: Colloquium, 1962. 139 pp.
5009. Hennig, Curt. Die Struktur der deutschen Reichsbank und ihre Geld- und Kreditpolitik unter der Herrschaft des Dawes-Planes 1924-1928. Die Haupttatsachen und Probleme deutscher Zentralnotenbankpolitik im Hinblick auf den Wiederaufbau unserer Geld- und Kreditwirtschaft. Diss. Königsberg, 1929. 203 pp.
5010. Hertz-Eichenrode, Dieter. "Reichskredite für die Ostsiedlung. Eine innenpolitische Streitfrage der Jahre 1925 bis 1927." Jahrbuch für die Geschichte Mittel- und Ostdeutschlands 27 (1978), 238-90.
5011. Hörster-Philipps, Ulrike. "Grosskapital, Weimarer Republik und Faschismus. Konzeptionen und Aktivitäten der deutschen Industrie und zur Errichtung der faschistischen Diktatur 1918-1933." in Die Zerstörung der Weimarer Republik. Cologne: Pahl-Rugenstein, 1977. pp. 38-141.
5012. Hörster-Philipps, Ulrike. Wer war Hitler wirklich? Grosskapital und Faschismus 1918-1945. Cologne: Pahl-Rugenstein, 1978. 388 pp.
5013. Holz, Kurt A. Die Diskussion um den Dawes- und Young-Plan in der deutschen Presse. 2 vols. Diss. Cologne, 1975. Frankfurt a. M.: Haag + Herchen, 1977.
5014. Hornung, Karl. Einflüsse auf die Gestaltung der Markdevise seit der Stabilisierung der deutschen Währung bis zur Neuordnung der Reparationsverpflichtungen durch das Inkrafttreten des Neuen Planes. Diss. Giessen. Giessen: Christ, 1933. 68 pp.
5015. Jacobson, Jon. Locarno Diplomacy. Germany and the West. 1925-1929. Princeton, NJ: Princeton University Press, 1972. 420 pp.

5016. James, Harold. The Reichsbank and Public Finance in Germany 1924-1933: A Study of the Politics of Economics During the Great Depression. Frankfurt a. M.: Knapp, 1985. 426 pp.

5017. Jordan, W. M. Great Britain, France and the German Problem, 1918-39. A Study of Anglo-French Relations in the Making and Maintenance of the Versailles Settlement. Oxford: Oxford University Press, 1943; rpt. London, 1971. 235 pp.

5018. Kayser, Jacques. Ruhr ou plan Dawes? Histoire des reparations avec une chronologie. Paris: A. Delpeuch, 1925. 103 pp.

5019. Keiser, Günter and Bernhard Benning. Kapitalbildung und volkswirtschaftliche Investitionen in Deutschland 1924 bis 1928. Berlin: R. Hobbing, 1931. 210 pp.

5020. Köhler, Henning. "Arbeitsbeschaffung, Siedlung und Reparationen in der Schlussphase der Regierung Brüning." Vierteljahrshefte für Zeitgeschichte 17 (1969), 276-307.

5021. Krohn, Claus-Dieter. "Helfferich contra Hilferding. Konservative Geldpolitik und die sozialen Folgen der deutschen Inflation 1918-1923." VSWG 62 (1975), 62-92.

5022. Krohn, Claus-Dieter. Stabilisierung und ökonomische Interessen. Die Finanzpolitik des Deutschen Reiches 1923-1927. Düsseldorf: Bertelsmann, 1974. 287 pp.

5023. Krüger, Peter. Deutschland und die Reparationen 1918/19. Die Genesis des Reparations-problems in Deutschland zwischen Waffenstillstand und Versailler Friedensschluss. Stuttgart: Deutsche Verlagsanstalt, 1973. 224 pp.

5024. Krüger, Peter. "Die Reparationen und das Scheitern einer deutschen Verständigungspolitik auf der Pariser Friedenskonferenz im Jahre 1919." Historische Zeitschrift 221 (1975), 326-72.

5025. Krüger, Peter. "Das Reparationsproblem der Weimarer Republik in fragwürdiger Sicht. Kritische Überlegungen zur neuesten Forschung." Vierteljahrshefte für Zeitgeschichte 29 (1981), 21-47.

5026. Lamont, Thomas W. "The Reparations Settlement and Economic Peace in Europe." Political Science Quarterly 45 (1930), 321-26.

5027. Lansburgh, Alfred. Die Politik der Reichsbank und die Reichsschatzanweisungen nach dem Kriege. Munich: Duncker & Humblot, 1924. 54 pp.

5028. Laubach, Ernst. Die Politik der Kabinette Wirth 1921/22. Lübeck: Matthiesen, 1968. 344 pp.

5029. Leuschen-Seppel, Rosemarie. Zwischen Staatsverantwortung und Klasseninteresse: die Wirtschafts- und Finanzpolitik der SPD zur Zeit der Weimarer Republik unter besonderer Berücksichtigung der Mittelphase 1924-1928/29. Bonn: Neue Gesellschaft, 1981. 312 pp.

5030. Link, Werner. Die amerikanische Stabilisierungspolitik in Deutschland, 1921-32. Düsseldorf: Droste Verlag, 1970. 704 pp.

5031. Lloyd George, David. The Truth About Reparations and War Debts. London: Heinemann, 1932; rpt. New York, 1970. 150 pp.

5032. Lüke, Rolf E. Das Geheimnis der deutschen Bankenkrise, 13. 7. 1931. Frankfurt a. M.: Knapp, 1981. 200 pp.

5033. McDougall, Walter A. "Political Economy Versus National Sovereignty. French Structure for German Economic Integration After Versailles." Journal of Modern History 51 (1979), 4-23.

5034. Meier, Ernst. Zeittafel der deutschen Reparation 1918-1932. 2nd ed. Erlangen: Palm & Enke, 1932. 146 pp.

5035. Moulton, Harold G. The Reparation Plan. An Interpretation of the Reports of the Expert Committee Appointed by the Reparation Commission. New York: McGraw-Hill, 1924; rpt. Westport, CT, 1970. 325 pp.

5036. Netzband, Karl-Bernhard and Hans-Peter Widmaier. Währungs- und Finanzpolitik der Ära Luther, 1923-1925. Basel: Kyklos, 1964. 286 pp.

5037. Neumark, Fritz. "Zur Finanzgeschichte der Weimarer Republik." Finanzarchiv, N.F., 35 (1976), 351-66.

5038. Northrop, Mildred B. Control Policies of the Reichsbank 1924-1933. Diss. Columbia University. New York: Columbia University Press, 1938. 405 pp.

5039. Palyi, Melchior. Zur Frage der Kapitalwanderungen nach dem Kriege. Munich: Duncker & Humblot, 1926. 100 pp.

5040. Petzina, Dietmar. "Staatliche Ausgaben und deren Umverteilungswirkungen--das Beispiel der Industrie- und Agrarsubventionen in der Weimarer Republik." in F. Blaich, ed. Staatliche Umverteilungspolitik in historischer Perspektive. Berlin: Duncker & Humblot, 1980. pp. 59-105.

5041. Reichardt, Wolfgang. "Kapitalbildung und Kapitalmarkt in Deutschland seit der Stabilisierung." in Probleme des deutschen Wirtschaftslebens. Erstrebtes und Erreichtes. Berlin: de Gruyter, 1937. pp. 568-618.

222   HISTORY OF FINANCE

5042. The Reparation Problem, 1918-1924. Washington, D. C.: Government Printing Office, 1924. 50 pp.
5043. Die Reparationen. Vom Waffenstillstand 1918 bis zum Hoover-Feierjahr 1931. Der Leidensweg des deutschen Volkes. Berlin: Verlagsanstalt des Deutschen Beamtenbundes, 1932. 164 pp.
5044. Ronde, Hans. Von Versailles bis Lausanne. Der Verlauf der Reparationsverhandlungen nach dem ersten Weltkrieg. Stuttgart: Kohlhammer, 1950. 210 pp.
5045. Rupieper, Herman J. The Cuno Government and Reparations, 1921-23. Politics and Economics. The Hague: M. Nijhoff, 1979. 289 pp.
5046. Salemi, Michael K. "Expected Exchange Depreciation and the Demand for Money in Hyperinflation Germany." Journal of Money, Credit and Banking 12 (1980), 592-602.
5047. Salemi, Michael K. Hyperinflation, Exchange Depreciation, and the Demand for Money in Post World War I Germany. Diss. University of Minnesota, 1976. 196 pp.
5048. Schacht, Hjalmar. The End of Reparations. London: J. Cape, 1931. 248 pp.
5049. Schacht, Hjalmar. The Stabilization of the Mark. London: Allen & Unwin, 1927; rpt. New York, 1979. 247 pp. (German: Stuttgart, 1927)
5050. Schiemann, Jürgen. Die deutsche Währung in der Weltwirtschaftskrise 1929-1933. Währungspolitik und Abwertungskontroverse unter den Bedingungen der Reparationen. Bern: Haupt, 1980. 358 pp.
5051. Schmidt, Royal J. Versailles and the Ruhr. Seedbed of World War II. The Hague: Nijhoff, 1968. 320 pp.
5052. Schnee, Heinrich et al., eds. Zehn Jahre Versailles. (1919-1929). 3 vols. Berlin: Brückenverlag, 1929-30.
5053. Schröter, Heinz. Konjunktur und Geldmarkt seit der Währungstabilisierung. Diss. Halle-Wittenberg. Halle a. d. S.: Klinz, 1934. 69 pp.
5054. Schuker, Stephen A. The End of French Predominance in Europe. The Financial Crisis of 1924 and the Adoption of the Dawes Plan. Chapel Hill: University of North Carolina Press, 1976. 444 pp.
5055. Schulz, Gerhard. "Reparationen und Krisenprobleme nach dem Wahlsieg der NSDAP 1930. Betrachtungen zur Regierung Brüning." VSWG 67 (1980), 200-22.
5056. Seegardel, Willi. Die Bilanzen der deutschen Kreditbanken, 1924-1928. Diss. Berlin. Berlin: W. Christian, 1930. 115 pp.
5057. Sering, Max. Germany under the Dawes Plan. Origin. Legal Foundations, and Economic Effects of the Reparation Payments. London: P. S. King, 1929. 251 pp.
5058. Skiba, Rainer and Hermann Adam. Das westdeutsche Lohnniveau zwischen den beiden Weltkriegen und nach der Währungsreform. Cologne: Bund-Verlag, 1974. 264 pp.
5059. Solmssen, Georg. Das deutsche Finanzwesen nach Beendigung des Weltkrieges. Berlin: H. R. Engelmann, 1921. 83 pp.
5060. Sommer, Albrecht. Sparkassen und Konjunktur. Berlin: C. Heymann, 1934. 191 pp.
5061. Soutou, Georges. "Die deutschen Reparationen und das Seydoux-Projekt 1920/21." Vierteljahrshefte für Zeitgeschichte 23 (1975), 237-70.
5062. Stucken, Rudolf. "Schaffung der Reichsmark, Reparationsregelungen und Auslandsanleihen, Konjunkturen (1924-1930)." in Währung und Wirtschaft in Deutschland 1876-1975. Frankfurt a. M.: F. Knapp, 1976. pp. 249-81.
5063. Takahashi, Susumu. "German Reparations Problem, 1920-1924. A Case Study of International Conflict." in Peace Research in Japan. Tokyo: Japan Peace Research Group, 1976. pp. 85-88.
5064. Trachtenberg, Marc. "Reparations at the Paris Peace Conference." Journal of Modern History 51 (1979), 24-55.
5065. Treviranus, Ralph. Die konjunkturpolitische Rolle der öffentlichen Haushalte in Deutschland während der grossen Krise 1928 bis 1934. Diss. Kiel, 1962. 139 pp.
5066. Vogt, Martin. Die Entstehung des Youngplans. Dargestellt vom Reichsarchiv 1931-1933. Boppard am Rhein: Boldt, 1970. 396 pp.
5067. Wandel, Eckhard. Die Bedeutung der Vereinigten Staaten von Amerika für das deutsche Reparationsproblem 1924-1929. Diss. Tübingen, 1970. Tübingen: Mohr, 1971. 332 pp.
5068. Weill-Raynal, Etienne. Les réparations allemandes et la France. 3 vols. Paris: Nouvelles Ed. Latines, 1938-47.
5069. Wheeler-Bennett, John. The Wreck of Reparations. Being the Political Background of the Lausanne Agreement, 1932. London: Allen & Unwin, 1933; rpt. New York, 1972. 295 pp.

5070. Wilhelmy, Rudolf. Geschichte des deutschen wertbeständigen Notgeldes von 1923-24. Diss. Berlin. Berlin: R. Wilhelmy, 1962. 172 pp.

5071. Wüest, Erich. Der Vertrag von Versailles in Licht und Schatten der Kritik. Die Kontroverse um seine wirtschaftlichen Auswirkungen. Zurich: Europa Verlag, 1962. 277 pp.

5072. Wuest, Eduard. Die Finanzierung der deutschen Lieferungen nach Sowjet-Russland in den Jahren 1925-1936. Diss. Heidelberg. Speyer: Pilger, 1938. 103 pp.

5073. Zimmermann, Heinrich. Die deutsche Inflation. (Historisch-kritische Betrachtungen zum deutschen Währungsverfall und zur Währungsreform). Berlin: Ebering, 1927. 120 pp.

5074. Zimmermann, Ludwig. Deutsche Aussenpolitik in der Ära der Weimarer Republik. Göttingen: Musterschmidt, 1958. 486 pp.

5075. Zwoch, Gerhard. Die Erfüllungs- und Verständigungspolitik der Weimarer Republik und die deutsche öffentliche Meinung. Diss. Kiel, 1951. 125 pp.

SEE ALSO: 937-38, 944-45, 950, 2411, 3667, 4399, 5086, 5088-90, 5093, 5097.

THIRD REICH--1933-1945

5076. "Die Änderungen in der Sozialversicherung und der Versorgung seit Beginn des Krieges." in Wirtschafts- und Sozialberichte. Berlin: Verlag der Deutschen Arbeitsfront, 1942. pp. 100-109.

5077. Blumhoff, Onno. Der Einfluss der deutschen Besetzung auf Geld- und Bankwesen in den während des zweiten Weltkrieges besetzten Gebieten. Diss. Cologne, 1961. 220 pp.

5078. Bopp, Karl R. Hjalmar Schacht: Central Banker. Columbia: The University of Missouri Studies, 1939. 91 pp.

5079. Ellis, Howard S. "Exchange Control in Germany." Quarterly Journal of Economics, Supplement, 54 (1940), 1-220.

5080. Emmendörfer, Arnulf. Geld- und Kreditaufsicht in den von Deutschland während des 2. Weltkrieges besetzten Gebieten. Eine völkerrechtliche Untersuchung über die geld- und kreditwirtschaftlichen Massnahmen. Diss. Mainz. Tübingen: Institut für Besatzung, 1957. 137 pp.

5081. Görlitz, Walter. Geldgeber der Macht: wie Hitler, Lenin, Mao Tse-tung, Mussolini, Stalin und Tito finanziert wurden. Frankfurt a. M.: Fischer-Taschenbücher, 1978. 256 pp.

5082. Halfmann, Dieter. Der Anteil der Industrie und Banken an der faschistischen Innenpolitik. Cologne: Pahl-Rugenstein, 1974. 48 pp.

5083. Klein, J. J. "German Money and Prices, 1932-44." in M. Friedman, ed. Studies in the Quantity Theory of Money. Chicago: University of Chicago Press, 1956.

5084. Lurie, Samuel. Private Investment in a Controlled Economy. Germany, 1933-39. New York: Columbia University Press, 1947. 243 pp.

5085. Mönch, Hermann. "Die Entwicklung der deutschen Sozialversicherung seit dem Jahre 1933." Jahrbücher für Nationalökonomie und Statistik 141 (1935), 53-74, 173-94.

5086. Muhlen, Norbert. Schacht, Hitler's Magician. The Life and Loans of Dr. H. Schacht. New York: Alliance Book Corp., 1939. 228 pp.

5087. Nathan, Otto. Nazi War Finance and Banking. New York: Financial Research Program, National Bureau of Economic Research, 1944. 97 pp.

5088. Pentzlin, Heinz. Hjalmar Schacht: Leben und Wirken einer umstrittenen Persönlichkeit. Berlin: Ullstein, 1980. 295 pp.

5089. Peterson, Edward N. Hjalmar Schacht. For and Against Hitler. A Political-Economic Study of Germany, 1923-45. Boston: Christopher, 1954. 416 pp.

5090. Poole, Kenyon E. German Financial Policies, 1932-1939. New York: Russell & Russell, 1969. 276 pp.

5091. Richter, Lutz. "Grundlinien zur Entwicklung der reichsdeutschen Sozialversicherung in den letzten vier Jahren." Schriftenreihe der Österreichischen Gesellschaft für Versicherungsfachwissen 22 (1937), 33-47.

5092. Sandberger, Martin. Die Sozialversicherung im nationalsozialistischen Staat. Grundsätzliches zur Streitfrage: Versicherung oder Versorgung. Diss. Tübingen. Urach: Bühler, 1934. 93 pp.

5093. Schacht, Hjalmar. Confessions of "the Old Wizard". Boston: Houghton Mifflin, 1956; rpt. Westport, CT, 1974. 484 pp.

5094. Schweitzer, Arthur. "Foreign Exchange Crisis of 1936." Zeitschrift für die gesamte Staatswissenschaft 118 (1962), 243-77.

5095. Schweitzer, Arthur. "Schacht's Regulation of Money and Capital Markets." Journal of Finance 3 (1948), II, 1-18.
5096. Seldte, Franz. Sozialpolitik im Dritten Reich. 1933-1938. Munich: Beck, 1939. 274 pp.
5097. Simpson, Amos E. Hjalmar Schacht in Perspective. The Hague: Mouton, 1969. 202 pp.
5098. Stuebel, Heinrich. "Die Finanzierung der Aufrüstung im Dritten Reich." Europa Archiv 6 (1951), 4128-36.
5099. Teppe, Karl. "Zur Sozialpolitik des Dritten Reiches am Beispiel der Sozialversicherung." Archiv für Sozialgeschichte 17 (1977), 195-250. (English summary)
5100. Teschner, Helmut. Die Entwicklung der Steuerpolitik 1933-1938 im Spiegel des Steueraufkommens. Diss. Breslau. Breslau: Ludwig, 1940. 91 pp.
5101. Wolfe, Martin. "The Development of Nazi Monetary Policy." Journal of Economic History 15 (1955), 392-402.

SEE ALSO: 3729, 3779, 3789.

GERMANY REDIVIDED--1945-1975

5102. Achterberg, Erich. "Bankgeschichte 1962 'en vogue'. Eine Sammelbesprechung." Tradition 8 (1963), 131-45.
5103. Arndt, Helmut. "Competition, Price and Wage Flexibility and Inflation: The German Experience." The Antitrust Bulletin 17 (1972), 859-83.
5104. Die Banken im Spannungsfeld von Notenbank und Bankenaufsicht. Frankfurt a. M.: Knapp, 1978. 63 pp.
5105. Baumgart, Egon, ed. Die Finanzierung der industriellen Expansion in der Bundesrepublik während der Jahre des Wiederaufbaus. Berlin: Duncker & Humblot, 1960. 89 pp.
5106. Biehl, Dieter et al. "Zu den konjunkturellen Effekten der Länder- und Gemeindehaushalte in der Bundesrepublik Deutschland 1960-1974." Die Weltwirtschaft (1974), 29-51.
5107. Bierich, Marcus. Dreissig Jahre Kapitalmarkt in der Bundesrepublik Deutschland. Frankfurt a. M.: Knapp, 1981. 248 pp.
5108. Blessing, Karl. Geld gestern und heute. Eine Dokumentation über Geldwesen und Währung in der Bundesrepublik Deutschland. 6th ed. Graz: Universal, 1969. 135 pp.
5109. Bloch, Max. "Social Insurance in Post-War Germany." International Labour Review 58 (1948), 306-44.
5110. Blum, Eugen. Die deutschen Kreditmärkte nach der Stabilisierung. Frankfurt a. M.: Keip, 1980. 210 pp.
5111. Bolster, David. "The End of Reparations." The Contemporary Review 178 (1950), 337-41.
5112. Bredemeier, Sonning and Winfried Harter. D.M. Geschichte einer Währung. Stuttgart: Deutscher Sparkassenverlag, 1981. 92 pp.
5113. Cholewiak, Stanislaw. "Reparations by the European Axis States After the Second World War." Studies on International Relations 2 (1973), 115-36.
5114. Christ, Eduard. Westdeutsche Bodenkreditanstalt (Westboden). Ihre Geschichte und ihr Aufgabengebiet. Frankfurt a. M.: Knapp, 1961. 146 pp.
5115. Cohen, Benjamin J. "Reparations in the Postwar Period. A Survey." Banca Nazionale del Lavoro 82 (1967), 268-88.
5116. Dreissig Jahre Kapitalmarkt in der Bundesrepublik Deutschland. Frankfurt a. M.: Knapp, 1981. 298 pp.
5117. Dumler, Georg. Die Kapitalrentabilität der deutschen Wirtschaft 1964-1980. Eine wirtschaftszweig- und rechtsformdifferenzierte Untersuchung unter besonderer Berücksichtigung von Gewinn. Diss. Marburg. Birkach: Ladewig, 1983. 399 pp.
5118. Einicke, Helga. Die geld- und währungspolitische Bedeutung des Goldes nach dem zweiten Weltkrieg. Diss. Marburg. Marburg: Nolte, 1959. 300 pp.
5119. Fehrs, Detlef. "Die Ausgaben für die soziale Sicherheit und ihre Deckung in den Jahren 1949 bis 1954." Bundesarbeitsblatt 18 (1955), 797-802.
5120. Fritsch, Ulrich. Die Eigenkapitallücke in der Bundesrepublik. Cologne: Deutscher Instituts-Verlag, 1981. 95 pp.
5121. Frowen, Stephen F. et al., eds. Monetary Policy and Economic Activity in West Germany. London: International Textbook, 1977. 268 pp.

5122. Gebhardt, Gerd and Klaus Kolloch. "Zur Entstehungsgeschichte der separaten Währungsreform in Westdeutschland." Zeitschrift für Geschichtswissenschaft 12 (1964), 1180-90.

5123. "German Reparations to Israel. The 1952 Treaty and Its Effects." The World Today 10 (1954), 258-74.

5124. Gerstenberg, Gerhard. "20 Jahre Sozialversicherung." Deutsche Finanzwirtschaft (1967), 20-22.

5125. Hockerts, Hans G. Sozialpolitische Entscheidungen im Nachkriegsdeutschland. Alliierte und deutsche Sozialversicherungspolitik 1945-1957. Stuttgart: Klett-Cotta, 1980. 463 pp.

5126. Jerchow, Friedrich. Deutschland in der Weltwirtschaft 1944-1947. Alliierte Deutschland- und Reparationspolitik und die Anfänge der westdeutschen Aussenwirtschaft. Düsseldorf: Droste, 1978. 512 pp.

5127. Keynes, John M. Activities 1941-1946. Shaping the Post-War World. Bretton Woods and Reparations. Ed. D. Moggridge. The Collected Writings of John Maynard Keynes, 26. London: Macmillan, 1980. 453 pp.

5128. Kindleberger, Charles P. "Germany's Persistent Balance-of-Payments Disequilibrium." in R. E. Baldwin et al. Trade, Growth and the Balance of Payments. Chicago: Rand McNally, 1966. pp. 230-48.

5129. Kleinewefers, Henner. "Die Politik der Deutschen Bundesbank in dem Konjunkturzyklus 1964 bis 1968." Kredit und Kapital 3 (1970), 31-81. (English and French summaries)

5130. Kloten, Norbert et al. Zur Entwicklung des Geldwertes in Deutschland. Tübingen: Mohr, 1980. 162 pp.

5131. Kuklick, Bruce. American Policy and the Division of Germany. The Clash with Russia Over Reparations. Ithaca, NY: Cornell University Press, 1972. 286 pp.

5132. Kuklick, Bruce. "The Division of Germany and American Policy on Reparations." The Western Political Quarterly 23 (1970), 276-93.

5133. Kumpf-Korfes, Sigrid. "Die ökonomische Expansion des deutschen Finanzkapitals in Bulgarien." Zeitschrift für Geschichtswissenschaft 17 (1969), 1427-41.

5134. Lebig, W. and Gerhard Gerstenberg. "Zehn Jahre einheitliche Sozialversicherung in der Deutschen Demokratischen Republik." Deutsche Finanzwirtschaft 11 (1957), 70-72.

5135. Linsenmeier, Heinz. Möglichkeiten und Grenzen der Konjunkturbeeinflussung durch aktive Bankpolitik, dargestellt am Konjunkturverlauf in der Bundesrepublik Deutschland seit 1948. Diss. Fribourg, 1964. 250 pp.

5136. Maunz, Theodor and Hans Schraft. Die sozialpolitische Gesetzgebung der Bundesrepublik auf dem Gebiete der Sozialversicherung 1950-1960. Berlin: Erich Schmidt, 1961. 91 pp.

5137. Möller, Hans, ed. Zur Vorgeschichte der deutschen Mark. Die Währungsreformpläne 1945-1948. Basel: Kyklos, 1961. 534 pp.

5138. Müller, Klaus. "Die Änderung der Währungsparität als Problem der innerstaatlichen Kompetenzverteilung." Der Betriebs-Berater 26 (1971), 726-29.

5139. Muhr, Gerd. "25 Jahre Selbstverwaltung der Sozialversicherung. Rückblick und Ausblick." Soziale Sicherheit 27 (1978), 161-66.

5140. "Die Nachkriegsentwicklung des mitteldeutschen Versicherungswesens." Wirtschaftsdienst 38 (1958), 155-59.

5141. Nathan, Eli. "Le Traité israelo-allemand du 10. IX. 1952." Revue générale de droit international public 58 (1954), 375-98.

5142. Nettl, Peter. "German Reparations in the Soviet Empire." Foreign Affairs 29 (1951), 300-07.

5143. Neumann, Manfred J. M. "Zur relativen Bedeutung fiskalischer und monetärer Impulse. Evidenz vom Konjunkturzyklus 1967-1971." WSI Mitteilungen. Wirtschafts- und Sozialwissenschaftliches Institut des Deutschen Gewerkschaftsbundes 26 (1973), 14-25.

5144. Paníc, M. "Gross Fixed Capital Formation and Economic Growth in the United Kingdom and West Germany 1954-1964." Bulletin of the Oxford University Institute of Economics and Statistics 29 (1967), 395-406.

5145. Pausch, Alfons. "Das Finanzamt im Wandel der Zeiten. Bericht über eine Ausstellung der Bundesfinanzakademie." Deutsche Steuer-Zeitung 62 (1974), 146-48.

5146. Piettré, André. "Les réparations allemandes (1945-1949)." Revue de science et de législation financières 42 (1950), 27-52.

5147. Pix, Manfred. "Veröffentlichungen zur Sparkassengeschichte in der Bundesrepublik Deutschland und in Berlin (West) von 1960 bis 1977." Bankhistorisches Archiv 3 (1977), 30-75; 4 (1978), 1-19.

5148. Pohl, Manfred. "Zerschlagung und Wiederaufbau der deutschen Grossbanken, 1945-1957."
Beiträge zu Wirtschafts- und Währungsfragen und zur Bankgeschichte 13 (1974), 21-32.
5149. "Le problème des réparations allemandes après la deuxième guerre mondiale." Chronique de
politique étrangère 2 (1949), 776-82.
5150. Raacke, Günter. Das gemeindliche Finanzsystem. Geschichtliche Entwicklung, gegenwärtige
Ausgestaltung und Reform. Mühlheim a. M.: Lutz, 1962. 105 pp.
5151. Radtke, Günter and Wolfgang Zschockelt. "Die Sozialversicherung in der DDR, sozialpolitische
Errungenschaft der Arbeiterklasse und Instrument der Finanzierung sozialer Prozesse."
Wirtschaftswissenschaft 28 (1980), 291-302. (English Summary)
5152. Die Reparationen in der Sowjet-Zone von 1945-1952. Bonn: Vorstand der Sozialdemokratischen Partei Deutschlands, 1954. 53 pp.
5153. Richter, Rudolf, ed. "Currency and Economic Reform. West Germany After World War II."
Zeitschrift für die gesamte Staatswissenschaft 135 (1979), special issue.
5154. Riehl, Hans. Die Mark. Die aufregende Geschichte einer Weltwährung. Hannover: Fackel-
träger, 1978. 276 pp.
5155. Rimlinger, Gaston V. "Social Change and Social Security in Germany." The Journal of Human
Resources 3 (1968), 409-21.
5156. Roeper, Hans. Die D-Mark. Vom Besatzungskind zum Weltstar. Eine deutsche Wirtschaftsgeschichte der Gegenwart. Frankfurt a. M.: Societäts-Verlag, 1978. 56 pp.
5157. Roeper, Hans. Geschichte der D-Mark. Frankfurt a. M.: Fischer, 1968. 176 pp.
5158. Sagi, Nana. German Reparations: A History of the Negotiations. Jerusalem: Magnes Press,
1980. 256 pp.
5159. Sahling, Claus. Die Reaktion des Aktienmarktes auf wesentliche Ausschüttungsänderungen.
Empirische Untersuchung zur Überprüfung der mittelstarken Form der Efficient Market-Theorie
für die Deutschen Börsen im Zeitraum 1971-1977. Diss. Hamburg, 1980. Schwarzenbek:
Martienss, 1981. 312 pp.
5160. Scherpenberg, Jens van. Öffentliche Finanzwirtschaft in West Deutschland 1944-1948.
Steuer- und Haushaltswesen in der Schlussphase des Krieges und den unmittelbaren Nachkriegsjahren. Frankfurt a. M.: R. G. Fischer, 1984. 544 pp.
5161. Schranz, Edgar. "Die Entwicklung des Sozialversicherungsrechtes in Westdeutschland seit
Kriegsende." Soziale Sicherheit 6 (1953), 234-37.
5162. Schwada, John W. Policies of the Western Allies Toward Postwar Germany: Development and
Evolution, 1941-1949. Diss. University of Texas, 1951. 382 pp.
5163. Schwarz, Hans-Peter, ed. Die Wiederherstellung des deutschen Kredits. Das Londoner
Schuldenabkommen. Stuttgart: Belser, 1982. 115 pp.
5164. Thude, Günther. Die Arbeiter und ihre Sozialversicherung. Aufbau und Leistungen der Sozialversicherung der Arbeiter und Angestellten in der DDR. Berlin: Tribüne, 1964. 118 pp.
5165. Veit, Otto. Grundriss der Währungspolitik. 3rd ed. Frankfurt a. M.: Knapp, 1969. 844 pp.
5166. Wadbrook, William P. West German Balance of Payments Policy. New York: Praeger, 1972.
340 pp.
5167. Wandel, Eckhard. Die Entstehung der Bank Deutscher Länder und die deutsche Währungsreform
1948. Die Rekonstruktion des westdeutschen Geld- und Währungssystems 1945-1949 unter
Berücksichtigung der amerikanischen Besatzungspolitik. Frankfurt a. M.: Knapp, 1980. 220 pp.
5168. Wandel, Eckhard. "Historical Developments Prior to the German Currency Reform of 1948."
Zeitschrift für die gesamte Staatswissenschaft 135 (1979), 320-31.
5169. Weidner, Alfred. Die Silberfrage in der Kriegs- und Nachkriegszeit. Diss. Göttingen.
Göttingen: Göttinger Handelsdruck, 1934. 122 pp.
5170. Wolf, Herbert. 30 Jahre Nachkriegsentwicklung im deutschen Bankwesen. Mainz: Hase &
Koehler, 1980. 180 pp.
5171. Wolkersdorf, Lorenz. "Zehn Jahre Deutsche Mark. Probleme und Möglichkeiten einer Politik
der Geldwertstabilisierung." Wirtschaftswissenschaftliche Mitteilungen 11 (1958), 141-50.
5172. Zorn, Wolfgang. "Neuerscheinungen zur deutschen Bankgeschichte 1956-1959." Tradition 5
(1960), 231-35.
5173. Zur Entwicklung der Sozialversicherung und des Krankenhauswesens in der UdSSR und in
Mitteldeutschland. Hamburg: Akademie für Staatsmedizin, 1959. 131 pp.

GERMAN REGIONS

Alsace-Lorraine

5174. Hynitzsch, Wolfgang. Die Währungsumstellung in Elsass-Lothringen 1870-71 und 1918-19. Diss. Mainz, 1959. 128 pp.
5175. Poidevin, Raymond. "Les banques alsaciennes entre la France et l'Allemagne de 1871 à 1914." in J. Schneider and K. E. Born, eds. Wirtschaftskräfte und Wirtschaftswege. Festschrift für Hermann Kellenbenz. Stuttgart: Klett-Cotta, 1978. pp. 461-73.
5176. Raffalovich, Arthur. "Banks of Alsace and Lorraine, After the Annexation." in A History of Banking in All the Leading Nations. New York: Journal of Commerce and Commercial Bulletin, 1898; rpt. New York: A. M. Kelley, 1971. III, 393-412.
5177. Widlöcher, Peter. Die öffentliche Finanzwirtschaft und das Finanzsystem Elsass-Lothringens 1870-1938. Diss. Frankfurt a. M., 1941. Borna-Leipzig: Noske, 1940. 91 pp.

SEE ALSO: 2448.

Baden-Württemberg

5178. Bahrfeldt, Max von. Das geprägte Notgeld der Gemeinden des Freistaates Baden 1916-1921. Halle a. d. S.: Riechmann, 1932. 83 pp.
5179. Breslauer, Berthold. Die Notenbanken in Württemberg 1876-1900. Diss. Heidelberg. Munich: J. Schweitzer, 1903. 52 pp.
5180. Buchenberger, Adolf. Finanzpolitik und Staatshaushalt im Grossherzogtum Baden in den Jahren 1850-1900. Heidelberg: C. Winter, 1902. 264 pp.
5181. Cahn, Julius. Münz- und Geldgeschichte der im Grossherzogtum Baden vereinigten Gebiete. Heidelberg: Winter, 1911. 460 pp.
5182. Cahn, Julius. Rappenmünzbund. Eine Studie zur Münz- und Geldgeschichte des oberen Rheinthales. Heidelberg: Winter, 1901. 218 pp.
5183. Elsas, Fritz. "Der Kampf um die Gründung einer Notenbank in Württemberg (1847-1871)." Schmoller 40 (1916), 1737-1819.
5184. Frank, Robert. Die Entwicklung der Sparkassen in Baden nach dem Kriege unter Berücksichtigung ihres Verhältnisses zu den Banken. Diss. Heidelberg. Wertheim a. M.: Bechstein, 1930. 66 pp.
5185. Goessler, Friedrich P. Das württembergische Kriegsnotgeld. Stuttgart: Württembergischer Verein für Münzkunde, 1920. 12 pp.
5186. Haas, Rudolf. Die Entwicklung des Bankwesens im deutschen Oberrheingebiet. Zur 100. Wiederkehr des Gründungstages der Rheinischen Creditbank Mannheim am 15. 6. 1970. Mannheim: Haas, 1970. 150 pp.
5187. Hecht, Felix. Die Mannheimer Banken 1870 bis 1900. Beiträge zur praktischen Bankpolitik. Leipzig: Duncker & Humblot, 1902. 153 pp.
5188. Hundertfünfzig Jahre städtische Sparkasse Karlsruhe 1813 bis 1963. Karlsruhe: Städtische Sparkasse Karlsruhe, 1963.
5189. Kaulla, Rudolf. Die Organisation des Bankwesens im Königreich Württemberg in ihrer geschichtlichen Entwicklung. Stuttgart: F. Enke, 1908. 60 pp.
5190. Keller, Rudolf. Staats- und Gemeindefinanzen in Württemberg in der grossen Inflation. Diss. Cologne, 1970. 245 pp.
5191. Kiener, Karl. Das Notgeld von Württemberg und Hohenzollern 1914-1922. Stuttgart: Meyer, 1922. 72 pp.
5192. Klein, Ernst. "Die Königlich Württembergische Hofbank und ihre Bedeutung für die Industrialisierung in der ersten Hälfte des 19. Jahrhunderts." Jahrbücher für Nationalökonomie und Statistik 179 (1966), 324-43.
5193. Kochendörfer, Jürgen. Die Finanzierung der Esslinger Maschinenfabrik. Eine Fallstudie über die südwestdeutsche Industrie im 19. Jahrhundert. Diss. Hohenheim, 1975. 209 pp.
5194. Loewenstein, Arthur. Geschichte des württembergischen Kreditbankwesens und seiner Beziehungen zu Handel und Industrie. Tübingen: Mohr, 1912. 244 pp.

5195. Longueville, H. P. de. "Geschichte des Sparkassenwesens in Württemberg und Baden im 19. Jahrhundert." in E. Maschke and J. Sydow, eds. Zur Geschichte der Industrialisierung in den südwestdeutschen Städten. Sigmaringen: Thorbecke, 1977.
5196. Meyer, Hermann. Die Entwicklung der württembergischen Kreditbanken in den letzten 25 Jahren (unter hauptsächlicher Berücksichtigung der Verhältnisse während des Krieges). Eine bilanzanalytische Studie. Diss. Tübingen, 1927. 336 pp.
5197. Ott, Wolf-Rüdiger. Grundlageninvestitionen in Württemberg. Massnahmen zur Verbesserung der materiellen Infrastruktur in der Zeit vom Beginn des 19. Jahrhunderts bis zum Ende des Ersten Weltkriegs. Diss. Heidelberg, 1971.
5198. Poinsignon, Heinrich. Kurze Münzgeschichte von Konstanz in Verbindung mit der der benachbarten Städte, Gebiete und Länder. Konstanz: Stadtarchiv, 1870.
5199. Reichle, Ottfried. Der Finanzhaushalt der Stadt Singen unter Berücksichtigung der wirtschaftlichen und demographischen Entwicklung. Diss. Fribourg, Switzerland, 1969. 166 pp.
5200. Reimer, Klaus. Das Steuerrecht in der Stadt Weinheim vom Beginn der Neuzeit bis zum Anschluss an Baden. Historisch-systematische Darstellung der in Weinheim erhobenen Steuern in materieller und verfahrensrechtlicher Hinsicht. Diss. Heidelberg, 1968. 271 pp.
5201. Schmeisser, Hermann. Der Gemeinde-Haushalt der Stadt Heidelberg von 1828 bis 1925. Diss. Heidelberg. Walldorf b. Heidelberg: Lamade, 1926. 193 pp.
5202. Schmitt, Peter. Die Münzstätte in Schwäbisch Hall, ihre Geschichte und Entwicklung sowie ihre Bedeutung für den wirtschaftlichen Aufstieg der Stadt. Diss. Tübingen, 1954. 419 pp.
5203. Schumann, Friedrich. Die Notenbankfrage in Württemberg seit 1847. Diss. Heidelberg. Gera: Fischer, 1909. 125 pp.
5204. Schumann, Friedrich. Die Privatnotenbanken. Ein Beitrag zu ihrer Geschichte und Lage. Die Bankfrage in Württemberg. Berlin: Puttkammer & Mühlbrecht, 1909. 125 pp.
5205. Schuon, Emil. Die württembergischen Kreditgenossenschaften im Weltkriege. Diss. Tübingen, 1923. 151 pp.
5206. Stange, Ewald. Geld- and Münzgeschichte der Grafschaft Ravensberg. Münster: Aschendorff, 1951. 211 pp.
5207. Wielandt, Friedrich. Badische Münz- und Geldgeschichte. 2nd ed. Karlsruhe: Braun, 1973. 573 pp.
5208. Wielandt, Friedrich. "Kleine Münzgeschichte von Mannheim." Mannheimer Hefte (1953), 22-25.
5209. Wysocki, Josef. Heidelberg: von Arbeit, Leben und Geld in 150jähriger Geschichte der Sparkasse. Stuttgart: Deutscher Sparkassenverlag, 1981. 242 pp.

SEE ALSO: 1814.

Bavaria

Bibliographic Reference

5210. Overbeck, Bernhard. Bibliographie der bayerischen Münz- und Geldgeschichte, 1750-1964. Wiesbaden: Harrassowitz, 1968. 114 pp.

Bavaria

5211. Bernhart, Max. Das Kriegsnotgeld in Bayern. Munich: Kuhn, 1919. 40 pp.
5212. Bing, Siegfried. Die Entwicklung des Nürnberger Stadthaushalts von 1806 bis 1906. Leipzig: Deichert, 1908. 176 pp.
5213. Ein Blick in die Geschichte der Zettelbanken in Europa und auf die Errichtung einer Nationalbank in Baiern. Nuremberg: Riegel & Wiessner, 1822. 26 pp.
5214. Cetto, Carl T. von. "Die Bayerische Landwirtschaftsbank, ihre Entstehungsgeschichte, Einrichtung und Geschäftsentwickelung." Schmoller 30 (1906), 1595-1638.
5215. Eibert, Georg. "Zur Finanzpolitik Nürnberger Maschinenbauunternehmer (1840-1914)." in Wirtschaftskräfte und Wirtschaftswege. Festschrift für Hermann Kellenbenz. 3rd ed. Stuttgart: Klett-Cotta, 1978. III, 387-415.

5216. Gutschmidt, Hans-Ulrich. Der Aufbau und die Entwicklung des Notenbankwesens in Bayern (1834-1881) unter Berücksichtigung der wirtschaftlichen Verhältnisse. Diss. Cologne, 1969. 329 pp.

5217. Hopfmann, Karl. Das Sparkassenwesen in Bayern. Diss. Erlangen, 1902. Erlangen: F. Junge, 1903. 46 pp.

5218. Hundertfünfzig Jahre Sparkasse Landshut 1823-1973. Landshut: Sparkasse Landshut, 1973.

5219. Krinner, Alfred. "Die Gesamt-Sozialversicherungsbeiträge seit 1957." Bayern in Zahlen 17 (1963), 272-75.

5220. Lieb, Ludwig. Die Entwicklung der Augsburger Effektenbörse (1815-1896). Augsburg: Selbstverlag der Stadt, 1930. 86 pp.

5221. Limburg, Hermann. Die königliche Bank zu Nürnberg in ihrer Entwicklung, 1780-1900. Nuremberg: Lippert, 1903. 183 pp.

5222. Meisner, Kurt. Die Entwicklung des Würzburger Stadthaushalts von 1806 bis 1909. Leipzig: Deichert, 1912. 190 pp.

5223. Putz, Max. Die neuere Entwicklung der ländlichen Zentral-Kreditgenossenschaften in Bayern. Diss. Jena. Munich: Gebele, 1928. 51 pp.

5224. Roettinger, Bruno. Das bayerische Kriegsnotgeld. Bamberg: B. Röttinger, 1922. 98 pp.

5225. Sachs, Karl L. "Die Nürnberger Girobank (1921-1927) im Rahmen der kontinentalen Bankgeschichte." in Eheberg-Festgabe. Beiträge zur Wirtschaftsgeschichte und Sozialtheorie. Leipzig: A. Deichert, 1925. pp. 139-61.

5226. Schmalisch, Oscar. Die Entwicklung der Gemeindefinanzen der Stadt Hof in der Zeit von 1818-1913. Diss. Erlangen. Kirchenlamitz: Seidel, 1927. 172 pp.

5227. Spiethoff, B. Ungewollt zur Grösse. Die Geschichte der bayerischen Sparkassen. Munich: M. Schmidt, 1958. 369 pp.

5228. Staub, Eduard. Die Entwicklung des Sparkassenwesens in Bayern unter besonderer Berücksichtigung der Zeit von 1924 bis 1927. Diss. Jena, 1928. Borna-Leipzig: Noske, 1930. 58 pp.

5229. Steffan, Franz and Walter Diehm. Die Bayerische Staatsbank 1780-1955. Geschichte und Geschäfte einer öffentlichen Bank. Munich: Bayerische Staatsbank, 1955. 458 pp.

5230. Theiss, Helmut. "Bayerische Hypotheken- und Wechsel-Bank." Revue Internationale d'Histoire de la Banque 1 (1968), 375-80. (French, Italian and English summaries)

5231. Trende, Adolf. "Die Geschichte des bayerischen Sparkassenwesens." Bayerland 70 (1968), 25-31.

5232. Troeltsch, Walter. "Beiträge zur Finanzgeschichte Münchens im 19. Jahrhundert. Der sogenannte Lokalmalzaufschlag." Finanz-Archiv 10 (1893), 1-159.

5233. Wysocki, Josef. "Kapitalbildungsprozesse ländlicher Regionen Bayerns im 19. Jahrhundert." Zeitschrift für Agrargeschichte und Agrarsoziologie 24 (1976), 202-13.

SEE ALSO: 3985, 3987.

Berlin

5234. Achterberg, Erich. Berliner Banken im Wandel der Zeit. Darmstadt: Hoppenstedt, 1956. 119 pp.

5235. Buss, Georg. Berliner Boerse von 1685-1913. Zum 50. Gedenktage der 1. Versammlung im neuen Hause. Berlin: Preussische Verlags-Anstalt, 1913. 155 pp.

5236. Fendler, Arnold. Kapitalkonzentration der Berliner Grossbanken von 1914-1923. Berlin: W. Christians, 1926. 109 pp.

5237. Grünert, Eberhard. Die preussische Bau- und Finanzdirektion in Berlin: Entstehung und Entwicklung 1822-1944. Cologne: Grote, 1983. 271 pp.

5238. Klebba, Walter. Börse und Effektenhandel im Kriege unter besonderer Berücksichtigung der Berliner Börse. Berlin: Haud & Spener, 1920. 152 pp.

5239. Köhne, Bernhard. Das Münzwesen der Stadt Berlin. Ein historischer Versuch. Berlin: Hayn, 1837. 84 pp.

5240. Latendorf, Otto. Die Entwicklung der städtischen Kassenorganisation Berlins von der Einführung der Städteordnung bis zur Gründung der Stadthauptkasse (1809-1843.) Berlin: Gsellius, 1931. 123 pp.

5241. Lesser, Ludwig. Zur Geschichte der Berliner Börse und des Eisenbahnaktien-Handels. Berlin: Klemann, 1844. 64 pp.
5242. Weber, Hanns. Bankplatz Berlin. Cologne: Westdeutscher Verlag, 1957. 246 pp.

SEE ALSO: 4600.

Brandenburg

5243. Schwarze, Hans. Die Finanzwirtschaft der Stadt Potsdam im Anfang des 19. Jahrhunderts. Eine Darstellung städtischen Finanzwesens in der Zeit vom Zusammenbruch des Preussischen Staates durch den Krieg von 1806 bis zur Wiederherstellung geordneter Verhältnisse nach der Einführung der Städteordnung. Diss. Giessen. Giessen: Eschenhagen, 1932. 140 pp.

Danzig

5244. Foltz, Max. Geschichte des Danziger Stadthaushalts. Danzig: Käfemann, 1912. 615 pp.
5245. Lilienthal, Wilhelm. Das Steuerwesen in der Freien Stadt Danzig 1920-1926. Leipzig: Noske, 1927. 89 pp.

East Prussia

5246. Bahrfeldt, Max von. Die Notmünzen der Provinzen Ost- und Westpreussen 1916-1921. Halle a. d. S.: Reichmann, 1930. 40 pp.
5247. Jerzembek, Gerhard. Die Entwicklung der Finanzen des Provinzialverbandes Ostpreussen vor dem Weltkrieg. Diss. Königsberg. Würzburg-Aumühle: Triltsch, 1940. 87 pp.
5248. Kapust, Wilhelm. Die Entwicklung der memelländischen Wirtschaft seit der Abtrennung vom Deutschen Reiche unter besonderer Berücksichtigung der Währungs- und Kreditverhältnisse. Diss. Marburg, 1929. 79 pp.
5249. Meinhardt, Günther. Die Einführung des Papiergeldes in Ostpreussen. Dortmund: O. E. Schulze, 1958. 27 pp.
5250. Meinhardt, Günther. Gemünzt zu Königsberg. Ein Beitrag zur Münz- und Geldgeschichte Ostpreussens. Leer: Rautenberg, 1977. 88 pp.
5251. Ortmann, Ewald. Die Finanzen des Provinzialverbandes Ostpreussen in den Jahren von 1919 bis 1932. Diss. Königsberg. Düsseldorf: Nolte, 1939. 108 pp.
5252. Schuch, Ernst. Die Entwicklung des Sozialversicherungsrechts im Memelgebiet. Diss. Leipzig. Dresden: Dittert, 1938. 70 pp.

Hansa Cities

5253. Achterberg, Erich. Kleine Hamburger Bankgeschichte. Hamburgische Landesbank. Girozentrale. Hamburg: Dingwort, 1964. 64 pp.
5254. Ahrens, Gerhard. "Das Ringen um eine Notenbank in Hamburg um die Mitte des 19. Jahrhunderts." Kredit und Kapital 7 (1974), 233-55. (English and French summaries)
5255. Beutin, Ludwig. Bremisches Bank- und Börsenwesen seit dem 17. Jahrhundert. Von der Wirtschaftsgesinnung einer Hansestadt. Bremen: Geist, 1937. 66 pp.
5256. Bremer Wertpapierbörse. 300 Jahre Bremer Börsenwesen. 1682-1982. Bremen: Bremer Wertpapierbörse, 1982. 20 pp.
5257. Heyden, Wilhelm. Die Hamburger Sparkasse von 1827. Hamburg: O. Meissner, 1893. 247 pp.
5258. Hinrichs, Walter. Die lübeckische Finanzpolitik 1867-1926. Diss. Berlin, 1929. Lübeck: Schmidt-Römhild, 1929. 66 pp.
5259. Jesse, Wilhelm. "Lübecks Anteil an der deutschen Münz- und Geldgeschichte." Zeitschrift des Vereins für Lübeckische Geschichte 40 (1960), 5-36.
5260. Lippmann, Leo. Mein Leben und meine amtliche Tätigkeit. Erinnerungen und ein Beitrag zur Finanzgeschichte Hamburgs. Hamburg: Christians, 1964. 720 pp.

5261. Molsen, Käthe. Die Handelsbank in Lübeck, 1856-1956. Hamburg: Verlag Hanseatischer Merkur, 1956. 141 pp.
5262. Schneider, Gerhard. Lübecks Bankenpolitik im Wandel der Zeiten 1898-1978. Lübeck: Schmidt-Römhild, 1979. 230 pp.
5263. Scholl, C. Franz and Walther Matthies. Hundert Jahre Vereinsbank in Hamburg, 1856-1956. Hamburg: Vereinsbank, 1956. 182 pp.
5264. Soetbeer, Adolf. Beiträge und Materialien zur Beurtheilung von Geld- und Bank-Fragen mit besonderer Rücksicht auf Hamburg. Hamburg: Herold, 1855. 135 pp.
5265. Weniger, Axel. Die Finanzverwaltung Lübecks im 19. Jahrhundert. Diss. Hamburg. Lübeck: Schmidt-Römhild, 1982. 183 pp.

SEE ALSO: 4018, 5270.

Hesse

5266. Achterberg, Erich. "Ein ereignisreicher Ausschnitt aus der Geschichte der Frankfurter Wertpapierbörse." Festschrift zum 70. Geburtstag seines Vorsitzers Herrn Hans Heinrich Hauck am 31. 8. 1960. Überreicht vom Vorstand der Frankfurter Wertpapierbörse. Frankfurt a. M.: Frankfurter Wertpapierbörse, 1960. 64 pp.
5267. Achterberg, Erich. Frankfurter Bankherren. 2nd ed. Frankfurt a. M.: Knapp, 1971. 144 pp.
5268. Berge, Otto. Fuldas öffentliches Bankwesen vorwiegend im 19. Jahrhundert. Fulda: Städtische Sparkasse und Landesleihbank, 1974. 312 pp.
5269. Bing, Hermann. Finanzgeschichte Waldeck-Pyrmonts von der Wende des 18. Jahrhunderts bis zum Jahre 1929. Eine Untersuchung aus Anlass des Aufgehens des Freistaates Waldeck in Preussen am 1. 4. 1929. Diss. Marburg. Marburg: Bing, 1929. 154 pp.
5270. Böhme, Helmut. Frankfurt und Hamburg. Des Deutschen Reiches Silber- und Goldloch und die allerenglischste Stadt des Kontinents. Frankfurt a. M.: Europäische Verlags-Anstalt, 1968. 387 pp.
5271. Cameron, Rondo E. "Founding the Bank of Darmstadt." Explorations in Entrepreneurial History 8 (1955-56), 113-30. [German: Tradition 2 (1957), 104-24.]
5272. Glück, Kurt. "Die Entwicklung des Banken- und Sparkassenwesens in Offenbach am Main." in E. Stein, ed. Tradition und Erneuerung. Erinnerungsgabe für Friedrich Hengst zum 80. Geburtstag. Frankfurt a. M.: Osterrieth, 1972. pp. 125-38.
5273. Heyn, Udo. "Banking, Entrepreneurship and Industrialization. The 'Paradox' of Frankfurt am Main." Bankhistorisches Archiv 2 (1976), 14-46.
5274. Heyn, Udo. Private Banking and Industrialization: the Case of Frankfurt am Main. 1825-1875. New York: Arno Press, 1981. 412 pp.
5275. Kämmer, Richard. Die Finanzwirtschaft der Stadt Marburg in den letzten 100 Jahren (1811 bis 1910) unter besonderer Berücksichtigung der Neuzeit (1890 bis 1910). Diss. Marburg, 1912. Marburg: Bauer, 1913. 70 pp.
5276. Kirchholtes, Hans-Dieter. Jüdische Privatbanken in Frankfurt am Main. Frankfurt a. M.: Kramer, 1969. 79 pp.
5277. Klötzer, Wolfgang. "Der Bankier und seine Stadt. Die öffentliche Verantwortung einer Führungsschicht am Beispiel der Stadt Frankfurt am Main." in H. H. Hofmann, ed. Bankherren und Bankiers. Limburg a. d. L.: Starke, 1978. pp. 1-26.
5278. Klüssendorf, Niklot. Papiergeld und Staatsschulden im Fürstentum Waldeck (1848-1890). Marburg: Elwert, 1984. 229 pp.
5279. Lauf, Friedrich. Im Zeichen des Bienenkorbes. Chronik der Frankfurter Sparkasse von 1822 (Polytechnische Gesellschaft), 1822-1981. Frankfurt a. M.: Kramer, 1984. 672 pp.
5280. Rahlson, Hellmut, ed. Zum Finanzwesen der Stadt Wiesbaden. Wiesbaden: Bergmann, 1908. 53 pp.
5281. Rompel, Josef. Die wirtschaftliche und finanzielle Entwicklung von Wiesbaden als Fremdenstadt seit Beginn der preussischen Herrschaft von 1867 bis 1907. Wiesbaden: Bergmann, 1910. 143 pp.
5282. Runkel, Wilhelm. Die Entwicklung des Sparkassenwesens im Grossherzogtum Hessen. Diss. Giessen, 1910. Frankfurt a. M.: Hauser, 1910. 109 pp.

5283. Schärffs, Walther. Die Reformen der veranlagten Staats- und Gemeindesteuern im Grossherzogtum Hessen (unter besonderer Berücksichtigung der Reformen seit 1899). Stuttgart:
Cotta, 1913. 211 pp.
5284. Schmitt, Edmund. Die Finanzwirtschaft der öffentlichen Verwaltung in Hessen vor und nach
dem Kriege. Diss. Giessen, 1930. Giessen: Prinz, 1931. 216 pp.
5285. Seidenzahl, Fritz. "Bismarck und die Gründung der Darmstädter Bank." Tradition 6 (1961),
252-59.
5286. Strube, H. Geschichte des Sparkassenwesens und der Sparkassen in Kurhessen 1819-1866.
Stuttgart: s. n., 1873.
5287. Wagner, Heinrich. Das Finanzwesen Giessens unter besonderer Berücksichtigung des 19. Jahrhunderts. Diss. Giessen. Leipzig: Fock, 1904. 102 pp.
5288. Weidemann, Johannes. Städtische Finanzwirtschaft im Wandel der Zeiten. Die Finanzgeschichte
der Stadt Kassel. Stuttgart: Kohlhammer, 1936. 171 pp.
5289. Westhäuser, Karl. Die Finanzentwicklung der Stadt Offenbach a. M. von 1890 bis 1919. Diss.
Giessen, 1926. Offenbach a. M.: Jacobi, 1927. 79 pp.
5290. Winterwerb, Rudolf. Die Frankfurter Bank 1854-1929. Frankfurt a. M.: Druck- und Verlags-
anstalt Frankfurt a. M., 1929. 254 pp.
5291. Wormser, Otto. Die Frankfurter Börse. Ihre Besonderheiten und ihre Bedeutung. Ein Beitrag
zur Frage der Börsenkonzentration. Tübingen: Mohr, 1919. 233 pp.

SEE ALSO: 4062, 4600.

Lower Saxony

5292. Augustiny, Waldemar. 75 Jahre im Dienste von Staat und Wirtschaft 1883-1958. Staatliche
Kreditanstalt Oldenburg-Bremen. Oldenburg: Stalling, 1958. 133 pp.
5293. Der Bankplatz Hannover. Börse und Banken in Hannover. Trautheim über Darmstadt: Mushake,
1962. 130 pp.
5294. Barth, Willy. Die Anfänge des Bankwesens in Hannover. Hannover: Geibel, 1911. 85 pp.
5295. Buck, Heinrich. Das Geld- und Münzwesen der Städte in den Landen Hannover und Braunschweig. Ein geschichtlicher Ueberblick mit Urkundenbeilagen und Münzfusstabellen. Frankfurt a.
M.: Hess, 1935. 83 pp.
5296. Fauteck, Otto. Die Finanzen der Stadt Lüneburg im 19. Jahrhundert. Eine finanzgeschichtliche
und finanzstatistische Studie. Diss. Jena. Lüneburg: von Stern, 1912. 115 pp.
5297. Hannoversche Landeskreditanstalt. Hundert Jahre im Dienste der niedersächsischen Landwirtschaft. 1840-1940. Hannover: Edler & Krische, 1940. 60 pp.
5298. Jesse, Wilhelm. Münz- und Geldgeschichte Niedersachsens. Braunschweig: Waisenhaus, 1952.
130 pp.
5299. Meinhardt, Günther. Münz- und Geldgeschichte der Stadt Göttingen von den Anfängen bis zur
Gegenwart. Göttingen: Vandenhoeck & Ruprecht, 1961. 249 pp.
5300. Sunder, Franz. Das Finanzwesen der Stadt Osnabrück von 1648-1900. Jena: Fischer, 1904.
219 pp.
5301. Thiede, Wolfgang. Auswirkungen der Gebietsreform im Bereich des kommunalen Finanz-
ausgleichs: empirische Untersuchung am Beispiel des Landes Niedersachsen. Diss. Hamburg.
Baden-Baden: Nomos, 1981. 365 pp.
5302. Wieden, Helge bei der. Die niedersächsische Bank. Ein Beitrag zur Geschichte der deutschen
Notenbanken. Mainz: Hase & Koehler, 1982. 184 pp.

SEE ALSO: 1228.

North Rhine-Westphalia

5303. Abs, Hermann J. "Die Anfänge des Bankwesens in Krefeld und seine Verbindung zur Textilindustrie." in Für Erich Selbach. zum 70. Geburtstag. 25. 7. 1975. Krefeld: Industrie- und
Handelskammer, 1975. pp. 13-20.

5304. Adamsen, Heiner R. <u>Investitionshilfe für die Ruhr. Wiederaufbau. Verbände und Soziale Markt-wirtschaft 1948-1952</u>. Wuppertal: Hammer, 1981. 294 pp.
5305. Bahrfeldt, Max von. <u>Die Notmünzen der Stadt Hamm (Westfalen) 1917-1919</u>. Halle a. d. S.: Riechmann, 1928. 16 pp.
5306. Berghaus, Peter. <u>Münzgeschichte der Stadt Dortmund</u>. Dortmund: s.n., 1958. 83 pp.
5307. Bieger, Helmut. <u>Das Finanzwesen der Stadt Köln unter preussischer Herrschaft bis zur Reichs-gründung 1871</u>. Diss. Cologne, 1968. 248 pp.
5308. Börner, Karl. <u>Die Entwicklung des münsterischen Bankwesens. Eine wirtschaftsgeschichtliche Studie im Rahmen der allgemeinen Bankenentwicklung</u>. Diss. Münster i. W. Münster i. W.: Krick, 1927. 36 pp.
5309. Dabritz, Walther. <u>Denkschrift zum fünfzigjährigen Bestehen der Essener Credit-Anstalt in Essen</u>. Essen: Credit-Anstalt, 1922. 318 pp.
5310. Dorn, Wolfram. <u>Der Rheinische Sparkassen- und Giroverband. 100 Jahre Sparkasseneinheit. 1881-1981</u>. Düsseldorf: Rheinischer Sparkassen- und Giroverband, 1981. 222 pp.
5311. Feldhege, Theodor. <u>Die Finanzwirtschaft der Stadt Buer der jetzigen Teilgemeinde der Gross-stadt Gelsenkirchen--vom Ausgangspunkt der stärkeren wirtschaftlichen Entwicklung (1895) bis zum Städtezusammenschluss (1928)</u>. Diss. Frankfurt a. M., 1929. Bigge a. d. Ruhr: Josefs-Druckerei, 1933. 355 pp.
5312. Haas, Ernst J. <u>Stadt-Sparkasse Düsseldorf. 1825-1972. Ein Beitrag zur Wirtschafts-geschichte der Landeshauptstadt Düsseldorf</u>. Berlin: Duncker & Humblot, 1976. 404 pp.
5313. Helten, Josef. <u>Die Kölner Börse 1553-1927</u>. Cologne: Kölner Verlags-Anstalt, 1928. 83 pp.
5314. Klersch, Joseph. <u>Die Sparkasse der Stadt Köln und ihre Stellung im rheinischen Sparkassen-wesen. 100 Jahre rheinischer Sparkassenentwicklung</u>. Cologne: Welzel, 1929. 401 pp.
5315. Klinker, Friedrich W. <u>Studien zur Entwicklung und Typenbildung von vier rheinisch-westfälischen Provinzialaktienbanken</u>. Karlsruhe: Braun, 1913. 129 pp.
5316. Krüger, Alfred. <u>Das Kölner Bankiergewerbe vom Ende des 18. Jahrhunderts bis 1875</u>. Essen: Baedeker, 1925. 231 pp.
5317. Kuske, Bruno. "Die Entstehung der Kreditwirtschaft und des Kapitalverkehrs." in B. Kuske. <u>Köln, der Rhein und das Reich. Beiträge aus fünf Jahrzehnten wirtschaftsgeschichtlicher Forschung</u>. Cologne: Böhlau, 1956. pp. 48-137.
5318. Leesch, Wolfgang. <u>Geschichte der Steuerverfassung und -verwaltung in Westfalen seit 1815</u>. Paderborn: Bonifatius, 1985. 181 pp.
5319. Martin, Paul C. "Monetäre Probleme der Frühindustrialisierung am Beispiel der Rheinprovinz (1815-1848)." <u>Jahrbücher für Nationalökonomie und Statisitik</u> 181 (1967/68), 117-50.
5320. Massmann, Friedrich. <u>Geschichte der Scheidemünze und Scheidemünzumlauf im Handels-kammerbezirk Dortmund</u>. Diss. Heidelberg. Heidelberg: Rössler & Herbert, 1911. 41 pp.
5321. Meier, Friedrich. <u>Die Trennung des Staats- vom Domanial-Haushalt in Lippe. Ein Beitrag zur Lippischen Wirtschafts- und Finanzgeschichte</u>. Diss. Frankfurt a. M., 1926. Gelsenkirchen: Münstermann, 1927. 168 pp.
5322. Perlitz, Uwe. <u>Das Geld-, Bank- und Versicherungswesen in Köln. 1700-1815</u>. Berlin: Duncker & Humblot, 1976. 399 pp.
5323. Reusch, Heinrich, ed. <u>100 Jahre westfälische Sparkassen</u>. Münster: Westfälischer Sparkassen- und Giroverband, 1934. 84 pp.
5324. Schneider, Ernst. <u>Die Entstehung der Selbstverwaltung und die Ordnung des Finanzwesens in der Rheinprovinz</u>. Diss. Heidelberg. Cassel: Landsiedel, 1909. 81 pp.
5325. Schröter, Hermann. "Essener Notgeld." <u>Tradition</u> 6 (1961), 1-21.
5326. Stange, Ewald. <u>Geld- und Münzgeschichte des Bistums Minden</u>. Münster: Aschendorff, 1915. 194 pp.
5327. Sunder, Franz. <u>Das Finanzwesen der Stadt Osnabrück von 1648-1900</u>. Jena: Fischer, 1904. 219 pp.
5328. Tilly, Richard H. <u>Financial Institutions and Industrialization in the Rhineland 1815-1870</u>. Madison: University of Wisconsin Press, 1966. 197 pp.
5329. Trippe, Anton. <u>Die Münzen von Medebach</u>. Braunschweig: Klinkhardt & Biermann, 1967. 88 pp.

SEE ALSO: 2599, 4126.

Pomerania

5330. Behnke, Franz. Die Finanzwirtschaft der Stadt Stettin unter besonderer Berücksichtigung der letzten fünf Dezennien. Diss. Greifswald, 1921. 122 pp.
5331. Conrad, Axel. Zur Entwicklung der Stralsunder Geld- und Kreditinstitute. Diss. Griefswald. Greifswald: Hartmann, 1926. 133 pp.
5332. Helfritz, Hans. Die Finanzen der Stadt Greifswald zu Beginn des neunzehnten Jahrhunderts und in der Gegenwart. Diss. Greifswald. Altenburg: Pierer, 1911. 297 pp.

Rhineland Palatinate

5333. Wagner, Georg. Münzwesen und Hausgenossen in Speyer. Diss. Heidelberg. Speyer: Jaeger, 1931. 156 pp.

Saarland

5334. Baschab, Lisbeth. Der Gemeindehaushalt der Stadt Zweibrücken. (1830-1930). Diss. Würzburg. Würzburg: Roll, 1932. 50 pp.
5335. "Die Entwicklung der Sozialversicherung im Saarland nach dem Zusammenbruch." Versicherungswissenschaft und Versicherungspraxis 1 (1947), 61-63.
5336. Klein, Ernst. "Die Bergmännische Sparkasse an der Saar (1835-1867)." Bankhistorisches Archiv 2 (1976), 1-13.
5337. Schömer, Wolfram. Die Entwicklung der Sozial-Versicherung im Saargebiet 1920-1935. Diss. Freiburg. Freiburg i. Br.: Weis, 1941. 228 pp.

Saxony

5338. Allendorf, Hugo. Das Finanzwesen der Stadt Halle a. S. im 19. Jahrhundert. Ein Beitrag zur Gemeinde-Finanz, -Statistik und -Politik. Jena: Fischer, 1904. 207 pp.
5339. Banck, Rudolf. Geschichte der sächsischen Banken mit Berücksichtigung der Wirthschaftsverhältnisse. Diss. Berlin. Dresden: Heinrich, 1896. 36 pp.
5340. Barduleck, Max. Die letzten Jahre der Münze in Dresden: Werksverzeichnis 1865 bis 1911. Berlin: Transpress, 1981. 184 pp.
5341. Boelcke, Georg O. M. Die Entwicklung der Finanzen im Grossherzogtum Sachsen-Weimar von 1851 bis zur Gegenwart. Diss. Jena. Jena: Fischer, 1906. 55 pp.
5342. Costabell, Otto. Die Entwicklung der Finanzen im Herzogtum Sachsen-Meiningen von 1831 bis zur Gegenwart. Jena: Fischer, 1908. 153 pp.
5343. Dietrich, W. M. "Die Landwirthschaftlichen Creditanstalten im Königreiche Sachsen." Jahrbücher für Nationalökonomie und Statistik 4 (1865), 219-48.
5344. Eicher, Hans. Die Finanzen des Kreiskommunalverbandes Delitzsch (1875-1928). Diss. Berlin, 1929. Berlin-Charlottenburg: Hoffmann, 1930. 175 pp.
5345. Fahrig, Rudolf. Das Finanzwesen der Stadt Eisleben in den Jahren 1880-1926. Diss. Leipzig. Eisleben: Schneider, 1928. 158 pp.
5346. Fischer, Martin. Die Finanzentwicklung der Stadt Stendal (1610-1910). Diss. Halle-Wittenberg. Stendal: Altmärkische Druck- und Verlagsanstalt, 1913. 66 pp.
5347. Huster, Franziska. Die Entwicklung des Magdeburger Bankgewerbes von 1875 bis zur Gegenwart. Halle a. d. S.: "Hallische Nachrichten", 1931. 171 pp.
5348. Kleine, Karl. Die Entwicklung des Halleschen Bankgewerbes. Jena: Fischer, 1910. 200 pp.
5349. Kunze, Arno. Der Frühkapitalismus in Chemnitz. Forschungsergebnisse aus dem Stadtarchiv Karl-Marz-Stadt und anderen deutschen Archiven mit Urkunden, Regesten, Plänen und Bildern. Karl-Marz-Stadt: Stadtarchiv, 1958. 178 pp.
5350. Meusch, Hans. Die Finanzwirtschaft der Stadt Weissenfels a. S. im 19. Jahrhundert. Ein Beitrag zur Gemeindestatistik. Halle a. S.: Kaemmerer, 1907. 268 pp.
5351. Moltke, Siegfried. Geschichte der Leipziger Maklerschaft. Leipzig: Deichert, 1939. 251 pp.

5352. Politz, August. Die Finanzwirtschaft der Stadt Dessau mit besonderer Berücksichtigung der Entwicklung seit 1882. Diss. Greifswald. Ballenstedt i. H.: Rühling & Paetz, 1926. 142 pp.

5353. Poschinger, Heinrich von. "Die Bankentwicklung im Königreich Sachsen nach amtlichen Quellen dargestellt." Jahrbücher für Nationalökonomie und Statistik 26 (1876), 296-356; 28 (1877), 73-129.

5354. Rummel, Bruno. Der Entwicklungsgang des Halleschen Bankgewerbes seit 1908. Diss. Halle-Wittenberg, 1928. Halle a. d. S.: John, 1929. 168 pp.

5355. Schönemann, Max. Die Entwickelung der anhaltischen Staatsfinanzen von 1863 bis zur Gegenwart. Diss. Halle-Wittenberg. Halle a. d. S.: Kaemmerer, 1908. 65 pp.

5356. Schreiber, Fritz. Die Sächsische Bank zu Dresden 1865 bis 1912. Ein geschichtlich- statistischer Beitrag zur Entwicklung des Notenbankwesens in Sachsen. Diss. Leipzig. Borna-Leipzig: Noske, 1915. 89 pp.

5357. Schröter, Karl. Die Steuern der Stadt Nordhausen und ihre Bedeutung für die Gemeindefinanzen. Jena: Fischer, 1904. 94 pp.

5358. Tobias, Georg. Die Entwicklung der Aktienbanken in Leipzig. Diss. Heidelberg. Leipzig: Hirschfeld, 1907. 133 pp.

5359. Trescher, Erich. Die Entwickelung des Steuerwesens im Herzogtum Sachsen-Gotha. Jena: Fischer, 1906. 111 pp.

5360. Walther, Kurt. Das Finanzwesen der Stadt Dresden von 1849 bis 1914. Leipzig: Heling, 1926. 125 pp.

Schleswig-Holstein

5361. Dorfmann, Bruno. Das Münz- und Geldwesen des Herzogtums Lauenburg und die Medaillen des Hauses Sachsen-Lauenburg. Lübeck: Reichmann, 1969. 144 pp.

5362. Ehlers, Franz, ed. Zoll- und Steuergeschichte Schleswig-Holsteins. Kiel: s.n., 1967. 549 pp.

5363. Geerkens, August, ed. Die Schleswig-Holsteinische Bank und ihr Arbeitsfeld im Lichte geschichtlicher Entwicklung. Festschrift zum 50jährigen Bestehen der Bank. Husum: Schleswig-Holsteinische Bank, 1926. 133 pp.

5364. Hinrichs, Hans. Die Sparkassen in der Provinz Schleswig-Holstein seit dem Jahre 1923. Diss. Hamburg, 1942. 129 pp.

5365. Otto, Frieda. Schleswig-Holstein im Finanzausgleich 1945-1952. Kiel: Institut für Weltwirtschaft, 1954. 378 pp.

5366. Waschinski, Emil. Währung, Preisentwicklung und Kaufkraft des Geldes in Schleswig-Holstein von 1226-1864. 2 vols. Neumünster: Wachholtz, 1959.

5367. Waschinski, Emil. "Währung und Preisentwicklung in Schleswig-Holstein von 1776-1864." in Aus Schleswig-Holsteins Geschichte und Gegenwart. Eine Aufsatzsammlung als Festschrift für Volquart Pauls. Neumünster: K. Wachholtz, 1950. pp. 113-32.

Silesia

5368. Bahrfeldt, Max von. Das geprägte amtliche Notgeld der Provinz Schlesien 1917-1921. Breslau: Hirt, 1935. 74 pp.

Thuringia

5369. Herting, August. Die Finanzwirtschaft der Stadt Mühlhausen in Thüringen von 1813-1913. Diss. Erlangen. Mühlhausen i. Th.: Mühlhauser Zeitung, 1927. 123 pp.

5370. Hertzer, Georg. Die Finanzwirtschaft der Stadt Weimar in ihrer Entwickelung. Halle a. d. S.: C. A. Kaemmerer, 1907. 177 pp.

5371. Horn, Wilhelm. Erfurts Stadtverfassung und Stadtwirtschaft in ihrer Entwicklung bis zur Gegenwart. Ein Beispiel zur Verfassungsgeschichte und Sozialpolitik der deutschen Städte. Jena: Fischer, 1904. 271 pp.

West Prussia

5372. Alfert, Werner. "Westpreussisches Papier-Notgeld 1914-1923." <u>Westpreussen-Jahrbuch</u> 24 (1973), 75-82.
5373. Meinhardt, Günther. "Das frühe Papiergeld in Westpreussen bis zur alleinigen Verwendung des Reichsgeldes 1891." <u>Beiträge zur Geschichte Westpreussens</u> 3 (1970), 72-87.

Author Index

Authors and editors are listed according to the entry number of their work (except for Roman numerals, which denote page numbers). Where an article appears in an edited work, only the author is listed, not the editor. (Note: *ä* is alphabetized as *ae*, *ö* as *oe*, and *ü* as *ue*.)

Bärtschi, Hans-Peter 1974
Bahr, Ernst 1192, 1389
Bahrfeldt, Max von 5178, 5246, 5305, 5368
Baicoianu, Constantin J. 4419
Bairoch, Paul 62,139, 1426, 1975, 2003,
    2671, 2727-29, 3040
Bakeless, John 199
Baker, James C. 4652
Baldwin, Robert E. 63, 2696
Ball, Joyce 1602
Ballod, Carl 796
Ballwanz, Ilona 1674
Balmer, Hans 3086
Baltzarek, Franz 515, 2080, 4430-31
Banck, Rudolf 5339
Bandera, V. N. 4270
Banderet-Lüdin, Elisabeth 588
Bandion, Erwin 3033
Banfield, Thomas C. 2289
Banik-Schweitzer, Renate 516, 2167
Bannock, Girolamo 2058
Banze, Angelika 797
Barbagallo, Corrado 2004
Barclay, David E. 798
Bardroff, Karl 1857
Barduleck, Max 5340
Bardy, Roland 388
Bark, Thomas 4753
Barkai, Avraham 978
Barkhausen, Max 1249
Barkin, Kenneth D. 2246, 2290
Barmeyer, Heide 1675
Barnes, Harry E. 64
Barnes, Thomas G. 200, 2005
Bartel, Otto 2208
Bartel, Walter 979
Bartels, Adolf 1606
Bartels, A. N. 1840
Bartens, Albert 1107
Barth, Alfred 3041
Barth, Anna 1526
Barth, Ernst 2291
Barth, Willy 5294
Barthel, Horst 1038-39
Barthelmann, Robert 3799-3800
Baruch, Bernard M. 4973
Basch, Antonin 418, 980
Baschab, Lisbeth 5334
Baschy, René 4441
Basler, Werner 4190
Batliner, Emil H. 4635
Battaglia, Roger von 3354
Baudis, Dieter 682, 799, 3216
Bauer, Felix 626
Bauer, Hans 532, 589, 3087, 4137, 4442
Bauer, Otto 1452
Bauert-Keetman, Ingrid 2247, 3355
Baumann, H. 3171

Baumgart, Egon 5105
Baumgart, Winifried 658
Baumgartner, Jean-Pierre 3042
Baumgartner, Otto 3117
Bauriedl, Ulrich 4653
Bausinger, Leopold 1209
Bay, Achim 3747
Bayer, Hans 389
Bayer, Kurt 271
Bazant, J. 2910
Beard, Miriam 2672
Beau, Horst 2538, 4085
Beaud, Michel 3801
Becher, Siegfried 2911
Bechler, Siegfried 4340
Bechtel, Heinrich 683-84, 3217
Beck, Bernhard 3088
Beck, Friedrich 1344, 4138
Beck, Joseph 3933
Beckenbach, Ralf 981
Becker, Anton 2539
Becker, Bernhard 2209
Becker, Carl 1330
Becker, Hans 4000
Becker, Heinrich 2540
Becker, Walter 931, 2374
Beckerath, Erwin 4654
Beckers, Hubertus 2541
Beckmann, Fritz 1607, 1764
Beer, Adolf 2730, 2912, 4341-4343
Beerli, Hans 2213
Behnke, Franz 5330
Behrendt, Richard F. 533
Beitel, Werner 3652
Bein, Louis 2618
Bell, Edward P. 4271
Bellagio, Andrea 2170
Below, Georg von 65
Benaerts, Pierre 2292
Bendicente, Francisco C. 4754
Benedikt, Heinrich 326, 2113-14, 2145,
    3356
Bengtson, John R. 3748
Bennathan, Esra 4655
Bennett, Edward W. 3653, 4974
Benning, Bernhard 5019
Benöhr, Hans-Peter 4755
Benthien, Bruno 1911
Bentler, Wilhelm 801
Bentzien, Ulrich 1887
Berber, Fritz 4975
Berdahl, Robert M. 1676
Berding, Helmut 685, 3218
Berend, Iván T. 201-2, 290, 438-40,
    2006-07, 2081, 2135-38, 2962, 4191
Berg, Volker vom 2542
Berg, Werner 802, 1251
Bergdolt, Wilhelm 1798

Coraggioni, Leodegar 4449
Cordes, Hans 4053
Cordey, Franklin 3142
Cornelius, Friedrich 701
Corni, Gustavo 1767
Cornwall, John 2814
Corsten, Hermann 702, 3389
Costabell, Otto 5342
Costas, Ilse 4776
Costigliola, Frank C. 936, 4279
Cottrell, Philip L. 2793, 4347
Cox, Ingrid 3807
Crämer, Rudolf 4777
Craig, Gordon A. 89
Crailsheim, Franz von 1822
Crandall, Ruth 49
Creanga, George D. 4231
Crew, David F. 2549
Cripps, T. F. 2815
Cristea, Gheorghe 467
Croner, Johannes 1686, 4778
Crook, James W. 4988
Croon, Helmuth 1900, 2550, 4086
Crouzet, François 90, 211, 2010, 4232
Crowley, Ronald W. 4196
Cruchon, Amédée 4526
Crüger, Hans 4008
Csató, Tamás 2888
Csöppüs, Istvan 1503
Cunow, Heinrich 91
Curth, Hermann 703, 4971
Curti, Giuseppe 3050
Curtiss, George B. 2011
Curtius, Julius 2977, 3235
Czada, Peter 2254
Czeike, Felix 517
Czekner, John Jr. 1467
Czichon, Eberhard 2397-98
Czoernig, Carl Freiherr von 335
Czollek, Roswitha 3753

Daems, Herman 2733
Dabritz, Walther 5309
Dahlmann, Friedrich C. 13
Dahrendorf, Gustav 3808
Dahrendorf, Ralf 704, 2303
Daigaku, Osaka S. 45
Daitz, Werner 92
Damianoff, Athanasius D. 1823
Dammang, Andreas 1504
Dane, Hendrik 3390
Daniels, Emil 4779
Dankelmann, Otfried 4140
Dankert, Jochen 2816
Danniger, Gerhard 3012
Dapper, Karl-Peter xiii, 1028
Darius, Rudolf 3391
Dascher, Ottfried 2551

Davis, Joseph S. 250, 937, 4233
Davis, Ralph 93
Dawes, Rufus C. 938
Dawson, Philip 2399
Dawson, William H. 820, 1687, 2304,
    3392-94
Day, Clive 94, 2677
Day, John P. 251
DeCecco, Marcello 4234
Deck, Helmut 1612
Decken, Hans 1613
Decken, S. Eberhard von der 1780
Decker, Franz 2552
Decoudu, Jean 4396
Deike, Ludwig 1878
Deininger, Heinz F. 1138
Deissmann, Gerhard 1204
DeJong, H. W. 1980
Dejung, Emanuel 631
Delbrück, Clemens von 821
Delena, W. 2161
Delle Donne, Ottavio 2778
Demmel, Karl 1824
Denil, Bernard 2817
Denison, Edward F. 2818
Denman, Donald R. 1392
Denoth, Caspar 4583
Denzler, Alice 2238
Dérobert, Eugène 3051
Dessauer, Lothar 2453
Dessauer, Marianne 3236
Dessmann, Günther 1947
Deutsch, Anton 4416
Deutsch, E. 4427
Diamant, Alfred 2917
Dickenmann, Heinz 3121
Dickler, Robert A. 1844-45
Diebold, William, Jr. 2820
Dieckmann, Jens 4665
Diefendorf, Jeffery M. 4087
Diehl, Alfred 3754
Diehl, Karl 1434, 4781
Diehm, Walter 5229
Dieterici, Carl F. W. 3396, 4782
Dieterle, Paul 2553
Dietrich, Hugo 3237
Dietrich, Richard 2508, 3397
Dietrich, W. M. 5343
Dietsche, Richard 2454
Dietschi, Erich 3091-93
Dietz, Alexander 4054
Dietz, Frederick C. 2012
Dietze, Constantin 1615
Dietze, Hugo 3238
Dietzel, H. 3398
Dietzel, Hans 3667
Dillard, Dudley 272
Dillen, J. G. van 4188

Hartwell, Ronald M. 216, 2020
Hasbach, Wilhelm 787
Haslehner, Werner 1544
Hasselmann, Erwin 3257-58, 3461, 3938
Hassinger, Herbert 2119, 2978
Hasslacher, F. Anton 2615
Hasslacher, Franz 394
Hattemer, Herman C. 600
Hauer, Joseph von 4357
Hauser, Albert 550, 634, 1438, 1563,
    1596, 3098-3100
Hauser, Benedikt 567
Hauser, Henri 2321
Hauser, Oswald 1269, 3686
Haushalter, -- 3967
Haushofer, Heinz 1402, 1627-29, 1820
Hausmann, Sebastian 1828
Haussherr, Hans 217, 837
Haver, Ursula 4060
Haverkamp, Frank 3939
Hay, Laszlo 2834
Heaton, Herbert 107
Hecht, Felix 5187
Hecht, Moriz 1112
Heckman, John H. 1407
Heckscher, Eli F. 108
Heeb, Friedrich 3194
Heeb, Walter 4534
Hegemann, Margot 3838
Heggen, Alfred 2322
Heilbroner, Robert L. 109
Heilig, Bernhard 421
Hein, John 3839
Heininger, Horst 3840-41
Heinrich, Walter 721, 2835
Heitger, Anneliese 5006
Heitz, Ernst 1707
Heitz, Gerhard 1708-09, 1789-90, 1914
Heizmann-Hauser, Fritz 4456
Helbich, Wolfgang J. 5007-08
Helbig, Herbert 4144
Held, Joseph 1511
Held, Max 3968
Helfferich, Karl T. 838, 4241-42, 4806
Helfritz, Hans 5332
Helg, Robert 3192
Helleiner, Karl F. 110, 2932
Heller, Sigmund 1176
Hellgreve, Henny 1270
Helling, Gertrud 1710-11
Hellinger, Kurt 3124
Hellwig, Fritz 1101
Helmreich, Ernst C. 839
Helmrich, Wilhelm 1271-72, 2560,
    4092
Helten, Josef 5313

Henderson, William O. 218, 947, 2021-23,
    2064, 2189, 2263, 2323-26, 2745-46,
    3259, 3462-75
Hennessy, Josselyn 277
Hennig, Curt 5009
Hennig, Eike 999
Henning, Friedrich-Wilhelm 722, 1273,
    1630, 2264, 2327-28, 2519, 3476,
    4677
Henning, Hansjoachim 1000, 2329, 3477,
    4093
Henning, Heinz 840
Henke, Rudolph 111
Henry, James A. 4243
Hentschel, Volker 723, 841-42, 1113,
    1374, 2747, 3478, 4094
Herbert, Walther H. 297
Herberts, Hermann 1274
Herbig, Rudolf 724
Herbst, Ludolf 1001
Hering, Gerhard 4075
Herker, Hellmuth 2561
Herker, Paul 3842
Herkner, Heinrich 219-20
Hermann, Eugen 635-36
Hermann, Franz-Josef 1852
Hermanns, Heinz 1275
Hermant, Max 948
Hermens, Ferdinand A. 949, 3687
Hermes, Peter 1791
Herms, Doris 2524
Herold, Hans 4457
Herrmann, Arthur R. 4678
Herrmann, Walther 843, 2562, 3843
Herting, August 5369
Hertner, Peter 4807
Hertz, Friedrich 298, 344
Hertz, Friedrich O. 2094
Hertz-Eichenrode, Dieter 1853, 3688, 5010
Hertzer, Georg 5370
Herwig, Christoph J. 3969
Herzig, Karl 1553
Hess, Mario W. 4535
Hesse, Albert 1195
Hesse, Friedrich 844, 950
Hesse, Helmut 3444, 3479
Hesse, Richard 1879
Heuberger, Max 3062
Heubner, Paul L. 4145
Heuer, Gerd F. 4808
Heumos, Peter 1491
Heussler, Heinz 3101
Heyd, Wilhelm 3940
Heyden, Wilhelm 5257
Heyn, Udo 5273-74
Heynicke, Hans 1184

ABOUT THE COMPILER

RICHARD D. HACKEN is European Studies Bibliographer at Brigham Young University. His previous publications include *The Religious Thought of Martin Opitz* and articles published in the *Review of Social Economy*.